The Second Interim Report of the Tribunal of Inquiry into Certain Planning Matters and Payments

BAILE ÁTHA CLIATH
ARNA FHOILSIÚ AG OIFIG AN tSOLÁTHAIR
Le ceannach d´reach ón
OIFIG DHÍOLTA FOILSEACHÁN RIALTAIS,
TEACH SUN ALLIANCE, SRÁID THEACH LAIGHEAN, BAILE ÁTHA CLIATH 2,
nó tr´d an bpost ó
FOILSEACHÁIN RIALTAIS, AN RANNÓG POST-TRÁCHTA,
51 FAICHE STIABHNA, BAILE ÁTHA CLIATH 2,
(Teil: 01 - 6476834/35/36/37; Fax: 01 - 6476843)
nó tr´ aon d´oltóir leabhar.

—————

DUBLIN
PUBLISHED BY THE STATIONERY OFFICE
To be purchased directly from the
GOVERNMENT PUBLICATIONS SALE OFFICE,
SUN ALLIANCE HOUSE, MOLESWORTH STREET, DUBLIN 2,
or by mail order from
GOVERNMENT PUBLICATIONS, POSTAL TRADE SECTION,
51 ST. STEPHEN'S GREEN, DUBLIN 2,
(Tel: 01 - 6476834/35/36/37; Fax: 01 - 6476843)
or through any bookseller.

—————

€1.00

Wt. —. 2,000. 9/02. Cahill. (M70755). G.Spl.

PREFACE

This is my Second Interim Report to the Oireachtas. I have, since my last Report, conducted what were in effect three separate Public Inquiries. They are referred to in this Report as the Brennan & McGowan Module, the Century Radio Module and the Gogarty Module. Public hearings on these issues took place between January 1999 and December 2001 and lasted 313 days, in the course of which 170 witnesses were heard. Where it has been possible, and is appropriate for me to do so, I now report my interim conclusions arising therefrom.

The subject matter of these inquiries extended to cover a period of more than 30 years and ranged over a number of topics, as diverse as: -
- Land rezoning;
- Radio broadcasting, and
- Offshore trusts and corporations.

The extent of the inquiries was dictated by the Terms of Reference which obliged me to investigate substantial payments made to Mr. Burke in the course of his long political career.

In reaching my conclusions in this Report, I have carefully considered the *viva voce* evidence of the witnesses who gave evidence on oath before me. I have considered the transcripts, which record their testimony and which extended to over 35,000 pages, and the exhibits referred to therein.

I have given full consideration to the points ably made by the legal representatives of the parties who appeared before me, and I have read and carefully considered the submissions, both oral and written, made by them at the conclusion of the public hearings of the issues in which they were involved. I reached the findings in this Report after much careful deliberation. I have sought in my Report to address the issues as I found them, so as to give a comprehensive and comprehensible report on the matters of concern to the Oireachtas which are encapsulated in my *Terms of Reference*.

In preparing this Interim Report, I was mindful of the vast volume of material which was considered by me in reaching my decisions, and the range of issues and arguments which were raised by the parties in their evidence and by their legal representatives in their submissions. I am conscious that a recital of each of the issues raised, and of the evidence/lack of evidence relating to them, would render this Report so voluminous and complex as to make it incomprehensible to its readers.

The absence, therefore, of specific references to the evidence given, or to each individual point raised, or to each argument advanced, is not to be taken as meaning that I have not given full and careful consideration to such evidence and/or submissions. I have fully considered all relevant matters on the issues, and I am satisfied that the conclusions reached by me in reporting my findings are fully borne out by the evidence heard.

All citizens have a duty to co-operate and assist a Tribunal and to tell the truth when summoned to appear at a public hearing. It is with considerable regret that I have concluded that I must report, as one of my findings, that certain parties who appeared before me chose not to co-operate with the Tribunal in its task and, further, having been duly sworn did not tell the truth.

The extent to which their actions may have involved them in breaches of the criminal law is a matter upon which the Director of Public Prosecutions has absolute and exclusive jurisdiction. I have decided to forward a copy of my Report to him to take such steps, and to do with it, what he, in his absolute discretion, considers appropriate.

I am very mindful of the significant costs which have been incurred in conducting the Inquiry to date. I have endeavoured to conduct the Inquiry in as economical a fashion as possible, having regard to the rights of those persons appearing before the Tribunal and my obligation to the Oireachtas.

In response to my request for information, the Revenue Commissioners and the Criminal Assets Bureau have informed me that, to date, in excess of €34,500,000 has been paid to these bodies in connection with inquiries into Revenue compliance issues arising directly or indirectly from this Tribunal. I believe that this is a significant consequence of the work of the Tribunal to date.

As this is an Interim Report only I am not at this time making any specific recommendations in relation to amendments to existing legislation in the areas of planning, local government, ethics in public office or otherwise.

The Honourable Mr. Justice Feargus M. Flood
September 2002

Introduction to the Second Interim Report of the Tribunal of Inquiry into Certain Planning Matters and Payments

This Tribunal was established by Ministerial Order, on the 4th November 1997, to inquire urgently into the matters of urgent public importance set forth in its original Terms of Reference (see **Appendix A**) and to report to the Clerk of the Dáil upon its findings.

The Tribunal is mindful of the desire of the House that the Inquiry be completed in as economical a manner as possible and at the earliest date consistent with a fair examination of the matters referred to it.

The original Terms of Reference enabled the Tribunal to report, on an interim basis, on any matters which the Tribunal believed should be drawn to the attention of the Clerk of the Dáil including any matter relating to the Terms of Reference. On the 26th February 1998, the Tribunal availed of this provision so as to request the Oireachtas to amend the original Terms of Reference by the deletion of the words, "committed on or after 20th June, 1985" from paragraph A. (5) of the original Terms of Reference. The proposed amended paragraph would have then read;

> "In the event that the Tribunal in the course of its inquiries is made aware of any acts associated with the planning process which may in its opinion amount to corruption, or which involve attempts to influence by threats or deception or inducement or otherwise to compromise the disinterested performance of public duties, it shall report on such acts and should in particular make recommendations as to the effectiveness and improvement of existing legislation governing corruption in the light of its inquiries."

Following upon this request, and in view of other significant developments which had taken place since the setting up of the Tribunal, the Oireachtas amended the Terms of Reference of the Tribunal by Instrument of the Minister for the Environment and Local Government dated the 15th July 1998. The full text of the amended Terms of Reference is appended to this Interim Report **(Appendix B).**

The amended Terms of Reference incorporated not only the original amendment sought by the Tribunal but also amendments which specifically required the Tribunal to inquire into the public life of a named former member of the House, Mr. Raphael Burke.

These amendments, provided for at paragraphs E1 and E2, were to greatly expand the Tribunal's task. In effect the Tribunal was obliged to investigate the entire public life of Mr. Burke from 1967 to 1997 to see whether any substantial payments were made or benefits provided to him which, in the opinion of the Tribunal, amounted to corruption, or involved attempts to influence or compromise the disinterested performance of public duties, or were made or provided in circumstances which may give rise to the reasonable inference that the motive for making or receiving such payments was improperly connected with any public office or position held by him, whether as Minister, Minister of State, or elected representative.

The amended Terms of Reference permit the Tribunal to report on an interim basis on any matters which the Tribunal believes should be drawn to the attention of the Clerk of the Dáil at that stage and to furnish such further interim reports as the Tribunal may consider necessary.

This Interim Report is provided at this time as the Tribunal considers it necessary to do so for the following reasons: -

1. The Tribunal has heard sufficient evidence in public to enable it to pronounce with finality upon certain payments made to Mr. Burke.

2. The likely duration of the public hearings of the matters which are the subject of current private inquiries being conducted by the Tribunal is such that a final report on these matters could not be delivered for at least two years from the present date.

3. In addition to those matters upon which decisions to go to public hearing have been taken, there are a number of additional matters currently under investigation by the Tribunal in its private investigative phase. It is not possible to forecast the likely duration of the public hearings on such matters should it be determined that they merit public hearings, and, consequently, the likely date for publication of a final report on all issues covered in the present Terms of Reference cannot be accurately forecast.

4. The Tribunal considers that the withholding of a report upon those matters which are capable of being determined at this time until the publication of the final report would be inconsistent with the Tribunal's obligation to report as soon as possible, consistent with fairness.

5. The Tribunal is being enlarged by the addition of two further members and, accordingly, it is considered appropriate that those matters upon which evidence was heard by the Sole Member Tribunal should, where possible, be the subject of a report which is independent of the reconstituted and enlarged Tribunal.

The Tribunal is in a position to report its conclusions in respect of the following matters:

● The acquisition by Mr. Burke of the dwellinghouse and lands at Briargate, Malahide Road, Swords, Co. Dublin.

● The payment of specific sums of money to Mr. Burke by Mr. Tom Brennan, Mr. Joseph McGowan, Mr. John Finnegan and/or their related companies.

● The payment of money to Mr. Burke by Mr. Oliver Barry.

● The payment of money to Mr. Burke at the meeting attended by Mr. James Gogarty and Mr. Michael Bailey at Briargate, Malahide Road, Swords, in June 1989.

The references to "payment" in this introduction extend to cover not only admitted payments but also alleged payments.

In addition to reporting upon the specific issues set out above this Interim Report contains a summary of the work carried out by the Tribunal to date in relation to:

1. Inquiries carried out into matters in respect of which it was determined that insufficient evidence existed to merit proceeding to public hearing.

2. Inquiries into complaints which, upon examination, were established not to fall within the Tribunal's Terms of Reference.

3. Inquiries into matters upon which, it was concluded by the Tribunal, there was no evidence to support the complaint.

The Report commences with a general background history of Mr. Burke's personal and professional details, in so far as they are relevant to the Tribunal's findings, and with a history of the events which culminated in his resignation from public life in October 1997.

The Report follows the chronological sequence of the events which are the subject of the report, rather than the sequence in which the Tribunal heard the evidence at public sessions.

TABLE OF CONTENTS

BRENNAN AND MCGOWAN MODULE

Payments made to Mr. Burke's offshore accounts attributed to Messrs. Brennan and McGowan, their related companies and associates

CENTURY MODULE

CHAPTER 8

GOGARTY MODULE

CHAPTER 12

The accounting and auditing procedures regarding the JMSE funds paid to Mr. Burke   89

CHAPTER 13

The reaction of those persons alleged to have been present at the meeting at Briargate, Swords in June 1989 to the publication of Mr. James Gogarty's allegations regarding payment to Mr. Ray Burke 103

CHAPTER 14

Challenges to the account of events given to the Tribunal by Mr. James Gogarty 116

CHAPTER 15

The participation proposal and payment of monies to Mr. Burke   134

SUMMARY / CONCLUSIONS

CHAPTER 18

Findings of the Tribunal in relation to the matters raised in Clause A, Sub-Clause 1, 2 and 3 of the Amended Terms of Reference of the Tribunal

CHAPTER 19

Other work of the Tribunal

APPENDICES

Chapter 1

Background to the Establishment of the Tribunal of Inquiry into Certain Planning Matters and Payments

BACKGROUND HISTORY OF MR. RAY BURKE OTHERWISE RAPHAEL P. BURKE

1-01   Mr. Burke was born on the 30th September 1943 in Donabate, Co. Dublin, the son of Patrick Joseph Burke and Catherine Mary Burke. His birth certificate records his full name as Raphael Patrick Burke. Prior to his marriage in November 1972, Mr. Burke resided at 251 Swords Road, Dublin 9, and subsequent to his marriage, he lived at Briargate, Malahide Road, Swords, Co. Dublin.

Political career details

1-02   Mr. Burke's father, Mr. P.J. Burke, was elected a member of Dáil Éireann in 1944, and served continuously until 1973 when he retired from active politics. Mr. Ray Burke entered public life as a Fianna Fáil councillor on Dublin County Council in 1967. He served as a member of the Council from 1967 until 1978. Between 1985 and 1987 he was Chairman of Dublin County Council. Mr. Burke was first elected to Dáil Éireann in 1973 upon the retirement of his father. He was a member of Dáil Éireann for the constituency of Dublin North from 1973 until his retirement on the 7th October 1997. Mr. Burke held the following ministerial offices during the course of his career:

- From January 1978 until October 1980, he was Minister of State at the Department of Industry, Commerce and Energy.

- From October 1980 until June 1981, he was Minister for the Environment.

- From March 1982 until December 1982, he was Minister for the Environment.

- From March 1987 until November 1988, he was Minister for Energy, and Minister for Communications.

- From November 1988 until July 1989, he was Minister for Communications and Minister for Industry and Commerce.

- From July 1989 to November 1991, he was Minister for Communications.

- From July 1989 until February 1992, he was Minister for Justice.

- From the 26th June 1997 to the 7th October 1997, he was Minister for Foreign Affairs.

On the 7th October 1997, Mr Burke retired both as Minister for Foreign Affairs and as a member of Dáil Éireann.

Professional career details

1-03   On the 4th October 1968, P.J. Burke (Sales) Limited was incorporated. Mr. Burke was a director of this company, which carried on the business of auctioneers and estate agents at Swords, Co. Dublin. The company made its last annual return on the 31st December 1980 and was dissolved on the 9th May 1989. On the 20th July 1984, Ray Burke & Associates Life & Pensions Limited was incorporated. Mr. Burke was a director and the secretary of the company. This company changed its name to Crown Insurance Brokers Limited with effect

1

from the 27th July 1987. Mr. Burke had resigned as a director and as the secretary of the company with effect from the 14th October 1986. Crown Insurance Brokers Limited filed its last annual return on the 31st December 1989, and was dissolved on the 26th September 1995.

BACKGROUND HISTORY OF EVENTS, WHICH PRE-DATED THE APPOINTMENT AND OF EVENTS WHICH PRE-DATED THE SUBSEQUENT RESIGNATION OF MR. RAY BURKE AS MINISTER FOR FOREIGN AFFAIRS AND AS A MEMBER OF DÁIL ÉIREANN

Publications in the print media

1-04   The following material was published in the print media and pre-dated Mr. Burke's appointment as Minister for Foreign Affairs in June 1997: -

- On the 3rd July 1995, a notice appeared in two Irish daily newspapers offering a £10,000 reward to persons providing information leading to the conviction of persons involved in corruption in connection with the planning process. Donnelly Neary Donnelly, Solicitors of Newry, Co. Down, placed this notice on behalf of unnamed clients. This notice was the subject of much public comment at the time of its insertion, and subsequently, both in the print media and in Dáil Éireann.

- On the 31st March 1996, the Sunday Business Post published an article by a journalist, Mr. Frank Connolly, under the heading, "Fianna Fáil Politician paid off by Developers." It was stated that a serving Fianna Fáil T.D. had been accused of receiving payments from property developers in Dublin in return for securing planning permission for housing. The article stated that an individual had claimed to the Newry Solicitors, Donnelly Neary Donnelly that, in 1989, he personally gave the politician, who was also a local councillor, cash and cheques worth £40,000 on one occasion and was present when a property developer handed over an equivalent amount. This person claimed that the money was in return for the promised rezoning of almost 1000 acres of land and was to cover payment for a number of named councillors who would support specific rezoning motions.

- On the 7th April 1996, in an article written by the same journalist in the Sunday Business Post it was stated that a former company executive had alleged that he was present in June, 1989 when £40,000 was handed to the politician by a director of his company, and that a further £40,000 was paid over by a property developer just days before a General Election. It was stated that the payment was in return for the promised rezoning of hundreds of acres of land in Dublin, which were owned by the company. It was stated that present at that meeting, in the politician's home, were the three directors of the company, including the man who made the allegations, the property developer, and the politician, according to the former executive who, it was stated, had said that he was prepared to restate his allegations in open court. It was stated that his understanding was that the rezoning would be achieved over a period of years at a cost to the developers of £1,000 per acre in payoffs. It was stated that the developer who organised the meeting indicated that the politician was anxious to get money urgently to cover election costs. It was stated that the payments were partly intended to cover the payment to other named councillors who would support rezoning of motions.

- On the 11th May 1997, the Sunday Business Post published an article by Mr. Frank Connolly in which he wrote that the former company director who had made serious allegations of planning corruption against a senior Fianna Fáil politician had indicated to the Gardaí that he would make a formal signed complaint if he was granted immunity from prosecution. It was stated that the company director said that the money, in two cheques of £40,000 each, were paid over by two persons active in the construction/property sector, neither of whom could be named in the article for legal reasons. It was stated that the two men alleged to have handed over the cheques were denying the allegations.

1-05   The following publications in the print media took place following the appointment of Mr. Burke as Minister for Foreign Affairs on the 26th June 1997 and prior to his resignation on the 7th of October 1997: -

- On the 20th July 1997, an article, in the Sunday Tribune newspaper by Mr. Matt Cooper, named Mr. Ray Burke T.D. as the person who had received £30,000 in electoral contributions from a property company called Bovale Developments in 1989. This article stated that the claimed payment of £30,000 to Mr. Burke was separate from the allegation of payment from other sources, which had been made by a former executive in a major property company.

- On the 27th July 1997, the Sunday Business Post published an article, written by Mr. Frank Connolly, headed "Burke Political Funds' Confusion Continues" in which he stated that confusion surrounded the amounts and nature of the monies given to the Minister for Foreign Affairs, Ray Burke, during the 1989 election campaign. It stated that Mr. Michael Bailey of Bovale Developments Limited had denied a report in the previous week's Sunday Tribune that he had handed Mr. Burke £30,000 before the election in 1989. The Tribune story had quoted unnamed Fianna Fáil sources as confirming Bovale had made such a contribution to Mr. Burke. The article stated that Mr. Bailey said that he was in Mr. Burke's home when a representative of Joseph Murphy Structural Engineers Limited (JMSE), a Santry firm, handed a large sum of money in bundles of cash to Mr. Burke in June 1989. The article stated that Mr. Bailey had insisted that the most he ever gave Mr. Burke in one electoral campaign was £1,000 and that he also assisted other parties.

1-06   The following publication took place following Mr Burke's first public statement refuting the allegations of Mr. James Gogarty on the 7th August 1997: -

- On the 10th August, 1997 the Sunday Business Post published an article written by Mr. Frank Connolly headed "The Other Side Of The Coin" in which Mr. Connolly claimed to talk exclusively to Jim Gogarty, the man identified by Foreign Minister, Ray Burke the previous Thursday as his chief accuser. In the article, Mr. Connolly stated that Mr. Gogarty informed him that two envelopes had been handed over to Mr. Burke. The article stated that the intention, as understood by Mr. Gogarty, was that Mr. Burke was to be given £80,000 of which £40,000 was to come from JMSE. The article stated that Mr. Gogarty said that Mr. Joseph Murphy Junior handed over the envelope containing the JMSE money to Mr. Burke and that Mr. Gogarty's understanding was that Mr. Bailey was matching this amount.

1-07   The following publication took place following Mr Burke's personal statement to the House on the 10th September 1997: -

- On the 25th September 1997, Magill Magazine published an article written by Mr. John Ryan which quoted part of the contents of a letter which had been written by Mr. Michael Bailey to Mr. James Gogarty on the 8th June 1989, in which Mr. Bailey stated that he would have to be offered a 50% stake in the Murphy lands in exchange for the procurement of planning permission and Building Bye-Law approval. It was stated that this would involve the procurement of a majority vote of a full Council meeting. The article stated that a few days later Mr. Gogarty and Mr. Bailey went to Mr. Burke's house and according to Mr. Burke an unsolicited political donation of £30,000 from JMSE was handed over by Mr. Gogarty.

PARLIAMENTARY QUESTIONS RAISED CONCERNING ALLEGATIONS MADE BY MR. JAMES GOGARTY

1-08   Deputy Thomas P. Broughan tabled the following parliamentary questions directed to the Minister for Justice on behalf of his constituent, Mr. James Gogarty between June 1995 and June 1996.

"Chun an tAire Dlí agus Cirt; to the Minister for Justice

Question: * To ask the Minister for Justice the action, if any, which will be taken by the Gardaí regarding the attacks and intimidation of a person (details supplied) in Dublin 13 between the years 1991 and 1994; and if so, when.

Thomas P. Broughan "

To which the following written answer was given on the 28th June 1995:
"Answer: I have requested a detailed report from the Garda Authorities in this matter and I will communicate with the Deputy once the Report is to hand."

"Chun an tAire Dlí agus Cirt; to the Minister for Justice

Question: * To ask the Minister for Justice the reason a file was not sent to the DPP in respect of the person (details supplied) in Dublin 13 following attacks on a home and cars, verbal phone threats and intimidation to which a Garda was a witness.

Thomas P. Broughan "

To which a written answer was given on the 2nd May 1996 as follows:

"Answer: I am informed by the Garda Authorities that having investigated this matter, they have found no basis for criminal prosecution."

"Chun an tAire Dlí agus Cirt; to the Minister for Justice

Question: To ask the Minister for Justice the allegations and background surrounding threats to and intimidation of a person (details supplied) in Dublin 13 in each of the years from 1989 to 1994; and the reason the investigation carried out by Gardaí have not been referred to the Fraud Squad in Harcourt Street, Dublin 2 in order to prepare a file for the Director of Public Prosecution, in view of the serious allegations of fraud made against a leading Dublin company (details supplied) in Dublin 9 in the Circuit Court on 8th March, 1994.

Thomas P. Broughan "

To which an oral answer was given on the 19th June 1996 as follows:

"Answer: I dealt with the allegation of intimidation in my response of 2nd May, 1996 to a previous parliamentary question tabled by the Deputy in this matter. As regards the allegations of fraud I am informed by the Garda Authorities that no such complaint has been received from the person in question. "

PUBLIC STATEMENTS BY MR. RAY BURKE T.D. ON THE 7TH AUGUST 1997 AND THE 10TH SEPTEMBER 1997

1-09   On the 7th August 1997, Mr. Ray Burke T.D., Minister for Foreign Affairs, issued a public statement in which he stated that he had been a target of a vicious campaign of rumour and innuendo during the previous two years. He stated that since his appointment as Minister for Foreign Affairs the campaign had intensified. He stated that the stories, which had appeared in the media in preceding weeks, were the culmination of a lengthy series of smears about him. He stated that the story kept resurfacing in different shapes and forms and that the repeated articles and comments of previous weeks had placed an unacceptable burden on his family and himself. While he resented having to dignify these allegations by responding to them at all, he believed that he was obliged to do so then.

1-10   In his public statement Mr. Burke stated:

(1) Mr. Michael Bailey of Bovale Developments Limited visited his home with a Mr. James Gogarty during the 1989 Election campaign;

(2) Mr. Bailey was well known to him, as he was a resident of North County Dublin and a long-term supporter of Fianna Fáil;

(3) He had not met Mr. Gogarty previously but that he was introduced by Mr. Bailey as an executive of Joseph Murphy Structural Engineers, (JMSE). Mr. Gogarty told him that JMSE wished to make a political donation to him and he received from him in good faith a sum of £30,000 as a totally unsolicited contribution;

(4) At no time during their meeting were any favours sought or given;

(5) He did not do any favours for or make any representation to anyone on behalf of JMSE, Mr. Michael Bailey, Bovale Developments Limited or Mr. James Gogarty either before or since 1989;

(6) He believed that Mr. James Gogarty might be the source of the allegations being made against him;

(7) He did not know of any motive which Mr. Gogarty would have in pursuing a vendetta against him. However, he believed that he had parted from his former employers, JMSE, in acrimonious circumstances. If Mr. Gogarty was the source of the allegations he was the author of a campaign of lies against Mr. Burke;

(8) He acknowledged that he had received a political contribution of £30,000 and not £80,000 as reported;

(9) He stated that the allegation that he had received £40,000 from Mr. Bailey or Bovale Developments Limited on that or any previous occasion was false;

(10) He stated that there were three persons present when he received the contribution from Mr. Gogarty, namely Mr. Gogarty, Mr. Bailey and himself and not five as reported;

(11) He stated that there was one JMSE executive present, Mr. Gogarty, and not two or three as variously reported;

(12) He stated that he was taking the opportunity to state unequivocally that he had done nothing illegal, unethical or improper. He found himself the victim of a campaign of calumny and abuse. He stated that it was totally unacceptable that the matter should be allowed to continue to fulfil an agenda which has nothing to do with election contributions or any other aspect of reasonable or reasoned political debate in public life;

(13) He stated that if any further untruths were published about him he would take all necessary steps to vindicate his good name and reputation.

1-11   On the 10th September 1997, Mr. Ray Burke T.D. availed of the opportunity of making a personal statement to Dáil Éireann. He indicated that he had come to the House to defend his personal integrity, the integrity of his party, of the Government and of the honour of the Dáil and to reassure the public, and in particular his constituents, that he had done nothing wrong. Mr. Burke reiterated the public statement, which he had made on the 7th August 1997, and elaborated upon it. He subjected himself to questions from members of the House.

1-12   Mr. Burke's statement to the Dáil revealed the following information in addition to that which had been contained in his public statement of the 7th August 1997;

(1) He said that the contribution was entirely in cash.

(2) He confirmed that he contributed £10,000 to the Fianna Fáil National Organisation during that election campaign. In addition, he handed over monies totalling approximately £7,000 to his local constituency organisation during the general election campaign in 1989. The remainder of the political contributions received by him, including the contribution Mr. Gogarty gave him during the meeting at his home was used to cover personal election campaign and subsequent political expenses.

(3) He said that as regards the contribution, £30,000 was the largest contribution he had received during any election campaign either before or since 1989.

1-13   In answer to questions put to him by members of the House, Mr. Burke provided the following information in relation to the payment referred in his statement: -

(1) He stated that in attempting to "recall and collect" details of particular allocations of funds, cheques or otherwise, during recent months in respect of the controversy he had no recollection of the denominations of the monies he received.

(2) He produced a letter dated the 8th September 1989, from Ulster Bank, Dublin Airport Branch, Swords Road, Cloghran, Co. Dublin from Mr. W. J. Moody, Senior Manager, Business Banking confirming that a bank draft No. 340804 in favour of Fianna Fáil in the sum of £10,000 was issued and duly lodged and paid by the bank on the 16th June 1989.

(3) He stated the sum given to his constituency organisation was confirmed as having been received in two drafts amounting to £2,000 and £5,000.

(4) He stated that the money given to him by Mr. James Gogarty was lodged to his personal account.

(5) He stated that his solicitors had received a letter from the solicitors acting for Joseph Murphy Structural Engineers Limited and Mr. Joseph Murphy Junior, stating that on the 8th June 1989, two consecutive cheques were drawn on the JMSE account in the AIB, Talbot Street Branch, one cheque for £20,000 and the second for £10,000. The cheque stubs in relation to both cheques said 'cash', they presumed that these cheques related to the £30,000 at issue, however, following inquiries with the AIB they had been unable to provide any details in relation to same and did have not have a record of paid cheques.

(6) He stated that in relation to records other than those relating to the £10,000 bank draft that went to Fianna Fáil headquarters, he had discovered something of which he was not aware, namely that banks did not keep records dating back eight or nine years. All records were stopped and it was practically impossible to find records. He had found as much as he possibly could and was trying to be as frank as possible.

(7) He stated that his recollection was that the money given to him was in two envelopes and that it was only after the people had left that the money was counted. He was not aware at the time of the sum he was receiving.

(8) He referred to a letter, of the 4th August 1989, from Ulster Bank, Dublin Airport Branch, Swords Road, Cloghran, Co. Dublin as evidence of an overdraft of £35,000, which he required at that time and as evidence of the financial straits in which he found himself after the campaign.

(9) He stated that because the money was given in cash, some of it would have been lodged and more of it would have been used on the ongoing daily expenses of the election campaign.

(10) He referred to alleged impropriety in relation to the acquisition of his home at Briargate, Swords and said that the land upon which his house was built was not purchased by his father from an inmate of the Mental Hospital in Portrane, Co. Dublin as alleged, but was bought by him in a normal commercial transaction from Oldpark(*sic*) Developments Limited. He said the house was built in the normal commercial manner when he was doing business with that company and that that transaction along with others was the subject of a Garda investigation in 1974.

1-14   The full text of Mr. Burke's statement and the questions and answers following upon his statement, are contained in the Dáil Report of the 10th September 1997 from paragraphs 616 to 638 inclusive and appears as **Appendix C** to this Report.

BACKGROUND TO THE RESIGNATION OF MR. RAY BURKE T.D. ON THE 7TH OCTOBER 1997 AND THE APPOINTMENT OF THE TRIBUNAL OF INQUIRY INTO CERTAIN PLANNING MATTERS AND PAYMENTS

1-15 Following Mr. Ray Burke T.D's statement to the members of Dáil Éireann on 10th September 1997, the following significant events occurred.

1-16 On the 11th September 1997, Mr. Pat Rabbitte T.D moved amendment No. 27 to the Report of Tribunal of Inquiry (Dunnes Payments) and Establishment of Tribunal of Inquiry: Motion (the Moriarty Tribunal Terms of Reference Debate) to provide for an amendment of the Motion so as to insert the following new subparagraph after sub paragraph (1):

> "(II) To carry out such investigation as it thinks fit, using all the powers conferred on it under the Acts, into the amount, source and circumstances of the financial donation received in 1989 by the Minister for Foreign Affairs, Mr. Ray Burke, which was the subject of a personal statement by him in Dáil Éireann on September 10th, 1997 in order to determine whether sufficient evidence exists to warrant proceedings to a full public inquiry into this matter."

1-17 This amendment, if passed, would have included the preliminary investigation into the payment of JMSE's money to Mr. Burke in the Terms of Reference of the Moriarty Tribunal. The amendment was rejected by 76 votes to 69.

1-18 On the 25th September 1997, Magill Magazine published excerpts from Michael Bailey's letter of 8th June 1989 to James Gogarty seeking a 50% interest in the Murphy lands in return for procuring planning permission and building bye-law approval for the development of the lands.

1-19 On the 1st October, 1997, in answer to Question 13 put to an Taoiseach by Mr. Pat Rabbitte T.D, an Taoiseach Mr. Bertie Ahern T.D. informed the House that the Government had decided that a new Tribunal would be established to investigate all matters relating to the parcels of land referred to in Mr. Bailey's letter and any related matters. He informed the House that the *Terms of Reference* had been the subject of discussion between the Whips and that the formal Motion would be put down for debate when those discussions were completed.

1-20 On the 7th October 1997, an Taoiseach advised the House that he had accepted, on behalf of the Government, the resignation of the former Minister for Foreign Affairs, Raphael P. Burke and had also accepted his decision to resign his seat as a member of Dáil Éireann.

1-21 On the 7th October 1997, Mr. Noel Dempsey T.D, Minister for the Environment and Local Government moved the Motion to set up this Tribunal which following debate was carried with agreed amendments. The full text of the debate is annexed to this Report and appears as **Appendix D**.

1-22 On the 4th November 1997, by Instrument of the Minister for the Environment and Local Government this Tribunal was established. The full text of the original Terms of Reference of the Tribunal appears as **Appendix A** to this Report.

Brennan & McGowan Module

Chapter 2

Mr. Ray Burke's involvement with Mr. Tom Brennan, Mr. Joseph McGowan and their related Companies and Associates

2-01   Mr. Tom Brennan and Mr. Joseph McGowan were both born in County Mayo in 1936 and 1944 respectively and were known to Mr. Ray Burke from the 1960's onward. Mr. Brennan and Mr. McGowan were friends of Mr. Burke's father, Mr. P.J. Burke, T.D. who had also been born and raised in Co. Mayo.

2-02   The Brennan & McGowan business relationship commenced as a partnership in 1965 when they started house building on a small scale in the Dublin area. They went on to form limited liability companies as their business increased and prospered. By the late 1970s they were amongst the largest house building companies in Ireland and both Mr. Brennan and Mr. Gowan were wealthy men.

2-03   The companies controlled by them included Grange Developments Limited, incorporated in May 1970, and Kilnamanagh Estates Limited incorporated in August 1972. In addition to the companies in which they had joint interests, Mr. Brennan also had building companies in which Mr. McGowan had no identifiable beneficial interest including a company called Oakpark Developments Limited, (Oakpark) which was incorporated in April 1970.

2-04   Oakpark's core business was the development of high-density housing estates in the Swords area. It did not build individual houses with one notable exception, a substantial detached house standing on one acre at Malahide Road, Swords, Co. Dublin which was built in 1972 and which was subsequently named "Briargate" by its first owner, Mr. Ray Burke.

2-05   From 1968 onwards, Mr. Burke was conducting an auctioneering and estate agency business in the Swords area through a company called P.J. Burke (Sales) Limited. This company acted as the sales agent for houses, which were being built by Brennan & McGowan connected companies.

2-06   In 1974, Mr. Burke's relationship with Messrs. Brennan and McGowan was the subject of a newspaper article written by Mr. Joe McAnthony, a journalist then with the *Sunday Independent*. In the course of the article, reference was made to a document, which had been sent to the Companies Office with the returns for Dublin Airport Industrial Estates Limited, a company connected with Messrs. Brennan and McGowan. The document contained a reference which stated "Ray Burke – planning - £15,000". As Mr. Burke was at that time both a County Councillor and a newly elected member of the Dáil, this article attracted widespread attention. A Garda investigation followed and at its conclusion did not recommend prosecution of any individual.

THE INVOLVEMENT OF MR. TOM BRENNAN AND MR. JOSEPH MCGOWAN WITH THE TRIBUNAL

2-07   In the course of his oral testimony before the Tribunal in July 1999, Mr. Burke gave evidence about the source of funds, which had been lodged to a bank account in Jersey, held in the name of a Jersey registered company called Caviar Limited. Mr. Burke had earlier disclosed the existence of this account in his affidavit of discovery provided to the Tribunal on foot of an order for discovery and production made by the Tribunal. He acknowledged that the Caviar account was his. Mr. Burke's evidence at that time was to the effect that there had been two lodgments to the account. Both lodgments were made in 1984. The first was a lodgment of stg.£35,000 made in April 1984, and the second a lodgment of stg.£60,000 made in October 1984. He gave evidence that these lodgments were the proceeds of political fundraising activities carried out in the UK by his political supporters previously identified to the Tribunal as Mr. Brennan and Mr. McGowan. He did not know the identity of the individual subscribers to these fundraising activities.

2-08   In correspondence with Messrs. Brennan and McGowan, the Tribunal sought to establish the full circumstances relating to all payments made by them to Mr. Burke. However, this correspondence did not produce the necessary information. The Tribunal invited Messrs. Brennan and McGowan to provide a written narrative account of their dealings with Mr. Burke but this invitation was declined. Accordingly, the Tribunal decided to call both Mr. Brennan and Mr. McGowan to give evidence at the public sessions of the Tribunal in April 2000.

2-09   The Tribunal's decision to do so was reached, having regard to the provisions of paragraphs E1 and E2 of the Tribunal's *Terms of Reference* and to the substantial payments received by Caviar with which Mr. Burke said that Messrs. Brennan and McGowan were associated.

2-10   The evidence provided by Mr. McGowan, in which he was supported by Mr. Brennan, in relation to the offshore fundraising activities conducted on Mr. Burke's behalf, was that fundraising events had taken place to coincide generally with horseracing events in the UK at which contributions were raised for Ray Burke/Fianna Fáil. This fundraising activity commenced in the 1970s. The funds estimated to have been raised during that period were in the region of stg.£110,000 to stg.£130.000. That was calculated on the basis of an average contribution of stg.£10,000 per annum and stg.£20,000 in one particular year. The evidence was that this fundraising activity ceased in or around 1984. The fundraising was on an informal basis and Mr. Ernest Ottiwell was said to have been the *de facto* treasurer of this fundraising group. Having received the evidence of Mr. Brennan and Mr. McGowan on the question of payment of monies to Mr. Burke, the Tribunal conducted further inquiries.

2-11   On the 28th June 2000, Mr. Burke revealed in correspondence that he had received a sum of stg.£50,000 in December 1982 from a company called Kalabraki. Mr. Burke, in later evidence, said that this payment was part of the offshore fundraising activities of Mr. McGowan/Mr. Ottiwell. Whereas his original testimony was that there were only two lodgments of stg.£35,000 and stg.£60,000 in April and November, 1984 attributable to this offshore fundraising, he now maintained that there were two payments, the first of which was for stg.£50,000 in December, 1982 and the second in November, 1984 for stg.£60,000. The lodgment of stg.£35,000 in April 1984 was now recategorised as part of the original stg.£50,000 donation made in December 1982.

2-12   The Tribunal made further inquiries of Messrs. Brennan and McGowan. The Tribunal identified to them the two payments that were now the focus of the Tribunal's investigation, namely:

    1. A payment of stg.£50,000 from Kalabraki in December, 1982, and

    2. A payment of stg.£60,000 to Caviar Limited in November 1984.

Messrs. Brennan and McGowan did not provide any additional information to advance the Tribunal's knowledge of either of these transactions.

2-13   On the 28th February and 1st March, 2001 Mr. Burke gave evidence to the Tribunal confirming that there had been only two payments attributable to the offshore fundraising activities conducted by Mr. McGowan/Mr. Ottiwell, namely the stg.£50,000 and stg.£60,000 payments already referred to above. He specifically rejected a suggestion that a lodgment of stg.£15,000 to the Caviar account on the 19th April 1985 represented a separate payment from the stg.£50,000 and the stg.£60,000. Mr. Burke's explanation for this lodgment of stg.£15,000 was that it was a relodgment of the same sum, which had been taken from the same account on the 9th April 1985.

2-14 The Tribunal's further inquiries established that this account of events could not be true. Mr. Burke's Jersey company, Caviar Limited, was administered through Bedell & Cristin, a firm of Advocates in Jersey. The Tribunal obtained their Caviar file which bore the reference C992. The Tribunal noted that this file also contained references to dealings involving file reference C758, a company subsequently identified as Canio Limited. The Tribunal provided this information to the Irish solicitors currently acting on Mr. Burke's behalf in his dealings with the Tribunal.

2-15 Although all correspondence was being conducted through our respective solicitors, on the 12th March 2001, Mr. Burke wrote a personal letter to me, in which he effectively retracted substantial parts of the evidence, which he had given to the Tribunal to date, concerning the source of the funds lodged to his offshore account.

2-16 On the 13th March, 2001 the Tribunal informed Messrs. Brennan and McGowan's Irish solicitors, Messrs. Miley & Miley, of its knowledge of the existence of Bedell & Cristin file reference C758, and its apparent connection with payments made by Messrs. Brennan & McGowan to Mr. Burke. On the following day, Miley & Miley contacted Bedell &Cristin in Jersey and were informed by them that, whilst the identity of the corporate entity behind file reference C758 was not known to the Tribunal, the Tribunal was now aware of the connection between that entity and Mr. Burke's account. They also advised that compulsory disclosure procedures existed in Jersey which they expected would be availed of by the Tribunal if the information sought was not provided voluntarily.

2-17 It transpired that file reference C758 was the Bedell & Cristin file of Canio Limited, a Jersey company that was two-thirds owned by Mr. Brennan and Mr. McGowan, the existence of which had not been disclosed to the Tribunal. Messrs. Brennan and McGowan now retracted a substantial portion of their evidence in relation to the payment to Mr. Burke. In particular, it was now acknowledged that:

1. Kalabraki was a company wholly owned by Mr. Tom Brennan and that its funds were paid to Mr. Burke in December 1982.

2. The payment of £60,000 to Caviar was made by Canio Limited, a Jersey registered company, which had funded the payment from borrowings raised on the security of lands at Sandyford, Co. Dublin, and

3. That the payment of £15,000 to Mr. Burke in April 1985 was a separate payment made by Canio. Messrs. Brennan and McGowan now maintained that these payments were political donations made to Mr. Burke, in addition to the fundraising efforts of Mr. McGowan/Mr. Ottiwell, which had previously been referred to in their evidence to the Tribunal.

In view of the contradictory evidence given by both Mr. Burke and Messrs. Brennan and McGowan, the Tribunal concluded that it was necessary to fully investigate the financial relationship of those parties from the commencement of their relationship.

2-18 The Tribunal is in a position to reach conclusions in relation to the activities of Mr. Burke, Messrs. Brennan and McGowan, their related companies and associates on the following matters:

1. The circumstances in which Mr. Burke came to own his dwelling house, "Briargate", Swords, Co. Dublin.

2. The circumstances in which Mr. Burke came to open and operate offshore bank accounts between 1971 and 1994.

3. The sources of the funds lodged to Mr. Burke's offshore accounts in the Isle of Man and Jersey.

BRIARGATE

Background

2-19   On the 15th March 1972, Oakpark Developments Limited (Oakpark) purchased approximately two acres of the land on Folio 17423 at Malahide Road, Swords from the estate of the late Joseph Coleman (deceased) for a consideration of £7,000.In late 1972, Oakpark commenced the construction of a substantial dwelling house on the lands, to the design of Mr. Jack Keenan, prepared at the request of Mr. Burke. On the 1st August 1973, the dwelling house was substantially completed and Mr. Burke signed a contract to purchase approximately one acre of the lands for £7,500. On the 10th October 1973, Mr. Burke occupied the house built on the lands by Oakpark.

2-20   By the 25th February 1974, the sale of the land was completed between Mr. Burke's then solicitor, Mr. Oliver Conlon, and Oakpark's then solicitor, Mr. Esmond Reilly. No money passed between them at the time of closing or at any time.

2-21   On the 10th September 1997, in the question and answer session which followed upon Mr. Burke's personal statement to the Dáil concerning the claimed payment by James Gogarty of £30,000 to him, Mr. Burke said the following in relation to Briargate: -

> "I have with me the Land Registry documentation relating to my home which clearly shows that, far from being bought from a hospital patient under his care, the house and site was transferred to me and I bought it in a normal commercial transaction from Oldpark (*sic*) Developments Limited. The house was built in the normal commercial manner. I was doing business with that company. That transaction along with others was the subject of a Garda investigation in 1974"

2-22   The Tribunal examined the circumstances of the acquisition of the land and the construction of the dwelling house thereon, in the light of the evidence of substantial payments having been made offshore to Mr. Burke by Messrs. Brennan and McGowan and companies related to them. In Mr. Burke's statement to the Dáil he said that: -

1.   He had bought Briargate in a normal commercial transaction;

2.   The house was built in the normal commercial manner, and

3.   The transaction along with others was the subject of a Garda investigation in 1974.

2-23   For the reasons set out hereunder, the Tribunal is satisfied that:-

1.   Mr. Burke did not buy his home in a normal commercial transaction.

2.   The house was not built in the normal commercial manner.

3.   Mr. Burke's acquisition of his house and site was never the subject of a Garda investigation in 1974.

The acquisition of the lands upon which Briargate was built

2-24   The directors and shareholders of Oakpark were Mr. Tom Brennan, Mr. Michael (otherwise Jack) Foley, Mr. William Brennan (a brother of Mr. Tom Brennan), Mr. Bernard Cooke and Mr. James Lyons. Mr. William Brennan, Mr. Bernard Cooke and Mr. James Lyons did not have any direct dealings with Mr. Burke in connection with the sale of the land or the construction of the house. The sale of the land and construction of the house were dealt with by Mr. Jack Foley and Mr. Tom Brennan for Oakpark and Mr. Burke on his own behalf. References hereinafter to the directors of Oakpark are deemed to refer to Mr. Jack Foley and Mr. Tom Brennan only.

Mr. Burke's evidence as to the acquisition of Briargate

2-25   In a statement furnished to the Tribunal, dated 24th May 2001, Mr. Burke said that to the best of his recollection, whilst not certain, the site cost £7,500 and the construction of the house cost £15,000. He stated that, as he was the auctioneer for Oakpark, he would have paid part of the purchase price through fees owed to him by the company, but he did not identify in his statement which portion was paid through fees. He stated that he obtained loan approval from the Property Loan & Investment

Company Limited (PLIC) for £15,000 but, having obtained loan approval, his circumstances changed. He said that he sold the goodwill of his insurance brokerage business for £8,545 and that he did not have to draw down the full loan. Fees owed by Oakpark would have helped finance the transaction. He was not aware as to whether the balance was drawn down from PLIC or through an overdraft at Bank of Ireland, Whitehall.

The evidence of Mr. Tom Brennan and Mr. Jack Foley

2-26   Neither Mr. Brennan nor Mr. Foley provided evidence of there having been an agreement to set off fees due by Oakpark to P.J. Burke (Sales) Limited in lieu of the consideration which was due by Mr. Burke to Oakpark for sale of the site. Whilst Mr. Foley acknowledged that this was a possibility, he had no recollection of any such agreement.

2-27   The evidence of Mr. Esmond Reilly, solicitor to Oakpark, was that he was first instructed regarding the sale of portion of the lands in Folio 17423 to Mr. Burke in 1973. He said that he was told, probably by Mr. Jack Foley, that no monies would be paid over on foot of the transaction. He was never made aware by Mr. Foley of any set-off or other arrangement between Oakpark and Mr. Burke or P.J. Burke (Sales) Limited although such a set-off would not of itself have been necessarily unusual. Mr. Reilly's functions terminated with the completion of the sale on the 25th February 1974. His evidence was that in June 1974, he received a telephone call from Mr. Conlon, the solicitor who had acted for Mr. Burke in the purchase of the lands, requesting him to either "bury or lose" the conveyancing file which related to the sale of the lands by Oakpark to Mr. Burke. He considered this to be an extremely unusual occurrence.

2-28   The communication from Mr. Conlon had followed the publication of the article by Mr. Joe McAnthony concerning the document containing the entry "Ray Burke – Planning - £15,000". Despite Mr. Conlon's evidence to the contrary, the Tribunal is satisfied that such a telephone call did take place and believes that it was made in the context that inquiries might be made of the relationship, which existed at that time, between Messrs. Brennan and McGowan and Mr. Burke. The only unusual feature of the transaction known to Mr. Reilly at that time was that he, as solicitor for the Vendor, had not received any payment from the solicitor for the Purchaser for the land, which he was conveying.

Contemporaneous documents in the possession of Mr. Burke

2-29   Mr. Burke had no documentation of his own or from P.J. Burke (Sales) Limited, which would evidence the fact that P.J. Burke (Sales) Limited was owed money from Oakpark which it had offset against a liability which Mr. Burke had to Oakpark, arising from the acquisition of the land at Briargate. Mr. Burke did not have any written document showing a reconciliation of the amounts which were owed by Oakpark to P.J. Burke (Sales) Limited nor did he have any documentation showing how P.J. Burke (Sales) Limited had dealt with an advance to him of the credit which it had given to Oakpark for its having provided him with the house and lands.

2-30   The Tribunal sought documentation elsewhere. Subsequent to the provisions of the written statement of Mr. Burke to the Tribunal and the evidence of Mr. Foley and Mr. Brennan on this issue, documentation, which had been in the possession of the Revenue Commissioners concerning the financial affairs of Oakpark, was made available to the Tribunal. This documentation established:-

1. That the sale of the land on the 25th February 1974 was not recorded in the books of account of Oakpark. Oakpark had produced financial statements to the Revenue for the two-year period ending on the 31st October 1975, in which the sale of the site should have been reflected. However consideration of this documentation revealed that the lands in question were still shown as an asset of the company at their original purchase price of £7,381, that is the consideration of £7,000 together with expenses of £381. As of this date, the accounts ought to have shown an appropriate credit of £7,500 since the land had supposedly been sold to Mr. Burke for that sum within the period covered in the accounts.

2. In the accounts for Oakpark for the three-year period to the 31st October 1978, the cost of the lands had been reduced by an amount of £3,690, presumably to represent the fact that only one acre remained of the two acres originally purchased at a cost of £7,381. The correspondence, which passed between the auditors of Oakpark and the Revenue at that time, stated that:

"One half of the cost of this plot of land has been transferred to the directors in equal proportions, as approximately one half in area of this plot was acquired by them".

2-31   This explanation did not reflect that one-half of the lands had been sold to Mr. Burke for £7,500 of which some or all was paid, by way of set-off of fees due by Oakpark, to his company, P.J. Burke (Sales) Limited. By letter of 12th November, 1979, the auditors wrote addressing further queries from the Revenue arising out of this disclosure to say: -

"The area involved is approximately 1 acre and the plot of land was given by the directors in lieu of sums due by them in respect of professional services."

2-32   This explanation suggests that the directors took ownership of the land in question from the company and then gave it to Mr. Burke in lieu of professional services. However, this ignores the fact that the contract for the sale of the land was entered into between Mr. Burke, in his personal capacity, and the company Oakpark and not its directors. Any professional fees due in respect of auctioneering or estate agency services were due not by the directors, but by the company, Oakpark, and were due not to Mr. Burke in his personal capacity, but to his company P.J. Burke (Sales) Limited.

2-33   The Tribunal is satisfied that the manner in which the directors of Oakpark dealt with the transaction in Oakpark's books of account was not one which could, in any circumstances, be called a normal commercial transaction.

The alleged payment of £15,000 to Oakpark Developments Limited by Mr. Burke for the construction of the house at Briargate

2-34   In 1974, Mr. Burke's bank account was held at the Bank of Ireland, Whitehall, and his full banking file was not available at the time that he provided his statement to the Tribunal on the issue as to how he had acquired Briargate, but subsequently became available in November 2001. This file contained a copy of a letter dated 20th August 1974, initialled by Mr. J.K. Delaney, then assistant manager of the Bank of Ireland, Whitehall and since retired, which stated that Mr. Burke was granted bridging facilities secured upon a letter of undertaking from Mr. Oliver Conlon, his Solicitor, in September 1973. It stated that, on the 12th October 1973, Mr. Burke transferred £15,000 from a joint deposit account held, with his father, at that branch of Bank of Ireland to the bridging loan account.

2-35   Mr. Burke told the Tribunal that this letter was written for the sole purpose of satisfying the Gardaí as to how he had paid for his house, and that this was as a result of an inquiry raised in the context of the Garda investigation, which followed upon the Joe McAnthony article. Mr. Burke said that the inference which the Tribunal should draw from this letter was either:-

1. That he had been granted and drew down a bridging loan from Bank of Ireland in September 1973, in the sum of £15,000 which he paid to Oakpark and which he subsequently repaid by way of transfer from the joint deposit account with his father, or

2. That he withdrew £15,000 from the joint deposit account in October 1973 and paid that sum to Oakpark.

2-36   Mr. Burke, in evidence, pointed to the fact that the withdrawal of the £15,000 from the joint deposit account in October 1973 accorded with the period in which he commenced occupation of the house on the 10th October 1973. Mr. Burke sought to use the letter from the Bank as corroboration of the fact that £15,000 had been paid from funds, either on deposit or borrowed from Bank of Ireland, to Oakpark. In so doing, however, Mr. Burke was offering an explanation, which had not been provided in his written statement to the Tribunal, in which the only identified sources of the payment to Oakpark were the proceeds of sale of his insurance brokerage business and a set-off of monies due by Oakpark to the auctioneering business.

2-37   The evidence of Mr. Jack Foley was not that the house was paid for in one £15,000 payment in October 1973, but that three cheques drawn on the Irish Permanent Building Society, totalling £15,500, had been paid during the course of construction of the house. He said that these payments arrived unannounced and unexplained to him and that he had not made any arrangements for obtaining payment for the house. There was, however, no other evidence of any involvement of Irish Permanent Building Society with this property.

2-38   Mr. Delaney gave evidence that, whilst a bridging facility was offered to Mr. Burke, he concluded, that it had never been taken up. The facility had been offered on the basis that Mr. Burke's solicitor, Mr. Oliver Conlon, had given an undertaking to lodge with the Bank of Ireland the proceeds of a loan cheque which would issue from PLIC. Mr. Delaney was satisfied that, if the bridging facility had been utilised by Mr. Burke, the cheque from Bank of Ireland would have issued only to Mr. Conlon and that this did not occur.

2-39   The Tribunal is satisfied that if borrowed monies had been used by Mr. Burke to acquire the property, the lenders would have insisted upon their interests being protected by appropriate undertakings from the solicitor holding the deeds or by registration of their interest as a burden on the Folio of the land. The Tribunal is satisfied that neither course was adopted and, consequently, that no financial institution was involved in providing a loan to Mr. Burke to acquire his interest in Briargate.

2-40   Mr. Delaney gave evidence that he was never asked by the Gardaí to explain how Mr. Burke had financed the purchase of his home and, consequently, his letter of the 12th August 1974 was not written in order to explain that transaction.

2-41   The Tribunal is satisfied that the coincidence in the figures of £15,000, between the newspaper article of Mr. McAnthony and the entry in the accounts of Mr. Burke recording a transfer of that amount, caused the Gardaí to seek an explanation for that entry, and that Mr. Delaney's response was specifically directed towards explaining that transaction. The Tribunal is satisfied that if the Gardaí inquiries were, as stated by Mr. Burke, directed towards establishing how he had paid for the house, the reply from the bank would have specifically addressed that issue. It did not do so. Mr. Delaney had no personal knowledge as to how Mr. Burke had financed his house and would not have been in a position to respond to such a query if he had been asked by the Gardaí. What limited knowledge he had was that a bridging facility had been extended to Mr. Burke, which was not taken up.

Acknowledgement of payment of monies by Mr. Burke to Oakpark in the books of account of Oakpark

2-42   It was accepted, by those of the directors of Oakpark who gave evidence on this issue, that the documentation discovered to the Tribunal from the Revenue Commissioners, which recorded the financial dealings of Oakpark between 1971 and 1978, did not reveal any record of any monies having been paid by Mr. Burke to Oakpark. The costs of the construction of the dwelling house at Briargate ought to have been recorded in the accounts provided by the company to the Revenue. However, the documentation provided to the Tribunal showed that none of the costs of the construction of Briargate were so recorded. The Tribunal considers that it follows that these costs of construction must have been allocated to other developments.

2-43   The Tribunal considers that what did take place, in relation to the acquisition and financing of Mr. Burke's home, was not what would have been expected in a normal commercial transaction. The Tribunal is satisfied that the transaction, under which Mr. Burke acquired his home and lands at Briargate, did not have the hallmarks of a normal commercial transaction. So far as the transfer of the site to Mr. Burke by Oakpark is concerned, it is clear that the auditors to Oakpark were not informed by the directors, Mr. Tom Brennan and Mr. Jack Foley, of a contract for the sale of the site to Mr. Burke for £7,500. They were not informed that it was intended that some or all of this consideration would be met by a set-off of funds due to Mr. Burke's company. No set-off of any account is shown in the books of account prepared by the auditors. The standard accounting entries, which should have applied in the reduction of the land value following on the set-off of fees, were not applied in connection with this transaction. These directors of Oakpark concealed the true nature of the transaction from Oakpark's auditors.

2-44   Notwithstanding that Mr. Burke was in possession of the dwelling house and lands since October 1973, the contract for the sale of the land was not completed until the 25th February 1974 without any consideration passing at the time of closing. The agreement under which the house was built does not have the hallmarks of a normal commercial transaction, because there was no signed contract entered into by the parties and there was no record of any payment made to the builders, either in the course of construction or on completion of the dwelling, as would be normal.

CONCLUSIONS ON THE ACQUISITION OF BRIARGATE

2-45   The Tribunal is satisfied that the probable explanation for the fact that there is no accurate record of either the amount paid by Mr. Burke to Oakpark, or the manner in which any such payment was made, lies in the fact that Mr. Burke and the directors of Oakpark, Mr. Tom Brennan and Mr. Jack Foley, had reached an agreement under which he would receive the property for a consideration which was less than open market value. The Tribunal is satisfied that Mr. Burke and these directors of Oakpark conducted their affairs in such a manner that no record of the actual consideration (if any) paid to Oakpark by Mr. Burke was available for scrutiny.

2-46   The Tribunal believes that, on the balance of probabilities, the true circumstances in which Mr. Burke acquired this property were such as to amount to the conferring upon him of a substantial benefit. The Tribunal is satisfied that Mr. Burke, Mr. Brennan and Mr. Foley have not given a truthful account of how Mr. Burke came to acquire this property. The Tribunal believes that the probable explanation for their failure to do so is the fact that the benefit thereby provided to Mr. Burke would not withstand scrutiny. The Tribunal believes, that the reasonable inference to be drawn from the facts proved, is that the motive for providing such benefit was an improper motive connected with Mr. Burke's position as an elected representative of Dublin County Council, a body with which Mr. Brennan's companies had extensive dealings at that time, and which could have been influenced by Mr. Burke. The Tribunal notes Mr. Burke's statement to the Dáil of the 10th September 1997, where he stated in the context of the JMSE payment to him that: "So far as the 1989 situation is concerned, there could have been some concern if I was a member of a local authority and in a position to influence any decision", as an acknowledgment by him of the apparent impropriety, which would result from his receipt of a substantial benefit from the directors of a building company, while he was a member of Dublin County Council.

OTHER COMMERCIAL DEALINGS BETWEEN MR. BURKE AND MESSRS. BRENNAN & MCGOWAN AND THEIR RELATED COMPANIES AND ASSOCIATES

Payments within the jurisdiction

2-47   While Mr. Burke was a member of Dublin County Council from 1967 onwards and an elected member of Dáil Éireann from 1973 onwards, he continued to conduct his auctioneering and estate agency business, P.J. Burke (Sales) Limited. The major clients of this company were companies in which Mr. Tom Brennan or Messrs. Brennan and McGowan had an interest. These companies were building houses in County Dublin which were being sold by Mr. Burke. Mr. Burke ceased his auctioneering business in 1982. Evidence established that between April 1975 and August 1982, the current account of P.J. Burke (Sales) Limited, at Bank of Ireland, Whitehall, was in receipt of a payment of £1,000 per month from Kilnamanagh Estates Limited, a Brennan & McGowan company.

2-48   Mr. Burke stated that these funds were probably lodged to the account on foot of an agreement, which he had reached with Mr. Tom Brennan regarding payment to P.J. Burke (Sales) Limited, for services rendered. Mr. Burke said that this arrangement provided for payment against the gross fees due to his company. There was no evidence of a formal balancing exercise ever having been carried out to establish whether or not these payments reflected the actual indebtedness of the Brennan & McGowan companies to his firm. There was no variation in the amount, paid monthly over a period of almost seven years, save for the final payment made in August 1982, which was for £2,000. The Tribunal considers this to be unusual, given that estate agents' fees are normally paid on a commission basis related to the value of the properties sold.

2-49   The Tribunal's consideration of the bank accounts of P.J. Burke (Sales) Limited, at Bank of Ireland, indicated that the vast majority of the sums lodged to this account were transferred on to the personal account of Mr. Burke. It is not clear how these transfers were treated in the books of account of P.J. Burke (Sales) Limited. However, it is apparent from the evidence of Mr. Burke that no reconciliation ever took place as between the work done by P.J. Burke (Sales) Limited and the amount due to P.J. Burke (Sales) Limited by Brennan & McGowan companies.

2-50   Accordingly the Tribunal concludes on the balance of probabilities that the £1,000 per month payment to the account of P.J. Burke Sales Limited was a retainer paid by the Brennan & McGowan companies and that Mr. Burke was the recipient of the majority of these funds.

2-51 The Tribunal concludes that whilst these were effectively substantial payments made to Mr. Burke by Brennan & McGowan companies through P.J. Burke (Sales) Limited, there is no evidence to establish that they were made for a corrupt purpose.

Chapter 3

Payments made outside the Jurisdiction

OFFSHORE BANK ACCOUNTS OPENED AND OPERATED BY MR. BURKE

3-01   Although Mr. Burke was at all times a resident of the Irish Republic, he opened and operated a number of bank accounts outside this jurisdiction from 1971 onwards. Between 1954 and 1992, Exchange Control legislation prohibited residents of the Republic of Ireland from opening or operating foreign currency accounts outside the State, save in limited circumstances that did not apply to Mr. Burke. Mr. Burke was aware of the Exchange Control regulations, both in his personal capacity as a citizen as he had sought Exchange Control permission to take limited funds out of the jurisdiction at the time of his marriage in 1972, and also as Minister for Justice, a position that he held from July 1989 until February 1992.

3-02   Mr. Burke, in his evidence, acknowledged that he had maintained accounts abroad which were in breach of the Exchange Control Regulations, but he offered as an explanation that these were matters of a "fairly technical application."

3-03   The Tribunal sought to establish how and why Mr. Burke had chosen to open and operate bank accounts in breach of the then current legislation. The Tribunal established in evidence the circumstances surrounding the opening and operation of a number of offshore bank accounts. The Tribunal endeavoured to trace the source of lodgments made to these accounts and the disbursements made from these accounts, in order to establish whether or not the monies lodged to the accounts amounted to corrupt payments.

3-04   The evidence heard before the Tribunal established that the following accounts were opened and operated by Mr. Burke in jurisdictions outside the Republic of Ireland from 1971 onwards: -

1. Foster Finance (NI) Limited
This account was opened on the 18th August 1971 in Belfast, and was operated until the 29th November 1972.

2. Bank of Ireland, Manchester
This account was opened on the 6th December 1974 in Manchester, and operated until the 28th December 1977.

3. AIB Bank (Isle of Man) Limited
This account was opened on 21st December 1982 in Douglas, and was operated until the 17th April 1984.

4. Allied Irish Bank, Bruton Street, London
This account was opened on the 30th November 1983 in London, and closed on the 5th December 1983.

5. Hill Samuel & Company (Jersey) Limited
This account was opened on the 19th April 1984 in St. Helier, and was operated until the 19th July 1994.

3-05   All of the above named accounts were sterling accounts. In addition to the above listed accounts, Mr. Burke indicated that he had operated an account at Allied Irish Bank, Bruton Street, London for a number of years. The evidence from Allied Irish Bank Bruton Street witnesses did not support Mr. Burke's evidence in this regard. The only recorded account, which existed at that branch, is that set out above as having operated between the 30th November 1983 and 5th December 1983.

MR. BURKE'S EXPLANATION FOR OPENING OFFSHORE ACCOUNTS

Foster Finance (NI) Limited

3-06 This account was opened through Bank of Ireland, Whitehall, where Mr. Burke had his account at the time. The account was opened in Mr. Burke's own name. Mr. Burke did not disclose the existence of this account to the Tribunal in his response to the written inquiries made of him by the Tribunal. His subsequent explanation to the Tribunal, for not doing so, was that he had forgotten about it. Mr. Burke was questioned as to the source of the sum lodged to this account, but was unable to give any evidence as to the source of the lodgment to this account. He assumed that the source of the lodgment was funds paid to P.J. Burke (Sales) Limited, the auctioneering company which had been founded by him. He had no adequate explanation as to why monies due to this company were lodged to his personal bank account maintained outside the State. The books of account of P.J. Burke (Sales) Limited were not available to the Tribunal, and it was not possible to establish if such sums were drawings from the company, or how such drawings by Mr. Burke had been treated in the books of account of the company. Mr. Burke stated that he believed that they would have been treated as directors' loans. The funds, standing to this account in Northern Ireland, were repatriated on the 29th November 1972, but Mr. Burke was not in a position to give evidence as to how these specific sum was expended. The Tribunal has concluded that Mr. Burke has not provided any reasonably comprehensible explanation for his having opened this account in Northern Ireland.

Bank of Ireland, Manchester

3-07 This account was opened in Manchester through Bank of Ireland, Whitehall, in Mr. Burke's own name. Lodgments to this account were made between December 1974 and February 1976. The existence of this account was not disclosed by Mr. Burke to the Tribunal, in response to the written requests made of him, to disclose all bank accounts both within and outside the jurisdiction. The funds lodged to this account remained offshore until the 28th December 1977, when £14,584.49 was repatriated to his personal account at Bank of Ireland, Whitehall. In correspondence, Mr. Burke was asked to account for the source of the lodgment of £14,584.49 to his personal account. In response to specific queries regarding the lodgment of this sum to his account, Mr. Burke was unable to identify the source of these funds.

3-08 The existence of the Manchester account was subsequently established by the Tribunal, as a result of documents produced by the Bank of Ireland. The Tribunal has not received any satisfactory explanation from Mr. Burke as to why monies, the property of P.J. Burke (Sales) Limited, were on deposit in accounts in his name in Manchester.

AIB Bank (Isle of Man) Limited

3-09 On the 21st December 1982, the sum of stg.£50,000 was lodged to Account No. 06472/00 at this bank. The documentary evidence established that the account was opened in the Isle of Man through the offices of Allied Irish Bank at Bruton Street, London. The account holder is named as Mr. Patrick D. Burke with an address at Bethany, 43 Church Lane, Holybourne, Nr Alton, Hampshire. Whereas there is no apparent connection between Mr. Raphael P. Burke of Briargate, Swords, County Dublin and Mr. Patrick D. Burke, of Hampshire, Mr. Ray Burke acknowledged in evidence that he is the account holder. The address, given at the time of opening the account, was an address occupied by his sister-in-law. The evidence established that A.I.B. Bank (Isle of Man) Limited was directed to communicate with Mr. Burke at the Hampshire address. Mr. Burke put in place a system whereby any such correspondence would be redirected by the occupant to him in Swords.

3-10 In his initial dealings with the Tribunal, Mr. Burke failed to disclose the existence of his account at AIB Bank (Isle of Man) Limited. Mr. Burke subsequently stated that the account was opened on his instructions with the intention of receiving a lodgment from Messrs. Brennan & McGowan, and that he gave Mr. McGowan and Mr. Ottiwell details which would allow them to lodge the funds into this account. No contemporaneous documentation created by the donor exists which identifies the lodgment as being one which was made as a result of a direction given by Mr. Burke.

3-11 No documentation exists to establish that a payment was made by Messrs. Ottiwell & McGowan as stated by Mr. Burke. In fact, the Tribunal established that the payment was made by a company called Kalabraki, a company which was wholly owned by Mr. Brennan and in which Mr. McGowan had no beneficial interest. No Kalabraki documentation identifying the nature of the payment to Mr. Burke has been made available to the Tribunal. No receipt or acknowledgement of payment was issued by Mr. Burke following the receipt of these funds to his account. No covering letter or confirmation of payment having been made was written by Mr. Brennan.

3-12   There were four withdrawals from the account during the currency of its operation, none of which coincide with the date of elections in which Mr. Burke was a candidate. Mr. Burke's explanation for opening this account was that it was for reasons of confidentiality and to receive political donations, which had been raised abroad. Apart from the opening lodgment of £50,000, the only other lodgment, interest apart, was a sum of £10,000, which was lodged to the fixed version of this account on the 9th December 1983. Mr. Burke claimed that this was a partial relodgment of a sum of £15,000, withdrawn by him on the 29th November 1983, from this account.

Allied Irish Bank, Bruton Street, London

3-13   The account opened by Mr. Burke at the Allied Irish Bank, Bruton Street, London was opened in the name of P.D. Burke, with the same address in Hampshire as had been given in respect of the Isle of Man account. Mr. Burke's claim that he had operated an account at this branch for years has not been substantiated. As with other accounts held abroad, Mr. Burke maintains that the account held at Allied Irish Bank, Bruton Street was held for purposes of confidentiality and also, in this instance, for convenience.

Hill Samuel and Company, Jersey

3-14   The bank account at Hill Samuel & Company, Jersey differed from the accounts held at Allied Irish Bank in London and the Isle of Man, insofar as the account was not opened in the name of Burke. The evidence established that this account was opened in the following circumstances:

3-15   In early 1984, Mr. Burke instructed Mr. Oliver Conlon, his Dublin solicitor, to arrange for the setting up of a Jersey registered company. The curiously named Caviar Limited (Caviar) was incorporated in Jersey on the 10th April 1984 by a local firm, Bedell & Cristin, Advocates of Normandy House, Grenville Street, St. Helier, Jersey, on Mr. Conlon's instructions. The registered office of the new company was the same address as the offices of Bedell & Cristin. By the 19th April 1984, a bank account was opened at Hill Samuel and Company (Jersey) Limited, in the name of Canio.

3-16   Bedell & Cristin were furnished with an instruction that all correspondence in connection with Caviar (which would automatically include bank statements) was to be placed in a sealed envelope and sent to Mr. A. Burke, c/o Mr. Oliver Conlon, solicitor in Dublin. Mr. Burke gave this instruction to Bedell & Cristin directly. Mr. Conlon stated that he forwarded some correspondence to Mr. Burke under this system. Mr. Burke confirmed that he received some correspondence under this system. There was, therefore, no direct communication between Hill Samuel and Company (Jersey) Limited and Mr. Burke in connection with the account of Caviar.

3-17   The Tribunal is satisfied that Mr. Burke gave this instruction to Bedell & Cristin for the purpose of ensuring that there would be no obvious direct or discernible connection between this company, Caviar, and its bank account and himself.

3-18   The Jersey Companies Office details record that the shareholders in Caviar were Laurence Anthony Wheeler, Alisdair Fraser McDonald and Howard Oke Dart, all of whom were members of the firm of Bedell & Cristin. Each one of these individuals, however, executed a Declaration of Trust in respect of the shares they held in Caviar, in which they declared, in private, that they held the issued shares as a nominee of, and trustees for, Mr. and Mrs. P.D. Burke of Church Lane, Holybourne, Nr Alton, Hampshire. This information was not publicly available. The directors of the company were Mrs. H. L.G. Gibson and Mr. Gerard King both of Sark, Channel Islands, and Mr. Laurence Wheeler of Bedell & Cristin.

3-19   It is noteworthy that the same firm of Advocates acted in a similar fashion in setting up companies which were either individually or jointly owned by Messrs. Brennan and McGowan or by Messrs Brennan and McGowan and Mr. John Finnegan. The beneficial owners of these latter companies were similarly protected from public scrutiny by the device of registering the members of the firm of Bedell & Cristin as shareholders, whilst they held their shares as nominees for the true owners.

3-20   Caviar was opened for the sole purpose of receiving funds for and on behalf of Mr. Burke. The company carried out no activity other than to be the account holder of a bank account at Hill Samuel to which funds were lodged including those which are the subject of detailed examination hereafter, namely stg.£35,000 in April 1984, stg.£60,000 in November 1984 and stg.£15,000 in April 1985, a total of stg.£110,000. By holding a bank account in the name of a company, in which he was not registered as either a director or a shareholder, Mr. Burke imposed an additional layer of secrecy over his offshore financial affairs.

3-21   The Tribunal concludes that the history of Mr. Burke's offshore financial dealings illustrates an increasing level of sophistication in the concealment of the existence of these accounts, proceeding from his holding accounts in his own name abroad, through holding accounts in false names with addresses other than his own address, and culminating in his holding an account through a corporate structure which could not be identified with him.

3-22   The Tribunal believes that Mr. Burke's accounts in the Isle of Man and in Jersey were not opened solely for the purpose of maintaining the confidentiality of Mr. Burke's affairs. Mr. Burke stated that the monies lodged to these accounts were the proceeds of political fundraising events conducted for his benefit abroad. The Tribunal is satisfied that, even if this were the true source of the funds, it would not afford an explanation for these monies being lodged and maintained in offshore accounts. Legitimate political donations, received by a politician, were not taxable in the hands of the recipient. If the funds were required for political purposes, it would have been reasonable to expect that regular withdrawals for that purpose would be shown in the accounts, whereas the operation of the Caviar account is consistent with the monies being maintained on long term interest bearing deposits.

THE EXTENT OF MR. BURKE'S OFFSHORE FINANCIAL ACTIVITY AS ESTABLISHED BY THE TRIBUNAL

3-23   The documentation considered by the Tribunal established that withdrawals totalling stg.£265,400.90 were made from Mr. Burke's offshore accounts, between November 1983 and July 1994. Mr. Burke claims that this figure includes a number of re-lodgments. In particular, he claimed that the stg.£15,000 deposited in his account at Allied Irish Bank in Bruton Street on the 30th November 1983 was one and the same as the stg.£15,000 withdrawn from AIB Bank (Isle of Man) Limited on the 29th November1983. Of this stg.£15,000 withdrawn from the Isle of Man on the 29th November 1983, he claimed that stg.£10,000 was re-lodged. Of the stg.£39,948.03 withdrawn from the Isle of Man account on the 17th April 1984, he claimed that stg.£35,000 was lodged to the Caviar account in Jersey. Based on acceptance of Mr. Burke's own figures, withdrawals from his offshore account amounted to stg.£205,400.90. In seeking to explain how these sums were expended, Mr. Burke indicated that all of the monies were brought back to Ireland in cash. The money was in sterling and he said that it was either kept in his safe or converted into Irish currency and spent for political purposes. Alternatively, it was lodged to Irish bank accounts and any withdrawals were subsequently spent on political purposes. Some of these monies remain in his accounts to this day.

3-24   On Mr. Burke's own figures, stg.£122,862.27 was lodged to bank accounts in Ireland and stg.£82,538.63 was dispersed in cash. Mr. Burke has not produced a single vouching document or established that any part of the stg.£82,538.63 was in fact expended for political purposes, nor has Mr. Burke produced any adequate documentation to establish, that any withdrawals from the accounts in which he says he lodged stg.£122,862.27 were expended for political purposes.

3-25   The Tribunal is not satisfied that Mr. Burke's evidence as to the amount of monies lodged to his accounts or the purpose for which he expended the monies is correct. The Tribunal does not accept that the monies gathered by Mr. Burke abroad, constituted a political fund. Mr. Burke did not reveal the existence of these monies to any member of his constituency organisation, nor did he inform his political party that he was maintaining such a fund at any time prior to his retirement from politics. Mr. Burke was asked in the Dáil on 10th September 1997 whether he held an offshore account, and he responded in the negative. Whereas his response may have been correct that day, insofar as the Caviar account had closed in 1994 and therefore he did not have an offshore account at that particular time, it did present an opportunity to Mr. Burke to reveal that he had maintained offshore accounts between 1982 and 1994 in which allegedly political funds were held. He chose not to do so. The Tribunal believes that in giving the response that he did, Mr. Burke seriously misrepresented the true position in relation to the subject matter of the questioning. Mr. Burke has laterally claimed that the proceeds of his offshore bank accounts constitute a political fund, which will be used for political purposes notwithstanding that he has retired from active politics.

3-26   The trustees of the shareholding in Caviar did not hold their shareholding in trust for any political party, political organisation or grouping, but declared they held their shareholding for the benefit of Mr. and Mrs. P. D. Burke.

3-27 The Tribunal considers it improbable that Mr. Burke would have established a political fund through a corporation the shareholding in which was secretly held by trustees for him and using a name and address which was not his own. Furthermore, if the fund was a political fund as claimed, it would be reasonable to assume that the trustees of the shares would have held their shares either for the local constituency organisation or the Fianna Fáil party.

3-28 In the course of his evidence, Mr. Burke offered as an explanation for his presence in Jersey in April 1985, the fact that he wished to ensure that his wife, Mrs. Ann Burke would have access to the Caviar account in the event of his death, as he described it "in the event of me being hit by the mythical bus". The Tribunal is satisfied that this explanation is untrue as the correspondence from Hill Samuel & Company dated 4th June 1985, addressed to Bedell & Cristin, informed them that the account was to be operated on the sole signature of Mr. P.D. Burke. It is clear therefore that no instruction was given to the bank in April 1985 by Mr. Burke to allow for access to the account by Mrs. Burke. However, the significance of this evidence is that Mr. Burke considered in his mind that the person who should have access to the account after his death was his wife, although it is clear that she did not have any role to play in the operation, or management of a political fund.

3-29 The Tribunal believes that Mr. Burke, at all times, treated the monies held in offshore accounts as his own funds to be expended as he wished, and that there is no question of these funds representing a political fund to be passed on to others engaged in politics upon his demise or retirement.

3-30 The Tribunal is satisfied that the monies lodged to Mr. Burke's offshore accounts were not the proceeds of political fundraising events as claimed. Insofar as the Tribunal has identified the source of monies paid to these accounts, such source was one of the following; Messrs. Brennan and McGowan, a company controlled by Mr. Tom Brennan solely or a company controlled by Mr. Brennan, Mr. McGowan and Mr. John Finnegan. The role of Mr. Brennan, Mr. McGowan and Mr. Finnegan in the context of their dealings with Mr. Burke is set out in detail hereafter.

CONCLUSION AS TO WHY MR. BURKE OPENED OFFSHORE ACCOUNTS

3-31 The Tribunal is satisfied that Mr. Burke opened offshore accounts so as to conceal the fact that he was the recipient of the funds contained in those accounts because the circumstances in which he came to be paid these sums would not withstand public scrutiny.

Chapter 4

Payments made to Mr. Burke's Offshore Accounts Attributed to Messrs. Brennan & McGowan, their related Companies and Associates

4-01   The Tribunal examined the circumstances surrounding four particular lodgments to Mr. Burke's offshore accounts, the first of which was made to his account at AIB Bank (Isle of Man) Limited and the remainder to the account of Caviar at Hill Samuel and Company (Jersey) Limited.

THE LODGMENT OF STG £50,000 TO AIB BANK (ISLE OF MAN) LIMITED ON THE 21ST DECEMBER 1982

4-02   While Mr. Burke had disclosed the existence of an offshore bank account held by him in Jersey, in the name of Caviar Limited, and gave evidence that the monies lodged to this account were the proceeds of political fundraising activities (earlier identified by him as simply having been carried out in the UK, and later identified by him to have been carried out by Mr. Joseph McGowan and Mr. Ernest Ottiwell) he did not reveal the existence of his Isle of Man bank account to the Tribunal until the 28th June 2000. Having done so, he revised the amount which he said was lodged to the Jersey account by stating that the stg.£35,000 lodgment made to that account in April 1984 was, sourced by way of a withdrawal of stg.£39,948.03, being the balance of the stg.£50,000 which had been lodged to the Isle of Man account in December 1982. The total of the payments from fundraising activities now admitted to by Mr. Burke, was stg.£110,000 and not stg.£95,000 as formerly stated on his behalf. Mr. Burke adopted Mr. McGowan's evidence, given in April 2000, as to how the UK fundraising activities were conducted, and he now attributed, albeit belatedly, the stg.£50,000 payment in December 1982 to such activities.

4-03   In the course of giving their evidence in April 2000, Mr. McGowan, in the presence of Mr. Brennan, denied operating offshore accounts in the Channel Islands or elsewhere. Mr. Brennan denied making any personal payment to Mr. Burke. He failed to disclose that his offshore company, Kalabraki, had paid stg.£50,000 to Mr. Burke in December 1982. Mr. McGowan claimed that the proceeds of their fundraising activities were dealt with by Mr. Ernest Ottiwell, a self appointed treasurer of the proceeds of these fundraising activities. It was said that Mr. Ottiwell handled the payment of the monies to Mr. Burke.

4-04   The Tribunal has established in evidence the following to be the true facts: -

1. Mr. Tom Brennan did operate offshore accounts in the Channel Islands.

2. Mr. Brennan was the sole beneficial owner of a company called Kalabraki Limited.

3. Kalabraki paid the stg.£50,000 to the account of Mr. Burke in the Isle of Man in December 1982.

4. Neither Mr. Joseph McGowan nor Mr. Ernest Ottiwell had any interest in Kalabraki.

5. The transfer to Mr. Burke's account was not effected through either Mr. McGowan or Mr. Ottiwell, but was made as a result of a direction given by Mr. Laurence Wheeler, Advocate, of Bedell & Cristin, Advocates, in Jersey to Jersey International Bank of Commerce Limited, which resulted in the funds being taken from the account of Kalabraki and paid to the account of Mr. P.D. Burke in the Isle of Man.

4-05   The Tribunal is satisfied that these facts establish that the sum of stg.£50,000, lodged to Mr. Burke's account in the Isle of Man in December 1982, was not the proceeds of any fundraising activity conducted by Mr. McGowan or Mr. Ottiwell, and that it represented a single payment of stg.£50,000 from Mr. Tom Brennan to Mr. Burke and was not an accumulated fund raised from individual subscribers in the UK.

4-06 The Tribunal is satisfied that Mr. Brennan was at all times aware that he had made such a payment to Mr. Burke, and that he knowingly misled the Tribunal in giving evidence on the 10th April 2000 to the Tribunal that he had not made any payment to Mr. Burke. The Tribunal rejects Mr. Burke's evidence that he first learned of the fact that Mr. Brennan was the payer of these monies in the year 2001. The money could not have been lodged into the account of Mr. Burke by Mr. Brennan through Mr. Wheeler, unless Mr. Burke had informed Mr. Brennan of the account into which it should be lodged. Mr. Brennan had no legitimate reason to conceal the fact that he had paid Mr. Burke stg.£50,000 in 1982. They were then, and have remained close friends. The information, provided by Mr. Burke, to enable the payment to be lodged to this account was in turn transmitted to Mr. Wheeler, who transmitted it to the bank official at Jersey International Bank of Commerce Limited who effected the actual transfer. This information was that the money should be credited to the account of Mr. Patrick D. Burke at Allied Irish Bank (Isle of Man) Limited.

4-07 The Tribunal believes that Mr. Burke and Mr. Wheeler were not known to each other at this time, and accordingly, the instruction to transfer the stg.£50,000 did not come directly from Mr. Burke. Mr. Wheeler would only have acted in relation to Kalabraki's affairs on the instructions of its owner, Mr. Brennan, and would only have disposed of that company's assets on the instructions of Mr. Brennan. The Tribunal is satisfied that the transfer was not made as a result of any instructions given by Mr. McGowan or Mr. Ottiwell. Mr. Brennan now maintains that the payment, which was made by Kalabraki to Mr. Burke, was a political donation to "Ray Burke/Fianna Fáil". The Tribunal rejects this evidence. As the identity of the recipient of the funds can only have been given to Mr. Wheeler by Mr. Brennan, it follows that Mr. Brennan knew that his stg.£50,000 payment was not being paid to "Ray Burke/Fianna Fáil", but was being paid to an account held in the name of Patrick D. Burke.

4-08 At the time of the payment in 1982, stg.£50,000 was an enormous sum. It represented three times the gross annual income of Mr. Burke. It was being paid offshore to an account, which Mr. Brennan, knew was not held in the true name of the intended recipient, Mr. Ray Burke. The active concealment of the existence of this payment, and the failure of Mr. Brennan to give an explanation for such payment when asked to do so by the Tribunal, are indicative of Mr. Brennan's wish to conceal this transaction from the Tribunal, which he knew was investigating Mr. Burke's offshore accounts.

4-09 The Tribunal concludes, on the balance of probabilities, that Mr. Brennan did not make the payment of stg.£50,000 in 1982 in the belief that he was making a legitimate political donation as claimed by him to "Ray Burke/Fianna Fail", but made it in the knowledge that it was a payment to Mr. Burke which would not withstand public scrutiny because, in the opinion of the Tribunal, it was a corrupt payment.

MR. BURKE'S EVIDENCE IN RELATION TO THE STG.£50,000 PAYMENT TO HIS AIB BANK (ISLE OF MAN) LIMITED ACCOUNT

4-10 Mr. Burke acknowledged that he opened this account to receive the payment. He said that the reason he used the name Patrick D. Burke was for confidentiality. The Tribunal is satisfied that Mr. Burke had not been given any reason to believe that the confidentiality of his Irish banking affairs was, at any time breached, and concludes that there was no valid reason for his using a name, other than his real name, to open an account if he intended to conduct his legitimate affairs through this account.

4-11 Mr. Burke said that the information necessary to allow Messrs. McGowan and Ottiwell to make the lodgment to this account was given by him to them. The Tribunal is satisfied that it is unlikely that this occurred in the manner described by Mr. Burke, as the donation was made by Mr. Brennan solely, and not by Messrs. McGowan and Ottiwell. For Mr. Burke's account of events to be true, it would have involved Mr. Brennan, Mr. Ottiwell and Mr. McGowan concealing from Mr. Burke the fact that the payment was made solely by Mr. Brennan. The Tribunal rejects this as implausible. The Tribunal is satisfied that Mr. Burke opened the account in a name other than his own and with an address other than his real address so as to ensure that the transactions which were conducted through this account remained secret. Mr. Burke had concealed the existence of this account from the Tribunal until the 28th June 2000. The Tribunal is satisfied that Mr. Burke made arrangements in 1982 with Mr.

Brennan to lodge stg.£50,000 to the account and that at the time of receipt of this money, neither of them believed that the payment was a political donation.

THE LODGMENT OF STG.£35,000 TO THE ACCOUNT OF CAVIAR ON THE 19TH APRIL 1984

4-12   When giving evidence to the Tribunal for the first time in July 1999, Mr. Burke disclosed an offshore account, which was maintained in Jersey, and into which lodgments were made of monies allegedly raised in political fundraising activities held in the UK, earlier identified to the Tribunal as having being conducted by Messrs. Brennan and McGowan. It had been put to Mr. McGowan, on Mr. Burke's behalf, that there were two payments only to this account, stg.£35,000 and stg.£60,000 respectively in April and November 1984. Once Mr. Burke revealed the existence of his second offshore account in the Isle of Man, he changed the explanation for this stg.£35,000 lodgment, saying that it represented part of the proceeds of the earlier deposit by Kalabraki of stg.£50,000 to the Isle of Man account. He still maintained, however, that this sum of stg.£35,000 represented the proceeds of the fundraising activities, involving Mr. McGowan and Mr. Ottiwell.

4-13   The Tribunal has established that the stg.£50,000 in question was not the result of political fundraising activities in the UK but rather was sourced from the resources of Mr. Brennan solely. Mr. Burke is incorrect in his evidence that this sum represented the proceeds of UK fundraising activities. In addition the Tribunal sought to establish whether, in fact the stg.£35,000 lodged to the Jersey account represents a withdrawal of the Kalabraki funds, or whether it represents a separate, distinct payment to Mr. Burke.

4-14   The bank records of A.I.B. Bank (Isle of Man) Limited established that a sum of stg.£39,948.03 was withdrawn in London from the account of Mr. P.D. Burke in the Isle of Man on the 17th April 1984. The withdrawal took place as a result of a written request for the debit of that sum which was lodged with Allied Irish Bank, Bruton Street, London, signed by Mr. Burke as Patk. Burke on the 17th April 1984. This written document was forwarded to AIB Bank (Isle of Man) Limited. The evidence established the transfer as being one involving "same day value", which means that Allied Irish Bank, Bruton Street received value on the same date as the actual debit, that is the 17th April 1984. Mr. Burke maintains that this stg.£39,948.03 was lodged to his account held at Allied Irish Bank, Bruton Street at that time. He said that stg.£35,000 was then transferred from this account at Bruton Street to the account of Caviar at Hill Samuel in Jersey on the 19th April 1984. He stated that the balance of stg.£4,948.03 would have been used by him for ongoing political expenses. This balance was probably taken in cash and there were no vouchers available.

4-15   Evidence was given to the Tribunal by the bank officials at Allied Irish Bank, that the normal procedure would have been for a transfer from an account in the Isle of Man to an existing account holder in Bruton Street, London would be by way of a credit transfer identifying the account in Bruton Street to which the funds were to be lodged. This was not the procedure adopted in respect of the withdrawal from Mr. Burke's account on the 17th April 1984, which was by way of a direct payment. Allied Irish Bank, Bruton Street had no record of Mr. Burke having held an account at that bank, but the records of that bank were incomplete, and they subsequently revised their position by stating that there had been an account opened for Mr. Burke, which was in operation for a one-week period between the 30th November 1983 and the 5th December 1983. Mr. Burke maintained that he had had a bank account at Bruton Street for some years.

4-16   The Caviar account at Hill Samuel Jersey branch bank records that on the 19th April 1984 a lodgment of stg.£35,000 was made to the account noting that it was made "per Allied Irish Banks". There was no further identification to indicate the name of an account holder in Allied Irish Bank from whose account this sum had been paid.

4-17   On Mr. Burke's account of events therefore, the monies, which were on deposit in the Isle of Man, were withdrawn in London and were dispatched by Allied Irish Bank, London to Hill Samuel in Jersey. If that were so, the Tribunal can see no reason why Mr. Burke would not have informed the Tribunal in the course of his evidence in July 1999 that the Hill Samuel account was opened with the proceeds of his Isle of Man account. The Tribunal would have expected that, if he was intending to transfer funds from an existing account in the Isle of Man to an ultimate destination in Jersey, the most direct route would have been to advise the bank in the Isle of Man to transfer that sum from the account to Hill Samuel in Jersey.

4-18 The Tribunal believes that the available documentation from AIB Bank (IOM) Limited indicates that the money was withdrawn in London from the Isle of Man bank account on the 17th April 1984 and that value was given for it that day. This suggests that the withdrawal did not go into a bank account in Allied Irish Bank, Bruton Street and could not have accounted for the reference "per Allied Irish Banks" in the Hill Samuel account statement unless Mr. Burke had first withdrawn and then re-lodged the money in Allied Irish Bank, Bruton Street for onward transmission to Jersey. The Tribunal rejects this scenario as improbable, because it would involve an unnecessary step, in what would otherwise have been a direct transfer of these funds to Jersey.

THE OPENING OF THE CAVIAR ACCOUNT

4-19 The evidence established that this account was opened as a matter of urgency. Mr. Burke's solicitor Mr. Oliver Conlon instructed Bedell & Cristin, Advocates, to form a company and, immediately following upon incorporation, to furnish documentation to Hill Samuel to facilitate the opening of a bank account in the name of the company. He stated that there was "considerable urgency" about this. The Tribunal fails to understand how there could have been considerable urgency, in the circumstances as described by Mr. Burke, as the effect of a re-lodgment of the monies withdrawn from the Isle of Man would have been merely to move monies which had been on deposit at one location for a period of a year and a half, to another location, where the evidence established the money also remained on deposit.

4-20 The Tribunal is satisfied that urgency could arise if fresh monies were being paid to Mr. Burke from sources other than his existing funds, and if Mr. Burke wished to place them in an account other than an account which he had used for other donations previously. Mr. Burke could not give any direct evidence as to the actual circumstances leading to the withdrawal of funds from his Isle of Man account, but did recollect, he said, that the source of the stg.£35,000 lodgment to his Caviar account was the withdrawal from his Isle of Man account. He offered to the Tribunal, as a process of deduction based on the available records, the fact that the stg.£35,000 in his Jersey account must have been part of the proceeds of the withdrawal of stg.£39,948.03, because of the proximity in the timing of the transactions, and because there was no other source of these funds. Insofar as this evidence is based on deductions, the Tribunal is not happy to accept Mr. Burke's deductions as sufficient evidence to establish the facts. Insofar as this evidence is based on Mr. Burke's claimed recollection, the Tribunal rejects the evidence as not being credible in view of his inability to recall the actual circumstances of the withdrawal.

4-21 The Tribunal considers that Mr. Burke ought to have been in a position to give positive and precise evidence as to the actual circumstances surrounding the stg.£35,000 lodgment to the Jersey account, since it was the opening balance in a new account which was being held in a different jurisdiction and through a different corporate structure than any previous accounts held by him to that date. The Tribunal does not accept that Mr. Burke could have been unclear as to the circumstances relating to the manner in which he had operated an Isle of Man bank account, prior to the operation of his Jersey account in the name of Caviar, and is satisfied that his failure to disclose the existence of the Isle of Man account, at the time of his evidence in July 1999, was a deliberate attempt to conceal the existence of the stg.£50,000 deposit of which he was aware at that time. The Tribunal is satisfied that Mr. Burke is seeking to utilise the proximity of dates between the withdrawal from the Isle of Man account and the lodgment in Jersey to make a connection between these funds, which does not in fact exist. The Tribunal is satisfied that the source of this lodgment of stg.£35,000 to Mr. Burke's Caviar account was not the withdrawal from the Kalabraki funds in the Isle of Man as claimed. The source of the lodgment remains unidentified in that the Tribunal cannot identify the bank account from which this sum was paid but the Tribunal is satisfied, on the balance of probabilities, that this payment was made by Mr. Tom Brennan and his associates.

PAYMENT OF STG.£60,000 TO THE ACCOUNT OF CAVIAR ON THE 21ST NOVEMBER 1984

4-22 As with the stg.£50,000 payment in December 1982, Mr. Burke maintained that the stg.£60,000 payment in November 1984 was a payment which had been made by Mr. McGowan/Mr.

Ottiwell as a result of their fundraising activities in the UK, as previously described by Mr. McGowan and Mr. Brennan to the Tribunal. He stated that it comprised an accumulation of individual donations made for political purposes which he chose to keep offshore. However as events transpired this explanation for the payment of stg.£60,000 to Caviar was totally false. The Tribunal's inquiries established that the stg.£60,000 paid to Mr. Burke's Caviar account, was not the result of individual political donations accumulated by Mr. McGowan and Mr. Ottiwell and lodged to Mr. Burke's Caviar account. It was a single payment made by a Jersey company called Canio Limited to Mr. Burke's Caviar account which had been sourced from funds borrowed from Lombard & Ulster Banking Ireland Limited. This borrowing was secured upon the interests of Canio in certain lands at Sandyford, County Dublin. These facts are now accepted by Mr. McGowan, Mr. Brennan and Mr. Burke, yet all three maintain that the payment of stg.£60,000 to Mr. Burke's Caviar account in November 1984 was a political donation.

4-23   Mr. McGowan now maintains that, whilst he was in error in significant portions of his earlier evidence given on the 10th April 2000, there had, in fact, been fundraising by Mr. Ottiwell which did raise funds of the order of stg.£120,000 over a ten year period, but that this fundraising was in addition to the separate and singular payments which were made to the Caviar account by Canio. If this evidence is correct it follows that Mr. Burke must have maintained other accounts either offshore or elsewhere, as the total of sums alleged to have been paid between Mr. McGowan/Mr.Ottiwell's fundraising activities and Canio's payments far exceeds the total of the amounts which can be identified as lodgments in the Isle of Man and Jersey accounts disclosed to date. Mr. Burke denies having any accounts other than those now disclosed to the Tribunal. If this is true, Mr. McGowan's account of the Ottiwell fundraising must be false.

4-24   The Tribunal is satisfied that Mr. Burke, on returning to give further evidence to the Tribunal in relation to the Canio payments, sought to distance himself from his earlier evidence, and to reduce the significance of the role previously attributed by him to Mr. Ottiwell. He stated, on this occasion, that Mr. Ottiwell's involvement was peripheral, and that he dealt in the main with Mr. McGowan. He now maintained that he only ever had two conversations with Mr. McGowan in connection with these monies, the first in connection with the stg.£50,000 Kalabraki payment in December 1982 and the other in connection with the stg.£60,000 Canio payment in November 1984. He continued to maintain, however, that he had given the account details for both the Kalabraki payment in December 1982 and the Canio payment in November 1984 to Mr. McGowan when Mr. Ottiwell was in his company. He also continued to maintain that it was his understanding at all times, based upon what Mr. McGowan had told the Tribunal and what he himself had known through the years, that these funds were sourced through the fundraising activities conducted by Mr. McGowan in England.

4-25   The Tribunal concludes that there was no reason for Mr. McGowan, Mr. Brennan or Mr. Ottiwell to have misled Mr. Burke as to the true source of the funds when the payments were being made to him in 1982 and 1984. If Mr. Burke's evidence is correct, it follows that Mr. McGowan lied to him as to the true source of the stg.£50,000 payment in 1982 and the stg.£60,000 payment in 1984. As is manifestly clear, the stg.£50,000 Kalabraki payment and the stg.£60,000 Canio payment were not accumulated funds sourced from individual donors but were payments from the accounts of companies controlled by either Mr. Tom Brennan solely or Mr. Brennan, Mr. McGowan and Mr. Finnegan.

4-26   The Tribunal can find no reason why Mr. McGowan would have given an explanation to Mr. Burke for such payments which was false. The Tribunal concludes that Mr. Burke was never informed by Mr. McGowan or Mr. Ottiwell that fundraising activities conducted by them had raised the stg.£50,000 or the stg.£60,000 for him as he claimed. The Tribunal is satisfied that the explanation given by Mr. Burke to the Tribunal for his receipt of these funds is false.

PAYMENT OF STG.£15,000 TO THE ACCOUNT OF CAVIAR ON THE 19TH APRIL 1985

4-27   The bank records established that on the 9th April 1985, the account of Caviar at Hill Samuel was in credit to the amount of stg.£89,448.32. On that date, stg.£15,000 was withdrawn by Mr. Burke, and collected in cash in Wood Street, London on the same date. On the 19th April 1985, a sum of stg.£15,000 was lodged to the Hill Samuel Caviar account by means of a cheque from Chase Bank and Trust Company (Channel Islands) Limited. Mr. Burke's evidence was this was a "contra", that it was a re-lodgment of the stg.£15,000 funds which had previously been withdrawn on the 9th April 1985, from the same account. Mr. Burke's evidence as to the sequence of events was as follows: -

1. On the 9th April 1985, he travelled to London and collected stg.£15,000 in cash from Hill Samuel at Wood Street London.

2. The stg.£15,000 collected at Wood Street, London was debited to the Caviar Hill Samuel account in Jersey on the same day.

3. He returned to Dublin with sterling cash of £15,000.

4. He placed the money in a safe in his house.

5. At some unidentified time later, he concluded that he did not require it and decided to re-lodge it.

6. On the 19th April he returned to London with £15,000 sterling in cash and on the same day he travelled from London to Jersey with this money.

7. In Jersey, he handed stg£15,000 to an employee of Bedell & Cristin, Advocates, who lodged the money to the account of Caviar at Hill Samuel, Jersey.

8. He recollected these events, because he had to go to Jersey to change the mandate on the account, so as to provide for his wife being able to draw from the account in the event of his untimely demise.

4-28   Neither Mr. Brennan nor Mr. McGowan had revealed in their earlier evidence to the Tribunal the existence of a payment of stg.£15,000 to Mr. Burke's Caviar account in April 1985.

4-29   The Tribunal's inquiries into this sequence of events established that the scenario so graphically described by Mr. Burke in his evidence could not have taken place.

4-30   The Bedell & Cristin files considered by the Tribunal confirmed that no member of staff of Bedell & Cristin had received stg.£15,000 in cash from Mr. Burke, as claimed by him, and that the stg.£15,000 lodgment did not come from cash provided by Mr. Burke, but came from the account of Canio.

4-31   Documents from the Bedell & Cristin Caviar file were furnished to Mr. Burke by the Tribunal following which Mr. Burke wrote a personal letter to me in the course of which he stated that he was incorrect in his recollection when he gave his earlier evidence in connection with the stg.£15,000 lodgment. He now accepted that the stg.£15,000 was in fact a separate payment made directly to Caviar, and that it was probably from the same source, as the stg.£60,000, which he identified as Messrs. Brennan and McGowan. He did not identify Mr. John Finnegan as the contributor of stg.£10,000 of that sum at that time nor did he do so subsequently.

4-32   When recalled to give evidence on this issue, Mr. Burke was unable to offer any satisfactory explanation to the Tribunal as to how he could recall events, which had not, in fact, ever occurred. The Tribunal is satisfied that Mr. Burke's response to the initial queries put to him regarding the stg.£15,000 clearly illustrate his ability to tailor his evidence to the documentation available, and to utilise this documentation as corroboration of an account of events, which was false. The Tribunal is satisfied that Mr. Burke's earlier evidence regarding the re-lodgment of the stg.£15,000 cannot be explained as an error of recollection on his part and that it was a deliberate invention. The Tribunal is satisfied that Mr. Burke deliberately misled the Tribunal as to the true circumstances surrounding this lodgment and that he did so with the assistance of Mr. Brennan and Mr. McGowan, so as to prevent the true nature and source of this payment being revealed.

CANIO LIMITED

4-33   Given that Canio Limited was the payer at stg.£60,000 to Mr. Burke in November 1984, and the apparent payer of stg.£15,000 in April 1985, it was necessary for the Tribunal to establish the identity of the beneficial ownership of Canio and the reasons for its payments to Mr. Burke.

4-34   The Bedell & Cristin file provided to the Tribunal established that the company had been incorporated in Jersey on the 1st December 1980. Bedell & Cristin recorded that its beneficial owners were Kalabraki Limited (beneficially owned by Mr. Tom Brennan), Gasche Investments Limited (beneficially owned by Mr. Joseph McGowan), and Foxtown Investments Limited (beneficially owned by Mr. John Finnegan). The information as to beneficial ownership was not publicly available through the Companies Office records. The records showed Canio was a company owned in turn by Ardcarn Limited, another Jersey registered company. Ardcarn's beneficial owners were privately stated in 1979 to be Mr. Tom Brennan, Mr. Joseph McGowan and Mr. John Finnegan, but by 1984 the beneficial owners were recorded as being the three corporate structures, namely Foxtown Investments Limited, Kalabraki Limited and Gasche Investments Limited.

FOXTOWN INVESTMENTS LIMITED

4-35   Foxtown Investments Limited (Foxtown) was a Jersey company incorporated on the 20th September 1972. It was a trust company established for Mr. John Finnegan by Mr. Des Traynor. Foxtown was wholly owned, through nominees, by College Trustees Limited, who were the trustees of the Amber Trust. The Amber Trust was a discretionary trust, whose named beneficiaries included the World Wildlife Fund, but whose trustees had the power to add or to delete beneficiaries at their sole discretion. College Trustees Limited was a subsidiary of Guinness Mahon Channel Islands Limited which was owned by Guinness & Mahon (Ireland) Limited. Management services for Foxtown were carried out by Sovereign Management Limited, which later changed its name to Credit Suisse Trust Limited.

4-36   The Tribunal is satisfied that Mr. Finnegan was the settlor of the Amber Trust, and sought documentation from Mr. Finnegan regarding the dealings of the trust and Foxtown. Mr. Finnegan claimed to be unable to obtain the documentation required of him from Credit Suisse. Mr. Finnegan is currently engaged in litigation in Guernsey (the trust having been moved to there) for recovery of documentation from Credit Suisse.

KALABRAKI LIMITED

4-37   Kalabraki Limited (Kalabraki) was a Jersey company incorporated through Bedell & Cristin for Mr. Tom Brennan. The Tribunal is satisfied that Mr. Brennan was the beneficial owner of the entire shareholding in Kalabraki.

GASCHE INVESTMENTS LIMITED

4-38   Gasche Investments Limited (Gasche) was a similar Jersey company incorporated through Bedell & Cristin for Mr. Joseph McGowan. The Tribunal is satisfied that Mr. McGowan was the beneficial owner of the entire shareholding in Gasche.

THE CONTRIBUTORS TO THE PAYMENT OF STG.£60,000 TO MR. BURKE'S COMPANY CAVIAR.

4-39   None of the three individuals involved with the three corporate structures which held one-third interests in Canio was able to provide any comprehensible and detailed explanation as to why Canio was established to acquire the Sandyford lands, and as to what their individual input into the company was other than an equal provision of funds to acquire these lands.

4-40   The Tribunal established that of the stg.£60,000 paid by Canio to Mr. Burke in November 1984, stg.£25,000 was paid by Kalabraki, stg.£25,000 was paid by Gasche and stg.£10,000 was paid by Foxtown. The proportions of their contribution to Mr. Burke did not match the proportions in which the individual contributors held their interests in Canio, one-third each.

4-41   The Tribunal established that the initial intention of Messrs. Brennan & McGowan was that each of the contributors would contribute stg.£20,000, but that Mr. Finnegan was prepared to pay only stg.£10,000, whereupon the shortfall of stg£10,000 in his contribution was funded equally by Mr. Brennan and Mr. McGowan's companies. To the point in time at which the existence of Canio was discovered by the Tribunal, Mr. Burke, Mr. Brennan and Mr. McGowan had not made any reference to the fact that stg.£10,000 of the money paid to Mr. Burke in November 1984 came from Mr. John Finnegan through Foxtown or that stg.£25,000 each came from Messrs. Brennan and McGowan through their corporate structures.

MR. JOHN FINNEGAN

4-42   Mr. John Finnegan is a well known Dublin auctioneer and estate agent who has been involved with the Dublin property market since the 1950s. In his evidence he claimed that he had never made a payment to Mr. Burke at any time. Mr. Burke confirmed that he had never received a payment attributable to Mr. Finnegan or Foxtown. Mr. Finnegan's explanation for the stg.£10,000 payment by Foxtown in November 1984 was that it had been a contribution towards a retention fund of stg.£30,000 which was set up by Canio to meet future expenses, including architects fees, in relation to its lands at Sandyford, Dublin. He understood that three contributions of stg.£10,000 each were made to this fund, one from each of the three beneficial owners.

4-43   Mr. McGowan said that the stg.£10,000 paid by Mr. Finnegan was in response to a request made by him of Mr. Finnegan for stg.£20,000 for a political donation to Fianna Fáil. He said that Mr. Finnegan was unwilling to pay stg.£20,000, but paid stg.£10,000 instead. He said that Mr. Brennan and himself made up the stg.£10,000 shortfall in Mr. Finnegan's contribution by additional payments of stg£5,000 each so as to bring their individual contributions to stg.£25,000 each and Mr. Finnegan's to stg.£10,000.

4-44   Mr. Finnegan in his evidence denied that he had ever been approached for a political donation by Mr. McGowan or that he had ever made any payment through Canio as a political donation to Mr. Burke or otherwise. Mr. Finnegan claimed to be totally unaware of the fact that Mr. Burke's company, Caviar, was paid stg.£60,000 from the funds of Canio in 1984. If Mr. Finnegan's evidence is correct, it follows that Mr. McGowan had obtained stg.£10,000 from him by false pretences and that stg.£10,000 intended by Mr. Finnegan to meet future expenses of the company, had been misappropriated and given to Mr. Burke without his knowledge.

4-45   The Tribunal considers that it is inherently implausible that Mr. Brennan or Mr. McGowan would have defrauded Mr. Finnegan of this relatively small sum. The Tribunal's inquiries established that these three parties had been connected financially to a series of land transactions, which had resulted in stg.£2,661,875.96 being transferred to Jersey and of that a sum of stg.£1,989,831.23 being distributed between the three participants. Mr. Finnegan's share of these monies was some stg.£633,994.85. To the date that the Tribunal commenced its inquiries into Mr. Finnegan's affairs, he had never alleged that any funds of his had been misappropriated by his former associates, Mr. Brennan and Mr. McGowan.

THE SOURCE OF THE STG£60,000 PAYMENT MADE BY CANIO TO CAVIAR IN NOVEMBER 1984

4-46   The Tribunal is satisfied that the evidence establishes that the ultimate source of the stg.£60,000 which was paid to Mr. Burke was a loan made by Lombard & Ulster Banking Ireland Limited to Canio in Jersey in November 1984. This loan facility was extended by Lombard & Ulster on foot of the security of land holdings, said to be unencumbered, belonging to Canio at Sandyford, Dublin. These lands were development lands through which it was intended that a motorway would, in time, be built.

4-47   The funds drawn down from Lombard & Ulster were not used to acquire these lands, which had already been acquired on foot of a contract entered into with the MacAogáin family in 1979 by a Mr. James J. Gleeson (in trust) the purchase monies for which had been provided equally from the resources of Messrs. Brennan, McGowan and Finnegan. The monies, subsequently borrowed from Lombard & Ulster in 1984, were borrowed with the intention that each of the three beneficial owners of Canio would receive an equal share of these funds.

4-48   The funds were received by Mr. Laurence Wheeler of Bedell & Cristin from Lombard & Ulster and with the consent of the Canio he deducted the professional fees due to his firm by Canio and by Ardcarn. From the balance of the funds he deducted sums of stg.£25,000 each from the interests of Kalabraki and Gasche, and stg.£10,000 from the interest of Foxtown, whereupon the sum of stg.£60,000 was sent by cheque to the account of Caviar. The distribution document prepared by Mr. Wheeler is at (**Appendix E**). The Tribunal is satisfied, on the balance of probabilities, that Mr. Wheeler would not have made such deduction or payment without the express authority of Canio and its owners.

THE ROLE PLAYED BY MR. DAVID BARRY OF COLLEGE TRUSTEES LIMITED

4-49   Mr. Finnegan appointed Mr. David Barry of College Trustees Limited to protect his interests (held through Foxtown) in Canio. Mr. Barry liaised directly with Mr. Laurence Wheeler who was administering the affairs of Canio in Jersey. Mr. Wheeler took the necessary legal steps to ensure that the paperwork in connection with Canio and its associated company Ardcarn reflected that Canio was owned by Ardcarn, that Ardcarn was owned one third each by Kalabraki, Gasche and Foxtown. By the 18ᵗʰ April 1984, Bedell & Cristin had dealt with the ownership of Canio and Ardcarn and had arranged for the issue of the necessary new blank share certificates and declarations of trust to be executed to reflect the above. Mr. Barry thereafter monitored the activities of Bedell & Cristin, and the Tribunal is satisfied that his client's interests were suitably protected by him.

4-50   The Tribunal is satisfied that Mr. Barry was aware that funds would be raised from Lombard & Ulster and that they would be distributed in equal proportions to the three owners of Canio. Accordingly, the Tribunal believes that any unexplained inequality in the amounts which the three individual owners received, would have been subject to comment by him in his dealings with Mr. Wheeler. The dealings of Canio clearly reflect that there was a disparity between the sums distributed to Mr. Brennan and Mr. McGowan through their corporate structures, and the sum paid to Mr. Finnegan through his corporate structure, and this reflected the fact that stg.£25,000 each had been deducted from their share, whereas only stg.£10,000 had been deducted from Mr. Finnegan's share.

4-51   The Tribunal is satisfied that at the time of the deduction of the stg.£10,000 from Mr. Finnegan's share held through Foxtown, Mr. Barry was in a position to know that this sum had been combined with the stg.£50,000 from Kalabraki and Gasche and sent to Caviar as a single payment of stg.£60,000.

4-52   The Tribunal is satisfied that Mr. Wheeler would not have withheld information from Mr. Barry about any transaction, which he, as a member of a firm of Jersey Advocates, had carried out on behalf of the company whose interests were represented by Mr. Barry. Mr. Barry had become a director of Canio by the 4th July 1984 and had full access to its documents. In these circumstances, the Tribunal does not believe that Mr. Wheeler would have been a party to diverting funds intended to be lodged to a retention fund for Canio, into the account of a company in which Canio had no beneficial interest, namely Caviar.

THE ORIGINS OF THE CLAIM THAT THE STG.£10,000 DEDUCTED FROM THE FOXTOWN SHARE BY MR. WHEELER WAS DEDUCTED FOR THE PURPOSE OF A RETENTION FUND FOR FUTURE EXPENSES SUCH AS ARCHITECT'S FEES

4-53   The Bedell & Cristin file recorded that, on the 14ᵗʰ November 1984, Mr. Wheeler sent a telex to Mr. Hugh Owens, a chartered accountant in Dublin, who was the financial adviser to two of the individuals who were Canio's beneficial owners, namely Messrs. Brennan and McGowan, which stated as follows: -

> "I briefly saw Mr. McGowan yesterday and he raised with me his wish and that of Mr. Brennan that each of the parties should reserve pounds 20,000 for possible future expenses (such as architect's fees) should the present negotiations not succeed. I put this to Barry of College Trustees Limited who said that this was not agreed. By the time I learned this I was not able to recontact Mr. McGowan but perhaps you would inform him and hopefully the three parties can agree in Ireland. In the meantime I am writing to Mr. Barry along the lines discussed with Mr. McGowan with the one proviso relating to the three pounds 20,000 retentions".

4-54   Mr. McGowan in his evidence agreed that he had had a meeting with Mr. Wheeler at which he had discussed the retention of stg£20,000 from each of the three parties, but says that he told him that this fund was for the purpose of making a political donation to Mr. Burke. Obviously, the telex to Mr. Owens does not reflect this fact and, on its face, the document supports Mr. Finnegan's subsequent claim to the Tribunal that his contribution was for future expenses such as architects' fees, and not as a political donation.

4-55   The Tribunal notes, however, that there was an element of urgency in the communication which passed between Mr. Wheeler and Mr. Owens, and it may be the case that Mr. Wheeler did not want to put in open correspondence that there was a dispute as to whether each of the three parties should pay stg.£20,000 to Mr. Burke. It is probable that each of the three parties, Messrs. Brennan McGowan and Finnegan, knew exactly what was in dispute between them and that the real purpose of the telex was to point out that the resolution of that dispute was a matter for the three participants in Dublin, without identifying what the dispute was.

4-56   The Tribunal is satisfied, on the balance of probabilities, that the factual position was that the decision-making power for Foxtown's decisions rested with Mr. Finnegan in Dublin, and not with his trustees in Guernsey, and that the decisions of Kalabraki and Gasche were effectively made by Mr. Brennan and Mr. McGowan and not by the directors of those companies in Jersey. No retention fund such as was envisaged in Mr. Wheeler's telex to Mr. Owens was ever set up by Canio, notwithstanding that there had been a deduction of stg.£10,000 from Foxtown's share of the Lombard & Ulster loan and deductions of stg£25,000 from the shares of Kalabraki and Gasche.

4-57   The Tribunal believes that Mr. Barry was vigilant in protecting Mr. Finnegan's interests, and that he must have been given an explanation for the deduction of this sum which met with the approval of Mr. Finnegan.

4-58   The Tribunal is satisfied, on the balance of probabilities, that Mr. Wheeler would not have told either Mr. Barry or Mr. Finnegan that the stg.£10,000 which he had deducted from the Lombard & Ulster funds and sent to Caviar, was a payment to a retention fund of Canio's since this was not the case, and could readily be demonstrated not to be the case. It follows, on the balance of probabilities, that Mr. Barry was aware that the stg.£10,000 was paid to Caviar and if so, the Tribunal believes that Mr. Finnegan was also aware of this fact.

4-59   The Tribunal believes that the fact that Canio did not have a retention fund with stg.£30,000 to its credit was obvious to Mr. Finnegan, and that, if he had had any genuine belief that his stg.£10,000 had been deducted for such a fund, he or Mr. Barry would have sought details of the fund. Any such request would have obliged Mr. Wheeler to respond, and the only information he could have given in response to such a request would have been that he had transferred the funds to Caviar. If Mr. Finnegan's account is true, this would involve an admission by Mr. Wheeler that he had transferred the funds without proper authority. Such a scenario is highly improbable. Mr. Wheeler was an experienced Jersey advocate administering funds for a company, in which members of his firm were nominees, and of which he was a director. The Tribunal is satisfied that he would have ensured that he had the consent of all the beneficial owners of Canio before paying out their funds to another company, Caviar.

4-60   Confirmation of the fact that no Canio retention fund existed can be reasonably inferred from the events which took place prior to the 28th September 1989. In that month, almost five years after the stg.£60,000 payment to Mr. Burke, and the alleged setting up of a retention fund for Canio according to Mr. Finnegan, a meeting took place in Mr. Finnegan's offices in Dublin. The meeting was attended by Mr. Brennan, Mr. McGowan and Mr. Finnegan, who was accompanied by his solicitor, Mr. Michael O'Shea. Mr. O'Shea took a note of what had transpired at this meeting in the course of which there was a discussion about what was noted to be possible planning costs and by-law application costs in respect of the Canio lands. To that point in time no development costs had been incurred by Canio which have been disclosed to the Tribunal. Mr. O'Shea's note further recorded that: -

> "The representatives agreed that the shareholders would have to make equal contributions to fund an application for the development of the lands".

4-61   This is precisely the type of expenditure which would have been funded from the type of retention fund referred to in Mr. Wheeler's telex, and which Mr. Finnegan says he believes had been created by his payment of the stg.£10,000 in November 1984. Since no such expenses had been incurred to that date, there ought to have been a fund available to the parties at the meeting in September 1989 of stg.£30,000 together with such interest as would have accrued on that retention fund from November 1984 to September 1989. None of the three parties present at this meeting, at which the creation of a retention fund was specifically discussed, made any reference to the fact that there had already been a retention fund created in 1984 for the purpose of meeting future expenses including architects' fees.

4-62   The Tribunal believes that this could not have been an oversight on the part of each one of the parties who were supposed to have contributed stg.£10,000 to such a fund. The Tribunal believes that if Mr. Finnegan had a genuine belief that his stg.£10,000 had been lodged to such a fund, he would have raised that matter at the meeting and that he would have instructed his solicitor as to its existence.

4-63   The question of making a contribution to a fund to pay for the development costs raised at the September 1989 meeting did not progress further in 1989. In 1990 negotiations took place as between Mr. Tom Brennan and Mr. Finnegan with a view to Mr. Finnegan's Canio interests being sold to Rushcliffe Limited (a company in which Mr. Tom Brennan had an interest). In order for this to take place, it was necessary to carry out a reconciliation or balancing exercise between the three parties involved in Canio.

4-64   The Tribunal is satisfied that if Mr. Finnegan had paid stg.£10,000 into a retention fund he would have sought credit for such payment or for a one-third share of the funds remaining in the account, in the balancing exercise which was undertaken. Mr. O'Shea, his solicitor, was carrying out this exercise on behalf of Mr. Finnegan, but he was never informed by Mr. Finnegan that he had made a payment to such a fund, and accordingly, Mr. O'Shea never sought a credit from Messrs. Brennan and McGowan for Mr. Finnegan in respect of that payment. Mr. O'Shea's evidence was that he was never informed by Mr. Finnegan that a retention fund had been created in Canio, with an initial payment by him of stg.£10,000. The Tribunal is satisfied, that if such a retention fund had been created, Mr. Finnegan would have so informed Mr. O'Shea.

4-65   The Tribunal is satisfied that the explanation for Mr. Finnegan's failure to refer to the existence of such a fund is accounted for by the fact that he was aware that no such fund was ever created, and that his stg.£10,000 was paid to Mr. Burke with his knowledge on foot of an instruction given by him to Mr. Barry or to Mr. Wheeler that such sum could be paid to Caviar. The Tribunal is satisfied that Mr. Finnegan gave a false and misleading account of the true circumstances in which his funds came to be paid to Mr. Burke through Caviar.

WHY WAS STG.£60,000 OF CANIO'S MONEY PAID TO MR. BURKE IN NOVEMBER 1984 AND A FURTHER STG.£15,000 PAID IN APRIL 1985?

4-66   In order to establish why Mr. Burke was paid these sums, the Tribunal sought to establish from Messrs. Brennan and McGowan, and Mr. Finnegan, why Canio was established, and what their individual input into the company was. Until such time as the existence of Canio was established by the Tribunal, Mr Brennan and Mr. McGowan had been falsely maintaining that the only payments (apart from some small payments from the Brennan and McGowan companies at election time) to Mr. Burke were from the accumulated fund being handled by Mr. Ernest Ottiwell, and Mr. Burke had supported this account of events.

4-67   Once Canio was revealed Mr. Burke claimed ignorance of any role that it may have had, and reasserted that his understanding had always been that these were funds raised through Mr. McGowan and Mr. Ottiwell's fundraising efforts. If true, this meant that Mr. Brennan and Mr. McGowan had for some un-explained reason borrowed stg.£60,000, paid it to Mr. Burke, and falsely represented to him that it was the proceeds of political fundraising activities. The Tribunal considers this to be utterly implausible, and rejects Mr. Burke's evidence that the Canio payments were ever attributed by Messrs. Brennan and McGowan to fundraising activities.

4-68   The Tribunal believes that the stg.£60,000 payment made to Mr. Burke in November 1984 was made on foot of an agreement reached with Mr. Burke whereby he was to receive that exact sum. The Tribunal does not know why Mr. Finnegan refused to pay more than stg.£10,000, or why Messrs. Brennan and McGowan conceded that this payment of stg.£10,000 was sufficient in circumstances where it appeared that each of the three of them ought to have paid stg.£20,000 so as to reflect their equal shareholding in Canio. This inability on the part of the Tribunal, to conclude what the true circumstances were in relation to this payment, stems from the fact that none of the principals involved namely Mr. Brennan, Mr. McGowan or Mr. Finnegan, has given any comprehensible account as to what their relationship was at that time.

4-69 The Tribunal's investigations established that the relationship of Mr. Finnegan with Messrs. Brennan and McGowan was not limited to the Canio transaction, but extended to cover a range of commercial transactions in Ireland which over time resulted in the transfer of stg.£2,661,875.96 to Jersey. Each of the parties shared substantially in these funds, yet each claimed to have an almost total ignorance of the circumstances which led to these funds being generated, or the role which each of them played in the transactions which led to them being so enriched.

4-70 It appears to the Tribunal that the corporate entities set up in Jersey were set up with the assistance of the lawyers, tax advisers and accountants to the parties to serve specific and identifiable functions which are capable of detailed explanation. The evidence adduced before the Tribunal established that the corporate structures involved were a labyrinth which stretched from Jersey and Guernsey to Tortola and the only common features were the involvement of Messrs. Brennan and McGowan and Irish land transactions which resulted in large sums of money being distributed between Messrs. Brennan, McGowan and Finnegan in Jersey.

4-71 The Tribunal believes that, on the balance of probabilities, a truthful explanation from Messrs. Brennan, McGowan and Finnegan for the existence of these companies, and the function which they were intended to perform would have assisted the Tribunal in establishing what the true purposes of the payments to Mr. Burke by Canio were, and that the failure on the part of these three participants to provide a comprehensible account of their dealings has hindered and obstructed the Tribunal in its ability to carry out its task.

4-72 The Tribunal does not accept that those who profess to be ignorant of these transactions were as ignorant as they claimed. The Tribunal finds that the claimed ignorance of the events in which these parties had participated and had profited so, is not credible. The level at which Mr. Finnegan was prepared to cooperate with the Tribunal's inquiries into the affairs with which he was so closely linked, can be measured from the submissions made on his behalf for the first time on the 21st September 2001, some four months after the Tribunal had commenced public hearings into the matters with which he was involved. On that day, it was first suggested to the Tribunal that Mr. Finnegan had made financial contributions in connection with the "Jersey part" of these transactions, but not in connection with the actual purchase of the lands involved. It was submitted by Counsel on his behalf as follows: -

> "He has given as much information as he possibly can, from his recollection of events. I explained, I think, yesterday that Mr. Finnegan, up until yesterday, was unable to instruct me in anyway in relation to these transactions, outside the bounds of the documents which had been furnished from this Tribunal to Messrs. Kennedy McGonagle Ballagh.* I have explained this. I have been at pains to explain this. I think I introduced this when I was cross-examining Mr. Brennan, that I had no further information than the Tribunal had in respect of these transactions"

* Messrs. Kennedy McGonagle Ballagh were Mr. Finnegan's solicitors.

And later: -

> "He has been unable to assist me or instruct me in respect of these transactions. Therefore I was unable until now to suggest that Mr. Brennan's testimony was untrue. I felt it was my professional standing not to contradict the witness who had given sworn testimony, unless I had a firm basis to do that"

4-73 The Tribunal believes that Mr. Finnegan's failure to engage with the issues raised with him by this Tribunal is consistent with a deliberate decision on his part to withhold any information, which might lead the Tribunal to establish the true circumstances, which led to Mr. Burke being paid monies by Canio, which were partly funded by him. The Tribunal is satisfied that as part of Mr. Finnegan's obstruction of the Tribunal, he challenged Mr. McGowan's evidence that he, Mr. Finnegan, was aware of the fact that the payment had been made as a political donation by representing that his money had been paid into a retention fund, when he was aware that this had not in fact taken place.

4-74 The Tribunal is satisfied that Messrs. Brennan and McGowan deliberately withheld from the Tribunal, any information which would allow the Tribunal to establish what the true relationship was as between them and Mr. Finnegan in relation to Canio, and that they failed to give a truthful account of the circumstances which led to Mr. Burke receiving funds from Canio.

CONCLUSIONS AS TO WHY MESSRS. BRENNAN, MCGOWAN, FINNEGAN AND RELATED COMPANIES PAID MONEY TO MR. BURKE'S OFFSHORE ACCOUNTS

4-75   The Tribunal is satisfied that the funds lodged to the offshore accounts of Mr. Burke which have been disclosed to the Tribunal, were not the proceeds of any fundraising or other activities conducted by Mr. Ottiwell, and that the fact that they were so attributed by Messrs. Brennan and McGowan, and by Mr. Burke, is indicative of collusion between Mr. Burke and Messrs. Brennan and McGowan to present an account of events to the Tribunal which they knew to be false.

4-76   The Tribunal is satisfied that each one of the Canio payments to Mr. Burke was made by the payers, whether Messrs. Brennan and McGowan in respect of the stg.£15,000 payment or Messrs. Brennan, McGowan and Finnegan in respect of the stg.£60,000 payment, for purposes other than as political donations to either Mr. Burke or to Fianna Fáil.

4-77   The Tribunal concludes that, in the absence of any legitimate commercial or other disclosed relationship existing between the payers and Mr. Burke, there was no legitimate explanation for the payment of such substantial sums to Mr. Burke.

4-78   The Tribunal concludes that the payments to Mr. Burke's offshore accounts in the Isle of Man and Jersey were made by the payers with the intention of securing some, as yet unidentified, benefit for them. These payments were substantial payments within the meaning of Clause E. 1 of the Tribunal's Amended Terms of Reference. As no legitimate explanation has been provided for these substantial payments, it is the opinion of the Tribunal and the Tribunal concludes that these payments were made in circumstances which give rise to a reasonable inference that the motives for making and receiving these payments were improper and that such payments were connected with the public office held by Mr. Burke. The Tribunal is satisfied, in all the circumstances, that these payments to the offshore accounts of Mr. Burke were corrupt payments.

Century Module

Chapter 5

Introduction to Century

INTRODUCTION

5-01   In the course of the Tribunal's inquiries carried out under the original *Terms of Reference*, it emerged that a lodgment of £39,500 had been made to one of Mr. Burke's bank accounts on the 31st May 1989.

5-02   Upon inquiry, Mr. Burke informed the Tribunal that the payment was an amalgam of political donations received by him, one of which was a donation in the sum of £35,000 from Mr. Oliver Barry, a businessman, who was involved in the entertainment business. At the date of payment Mr. Barry was centrally involved with a company called Century Communications Limited (Century), which in January 1989, had been awarded the first independent National Sound Broadcasting Contract in the State.

5-03   As the Minister for Communications at the date of payment, Mr. Burke was responsible for matters relating to the granting of broadcasting licences, although the power to award sound broadcasting contracts was not within his remit but rested with the Independent Radio and Television Commission (IRTC), an independent statutory authority.

5-04   In March 1989, some months prior to the payment in question, Mr. Burke, in his capacity as Minister for Communications, had issued a Directive which fixed the level of transmission fees payable by Century to Radio Telefís Éireann (RTÉ), the national broadcaster. Mr. Burke's Directive resulted in Century paying RTÉ considerably less than RTÉ had sought for the use of its facilities. In 1990, the year following the payment, Mr. Burke promoted legislation which, inter alia, restricted RTÉ's income from advertising in anticipation that independent broadcasters would benefit.

5-05   Clauses E1 and E2 of the *Amended Terms of Reference* provide, that:

"The Tribunal shall … inquire urgently into …
1.   Whether any substantial payments were made or benefits provided, directly or indirectly to Mr. Raphael Burke which may, in the opinion of the Sole Member of the Tribunal, amount to corruption or involve attempts to influence or compromise the disinterested performance of public duties or were made or provided in circumstances which may give rise to a reasonable inference that the motive for making or receiving such payments was improperly connected with any public office or position held by Mr. Raphael Burke, whether as Minister, Minister of State or elected representative.

2   Whether, in return for or in connection with such payments or benefits, Mr. Raphael Burke did any act or made any decision while holding any such public office or position which was intended to confer any benefit on any other person or entity making a payment or providing a benefit referred to in paragraph 1 above, or any other person or entity, or procured or directed any other person to do such an act or make such a decision."

5-06   Having regard to the foregoing and to the relationship between the promoters of Century and Mr. Burke, the apparent benefits which accrued to Century from his actions and the magnitude of the payment involved, the Tribunal was obliged to inquire into the circumstances surrounding the payment of £35,000 to Mr. Burke. Ultimately, it sought to determine at whose behest, and on whose behalf, this payment was made, whether it represented a political donation or an improper payment as defined by the *Amended Terms of Reference* above, and, if satisfied it constituted the latter, what benefit, if any, was procured by such inducement.

5-07   The following three substantive areas became the focus of inquiry, namely:

1.   The circumstances surrounding the payment itself;

2.   The issuing of a Directive by Mr. Burke as Minister for Communications under Section 16 of the Radio and Television Act 1988, which prescribed a series of tasks for performance by RTÉ in return for certain payments by Century at an amount fixed by him;

3.   The circumstances surrounding Mr. Burke's relationship with Century's promoters in 1989 and 1990 when it was in serious financial difficulty and in particular

(a)   The promotion and ultimate enactment of the Broadcasting Act 1990, which restricted RTÉ's advertising revenue;

(b)   Attempts to divert part of RTÉ's licence fee income to the IRTC for onward transmission to independent broadcasters; and

(c)   The proposal to change the role of 2FM programming, announced by him in the Dáil on the 29th May 1990.

BACKGROUND

Legislative history leading to the passing of the Radio and Television Act 1988

5-08   The radio frequency spectrum is a natural resource used for a number of functions, including broadcasting. It is allocated internationally by the International Telecommunications Union. Until the late 1980s the Wireless and Telegraphy Act 1926 governed the national grant of licences in respect of the radio frequency spectrum, including broadcast licences. In 1988 RTÉ, the national broadcaster, was the sole public radio broadcaster in the State.

5-09   During the 1970s a number of unlicensed broadcasters, commonly known as "pirates", came into existence. These unlicensed broadcasters were considered a danger as their existence could have led to an interference with emergency services which also used the spectrum. Attempts were made from the late 1970s to introduce legislation to shut down unlicensed broadcasters and from the early 1980s to provide for a licensing system for local independent broadcasters, but legislation was not enacted until 1988 in the form of the Broadcasting and Wireless Telegraphy Act 1988, and, later, the Radio and Television Act in 1988.

5-10   In September 1987, Mr. Burke, as Minister for Communications, sought Government approval for the introduction of new legislation to provide for the licensing of local and community sound broadcasting services together with the re-introduction of the Broadcasting and Wireless Telegraphy Bill 1985 (Broadcasting and Wireless Telegraphy Bill 1987). The Bills proposed to strengthen the Minister's powers to deal with illegal broadcasting and other illegal uses of wireless telegraphy. Since 1979 three Bills, one in 1981 and two in 1983, had been introduced in an effort to establish a statutory regime for local radio, but none of these had been promulgated into law.

5-11   By November 1987, in accordance with Government approval received earlier that year, the text of the Sound Broadcasting Bill 1987 was in place. In the Memorandum to Government seeking approval for the text of the Bill, Mr. Burke reminded the other Ministers that, when the scheme of the Bill was being considered in October, he had drawn their attention to the fact that the Bill had been constructed in a sufficiently flexible manner so as to accommodate the licensing of an independent national radio service. It was suggested that, from a technical point of view, the frequencies for such a service were immediately available on VHF and there was a favourable prospect that a medium wave frequency would be available within nine months. The Minister considered that this development was timely and accorded with the general thrust of broadcasting policy, both in Ireland and internationally, to provide diversity and choice of service to the public, relaxing the state monopolies which existed in the broadcasting sector, and allowing greater competition. The Minister held strong views that it was important that there should be an alternative to RTÉ services in the areas of news, information, current affairs and public interest programming, given that for many people the broadcasting services were the main, if not the only, source of such information.

5-12 These Bills were duly introduced into Dáil Éireann on the 8th December 1987, and the second stage was passed on the 10th February 1988. The initial approach of the Government, as evidenced by the Sound Broadcasting Bill, was that the selection of licensees and the granting of licences would be made by the Minister on the basis of stated criteria and having regard to advice from a proposed Advisory Committee. In the course of the second stage debate, however, the opposition strongly objected to the proposed ministerial power to grant licences in view of the possible abuse of such a power.

5-13 A Memorandum for Government, on the 12th May 1988, sought Government approval for a number of amendments to the Bill, including the establishment of a new regulatory body to be entitled the Independent Radio and Television Commission. The amendments, in effect, led to the creation of a new Bill, known as the Radio and Television Bill 1988, which became the Radio and Television Act, 1988 (the 1988 Act).

CENTURY COMMUNICATIONS LIMITED

The origins of Century

5-14 Century Communications Limited (Century) was incorporated in Ireland on the 30th November 1988. The company was established to apply for and operate an independent commercial sound broadcasting service licence as provided for by the Radio and Television Act 1988.

5-15 The evidence in relation to the origins of Century was broadly consistent. It appears that, some time in mid to late 1987, Mr. Oliver Barry approached the broadcaster, Mr. Gay Byrne, telling him of his idea to set up an independent radio station and asking Mr. Byrne if he would be interested in the project. In late 1987 Mr. Barry met an acquaintance of his, Mr. John Mulhern, while travelling to Cork on a train and a discussion ensued concerning a newspaper article referring to a proposal to issue broadcasting licences. Mr. Barry mentioned that he had had discussions with Mr. Byrne on the subject and that they were considering getting involved in independent broadcasting. Mr. Barry asked Mr. Mulhern if he would be interested in getting involved in the project and Mr. Mulhern confirmed that he would. Subsequently Mr. Mulhern introduced Mr. James Stafford to Mr. Barry. Ultimately, Messrs. Stafford, Barry and Mulhern became the promoters of Century.

5-16 Although the promoters of Century were focused on the establishment of a national radio service, Mr. Byrne advocated the establishment of a local station, as he believed this latter option would involve less investment. However, he told the Tribunal that the other promoters dismissed this idea out of hand as they were "imbued with a fervour for a national licence" rather than a local one.

5-17 Various figures and projections were presented at meetings in late 1987 and early 1988. Mr. Byrne said it appeared that the promoters strongly felt that if the venture were successful there would be considerable profits to be made, but even in the worst case scenario, "if all the wheels came off and the audience was not as great as expected and the advertising revenue was not as great as expected," there was still a profit to be made and a large profit would perhaps just take a little longer.

5-18 It was not envisaged that Mr. Byrne would become an investor in the project, but there was a suggestion that he would be given a small shareholding. Although he had not entirely dismissed an involvement with the venture, as time progressed Mr. Byrne's confidence in the project declined and he ceased attending meetings.

5-19 At some stage, probably towards the end of 1988, Mr. Barry called to Mr. Byrne's home with an envelope, which, Mr. Barry said, contained a bank draft. Mr. Byrne assumed that the draft was for an amount that had been discussed between the two of them in respect of his taking up a three-year contract with Century. Mr. Barry confirmed that the draft was for the sum of £1million. Mr. Barry sought an answer from Mr. Byrne as to whether or not he was going to join Century. Having considered the matter Mr. Byrne decided not to take up the Century offer and renewed his contract with his then employer, RTÉ, on the 16th January 1989.

THE PERSONALITIES BEHIND CENTURY

Mr. Oliver Barry

5-20   In 1988 Mr. Oliver Barry was involved in the entertainment business. He had been a promoter of musical events and manager of artistes for some twenty-five years. Prior to the inception of Century, Mr. Barry had been a member of the RTÉ Authority for approximately three years.

Mr. John Mulhern

5-21   In 1988 Mr. Mulhern was a successful businessman and the son-in-law of the then Taoiseach, Mr. Charles J. Haughey. Mr. Mulhern was a director and a major shareholder of Clayton Love Distribution Limited, from which Mr. Mulhern withdrew funds for investment in Century. It would appear that Mr. Mulhern did not take an active role in the day-to-day running of Century.

Mr. James Stafford

5-22   Mr. Stafford was approached by Mr. Mulhern, in late 1987 or early 1988, who asked him if he would be interested in becoming involved with the venture. At that time Mr. Stafford and Mr. Mulhern were friends and had had dinner together once a month for the previous twenty-five years. Mr. Stafford was also a friend of the then Taoiseach, Mr. Haughey, and was best-man at the wedding of Mr. Mulhern to Mr. Haughey's daughter.

Mr. Laurence Crowley

5-23   In or about September 1988, Mr. Stafford asked Mr. Crowley to become Chairman of what was to be Century. Mr. Crowley was an accountant with KPMG Chartered Accountants and had specialised in insolvency work with that firm. He was co-opted as Chairman of the Board of Century in 1989. Mr. Crowley informed the Tribunal that he was a non-executive Chairman. Although not an investor in the company, Mr. Crowley was given share options that he did not ultimately exercise.

Chapter 6

The Ministerial Directive

6-01   The Broadcasting and Wireless Telegraphy Act 1988 envisaged that the illegal operators would be closed down and the Radio and Television Act 1988 provided that the Independent Radio and Television Commission (IRTC) would award a number of sound broadcasting contracts including one for an independent national sound broadcasting service.

6-02   It was determined that it was appropriate to grant the franchise for the national radio licence in advance of the local radio licences. The IRTC fixed the 16th December 1988 as the last date for acceptance of written submissions by interested parties for the national licence, and conducted oral hearings in January 1989 where potential franchisees were given the opportunity of making their submissions to the Commission in public. Having considered the submissions made, on the 12th January 1989, the IRTC decided to grant the franchise for the independent national radio service to Century on the 18th January 1989. The successful franchisee was entitled to enter into a seven-year renewable sound-broadcasting contract for the provision of a national independent commercial radio broadcasting service. As appears from the history of events set out in this Report, the contract to deliver this service was not signed until the 21st July 1989 notwithstanding that Century was declared the successful applicant on the 18th January 1989.

6-03   The capital costs involved in setting up a separate transmission service to broadcast independent commercial radio envisaged by the Act would have been prohibitively expensive, and it would have taken an inordinately long period of time to construct and to commission such a service. It was anticipated that the franchisee who would provide the independent national radio broadcasting service might seek to use the existing transmission network, which was at that time vested in RTÉ as the national broadcaster, to transmit its signal.

RTÉ TRANSMISSION CHARGES

6-04   RTÉ was aware that the successful franchisee for the new service would, in all probability, utilise its facilities. The evidence adduced before the Tribunal established that it was RTÉ policy to share its facilities with the successful independent broadcasting applicants, including the national broadcasting applicant, where requested to do so and that it was its policy to co-operate with each of the applicants to that end. As early as the 16th March 1988, Mr. Robert K. Gahan, Assistant Director General of RTÉ, had written to the Department of Communications confirming that RTÉ had no objection in principle to giving access to its sites to the independent broadcasters, or to the installation of separate facilities at a reasonable rent, provided all regulations were met and all extra costs incurred by RTÉ, including extra security costs, were reimbursed to it. Not unreasonably, RTÉ anticipated that a benefit would ensue to it from such an arrangement. RTÉ understood and believed that it would receive a commercial return on such activity, as it was always understood that any co-operation would be rendered on a commercial basis.

6-05   Mr. Burke, as Minister for Communications, had expressed the same view. In reply to a question put in the Seanad concerning the operation of Section 16 of the 1988 Act, he acknowledged that RTÉ's co-operation would necessarily be rendered on a commercial basis. On the 1st June 1988 in the Dáil, he had stated that the thrust of Section 16 of the 1988 Act was that there should be "this type of co-operation, any such co-operation should be rendered on a commercial basis." The Tribunal is satisfied that it was Government policy that the independent radio broadcasters would not receive a subsidy, directly or indirectly, from RTÉ in providing its service.

6-06   Section 16 of the 1988 Act provides as follows: -

"(1) The Minister may, at the request of the Commission and after consultation with Radio Telefís Éireann, require the latter to co-operate with sound broadcasting contractors in the use of any mast, tower, site or other installation or facility needed in connection with the provision of transmission facilities for sound broadcasting services to be established under this Act.

(2) A sound broadcasting contractor shall make to Radio Telefís Éireann such periodical or other payments in respect of any facilities provided in pursuance of sub-section (1) as the Minister, after consultation with Radio Telefís Éireann and the Commission, directs."

6-07   The effect of this section was to confer upon the Minster the power to order RTÉ to make its transmission facilities available to the independent national broadcaster and the power to fix the payments which the independent national broadcaster would pay to RTÉ for such facility. The 1988 Act envisaged that the Minister's power was to be exercised at the request of the IRTC and after consultation with RTÉ.

6-08   As events transpired, on the 14th March 1989 the Minister exercised his power under Section 16 of the 1988 Act to fix the level of charges which were to be paid by Century to RTÉ for the use of the RTÉ transmission facilities, and to direct RTÉ to acquire the necessary equipment to enable Century to broadcast its signal. The Directive of the Minister effected a considerable saving to Century over the amounts that were being sought by RTÉ for the provision of its services.

6-09   The Tribunal has sought to establish the circumstances leading to the making of this Directive and Mr. Burke's motive in so doing.

THE POSITION OF RTÉ

6-10   In 1988 RTÉ sought to establish the cost of the provision of transmission network facilities and services to third party broadcasters. In doing so it sought to: (a) ascertain the overall cost of the operation of the network, and (b) devise a formula for the apportionment of the network's operation costs as between the various services using it, and applying that formula to work out the appropriate charge for a third party wishing to use the network for a new radio service. RTÉ provided not only radio services but also television services within the State and, consequently, it was necessary for the purpose of its accounting exercise to apportion the cost of services as between these different media. As the names of some of those services changed, they shall, for ease of reference, be described hereinafter as Radio 1, 2FM, Raidio na Gaeltachta, RTÉ 1 and Network 2.

6-11   Initially, RTÉ's Finance Department apportioned $^4/_7$ths of costs to television and $^3/_7$ths of costs to radio on the basis that two television services equated with four radio services. Accordingly RTÉ's two television services, that is RTÉ 1 and Network 2, equated to four services and Radio 1, 2FM and Raidio na Gaeltachta brought the total complement of services up to an equivalent of seven radio services.

6-12   The cost associated with the provision of a single service could be calculated by dividing the relevant total cost of the provision of facilities and services by seven. This formed the basis of RTÉ's method for calculating the appropriate transmission charges to independent third parties. RTÉ, in evidence, maintained that this method of calculating the appropriate charges was transparent. It was designed, they maintained, to be fair and reasonable although the calculations, of necessity, contained subjective elements such as, for example, equating one television service with two radio services. RTÉ told the Tribunal that this apportionment allowed for some "headroom" in anticipation of future negotiations. Later, further analyses of the apportionment of costs resulted in a decision to abandon the subjective $^4/_7$: $^3/_7$ ratio and to divide all costs evenly among television and radio services. Costs were thus to be divided among six services, i.e. the five RTÉ services and the new national independent radio service. These costs would be divided further as more new local licensees would seek to use RTÉ facilities.

6-13   RTÉ's calculations were made in advance of the anticipated negotiations with any of the national/local-broadcasting applicants and were not produced solely with Century in mind.

6-14   The Tribunal has concluded that RTÉ's method of arriving at its charge for its services was reasonable. The Tribunal further concludes that RTÉ would have been in breach of its statutory duty to maximise its revenues were it, for any reason, to decide unilaterally to undercharge for the use of its facilities or for the provision of its services. The figures identified by RTÉ as the cost of staff, power, spares, insurance, etc., were, in the opinion of the Tribunal, all derived from the actual budget of RTÉ. No additional costs were added on in any way to these figures. The Tribunal is equally satisfied that any surplus which existed in RTÉ's figures, arrived at from the apportionment formula referred to above between radio and television, would inevitably be identified by the negotiating independent broadcasters who would seek to have any surplus removed and would, accordingly, form the basis of any negotiations on these proposed charges.

CENTURY'S POSITION REGARDING RTÉ'S TRANSMISSION CHARGES

6-15   Once Century was awarded the franchise on the 18th January 1989, the Tribunal considers that it would have been reasonable to have expected its promoters to have immediately commenced negotiations with RTÉ with a view to reaching a mutually acceptable level of charge for the transmission services which they, at all times, recognised would have to be availed of in order to broadcast the Century signal.

6-16   The Tribunal is satisfied from the history of events recounted at the Tribunal that Century never negotiated or attempted to negotiate with RTÉ over the level of transmission charges which it would have to pay.

6-17   Whilst RTÉ could not know the exact requirements of the incoming broadcaster until such time as the details of the service required were agreed between them, it had, nonetheless, carried out certain projections which it incorporated in a document, headed 'National FM Radio Coverage – Outline Proposals and Costs', which was sent to Mr. Barry with a covering letter on the 2nd November 1988 (**Appendix F**). Included in this document was a calculation for the provision of an "all-in" service for FM signal distribution, which was referred to in the evidence as a "turn key" operation. This was costed at £1.14 million and included the acquisition by the commercial operator of the necessary capital equipment over a five-year primary leasing period. This scheme envisaged the operator using the FM service and having 98.5% national coverage from the end of the third year. From their meeting on the 2nd November 1988 with RTÉ, Mr. Barry and Mr. Stafford were aware of RTÉ's estimated cost of the service on this basis.

6-18   In making their written submission to the IRTC in December 1988, Century included a figure of £375,000 for its transmission costs. The origin of this figure is unclear, and although Century subsequently sought to attribute it to a costing exercise of its consultants, the Independent Broadcasting Authority (IBA), the Tribunal is satisfied that it did not originate from any scientific costing exercise and that it had its origin in the financial costings considered in progressing a business plan for Century. It was, at its highest point, a figure which the promoters felt should be paid to RTÉ, as it was within Century's financial projections and was a figure their experts would not dispute having regard to the brief they had been given by Century. This figure was never put to RTÉ's representatives by Century prior to the award of the licence.

6-19   Meetings had taken place between Century and RTÉ, on the 2nd November 1988, the 8th November 1988, and the 18th November 1988, at which RTÉ's costs were discussed. In the course of those meetings, RTÉ's figures had been revised downward to £914,000, but Century had not responded with any alternative figures. As of the 8th December 1988, Mr. Stafford was preparing a document headed 'Brief to the Minister' in which it set forth Century's figure of £375,000 as against a claimed £1.25 million from RTÉ. It is not clear from the evidence whether this brief was actually provided to Mr. Burke as no copy of it appears on any of the Department files. However, the Tribunal is satisfied that Mr. Burke and Mr. Barry were in regular contact at that time and concludes that it is probable that Mr. Burke was made aware by Mr. Barry of Century's disquiet at the level of transmission charges being sought by RTÉ, and that he was also made aware of Century's figures.

6-20   The IRTC was aware of the concern about RTÉ's proposed level of transmission charges that had been expressed by each of the three applicants for the national broadcasting licence intending to use terrestrial based systems. Whilst all considered RTÉ's charges to be excessive, Century's estimate for the charges was half that which the other applicants were prepared to pay.

6-21   The IRTC did not consider that it was its function to establish what the appropriate rate of charge for access to the RTÉ transmission service should be. It was aware, before the award of the licence to Century, that the Department of Communications and RTÉ had agreed, on the 10th January 1989, that a sum of £692,000 per annum was the appropriate charge for provision of the FM service.

6-22   On the 13th January 1989, the day after Century's oral presentation to the IRTC, the Chairman and Secretary of the IRTC met with Mr. Stafford. According to a fax sent by Mr. Stafford later that day to Professor Hills, one of Century's specialist consultants, Mr. Stafford claimed that the Chairman and Secretary required as much information as possible to challenge the RTÉ figures and justify £300,000 as the correct charge. Century endeavoured to provide this information as a matter of urgency, but in fact provided little significant independent support for their figure despite the best efforts of Professor Hills to obtain a report from the IBA. Professor Hills noted with disappointment the response that had been provided by his former colleague in the Independent Broadcasting Authority Consultancy Service (IBACS) . The IRTC however concluded that the resolution of the transmission charges issue was one for Century and RTÉ to resolve in negotiation.

6-23   In fact Century never embarked upon the process of negotiation with RTÉ at any time prior to the award of the licence but instead directed considerable energy towards ensuring that the Minister, Mr. Burke, would make the ultimate decision as to the cost of the provision of services by RTÉ.

6-24   The Tribunal finds as a fact that Century's failure to commence negotiation with RTÉ as to the level of charges is explained by the fact that Mr. Burke had given Century's promoters to understand that he would resolve the dispute in their favour. Mr. Stafford and Mr. Barry were in a position to tell their solicitors, Arthur Cox & Co., on the 14th February 1989 that the Minister would give a Directive in their favour, notwithstanding that no application for a Directive had yet been made by the IRTC to the Minister.

6-25   Mr. Stafford acknowledged that, at a meeting with Mr. Burke, he had been informed by Mr. Burke that he did not have the power to fix the level of transmission charges unless the matter was referred to him by the IRTC. In its efforts to have the matter referred by the IRTC to the Minister, Century had engaged in correspondence with the Chairman and Secretary of the IRTC expressing dissatisfaction with the level of charge being sought by RTÉ and seeking to create the impression that negotiations with RTÉ were log -jammed.

6-26   Mr. Connolly, the Secretary to the IRTC was apparently impressed with Century's arguments and wrote to the Department of Communications on the 6th February 1989, endorsing their views (**Appendix G**). The Department had independently been endeavouring to impress on RTÉ the need to reduce its level of charges. The variation in the charges proposed by RTÉ was as follows:

On the 2nd November 1988, an all-in annual rental figure for FM services of £1.14m was proposed in the document headed *"National FM Radio Coverage-Outline Proposals and Costs."* (**Appendix F**). This figure was to be payable once 98.5% coverage was achieved in the 3rd year of operation. In year 1, the initial rent was to commence at £600,000 per annum and progress to £840,000 per annum as coverage increased.

On the 18th November 1988, a figure of £914,000 for an annual charge for the all-in service was proposed (**Appendix H**).

By the 10th January 1989, an annual charge of £692,000 for the provision of an FM service and a figure of £112,000 for AM services (Dublin and Cork) together with figures for FM and AM project management and installation of £230,000 were agreed between RTÉ and the Department of Communications and the Minister, Mr. Burke (**Appendix I**).

On the 14th February 1989, following a further meeting between the Minister and the Director General of RTÉ, RTÉ was prepared to accept an annual sum of £614,000 for the FM service charge previously agreed at £692,000 (**Appendix J**).

6-27   This final figure was at that time acceptable to the Minister and the IRTC was so informed on the 16th February 1989, by letter, wherein the Minister stated that a sum of £614,000 was not unreasonable in Irish circumstances (**Appendix K**).

6-28   The response of Century to this information was to write to the IRTC on the 17th February 1989 and on the 20th February 1989. The first of these letters (**Appendix L**) was signed by Mr. Barry and Mr. Stafford, the second by the Chairman of the company, Mr. Laurence Crowley (**Appendix M**). In the first letter, Messrs. Barry and Stafford stated: -

"The Board meeting reviewed the question of transmission charges. They were of the unanimous opinion that the £375,000 offered to RTÉ for a full transmission service was, given the advice they had from the IBA, fair and reasonable. Furthermore they were of the unanimous view that they were not prepared to negotiate or to increase that offer as it would effect the viability of the service."

6-29   Their letter of the 17th February 1989 was accompanied by a schedule setting out the headings under which they calculated the £375,000 charge. The letters written by Century on the 17th and 20th February 1989 to the IRTC seriously misrepresented the factual position pertaining at that time. The Tribunal is satisfied that there had never been an offer by Century to RTÉ of £375,000 or any other sum. The Tribunal is satisfied that the IBA never costed the provision of eight transmitters and six boosters over four years to provide a national coverage of 98.5% at £300,000. The Tribunal is satisfied that RTÉ never quoted Century a rate of 7% on the combined investment over a twenty-year plan as claimed. The Tribunal is satisfied that there was never a Board meeting at which Century resolved that the £375,000 was the figure above which their plan was not viable. The Tribunal is satisfied that the notes taken at the Century meeting of the 14th February 1989 accurately reflect the true position; namely that Century considered transmission charges at a cost of £375,000 would represent 'a steal' and that the company was prepared to pay £520,000. The Tribunal is satisfied that these letters were written and the meeting with the Chairman of the IRTC arranged so as to convince the IRTC that the only possible resolution of the matter lay in the hands of the Minister, in circumstances where an impasse had arisen as between negotiating parties, whereas the true position was that no negotiation at all had taken place.

6-30   The Tribunal is satisfied, on the balance of probabilities, that Century would not have insisted on the matter being referred to the Minister unless its promoters believed that he would resolve the matter in their favour.

MR. BURKE'S CONSIDERATION OF THE IRTC LETTER OF THE 20TH FEBRUARY 1989 AND ITS ENCLOSURES

6-31   The Chairman of the IRTC wrote to Mr. Burke on the 20th February 1989 in the following terms:

> "*Re: Transmission Charges for National Independent Radio.*
>
> Dear Minister,
>
> Please see the enclosed copy of a letter received today from Century Communications concerning the charges being sought by RTÉ for the provision of transmission facilities for the new independent national radio station.
> Please note that Century Communications are seeking a Ministerial Directive under Section 16 of the Radio and Television Act 1988.
> It would appear that a contract with Century Communications cannot be entered into until this matter is cleared up.
> I look forward to hearing from you at your convenience.
>
> Yours sincerely."

Mr. Burke chose to treat this letter as a reference under Section 16 of the 1988 Act by the IRTC, although the letter itself expressly noted that Century was seeking the Ministerial Directive.

6-32   Although there had not been a formal Board decision of the IRTC to refer the matter to the Minister for a Directive under Section 16 of the 1988 Act, the Chairman stated in evidence that he was quite sure, with the benefit of hindsight, that the Commission was in agreement with the request. He also stated that he never heard it said that the Commission did not make a request for a Directive under Section 16 of the Act. The Tribunal accordingly finds that Mr. Burke was entitled to treat the Chairman's letter as a request by the IRTC to him for a Directive under Section 16 of the 1988 Act.

6-33   The section provides that, after consultation with RTÉ, the Minister may require it to act. Mr. Burke agreed that there had been no communication with RTÉ between the date of receipt of the IRTC's letter on the 20th February 1989 and the date upon which he issued his Ministerial Directive, the 14th March 1989. In evidence Mr. Burke stated that he considered that he had already carried out the consultation process which was envisaged in the section, insofar as he had considered RTÉ's position, both in consultation with RTÉ and with his own departmental advisors, on a number of occasions from January onwards.

6-34   It is true to say that Mr. Burke had considered RTÉ's figures on a number of occasions but it is also the case that in so doing he had considered the Century figures and their arguments, and rejected them in favour of RTÉ's figures. In reaching his decision that £614,000 was a reasonable annual charge to make for the FM transmission services, Mr. Burke had considered the Century figure of £375,000 and had rejected it in holding that £614,000 was the appropriate figure. He must also, of necessity, have rejected the arguments in favour of Century's £375,000 figure which were advanced by the Secretary to the IRTC in his letter to the Minister of the 6th February 1989 which, in turn, enclosed the only independent documentation which had been proffered to support Century's figures; namely the fax prepared by the IBACS the contents which had been found wanting by Professor Hills.

6-35   In his direct dealings with the Director General of RTÉ, Mr. Burke advanced to him the arguments that were contained in Mr. Connolly's letter of the 6th February 1989 for his response. Since he went on to hold in favour of the RTÉ figures over the Century figures, it follows that he must have preferred RTÉ's argument at that time.

6-36   Notwithstanding the letter and enclosure received from the Chairman of the IRTC on the 20th February 1989 it is difficult to conclude that there was sufficient additional information which would have allowed for the Minister to reach a conclusion as to the appropriate transmission charge other than that which he had expressed four days earlier, namely that £614,000 was the appropriate charge for use of the RTÉ transmission facilities for the FM service.

6-37   The IRTC's letter and its enclosure were considered in the Department of Communications, and, on the 23rd February 1989, an Aide-Memoire (**Appendix N**) was prepared for the Minister by his department and provided to him by the then Secretary of the Department, Mr. McDonagh. This document reviewed the issues surrounding the application for the Directive and analysed the main arguments advanced by Century and by RTÉ in relation to their respective positions. It concluded that Century had seriously underestimated the costs involved in matching RTÉ's FM service.

6-38   It stated that the IBA service in the United Kingdom and in Northern Ireland was not comparable with the RTÉ service and that the UK charges, quoted by Century and used as the basis for the provision of services in Ireland, were not supported by any examination. It stated that Century in its submissions to the IRTC had ignored the project management and installation costs totalling £375,000.

6-39   On the issue of the purchase of capital equipment, it highlighted Century's claim that RTÉ had quoted an interest rate of 7% per annum and that the equipment had a life expectancy of twenty years and that Century claimed that the costs should be written off over twenty years at an interest rate of 7% per annum. The document noted, however, the RTÉ response that there was no possibility of being able to borrow money at a fixed rate of 7% over 20 years and that RTÉ's own Exchequer Borrowings were costing an average of 12% per annum.

6-40   The Aide-Memoire drew attention to the fact that Century had ignored the costs of the AM service completely and had assumed that they were included in the FM charges.

6-41   Appended to the Aide-Memoire was a memorandum that recorded a discussion which had taken place between Mr. Michael Grant of the Department and Mr. Ivan Tinman, Managing Director of Downtown Radio, in which it was stated that Mr. Tinman had expressed the view that a charge of stg.£800,000 would not be unreasonable for a fourteen station national FM network, covering the twenty-six counties. The Tribunal is satisfied that Mr. Grant's contact with Downtown Radio was prompted by Century's letter of the 17th January 1989 to Mr. Connolly stating that the figures paid by Downtown Radio to the IBA in the North of Ireland were supportive of the figures which it was prepared to pay to RTÉ.

6-42   A further memorandum was attached to the Aide-Memoire, which recorded the contact by the department with a representative of the IBA in which it was stated that this representative had said that the IBA's costing methodology would be of little help in determining the appropriate way of apportioning costs in Ireland for the reasons set out therein.

6-43   The Minister's Directive of 14th March 1989 (**Appendix O**) required RTÉ to provide its facilities to Century on the following basis:

1. RTÉ was to provide access to its 14 FM sites and two AM sites (Dublin and Cork) at an annual cost of £35,000.

2. Maintenance charges in relation to Century's equipment was to be levied at: £30,000 per annum to cover the first thirty visits, £1,000 per visit for each of the next 40 visits; and additional visits to be charged at actual cost plus 25%.

3. Power and spares to be charged on an actual cost basis.

4. RTÉ would acquire the necessary transmitting and associated equipment and the cost would be financed at the best available terms over 14 years. The capital cost and interest charges would be paid by Century over the 14 year period and the residual value of the equipment at the end of the period would accrue to Century.

5. Annual charges would be increased in line with the Consumer Price Index and 5% for overheads would be paid

6. A once-off installation and project management fee of £250,000 would be paid by Century to RTÉ for the AM and FM facilities.

6-44   These figures were radically different from what had been agreed with RTÉ by the Minister in February 1989, when £252,000 *per.annum* was agreed as the appropriate figure for access, whereas Mr. Burke had now directed that access be provided for £35,000 per annum. £355,000 had been agreed as the appropriate figure for maintenance, whereas Mr. Burke was now directing that RTÉ provide this service for £30,000 on the basis of 30 visits, with £1,000 for each subsequent visit (up to 40), and additional visits to be charged at actual cost plus 25%.

6-45   The Tribunal is satisfied that, as of the date upon which Mr. Burke elected to make his Directive, he had no fresh evidence to justify altering his decision of the 16th February 1989 and that he had compelling evidence to show that Century's figures were unsustainable. Notwithstanding this Mr. Burke went on to give a Directive which totally reversed his earlier decision and which directed RTÉ to provide its services to Century at a cost which had never been discussed with them either by the Minister or by Century. Mr. Burke's Directive was a total reversal of the previous position. It was contrary to the advices of his Department and was unsupported by any independent evaluation of the argument advanced by Century. It conferred a substantial financial benefit upon Century. The saving to Century achieved by the Minister's Directive over the previously agreed figure of £614,000 per annum would have amounted to almost £2 ½ million over years four, five, six and seven alone of the seven–year contract period. The Tribunal is satisfied that Mr. Burke's Directive was heavily weighted in Century's favour in circumstances where there was clearly insufficient evidence available to the Minister to support Century's contentions.

MR. BURKE'S JUSTIFICATION FOR HIS DECISION

6-46   Mr. Burke sought to justify his decision on the following grounds: -

• The transmission charges as fixed by him, although lower than those sought by RTÉ, were what he considered to be 'fair and reasonable'.

• The charges as fixed by him did not involve a subsidy to anybody as was confirmed at his meeting with RTÉ on the 31st March 1989. He had agreed with RTÉ that maintenance charges would be reviewed after 18 months so as to ensure that there was no question of subsidy.

• The amount being asked by RTÉ was not an amount which was going to be paid by Century and accordingly, if the station was to be got up and running, he was obliged to take the course of action which he did.

• He had no option but to issue a Directive since he had been requested to do so by the IRTC in their letter of the 20th February 1989.

6-47   The Tribunal does not accept Mr. Burke's explanation for his decision and is satisfied that: -

• There was no evidence which would allow him to conclude that the charges he fixed were fair and reasonable.

● He could not have believed that the figures set by him did not amount to a subsidy to Century given that he had earlier agreed that a figure of £614,000 per annum was a reasonable figure to pay in the circumstances.

● RTÉ never accepted that the charges fixed by the Minister did not subsidise the independent broadcaster, as was stated by Mr. Burke.

● Mr. Burke had no reasonable grounds for believing that Century would not enter into a contract with RTÉ other than on the terms which he fixed in his Directive.

● The fact that he was requested to give a Directive by the IRTC did not mean that he necessarily had to direct that the service would be provided at a rate lower than that already found by him to be appropriate.

CONCLUSION AS TO MR. BURKE'S REASONS FOR ISSUING A DIRECTIVE PURSUANT TO SECTION 16 OF THE RADIO AND TELEVISION ACT 1988

6-48   The Tribunal is satisfied, that in giving his Directive, Mr. Burke did not act in the public interest but was acting to serve the private interests of the promoters of Century Radio.

Chapter 7

Payment of £35,000 to Mr. Ray Burke by Mr. Oliver Barry on the 26th May 1989

7-01   On the 26th May 1989, £35,000 in cash was handed to Mr. Burke by Mr. Barry in the Minister's office in Kildare Street, Dublin 2. In March 1989, Century Radio had been the beneficiary of a Ministerial Directive under Section 16 of the Radio and Television Act 1988, which obliged RTÉ to provide equipment and transmission facilities to Century at a figure which was considerably lower than that which RTÉ considered appropriate and also considerably lower than that which had been previously agreed by the Minister. Century had yet to sign the broadcasting contract with the IRTC and, as of May 1989, was in dispute with RTÉ as to the extent of the obligations which were imposed upon RTÉ by the Ministerial Directive.

7-02   Century had yet to go on air and would not do so for a further four months. Mr. Barry and Mr. Burke met regularly and discussed Century's progress and its difficulties. The circumstances in which the admitted payment of £35,000 came to be made are disputed in the accounts of events given to the Tribunal by the donor, Mr. Barry, and by the recipient, Mr. Burke.

7-03   On Mr. Barry's account of events, Mr. Burke had asked him for £30,000 as a contribution to the Fianna Fáil party and had specified that the payment should be made in cash. If such were the circumstances in which the payment came to be made, the Tribunal considers that it was an improper demand and that it was an abuse of Mr. Burke's position as a Minister of Government to have received the payment in those circumstances. The exercise of Mr. Burke's ministerial functions to that date had involved him in making decisions which affected the commercial viability of a company with which he knew Mr. Barry to be closely linked. It was clear that if Mr. Burke were re-elected and again held that office, he would continue to have a role in the affairs of Century. The Tribunal considers that had such a 'request' been made by the Minister it would, in effect, have constituted a demand for payment, which could not have been refused by Mr. Barry given his company's ongoing relationship with the Department of Communications.

7-04   Mr. Burke, however, denied that these were the circumstances in which he came to receive the money. He said that Mr. Barry had, of his own volition, proffered the sum of £35,000 in cash by way of an unsolicited political donation. He said that they had been discussing the political campaign that would precede the General Election, which was to take place on the 15th June 1989, and that Mr. Barry had volunteered the payment with the object of assisting in the retention of the second seat in Mr. Burke's constituency of Dublin North. Mr. Barry, he said, was a personal friend and a constituent who had helped him in past election campaigns.

7-05   If this was the true sequence of events leading to the payment, the Tribunal considers that it was, at a minimum, imprudent of Mr. Burke to have accepted the money proffered by Mr. Barry, given the ongoing relationship between Century, the Minister and his Department. The Tribunal considers that the payment of such a substantial sum of money to a Minister was such as to bring into question any subsequent decision which might be taken by him in the course of those of his public duties that involved the donor or his company. In these circumstances, the Tribunal considers that any such donation ought to have been refused by Mr. Burke.

7-06   The Tribunal considers that the first issue to be determined is whether or not the payment was sought from Mr. Barry by Mr. Burke, or whether it was volunteered by Mr. Barry to Mr. Burke.

7-07   Despite being a personal friend of Mr. Burke's and a long time supporter of the Fianna Fáil party, Mr. Barry had never before made a payment approaching £35,000 to either. In the course of the political campaign in which Mr. Burke received his payment, Mr. Barry made payments of £5,000 to the Fianna Fáil party and a similar sum to Mr. Charles J. Haughey, then an Taoiseach. The payment to Mr. Burke was seven times greater than that which was made to the party or to an Taoiseach. The Tribunal is satisfied, on the balance of probabilities, that such a payment to Mr. Burke would not have been made by Mr. Barry on his own initiative. The amount handed over was enormous. In the context of Mr. Burke's then income, it represented a sum which almost equated to his gross income as the holder of two ministerial offices and certain additional private income. Mr. Barry's financial circumstances at that time were not such that he could make a payment of £35,000 at will. As indicated later in this report, Mr. Barry sought reimbursement of this payment from Century. The Tribunal has concluded that it is inherently improbable that Mr. Barry would have made such a large payment to Mr. Burke unless Mr. Burke had specified the sum that he required.

7-08   Support for Mr. Barry's contention that Mr. Burke sought the money from him, and that it was not volunteered by Mr. Barry, came from the evidence of Mrs. Maeve McManus, a former employee and subsequently a director of Mr. Barry's company, Quality Artistes Management Limited (QAM). She recollected Mr. Barry telling her that Mr. Burke was looking for a large donation from him and, while she gave conflicting accounts as to whether or not the sum of £30,000 was expressly referred to by Mr. Barry in his conversations with her, she is clear that she was aware that such a demand was made of Mr. Barry prior to the actual payment being made. Mr. Barry's own account of events was that he was rather taken aback by the amount of money which was being solicited from him. The Tribunal considers that it is probable that this significant event was discussed between Mr. Barry and Mrs. McManus at that time. The Tribunal is satisfied that the £35,000 paid to Mr. Burke was paid following upon his having sought a payment of £30,000 in cash, nominally for Fianna Fáil, from Mr. Barry, as claimed by Mr. Barry, and that the sum was not volunteered by Mr. Barry as claimed by Mr. Burke.

CONCLUSIONS ON MR. BURKE'S TESTIMONY CONCERNING THE £35,000 CASH PAYMENT BY MR. BARRY

7-09   The Tribunal concludes that Mr. Burke has endeavoured to conceal from the Tribunal the true nature of the payment made to him. On Mr. Burke's own admission no part of the £35,000 received from Mr. Barry went directly to the Fianna Fáil party although the Tribunal is satisfied that this was the stated reason given by him when the demand for payment was made of Mr. Barry. The Tribunal is satisfied that the sum was paid in cash because Mr. Burke had specifically sought to be paid in that form and rejects Mr. Burke's denial that that was so. The Tribunal sets out its conclusions below in relation to Mr. Barry's actual motives in paying Mr. Burke.

7-10   Mr. Burke has given evidence to the Tribunal that the £35,000 received from Mr. Barry formed part of a £39,500 lodgment made to one of his accounts on the 31st May 1989, five days after its receipt. Mr. Burke was not in a position to identify the source of the remaining £4,500. Mr. Burke's evidence on this issue cannot be verified at this time. No contemporaneous documentation was produced to the Tribunal to prove that the monies lodged to this account on the 31st May 1989 comprised any part of the £35,000 received from Mr. Barry five days earlier. Mr. Burke was not in a position to produce any adequate documentation to vouch the expenditure of this sum on political expenses, either in the 1989 election or otherwise.

7-11   If it was the intention of Mr. Burke to apply these funds towards the campaign so as to ensure the re-election of a second candidate for Fianna Fáil in his constituency, as claimed, the Tribunal would have expected that the existence of this donation would have been made known to Mr. Burke's constituency organisation at the time, and that there would be evidence of expenditure of that sum, or a substantial part thereof, during the campaign. Mr. Burke accepts, however, that he did not inform any person in Fianna Fail of the fact that he had received this sum from Mr. Barry. The Tribunal believes that the manner in which Mr. Burke dealt with this payment is inconsistent with it having been acquired for any legitimate political purpose. The Tribunal is satisfied that Mr. Burke treated this money as his own, to do with as he pleased, and that he had solicited the payment from Mr. Barry on that basis.

MR. BARRY'S MOTIVE IN MAKING

THE PAYMENT TO MR. BURKE

7-12   Mr. Barry's evidence was that he made the payment to Mr. Burke on behalf of Century because he felt that it was in the company's best interests so to do. Mr. Burke had been Minister for Communications in the outgoing Government and he had introduced commercial broadcasting in the State. Mr. Barry felt that it would have been disadvantageous to his investment in Century if Fianna Fáil did not get back into power. Whilst Mr. Burke had made a demand of him for £30,000, he felt that it was in the Century's interest to make a payment to Mr. Burke in the sum of £35,000. It is clear from his evidence that, whilst the demand was made of him personally by Mr. Burke, it was his decision to make the payment on behalf of Century. In so doing, he claimed that it was less of a financial burden on him as the other two promoters would share in the contribution.

THE TREATMENT OF THE £35,000 PAYMENT TO MR. BURKE IN THE BOOKS OF ACCOUNT OF MR. BARRY, QUALITY ARTISTES MANAGEMENT LIMITED AND CENTURY COMMUNICATIONS LIMITED.

7-13   Since Mr. Barry stated that the payment to Mr. Burke was a legitimate political donation made by him on behalf of Century, the Tribunal would have expected that this payment would be so reflected in the books of account of Century, and of any other company involved in the payment. However, this is not the case. The payment can be identified in the financial memoranda of Mr. Barry as 'deposit' and as 'donation' and as 'cash payment' but nowhere is there an unequivocal statement that it was a political donation much less that it was a payment made to Mr. Ray Burke, T.D.

7-14   Mr. Barry gave no explanation to the Tribunal as to why details of the admitted £35,000 payment made by him to Mr. Burke were not provided by him to the relevant accountants in order to allow for the payment to be recorded in any one of the accounts of QAM, or the accounts of Century, or his own personal records.

7-15   The evidence established that the cash handed to Mr. Burke, on the 26th May 1989, was sourced from an account called the '*Oliver Barry/Frank Sinatra savings account*' at the Bank of Ireland at 28 Lower O'Connell Street, Dublin 2. Century had no connection with this account, which was the account of a company solely owned by Mr. Barry. Mr. Barry sought to have his expenditure reimbursed by Century. His first attempt to do so was by reducing the amount he was obliged to pay to the Century's share capital account, thus giving himself a credit for the payment. In July 1989, Mr. Barry made a payment of £148,334 to the share capital account. This payment brought his contributions to that date to £215,000, which was £35,000 short of the £250,000 which had been paid by that date by Mr. Stafford. Mr. Stafford's area of expertise lay in the field of corporate finance and the Tribunal is satisfied that, as of July 1989, Mr. Stafford must have been aware that Mr. Barry had given himself credit for £35,000, in his dealings with Century, by paying a reduced contribution to the share capital account.

7-16   Ms. Noreen Hynes, a Chartered Accountant, was the Head of Administration and Finance in Century from June 1989 until August 1990. She was never made aware by Mr. Barry or Mr. Stafford of the fact that Mr. John Mulhern was entitled to any shareholding in the company. She understood the payments into the company's share capital account to come from Mr. Barry and Mr. Stafford, although she was not able to distinguish which of them made any particular payment, as the monies were merely lodged to the account without any indication to her as to identity of the contributor.

7-17   While Mr. Barry sought to give himself credit for the £35,000 payment to Mr. Burke, by withholding an equivalent amount from the share capital account, he provided no documentation to support this expenditure, nor did he inform Ms. Hynes that he was adopting that course. When the first annual audit of the company was performed in March and April 1990, Ms. Hynes recorded in a memorandum addressed to Mr. Stafford and Mr. Barry, that there was a shortfall in the share capital account of £122,695. These figures were calculated without reference to any credit being given to Mr. Barry for a £35,000 payment. Mr. Stafford, at this time, informed her that there were expenses of the company which had been met by the directors personally for which credit should be given to them in this account and for which invoices would be produced. By the 31st of December 1989, the end of the financial period for Century, the shortfall in the share capital account was £120,225 despite the efforts of Ms. Hynes to have the directors vouch the claimed credits at the time of the signing off of the accounts.

7-18   Ms. Hynes prepared a memorandum to that effect and circulated it to Mr. Barry and Mr. Stafford. It ought to have been clear to Mr. Barry from that memorandum that he was not being allowed to take credit for the £35,000 shortfall. The reason why Mr. Barry was not allowed credit for that sum was because it had not been vouched. Had Mr. Barry produced a receipt from Mr. Burke for the £35,000 which was paid to him in May 1989, Mr. Barry would have been allowed full credit for this expenditure. The Tribunal is satisfied that, instead of obtaining such a receipt from Mr. Burke, Mr. Barry set about trying to seek reimbursement of this expenditure from the company through other means.

7-19   Having failed in his attempt to recover the expenditure via a credit in the share capital account, he then tried to recover it on the basis of it having been a loan to the company from him. By mid-1990, Century was in serious financial difficulties and the directors of the company were themselves funding the company's expenditure, including its wage bill.

7-20   A financial restructuring of the company took place, which involved the acquisition of a substantial shareholding by the United Kingdom based company, Capital Radio Plc, and the injection of additional finance by the original promoters. It was agreed that the directors were to be allowed credit for the loans they had provided to the company.

7-21   In the course of the due diligence exercise carried out prior to the completion of the agreement with Capital Radio, Mr. Barry and Mr. Stafford advanced a claim to offset the sum of £302,094.16 on the basis of loans made to Century by them. Of this sum, £260,853.63 could be vouched as expenses incurred in funding the wages account of Century and in lodgments to Century's bank account. The un-vouched element of the claim amounted to £40,686.04, of which the Tribunal is satisfied £35,000 was represented by the payment which had been made by Mr. Barry to Mr. Burke. Given the absence of vouching documentation for this expenditure, Capital was unwilling to give credit to the directors for this sum, with the result that the agreement closed on the basis of the directors' loans being quantified at £260,853.63. The second attempt to have Mr. Barry's £35,000 payment to Mr. Burke paid back to him thus failed.

7-22   Having failed to recover the £35,000 through the directors' loan stratagem, Mr. Barry sought to have the money paid out on the basis that his company QAM, had provided services to Century between January 1990 and July 1990 at a rate of £1,600 per week. No such claim had been made by QAM to that point.

7-23   Ms. Noreen Hynes confirmed in her evidence that she had made all of the directors, including Mr. Barry, aware of their responsibility to ensure that all known liabilities of Century were fully disclosed to Capital Radio as part of the due diligence exercise. Yet Mr. Barry never indicated to her that he or QAM were owed any money for services rendered. Had he done so, she would have entered QAM as a creditor in the accounts that were prepared prior to closing the agreement with Capital Radio Plc.

7-24   The Tribunal is satisfied that there was no such liability on Century to pay £40,000 to QAM and this was merely a device contrived to ensure that the monies paid to Mr. Burke by Mr. Barry were reimbursed by Century. Mr. Taylor, Financial Director of Capital Radio and a director of Century, was not prepared to sanction this payment, but Mr. Stafford was insistent that the matter be referred to the Board for discussion and, at a Board Meeting on the 10th January 1991 it was resolved "that the matter be agreed between Mr. Barry and the company." Subsequently a cheque dated 19th February 1991, for £40,000 was issued by Century to QAM. The Tribunal is satisfied that, of this sum, £35,000 was to recompense Mr. Barry for the expenditure of £35,000 incurred in paying Mr. Burke in May 1989. The balance represented monies that Mr. Barry claimed to have paid on behalf of Century by way of bonus payments to RTÉ staff for their work in enabling Century to get on air in September 1989.

7-25   The extraordinary lengths which were gone to in order to achieve this repayment, were necessitated by the fact that there was no supporting documentation to record that Mr. Burke had been paid £35,000 by Mr. Barry. Had such documentation been available, Mr. Barry would have been reimbursed without further ado. The accountants for Century properly insisted upon vouchers being produced for any expenditure sought to be attributed to expenses paid by the directors on behalf of the Century.

7-26   The Tribunal is satisfied that Mr. Barry's reluctance to provide documentary evidence of this payment stems from the fact that he was aware that the payment was a corrupt payment for which Mr. Burke would not issue any formal acknowledgement or receipt. If the payment to Mr. Burke had been a legitimate payment, there would have been no impediment to Mr. Burke issuing a receipt for that sum to Mr. Barry, which he in turn could have provided to the accountants and auditors and claimed the reimbursement. The Tribunal is satisfied that, at the time of the payment of the monies to Mr. Burke, Mr. Barry knew that the sum was a payment to Mr. Burke to be used for his own purposes and that it was not a political donation either to Fianna Fáil or to Mr. Burke, although Mr. Burke used those words in making his demand of Mr. Barry for £30,000 in cash.

MR. STAFFORD'S KNOWLEDGE OF THE PAYMENT TO MR. BURKE

7-27   Mr. Stafford, in his evidence, emphatically denied that he had any prior knowledge of the payment or that he had consented or given instructions regarding the payment of any money to Mr. Burke. He maintained that no monies were paid on his behalf to Mr. Burke and he did not reimburse Mr. Barry for this payment at any time. He claimed he was aware of only two political payments made by Century, one in the sum of £5,000 to Fianna Fáil and one in the sum of £2,000 to Fine Gael. The Tribunal rejects Mr. Stafford's evidence on this issue.

7-28   The Tribunal accepts the evidence of Mr. Stafford's accountant, Mr. Thomas Moore, who stated that, on a date unknown in 1989, Mr. Stafford informed him, in the course of a conversation, that Mr. Barry was contemplating making a payment to Mr. Burke. Mr. Moore said in evidence, " Mr. Stafford said that he was appalled at the idea, it wasn't the way he did business and he didn't want Century Communications involved in it, in a transaction of that nature." Mr. Moore said that Mr. Stafford informed him that he would advise Mr. Crowley, the Chairman of the company, of what was being proposed and Mr. Moore agreed with this course of action.

7-29   The evidence of Mr. Laurence Crowley confirmed that Mr. Stafford had informed him, in the summer of 1989, that Mr. Barry had made a payment of £35,000 to Mr. Burke. The evidence of Mr. John Mulhern was that Mr. Stafford informed him of the payment in 1989. The Tribunal is satisfied that Mr. Stafford was aware from July 1989 that Mr. Barry was seeking to reimburse himself for the £35,000 expenditure to Mr. Burke by withholding an equivalent amount from the share capital account contribution that was due by him at that time.

7-30   In Mr. Stafford's interview with the Tribunal legal team prior to giving evidence before the Tribunal, he claimed that he did not actually know of such a payment having been made until he read it in a report of the Tribunal's proceedings in the newspapers. He subsequently endeavoured to qualify this, in his oral evidence before the public sessions of the Tribunal, by stating that whilst he was made aware of a claim for £35,000 reimbursement by Mr. Barry in March 1991, he did not actually believe that the original payment had ever been made and, consequently, he claimed that this allowed him to state that he did not actually know of the payment until he read of it in the newspapers. The Tribunal rejects Mr. Stafford's evidence in this regard.

7-31   The Tribunal is satisfied that Mr. Stafford had, at all times since the payment was made public, endeavoured to distance himself from any association with the payment made by Mr. Barry to Mr. Burke and that the reason for so doing is that he knew that the payment to Mr. Burke was a corrupt payment.

7-32   The Tribunal does not believe that Mr. Barry would have expended £35,000 of his own monies in paying Mr. Burke without being satisfied that he would be reimbursed by his fellow promoters of Century for such payment.

7-33   The Tribunal is satisfied that Mr. Barry was so reimbursed with the assistance of Mr. Stafford and the knowledge of Mr. Mulhern. Mr. Stafford himself acknowledged his awareness of the fact that Mr. Barry was endeavouring to recoup certain cash payments amounting to £40,000, which he said were made without him being informed. In communication with his own solicitor, in February 1993, in connection with a claim he was then processing against Mr. Barry, he said: -

> "Mr. Barry maintained that he was entitled to a sum of £40,000 in respect of certain payments he had made. He maintained that these payments were in cash, no invoices were issued, and no receipts ever obtained. These payments allegedly on behalf of Century were made without my being consulted or informed and when I was put on notice of their nature I refused to accept them, or indeed to be associated with them in any manner. However Mr. Barry pressed his claim against Century in October/November for £40,000 but on the basis of his own staff costs and following exchange of correspondence with Patrick Taylor of Capital Radio plc on the 20 and 21 December 1990 he was paid the following February."

Mr. Stafford stated in evidence that these instructions to his solicitors in 1993 were incorrect. He said that he assisted Mr. Barry in obtaining these legitimate expenses from Century.

7-34   The Tribunal rejects Mr. Stafford's claim that these instructions to his solicitors were incorrect. The Tribunal is satisfied that Mr. Stafford was equating the payment to Mr. Barry of the £40,000 in February 1991 with the recovery by Mr. Barry of his payment to Mr. Burke in May 1989.

The Tribunal considers it significant that Mr. Stafford held this view of the claim for the recovery of the £40,000. The Tribunal concludes that Mr. Stafford was at all times aware that the claim by Mr. Barry for the recovery of this sum of £40,000 from Century was an attempt by him to recover the monies paid to Mr. Burke. The Tribunal is equally satisfied that Mr. Stafford assisted Mr. Barry in recovering this money and, therefore, was complicit in the deception of Century and Capital Radio at this time.

MR. MULHERN'S KNOWLEDGE OF THE £35,000 PAYMENT BY MR. BARRY TO MR. BURKE

7-35   Mr. Mulhern claimed to have first learned of this payment only after the event, and infers that he would not have given his consent to such payment being made had he learned of it in advance. He acknowledged that he became aware of the payment "before the end of 1989" and said that he had been made aware of the payment by Mr. Stafford.

7-36   The Tribunal has already concluded that Mr. Stafford was in fact aware of the payment in 1989, despite his claim to the contrary. The Tribunal is satisfied that the payment of £35,000 in 1989 was a substantial outlay, and considers that it is improbable that Mr. Barry would have taken it upon himself to make such a payment from his own funds unless he had reasonable grounds for believing that he was going to be recompensed by his fellow promoters of Century for this expenditure or given credit for this payment in some way.

7-37   The Tribunal considers it unlikely that Mr. Barry would have assumed that he would have been recompensed by them as a matter of course, and that it is more probable that he would have made his fellow promoters aware of his intention to make the payment before so doing. Mr. Barry was vague in his evidence as to how he made his fellow promoters aware of his intention to pay the money, but says that it was his belief that the payment was made with their prior knowledge and approval. As with Mr. Stafford, Mr. Mulhern has denied prior knowledge of the payment.

7-38   The Tribunal believes that Mr. Barry would have shared his knowledge of company matters with Mr. Stafford and Mr. Mulhern equally, and that there are no circumstances in which he would have kept from Mr. Mulhern information concerning Century which he had imparted to Mr. Stafford. All three promoters of Century had very vague recollections of the circumstances surrounding the making of this payment to Mr. Burke and their knowledge of the payment.

7-39   The Tribunal is satisfied, having regard to the size of the payment, that it was a matter which must, at some point in time, have been discussed specifically by all three promoters of Century and that on the balance of probabilities such discussion took place prior to the payment to Mr. Burke. Any reimbursement of Mr. Barry's payment would have to have been made with the consent of all three.

7-40   Although Mr. Mulhern's involvement as a shareholder in Century was disguised from both the IRTC and the stockbrokers who had placed Century's shares, the Tribunal is satisfied that Mr. Mulhern was kept abreast of affairs within the company by Mr. Stafford and Mr. Barry. The Tribunal is satisfied that, having regard to the nature of the relationship which existed between Mr. Barry and Mr. Burke, Mr. Barry would have made Mr. Burke aware of Mr Mulhern's involvement with Century. Mr. Mulhern acknowledges that he was aware of the payment in 1989. He said that he had been made aware of it by Mr. Stafford before the end of 1989, either some weeks or indeed months, after the payment had been made. He said that he came from a 'different school' to Mr. Barry and, in his opinion, it should not have been paid as this was an infant business and, having regard to the size of the donation, the company could not afford this disbursement. He took the view that once it had been done, he could not change it and stated that he may have expressed his displeasure to Mr. Barry that the payment had been made.

7-41   The Tribunal is not satisfied that this affords the explanation for Mr. Mulhern's unhappiness with the payments. The Tribunal believes that, on the balance of probabilities, Mr. Mulhern would, in those circumstances, have sought to know the full details of how and why a payment was made to Mr. Burke, what the motivation of Mr. Barry in making the payment on behalf of Century was, and Mr. Barry's explanation for not informing him in advance that he intended to make the payment. Apparently none of these issues were raised by Mr. Mulhern with Mr. Barry.

7-42   The Tribunal believes it probable that Mr. Barry would have informed Mr. Mulhern that the request had been made of him by Mr. Burke for the money and, if such is the case, it must have been clear to Mr. Mulhern that this was an improper payment, not only because of its size, but because it had been effectively demanded of Mr. Barry in circumstances where Century and Mr. Burke had unfinished business.

7-43   The Tribunal is not satisfied that Mr. Mulhern's account of his knowledge of this payment is full or accurate and believes on the balance of probabilities that he was made aware of the fact that a payment was sought prior to it having been made and that he acquiesced in the payment, albeit reluctantly.

CONCLUSIONS

7-44   In relation to the £35,000 the Tribunal concludes that: -

1. Mr. Burke solicited £30,000 in cash from Mr. Oliver Barry in May 1989.

2. Mr. Barry brought this demand to the attention of his associate in Quality Artistes Management Limited, Mrs. McManus, and also to the attention of his fellow promoters in Century, Mr. James Stafford and Mr. John Mulhern prior to making the payment of £35,000 to Mr. Burke on the 26th May 1989.

3. It was agreed by Mr. Stafford and Mr. Mulhern that a payment of £35,000 to Mr. Burke would be financed by Century although the actual payment over of the sum in cash was to be made by Mr. Barry through funds at his disposal.

4. The payment to Mr. Burke was not made as a contribution towards election expenses in Dublin North, but was made in response to his request for money at a time when the promoters believed that it would assist their private interests if the money was paid to Mr. Burke, as Mr. Burke would act in Century's interests when performing his public duties both as the Minister for Communications and a member of the Government.

5. The money was received by Mr. Burke, not as a political contribution, but as a bribe.

6. Various attempts were made by Mr. Barry, with the support of Mr. Stafford and the knowledge of Mr. Mulhern, to reimburse Mr. Barry for the payment made to Mr. Burke from the funds of Century.

7. The delay in reimbursement of the funds to Mr. Barry stemmed from the fact that the accountants to Century were not prepared to sanction a payment of company funds without appropriate documentation to vouch the payment.

8. No vouching documentation was sought from Mr. Burke by Mr. Barry because it was known that the payment was an illicit payment which would not be acknowledged by Mr. Burke in writing.

Chapter 8

Mr. Burke's Relationship with Century's Promoters in 1989

8-01   On the 15th September 1989, at the instigation of the IRTC, a lunch meeting with Century management personnel was held at the Grey Door Restaurant. The objective was to improve relations between the parties. A note of the meeting was taken by Mr. Laffan of Century and the content of the comments attributed to Mr. Connolly, the Secretary of the IRTC, were confirmed subsequently by Mr. Connolly who informed the Tribunal that the views expressed were those of the Commission.

8-02   The document noted Mr. Connolly's comment that the promoters of Century Radio were "too highly politicised" and that they felt "empowered to enlist the help of Ministers wherever and whenever they chose." The Ministerial Directive of the 14th March 1989 was highlighted as an example of this claim. Mr. Connolly had also referred to "the almost daily consultation with the Minister on matters which properly belonged to discussion and negotiations between Century, the IRTC and RTÉ." The Tribunal believes that the views expressed by Mr. Connolly at that time were an accurate summation of the relationship which existed between Century and the Minister.

STEPS TAKEN BY MR. BURKE TO ASSIST CENTURY FROM DECEMBER 1989

The Broadcasting Act 1990

8-03   The Tribunal inquired into the circumstances surrounding the origin, preparation and ultimate enactment of the Broadcasting Act 1990. This Act restricted the sale of advertising time by RTÉ, which in turn led to the substantial reduction in its overall income. Mr. Burke, as Minister for Communications, was centrally involved in promoting this legislation.

8-04   The Tribunal also inquired into a proposed amendment to the Broadcasting Bill, as it made its way through the Oireachtas. The suggested amendment was announced by Mr. Burke in the Dáil on 29th May 1990 and, if enacted, would have diverted a portion of RTÉ's licence fee income to the IRTC for onward distribution to the independent broadcasting sector. By the 7th June 1990 however, Mr. Burke informed the Dáil of the Government's intention not to proceed with this proposal.

8-05   The Tribunal was also concerned to inquire into the contents of a speech made by Mr. Burke to the Dáil, on 29th May 1990 where, having set out the original rationale for the development of 2FM, he queried whether in its then format (music based) it represented the best use of a "scarce and valuable natural resource." He there stated that the Government's intention was to ask the RTÉ Authority, as a matter of priority, to develop plans for an alternative use of 2FM which would be more in keeping with the public service mandate of RTÉ.

8-06   The effect of this latter proposal, if implemented, would have been to change the focus of programming within 2FM, thereby making it a less attractive medium for advertising. This could have had a significant adverse effect on RTÉ's advertising income and could have had a major benefit to Century, since 2FM was in direct competition with Century for advertising.

8-07   The Tribunal sought to establish whether these proposals and the ultimate introduction of the legislation constituted a proper exercise by Mr. Burke of his ministerial powers as Minister for Communications, and whether he was bringing forward proposals which reflected his own and the Government's policy, or whether his actions were motivated by a desire to rescue Century from financial ruin - particularly since Century had made a substantial payment to him in May of the previous year.

THE PERCEIVED CAUSES OF CENTURY'S FINANCIAL DIFFICULTIES

8-08   Mr. Barry and Mr. Stafford accepted in evidence that, by the end of 1989, after approximately three months on air, the Company was in serious financial crisis and was facing liquidation. Both Mr.

Barry and Mr. Stafford diverged, to some extent, in their evidence as to the cause of Century's malaise. The Tribunal's assessment of the various reasons offered for Century's failure by the main participants is as follows:

Mr. Stafford's perception of the cause of Century's difficulties

8-09   Mr. Stafford blamed RTÉ for Century's difficulties. He criticised the lack of transmission coverage afforded to Century by RTÉ, and claimed that it was in breach of its contractual obligations to Century. He also criticised the manner in which RTÉ restructured its own advertising strategy both prior to and after the launch of Century.

Mr. Barry's perception of the cause of Century's difficulties

8-10   Mr. Barry informed the Tribunal that he was of the view that Century's problems were attributed to a combination of internal factors including high start-up costs, salaries, and programming problems. He also identified difficulties with the transmission service provided by RTÉ as part of the problem claiming that there were large pockets of the country where Century did not have coverage. This complaint, however, must be viewed in the light of the fact that Mr. Barry was prepared to pay a sum, he said, of £5,000 in cash, by way of bonus payments to RTÉ staff for the work which they had carried out in enabling Century to get on air in September 1989.

RTÉ's perception of the cause of Century's difficulties

8-11   RTÉ disputed that it was in any way responsible for Century's financial difficulties. It pointed out that the transmission agreement, signed on the 28th July 1989, set out a time schedule for the installation of facilities for Century's FM transmission. It stated that under this contract the third quarter of 1990 was the earliest commencement date envisaged for the full transmission service. Century's financial woes were manifest in the first quarter of its operation, in December 1989. RTÉ was, in fact, ahead of schedule in the performance of its contractual obligations and had provided temporary installation for transmission facilities.

8-12   An RTÉ generated document, dated 29th September 1989, headed *"Temporary Installation, Primary and Fringe Coverage for FM only"* shows that, as of that date, RTÉ had provided Century with 45.6% coverage nationally. The memorandum went on to state that it was intended that, by the end of November, that figure would increase to 48.9%, reaching 68.3% by 15th December 1989.

8-13   In a memorandum to the staff of Century, dated 18th October 1989, Mr. Laffan noted that the level of developments in the transmission system was such that Century would have in excess of 70% coverage of the national population by the end of November 1989, and in excess of 75% by the end of that year. Furthermore, in an internal bank memorandum of 7th December 1989, Century's bankers recorded that Messrs. Stafford and Barry informed them that Century, at that date, had a broadcasting coverage of 70 – 75%.

Capital Radio's perception of the cause of Century's difficulties

8-14   Mr. Taylor of Capital Radio attributed Century's difficulties to two things. First, Century had made commitments to advertisers in relation to audience levels which had not been fulfilled, as a result of which the revenues generated did not match the cost of the station. And, second, the station was set up with a significant level of costs, particularly in respect of personnel. He believed that it was clear from the way in which the station was structured initially that it was non-viable in the medium term.

The view within the Department of Communications as to the cause of Century's difficulties

8-15   Mr. Grant of the Department said of Century that:

> "My recollection is that there was a view that the station was unfocused in the audience it was intending to reach. There was a view, I think, that it had spent a lot of money on high profile presenters, and that high profile presenters did not necessarily bring in the audience and of course, the two issues that were crucial to the success of any National Radio Service was the extent of its coverage and the popularity of its programming, if we are not talking about pure public service programming. I don't know whether we coined the phrase, but certainly we wrote it a number of times, that advertising follows audience and until such time as Century Radio had developed a significant or relatively significant

audience share, it was going to be difficult to persuade advertisers to spend a significant amount of money on the station. I do recollect that there was a view that the advertising sector was favourably disposed towards Century because they were naturally anxious, in the interest of bringing pressure, presumably on RTÉ to bring down their advertising rates, to a viable competitive alternative to RTÉ."

THE SEARCH FOR A SOLUTION TO CENTURY'S FINANCIAL DIFFICULTIES

8-16   Shortly after Century went on air it became apparent that it was not generating the projected income and that its costs were in excess of its revenue to the extent that, unless significant savings could be made in running costs and significantly increased advertising sold, it would be insolvent. Accordingly, Century explored all of the available options open to it to limit its costs and increase its revenue including limiting its public service content which was fixed at 20% of air time.

Legal advice

8-17   Mr. Eugene Fanning, solicitor of Arthur Cox & Co., faxed Mr. Michael Laffan, Chief Executive of Century, on the 30th November 1989, in connection with advertising on RTÉ radio and television. This fax followed a telephone conversation which had taken place the previous day between Mr. Laffan and Mr. Fanning, where advice was sought as to what leeway or freedom Century could obtain from the IRTC as regards the 20% public service content requirement imposed on them as a condition of its broadcasting licence. The advice given detailed the national and European legislation, as regards RTÉ and Century's advertising entitlements, and the Minister's power to regulate in that area. Prior to December 1989 there were no discussions or proposals within the Department of Communications which in any way suggested curtailing RTÉ's advertising time. Representations had been made over time to the Minister and to the Department by the print media and their lobbyists that such curbs be introduced. However, this was not in the context of independent radio broadcasting.

The involvement of the Minister, Mr. Burke

8-18   Mr. Burke was approached by Messrs. Barry and Stafford, in relation to the precarious financial situation, which had developed in Century by early December 1989. Two meetings took place on the 19th December 1989, involving these parties. On the 19th December a copy of the legal advices, which had been furnished by Mr. Fanning to Mr. Laffan on the 30th November, were faxed to Mr. Stafford at his request. The covering page of the fax transmission drew attention to Section 20(3) of the Broadcasting Act 1960 suggesting that this enabled the Minister for Communications to regulate advertisements in RTÉ and that the total daily time allocated to advertising and distribution of advertisements throughout the day was a matter which was subject to ministerial approval, thereby clearly suggesting that the Minister could unilaterally control RTÉ's advertising strategy.

8-19   In evidence Mr. Burke said that he could not recall being given these advices nor did he have any recollection of receiving the fax. However, a copy of the fax was found in the documentation discovered to the Tribunal by the Department of Communications. The Tribunal is satisfied that this document was probably given to Mr. Burke by Mr.. Barry or Mr. Stafford at the time of their first meeting on 19th December 1989, and that it was considered by him at that time.

8-20   Of the two meetings attended by Mr. Burke, Mr. Barry, and Mr. Stafford, on the 19th December 1989, the first took place in the morning and the second later that afternoon. There was no civil servant present at the first meeting. The meeting was quite short and Messrs. Barry and Stafford were to return again that afternoon. In the course of the meeting, Mr. Burke was advised of Century's perilous financial position and of Mr. Stafford's view that this had been brought about by the abuse of a dominant position within the broadcasting industry by RTÉ. Mr. Barry and Mr. Stafford claimed that a levelling of the playing pitch in advertising was necessary, and they sought Mr. Burke's assistance in this regard. Mr. Burke informed the Tribunal that there was anecdotal evidence from local stations as well as a general perception that this was in fact the case. He acknowledged, however, that no evidence, documentary or otherwise, was introduced at this meeting to support this contention. As Century was broadcasting for no more than three months at this time, the Tribunal considers that its directors' capacity to pronounce with any certainty upon the cause of its financial ills being related to RTÉ's activities must, at a minimum, have been considered speculative.

8-21   The second meeting took place on the afternoon of the 19th December 1989 and, in addition to those who had attended the earlier meeting, the Minister was accompanied by Mr. Bernard McDonagh,

Secretary General to the Department of Communications. The Tribunal sought to establish whether any minutes of this important meeting existed, but no departmental documentation recording what had transpired at that meeting was available to the Tribunal. From the evidence of those who attended the meeting, the Tribunal is satisfied that Mr. Barry and Mr. Stafford threatened to liquidate Century unless the Minister found a solution to their difficulties. Whilst Mr. Burke does not recollect the meeting, he does not dispute that such a meeting took place or that he was in attendance. He had a recollection of complaints being brought to his attention by Mr. Barry or Mr. Stafford about unfair competition and the treatment of Century at the hands of RTÉ.

8-22   Mr. Stafford maintained that certain assurances were given by the Minister at the afternoon meeting, and, as a result of these assurances, both he and Mr. Barry temporarily shelved their decision to liquidate Century.

8-23   The Tribunal accepts that, at the afternoon meeting, Mr. Burke gave a direction to Mr. McDonagh to take steps to cap the level of RTÉ's advertising time. The Tribunal accepts that Mr. Stafford's letter to Mr. Burke, of 26th February 1990, is confirmatory of this fact. There was subsequently a dispute as to whether Mr. Burke had given an assurance to Century's promoters that RTÉ's advertising time would be reduced by 50% or by a lesser proportion. Mr. Burke, however, denied that he had ever given any such assurance.

8-24   Further support for Messrs. Barry and Stafford's contention that assurances had been given to them at that meeting to curtail RTÉ's advertising revenue can be gleaned from a memorandum prepared within the Department of Communications, on the 3rd January 1990. Mr. McDonagh, Secretary General in the Department, had delegated to Mr. Ó Móráin, Principal Officer in the Department, the task of obtaining advices from the Office of the Attorney General as to how the Minister could reduce the total daily advertising time allowed to RTÉ. In the course of this memorandum Mr. Ó Móráin noted, "the more fundamental question of cutting back RTÉ's limit to 5% to help Century…." The Tribunal believes that it is clear from this memorandum that Mr. Ó Móráin had been instructed that the intended action was directed towards helping Century. As Mr. Ó Móráin had not himself attended this meeting, he could only have obtained this information from either Mr. McDonagh or from the Minister. The reference to cutting back RTÉ's limit to 5% refers to the percentage of advertising time per broadcasting hour that was allowed under the regulation. The result of reducing advertising time to 5% would effect a 50% cut in the total advertising time available to RTÉ.

8-25   Still further support for Messrs. Barry and Stafford's contention that the Minister had given an assurance that he would reduce RTÉ's advertising times, comes from a memorandum prepared by Mr. Paul McHale, a bank official, to whom Mr. Stafford and Mr. Barry had recounted details of their meeting with Mr. Burke on the day following the meeting. Mr. McHale's memorandum, of 20th December 1989, records as follows:

> "The following information was advised in confidence by James Stafford and Oliver Barry at the Century meeting:
>
> The Minister for Communications has confirmed to Oliver Barry and James Stafford that with almost immediate effect RTÉ will be required to operate on an equal basis in future. This stipulation will be issued by way of regulation, Directive or legislation if necessary. The major benefit to the independent sphere will be that advertising time available to RTÉ1 and 2 will in future be the same as that available to Century themselves. Century estimated that this will reduce RTÉ income by approximately 25%. Oliver Barry suggested that the decision may in effect bring about closure of RTÉ 2.
>
> The decision has full Cabinet support, which is totally committed to the concept of independent radio and its success.
>
> The decision it would appear has come about as a result of pressure from all of the independents whose viability is in question as a result of RTÉ's strength and its ability to cross fund Radio 2 from Radio 1.
>
> Barry and Stafford advised that the Minister would be pleased to meet with a representative from the bank to offer reassurance on the above…"

MEETING BETWEEN CENTURY'S BANKERS AND MR. BURKE

8-26   The Bank took up the offer to meet the Minister. Mr. Burke met with Century's bankers on the 22nd December 1989. The meeting was attended by Messrs. Burke, Stafford, Barry and three senior officials from Bank of Ireland. No civil servants were present at this meeting, which took place in one of the Minister's offices, the exact location of which is not clear. One of the bank officials believed that it took place "just up from the corner of Earlsfort Terrace."

8-27   Other than a manuscript note prepared after the meeting by Mr. Michael Connolly, one of the bank officials, no other written record appears to have existed of what was discussed and agreed with the Minister at this meeting. Mr. Connolly's note gives further corroboration of the evidence of Messrs. Barry and Stafford regarding the assurances given to them at the second meeting of the 19th December 1989. The note records :

> "Minister confirmed:

> 1. Government's commitment to independent radio and intention to eliminate RTÉ 'excesses' in recent months. Will limit their advertising – either by way of Ministerial order (Attorney General examining this at the present) or legislation. Legislation will be initiated immediately post-Christmas; will try to get it through by Easter but at worst by summer recess.

> 2. Talking to radio authority re sharing of news between independent stations. Aware of costs impact on Century of present "stand alone" system.

> 3. We asked Stafford/Barry to leave meeting for a few minutes. During this – Minister confirmed commitment to Century (rather than just all independent stations in general)."

8-28   Century was, at this time, considerably indebted to the Bank of Ireland and, whilst there was no offer of money made by Century to the bank at that time, the bank personnel gave evidence that they took some comfort from the fact that a Cabinet Minister was meeting with them on behalf of Century in Christmas week. The bankers maintained, however, that they were not influenced in the operation of the account as a result of whatever steps the Minister took. Mr. O'Donoghue, another of the bank's officials, said that there so many strings attached to the Minister's assurance that the meeting really did not have a major influence, and he would not comment as to whether or not the bank would have appointed a receiver in the absence of the Minister's assurances.

Mr. Burke's evidence in relation to the meeting with Century's bankers

8-29   The Tribunal considers it important to note that Mr. Burke himself accepted in evidence that at this time, no issue relating to RTÉ's claimed "excesses" in the advertising market had been brought to Government, nor had any decision been taken concerning a change in the then current legislation. Accordingly, contrary to what is recorded in the memoranda, the Government had not given any commitment to the course suggested by Mr. Burke. Although Mr. Burke denied that he had used the word "excesses" when referring to RTÉ as is recorded in the bank memorandum, he said that he did have a different view to his Department staff as to whether or not there were excesses on the part of RTÉ.

8-30   Mr. Burke maintained that he was not telling the bankers about the Government's view regarding RTÉ, but was merely expressing his own view, as he was not in a position to express the Government's view. He stated he would not have informed anybody of the Government's intention, particularly at a time when he had not put anything before the Government. His explanation was that the bankers must have misinterpreted what he had said to them, and that they were obviously linking the Government's commitment to independent radio to his personal intention to bring forward legislation to cap advertising. The Tribunal notes that Mr. Burke's interpretation of what had taken place in this meeting is not supported by any other documentation discovered from Century, the Bank, or the Department.

The meeting with the bankers in the absence of Messrs. Stafford and Barry

8-31   The Tribunal considers it significant that the bankers requested their clients to leave the meeting whilst they discussed the matter further with the Minister. The Tribunal considers this to be a significant indicator of the importance which the bank was placing upon the Minister's assurances. The Tribunal believes that the purpose of continuing the meeting in the absence of the clients was to allow the bankers the opportunity of testing Mr. Burke's commitment. If the clients were not present, it allowed Mr. Burke the opportunity of putting whatever qualification he wished upon the assurances that he had already given. The Tribunal is satisfied that Mr. Burke did not qualify his commitment in any way, but assured the bankers in terms that allowed them to report that the commitment of Mr. Burke, the Minister, was a commitment to Century in particular rather than to the independent broadcasting industry as a whole. The Tribunal does not accept Mr. Burke's evidence to the effect that he gave the bankers no guarantees or comfort other than to say what he had previously said to them in the presence of its clients, namely that the Government was committed to the independent broadcasting sector and since Century was a major part of the whole of this sector the Government was committed to them.

Century's credit status with its bankers prior to the meeting with the Minister of the 22nd December 1989

8-32 In October 1989, the Bank of Ireland offered facilities to Century which comprised an overdraft of £1 million, a term loan of £1 million, and letters of guarantee in favour of RTÉ in an amount of £282,000 and to Telecom Éireann in the sum of £20,000. The overdraft facility was repayable on demand and the term loan was repayable in four equal instalments, the first of which was to be paid on the 31st December 1992. These facilities were accepted by Century. By the 7th December 1989, it was apparent to the bankers that Century was in breach of its covenants undertaken at the time of taking out the loan. Instead of having a net worth of approximately £1.2 million in line with its original forecast, the net worth was £554,000 as of the 26th November 1989, and its net current liabilities were £883,000 as opposed to the £214,000 forecast.

8-33 The Tribunal is satisfied that this marked change in the financial situation prompted the bank to revise its approach to Century. Under the terms of its loan facility it would have been entitled to call in its loan to Century at that time. The Tribunal is satisfied that, on the 22nd December 1989, the bank verbally notified Mr. Barry and Mr. Stafford that it was altering the existing facility and offering in lieu an overdraft facility of £2 million, which was verbally accepted by Mr. Barry and Mr. Stafford. Whereas the parties subsequently disputed the precise conditions which should attach to this loan offer, the Tribunal is satisfied on the balance of probabilities that the bank's decision to offer this new facility to Century was influenced by the assurances given by Mr. Burke that he would effect the regulatory or legislative change necessary to limit RTÉ's advertising.

The Tribunal's conclusions from Mr. Burke's meetings with the Bankers

8-34 The Tribunal is satisfied that Century's bankers received an assurance from Mr. Burke, as Minister for Communications, that he would introduce the necessary regulation or legislation to curb RTÉ's revenue from advertising. The intended consequence of this action was clearly to improve Century's financial prospects. The Tribunal is satisfied that the fact of such assurance being given to the bank by a Cabinet Minister influenced the bank in their decision to continue providing finance to Century.

PRESSURE EXERTED UPON MR. BURKE TO DELIVER UPON HIS COMMITMENT TO CAP RTÉ'S REVENUE

8-35 After the December meetings, Mr. Stafford wrote to Mr. Burke at his department, strongly urging him to implement the solution in accordance with his agreement at their meeting and the meeting with Century's bankers. None of this correspondence was found within the Department files, where it could be expected that such communication would be retained.

8-36 The first letter regarding this issue was dated the 26th February 1990. It advised that Century's losses for January and February 1990 were the greatest of any month to date. It further advised that Century's bankers were very concerned that the solution proposed had not been implemented, and that Century could not expect the bank to tolerate a further dilution of its security, unless the solution was implemented quickly. Mr. Stafford's letter set out the position thus:

> "I refer you to our meeting held on the morning of the 19th December 1989 when both Oliver Barry and I advised you of the difficulties being encountered by Century and to our subsequent discussion that afternoon. On the basis of your assurance that you would

cut approximately 50% of RTÉ's total advertising time and revenue to be spread equally across all its services, along with all the various safeguards discussed, both Oliver and I have continued to support Century. Both of us were greatly reassured by your instructing the Secretary of your Department in our presence that such measures be brought into effect immediately by direction or legislation if necessary. We were further reassured that if it were necessary to bring in legislation that the latest date of implementation of the solution would be the end of February."

8-37 Mr. Stafford again sent a letter on the 18th April 1990. This letter was sent following a meeting which had taken place between Mr. Stafford, Mr. Barry and Mr. Burke on that day. It was addressed to Mr. Burke at the Department of Communications, Scotch House, Hawkins Street, Dublin 2. This letter set out a number of Mr. Stafford's complaints with regard to what was being proposed at that time by Mr. Burke in the draft legislation, namely: -

(a) He complained that what was being proposed by Mr. Burke at this point was not consistent with what had been sought and promised by Mr. Burke to Century and its bankers in December/January, in that the net effect of the proposed legislation was to reduce RTÉ's advertising time by 25% whereas Mr. Burke had earlier agreed to a reduction of 50%.

(b) He complained that the proposed solution for capping RTÉ's revenue at 75% of its licence fee still allowed RTÉ to sell advertising at a significant discount to actual costs.

(c) He proposed a solution which he felt was one which would have been acceptable to all parties, subject to certain safeguards, as follows: -

> "To be constructive, I would suggest that an acceptable solution to all parties must be that RTÉ's total licence fee for the last year as a percentage of RTÉ's total running costs, both TV and radio, be deemed to be a purchase by the licence payers of a corresponding percentage of their total allowable advertising time of 6 minutes."

8-38 Mr. Burke accepted in evidence that both of these letters had been written to him. He insisted, however, that what Mr. Stafford was reminding him of was what he, Mr. Stafford, perceived to have been given by way of an assurance of the meeting in December 1989, whereas Mr. Stafford was in fact wrong in his perception. He endeavoured to explain Mr. Stafford's remarks on the basis that Mr. Stafford was under considerable pressure at the time. Mr. Burke stated that he had never contemplated cutting RTÉ's advertising by 50%, as stated by Mr. Stafford and that Mr. Stafford was, in effect, writing in hope rather than in expectation. He acknowledged that the letters were an attempt by Mr. Stafford to pressurise him into a course of action, but he was adamant that Mr. Stafford did not succeed in so doing.

8-39 The Tribunal believes that Mr. Burke received both letters, notwithstanding that no acknowledgement issued from his Department. The Tribunal concludes that these letters were retained by Mr. Burke because their contents confirmed that he had given assurances to Century's promoters which were improper in the circumstances and which would have been politically damaging to him had the contents of the letters been publicly aired.

THE STEPS TAKEN BY THE DEPARTMENT OF COMMUNICATIONS TO IMPLEMENT MR. BURKE'S WISH TO CONTROL RTÉ'S ADVERTISING

8-40 The advent of Independent Radio was a period of transition for the Department because, for 30 years or more, they had a relationship with only one broadcaster, but were now required to work with a number of broadcasters including RTÉ.

8-41 After Mr. Burke had given the commitment to Century to regulate RTÉ's advertising, the Department was faced with the problem of ensuring that the implementation of this wish by the Department did not infringe any legal entitlement of others. Some years beforehand, when RTÉ was the only national broadcaster, RTÉ's advertising limits were set at 10% of broadcasting time per day, subject to a maximum of 7.5 minutes in any one broadcasting hour.

8-42   Mr. Ó Móráin of the Department contacted the Attorney General's office by letter, on the 2nd January 1990, seeking advice as to whether the Minister could unilaterally withdraw his approval of the advertising limits which were in existence and seek to establish new and lower levels either directly or indirectly by refusing to approve anything other than the lower limits which he had in mind.

8-43   Mr. Ó Móráin's memorandum of the 3rd January 1990, directed to the Secretary of his Department, contains a contemporaneous record of what the Department believed the Minister had in mind at that time. The memorandum records the objective of the Department, as directed by Mr. Burke, was the "cutting back [of] RTÉ's limit to 5% to help Century." The memorandum envisaged, by reducing the level to 5%, approximately £7 million of advertising revenue would be displaced - although there was no evidence that this displaced advertising would go to Century. Whilst Mr. Ó Móráin understood the objective of the reduction in advertising time was to help Century, he was less than certain that the proposed course of action would achieve the desired outcome. He recorded: -

> "(b)   In the IRTC's view the most of it will be picked up by local stations who, in comparison to Century, have been significantly exceeding revenue targets to date. Century's basic problem in the IRTC view is its lack of identity and programming appeal.
>
> (c)   Advertising follows audience. Even with a 5% limit RTÉ will probably be able to retain a reasonable share of the 'displaced' advertising by simply increasing price."

8-44   Despite the view expressed by his civil servants, Mr. Burke was not to be deterred in the course of action which he had chosen, and the Department continued its liaison with the Attorney General's office on this complex issue. While Mr. Burke's department was considering actions which would radically affect RTÉ's operations, no official communication of the Minister's intentions was made known to RTÉ. The Department and RTÉ had, for years, conducted regular informal meetings to discuss and resolve, where possible, matters of mutual interest. The understanding was that these meetings took place under, what was described in evidence as, the '*Chatam House Rules*', which the Tribunal understood to mean that no note or memorandum of the contents of these meetings were to be prepared of the matters discussed at such meetings.

8-45   Despite this understanding a note was prepared within RTÉ, on the 6th February 1990, following one such meeting, from which it is apparent to the Tribunal that RTÉ became informally aware of moves afoot to assist Century. The memorandum in question records as follows: -

> "Century Communications: Department officials advised that the political will was that Century had to succeed and therefore be given whatever support was necessary to achieve this. Consideration had already been given to a restriction on advertising time on RTÉ Radio but this was being ruled out as it would be of greater assistance to the other independent radio stations, as Century did not have the product at present to attract audience levels justifying increased advertising spend. The question of a subvention from the television licence fee had been raised but this would require legislation and would also lead to demands for equal treatment by the other independent radio stations and, in time, TV3.
>
> RTÉ providing free transmission facilities would not be a great [*sic*] cash flow assistance due to low level of these charges already.
>
> Department officials requested RTÉ to give the matter serious thought as it was probable that at short notice, RTÉ would be requested to assist Century – ideally whatever assistance being given, should be capable of being withdrawn if/when Century became financially viable ."

8-46   The issue of the diversion of RTÉ licence fee income and the subsidisation of Century by RTÉ was raised in the Dáil on 27th February 1990 by a number of deputies, following a press release issued by Mr. Jim Mitchell, T.D. on the 12th February 1990. In the course of debate on this issue, Mr. Burke replied as follows to the Dáil: -

> "Neither I nor my Department have made any proposals, formal or informal, to RTÉ to divert income to any independent radio station.

…I take this opportunity to say again; in case there is any misunderstanding, that neither my Department nor I have made any proposals, formal or informal, to RTÉ to divert income to any independent radio station. Not only am I saying that but I note that the Director General of RTÉ has confirmed the situation."

8-47   Whilst it is true to say that Mr. Burke had not formally approached RTÉ, it is also abundantly clear that he did have plans to curtail RTÉ's revenue by capping its advertising revenue and also that he had considered the question of a subvention from the licence fee income which had been informally disclosed to RTÉ by his department on the 6th February 1990.

8-48   The Tribunal considers that the Minister's lack of consultation with RTÉ, on a matter which was to cause it a significant reduction in its available income, was remarkable. It was estimated that the proposals could amount to a reduction of up to £14 million in RTÉ's income from advertising on the basis of the 1989 figures of £55.2 million.

8-49   As late as March 1990, Mr. Burke had yet to consult with RTÉ. As of the 13th March 1990, Mr. Grant of the Department had prepared a document in which he indicated a method whereby RTÉ's advertising time could be capped by linking the same to the licence fee of the previous year on a percentage basis. This formula ultimately found its way into the legislation. In his memorandum Mr. Grant said that this approach could go a long way to eliminating the possibility of endless and inconclusive rows with the independent broadcasting sector and the newspaper industry which could be expected if the restriction were to be expressed as a percentage of broadcasting time to be devoted to advertising. He suggested this approach would also enable RTÉ to promote its own activities including the sale of TV licences, the *"RTÉ Guide"*, etc.

8-50   No research had been done within the Department to ascertain whether there was a distorted media spend or whether RTÉ was abusing its dominant position. Yet the Department's own rough calculations showed a possible reduction in RTÉ's income as a result of these proposals to be in the order of £12-14 million per annum. The Department appreciated that the reduction in income would result in curtailment and reduction in programme quality, reduction in output and possible staff redundancies. This was of concern to the Department and the civil servants felt it necessary to formally record that the Department had not consulted RTÉ in regard to the consequences for programming or on the estimate of income diverted.

THE AIDE-MEMOIRE TO THE GOVERNMENT

8-51   An Aide-Memoire was circulated at the Government meeting of the 22nd March 1990 in which the Minister proposed an amendment to Section 20 of the Broadcasting Act 1960, so as to provide that the total daily time for broadcasting advertisements on RTÉ should not exceed 7.5% (as opposed to 10%) of broadcasting time per day. The maximum advertising in any one hour was to be limited to 4.5 minutes (as opposed to 7.5 minutes). The stated purpose of this measure was to provide "a fairer competitive environment for the independent broadcasting sector, and to address to some degree the concerns of the newspaper industry," The proposed lower limit was the equivalent to half the time allowed to the independent sector.

8-52   Mr. Burke received Government authority to arrange for the drafting of legislation along the lines proposed by him in his Aide-Memoire and his department set about giving consideration to the details of the "Heads of Bill" likely to be required to give effect to the proposals in the original Aide-Memoire.

8-53   On the 29th March 1990, Mr. Burke spoke directly with the Attorney General concerning the urgent preparation of the legislation as authorised by Government. The telephone conversation with the Attorney General was followed up on the following day by a letter from Mr. O'Morain enclosing the Aide-Memoire sent to Government, together with draft legislation which he had been instructed to prepare by the Minister. The draft legislation, with the words *"final copy"* written thereon, was approved by the Minister and sent to the Attorney General's office.

8-54   A memorandum, prepared by Mr. Grant for discussion within the Department, was entitled "Comments and suggestions on the draft of Broadcasting and Wireless Telegraphy." In it, Mr. Grant had suggested that RTÉ be allowed a limited form of flexibility by inserting the words "on average" after "7.5%" in the proposed legislation. Mr. O'Morain noted the Minister's views concerning this proposal as follows: -

"Minister was adamant, definitely not."

8-55   Mr. Burke in evidence said he had no recollection as to what was meant by this note. He rejected the suggestion that this position had been adopted because Mr. Stafford had indicated that he did not want any flexibility given to RTÉ.

8-56   Despite Mr. Burke's assertions to the contrary, the Tribunal is satisfied that, at this time, Mr. Stafford and Mr. Barry were in regular communication with Mr. Burke in view of the worsening financial crisis developing in Century and that pressure was being applied upon Mr. Burke to deliver upon his assurances. Mr. Stafford did not dispute that he was applying pressure for that purpose.

Chapter 9

The Extent to which the Proposed Legislative Changes were dictated by Century's Demands of the Minister for Communications

THE CAPPING OF RTÉ'S ADVERTISING

9-01   There were no plans in the Department of Communications in December 1989 to cap RTÉ's advertising. There was no evidence in the Department to indicate that independent broadcasters as a whole felt that RTÉ's advertising strategy was harming the industry. The complaints that there was not a level playing pitch and that there was an abuse of its dominant position by RTÉ, were developed by Mr. Stafford. Whilst Mr. Burke in evidence maintained that there was anecdotal evidence available to him that RTÉ was abusing its position, the Tribunal is satisfied that no such evidence was made available to the Department of Communications and that no investigation by the Minister was directed to establish whether or not there was, in fact, such abuse.

9-02   The Tribunal is satisfied that Mr. Stafford's complaints to Mr. Burke formed the basis of his direction to the Secretary-General of his department to proceed to reduce RTÉ's advertising capacity by 50%, either by Directive or by legislation.

9-03   The Tribunal is satisfied that Mr. Burke adopted Mr. Stafford's views without any proper analysis of the issue, and without commissioning any study into the possible adverse consequences which would follow in the event that Mr. Stafford's suggestion was implemented.

9-04   The Tribunal is satisfied that the genesis of the legislation to curb RTÉ's advertising costs was Mr. Stafford's request of Mr. Burke that such curbs be imposed.

THE PROPOSAL TO RE-DIRECT A PROPORTION OF THE LICENCE FEE INCOME

9-05   Prior to January 1990 there were no proposals extant in the Department of Communications to redirect any portion of the licence fee income which had to that date been paid to RTÉ. Century, however, sought Counsel's opinion on the 19th January 1990 and amongst the issues addressed was the question of the discretionary nature of the licence fee payments to RTÉ. Following receipt of counsel's advice Arthur Cox & Co., solicitors to Century, wrote to Century stating that:

> "Century could usefully consider approaching the Minister about the axing of some or all of the licence fee income received by RTÉ."

9-06   Counsel's view was that the Minister would be obliged to give RTÉ notice of his intention to axe some or all of the licence fee income, and that a 12 month period might be required. The solicitors offered the view that closer investigation of the deregulation situation could lead to the view that the period of notice could be considerably shorter than that. The Tribunal believes that it was only following these advices that consideration of the diversion of licence fee income to independent broadcasters was considered in the Department.

9-07   Some RTÉ personnel learned of a proposal in an informal way at the meeting which took place, on 6th February 1990, with the Department officials. On the 27th February 1990 the matter was raised specifically in the Dáil by Deputy Mitchell, and responded to by Mr. Burke in a manner which could only be interpreted as a denial that any such plans were afoot. A proposal to divert licence fee income was contained in proposed legislation which Mr. Burke laid before the Dáil on the 29th May 1990, (**Appendix P**). The criteria therein, to be applied in determining the entitlement of the independent broadcasters to share in the diverted licence fee, were such that Century was likely to be the main beneficiary of this legislation.

9-08   The Tribunal is satisfied on the balance of probabilities that Messrs. Barry and Stafford were the instigators of this proposal. The Tribunal considers that the speed with which Mr. Burke adopted this proposal is indicative of his overriding desire to assist Century's promoters. The Tribunal believes that Mr. Burke's decision to do so was taken without due consideration of the adverse consequences which might result to RTÉ from his decision, and that the explanation for his so doing was the payment made by Mr. Barry on Century's behalf.

THE PROPOSAL TO ALTER THE STATUS OF 2FM

9-09   In his speech to the Dáil, on the 29th May 1990, Mr. Burke set out the main rationale for the development of 2FM, and queried whether in its then format, which was music based, it represented the best use of a "scarce and valuable national resource." He stated that the Government's intention was to ask the new RTÉ Authority, as a matter of priority, to develop plans for alternative uses of 2FM, which would be more in keeping with the public service mandate of RTÉ. This issue had not formed part of any recorded deliberations of the civil servants in the Department of Communications to that point in time.

9-10   The Tribunal is satisfied that 2FM's position as a competitor of Century was a concern which had been specifically addressed by Century's public relations firm, Wilson Hartnell. The conclusions contained in a memorandum of a meeting on the 29th March 1990 between Century personnel and Mr. Frank Young of Wilson Hartnell included the following:

> "The most practical and beneficial solution based on the information available to us is to convince the Minister that the transfer of 2FM to Century is both in the best interests of Radio 1 and Century. It allows Radio 1 to compete in the open market with Century."

9-11   By 29th May 1990 Mr. Burke was in a position to make his Dáil speech concerning 2FM, and the possibility that its role would be altered. The Tribunal is satisfied that Mr. Burke had, by that time, discussed the matter both with Mr. Stafford, and with Mr. Barry, and that he had given them to understand that 2FM's role would not continue as theretofore.

9-12   In the absence of any investigation being carried out within his own department to establish the viability and consequences of moves to alter 2FM's programme content, the Tribunal is satisfied that the only factors which caused this matter to be raised in Dáil Éireann were the persistent attempts by Mr. Stafford and Mr. Barry to have the Minister alter the status of 2FM to their company's advantage.

CONCLUSIONS AS TO MR. BURKE'S EFFORTS TO ASSIST CENTURY FROM DECEMBER 1989 ONWARDS

9-13   The Tribunal concludes that the payment of £35,000 to Mr. Burke by Mr. Barry in May 1989 had the effect of ensuring that decisions made by Mr. Burke, in his capacity as Minister for Communications, would reflect favourably upon those who had paid him this sum.

9-14   The Tribunal concludes that the assurances given to Century's bankers were given to advance the private interests of Century's promoters, and not to advance the public interest.

9-15   The Tribunal is satisfied that Mr. Burke's decisions in relation to the proposed capping of RTÉ's advertising income, the diversion of licence fee income from RTÉ, and the possible reorganisation of 2FM, were all motivated by a desire on his part to benefit those who had paid monies to him, and that proposals on such issues would not have been advanced by Mr. Burke at that time were it not for the fact that he had been paid £35,000. In all the circumstances the Tribunal concludes that the payment made to Mr. Burke was a corrupt payment.

Chapter 10

Mr. P.J. Mara and the Promoters of Century Radio

BACKGROUND

10-01 Mr. P.J. Mara was Press Secretary to Fianna Fáil between 1983 and 1987. In 1987 he was appointed Government Press Secretary, and he held this position until February 1992, when he left the Public Service to move into the private sector.

10-02 During the course of his employment as a Press Secretary, his financial remuneration was not sufficient to meet his immediate financial requirements, and he experienced financial difficulties. He said he received assistance from his friends, Mr. Oliver Barry and Mr. Dermot Desmond, in the form of loans. There was no formal structure to these loans. There was no interest charge, nor was there any fixed schedule for repayment. Those making the loans did not intend that the sums advanced would be treated as gifts by Mr. Mara, but were content to receive their money back, once Mr. Mara was in a position so to do.

10-03 Mr. Oliver Barry remembered lending Mr. Mara a sum of £2,000 on one occasion between 1982 and 1984, and Mr. Desmond believed that he advanced sums in the region of £46,000 to Mr. Mara between 1986 and 1989. Mr. Desmond did not produce any formal record of such payments, but said that they had been made by cheque and that, these cheques were a record of the loan having been made.

MR. P.J. MARA'S INVOLVEMENT WITH THE TRIBUNAL.

10-04 The Tribunal became involved in inquiring into Mr. Mara's role with the promoters of Century because it had received information from Mr. James Stafford to the effect that: -

1. Mr. Oliver Barry had informed him in 1988, prior to the issue of the franchise to Century by the IRTC, that there was a rumour at the time that Mr. Burke and Mr. Mara expected to receive payment of £90,000 for the independent television licence, £75,000 for each of the Dublin radio licences, and £25,000 each for the local radio licences;

2. Mr. Stafford had indicated that Mr. Barry informed him in 1990 that Mr. Mara was seeking a sum of £30,000 from Century; and

3. Mr. Stafford had been requested to pay £30,000 to Mr. Mara by Mr. Dermot Desmond in September 1990.

10-05 The amended statement of evidence of Mr. Stafford, in which these allegations were contained, was circulated to all affected parties, and, at the opening of the module of evidence in which Mr. Stafford's allegations were addressed, on the 18th July 2000, Mr. Mara's rejection of the allegations, insofar as they affected him, was publicly aired.

10-06 In its private inquiries the Tribunal sought to establish whether or not Mr. Mara had in fact received monies which could be attributed to payments made by the licence holders of the franchises to provide independent broadcasting services in the State.

10-07 These inquiries included the making of an Order for Discovery and Production on the 7th December 2000, directed to Mr. Mara, requiring him to make discovery on oath of and to produce to the Tribunal, all documents in relation to any account of his, either within or outside the State, from 1988 onwards.

10-08 Mr. Mara's first affidavit of discovery, in purported compliance with the Order, was deficient insofar as the documentation provided was not properly scheduled, and did not provide adequate attribution of certain specific payments referred to therein. The second affidavit of discovery sworn by him purported to "tidy up matters not scheduled properly."

10-09   In correspondence which passed between the Tribunal and Mr. Mara's solicitors in March 2001, Mr. Mara stated that the only business activities carried out by him were carried out through Mara Communications Limited, and that the amounts received for such services were lodged to the accounts disclosed to the Tribunal.

10-10   Mr. Mara initially failed to disclose to the Tribunal the fact that he was the beneficial owner of an account held in the Royal Bank of Scotland, in the Isle of Man, by a company called Pullman Limited (Pullman). This was an Isle of Man company.

10-11   The details of this company available for inspection by the public at the Companies Office would not have revealed any connection between this company and Mr. Mara. However, it was the case that Mr. Mara was the beneficial owner of this company and that his interest was held in trust for him by a trust company called Europlan Trust Company (Isle of Man) Limited (Europlan Trust).

10-12   Europlan Trust transferred funds from the Isle of Man to the account of Mr. Mara and his wife, at Bank of Ireland Private Banking, and it was named as the transferor in the record of this transfer, which appeared in the body of his Bank of Ireland monthly statement of account for the month of March 1994. This statement was included in the documentation which had been provided to the Tribunal, not only by Mr. Mara, but also independently by Bank of Ireland.

10-13   The existence of Mr. Mara's offshore account in the Isle of Man had not been revealed in either of the affidavits of discovery sworn by him, or in subsequent correspondence. The first acknowledgement by Mr. Mara of the existence of the Pullman account was ultimately made to the Tribunal in the days leading up to the taking of his oral testimony before the Tribunal in July 2001. By way of explanation for his prior non-disclosure of this account, Mr. Mara told the Tribunal that he had forgotten about it, and was reminded of it by the Europlan Trust reference in his Bank of Ireland monthly statement.

10-14   In view of the specific requirement imposed on Mr. Mara by the Order made against him for discovery of documents in connection with offshore accounts, the Tribunal believes that it is unlikely that he could have forgotten about the existence of an account which had been opened by him in the Isle of Man. This is manifestly so given the steps which would have had to be taken to form a company there and to maintain an account in that jurisdiction, given the level of turnover in the account between August 1993 and October 1997 and given the fact that Mr. Mara had used Pullman as a vehicle to bill for services within the jurisdiction as late as September 1997. The Tribunal does not accept Mr. Mara's explanation for his failure to disclose this account to the Tribunal. In its review of the documentation discovered to the Tribunal by Mr. Mara, the Tribunal did not find any link between Mr. Mara's financial affairs and any payment to him, which could be attributed to the franchisees of licenses issued for independent broadcasting from 1988 onward.

THE ALLEGED 1988 RUMOUR CONCERNING PAYMENT FOR LICENCES

The oral testimony offered by the witnesses in relation to the alleged rumour

10-15   Mr. Burke, through his counsel, denied the substance of any rumour to the effect that he and Mr. Mara expected payment in respect of broadcasting licences. Mr. Mara denied any knowledge of such a rumour, and further denied that there was any substance in Mr. Stafford's allegation.

10-16   Mr. Oliver Barry denied that he had any knowledge of such a rumour, or that he had brought the existence of such a rumour to the attention of Mr. Stafford in 1988. He considered that it would have been a significant matter if there was such a rumour, and that he would have remembered it, and would have remembered telling Mr. Stafford of it, if there had in fact been such a rumour at the time.

10-17   Mr. Stafford was adamant that this rumour had been brought to his attention by Mr. Barry, and said that he had raised the matter with Mr. Laurence Crowley, the subsequent Chairman of Century. Mr. Crowley had no recollection of the matter being raised with him by Mr. Stafford. Mr. Crowley pointed out that at the time that it was stated that Mr. Barry had communicated with Mr. Stafford on the issue, he, Mr. Crowley, had no involvement with Century.

10-18   In view of the total conflict in the evidence between Mr. Barry and Mr. Stafford, and the absence of any independent evidence to support one or other account of events, the Tribunal is not in a position to pronounce with any degree of certainty on the issue as to whether or not Mr. Barry did in fact tell Mr. Stafford of the existence of such a rumour, much less reach any determination as to whether there was any such rumour abroad in 1988.

THE DEMANDS FOR £30,000 ALLEGED BY MR. STAFFORD TO HAVE BEEN MADE ON BEHALF OF MR. MARA

Mr. Stafford's account of events

10-19   Mr. Stafford gave evidence to the Tribunal to the effect that in or about March 1990 Mr. Oliver Barry informed him that Mr. Mara was seeking a sum of £30,000 from Century. On questioning Mr. Barry as to why this payment was being sought Mr. Stafford said that he was told that there was no explanation, but that Mr. Mara expected the money. Mr. Barry confirmed to him that there had been no agreement made with Mr. Mara under which Mr. Mara was entitled to this sum.

10-20   Mr. Stafford said that Mr. Barry brought the matter to his attention on a number of occasions. He said that he was suspicious, unhappy, and anxious about the claim. On one occasion upon which it was raised with him, he brought the matter to the attention of both Mr. Mulhern and Mr. Crowley, who was at that time chairman of the company.

10-21   He said that both Mr. Mulhern and Mr. Crowley shared his view that Century should in no circumstances pay money to Mr. Mara. Mr. Stafford said that Mr. Barry informed him that he was becoming increasingly embarrassed by the situation, and asked whether Mr. Stafford would deal with it by attending a meeting with Mr. Mara to discuss the matter. He agreed to do so and attended a meeting at the offices of Mr. Dermot Desmond at Mount Street, Dublin. He could not fix a precise date for this meeting, but thought it was in the middle of 1990 or earlier. He said that the meeting was a relatively brief one, lasting in all less than five minutes, and that the respective speakers at the meeting were Mr. Desmond and himself.

10-22   He stated that at the outset Mr. Desmond indicated to him and to Mr. Barry that, "you owe Mr. Mara £30,000", by which Mr. Stafford understood that this was a claim being made against Century of which both he and Mr. Barry were directors. He stated his response to Mr. Desmond was to say "we do not owe Mr. Mara £30,000", to which Mr. Desmond responded, "Well, you owe him £30,000. I have lent him £100,000 and this is part of the repayment, and as far as I am concerned, you have to pay it."

10-23   Mr. Stafford said that he responded by saying that there was no contract or other obligation on Century which would require them to make this payment and after expressing the view to those present that he thought the demand was possibly improper and that he was not prepared to have any part in it, the meeting terminated.

Mr. Barry's account of events

10-24   Mr. Barry's evidence as to what had taken place at this admitted meeting, and its purpose, was remarkably vague. His initial recollection was that Mr. Mara was not present at the meeting, but he accepted that his belief in this regard was certainly incorrect. He said that the background to the meeting was that Mr. Mara, who was a long time friend of his, had indicated his unhappiness about his position in the public service, and that he had felt that he should move into the private sector.

10-25   Mr. Barry said this subject probably arose in the course of a meal where they were talking about the respective hard times they were both going through at that time. He said that he suggested to Mr. Mara that he might consider some involvement with Century. At the time he felt that Mr. Mara might be a useful ally and a good consultant to Century, and that he might help its corporate image given the expertise that he had gained over his career to date.

10-26   Mr. Barry said he believed that Mr. Mara had good contacts with major advertising agencies, and in the business community and that he might be able to "land" Century with an investor. In essence he felt that he might have a role which would have helped Century financially. The position he envisaged Mr. Mara taking up with Century was as a consultant rather than as a full time employee. His idea was that Mr. Mara would be taken on an annual retainer of £30,000, but he said there was no question of this sum being paid as an upfront payment.

Mr. Mara's account of events

10-27 Mr. Mara's evidence was that he was considering a change of career at the time. He believed that an Taoiseach under whom he served was considering stepping down at the end of 1990, when Ireland handed over its presidency role in the European Council. His aspiration was that he would set up his own PR consultancy. He said that the only significant effort he made to advance his plan was to discuss the matter with Mr. Barry in early 1990, and that these discussions culminated in a meeting at Mr. Desmond's office, probably before the end of March 1990.

10-28 He stated that he felt obliged to remain in his position as a result of the political climate. He said that he temporarily abandoned his notion of moving from the public service, and he remained on as Government Press Secretary until February 1992. He said that he had never any direct contact with Mr. Stafford regarding his potential engagement by Century until the meeting in Mr. Desmond's office. Mr. Mara said that he was discussing rates of remuneration of between £60,000 and £70,000 per annum and stock options, and that there had been detailed discussion on this issue with Mr. Barry. He required half of whatever sum was agreed, "upfront."

10-29 He said that he had a number of conversations with Mr. Barry, but the matter did not reach finality because Century was not willing to pay him the kind of remuneration package he was seeking. He met regularly with Mr. Dermot Desmond, a number of times per week on average, and Mr. Desmond suggested a meeting to bring the matter to a head. He went to the meeting in the knowledge that it was unlikely that anything was going to happen. It was a short meeting at which he spoke, Mr. Dermot Desmond spoke and Mr. Stafford spoke. He described this as a friendly, informal meeting, and he denied that Mr. Desmond spoke the words which Mr. Stafford attributed to him or that Mr. Stafford had indicated that the demand was possibly an improper one.

Mr. Desmond's account of events

10-30 Mr. Dermot Desmond's evidence was that he had instigated the meeting with Mr. Stafford and Mr. Barry with the intention that it should bring to a close the discussions about the provision of consultancy services which had been taking place between his friend, Mr. Mara and Century.

10-31 He believed that the negotiations were at an advanced stage and that Mr. Mara was seeking from him, in that context, advice on the stock options which would be open to him. He believed that what Mr. Mara was to provide to Century was public relations and consultancy services. He had not assisted Mr. Mara in the negotiation stage, but was aware of the negotiations and of the fact that Mr. Stafford was considered a stumbling block in the negotiations. He understood that Mr. Barry was supportive of Mr. Mara's desire to move from the public service, and that Mr. Barry was agreeable to Mr. Mara joining the company.

10-32 Mr. Desmond took credit for having advised Mr. Mara to seek a signing-on fee and he said that it was not unusual for one joining a firm to talk about obtaining stock options. He was not, however, aware of the size or capital structure of Century at this stage and was not in a position to advise Mr. Mara as to what stock options to seek.

10-33 He understood his role at the meeting to be one where he would endeavour to establish the nature of the impasse preventing Mr. Mara's recruitment to Century. He understood that the meeting commenced with him asking questions along the lines of "can we resolve the impasse which exists between Century and Mr. Mara and get this sorted out?", to which Mr. Stafford responded that he did not see any way in which they were going to transact business with Mr. Mara. Thereupon Mr. Desmond said he terminated the meeting by saying "well if that's the case, if that's your firm view on this here, there is no point in carrying the discussion any further." Mr. Desmond believed that the meeting was finished within a minute and a half.

10-34 He stated that there was no discussion at the meeting as to whether Mr. Mara owed Mr. Desmond money or otherwise. He said the meeting terminated in an air of anger, as evidenced by the fact that none of those present exchanged pleasantries before leaving. Mr. Desmond had no recollection of figures being discussed at the meeting.

CONFLICTS OF EVIDENCE

10-35 It was apparent to the Tribunal that there were very wide divergences in the accounts of what had taken place at the meeting in the testimony of each of the witnesses who attended the meeting and that the only common facts were: -

- That there was a meeting in Mr. Desmond's office, which probably took place in March 1990.

- That Mr. Mara and Mr. Desmond represented one faction, and Mr. Stafford and Mr. Barry the other.

- That Mr. Desmond was supporting Mr. Mara's appointment to Century.

- That Century, and in particular Mr. Stafford, was unwilling to grant what was being sought by Mr. Mara.

10-36   The essential differences which existed between the parties were: -

- That Mr. Stafford maintained that the meeting was held in the context of an ongoing demand for £30,000 being made by Mr. Mara in circumstances where Century had no contractual or other obligation to pay that sum to him, and where he was giving no explanation as to why this sum was due.

- Mr. Barry, Mr. Mara and Mr. Desmond's contention that the meeting had been scheduled in the context of ongoing discussions taking place between Mr. Mara and Mr. Barry on behalf of Century, on the subject of the possible engagement of Mr. Mara as a PR Consultant to Century.

10-37   In endeavouring to reach its conclusion as to the true purpose of the meeting, the Tribunal had regard to the circumstances pertaining in Century in March 1990. The situation can be summarised thus:

- As of late December 1989, Century's financial targets were not being met, and the question of liquidation of the company was considered by its promoters.

- As of late December 1989, an assurance was given by the Minister, Mr. Burke, to Century and its bankers, that RTÉ's advertising capacity would be reduced by 50% in order to help Century. This had the effect of extending Century's credit facilities, which were for review on the 30th March 1990.

- The hoped-for curb on RTÉ's advertising capacity did not take place within the first quarter of 1990, and the losses of the company accelerated to the point that up to 40 staff, including the Chief Executive of the company, were let go. The losses in February and March were the worst to that time.

- No further credit facilities were available from the bank and the promoters of Century were funding the wages bill from their own pockets. Mr. Barry had moved in with his staff to Century, and the remaining Century staff had accepted reduced wages in an effort to keep the operation going.

10-38   It is in this context that Mr. Mara's evidence that he was in negotiation with Mr. Barry for a position within Century must be considered. It would not be an exaggeration to say that up to that time, the Century project had proved a financial disaster to its promoters and that the prospects for the future seemed bleak. If Mr. Mara was to leave his public service job in the expectation of receiving an income from Century it was a very high-risk strategy indeed. It seems to the Tribunal that if Mr. Mara were to have done so, he would have been attaching his future to a sinking ship. The evidence established that Mr. Barry and Mr. Mara were close friends and, in those circumstances, the Tribunal finds it difficult to understand how Mr. Mara could have received any assurance from Mr. Barry that a move from the public service would be in his best interests.

10-39   Any decision to make a payment of £60,000 to £70,000 to a PR consultant, who was untried in that field, would appear to the Tribunal to be a decision which could only have been taken by Century after very careful consideration in any circumstances, and particularly where the company's finances were stretched. Mr. Barry did not say that he ever discussed the details of any contract which would be given to Mr. Mara by Century with Mr. Stafford. He, Mr. Barry, rejected Mr. Mara's evidence that the figures they were considering in their discussions were in the range of £60,000 to

£70,000. On Mr. Barry's evidence the figure was £30,000, and there was no question of this amount being paid upfront.

10-40 £30,000 was the figure which Mr. Stafford maintained had always been sought of Century by Mr. Mara. However £30,000 was not a figure which featured in the accounts of events of the other participants at the meeting. Mr. Barry was the only other attendee whose evidence specifically referred to a sum of £30,000, albeit in the context of an annual payment to Mr. Mara. Mr. Mara's account dealt with figures of £60,000 to £70,000, of which he required 50% upfront - thereby suggesting that figures up to £35,000 could have featured in their discussions. Mr. Desmond says that specific figures were not discussed at all by him.

10-41 The Tribunal considers that it is highly improbable that Century would have considered paying £60,000 to £70,000 per annum to Mr. Mara in March 1990. Mr. Mara said that his public service earnings at that time were £47,000 to £48,000 and, accordingly, there was no question of his agreeing to work for £30,000, which was the figure which Mr. Barry says was discussed between them. There was no documentary evidence to establish that any negotiations had in fact taken place between the parties, and, whilst the Tribunal accepts that three of the parties were well known to each other, it nonetheless would have expected some documents to have been generated in the course of the negotiation, or in anticipation of the meeting which is known to have taken place involving the four parties.

10-42 It is clear that any upfront payment contemplated in March 1990 would have had to come directly from the personal funds of the three Century promoters. In those circumstances the Tribunal concludes that any proposal involving a payment of that nature would have to have been the subject of discussion involving Mr. Barry, Mr. Mulhern, and Mr. Stafford.

10-43 However, Mr. Mulhern says that he was never made aware of Mr. Mara's interest in becoming involved in Century. If there was any plan to engage Mr. Mara, the Tribunal considers that Mr. Mulhern's prior consent to such a course would have been sought, given that he would be paying one-third of Mr. Mara's salary until such time as Century became viable.

10-44 The Tribunal considers that it is inherently unlikely that Century would have engaged the former Government Press Secretary as its PR consultant at a time when it was aware that the Minister for Communications, Mr. Burke, intended to introduce legislation to cap RTÉ's advertising. The Tribunal considers that Century's promoters must have been aware that such legislation was likely to result in criticism of the Minister on the basis that he was favouring Century. Such in fact transpired to be the case when the legislation was introduced. The Tribunal considers that it would have been obvious to Century's promoters that the engagement of the former Government Press Secretary as its PR consultant could have been damaging to their interests, insofar as it might have linked Century Radio with Fianna Fáil, and thereby made the passing of the legislation more difficult.

10-45 The Tribunal is satisfied, on the balance of probabilities, that the promoters of Century did not meet to consider the possible appointment of Mr. Mara as a public relations consultant to the company at any time prior to the meeting which took place at Mr. Desmond's offices in March 1990. If there was any discussion on this issue it was one which involved Mr. Barry and Mr. Mara only. Insofar as Mr. Barry may have discussed the matter with Mr. Mara, he could only have done so in his personal capacity, and not on behalf of Century. The Tribunal accepts that the possibility exists that Mr. Barry expressed to Mr. Mara his own personal desire to have him act as a consultant to Century, but is also satisfied that had any such discussion taken place there could not have been any discussion as to Mr. Mara receiving either an upfront payment of £30,000 or remuneration of between £60,000 and £70,000 per annum.

THE ROLE OF MR. DERMOT DESMOND AT THE MARCH 1990 MEETING

10-46 It is accepted that Mr. Desmond suggested the meeting at his office in March 1990, and that he did so in order to bring to finality to whatever issue existed between Mr. Mara and the promoters of Century. If Mr. Stafford's account of events is correct, Mr. Desmond was engaged in a blatant attempt to extort money from Century's promoters for Mr. Mara. On his own account Mr. Desmond was seeking to resolve an impasse in negotiations in which his particular involvement was to advise Mr. Mara on the question of stock options and the advisability of seeking an upfront payment. These were matters which Mr. Stafford said were not mentioned at all at the meeting in his office.

10-47   The Tribunal accepts that the lapse of time between the date upon which the witnesses gave evidence and the occurrence of the events they were recalling can account for some divergences in the evidence of the parties. However, in this instance, the accounts of events given are so radically different that it follows that one or more of the attendees at this meeting deliberately set out to give a false account of what had taken place and of the true purpose of the meeting.

10-48   The Tribunal's inquiry has been hampered by the fact that none of the parties kept any contemporaneous record of what had in fact taken place at the meeting. There is no documentation in existence which independently supports one or other version of events.

10-49   It was Mr. Desmond's belief, that prior to the meeting, he had funded Mr. Mara by giving him loans of approximately £46,000, between 1986 and 1989. However, details of Mr. Mara's bank accounts provided to the Tribunal did not reveal that such payments had, in fact, been made within that period. Mr. Desmond's evidence on this issue was not challenged by Mr. Mara.

10-50   Mr. Mara, in his second affidavit of Discovery, attributed three payments by Mr. Desmond totalling approximately £36, 200, but none of these had taken place between 1986 and 1989. The first of the payments, attributed by Mr. Mara to Mr. Desmond, was a payment of £15,000 on the 15th March 1990. As the date of the meeting in Mr. Desmond's office cannot be fixed with certainty by any of the parties present, it is not clear whether this was a payment which took place immediately prior to the meeting or subsequently, but, in either event, it could not have been any part of the sum which was in Mr. Desmond's contemplation when he informed the Tribunal that £46,000 had been paid to Mr. Mara between 1986 and 1989.

10-51   The second payment was a payment in the sum of £10,567.47, made on the 6th February 1992. This payment represents a payment of stg.£10,000 which was converted to Irish currency at the appropriate rate on the day. The third payment is a payment of £10,632.64, on the 24th February 1992, and is likely to have been a similar payment in sterling, converted as of that date.

10-52   None of the payments attributed by Mr. Mara to Mr. Desmond fall within the timescale in which Mr. Desmond indicated the payments had been made to Mr. Mara. While Mr. Desmond believed that all payments had been made by cheque, it would appear that at least two of the payments were made in sterling and therefore are unlikely to have been recorded in any Irish bank account.

10-53   The Tribunal has been unable to determine whether Mr. Desmond's evidence as to payments to Mr. Mara is correct, insofar as he claimed to have made payments of approximately £46,000 between 1986 and 1989 by cheque, and no payments after mid-1990, or whether the evidence of Mr. Mara is correct in so far as he claimed that the loans made by Mr. Desmond were made between 1990 and 1992

10-54   The Tribunal cannot reconcile the evidence of the four participants at the meeting in March 1990, nor can it pronounce with any degree of certainty on the likely explanation for the meeting which took place in Mr. Desmond's office. The Tribunal is not satisfied that Mr. Stafford's allegation that £30,000 was demanded of Century for Mr Mara has been substantiated having regard to the standard of proof required to make such a finding.

MR. STAFFORD'S CLAIM THAT MR. DESMOND MADE A FURTHER DEMAND FOR £30,000 FOR MR. MARA IN SEPTEMBER 1990

10-55   Mr. Stafford gave evidence that, while he was attending a post wedding reception at the home of Mr. Charles J. Haughey at Kinsealy, Co. Dublin, in September 1990, he was approached by Mr. Dermot Desmond who again claimed that Mr. Mara was owed £30,000. Mr. Stafford said that he threatened to bring the matter to the attention of Mr. Haughey, whereupon Mr. Desmond left his company.

10-56   Mr. Desmond acknowledged that he was in attendance in Kinsealy at the reception referred to by Mr. Stafford, but had no recollection of having any conversation with Mr. Stafford. It did not happen as far as he was concerned. He had no memory of Mr. Stafford being present at all, but was certain that he would have remembered a threat to bring the matter to the attention of Mr. Haughey if such a threat had been made.

10-57   In these circumstances the Tribunal is unable to resolve this conflict of evidence.

GOGARTY MODULE

Chapter 11

Payment of Money to Mr. Ray Burke T.D at his Home at Briargate, Swords, Co. Dublin in June, 1989 at a Meeting Attended by Mr. James Gogarty

CORE ALLEGATION MADE BY MR. JAMES GOGARTY AGAINST MR. BURKE, MR. MICHAEL BAILEY AND MR. JOSEPH MURPHY JNR.

11-01 Mr. James Gogarty claimed to have witnessed the handing over of two envelopes, said to contain £40,000 each, to Mr. Burke at a meeting which took place at his home at Briargate, Swords, Co. Dublin shortly before the General Election, which took place on 15th June 1989. Mr. Burke was at that time Minister for Industry and Commerce. Mr. Gogarty claimed that the payments were made to Mr. Burke in order to secure his support and political influence on councillors so as to achieve the rezoning and planning changes required to alter the status of approximately 700 acres of land owned by the Murphy companies (**Appendix Q**) in North County Dublin which were the subject of a joint development proposal involving Mr. Michael Bailey and his Companies and the Murphy interests (**Appendix R**).

THE BACKGROUND TO THE PAYMENT OF MONIES TO MR. BURKE ACCORDING TO MR. JAMES GOGARTY

11-02 Mr. Gogarty gave evidence that his former employer, Mr. Joseph Murphy Snr., had acquired various lots of land in North County Dublin from the 1960s onwards. These lands were mainly zoned for agricultural use, but it was Mr. Murphy's belief that in time they would have development potential as Dublin City expanded. Where lands had been rezoned and planning permission obtained, houses were built on the lands and sold to individual householders who became tenants of the Murphy land owning companies which remained the ground landlords. Initially the dwelling houses were built by a building firm, O'Shea & Shanahan Limited in which Mr. Joseph Murphy Snr. held a one-third interest. This firm had built housing estates in North County Dublin in the 1970s. In addition to their joint ownership of this company the directors of O'Shea & Shanahan Limited owned licensed premises in Swords known as the Harp Inn.

11-03 The relationship between Mr. Murphy Snr. and his fellow directors of O'Shea & Shanahan deteriorated due to disputes as to the price to be paid for house sites with the result that in 1978 Mr. Murphy Snr. disposed of his $^1/_3$ interest in O'Shea & Shanahan to the remaining directors, and he also disposed of his interest in the Harp Inn. Thereafter Mr. Murphy Snr. did not have a shareholding in any active house building company in Ireland, although limited building operations were carried out through the Grafton Construction Company Limited, Reliable Construction Limited at the Gaiety Theatre and also in the refurbishment of a private house on Anglesea Road, Dublin. By the late 1980s the portfolio of property owned by the Murphy family, and Companies owned by them, included, the six lots of land referred to in the *Terms of Reference* of the Tribunal, lands at Forrest Road, Swords, Co. Dublin which had the benefit of planning permission for development, the Gaiety Theatre, an office building in Baggot Street, Dublin, farm lands at Abbeycarton, Co. Longford, and a mews house at Wilton Place, Dublin. A Murphy company, Joseph Murphy Structural Engineers Limited owned and operated a steel fabrication facility at Shanowen Road, Santry, Dublin.

11-04 The Murphy properties were held by limited liability companies registered in Ireland which were in turn part of a holding company, Lajos Holdings Limited, which was in turn owned by General Agencies Limited, an Isle of Man registered company. The Murphy companies were held in overseas trusts, and the class of beneficiaries of these trusts included members of Mr. Murphy Snr.'s family. The Tribunal is satisfied that the ultimate control of the Murphy companies at all times was exercised by Mr. Joseph Murphy Snr., through the professional trustees appointed by him.

11-05   The management of the Murphy companies changed in June 1988, and Mr. Gogarty gave evidence that in early 1989 he was requested by Mr. Joseph Murphy Snr. to obtain a valuation of the companies' North Dublin lands with a view to selling these properties. Acting on these instructions he obtained a valuation of the lands from Duffy Mangan Butler, a firm of auctioneers and estate agents who had managed the conacre letting of these lands from the date of their acquisition.

11-06   Mr. Gogarty stated that he furnished a copy of a Valuation Report prepared by Duffy Mangan Butler dated the 28th March, 1989 to Mr. Murphy Snr., and that he subsequently received instructions from him to place the properties on the books of Duffy Mangan Butler for sale. The valuation prepared by Duffy Mangan Butler had attributed some development potential value to portion of the lands. However, Mr. Murphy Snr. was prepared to sell the lands, discounting any such potential value. All of the lands were zoned agricultural and were offered for sale on that basis.

11-07   Mr. Gogarty stated that Mr. Murphy Snr.'s wish to sell the lands for agricultural value ran counter to the wishes of his son, Joseph Murphy Jnr. and of Mr. Frank Reynolds, the Managing Director of JMSE. He said they believed that the lands should be retained for their development potential rather than being sold off at mere agricultural value. Mr. Gogarty said that he was asked by Mr. Murphy Jnr. and Mr. Reynolds to use his influence with Mr. Murphy Snr. so as to ensure that the lands were retained rather than sold.

11-08   Mr. Michael Bailey, a builder and property speculator, who had purchased the Murphy Forrest Road lands at Swords, Co. Dublin for £1.45 million earlier that year, expressed an interest in acquiring the balance of the North Dublin lands. Mr. Bailey wrote the letter of the 8th June 1989 (which is appended to the Terms of Reference) to Mr. Gogarty, in which he set out in detail his various proposals in relation to the Murphy lands. These included proposals for:

>   1. An outright purchase whereby he would acquire the entire of the lands over a specified time scale;

>   2. A participation proposal under which, *inter alia*, he would receive 50% of the lands in return for procuring planning permission and bye-law approval and;

>   3. An equity retention proposal whereby he would purchase the lands but would allow the Murphys to retain an equity in the lands if they so wished.

11-09   Mr. Gogarty claimed that the payment of the money to Mr. Burke between the 8th June 1989 and 15th June 1989 followed upon agreement having been reached between the Murphy interests and Mr. Bailey to advance the participation proposal which was outlined in the letter of the 8th June 1989. Mr. Gogarty alleged that a meeting had taken place some days prior to the 8th June 1989 at which Mr. Michael Bailey had outlined the method by which he would ensure that the Murphy lands were altered from their then existing agricultural status, to the status of development land. He said that Mr. Bailey informed those present at the meeting that there were five or six councillors who could organise, or maximise the votes on Dublin County Council to ensure that a majority vote could be achieved so as to alter the zoning status of the lands. He claimed that Mr. Ray Burke could use his influence on politicians and councillors to achieve this end. He stated that he, Michael Bailey, could cross the political divide, and that he had a close liaison with County Council Officials, including Mr. George Redmond, the Assistant City and County Manager and certain planning officials.

11-10   Mr. Gogarty maintained that the letter of the 8th June 1989 encapsulated Mr. Bailey's proposal as stated at the meeting, albeit that it did not detail the methodology by which the intended change in zoning/planning status would be achieved through Mr. Burke's political influence. Mr. Gogarty stated that the contents of Mr. Bailey's letter of the 8th June 1989 were read to him over the telephone by Mr. Frank Reynolds on the 8th June 1989, and he was requested by Mr. Reynolds to attend the JMSE offices that afternoon. Mr. Gogarty stated that when he arrived at the JMSE offices on the afternoon of the 8th June, 1989, there was a sum of £30,000 in cash in the office which he was informed had been obtained by Mr. Joseph Murphy Jnr. and Mr. Frank Reynolds, but that a further £10,000 was required, whereupon a cheque in that amount was produced for his signature and he duly signed it. He said that he was informed by Mr. Joseph Murphy Jnr. and Mr. Reynolds at this meeting that an agreement had been reached with Mr. Bailey whereby the sum of £80,000 would be paid to Mr. Burke, and that this sum was required forthwith, in view of the impending General Election. He was told that £40,000 each would be advanced by the Murphy interests, and by Mr. Bailey, to Mr. Burke.

11-11   Mr. Gogarty stated that he counted out the bundles of cash and was reasonably satisfied that there was £30,000 in cash available on that date, to which the cheque for £10,000 was added. He understood the intention was that he would accompany Mr. Michael Bailey to meet Mr. Burke that day, and hand over the money to him, but for some reason, unknown to Mr. Gogarty, this plan was cancelled.

11-12   Mr. Gogarty said that some days later, he received a telephone call from Mr. Frank Reynolds to attend at the JMSE offices, and when he got there, he met with Mr. Joseph Murphy Jnr., who informed him that Mr. Michael Bailey was going to take them to Mr. Burke's house that day to make the payment. He said that it was intended that Mr. Reynolds would accompany them, but at the last moment, Mr. Reynolds indicated that he had other commitments. Accordingly, Mr. Gogarty, Mr. Joseph Murphy Jnr., and Mr. Michael Bailey, travelled in Mr. Bailey's car to Mr. Burke's house to make the payment. Mr. Gogarty stated that in the course of this journey he inquired of Mr. Bailey as to whether they would receive a receipt from Mr. Burke for their payment to which he received a colourful and dismissive response in the negative.

THE MEETING AT BRIARGATE ACCORDING TO MR. GOGARTY

11-13   Mr. Gogarty stated that when they arrived at Mr. Burke's house he was carrying the envelope in which the JMSE contribution was contained. He said that Mr. Bailey took a similar size package from the glove box of his car, and they went to the front door of the house where they met with Mr. Burke who was introduced to both Mr. Joseph Murphy Jnr. and himself by Mr. Bailey. He said that they were brought into a room in the house where the hand over of the funds took place, Mr. Joseph Murphy Jnr. handing over the JMSE contribution, and Mr. Bailey handing over his envelope thereafter.

11-14   Mr. Gogarty stated that at this meeting he offered Mr. Burke a copy of the letter of 8th June 1989 which had been written to him by Mr. Bailey, but that Mr. Burke declined this, indicating that he had already seen it, and knew of its contents. He said that he also produced a schedule of the lands, but Mr. Burke also declined this, saying that he had already seen a copy of it. Mr. Gogarty's evidence was that he had expressed a concern to Mr. Burke that a substantial payment was being made against an open-ended commitment, and that he, Mr. Gogarty, was anxious that he should be able to allay Mr. Murphy Snr.'s. anxiety about paying over this money. He stated that Mr. Burke responded that both Mr. Murphy Snr. and Mr. Bailey were well aware of how he had honoured his commitments in the past. Mr. Gogarty said that he did not pursue the matter further, because both Mr. Bailey, and Mr. Murphy Jnr., gave him to understand that it was not necessary to go further. Mr. Bailey suggested that he leave the matter with himself and "Ray", and Mr. Murphy Jnr. indicated that he would discuss the matter with his father.

EVIDENCE OF MR. BURKE RELATING TO THE ALLEGATIONS MADE BY MR. GOGARTY

11-15   Mr. Burke acknowledged in evidence that on a date unknown prior to 15th June, 1989, a meeting took place at his home at Briargate, Swords, Co. Dublin, which was attended by Mr. Michael Bailey and Mr. James Gogarty. He denied that Mr. Joseph Murphy Jnr. was present at this meeting. He stated that the meeting had been arranged by Mr. Michael Bailey by telephone, the day before. Mr. Bailey had informed him on the telephone that he wished to assist him in regard to the forthcoming General Election and Mr. Burke interpreted this as being a desire on Mr. Bailey's part to make a financial contribution to him. He said that no mention was made of Mr. Gogarty, or of JMSE at the time the meeting was arranged. Mr. Burke said that he knew Mr. Michael Bailey, because he was engaged in house building in the locality of Mr. Burke's home in Swords at that time, and he knew him to be involved in Fianna Fáil affairs, to the extent that he had attended Fianna Fáil race nights in the constituency in 1988. He stated that when Mr.

Gogarty was introduced to him he indicated his wish to make a political donation to Mr. Burke on behalf of his employers, and he proceeded to do so in the presence of Mr. Bailey. Mr. Burke believed that he had received two envelopes from Mr. Gogarty.

11-16 Mr. Burke stated that he did not know Mr. Gogarty prior to this meeting, and that he had never received a political donation prior to that date from JMSE, or from any other Murphy company. He had never met any member of the Murphy family, and he never received any donations from them. He was aware of the existence of JMSE, as its manufacturing premises was located in proximity to his former home at 251 Swords Road, Santry, and was on the boundaries of his constituency.

11-17 Mr. Burke denied that any copy of the letter of the 8th June 1989 was produced at the meeting by Mr. Gogarty, nor was any schedule of the lands produced. He denied that Mr. Gogarty had sought any assurances from him, or that he had given any to Mr. Gogarty. Mr. Burke stated that he had never made any representation on behalf of Mr. Bailey, or his Companies, to any person, nor had he done so in respect of the Murphy companies. He stated that he actively opposed proposed rezonings in 1993 and had led a delegation to the then Minister for the Environment urging him to reject certain zoning applications, and to follow the Development Plan.

EVIDENCE OF MR. MICHAEL BAILEY IN RESPONSE TO THE ALLEGATIONS MADE BY MR. GOGARTY

11-18 Mr. Michael Bailey stated that he had developed a relationship with Mr. Gogarty in the course of negotiating the acquisition of the Murphy company lands at Forrest Road, Swords in 1988. In April/May, 1989 he began to negotiate with Mr. Gogarty over the possible acquisition of the remainder of the Murphy's North Dublin land holdings. He stated that, in the course of his meetings with Mr. Gogarty, Mr. Gogarty asked him for a recommendation as to whom he should make a political donation to, on behalf of his employers, JMSE. Mr. Bailey said that he recommended that the payment should be made to Mr. Ray Burke, then a Government Minister in his local constituency. He offered to set up a meeting with Mr. Burke, if Mr. Gogarty wished him to do so. He stated that Mr. Gogarty asked him to arrange for such a meeting, and accordingly he telephoned Mr. Burke, and made the appointment. He believed that he had made it clear to Mr. Burke that the meeting was one at which Mr. Gogarty was to make the contribution.

11-19 Mr. Michael Bailey stated that on the day of the meeting, Mr. Gogarty drove to the Bovale building site at Carlton Court, Swords, where they met and they then travelled a short distance from the building site to Mr. Burke's home. He did not collect Mr. Gogarty at the JMSE premises as claimed by Mr. Gogarty. Mr. Tom Bailey stated that he was present at Carlton Court when Mr. Gogarty arrived, and he confirmed that Mr. Gogarty, and Mr. Michael Bailey, left for Mr. Burke's house from Carlton Court. Mr. Michael Bailey has stated that after he had introduced Mr. Gogarty to Mr. Burke, Mr. Gogarty indicated to Mr. Burke that he wished to make a donation on behalf of his employers, and handed it over to him. Mr. Michael Bailey said that he was surprised by the amount of the donation. He said that he had not asked Mr. Gogarty, at any time, what the amount of the intended donation was, and after the donation was made he did not inquire from him as to why he had made such a large donation. At the conclusion of their brief meeting with Mr. Burke, Mr. Bailey said that he drove Mr. Gogarty back to Carlton Court.

11-20 Mr. Michael Bailey denied that there was any connection between the proposals contained in his letter of the 8th June 1989, and the subsequent meeting with Mr. Burke. He stated that he had never met Mr. Joseph Murphy Jnr. in 1989, and that all negotiations in relation to the possible acquisition of the North Dublin lands were conducted solely with Mr. Gogarty. He claimed that he had not agreed to be part of a plan to pay Mr. Burke £80,000. He stated that, Mr. Joseph Murphy Jnr. was not present at the meeting at Mr. Burke's house, there was no discussion at the meeting in Mr. Burke's house regarding the Murphy lands, and no schedule of the lands was produced by Mr. Gogarty to Mr. Burke, nor was any copy of the letter of the 8th June, 1989 produced to him. He stated that Mr. Burke had not said that Mr. Murphy Snr., and Mr. Bailey, knew that he had honoured his commitments in the past.

EVIDENCE OF THE MURPHY INTERESTS IN RELATION TO MR. GOGARTY'S ALLEGATIONS OF PAYMENT TO MR. BURKE

11-21 It was stated that Mr. Gogarty was in exclusive charge of the lands owned by the Murphy companies in Ireland. Mr. Joseph Murphy Snr. claimed to be unaware of the instructions given to Duffy Mangan Butler regarding the sale of the North Dublin lands, although he accepted that any decision as to whether the lands would be sold was ultimately a matter for him. He denied that there was any conflict as between himself, and his son, as to whether the lands should be sold, or retained. Both Mr. Murphy Snr. and Mr. Murphy Jnr. denied any knowledge of any political donation being made to Mr. Burke in 1989 until mid-August 1997. Both denied any knowledge of any proposals being advanced by Mr. Michael Bailey in relation to the alteration of the planning status of the lands. Mr. Joseph Murphy Jnr. said that he did not meet with Mr. Michael Bailey at any time in 1989, and that he was unaware of the content of the letter of the 8th June 1989, until he saw extracts from it printed in Magill Magazine in September, 1997. Mr. Joseph Murphy Jnr. denied that he had met with Mr. Gogarty at the JMSE offices on the 8th June 1989, and/or that he had any knowledge of the assembly of the funds that were to be paid to Mr. Burke. He denied attending any meeting at Mr. Burke's home in June 1989, and claimed never to have met with Mr. Burke at any time either prior, to or subsequent to, that date.

11-22 Mr. Frank Reynolds denied any knowledge of Mr. Bailey's proposals as contained in the letter of 8th June 1989. He denied any meetings with Mr. Bailey in connection with the proposed sale of the North Dublin lands to him. He denied that he had expressed any views regarding the sale, or otherwise, of the Murphys' North Dublin lands. He denied that he was aware of any meeting with Mr. Burke or any payment to Mr. Burke in 1989.

THE TRIBUNAL'S ASSESSMENT OF ITS TASK IN THE LIGHT OF THE EVIDENCE OF MR. GOGARTY AND THE RESPONSES TO HIS ALLEGATIONS BY MR. BURKE, THE MURPHY INTERESTS AND THE BAILEY INTERESTS

11-23 The Tribunal concluded that the conflicts which are apparent from consideration of the evidence of the parties, could not be explained on the basis that they were innocent failures of recollection, mistakes, or misinterpretation of the true facts. The Tribunal concluded that the divergences in the accounts given by the parties could only be explained on the basis that some party, or parties, had deliberately set out to mislead the Tribunal as to the true circumstances leading to the meeting with Mr. Burke, and the payment of monies to him. In broad terms the issue arising was whether the account given by Mr. Gogarty was true or whether the accounts given by all of the other persons present in Mr. Burke's house at the time of the meeting were true. Certain facts were common case, namely (1) a meeting did in fact take place at the home of Mr. Burke in June, 1989, (2) Mr. Gogarty, Mr. Michael Bailey and Mr. Burke were present, (3) a substantial sum of money, amounting to not less than £30,000, was paid to Mr. Burke at this meeting partly in cash, and partly by cheque, and the majority of which was in cash. The essential disputes between the parties arising from the evidence in relation to the JMSE funded payment were (1) whether this payment was made as a political donation, or as a bribe, (2) whether this payment was made with the knowledge of the Murphy interests or not.

THE INDIVIDUALS NAMED IN THE ALLEGATION AND THE UNIQUE FEATURES OF THE PAYMENT

11-24 The Tribunal examined the apparent relationship between the parties in June 1989 in an effort to establish what was the probable explanation for the payment of JMSE monies to Mr. Burke.

Mr. James Gogarty

11-25 Mr. Gogarty had no known political preferences. He was not a member of any political party. He was not resident in Mr. Burke's constituency, he had never made a political payment to Mr. Burke at any time prior to 1989.

Mr. Michael Bailey

11-26   Mr. Bailey's relationship with Mr. Gogarty was purely commercial. On his account of events they had never discussed politics, save on the occasion when he was asked to nominate a suitable recipient for a political donation by JMSE. He was a member of Fianna Fáil, and had made modest contributions to constituency events hosted in Mr. Burke's constituency, but he never made a personal donation to him. He was not a fundraiser for Mr. Burke in the 1989 General Election campaign.

Mr. Ray Burke

11-27   Mr. Burke was the outgoing Minister for Industry and Commerce, and also the Fianna Fáil T.D. for the Constituency of Dublin North, a position which he had held since 1973. He had no business dealings with JMSE, or the Murphy companies. He did not know Mr. Gogarty, he had limited knowledge only of Mr. Michael Bailey, which was based on the fact that Mr. Bailey was working in the Swords area at the time, and was known to have made some small contribution to Fianna Fáil fundraising events within the constituency.

The Murphy interests

11-28   The Murphy family, and their Companies, had not been contributors of any significant amounts to any political party in Ireland at any time prior to June 1989. They had no business, or other relationship, with Mr. Burke. Their relationship with Mr. Bailey was limited to the fact that he was the purchaser of their Forrest Road lands in 1988, and was actively negotiating to purchase their North Dublin lands in 1989. Their relationship with Mr. Gogarty was that he was a long serving member of their staff, with whom an agreement in principal had been reached in May 1989 under which he was to retire from all positions within the company, and to provide his services as a consultant for 5 years thereafter, if so required.

The Tribunal considered that if the relationship between these parties was as set out above, it did not provide any apparent explanation as to why a substantial sum of Murphy company money should be paid to Mr. Burke.

THE UNUSUAL FEATURES ATTACHING TO THE ACKNOWLEDGED RECEIPT BY MR. BURKE OF JMSE FUNDS

11-29   Irrespective of what the actual intention of the donor of the money was, the transaction in which Mr. Burke received these funds has the following unusual features: -

The amount of the donation.

11-30   In June 1989 £30,000 was an extraordinarily large donation for any individual or company to make to a politician. Mr. Burke acknowledged this fact.

The form in which the donation was made.

11-31   There is a conflict as to whether the admitted payment of JMSE sourced money to Mr. Burke comprised £30,000 in cash, accompanied by a £10,000 cheque, or £20,000 in cash and a £10,000 cheque. Irrespective of whether the cash element of the JMSE sourced payment was £30,000, or £20,000, the Tribunal considers it extraordinary that a senior political figure would accept such a large sum in cash, particularly if it was expressed to be a corporate donation, since such payment could have been made entirely by way of cheque.

The relationship between the donor and the recipient.

11-32   It was accepted by Mr. Burke, and by the Murphy interests, that no prior political donation was ever made to Mr. Burke by the Murphy companies or their directors, either on their own behalf, or on behalf of any of the Murphy companies. It was accepted by Mr. Burke that Mr. Gogarty had never made any prior political donation to him, and that he was unknown to him, prior to the payment in June 1989.

The Tribunal considers it extraordinary that, despite the absence of any prior relationship whatsoever between the donor and the recipient, a very substantial sum in cash, was paid to Mr. Burke.

Response of the recipient.

11-33   It was agreed by all the parties who acknowledged their presence at the meeting that the packaging in which the JMSE monies were contained was not opened by Mr. Burke at the meeting. The Tribunal has concluded that it was clear to all persons then present, that a substantial sum in cash was involved in the handover. Whether the JMSE money was contained in one or two envelopes, and whether it comprised £20,000 in cash, or £30,000 in cash, it must, of necessity, have been a bulky and obviously large donation. Mr. Michael Bailey, who was on his evidence a disinterested observer, noted the handover to Mr. Burke. He could conclude from the size of the packaging that a large donation in cash was being made to Mr. Burke. The Tribunal believes that the same conclusion was capable of being drawn by Mr. Burke at that time. While on his account to the Tribunal he claimed that he was not to know of the exact amount of the donation until later that day, when he opened the envelope, the Tribunal has concluded that it must have been apparent to Mr. Burke at the time of the receipt of the package, or packages, that he was being given a substantial sum in cash. The Tribunal considers it extraordinary that, if his version of what took place is true, Mr. Burke did not take immediate steps to establish from the donor the amount of the donation, the reason for its being in cash, and the reason why he had been selected as the recipient for such a large sum at that time.

The absence of an appropriate acknowledgement by Mr. Burke for the payment of £30,000.

11-34   Mr. Burke states that he expressed thanks orally to the donor at the time of the receipt of the donation. He said he was unaware at the time of the enormity of the payment. A substantial payment of this nature ought to have earned an effusive expression of appreciation, and gratitude, from the recipient. None such was offered to Mr. Gogarty in the account of events given by Mr. Burke, or Mr. Bailey. The Tribunal believes that the reaction of any person, who had discovered to his surprise, that he was the recipient of a £30,000 donation in 1989, would have been to contact the donors to specifically thank them for this donation, particularly where only an oral acknowledgement of the donation had been made at the time of the handover. The Tribunal concludes that, it is unusual that, once Mr. Burke discovered the enormity of the donation, he did not contact either Mr. Gogarty, or JMSE, to express his gratitude for this generosity.

The failure to account for the payment.

11-35   Mr. Burke did not issue a receipt to the donor at the time of the handover, nor did he subsequently provide any written acknowledgement. He did not disclose the fact that he had received this substantial donation to any person in his political organisation at local constituency level, or at Party level. The Tribunal considers it unusual that Mr. Burke failed to disclose the fact of the payment to any person connected with the finances of his political campaign if he believed that the payment had been made to him for political purposes.

The expenditure of the money.

11-36   Mr. Burke was not in a position to produce any evidence to the Tribunal to show that any portion of this particular donation was expended for a political purpose. He concluded from sight of the JMSE financial records provided to him by the Tribunal that the £10,000 cheque element of the payment had been lodged to an account of his. The account referred to by Mr. Burke was an account in the joint names of himself and his wife which was apparently opened by the lodgment of this cheque. There was no evidence that any sum from that account was spent in that election campaign, or at any later stage, for political purposes.

The absence of any subsequent request for funds by Mr. Burke.

11-37   Mr. Burke acknowledged that he never again made contact with either Mr. Gogarty or JMSE to seek their support in any of the election campaigns which followed the 1989 campaign. The Tribunal considers that Mr. Burke could hardly have forgotten the apparent generosity of JMSE in 1989, and that his failure to seek further donations from them was not satisfactorily explained.

CONCLUSION AS TO THE CIRCUMSTANCES SURROUNDING THE JMSE PAYMENT

11-38   Having considered all the evidence relating to the manner in which the admitted receipt of £30,000 of JMSE funds was dealt with by Mr. Burke, the Tribunal has concluded that the payment did not have the hallmarks of a legitimate political donation, but that it did have the hallmarks of a secret payment made other than for legitimate political purposes.

WHY WAS MR. BURKE PAID A SUM OF NOT LESS THAN £30,000 FROM THE FUNDS OF JMSE?

11-39   Mr. Burke said that he believed that the payment was made to him as a contribution towards his election expenses for the 1989 General Election. The Tribunal is satisfied that, irrespective of whether Mr. Burke held this belief or not, the payment was not in fact a political donation. Whether the payment was made by Mr. James Gogarty, as claimed by Mr. Bailey and Mr. Burke, or by Mr. Joseph Murphy Jnr. as claimed by Mr. Gogarty, there is no evidence to establish that the donor's motive was to make a political contribution.

11-40   The Murphy interests acknowledged that they had never made a prior political donation to Mr. Burke. The evidence established that in the 21 years in which Mr. Gogarty was involved in the Murphy companies, he had never made any other substantial payment to any politician, or political party. The Tribunal is satisfied that, whatever the purpose of the payment to Mr. Burke was, it was not for political purposes. Mr. Gogarty has maintained that the money was paid as a bribe. The Murphy interests offer no alternative explanation for the payment, but contend that Mr. Gogarty's explanation is false, and that his evidence should be rejected in total. They now concede that £30,000 of their money was paid to Mr. Burke but say that it was done without their knowledge by Mr. Gogarty.

11-41   The Tribunal examined the evidence to establish whether there was any identifiable reason for Mr. Gogarty to have paid at least £30,000 of his employer's monies to Mr. Burke. The Tribunal has rejected the suggestion that the payment was a political donation, and has not identified any personal benefit which would have accrued to Mr. Gogarty, had he made a £30,000 payment to Mr. Burke, as claimed in the account of events given by Mr. Burke and Mr. Bailey. It is agreed by those who admit to being present at the meeting that Mr. Gogarty made no demand for favours of Mr. Burke at the time of payment. Mr. Burke acknowledges that Mr. Gogarty never sought any benefit from him at any time after the payment of the £30,000 to him. The Tribunal has not identified any possible advantage or benefit which would have flowed from Mr. Burke to Mr. Gogarty as a consequence of a payment of £30,000 to him.

11-42   If it was the case that Mr. Gogarty had made an unauthorised payment of his employer's funds to Mr. Burke the potential adverse consequences which would follow, in the event that this payment was discovered, would include:

> 1. Instant dismissal from his position within the Murphy group, and the revocation of the pension agreement entered into by Joseph Murphy Snr. with Mr. Gogarty on the 22nd May 1989.

> 2. A criminal prosecution for theft, or embezzlement, being brought against him at the instigation of the Murphy companies, whose funds he had misappropriated.

> 3. Penury for himself and his family, whose sole source of income would be his old age pension, and social welfare payment, as he was entirely financially dependent upon his pension from JMSE to support his wife and young family.

11-43   The Tribunal considers that, given the absence of any identifiable benefit flowing to Mr. Gogarty and the obvious adverse consequences which would follow if he had misappropriated his employer's funds, on the balance of probabilities Mr. Gogarty would not have made such a payment to Mr. Burke and that he did not misappropriate these funds. If Mr. Gogarty had intended to make an unauthorised payment of £30,000 to Mr. Burke from the funds of his employer the Tribunal believes that on the balance of probabilities he would not have involved the financial director of the company in sourcing the money as is claimed by the Murphy interests. The Tribunal considers that it is manifestly improbable that Mr. Gogarty would have misappropriated £30,000 of his employer's money, with the prior knowledge of the company's financial director, and that he would then have handed this money to a politician with whom he had no prior dealing in circumstances where no discernable benefit resulted to him. Detection of any such unauthorised activity was inevitable, and the consequences for him and his family catastrophic.

THE POSSIBILITY THAT MR. GOGARTY MADE THE PAYMENT TO MR. BURKE IN ORDER TO DAMAGE THE MURPHY INTERESTS

11-44   The Tribunal is satisfied that there was no material benefit to Mr. Gogarty in paying money to Mr. Burke, and addressed the converse, whether the payment was made by Mr. Gogarty for the purpose of damaging their legitimate interests.

11-45   The Tribunal believes, on the balance of probabilities that, a payment of £30,000 from the funds of JMSE would not have been made by Mr. Gogarty for the purpose of damaging his employer's interests for the following reasons:

1 There is nothing inherently wrong in a company making a political donation to a politician, and consequently a subsequent public revelation that such a donation had been made would not of itself necessarily harm the Murphy interests.

2 If Mr. Gogarty was endeavouring to "set up" Mr. Burke and/or the Murphy interests he would not have arranged for the attendance of a witness, Mr. Bailey, whose evidence would be that he had witnessed a handing over of a legitimate political donation.

3 In making such a payment to Mr. Burke Mr. Gogarty could not have assumed that Mr. Burke would not have issued a receipt, and/or written to thank JMSE acknowledging the payment, thus bringing it to the immediate attention of JMSE directors.

4 Mr. Gogarty could not have assumed that Mr. Burke would not have followed the procedures which would have given that the payment the *indicia* of a legitimate political donation, for example, by issuing a receipt, recording it in the books of account of the constituency, disclosing it to his constituency organisation, and/or his political party.

5 It is improbable that if a scheme was being devised to damage the Murphy interests that it would be as convoluted, complex, and dependent on matters outside the control of Mr. Gogarty, for its success.

6 The fact that it took almost seven years for the matter to be disclosed publicly indicates the improbability of it being part of a scheme, devised in 1989, to damage the Murphy interests.

7 The Tribunal considers it inherently improbable that Mr. Gogarty would have pitted himself against persons of considerable standing within the community, including a serving Government Minister, and a retired senior figure in local government, if he had a plan solely to damage his employer's interests. There was no apparent or obvious reason for his making allegations of wrong-doing on the part of persons other than his employers. If he had a scheme to damage his employer's interests the joinder of these parties could only have made his task more difficult.

8 The Tribunal is satisfied that if Mr. Gogarty had devised a scheme to "set up" his employers it would not have been one in which he was essentially relying on his word against the word of many others.

MR. GOGARTY'S ADMITTED HATRED OF MR. JOSEPH MURPHY JNR. AS A POSSIBLE EXPLANATION FOR HIS MAKING ALLEGATIONS AGAINST MR. BURKE AND THE MURPHY INTERESTS

11-46   In the course of the Tribunal hearings, it became manifest that Mr. Gogarty had an abiding hatred and contempt for Mr. Joseph Murphy Jnr., which was matched only by the hatred and contempt which Mr. Joseph Murphy Jnr. had for Mr. Gogarty. The Tribunal has been invited to conclude that the allegations made by Mr. Gogarty are a fabrication on his part motivated out of a desire to damage the legitimate interest of the Murphy family and that Mr. Burke has been drawn into this conflict which was not of his making. The Tribunal has examined all of the evidence relating to the admitted deterioration in the relationship which had formally existed between Mr. Gogarty and the Murphy interests in order to establish whether it affords an explanation for Mr. Gogarty making his allegations against Mr. Burke and the Murphy interests.

MR. GOGARTY'S HISTORY, 1917 - 1968

11-47   Mr. James Martin Gogarty was born in 1917 in Kells, Co. Meath where his father was a small building contractor. He attended National School and Secondary School before being apprenticed as a bricklayer/plasterer. At the outbreak of the Second World War he joined an auxiliary force of an Garda Síochána. He subsequently joined an Garda Síochána and was stationed at Clontarf. While a member of an Garda Síochána he pursued night studies and matriculated to the National University of Ireland where he studied for a degree in engineering while still serving as a member of an Garda Síochána. He found that he could not successfully combine both activities and took leave from U.C.D. prior to the date of the second year engineering examinations. He subsequently returned to U.C.D. years later to complete his engineering studies and obtained a degree in engineering.

11-48   After graduation he was employed in the architect's firm of Higginbotham and Stafford, which at that time was engaged in the design of housing estates in the emerging Dublin suburbs. In the course of this work he came to know Mr. Batt O'Shea and Mr. Tom Shanahan who were the principal directors of the firm of O'Shea and Shanahan Limited. This firm had commenced operations as shop fitters and had moved to being house builders in North Dublin and elsewhere. Mr. Batt O'Shea was born in Kerry. He was a friend and contemporary of Mr. Joseph Murphy Snr., who was born in Caherciveen, Co. Kerry. Mr. Joseph Murphy Snr. became a director and a one third owner of the shareholding of O'Shea and Shanahan Limited although the operations were managed on a day-to-day basis by the other directors. Mr. O'Shea advised Mr. Murphy from time to time in relation to land purchases in Ireland, and in due course O'Shea and Shanahan Ltd came to build on lands owned by Mr. Murphy's wholly owned land-owning companies.

MR. GOGARTY'S INVOLVEMENT WITH JMSE, 1968 - 1982

11-49   In 1968 Mr. Murphy acquired an interest in an ailing steel company based in Santry then known as George Milner and Sons Limited. He sought to appoint a joint managing director to this company to protect his interests. Mr. O'Shea recommended Mr. Gogarty for the position and Mr. Gogarty was duly appointed. In 1969 Mr. Murphy acquired the entire shareholding of George Milner and Sons Limited and renamed it Joseph Murphy Structural Engineers Limited (JMSE) whereupon Mr. Gogarty was appointed its sole managing director. Mr. Gogarty held this position until 1982. During the period of his stewardship the company was turned around from being virtually insolvent to being a major player in the steel contracting business in Ireland, concentrating on semi-state companies' projects. During this period Mr. Gogarty worked closely with Mr. Joseph Murphy Snr. and both parties had a mutual respect for each other's abilities. Mr. Gogarty was 51 years of age at the time of his appointment, and in 1982 he reached the age of 65, whereupon, at Mr. Murphy Snr.'s request, he retired from the position of Managing Director, and remained on as non-executive Chairman of the company.

MR. GOGARTY'S INVOLVEMENT WITH JMSE, 1982 – 1988

11-50   In 1982 Mr. Murphy Snr. had decided to appoint Mr. Liam Conroy, a member of the firm of Dublin architects, Conroy Manahan, as the Acting Chief Executive of his Companies, both in Ireland and

England. Mr. Murphy was 65 years of age, and wished to play a lesser role in the management of his Companies. In this transition Mr. Gogarty was invited to resign as Managing Director and to be appointed as Chairman of JMSE.

11-51 Mr. Gogarty's evidence was that he had been asked by Mr. Murphy Snr. to serve as Chairman for the next two years or so, and was promised that he would be provided with a capital sum to be used to purchase a pension for himself and his wife on his retirement at the conclusion of this period. In the interim he was to continue to receive his salary. Mr. Gogarty said that he agreed to Mr. Murphy's proposal but that the anticipated retirement did not take place as intended two years later. Upon being appointed chief executive of the Murphy companies Mr. Conroy replaced the existing management with his own nominees and moved to London where he exercised overall control of the Murphy companies, both in Ireland and in England. Mr. Gogarty had a limited role in the affairs of JMSE once Mr. Conroy was appointed, and did not enjoy a cordial relationship with either Mr. Conroy, or the new directors. Mr. Murphy Snr. was initially satisfied with Mr. Conroy's performance, but relationships between Mr. Conroy and his executives, and Mr. Gogarty were strained from the start. The promised pension did not materialise after two years.

11-52 In 1987 Mr. Gogarty was still acting as chairman of JMSE, and Mr. Joseph Murphy Snr. began to have concerns about the manner in which Mr. Conroy was managing his operations. Mr. Murphy shared his concern with Mr. Gogarty, and ultimately came to seek his assistance in the removal of Mr. Conroy from the Murphy companies and trusts. In mid-1988 Mr. Murphy resolved to remove Mr. Conroy from all positions of authority, and with the assistance of his legal and financial advisers, he mounted a coup to regain control of his trusts and companies. He succeeded in doing so in June 1988, but for some years thereafter, he was the subject of legal proceedings, which had been commenced by Mr. Conroy and his trusts in various jurisdictions. During the currency of these legal proceedings from June 1988 onwards JMSE was under the management of new directors appointed by Mr. Joseph Murphy Snr.

MR. GOGARTY'S INVOLVEMENT WITH JMSE, JUNE 1988 – JULY 1989

11-53 Mr. Gogarty remained on as Chairman of JMSE after the removal of Mr. Conroy but his role did not increase. The day-to-day management of JMSE was conducted by Mr. Frank Reynolds and Mr. Gabriel Grehan, new directors appointed by Mr. Murphy Snr. on the recommendation of Mr. Gogarty. The overall charge of the company was exercised by Mr. Joseph Murphy Snr., with the advice of his strategy committee, comprising: Mr. Edgar Wadley a former chartered accountant then acting as a financial adviser, Mr. Christopher Oakley an English solicitor and Mr. Roger Copsey, a chartered accountant in Ireland. Mr. Copsey was formerly a partner in the accountancy firm, Midgeley Snelling, with Mr. Wadley.

11-54 Whilst Mr. Gogarty had been of assistance to Mr. Murphy in regaining control of his companies he did not play any significant role in the management of JMSE after it had reverted to Mr. Murphy's control. Mr. Gogarty was at that time 71 years of age, and his primary interest was to secure his pension. Mr. Gogarty's pension was not a priority issue for Mr. Murphy Snr. The removal of the Chief Executive Mr. Conroy and the majority of Board Members of the Murphy companies had caused considerable disruption, and was of concern to the companies bankers. Mr. Murphy's priorities were directed towards consolidating his company's financial position. On the 22nd May 1989, however, a meeting took place between Mr. Murphy Snr. and Mr. Gogarty in London, which resulted in heads of agreement for the pension being reached, and on the 6th July 1989 Mr. Gogarty retired from all positions in the Murphy companies. As part of the terms of his pension he continued to provide services to the companies as a consultant.

MR. GOGARTY'S PENSION FROM JMSE, 1968 - 1989

11-55 It was not a term of Mr. Gogarty's initial employment with JMSE that he would receive a pension after his retirement. Had he fully retired at 65 years of age in 1982 he would have been dependent solely upon state assistance. He had married his wife who was 20 years his junior and they were the parents of six children who were financially dependent upon him. The Tribunal accepts that Mr. Gogarty was promised a pension by Mr. Murphy Snr. in 1982. On foot of that arrangement some money was lodged to an account opened for him by Mr. Murphy Snr. in the Channel Isles in 1982. This lodgment was not declared to the

Irish Revenue authorities at the time, but was subsequently repatriated by Mr. Gogarty, and declared to the Revenue under the terms of the tax amnesty then prevailing.

11-56   When Mr. Liam Conroy was appointed as Chief Executive of the Murphy companies in 1982, Mr. Gogarty's pension position received low priority from him. In view of Mr. Gogarty's advanced years at that time, it would have required a sizeable capital sum to be invested to secure an annuity for him, and an even larger sum if it was also to provide support for his wife after his death given the difference in their ages. Over the succeeding years Mr. Conroy was unsuccessful in his attempts to secure Mr. Gogarty's voluntary retirement on pension. Mr. Gogarty's continuing involvement with the company was considered by Mr. Conroy to run counter to the best interests of the company, and he accordingly resolved in June 1988 to have him dismissed by resolution of the Board. A Board Meeting was convened to take place in Dublin on the 7th June 1988 for that purpose. At this time Mr. Murphy Snr. and Mr. Conroy were in dispute as to the control of the companies, and Mr. Conroy's attempt to remove Mr. Gogarty was used by Mr. Murphy Snr. as one of the grounds to remove Mr. Conroy from office.

11-57   After the successful removal of Mr. Conroy from all positions of authority in June 1988 Mr. Gogarty believed that his pension issue would be satisfactory resolved by Mr. Murphy Snr.. However, it was not until February 1989 that Mr. Copsey was deputed by Mr. Murphy Snr. to discuss Mr. Gogarty's pension with him. Mr. Copsey and Mr. Gogarty failed to agree on mutually acceptable terms, and their meeting ended with Mr. Gogarty becoming quite emotional on the issue, according to Mr. Copsey.

11-58   Direct negotiations later took place between Mr. Murphy Snr. and Mr. Gogarty at the Bonnington Hotel in London on the 22nd May, 1989, and on that occasion, the parties reached mutually acceptable heads of agreement which were to be given legal effect through documents to be drawn up by their respective solicitors. The terms of the pension package negotiated by the parties in May, 1989 were that:-

1. A capital sum of £300,000 would be used to purchase a pension for life for Mr. Gogarty and for his wife after his death.

2. Mr. Gogarty would continue to be paid a sum equivalent to his then salary in return for his acting as a consultant to the Murphy companies for a period of five years after his retirement.

3. Mr. Gogarty and JMSE would share equally in the proceeds of an unresolved claim for extras which was being pursued by JMSE against ESB for work which had been carried out by JMSE years beforehand at the Moneypoint Power Station project. This sharing agreement was in respect of all sums above a base figure which was initially fixed at £40,000, and subsequently revised to £130,000.

4. Mr. Gogarty would be given the use of a company car and expenses.

11-59   This pension arrangement was in excess of what Mr. Murphy Snr. had been advised by Mr. Copsey to pay and was approximately equal to that which had been sought by Mr. Gogarty in the course of his failed negotiations with Mr. Copsey.

11-60   The Tribunal concludes on the balance of probabilities that Mr. Gogarty's outstanding pension issue had been resolved to the satisfaction of all parties on the 22nd May, 1989, and accordingly it could not have been the basis of any dispute which could account for a payment of money being made to Mr. Burke three weeks later, in June 1989. The Tribunal is satisfied that at the end of May, and in early June, 1989 the relationship of Mr. Gogarty and Mr. Murphy Snr. was at its zenith. The long unresolved pension issue, extending back to 1982, had been resolved to everybody's satisfaction, and Mr. Gogarty had no other identifiable grievance, or concern with his employer at that time. The Tribunal concludes that Mr. Gogarty's attendance at the meeting at Mr. Burke's house three weeks later was not in furtherance of any scheme devised by Mr. Gogarty to damage the Murphy interests.

THE DETERIORATION IN THE RELATIONSHIP BETWEEN MR. GOGARTY AND THE MURPHY INTERESTS

11-61   In late June 1989, a number of matters of concern to Mr. Gogarty arose from the manner in which the affairs of the Murphy companies were being conducted. He became aware of the fact that consideration was being given by Mr. Murphy Snr. and his advisers to the separation from JMSE of its English sister company, AGSE. If this separation was implemented, it would have resulted in JMSE being an unsecured creditor of AGSE's. AGSE was at that time indebted to JMSE for approximately £1.8m worth of steel and services which had been provided to AGSE by JMSE in connection with its English contracts. In the event that AGSE did not discharge its debt in full to JMSE, JMSE would be insolvent and consequently would be unable to fund the pension package already agreed with Mr. Gogarty.

11-62   The annual accounts for JMSE for 1988 had not been signed off by the directors. Mr. Copsey, the Financial Director of JMSE, was insistent that Mr. Gogarty sign off on these accounts. Mr. Gogarty was concerned that the draft accounts had been prepared on the basis of information generated during the period in which Mr. Conroy was in control of the company. He was unhappy about the manner in which Mr. Conroy had conducted the affairs of the Company and was unwilling to accept the accuracy of these accounts. Mr. Gogarty expressed his concern to the other Irish directors, Mr. Frank Reynolds and Mr. Gabriel Grehan, who were equally concerned that they were being requested to sign off on accounts covering a period prior to their appointment as directors, and for a period when Mr. Conroy was in control of the company. Despite Mr. Copsey's urgings they sought independent legal advice as to their position as directors and, having done so, remained unwilling to sign off on the accounts.

11-63   At the insistence of the Irish directors, a Board Meeting for JMSE was convened to take place in Dublin on the 3rd July 1989. The Irish directors had expressed the concern to Mr. Copsey that JMSE was being run by an elite group in the UK without consultation with the Irish directors, and that Board Meetings of the Company had not been held to that date. Accordingly, Mr. Joseph Murphy Snr. travelled to Dublin and attended the meeting of the 3rd July, 1989. Amongst the issues discussed at the meeting was the ongoing failure of the Irish directors to sign off on the 1988 accounts of JMSE. The Tribunal is satisfied that this was a heated meeting, and that, as a result of what was said, Mr. Gogarty came away from the meeting with the belief that his pension entitlement was again in jeopardy in the event that he did not sign off on the accounts, and that he did not assist Mr. Murphy Snr. by furnishing a Replying Affidavit to the then current proceedings which had been launched by Mr. Conroy against the Murphy interests in the Isle of Man. As Mr. Gogarty was unwilling to comply with either of these requests he tendered his resignation from JSME with effect from the 6th July 1989. He continued, however, to provide his services to the Murphy companies in a consultancy capacity as was envisaged in the pension package negotiated with Mr. Murphy Snr. in May 1989.

THE ESB EXTRAS CLAIM DISPUTE

11-64   From March 1989 onwards Mr. Gogarty's attentions had been focused on finalising the ESB extras claim on the Moneypoint contract. The heads of agreement on the pension issue had been agreed with Mr. Murphy Snr., on the 22nd May 1989, but at the date of Mr. Gogarty's resignation, on the 6th July 1989, had not yet been reduced to a formal written agreement signed by both parties. Mr. Gogarty was concerned that JMSE's affairs might be conducted in a manner which would leave the company without sufficient funds to purchase his agreed pension. He resolved, after taking legal advice on the matter, to place the proceeds of the settlement of the ESB extras claim in an escrow account in the name of JMSE and his solicitors, McCann Fitzgerald, pending the satisfactory completion of his pension arrangements.

11-65   While Mr. Gogarty had resigned without complying with Mr. Murphy's request in relation to signing off on the 1988 accounts, and without swearing the Affidavit in the Isle of Man proceedings, their relationship was still relatively cordial. This is evidenced by the fact that Mr. Gogarty continued to be engaged in progressing the ESB extras claim, and also in negotiating the sale of the Murphy's North Dublin lands to Mr. Bailey. When Mr. Gogarty implemented his plan to secure his pension and placed the proceeds of the ESB extras claim in the escrow account the Murphy's relationship with Mr. Gogarty became strained.

11-66   The Tribunal is satisfied that while Mr. Joseph Murphy Jnr. came to view Mr. Gogarty's actions in relation to the ESB funds as tantamount to fraud, the strategy adopted by Mr. Gogarty was no more than a method of ensuring that Mr. Murphy Snr. would honour his existing commitment to Mr. Gogarty in relation to his agreed pension and that JMSE would have sufficient funds in its accounts to do so. While legal proceedings were instituted against Mr. Gogarty and against McCann Fitzgerald Solicitors by JMSE, notwithstanding that Mr. Gogarty had offered to pay over to them all sums in excess of the cost of the pension agreed, the proceedings were ultimately settled on the basis that Mr. Gogarty was allowed to retain a sufficient sum of money from the escrow account to meet his already agreed pension entitlement. This was all that Mr. Gogarty had ever sought to achieve by adopting this course.

11-67   Despite the fact that the ESB money dispute had resulted in litigation against him, Mr. Gogarty was called upon by the Murphy interests to attend a meeting with Mr. Michael Bailey and Mr. Tom Bailey at the Swiss Cottage public house in mid-1990, in an effort to resolve the dispute which was delaying the closing of the contract for sale of the North Dublin lands which was to have taken place in April 1990. Mr. Murphy Snr. retained his confidence in Mr. Gogarty. He considered him to be the best person to negotiate the extras claim on behalf of AGSE in respect of another contract, the Sizewell contract, which was still outstanding. The Tribunal concludes that Mr. Gogarty had retained Mr. Murphy Snr.'s trust, despite their dispute at the Board Meeting of the 3rd July 1989 and the subsequent ESB monies dispute.

THE CLAIMED OVER-PAYMENT OF EXPENSES TO MR. GOGARTY

11-68   Mr. Joseph Murphy Jnr.'s relationship with Mr. Gogarty was less sanguine. From the date of his retirement in July 1989 Mr. Gogarty had been providing consultancy services to the Murphy companies, but increasingly disputes arose between himself and Mr. Murphy Jnr. Mr. Murphy Jnr. had assumed an increasingly important role in the management of the Murphy companies from June 1988 onwards, ultimately culminating in his control of both the Irish and the English operations by 1991.

11-69   Mr. Murphy Jnr. came to dispute the level of expenses being charged by Mr. Gogarty and their relationship deteriorated to the point that Mr. Gogarty was discharged by Mr. Joseph Murphy Jnr. from any further obligations to provide services to the Murphy companies - notwithstanding that the companies remained obliged to pay him consultancy fees for the remainder of the five year period from the date of his resignation. At the expiry of the consultancy period of five years, the Murphy companies instituted Court proceedings to recover circa. £1,500 from Mr. Gogarty, which they indicated had been an over-payment to him. These proceedings were successfully defended by Mr. Gogarty in the District Court which dismissed the Murphy claim against him.

THE P.60 DISPUTE

11-70   When it came to implementing the pension agreement, which was eventually signed by the parties the consent of the Revenue to the proposed scheme was necessary. One of the Revenue requirements was that a P.60 Form would be provided by Mr. Gogarty's former employers. The Murphy companies sought to issue P.60 Forms from a number of companies in the Murphy Group, including the land owning companies of which Mr. Gogarty had been a Director, but from which he had not received any salary or remuneration. Mr. Gogarty believed, and was so advised, that the issue of such forms from companies which had not paid him any wages could jeopardise his position with the Revenue authorities, and accordingly he insisted on receiving a single P.60 Form from the company which had, in fact, paid him wages - JMSE.

11-71   It would have been more advantageous from a tax point of view for the Murphy companies to have followed their intended course by issuing a number of P.60s from their various companies rather than a single P.60 from JMSE. Mr. Joseph Murphy Jnr. considered that Mr. Gogarty's refusal to agree to this course was motivated solely by a desire to increase the cost to the company of providing his pension, rather than to reflect any legitimate concern which he had regarding his tax status had he followed their proposal.

11-72   In order to resolve this impasse, Mr. Gogarty instituted proceedings in the Dublin Circuit Court seeking, *inter alia*, a declaration that he was entitled to receive his P.60 from his former employer, JMSE, only. This litigation was protracted and was ultimately heard in Dublin Circuit Court on the 8th March,

1994, when judgement in favour of Mr. Gogarty was decreed against JMSE. The Murphy interests were dissatisfied with this judgement, and appealed it to the High Court, but subsequently withdrew their appeal.

11-73   The Tribunal is satisfied on the evidence that Mr. Joseph Murphy Jnr. developed a deep hatred for Mr. Gogarty from 1989 onwards. Mr. Gogarty had successfully negotiated a pension which Mr. Joseph Murphy Jnr. felt to be overgenerous. He had successfully secured his pension by depositing the ESB monies into the escrow account. He had successfully defended the Murphy's claim against him for claimed overpayment of expenses. He had successfully concluded the P.60 dispute with the result that the Murphy companies were deprived of the opportunity of offsetting some of the costs of Mr. Gogarty's pension against the tax payable on the profits of their land owning companies.

THE LAST STRAW

11-74   Mr. Joseph Murphy Jnr.'s hatred of Mr. Gogarty manifested itself in two telephone calls made to Mr. Gogarty's home, in the early hours of the morning of the 20th June 1994, in which he verbally abused Mr. Gogarty and threatened him with physical violence. The Tribunal believes that these intemperate outbursts were probably fuelled by excessive alcohol consumption on Mr. Joseph Murphy Jnr.'s part, and does not believe that Mr. Joseph Murphy Jnr. had the actual intention of inflicting physical harm upon Mr. Gogarty at that time or subsequently. The outbursts, however, establish the intensity of his feelings towards Mr. Gogarty.

11-75   The Tribunal accepts that Mr. Murphy Jnr. subjected Mr. Gogarty to a shocking and frightening experience. Mr. Gogarty was, at that time, 77 years of age and in poor health, suffering from a number of serious ailments. The Tribunal is satisfied that the reaction of Mr. Gogarty to the abuse by Mr. Joseph Murphy Jnr. was to crystallise the latent hostility, which had been simmering between them over the previous five years, into a fixed hatred for Mr. Murphy Jnr. This was to have a profound effect on Mr. Gogarty, and his relationship, not only with Mr. Joseph Murphy Jnr., but with Mr. Joseph Murphy Snr. and the Murphy interests.

MR. GOGARTY'S CAMPAIGN AGAINST MR. MURPHY JNR.

11-76   From the 20th June 1994 onwards Mr. Gogarty conducted a campaign against Mr. Murphy Jnr. The purpose of his campaign was to ensure that Mr. Murphy Jnr. was suitably punished for his behaviour to that date, and that he was restrained from further similar acts. Mr. Gogarty lodged a formal complaint with the Gardaí against Mr. Murphy Jnr. in the expectation that a criminal prosecution would follow. His expectation in this regard was not fulfilled. Detective Sergeant Sherry decided not to prosecute Mr. Joseph Murphy Jnr. arising from the telephone incidents. The Tribunal accepts that Detective Sergeant Sherry's decision was taken for sound operational reasons. The perpetrator was not an Irish resident, proof of the threat element of the telephone calls could prove difficult, the parties were already engaged in civil litigation at that time arising from the P.60 issue, and the chances of a repetition of the abuse seemed slight.

11-77   Although advised by his own solicitor of the Garda decision not to prosecute, and of the reasons for the decision, Mr. Gogarty would not accept that it was a valid decision and maintained that the Gardaí had been corrupted by the Murphy interests. Whilst Mr. Gogarty persisted with his allegation over time in his dealings with journalists and with politicians, he did not pursue that allegation at the Tribunal hearing, and the Tribunal was satisfied that the reputation of the Gardaí involved did not require vindication.

11-78   The Tribunal has been urged to draw the conclusion that the making of the allegation against the Gardaí was evidence of reckless malice on the part of Mr. Gogarty, and of a tendency to make unsubstantiated allegations against any person who might disagree with his point of view. The Tribunal is not satisfied that this is the case. If it were the case that Mr. Gogarty had witnessed the bribery of a senior politician by the Murphy interests, as claimed by him, his conclusion, that the perpetrator of the threatening phone calls, had also used his influence to forestall a prosecution would be neither wild nor far-fetched.

11-79   When Mr. Gogarty's complaint to the Gardaí failed to produce the desired result Mr. Gogarty instituted civil proceedings in the High Court against Mr. Joseph Murphy Jnr. His ability to bring these proceedings to fruition was thwarted by the inability of the Summons Server to locate and personally serve the defendant, Mr. Joseph Murphy Jnr. None of the solicitors who performed work for the Murphy companies in Ireland received any instructions from Mr. Joseph Murphy Jnr. to accept service of the proceedings on his behalf, notwithstanding that he was in *de facto* control of the companies which instructed them. Mr. Gogarty ultimately sought an Order from the High Court for substituted service.

CONCLUSIONS

11-80   The Tribunal believes that Mr. Gogarty became frustrated and obsessed with the belief that he had been sorely wronged. He was determined to punish those whom he perceived had wronged him. In his review of his dealings with Mr. Joseph Murphy Jnr. he came to conclude that various acts of malicious damage caused to his property in the years after his retirement, and prior to Mr. Murphy's telephone call in 1994, were the work of Mr. Joseph Murphy Jnr.

11-81   The Tribunal is satisfied that there is no substance in these beliefs and that Mr. Murphy Jnr. had no hand, act, or part in damaging Mr. Gogarty's car, or in firing shots at his window, as claimed by Mr. Gogarty. However, the Tribunal does not believe that the incidents described are inventions on Mr. Gogarty's part. His property was in fact damaged at the time he claimed, but not by Mr. Murphy Jnr. The Tribunal concludes that his subsequent connection of these incidents with Mr. Murphy Jnr. was irrational and was the result of the blind hatred that had developed between them.

11-82   In considering all of the evidence which charted the established deterioration of the relationship between Mr. Gogarty and the Murphy interests, and *vice versa*, the Tribunal has concluded that this deterioration took place at a time after the date of payment of the monies to Mr. Burke in June 1989. The deterioration of the relationship with Mr. Joseph Murphy Jnr. undoubtedly led to the public airing of Mr. Gogarty's grievances against the Murphys, which in turn led to the revelation of the details of the meeting at which Mr. Burke was undeniably paid at least £30,000 of JMSE's money. However, it is not an aid to establishing why Mr. Burke was paid money on that occasion, nor does it provide a motive for Mr. Gogarty's actions in 1989.

Chapter 12

The Accounting and Auditing Procedures regarding the JMSE Funds paid to Mr. Burke

12-01 The evidence offered on behalf of the Murphy interests was that they were unaware, until mid-August 1997, that any of their funds had been paid to Mr. Burke in 1989, and that Mr. Gogarty had made the payment without their knowledge. It was conceded that £30,000 of JMSE money paid to Mr. Burke had been sourced through their bank account and had been accounted for, to some extent, in the company's books of account.

12-02 The Tribunal sought to establish from the involvement of JMSE personnel, other than Mr. Gogarty, with these funds, whether there was any evidence to support or to disprove the contention that Mr. Gogarty was acting on his own behalf, and without the knowledge of his employers, when he attended the meeting at Mr. Burke's house, in June 1989, at which the money was handed to Mr. Burke.

MR. ROGER COPSEY'S INVOLVEMENT IN THE ASSEMBLY OF FUNDS FOR PAYMENT TO MR. BURKE

12-03 Mr. Roger Copsey was the Financial Director of JMSE, in June 1989, and he is the only witness in that organisation who acknowledged in evidence that he was aware, prior to the event, that £30,000 of Murphy company funds was to be paid as a political contribution in the lead up to the 1989 General Election. Mr. Copsey's involvement in the assembly of the funds for that purpose was independently noted in the written attendances kept by the late Mr. Denis McArdle, the conveyancing solicitor to the Murphy companies, and in those of his secretary, Eilish.

12-04 On the morning of the 8th June 1989 a written attendance was taken by Mr. Denis McArdle, which recorded a telephone contact made with him by Mr. Roger Copsey. Mr. Copsey is noted as having sought from Mr. McArdle that day £30,000, preferably £20,000 in cash and £10,000 by way of cheque, for the purpose of a political donation in connection with the forthcoming General Election taking place on the 15th June 1989. The attendance memorandum recorded a question mark after the word "donation". Mr. McArdle died prior to giving evidence to the Tribunal. Mr. Copsey's evidence regarding this contact with Mr. McArdle was that he had been contacted by Mr. Gogarty sometime earlier that day. He said that Mr. Gogarty told him he was seeking these funds in order to make a political donation. Mr. Copsey's evidence was that he was implementing Mr. Gogarty's request by contacting Mr. McArdle. Mr. Copsey said that he did not wish the payment to be made from funds of the trading company, JMSE, but rather from Grafton Construction Company's funds, which were on deposit through Mr. McArdle in an account at the ICC Bank.

12-05 Mr. Gogarty, in his evidence, emphatically denied that he had ever contacted Mr. Copsey that day, or that he had given him any instruction to obtain money from Mr. McArdle for a political donation or otherwise. Mr. Copsey's evidence was to the effect that Mr. Gogarty's request was considered by him to be an unusual one because, in his experience, the companies had never made a political contribution, or donation, of this magnitude before. He said Mr. Gogarty did not name the intended recipient of the funds when he made the request of him. Mr. Copsey did not put any procedure in place whereby he would receive a receipt or an acknowledgement of the donation from the recipient. Mr. Copsey did not ask Mr. Gogarty why a political donation was being made at that time, nor did he ask him to name the intended recipient, nor did he establish whether it was being paid to an individual, or to a political party.

12-06 Mr. Copsey's belief was that he had instructed his subordinate, Mr. Tim O'Keeffe, to account for this transaction in the books of JMSE as an inter-company loan. But he did not tell him what the purpose of this loan was, nor did he instruct him as to how to record the transaction in the books of The Grafton Construction Company Limited (Grafton) which was the ultimate source of the funds. Mr. Copsey did not prepare any written attendance of his meeting with Mr. Gogarty, or of his request to Mr. McArdle, nor did he prepare any memorandum or ledger entry for the Grafton files which would identify this expenditure either as a political donation or otherwise. Mr. Copsey took no steps to record the transaction in the books of account of Grafton. He did not contact Mr. Joseph Murphy Snr. to establish whether the intended political payment was authorised by him. He did not follow up the matter with Mr. Gogarty after his retirement. This evidence must be viewed against the history of Mr. Copsey's appointment to the Murphy companies in 1988.

12-07   During the period prior to June 1988, when Mr. Liam Conroy was in charge of JMSE, Mr. Gogarty was levelling criticism against the Conroy appointed directors - centering upon his belief that the company funds were being misappropriated by them. Once Mr. Murphy Snr. had regained control of the companies, and upon the appointment of Mr. Copsey as Financial Director of JMSE in June 1988, Mr. Copsey found that there was a want of proper accounting procedures to vouch managerial expenditure. Accordingly, on the 2nd August 1988, the Company formally resolved to put in place a system whereby all cash expenditure had to be vouched by appropriate receipts.

12-08   While Mr. Copsey did not accept that Mr. Gogarty's allegations of financial impropriety on the part of the former managers of JMSE were soundly based, the Tribunal considers that he must have been mindful of the fact that similar allegations could be made against him by Mr. Gogarty if he failed to follow the accounting procedures which he himself had set up to record cash expenditure. Mr. Copsey admitted that this was an extraordinary payment, yet it is clear that he failed to maintain appropriate records for such payment. The Tribunal would have expected that any request made of Mr. Copsey by Mr. Gogarty would have been fully documented by Mr. Copsey, and that at a minimum he would have requested a written confirmation or acknowledgement from Mr. Gogarty of this request for his own protection.

12-09   The Tribunal also believes that it is unlikely that Mr. Copsey would have accepted Mr. Gogarty's bald assertion that this substantial sum of money was required for a political purpose without obtaining confirmation from Mr. Murphy Snr. that he had authorised such payment. The fact that £20,000 of the donation was being sought in cash form must have immediately alerted Mr. Copsey to a possible accountancy problem. His function was to account for the company's expenditure and to be in a position to explain all financial dealings by the company to its directors. Without any invoice, receipt or written acknowledgment for such payment, Mr. Copsey must have known that he could not properly account for such payment.

12-10   The Tribunal is satisfied that Mr. Gogarty's role in JMSE in June 1989 was not such as would have allowed him to unilaterally direct the Financial Director to provide him with £30,000 cash or its cash/cheque equivalent. If such a demand had been made by Mr. Gogarty he could not reasonably have anticipated that Mr. Copsey would not have immediately brought this matter to the attention of Mr. Murphy Snr. Accordingly, if the payment had not been authorised, as is now claimed by the Murphy interests, Mr. Gogarty would have immediately found himself subject to severe sanction for having endeavoured to obtain this substantial sum of money from the company for his own unauthorised purposes.

12-11   Mr. Copsey and Mr. Gogarty did not enjoy a cordial relationship in 1989. Mr. Gogarty did not trust Mr. Copsey from the time of his appointment as Financial Director, and their relationship was strained, particularly after their unsuccessful attempts to negotiate pension terms in February 1989. In June 1989, Mr. Copsey and Mr. Murphy Snr. were in regular contact by telephone in relation to the financial affairs of JMSE. At that time Mr. Copsey specifically liaised with Mr. Murphy Snr. on the question of his own professional fees and he received authority by telephone from Mr. Murphy Snr. to seek £16,500 from the same source of funds held by Mr. McArdle at ICC Bank - a fact that is recorded both in the written attendance prepared by Mr. McArdle and also in correspondence from Mr. Copsey. Mr. Copsey's stated reason, for not raising the issue with Mr. Murphy Snr. as to whether the JMSE payment to Mr. Burke was sanctioned by him, was expressed to be a belief that politics in Ireland were a private matter, and accordingly he had a reluctance to inquire into Mr. Murphy Snr.'s politics.

12-12   The Tribunal considers it improbable that Mr. Copsey would not have contacted Mr. Murphy Snr. to seek his consent to any payment of £30,000 in cash, or cash equivalent, at the request of Mr. Gogarty, particularly if the request originated with Mr. Gogarty and was unsupported by any documents either recording or authorising the request. The Tribunal considers Mr. Copsey's explanation for not so doing to be unconvincing given that an appropriately worded inquiry of Mr. Murphy Snr. could have been made which would have elicited whether the payment was authorised or not, without encroaching upon the personal political preferences of Mr. Murphy Snr. On Mr. Copsey's account he was already aware of the fact that the £30,000 was to be paid for a political donation. It was not necessary for him to establish the motive for such payment, or the identity of the intended recipient, in order to establish from Mr. Murphy Snr. whether such payment was sanctioned by him.

12-13 The Tribunal concludes that it is inherently improbable that Mr. Copsey, as a chartered Accountant and the Financial Director of JMSE, would have allowed himself to be instrumental in seeking to procure £30,000 of Murphy company funds at the sole request of Mr. Gogarty, and rejects the evidence of Mr. Copsey on this issue. A request was undoubtedly made of Mr. McArdle by Mr. Copsey on the 8th June 1989, but the Tribunal is satisfied that it was not made as a result of any request made by Mr. Gogarty of Mr. Copsey. The Tribunal concludes that, on the balance of probabilities, Mr. Copsey's request of Mr. McArdle for £30,000 was expressly authorised by Mr. Murphy Snr., and that he was authorised to assemble the funds without recording in writing the name of the recipient or the purpose for which the sums were to be expended.

MR. TIM O'KEEFFE'S INVOLVEMENT IN THE ASSEMBLY OF FUNDS PAID TO MR. BURKE

12-14 In 1988, Mr. O'Keeffe was a recently qualified Accountant in the firm of Copsey Murray & Co. He was appointed Financial Controller of JMSE and held that position until he was replaced by Mr. John Maher in September 1989. He recalls attending the AIB Branch at Talbot Street, Dublin, in June 1989 to collect a sum of £20,000 in cash. He believes that he was driven to the bank by Mr. Frank Reynolds, who waited in the car while the £20,000 was counted out to him by a bank official. He then returned with Mr. Reynolds to the JMSE offices, where he said he handed over the £20,000 cash to Mr. Gogarty. Mr. Gogarty disputes the entirety of Mr. O'Keeffe's evidence in this regard.

MR. FRANK REYNOLD'S INVOLVEMENT IN THE ASSEMBLY OF FUNDS PAID TO MR. BURKE

12-15 Mr. Frank Reynolds was Managing Director of JMSE and had no particular recollection of driving Mr. O'Keeffe to the Bank in June 1989, but acknowledged that he did so from time to time. He was not aware that Mr. O'Keeffe had collected £20,000 in cash in the bank on the 8th June 1989, and says that no discussion between himself and Mr. O'Keeffe took place regarding any such sum. He had no special recollection of counter-signing a cheque for £10,000 at Mr. Gogarty's request.

CONCLUSION ON THE INVOLVEMENT OF MR. O'KEEFFE AND MR. REYNOLDS IN THE ASSEMBLY OF FUNDS PAID TO MR. BURKE

12-16 The Tribunal considers it improbable that Mr. O'Keeffe would not have discussed the assembly of £20,000 in cash with Mr. Reynolds in the course of their journey, or subsequently in the JMSE premises, when the cheque for £10,000 was drawn, if such was the case, as he was responsible to the company's owners for accounting for this expenditure. The Tribunal considers it improbable that Mr. Reynolds would not have recollected the circumstances in which he drove Mr. O'Keeffe to collect £20,000 in cash from the company's account.

THE ACCOUNTANCY TREATMENT OF THE TRANSACTIONS RELATED TO THE PAYMENT OF THE £30,000 OF JMSE FUNDS TO MR. RAY BURKE IN JUNE 1989

12-17 The Tribunal sought to establish how the payment had been accounted for, and found that none of the documents, prepared by the accountancy personnel, dealing with the funds used to pay Mr. Burke £30,000 record the fact that the money was paid to him. None of the documents prepared by the accountancy staff record that any political donation of £30,000 was made by any Murphy company in the year 1989. The fact that £30,000 was expended by JMSE in June 1989 is evidenced by the monthly bank statement on the JMSE Current Account at AIB, Talbot Street, Dublin.

12-18   The opportunities for recording Mr. Burke as the recipient of the fund existed at the time when the cheques were drawn on the 8th June 1989, when the cheque stubs were completed on the same date, when the details of the cheques were entered in the JMSE cheque payment journal for June 1989, when the nominal ledger entry explaining the Grafton/JMSE transaction was prepared, when the annual accounts were being prepared and when the auditor was preparing his working papers.

12-19   The explanation offered to the Tribunal by the Murphy interests for the absence of any record of the monies being paid to Mr. Burke was that no-one, other than Mr. Gogarty, knew the identity of the recipient of the funds, and no-one, other than Mr. Copsey, knew that any political donation was to be made by Mr. Gogarty. The Tribunal has reviewed all of the documents generated in the course of the recording of the transaction and the evidence of those who prepared the entries.

JMSE RECORDS

12-20   The documentary evidence available to the Tribunal commences with the cheque stubs for two cheques drawn sequentially on the JMSE account at AIB, Talbot Street, Dublin, both dated the 8th June 1989. These cheque stubs record amounts of £20,000 and £10,000 respectively with the words, "re; Grafton cash" on each stub - thus indicating that these cheque payments by JMSE were made to, or on the behalf of, Grafton. The JMSE cheque payment journal completed by the in-house accountancy staff in JMSE, for the month of June 1989, records the two cheque payments as having been made on the 8th June 1989, and attributed them to "Grafton Construction". The AIB bank statement for the month of June 1989 records that the cheques for £20,000 and £10,000 had been debited to the company's account in June 1989. A nominal ledger entry was prepared by the accountants showing that the expenditure of £30,000 incurred by the cheques for £20,000 and £10,000 respectively in June 1989 was re-imbursed by a £30,000 payment from Grafton some days later.

McARDLE AND CO. RECORDS

12-21   The apportionment account prepared by Mr. McArdle, solicitor, in relation to the proceeds of the sale of the Forrest Road lands, records that on the 13th June 1989 £30,000 was paid from the funds of Grafton to JMSE. The correspondence from Mr. McArdle to JMSE, in June 1989, indicates that a £30,000 cheque drawn on ICC Bank was being forwarded to "Jim" in response to Mr. Copsey's telephone request for £30,000 made on the 8th June 1989 and that "Jim" (Mr. Gogarty) had responded that he did not need it. Thereupon Mr. McArdle sought further instructions from Mr. Copsey who then instructed Mr. McArdle to send it to Mr. O'Keeffe at JMSE.

GRAFTON RECORDS

12-22   Grafton did not write its own cheque to re-imburse JMSE. The payment was made from Mr. McArdle's Solicitor/Client account at ICC Bank. Accordingly there was no independent Grafton-generated record of the transaction – it was recorded in Mr. McArdle's Grafton file and his apportionment account was in turn enclosed in the Grafton financial file maintained at JMSE premises at Shanowen Road. Since the accounts of Grafton do not record the receipt by Grafton of the proceeds of either of the cheques for £20,000 or £10,000 drawn upon the JMSE account which are attributed in JMSE's cheque journal to them, it is therefore apparent from the available records that JMSE paid some third party, or parties, the cheques or their proceeds on behalf of Grafton and that this expenditure was reimbursed within days to JMSE by Grafton through the cheque for £30,000 drawn on the Solicitor/Client Account of Mr. McArdle at ICC Bank.

THE ACCOUNTING REQUIREMENT CREATED BY THE EXPENDITURE OF JMSE FUNDS AND THE REIMBURSEMENT OF THE EXPENDITURE FROM THE FUNDS OF GRAFTON

12-23 In the accounts of JMSE, it was sufficient to record the mechanics of the transactions without necessarily recording the nature of the transactions as the role of JMSE was as facilitator only for Grafton, a sister company in the Lajos Holdings Limited group. Since the payment out by JMSE of cheques for £20,000 and £10,000 on the 8th June 1989 was reimbursed in full on the 13th June 1989, it did not involve any expenditure of JMSE funds which would have to be reflected in the company's annual accounts. It was sufficient to prepare a nominal ledger for the JMSE monthly accounts, recording the expenditure and reimbursement of this sum. Such nominal ledger was prepared by the in-house JMSE accounting staff. **(Appendix S)**.

12-24 The accounting requirement in relation to Grafton's account was different it had made a payment out of £30,000 to reimburse JMSE, which would have to be explained in its accounts. Unlike JMSE, it had not been reimbursed this sum from any other company within the Murphy Group. Grafton was a land-owning company which was engaged in a limited number of financial transactions in any one year. The accountancy functions for Grafton were carried out by the same office staff who performed the accountancy functions for JMSE. Unlike JMSE's accounts, it was sufficient for Grafton's purposes to prepare annual accounts as opposed to the various weekly, monthly and quarterly accounting exercises involved in JMSE's business activities. It was nonetheless important that all expenditure by the company would be properly vouched and accounted for.

12-25 In February 1989, Grafton, and its sister company Reliable, were paid the outstanding balance of the £1.45m sale price of the Forrest Road lands which had been sold to Mr. Michael Bailey. Much of Grafton's actual expenditure for the years 1989 and 1990 was doubly accounted for because these cash assets of Grafton were held on deposit in the Solicitor/Client account of Mr. McArdle at ICC Bank. Any funds that were withdrawn from this account were recorded by McArdle & Co. independently of any internal accounting by JMSE/Grafton's accountants. McArdle & Co. accounted to Grafton for the fund which had passed through its client account, and this included the £30,000 which had been paid by Grafton to JMSE on the 13th June 1989 by an ICC cheque requested by Mr. McArdle on the 8th June 1989.

THE GRAFTON ACCOUNTS FOR THE YEAR ENDED THE 31ST MAY 1990

12-26 The annual accounts of Grafton were prepared by Mr. Bates, the Auditor of the Irish Murphy companies, based upon the financial records and information provided to him by the JMSE accounting staff. The internal accountancy staff in JMSE retained the relevant financial information, and supporting documentation, which was generated in the course of the financial year in anticipation of the ultimate preparation of the annual accounts by Mr. Bates. Mr. Bates was familiar with the Grafton accounts, having prepared this company's accounts for some years previously.

12-27 The various Murphy land-owning companies in Ireland had carried out limited financial activities in the course of the financial year ended the 31st May 1990. The extent of those activities was such that the financial records for three companies namely Grafton, Reliable and Wexburn, were contained within one lever arch file. This file was discovered to the Tribunal; it was internally divided so as to separate the documents between the three companies involved, and was further divided so as to separate the individual company's receipts from expenditure.

12-28 In the section of the file relating to Grafton, headed "General", there were a small number of original documents, which record or explain certain financial transactions engaged in by the Company during the financial year commencing the 1st June 1989 and ending the 31st May 1990. In this section of the file was to be found the apportionment account of McArdle & Co., **(Appendix T)** which confirms, inter alia, the payment of £30,000 from Grafton to JMSE on the 13th June 1989. Mr. McArdle's accounting obligation to his client ceased with the preparation of this apportionment account. He was not obliged to inquire as to whether this payment was ultimately utilised for any particular purpose, although he may have been aware of such purpose. Those preparing the annual accounts for Grafton had the obligation to account for this expenditure.

12-29   Until the 14th August 1990, Copsey Murray & Co. had been providing accountancy services to JMSE. In June 1989 Mr. O'Keeffe was the Financial Controller and in-house accountant having been seconded from Copsey Murray & Co. to work for the Murphy companies. He reported directly to Mr. Copsey, the Financial Director. The Tribunal is satisfied that it would have been Mr. O'Keeffe's responsibility to account for the Grafton expenditure of the £30,000 to JMSE in June 1989.

12-30   Mr. O'Keeffe's role as in-house accountant ceased with the appointment of Mr. John Maher in September 1989, but he continued to provide his accountancy services to the Murphy companies until the 14th August 1990. In 1990, at the request of Mr. Copsey, he prepared a document headed "Grafton/Reliable Cash Balance", in which he sought to establish the balance of the funds which would be available to Grafton from the proceeds of sale of the Forrest Road lands after deduction of all outlay and expenses. This document was contained within the general section of the Grafton file to year-ending the 31st May 1990, prepared for the Auditor (**Appendix U**). This document set out the relevant figures, involving both accretions and deductions, under various headings, which were in turn sub-divided into categories in which the individual items were separately listed. The accretions shown therein comprised; a deposit, the balance of the purchase money, and a draft received in respect of the sale of Forrest Road land. The deductions shown were in respect of the costs, disbursements, purchase of land and repayment of inter-company loans and tax.

12-31   Within the heading "Costs" there were two sub headings, "Planning Permission" and "Fees". Immediately above the category "Fees" there was one blank line effectively dividing these two categories from one another. There is only one recorded expenditure of £30,000 appearing on this document and it is entered in the section headed "Costs". On its plain and obvious reading this document attributed the payment of £30,000 to planning permission.

12-32   Mr. Copsey is an experienced accountant who has for many years dealt with financial documentation prepared by his colleague, Mr. O'Keeffe. Mr. Copsey confirmed in the course of his evidence that the £30,000 entry shown on the Grafton/Reliable Cash Balance document was a cost referable to planning permission. In the course of his being questioned on this document, he did not suggest that the £30,000 reference appearing therein was anything other than a reference attributing the £30,000 payment to planning permission.

12-33   The author of the document, Mr. O'Keeffe, when called to give evidence some days later disputed that the reference in the document attributed the expenditure to "planning permission". His evidence was that the planning permission entry referred solely to the figure appearing on the same line, that is £80,258.00 and did not apply to the £30,000 entry appearing on the line below. He maintained that he would have inserted letters "DO", (meaning Ditto), beneath the words "planning permission" referred to in the line above had he intended to record that both entries referred to expenditure in relation to planning permission. He sought to distinguish the "planning permission" reference on the first line from the entry on the immediately following line by pointing out that a colon does not follow the words "planning permission", and, therefore, the reference is to one item only - namely the £80,258.00 entry recorded on that same line.

12-34   In fact there is no consistent usage of the colon in this document to indicate series and the letters "*DO*" do not appear beneath descriptions of like expenditure, for example under the heading "disbursements". Significantly, no dividing line appears between the two entries which record the expenditure of £80,258, which Mr. O'Keeffe accepted as referring to planning permission, and of £30,000 which he stated appeared in the document as an unattributed expenditure. It is noted that, in every other instance of separate groupings of figures in the document, at least one line divides each category from its succeeding category, thereby readily distinguishing the respective categories of expenditure.

12-35   The Tribunal considers that Mr. O'Keeffe's explanation of the £30,000 as unattributed expenditure does not withstand critical examination. If Mr. O'Keeffe was, as he says, unaware at the time of the preparation of this document as to what the expenditure of £30,000 related to, he had no basis for including the payment under the heading of "Costs" at all. For all he knew it could have been for expenditure for purposes other than costs, including for purposes which may have properly resulted in the expenditure being categorised under any one of the other different headings appearing elsewhere in the document, including "inter-company loan".

12-36 The Tribunal concludes that the probable explanation for the entry of the £30,000 in the category of planning permission under the heading "Costs" was that Mr. O'Keeffe had learned that this expenditure was incurred in respect of a transaction which was in some way related to planning permission. Clearly, if a bribe was in fact paid, it could never be recorded in the accounts as such, but at the same time the accounting obligation remained. The obvious expenditure of £30,000 by JMSE would have to be accounted for in some way, as it had been sourced from that company's bank account at AIB, and was there recorded. Furthermore, it had been re-imbursed from a solicitor/client bank account which would also be recorded in the solicitors' apportionment account. This account would be furnished to Grafton as a matter of course and would be retained as part of the Grafton record of the expenditure of the proceeds of sale of that company's major asset. The Tribunal concludes that the description "planning permission" was a cynical use of these words, which allowed those who knew of the bribe to identify the source of the funds used to make it, whilst at the same time appearing to be a legitimate heading of expense to any person who was unaware of the bribe.

MR. ROGER COPSEY'S CONSIDERATION OF THE GRAFTON/RELIABLE CASH BALANCE DOCUMENT

12-37 Mr. Copsey considered this document in his capacity as Mr. Murphy Snr.'s. Financial Advisor. He did so in order to be in a position to advise Mr. Murphy Snr. as to the net balance of funds available to him from the proceeds of sale of the Forrest Road lands. It is inherently improbable that, in considering this document, Mr. Copsey would not have carefully considered the individual items which led to the bottom line figure. The Tribunal rejects Mr. Copsey's evidence that he was only interested in the bottom line figure, and that he was not concerned with the financial calculations which led to it.

12-38 When Mr. Copsey first considered this document a relatively short period of time had elapsed from the date of his involvement in seeking the £30,000 from Mr. McArdle as a claimed political donation. Mr. Copsey was therefore aware that a £30,000 payment had been made in June 1989, and that it had been funded from the Grafton/Reliable deposit at ICC Bank which was the subject of the analysis in the Cash Balance document. It should, therefore, have appeared as an item of expenditure in the document he was considering. In considering this document he only had to consider fourteen items of expenditure, of which only one referred to a sum of £30,000. The Grafton/Reliable Cash Balance document prepared by Mr. O'Keeffe contained no reference whatsoever to any expenditure on a political donation having been funded from the proceeds of the sale of the Forrest Road lands on deposit at ICC Bank. The correct designation of the £30,000 payment was necessary to ensure that the bottom line figure was correct. If an expenditure on a political donation were incorrectly entered as a tax deductible expense, the bottom line figure would be wrong.

12-39 If Mr. Copsey's version of events were true it ought to have been readily apparent to him at that time that the bottom-line figure was incorrect, because Mr. O'Keeffe had wrongly attributed a payment which Mr. Copsey knew to be a £30,000 political donation as a payment for planning permission which was a tax deductible expense, whereas Mr. Copsey knew the payment was made for a non tax deductible expense. Even if Mr. Copsey did not check whether the correct tax status had been allowed for by Mr. O'Keeffe it was clear from the document that Mr. O'Keeffe had not made any reference to the expense being a political donation, but had apparently treated the payment as one related to planning permission. On his version Mr. Copsey knew that £30,000 had been expended as political donation, yet there was no record of any such expense in the Cash Balance document. It ought to have been apparent to him at that time that there was a manifest error in Mr. O'Keeffe's document.

12-40 Although this document was not specifically prepared for the purpose of the annual audit, it was one which would find itself in the audit file of Grafton documents in the normal course. If there was any mistake, ambiguity, or lack of clarity in this document it was incumbent upon Mr. Copsey to correct the entry so as to reflect the true position. Mr. Copsey could not know, at the time of the consideration of the document in 1990, that Mr. O'Keeffe was subsequently to qualify the "planning permission" reference in 1999 so as to exclude the £30,000 entry from that category, and to claim that it stood alone as unattributed expenditure. Mr. Copsey made no attempt in 1989 or 1990 to remedy what to him must have been an obvious error in the face of this document (if such in fact was the case).

12-41   The Tribunal concludes that the probable explanation for the fact that the Cash Balance document entry of £30,000 remained unaltered is that the attribution of £30,000 to planning permission was acceptable to Mr. Copsey because he knew that this reference was to cover the fact that this was the sum paid to a politician in June 1989, and he knew that it was paid in connection with planning permission. Independently of the existence of the Grafton/Reliable Cash Balance document, it is clear that Mr. Copsey must have given consideration in June 1989 to the manner in which the political payment of £30,000, of which he was aware, would be reflected in the accounts of Grafton.

12-42   Mr. Copsey's evidence on this issue was that he believed that he had instructed Mr. O'Keeffe to treat the matter as an inter-company loan between Grafton and JMSE. If that was the limit of his instructions it singularly failed to address the question of how the payment was to be accounted for. With that limited information Mr. O'Keeffe could not account for the expenditure, because he had not been given the necessary information to enable him to do so. The Tribunal believes that it is highly improbable that Mr. Copsey would have given such an ineffectual instruction to his subordinate, or that Mr. O'Keeffe would not have sought meaningful instructions from his superior if such a meaningless instruction was given. Upon ceasing to act for the Murphy companies in August 1990, Mr. Copsey must have been aware of the fact that the £30,000 political donation had not been recorded by him in any of the financial records of Grafton or JMSE. He must have known that he personally would have to advise Mr. O'Keeffe's successor, the in-house accountant Mr. John Maher, of the nature and purpose of this expenditure so that it could be properly accounted for in the companies' books of account. However, if Mr. Copsey's evidence is to be accepted, it follows that he took no steps whatsoever to ensure that this substantial cash payment of £30,000 was accounted for in any way, either at the time of its making, or for the fourteen months thereafter, during which time he was Financial Director of the Company.

12-43   The Tribunal believes that this is improbable and concludes that it is likely that Mr. Copsey was, at all times, aware of how the expenditure had been treated in the books of account of the companies, JMSE and Grafton. The Tribunal is satisfied that he would not have left the sum of £30,000 unaccounted for without advising the directors of that fact.

THE INVOLVEMENT OF MR. O'KEEFFE IN ACCOUNTING FOR THE £30,000 EXPENDED IN JUNE AND REIMBURSED BY GRAFTON

12-44   In his evidence Mr. O'Keeffe said that he assumed that he was given instructions by Mr. Copsey as to how to account for the transaction. The Tribunal would have expected, given its unique nature, that Mr. O'Keeffe would have been in a position to give evidence as to exactly what he was told by Mr. Copsey at the time. However, he was not in a position to do so. On Mr. O'Keeffe's recollection of events, he was not given any explanation from either the Managing Director, Mr. Frank Reynolds, or from the Chairman of the Company, Mr. James Gogarty, as to why the money was assembled. He merely collected £20,000 in cash at the bank as instructed, and handed it over to Mr. Gogarty on his return to the JMSE offices on the 8th June 1989. Mr. Gogarty disputed Mr. O'Keeffe's evidence and said that the cash was already in the office prior to his arrival on the afternoon of the 8th June 1989. Mr. O'Keeffe was a trained Accountant, he was the Financial Controller of the company from whose bank account this money was being taken. He knew that this expenditure would have to be accounted for by him both in the books of JMSE and its sister company, Grafton.

12-45   The Tribunal does not consider it credible that Mr. O'Keeffe would have accepted an instruction from Mr. Copsey to treat the transaction as an inter-company loan in the books of JMSE as sufficient to account for this expenditure. The manner in which the payment was to be treated did not afford an explanation that was sufficient to identify the purpose for which the money was spent. Hence, it could not be accounted for. The Grafton financial file assembled over the course of the financial year from June 1989 to May 1990 would in all probability have been complete, or at least substantially complete, before Mr. O'Keeffe left the employment of JMSE on the 14th August 1990.

12-46   The Tribunal considers that it must have been obvious to Mr. O'Keeffe that there was a serious omission in the documentation available to the accountant/auditor for the preparation of the year-end accounts for the year ended the 31st May 1990, as a very large sum, including the £20,000 in cash which he said he handed to Mr. Gogarty, was unaccounted for. The Tribunal considers it highly improbable that Mr. O'Keeffe would have allowed this situation to continue, and that he would not have taken steps to address what were obvious omissions in the proper accounting for a substantial cash withdrawal, during his tenure as Financial Controller, with which he was clearly identified. If the account given by Mr. O'Keeffe was true this would have constituted an extraordinary omission on Mr. O'Keeffe's part, for which there is no reasonable explanation.

12-47 The Tribunal considers Mr. O'Keeffe's account of events to be improbable. During the currency of Mr. O'Keeffe's tenure as Financial Controller, and subsequently as Accountant to JMSE, the dispute with Mr. Gogarty over the ESB monies had resulted in litigation being pursued against Mr. Gogarty for the return of these funds. The Tribunal considers it highly improbable that, in circumstances where Mr. Gogarty's integrity was apparently in issue, Mr. O'Keeffe would not have brought to the attention of the directors of the company the fact that he had handed over £20,000 in cash to Mr. Gogarty for which Mr. Gogarty had not given him any receipt or other explanation, and for which there was no vouching documentation, if that were the case.

12-48 The Tribunal is satisfied that in his preparation of the Grafton/Reliable Cash Balance document in 1990 Mr. O'Keeffe consciously attributed the £30,000 expenditure to planning permission in the knowledge, at that time, that this expenditure had been incurred in connection with some intended changes to the planning status of the Murphy lands, and that the reference to "planning permission" would allow Mr. Copsey to identify this entry as referring to the £30,000 which he, Mr. Copsey, knew had been paid to a politician in June 1989.

THE AUDITORS' TREATMENT OF THE £30,000 EXPENDITURE OF GRAFTON FUNDS IN THE ACCOUNTS OF GRAFTON FOR YEAR ENDED THE 31ST MAY 1990

12-49 In the latter part of 1990, it fell to Mr. John Bates, the Auditor, to prepare the annual accounts for the Murphy land-owning companies. Prior to so doing, he had the benefit of conducting an audit upon the more complex accounts of JMSE. He had noted that there was a nominal ledger prepared which showed an inter-company loan as between JMSE and Grafton in June 1989 and involving the expenditure of £20,000 and £10,000 by way of two cheques from JMSE, which sums were reimbursed by a £30,000 cheque payment from Grafton to JMSE on the 13th June 1989.

12-50 In preparing the accounts for Grafton, Mr. Bates sought to establish to what this £30,000 expenditure related. In his evidence he stated that, in performing the audit, he had been unable to identify the purpose for which the expenditure had been incurred as the expenditure was un-vouched in the company's financial records considered by him. He stated that, in 1990, he made inquiries of the JMSE in-house accounting staff to establish what the £30,000 was expended for, but without success. He specifically recalled asking Mr. John Maher, the in-house accountant, and Mr. Frank Reynolds, the Managing Director, but neither could assist him.

12-51 Mr. Bates was aware that Copsey Murray & Co.'s involvement as accountants to the companies had ceased in August 1990, and that Mr. Copsey and Mr. O'Keeffe were no longer employed by the companies. He said he felt that there was a certain coolness in the relationship between JMSE and the members of Copsey Murray since their removal from office. Accordingly, he said he did not pursue the matter with them other than to make a telephone inquiry to the office of Copsey Murray. He was aware that Mr. O'Keeffe had been seconded from Copsey Murray to the accounts department of JMSE, and that he was JMSE's in-house accountant in June 1989 - the relevant period in which the unaccounted for expenditure had been incurred. However, he claimed to be unable to make personal telephone contact with either Mr. Roger Copsey or Mr. Tim O'Keeffe when he was preparing the accounts in 1990. Mr. Bates believed that he did receive information by telephone from an unknown member of staff in Copsey Murray & Co. who suggested that the payments might have been a finder's fee or auctioneers fee, but he said that he rejected this explanation in the absence of any supporting documentation.

12-52 Mr. Bates gave evidence that he concluded that the un-vouched £30,000 expenditure must have been expended for a purpose which had enhanced the value of the land owned by the company, and he so treated the expenditure in the financial accounts of Grafton which were presented by him to the company's directors for approval and signature in February 1991. In those accounts he added the £30,000 to the expenditure of £65,273 involved in acquiring additional lands, at Poppintree, so as to record the enhancement expenditure as £95,273 (**Appendix V**). Mr. Bates said that he was at all times conscious of the fact that he had received no explanation for the £30,000 expenditure from the directors or staff in JMSE or Grafton. He had seen no vouching documentation to identify the recipient or recipients of those funds. Consequently he said that, at the time, he told both of the directors, Mr. Murphy Jnr. and Mr. Reynolds, and also the in-house accountant, Mr. John Maher, that his audit inquiries to that date had revealed that there was an un-vouched expenditure of £30,000 in the Grafton accounts. He said that, notwithstanding the absence of any explanation or supporting documentation for this expenditure, the directors signed off on the accounts for year ended the 31st May 1990. The evidence of Mr. Bates, if true, indicates a most unusual state of affairs. The Tribunal considers it improbable that the auditor of a company would have taken it upon himself to attribute a substantial un-vouched cash payment to a specific heading of expenditure without any factual basis for doing so, save his belief that since the company owned land any unaccounted for expenditure must have enhanced the value of that land.

THE AUDIT TRAIL AVAILABLE TO MR. BATES TO FOLLOW

12-53   Despite the fact that Mr. Bates said that his audit queries left him unable to account for the expenditure of £30,000, the Tribunal believes that there was a readily apparent audit trail which would, in all probability, have allowed him to identify the recipient of the un-vouched £30,000, had he chosen to follow it. Mr. Bates had the Grafton accounting file before him which contained Mr. McArdle's apportionment account showing that the £30,000 of Grafton money expended on the 13th June 1989 was attributed to JMSE. He knew, or could ascertain from the JMSE nominal ledger account, that the £30,000 expenditure by Grafton on the 13th June 1989, was to reimburse JMSE for the two cheques for £20,000 and £10,000 respectively, written on the 8th June 1989. He knew therefore that the bank account maintained by JMSE, at AIB Talbot Street, funded the expenditure which was un-vouched in the accounts of Grafton. The cheque payments journal maintained by JMSE for the month of June 1989 showed Grafton as the payee of the £20,000 cheque, number 011546, and the £10,000 cheque, number 011547, thus confirming that this expenditure by JMSE was stated to be in relation to Grafton. This journal was available to Mr. Bates.

12-54   Armed with this knowledge Mr. Bates could have checked the two cheque stubs, which were in the possession of JMSE, and the relevant bank statement for the month of June 1989, from which he could have readily established the following relevant information:

> 1 The £30,000 expenditure was sourced from the JMSE account at AIB, Talbot Street, by means of two cheques, the stubs for which referred to "8th June 1989 …re Grafton cash"

> 2 The £20,000 cheque, number 011546, was debited to the JMSE account at AIB, Talbot Street, on the 8th June 1989 - the date upon which it was written, and was therefore, in all probability, exchanged for cash at that branch on that date.

> 3 Mr. Tim O'Keeffe was the person who had written out the cheque stubs and was therefore, in all probability, the person who had completed the cheques.

12-55   With this information, Mr. Bates could have sought details from the Manager of AIB, Talbot Street, as to the circumstances in which the £20,000 cheque was negotiated at his branch on the 8th June 1989. He could have sought the return of the original cheques or sight of copies of the cheques from the bank. Perusal of either would have allowed him to establish the identity of any payee shown on the cheque. He could have identified the cheque signatories to each cheque, the identity of any person who may have endorsed either of the cheques, and, possibly, the account into which the £10,000 cheque was lodged.

12-56   Copies of these cheques ought to have been readily available to Mr. Bates in 1991 as his inquiries were being made within two years of the date upon which the cheques had been written. The cheque stubs for these cheques were in the JMSE premises, where the Grafton documentation was also retained, pending audit. The cheque stubs ought to have been readily available to Mr. Bates in 1991, as they were relevant to the preparation of the financial year statements for JMSE for the same period. Had Mr. Bates viewed the cheques or copies, he would have been in a position to approach the payees if they were named thereon. Even if the cheques were made out to cash, he would have been in a position to approach the signatories to the cheques to obtain details from them of the purposes for which the cheques were written. Even if Mr. Gogarty were a signatory on both cheques, the cheques required two directors' signatures and, consequently, if he were reluctant to approach Mr. Gogarty directly he could have approached the other signatory. Even if the cheques showed the payees as "cash", it should have been possible for the bank to trace the account into which the £10,000 cheque was lodged.

12-57   Inquiries of the Manager of AIB, Talbot Street, would in all probability have confirmed that the £20,000 was negotiated for cash at that bank on the 8th June 1989. Given the relatively unusual nature of the transaction in the context of JMSE's accounts, it is probable that some member of staff would have recalled paying £20,000 in cash to Mr. O'Keeffe on that date. Even if such a staff member could not be identified, the bank would surely have been in a position to produce a receipt or acknowledgment signed by the recipient of these funds, had an inquiry been made of them in 1991. However, even if it were the case that the bank could not assist in identifying the recipient of the £20,000 in cash or of the £10,000 cheque, it ought to have been abundantly clear to Mr. Bates that Mr. Tim O'Keeffe could assist him in his quest for information. The events surrounding the writing of these cheques and their presentation ought to have been fresh in the mind of all parties who dealt with the cheques at the time when Mr. Bates was carrying out his audit at the end of 1990 and the beginning of 1991.

12-58   The Tribunal considers it extraordinary that Mr. Bates did not follow the obvious audit trail to its conclusion. The Tribunal considers it inconceivable that any auditor concerned with the tracking down of this un-vouched expenditure of £30,000 would not have followed the basic steps in endeavouring to pursue the money trail. The Tribunal considers it equally improbable that the auditor would have reported to the directors of the company that he had been unable to trace this cash expenditure when he had not, in fact, even sought the return of the paid cheques by which he knew the expenditure was incurred.

THE MATERIAL ACTUALLY AVAILABLE FOR CONSIDERATION BY THE AUDITOR IN THE GRAFTON FILE FOR YEAR ENDED THE 31ST MAY 1990

12-59   Mr. Bates had before him the file that contained all the financial records for Grafton to year ended the 31st May 1990. This file contained the apportionment account prepared by Mr. Denis McArdle, from which it was clear that the un-vouched £30,000 had passed through Mr. McArdle's account. Yet there was no evidence that Mr. Bates inquired of Mr. McArdle as to whether he knew what this expenditure related to. Had Mr. Bates made the inquiry in 1990/1991, Mr. McArdle would in all probability have been in a position to inform him that he had been asked by Mr. Copsey on the 8th June 1989 for £30,000 - £20,000 of which was to be in cash, and the balance a cheque, for the purpose of making a political donation. Mr. McArdle could have informed him that this £30,000 was sent by him to JMSE, on the 13th June 1989, and subsequently recorded in his apportionment account as a payment to JMSE. The Grafton/Reliable Cash Balance document in the handwriting of Mr. O'Keeffe which appeared on its face to attribute a £30,000 expenditure to "planning permission", was in the file. If this document was considered in conjunction with Mr. McArdle's apportionment account, it would be clear that the £30,000 expenditure which was incurred on the 13th June 1989 and shown on the apportionment account as "To JMSE" was probably the £30,000 shown as the cost incurred in relation to planning permission.

12-60   The Tribunal considers it inconceivable that, having considered Mr. O'Keeffe's Cash Balance document, Mr. Bates could have concluded that the reference to £30,000 in the Cash Balance document meant anything other than that the £30,000 expenditure for which he was seeking an explanation was attributed in this document as having been made in connection with planning permission. Whilst it is true that there was no back-up documentation in the Grafton file to vouch that the £30,000 had in fact been paid in respect of planning permission, there was no other documentation on file which suggested that the £30,000 had been expended for any purpose other than for planning permission.

12-61   In these circumstances the Tribunal considers it inconceivable that Mr. Bates would have chosen to reject or disregard the apparent attribution of £30,000 to "planning permission" and substitute his own surmise when preparing his final accounts. Whilst Mr. Bates in evidence initially stated that he believed that he had not considered the Grafton/Reliable Cash Balance document in preparing his accounts, he later conceded that he had in fact done so, and a copy of the document was found in his audit working papers which confirms this to be the case. At a minimum it must have been clear to Mr. Bates that Mr. O'Keeffe, the identifiable author of the Grafton/Reliable Cash Balance document, had information which had apparently caused him to conclude that the transaction giving rise to the £30,000 expenditure related to planning permission.

12-62   In these circumstances the Tribunal considers that it is improbable that Mr. Bates would have gone to the directors to say that he could not identify how this sum was expended. If Mr. Bates was genuinely seeking an explanation as to how the £30,000 was expended, the Tribunal considers that the minimum steps he would have taken would have been to send a copy of the Grafton/Reliable Cash Balance document to Mr. O'Keeffe to seek his explanation for his apparent attribution of the expenditure to planning permission. He did not do so.

12-63   In his working papers for the accounts for year ended the 31st May 1990, Mr. Bates dealt with the un-vouched expenditure of £30,000. He entered the expenditure under the journal heading 'Audit Adjustments.' It is there recorded by him as two separate payments, one of £20,000 and one of £10,000, identified as "enhancement expenditure". (**Appendix W).** Under the heading, 'Development Property', he recorded two items of enhancement expenditure, one of £65,273 related to land at Poppintree, and one of £30,000 headed simply 'Cash'. (**Appendix X).** The only document in the Grafton file which would have allowed him to reach the conclusion that the £30,000 expenditure had been expended in enhancing the value of the land was the Grafton/Reliable Cash Balance document which had been prepared by Mr. O'Keeffe and which, on its face, showed a payment of £30,000 attributed to planning permission. (**Appendix U).**

12-64   Mr. Bates in his evidence denied that this was the basis for his attribution. His evidence was that he attributed the expenditure to 'Land Enhancement' because the company was primarily a land-owning company and, consequently, the expenditure was probably incurred in enhancing the value of the company's land holding. However, only those expenses incurred in the enhancement of the value of the company's property portfolio could properly be so described. Other than the purchase of the Poppintree lands recorded in the Cash Balance document, there was no documentation in the file for the year ended the 31st May 1990 to suggest that any further lands had been acquired that year. It was clear from the accounts file that Grafton/Reliable had sold their major land holding at Forrest Road, Swords, so that there was a translation of the companies' assets from land to cash, which in turn was placed on deposit with ICC bank from February 1989 onwards.

12-65   In making the attribution "cash-land enhancement", on the basis upon which he claims to have done, Mr. Bates would have had to have ruled out the possibility that the un-vouched expenditure may have been incurred under any one of the other headings of expense under which the company had in fact incurred expenditure during that year. The other documents which he had on file showed that, notwithstanding that Grafton was a land-owning company, it had nonetheless expended over £100,000 that year on expenses which did not enhance the value of the company's property portfolio. Having considered the documents in the Grafton file, Mr. Bates had prepared accounts which showed that the expenditure of over £100,000 had been incurred under such headings as legal fees, professional fees, directors fees, travelling expenses, etc. None of these enhanced the value of the land and, consequently, he had no valid basis for assuming that the un-vouched expenditure had to be reflected as an enhancement of the company's land.

12-66   The only documents in the Grafton file which recorded the expenditure of a specific amount of £30,000 by Grafton were the apportionment account of McArdle & Co. Solicitors, which showed that £30,000 was paid to JMSE, and the Grafton/Reliable Cash Balance document, which showed that £30,000 was attributed to planning permission. If Mr. Bates accepted these documents at face value, he could legitimately attribute the expenditure as "cash-land enhancement", albeit that he would not be in a position to produce a voucher from the recipient of the money to prove that this expenditure was incurred for that purpose.

12-67   The Tribunal rejects Mr. Bates evidence that his attribution of the £30,000 expenditure to land enhancement was based upon a belief that expenditure incurred by a land-owning company, which could not be vouched otherwise, must have enhanced the value of the land.

12-68   The Tribunal believes that the actual basis for his attribution was his consideration of the Cash Balance document and the response of the directors to his inquiries. The Tribunal considers it highly probable that Mr. Bates brought to the attention of the in-house accountant and to the directors of JMSE, Mr. Murphy Jnr. and Mr. Frank Reynolds, the fact that the £30,000 expenditure, although attributed to 'planning permission' in Mr. O'Keeffe's Cash Balance document on file, was not in fact vouched by any receipt or invoice, so that the identity of the recipient of the funds was unknown to him.

12-69   Whilst Mr. Bates has given evidence that what he drew to the attention of the directors, Mr. Murphy Jnr., and Mr. Reynolds, in 1991 was the fact that the £30,000 payment was un-vouched. Both Mr. Murphy Jnr. and Mr. Reynolds deny that they were so informed by him. The Tribunal rejects the evidence of Mr. Reynolds and Mr. Murphy Jnr. that they were not made aware of the fact that there was un-vouched expenditure of £30,000 in the accounts of Grafton for that year. The auditor could hardly have done otherwise than to draw the attention of the directors to the obvious fact that this expenditure was un-vouched, particularly where it appeared to have been substantially taken out in cash.

12-70   The Tribunal is satisfied that Mr. Murphy Jnr. and Mr. Reynolds were aware at the time of signing off of the accounts for the year ended the 31st May 1990 that there was no vouching documentation for the £30,000 expended by Grafton in June 1989. Since this expenditure was incurred shortly prior to the resignation of Mr. Gogarty, and since Mr. Murphy Jnr. was of the opinion in 1990 that Mr. Gogarty had defrauded JMSE in his dealings concerning the ESB monies in October 1989, it is inconceivable that Mr. Murphy Jnr. would not have questioned the Auditor as to what steps he had taken to trace this un-vouched expenditure if he was not already aware of how this sum had been expended.

12-71   The Tribunal concludes that the probable explanation for the auditors' failure to take the basic steps to establish the identity of the recipient of these monies was because he gathered from the directors that it was not necessary for him to do so. The Tribunal believes that Mr. Bates real difficulty in the finalisation of the Grafton accounts for the year-ended May 1990 was not, as he claimed in evidence, that he could not obtain an explanation for the established cash expenditure of £30,000, but that he had an explanation for which there was no vouching documentation on file.

12-72   The Tribunal believes that the concern which he brought to the attention of the in-house accountant and the directors of the company, was that the established expenditure of £30,000, which was attributed to a payment in respect of planning permission, was un-vouched.

12-73   The Tribunal considers it improbable that the directors of the company would have signed off the annual accounts of Grafton unless they were satisfied with the manner in which the un-vouched expenditure of £30,000 was treated in the accounts prepared by Mr. Bates. Once Mr. Bates had informed them of the lack of vouching documentation for this expenditure, the directors must have been aware that to have signed off the accounts without explanation for this expenditure would have left unresolved the possibility that some person had misappropriated £30,000 of the company's money in the financial year 1989/90. The Tribunal is satisfied that the directors would not have allowed this possibility to remain open and that they signed off on the accounts because they were aware that the £30,000 was paid to a politician so as to achieve a change in the planning status of their lands and that no vouching documentation would be forthcoming from that source.

12-74   The Tribunal concludes that the accounting treatment of the monies paid to Mr. Burke in the financial records of the Murphy companies is not consistent with the recording of a payment of a legitimate political donation to him, but is wholly consistent with a clandestine payment made with the knowledge of the directors of JMSE, Mr. Murphy Jnr. and Mr. Reynolds, and actively concealed by them with the assistance of their accountants.

CONCLUSIONS

12-75   The Tribunal concludes that the following is the probable sequence of events in relation to the assembly of the JMSE monies which were paid to Mr. Burke, and in relation to the subsequent accounting for such expenditure in the accounts of JMSE and Grafton:

1. The directors of JMSE, including Mr. Joseph Murphy Snr., Mr. Joseph Murphy Jnr., Mr. Roger Copsey, and Mr. Frank Reynolds, were at all material times aware that Murphy funds were to be paid to Mr. Burke in connection with his support for the intended re-zoning and changes in the planning status of the Murphy's North Dublin lands, as envisaged in Mr. Michael Bailey's participation proposal as set out in his letter of the 8th June 1989.

2. The advice of Mr. Roger Copsey was sought by directors of JMSE, other than Mr. James Gogarty, as to how such payment should best be funded from the Murphy assets in Ireland, and he advised that £30,000 of the intended payment should be sourced from the funds on deposit at ICC Bank. Because the funds could not be obtained in cash that day from Mr. Denis McArdle, the plan was altered so that the cash would be collected from the JMSE account at AIB, Talbot Street, that day.

3. Mr. Frank Reynolds was aware of the fact that the cash would be collected from AIB, Talbot Street, and brought Mr. Tim O'Keeffe to the bank for that purpose. Mr. James Gogarty was not made aware that £20,000 in cash had been sourced from the JMSE account.

4. Mr. James Gogarty signed a cheque for £10,000 on the JMSE account which was counter-signed by Mr. Frank Reynolds, not because cash could not have been obtained in the bank on that date as stated to him, but because the Murphy interests or Mr. Burke wished £10,000 of the payment to Mr. Burke to be in the form of a cheque.

5. Mr. Roger Copsey directed that the payment of the funds by JMSE be treated as an inter-company loan to Grafton in the expectation that an inter-company transaction would not be subject to outside scrutiny.

6. The attribution of the words "planning permission" to this payment by Mr. Tim O'Keeffe was made so as to allow Mr. Roger Copsey to identify this payment without naming Mr. Burke as the recipient.

7. Mr. Roger Copsey and Mr. Tim O'Keeffe deliberately left the payment to Mr. Burke unaccounted for in the accounting records prepared for JMSE and Grafton's annual accounts for the year ended the 31st May 1990.

CHAPTER 13

The Reaction of those Persons Alleged to have been present at the Meeting at Briargate, Swords in June 1989 to the Publication of Mr. James Gogarty's Allegations regarding Payment to Mr. Ray Burke

13-01   The Tribunal examined the evidence in relation to the manner in which Mr. Burke, Mr. Bailey, and the Murphy interests, dealt with the allegations being made against them by Mr. Gogarty in order to establish whether these reactions were consistent or inconsistent with the Murphys' claimed lack of knowledge of any payment having been made to Mr. Burke until mid-August 1997.

13-02   Mr. Gogarty allegations were first publicly aired in March 1996 in the *Sunday Business Post*, although Mr. Burke was not named as the politician involved. Mr. Burke's first acknowledgement that he had received £30,000 of JMSE's money was made on the 7th August 1997, almost 17 months later. Immediately prior to the publication of the first article in the *Sunday Business Post* of the 31st March 1996 the journalist, Mr .Frank Connolly, had attended a pre-arranged meeting at the head office of JMSE at Shanowen Road, Santry, where he met with Mr. Frank Reynolds, the managing director, and with Mr. John Maher, the in-house accountant.

13-03   In the course of that meeting Mr. Connolly made them aware of the details of Mr. Gogarty's allegation in relation to the payment of Murphy company monies to Mr. Ray Burke in June 1989. The Murphy representatives present denied that there was any truth in the allegations that there had been such a payment, and gave Mr. Connolly to understand that they believed that Mr. Gogarty was making false allegations against the company because he was a disgruntled ex-employee with a grudge against his former employers.

13-04   Mr. Connolly went on to publish two articles on the 31st March 1996 and the 7th April 1996, from which it was clear to those who had attended the earlier meeting with Mr. Connolly, that the essential elements of Mr. Gogarty's allegations included allegations that:

> 1. The alleged payment by the Murphy company's was £40,000, made up in part by cash, and the balance by cheque.
> 2. The payment was made to Mr. Burke by a director of the company other than Mr. James Gogarty.
> 3. The payment of £40,000 was matched by an equal payment made at the same time by a property developer.
> 4. The handover of the money took place at Mr. Burke's home just days before the General Election of June 1989.
> 5. The meeting had been organised by the property developer who was present with Mr. Gogarty at this meeting.
> 6. The payment was a bribe intended to achieve the rezoning of approximately 1,000 acres of land.

Mr. Reynolds in his evidence acknowledged that he understood the *Sunday Business Post* articles to refer to the allegations which Mr. Connolly had attributed to Mr. Gogarty, and which had been discussed with Mr. Connolly at their meeting prior to publication.

THE REACTION OF THE MURPHY INTERESTS

13-05   Immediately following the publication of these articles Mr. Reynolds and Mr. Joseph Murphy Jnr. discussed their content, and the company sought legal advice from its solicitors as to whether or not the articles gave them a basis for suing for defamation. It was clear therefore that these allegations were being considered very seriously by JMSE's directors and managers from the start.

13-06   Notwithstanding the publication of the articles the Murphy interests at that time took no steps to ascertain whether or not there was any substance in any of the allegations attributed to Mr. Gogarty. The explanation for this, proffered by Mr. Murphy Jnr., was that because he knew that he was not present at any such meeting it was obvious that Mr. Gogarty's allegations were false, and it was therefore unnecessary to investigate the matter further. The Tribunal does not accept this as a credible response.

13-07   If these allegations were believed by the Murphy interests to be without foundation, they could easily have confirmed the factual situation by making very specific inquiries based on what they had been told by Mr. Connolly, and what was contained within the articles. From the information then available they knew the amount of the claimed payment, the composition of the claimed payment, and the approximate date of the claimed payment. Very specific inquiries could have been made in the accounts department of JMSE which could have established the factual position regarding payments by the company in 1989. The identity of the unnamed property developer referred to in the articles could easily be deduced since the only development land sold by the Murphy companies in 1989 was sold to Mr. Michael Bailey.

13-08   They knew from their meeting with Mr. Connolly that the alleged recipient of the funds was Mr. Burke, yet no contact was made by the Murphy interests with either Mr. Bailey or Mr. Burke to establish whether there was any substance in the allegation, or to adopt a joint strategy to ensure that no further publication of these claimed false allegations took place. At the time of the publication in 1996 the Murphy interests and Mr. Gogarty were no strangers to litigation. The Murphy interests had previously sued Mr. Gogarty for as little as £1,500, yet they took no steps in this instance to write to Mr. Gogarty either to establish the basis upon which he was making the allegations to Mr. Connolly, or to require him to desist from making further allegations.

13-09   Apparently no attempt was made by the Murphy interests to contact Mr. Burke to establish whether in fact any Murphy company monies had been paid to him by Mr. Gogarty, or whether any meeting had taken place at his home attended by representatives of the Murphy companies and Mr. Bailey. No contact was made with Mr. Bailey to establish whether he had been present at any meeting in Mr. Burke's house in June 1989 when JMSE money was paid to Mr. Burke.

THE REACTION OF MR. BURKE

13-10   If the allegations contained in the articles were untrue, and if Mr. Burke was perceived to be the un-named politician involved, he would be the person most seriously affected. On his account of events to the Tribunal he had received a surprisingly large political donation with no strings attached from Mr. Gogarty. The allegation was now being made seven years later that this was a corrupt payment and a bribe. Yet Mr. Burke never contacted Mr. Gogarty to seek an explanation for Mr. Gogarty's apparently bizarre behaviour in seeking to falsely attribute a sinister motive to what Mr. Burke believed was a legitimate payment.

13-11   Mr. Burke did not contact Mr. Bailey to see whether he would support Mr. Burke's account of the events which led to the payment being made to him and whether he had any explanation for Mr. Gogarty's behaviour. Mr. Burke did not contact JMSE to seek confirmation that their money was paid to him as a legitimate political donation, or to establish whether they had any explanation for their former Chairman's bizarre behaviour in alleging that the donation was a bribe.

13-12   The Tribunal accepts the evidence of Mr. Connolly that Mr. Burke's reaction to an inquiry made of him by Mr. Connolly in 1996, as to whether he had received JMSE money, was to abruptly terminate the conversation, once the issue of the alleged payment had been raised.

13-13   It was not until one year and five months later in August 1997 that Mr. Burke made his first acknowledgment of having received £30,000. This statement was only made after he had been publicly named in the national press as the politician who had received £30,000 in June, 1989.

13-14   In his Dáil statement a month later on the 10th September 1997 he disingenuously suggested that of the £30,000 which he acknowledged he had received from JMSE, £10,000 was paid directly to Fianna Fáil, and a further £7,000 was paid by way of two drafts to his constituency organisation. He acknowledged before the Tribunal that his Dáil statement in this regard was incorrect, and that the £10,000 which he had given to Fianna Fáil was not part of the JMSE money. This was a fact which had already been independently established in 1998, and had led to the enlargement of the Tribunal's Terms of Reference.

13-15   In giving his evidence to the Tribunal Mr. Burke suggested that he had never intended that his Dáil colleagues would relate his reference in the Dáil to the payment of £10,000 to Fianna Fáil as referring to the JMSE contribution, but rather that it was intended and understood to mean that in the course of that election he had paid £10,000 to Fianna Fáil from other contributions. The Tribunal rejects this evidence.
Mr. Burke also acknowledged in his evidence to the Tribunal that he was incorrect in telling the Dáil that he had paid two drafts for £2,000 and £5,000 respectively to his constituency organisation. In evidence before the Tribunal, he suggested that his donation was in fact considerably more, albeit not in the form of drafts as stated in the Dáil. Mr. Burke was unable to produce any evidence to support any personal expenditure by him in the 1989 election save a receipt for payment to the Harp Inn, Swords where he hosted a victory celebration for his supporters at a cost of £1,027.

13-16   In this public statement on the 7th August 1997 Mr. Burke claimed that he had been the victim of a two year campaign of falsehood and innuendo, yet during that period he had taken no steps whatsoever to contact either JMSE, or Mr. Bailey, or Mr. Gogarty, to establish why Mr. Gogarty was making what he claimed were false allegations against him, nor did he take any steps to restrain Mr. Gogarty from any further repetition of these supposedly false allegations. The Tribunal concludes that Mr. Burke's inaction was the result of his having taken a conscious decision not to make any public statement on the matter in the hope that the story would die.

13-17   The Tribunal considers that if Mr. Burke's public statement of the 7th August 1997 was a truthful account of events there was no reason for him to have subjected himself to two years of rumour and innuendo before making such a statement. Having waited so long to make such a statement the Tribunal considers it remarkable that Mr. Burke was not scrupulous in ensuring that the statement he made was accurate and truthful, and that the responses which he chose to give to the questions put to him in Dáil Éireann arising therefrom were likewise true, and accurate.

13-18   The Tribunal considers it significant that Mr. Burke's statement in Dáil Éireann, and his responses to the questions put to him, were not accurate. The Dáil statement was intended by Mr. Burke to silence his critics. It concluded with a threat to those making allegations against him that any further repetition would result in legal proceedings being issued against them. Had this threat had its desired effect the record of the House would have stood as evidence of the fact that of the £30,000 received by Mr. Burke from JMSE, drafts to a total of £17,000 had been paid over to Fianna Fáil and to his local constituency organisation, whereas this was untrue.

13-19   The Tribunal is satisfied that this was a deliberate attempt by Mr. Burke to forestall any further investigation into his affairs by attempting to minimise the proportion of the payment which was in fact retained by him, and by inferring that the payment had been brought to the attention of his political party and members of his constituency staff at the time when it was made, thus rendering it an apparently transparent transaction, whereas in fact this was not the case. Mr. Burke acknowledged in his evidence to the Tribunal that he did not inform any member of his constituency team, or any of his Party's fundraisers in 1989, that he had received a £30,000 donation from JMSE.

THE BAILEY REACTION

13-20   Although made aware of Mr. Gogarty's allegations by Mr. Frank Connolly, Mr. Bailey took no steps to challenge Mr. Gogarty on his account of what had taken place in Mr. Burke's home in June, 1989. In his evidence he claimed that subsequent to the publication of the Sunday Business Post articles in March/April, 1996 Mr. Gogarty continued to demand money from him in relation to the a £150,000 finder's fee, and he continued to pay him. The Tribunal considers this evidence preposterous. The Tribunal is satisfied that Mr. Michael Bailey's reaction to the publication of details of the meeting at Mr. Burke's house was to lie to Mr. Connolly, initially denying that any meeting had in fact taken place.

13-21 If it was the case that Mr. Gogarty's published account of the circumstances surrounding the payment of monies to Mr. Burke was false, Mr. Burke, the Murphy interests, and Mr. Michael Bailey, had a mutual interest in ensuring that these unfounded allegations should cease forthwith, yet no steps were taken by any one of them to challenge Mr. Gogarty's account of events, or to restrain further publication, or to give an account of what had actually taken place at the meeting.

CONTACTS BETWEEN THE BAILEY AND MURPHY INTERESTS POST PUBLICATION OF THE GOGARTY ALLEGATION

13-22 Mr. Michael Bailey was in contact with Mr. Joseph Murphy Jnr. by telephone at the JMSE offices in 1996, and also with Mr. Roger Copsey from 1996 onwards, yet it is claimed that he never once discussed with them the then current allegation that he had attended the meeting at Mr. Burke's house with Mr. Gogarty in 1989, at which a bribe was paid to Mr. Burke in his presence.

13-23 Mr. Joseph Murphy Jnr. and Mr. Michael Bailey met at the Burlington Hotel in 1996 for over an hour on the subject of Mr. Gogarty, and whilst they say that they discussed general matters they both claim that no mention was made of the matter which ought to have been of significant concern to both of them, namely the Gogarty allegation that they were jointly involved in bribing a senior government minister. Since the claimed purpose of this meeting was to endeavour to resolve Mr. Gogarty's ongoing dispute with the Murphy interests, it is all the more incredible that these parties would not have sought to establish why he was making false allegations against both of them and Mr. Burke, if the allegations were false. The Tribunal is satisfied that evidence given by both Mr. Bailey and Mr. Murphy Jnr., as to the purpose of their meeting at the Burlington Hotel and the subject of their discussions is false, and believes that the true position is that the meeting was set up in order to persuade Mr. Gogarty to desist from making further allegations, which they both knew to be true.

MR. JOSEPH MURPHY JNR.'S KNOWLEDGE OF THE 1989 PAYMENT OF JMSE MONIES TO MR. RAY BURKE

13-24 The Tribunal rejects as improbable the evidence of Mr. Joseph Murphy Jnr. that he first learned in mid-August 1997 of the fact that his company's monies were used to pay Mr. Ray Burke in June, 1989. Mr. Joseph Murphy Jnr. had been interviewed in London on the 24th June 1997 by Mr. Dermot Ahern T.D. at the request of Mr. Bertie Ahern T.D. and had specifically denied any knowledge of any payment to Mr. Burke in June 1989. A week later on the 1st July 1997 Mr. Joseph Murphy Jnr. informed Mr. Dermot Ahern that he had had a long telephone conversation with Mr. Michael Bailey on the 30th June 1997 when Mr. Bailey informed him that he had had a meeting with Mr. Burke during which he, Mr. Bailey, had informed Mr. Burke that he was being drawn into a dispute between two old men – Mr. Gogarty and Mr. Murphy Snr. Despite the fact that Mr. Gogarty, Mr. Burke and Mr. Bailey were all mentioned in this telephone conversation with Mr. Joseph Murphy Jnr. on the 1st July, Mr. Murphy Jnr. still maintained that he was unaware that there had in fact been a meeting in Mr. Burke's house in 1989 which was attended by Mr. Bailey and Mr. Gogarty until mid-August, 1997.

13-25 The Tribunal considers it inconceivable that Mr. Gogarty's allegations involving Mr. Burke, JMSE and Mr. Bailey were never discussed between Mr. Murphy Jnr. and Mr. Bailey at any time between 1996 and mid-August 1997 as claimed by Mr. Murphy Jnr. Clearly any discussion whatsoever on this topic would have immediately resulted in Mr. Murphy Jnr. being made aware by Mr. Bailey of the fact that there was such a meeting, that he and Mr. Gogarty had attended it, and that JMSE company funds were used to pay Mr. Burke.

13-26 The Tribunal considers it significant that Mr. Murphy Jnr.'s claimed lack of knowledge of the payment extended beyond the 7th August 1997, the date when Mr. Burke had publicly announced that he had in fact received £30,000 of JMSE's money at a meeting attended by Mr. Gogarty and Mr. Bailey in June 1989.

Even after Mr. Burke's statement in Dáil Éireann on the 10th September 1997 the Murphy interests never contacted Mr. Burke to establish whether their surmise that the £30,000 payment acknowledged by him was represented by the cheques for £20,000, and £10,000 respectively, was correct. They never requested him to return their money on the basis that the funds had been misappropriated by their ex-employee Mr. Gogarty as they now claim.

13-27   If the accounts of events given by Mr. Joseph Murphy Jnr., and Mr. Frank Reynolds are true, Mr. Burke's public acknowledgement of receipt of the JMSE funds of £30,000 ought to have been a major surprise to them, as they were allegedly unaware up to that date of any such payment, and had supposedly diligently searched their records for evidence of any such payment, without success. Mr. Burke's revelation on the 7th August 1997, however did not elicit any response whatsoever from them. It was not until the 4th September 1997 when Mr. Burke's solicitors wrote to their solicitors in the context of Mr. Burke issuing proceedings for defamation against Mr. Gogarty, that the Murphy interests communicated with Mr. Burke for the first time. Mr. Burke's solicitors letter sought responses to three specific queries which were framed as follows:

> "Whether Mr. Joseph Murphy Jnr. was present in our client's house at the time James Gogarty handed a political contribution of £30,000 to our client?
>
> Whether Mr. Joseph Murphy has ever met with our client and if so when and on what basis?
>
> We would be very much obliged if you would let us know whether your client has been able to identify the source of the payment to our client, and whether there are any records of these payments, and if so, you might be good enough to let us have a breakdown of the record of the payments".

13-28   Notably no questions were directed to establish whether the Murphy interests had any possible explanation as to why their former chairman was now alleging that the "political donation" received by their client, Mr. Burke, was a bribe.

13-29   The Tribunal considers it extraordinary that Mr. Burke was seeking to establish from the Murphys whether Mr. Joseph Murphy Jnr. was in his house at the time of the handover, or whether Mr. Murphy Jnr. had ever met with him, and if so when and on what basis, given his persistent denial of ever having met Mr. Murphy Jnr. either in his home or elsewhere. If it is the case that Mr. Joseph Murphy Jnr. was not present at the meeting at Mr. Burke's house that fact was either known to Mr. Burke in 1997 in which case he did not require to establish that fact from Mr. Murphy Jnr. or alternatively Mr. Burke was unaware of who was at the meeting until he received confirmation of that fact from Mr. Murphy's solicitors on the 8th September 1997.

13-30   On the 8th September 1997 the solicitor representing the Murphy interests responded to Mr. Burke's solicitors query of the 4th September by stating:

> "1 Our client was not present in your clients home when your client met with Mr. James Gogarty.
>
> 2 No.
>
> 3 Two consecutive cheques were drawn on the JMSE account on the AIB Talbot Street branch, one cheque for £20,000 and the second for £10,000. The cheque stubs in relation to both cheques say "cash". We presume that these cheques relate to the £30,000 at issue. However, following inquiries with the AIB they have been unable to provide any details in relation to the same and do not have a record of paid cheques".

The assumption made by the writer of that letter has proved to be correct, in that the two cheques referred to did provide £30,000 as acknowledged by Mr. Burke as having been received, however at the time of the writing of the letter it was surmise on the part of the writer.

13-31   The Tribunal considers it significant that no questions were asked by the Murphy solicitors of Mr. Burke's solicitors regarding the transaction in which Mr. Burke was now an acknowledged participant. He was not asked whether he had in fact received either of these cheques or whether he had received cash. He was not asked whether he had presented either of these cheques to his own bank for encashment or whether he had lodged either of these cheques to his account, or to the account of his constituency organisation, or his political party. He was not asked whether he had kept any record which might be of assistance in identifying these payments.

13-32 If the evidence of the Murphy interests adduced before the Tribunal was correct, the Murphy interests had spent a considerable period of time endeavouring to trace any payment out of their account to Mr. Burke without success. Some time after Mr. Burke had publicly acknowledged the receipt of £30,000 of JMSE's monies the assumption had been made by Mr. Joseph Murphy Jnr. that these two cheques were related to the payment to Mr. Burke, yet no steps were taken to establish from Mr. Burke whether that assumption was in fact correct, although the opportunity for doing so was clearly presented.

13-33 Once it had been established that Mr. Burke had in fact received at least £30,000 of JMSE's funds, in circumstances where the Murphy interests had denied such a transaction since March 1996, it would have been reasonable to assume that they would wish to establish all of the circumstances which led to this payment being made to Mr. Burke. Yet no request was made to Mr. Burke to provide any account or statement as to what had taken place at the meeting at his house in June 1989. No inquiry was made of Mr. Burke by the Murphy interests to establish what Mr. Bailey's role was at this meeting. No inquiry was made of Mr. Burke to establish whether he had any explanation for Mr. Gogarty's behaviour.

13-34 Despite the frequent contact which had taken place between Mr. Michael Bailey and the Murphy interests over the previous eighteen months regarding Mr. Gogarty, during which period it is claimed that he never revealed to Mr. Joseph Murphy Jnr. the fact that he had attended the meeting at which Mr. Burke was paid, no contact was made by the Murphy interests with Mr. Bailey to establish what had happened at this meeting.

13-35 At that point it had apparently been established to the satisfaction of Mr. Joseph Murphy Jnr. and Mr. Reynolds that they had been wrong in their belief that there had not been a meeting at Mr. Burke's house at which substantial sums of JMSE money were paid over to Mr. Burke. Whilst Mr. Burke denied that the sum was a bribe, and claimed that it was a political donation, they knew that JMSE did not make political donations to Mr. Burke, and they equally knew that Mr. Gogarty had never made a political donation from JMSE funds before, and therefore it was most unlikely that the payment to Mr. Burke was in fact a political donation, despite his claimed belief that it was. Mr Burke's revelation had put the Murphy interests on notice that their money had been handed over in the presence of Mr. Bailey.

13-36 The Tribunal considers it inconceivable that if their version of events was correct, that is if they did not know of the meeting at which Mr. Burke was paid £30,000 of their money until August, 1997, that they would not have immediately contacted Mr. Michael Bailey who was a witness to these events, to establish, firstly, why he had not informed them at any time over the previous eighteen months of the fact that he had attended the meeting, and witnessed the handover of their funds to Mr. Burke, and secondly, to inquire whether he had any information which would assist them in establishing whether the payment was in fact made as a political donation as claimed by Mr. Burke, or as a bribe as claimed by Mr. Gogarty .

13-37 The Tribunal considers it extraordinary that, having been made aware of the fact that Mr. Gogarty had handed over their funds to Mr. Burke, the Murphy interests did not immediately demand re-payment from Mr. Gogarty on the basis that it was an unauthorised payment, or that they did not forthwith institute proceedings against him for the recovery of these sums, if they honestly believed that he had misappropriated their funds.

13-38 None of the parties at that time were to know that a Public Inquiry would be commenced into the circumstances of the payment, and therefore the subsequent establishment of this Inquiry in November, 1997 does not afford an explanation for the inaction on the part of Mr. Burke, Mr. Bailey and the Murphy interests, following upon Mr. Burke's acknowledgement in August 1997 of receiving JMSE's funds in June 1989.

13-39 The Tribunal considers that the reaction of the Murphy interests to the public acknowledgement by Mr. Burke of the receipt of their funds is not consistent with their claimed lack of knowledge of such payment.

The Tribunal is satisfied that Mr. Joseph Murphy Jnr. was aware that his company's money had been paid to Mr. Burke and that his claim that he first became aware that the money was paid in mid –August 1997, is untrue.

THE EFFORTS ALLEGED TO HAVE BEEN MADE BY THE MURPHY INTERESTS AND MR. JOHN BATES IN 1997 TO ESTABLISH WHETHER THERE WAS ANY EVIDENCE OF THE PAYMENTS TO MR. BURKE IN THE ACCOUNTS OF THE MURPHY COMPANIES

13-40   Whilst the explanation offered for the failure to carry out any search of the financial records of the Murphy companies in 1996 was Mr. Joseph Murphy Jnr.'s claimed belief that the allegations were untrue and therefore did not merit further investigation, it was conceded that in 1997, in view of the persisting allegations being made, an investigation of the financial records took place in JMSE. This is said to have been conducted by Mr. Joseph Murphy Jnr. and Mr. Frank Reynolds. Mr. John Maher the in-house accountant in JMSE said he was not involved in this exercise.

13-41   Mr. Frank Reynolds's evidence was that his efforts were directed towards establishing whether there was evidence of a £40,000 payment to Mr. Ray Burke in the accounts of the Murphy companies. Any inquiry which was narrowed to a search for a single payment of £40,000 to a named individual namely, Mr. Ray Burke, could not have revealed the documentary evidence, which established that Mr. Burke could in fact have been paid at least £30,000 of JMSE's money.

13-42   The Tribunal is satisfied that there was no basis for Mr. Reynolds' conducting an inquiry limited to seeking evidence of a £40,000 payment to Mr. Ray Burke, given that the allegation made by Mr. Gogarty was that the payment was made partly in cash, and partly by way of cheque. Any person seeking to establish the truth or otherwise of this allegation, therefore, would be searching not for a single payment of £40,000, but for cheques and cash payments which might have totalled £40,000.

13-43   The Gogarty allegation was that the payment had been made in the days prior to the General Election in June 1989. The obvious first port-of-call in any search of the financial records would have been to consider the JMSE cheque payments journal for that period as JMSE was the trading company through which the majority of Murphy companies banking activity was conducted in Ireland. Consideration of this document would immediately have revealed the existence of the two cheques drawn on the 8th of June 1989 totalling £30,000, which were attributed to Grafton. The mere fact that Mr. Burke's name was not recorded in the cheque journal as the recipient of these cheques was not a ground for ruling out the possibility that these cheques might have formed part of the cash and cheque payments allegedly made to Mr. Burke. Since the allegation was that the money was paid to Mr. Burke as a bribe it would be reasonable to assume that his name would not be revealed in the record, but that identity of the recipient would be concealed in some way.

13-44   The Tribunal considers that it ought to have been immediately apparent to any person with knowledge of the JMSE accounting system who was conducting a bona fide search for evidence of a bribe, that the two entries in the cheque journal for the 8th June 1989 showing payment to Grafton could possibly have been the source of the claimed payment to Mr. Burke, and that it was a relatively simple exercise to trace these two cheque entries to the Grafton expenditure of £30,000 for which there was no vouching documents in the accounts.

13-45   When Mr. John Bates, the auditor, was re-engaged in 1997 to review the books of account of JMSE in order to establish whether there was any substance in the Gogarty allegations, he was seeking evidence of payments of £30,000 or £25,000. He stated that within a short time of his engagement he recollected that £30,000 of the expenditure on the part of Grafton in 1989 had been un-vouched, and that this fact had been brought to the attention of the directors at the time of preparation of the year-end accounts to the 31st May 1990. He said that in early 1997 he therefore brought this fact to the attention of Mr. Reynolds. In evidence Mr. Reynolds denied that this was the case.

13-46   The Tribunal rejects Mr. Reynolds evidence on this point and is satisfied that Mr. Bates's recollection that there had been un-vouched expenditure of £30,000 in 1989 was known to both Mr. Reynolds and Mr. Murphy Jnr. by May 1997.

13-47   The Tribunal considers that it was a relatively simple exercise on the part of an accountant to establish that the two JMSE cheques written on the 8th June 1989 represented the expenditure which was not vouched in the accounts of Grafton, and that an accountant who had noted this lack of vouching documentation in the preparation of the accounts to year ended the 31st May 1990 would swiftly recollect this fact on reviewing the same documentation in 1997.

13-48   From its review of the financial documentation which was available to Mr. Bates, to Mr. Joseph Murphy Jnr. and to Mr. Frank Reynolds in 1997, the Tribunal has concluded that the connection between the un-vouched £30,000 expenditure in 1989, and the possible payment of £30,000 to Mr. Burke, was one which was readily discernible to any person with knowledge of the accounting system of Grafton and JMSE.

13-49   The evidence of Mr. John Maher, the in-house accountant, was that Mr. Bates's activities were confined to carrying out the necessary audit adjustments which followed upon the claimed discovery by Mr. Reynolds and Mr. Murphy Jnr. that the unvouched £30,000 payment in the year ending 31st May 1990, was probably paid to Mr. Burke.

13-50   The Tribunal rejects this evidence, and accepts the evidence of Mr. Bates, that he was specifically engaged in the early part of 1997 to establish whether there was any evidence in the books of account of the Murphy companies which might support Mr. Gogarty's allegation. While it is undoubtedly correct that Mr. Bates did in fact submit amended returns in September 1997 to the Revenue, which reflected the change in the companies' tax liability, which was consequent upon his re-designation of the £30,000 payment from "land enhancement" to "political donation", this function was carried out in September 1997, whereas Mr. Bates had commenced his investigation of the records in April 1997.

13-51   At his initial meeting with Mr. Dermot Ahern, T.D. in London on the 24th June 1997, Mr. Joseph Murphy Jnr. categorically stated that he had checked the records of the companies and was satisfied that no payment to Mr. Burke had been made with Murphy company funds. He was specifically asked whether or not it was possible that any money could have been taken out of the Irish companies without the company being aware of this fact, and he categorically stated that this could not have happened. He was subsequently to reaffirm this statement in the second meeting with Mr. Dermot Ahern T.D. in Dublin on the 1st July 1997.

13-52   The Tribunal is satisfied that Mr. Joseph Murphy Jnr. was aware prior to his meetings with Mr. Dermot Ahern that Mr. Bates's investigation from April 1997 onwards confirmed that there was un-vouched expenditure of £30,000 in June 1989 by one of the Murphy companies.

13-53   Even if, as he claims, Mr. Joseph Murphy Jnr. was unaware of any meeting at Mr. Burke's house in 1989 at the time of his meeting with Mr. Dermot Ahern in June 1997, he could not legitimately have given the assurance to Mr. Ahern that no such payment could have been made from the Murphy companies in the light of the knowledge which he had at that time of the unvouched £30,000 in the 1989 accounts.
The Tribunal is satisfied that the explanation for Mr. Joseph Murphy Jnr.'s. failure to disclose the fact that there was an un-vouched expenditure of £30,000 by the Murphy companies in June 1989 was that he was aware at all times that these monies had been paid to Mr. Burke and he wished to conceal this fact.

THE SUBMISSIONS MADE ON BEHALF OF THE MURPHY INTERESTS IN RELATION TO THE MANNER IN WHICH THE £30,000 PAYMENT OF MURPHY COMPANY FUNDS WAS DEALT WITH IN THE FINANCIAL DOCUMENTATION WHICH CAME INTO BEING SUBSEQUENT TO THE PAYMENT

13-54   At the conclusion of the hearing of the oral evidence submissions were invited from those parties who had been granted legal representation before the Tribunal. In dealing with the evidence given in relation to the accounting records it was submitted on behalf of the Murphy interests that the financial documentation actually prepared following the transaction was consistent with the payment being properly recorded, but being inadequately or incorrectly described, because those attributing the descriptions to them did not know what the payments were for.

13-55   It was further submitted that these records would not have been prepared at all if those recording the payments had been involved in a corrupt enterprise. The Tribunal rejects these contentions. Once it had been decided to source the monies through the bank accounts of JMSE a record of the fact of such withdrawals existed independently of any record keeping exercise by JMSE. The bank statements themselves showed a £30,000 expenditure, which would have to be explained in the accounts of the company in order to complete the annual audit. Records had to be prepared, it was not a matter of choice for the accountants as to whether they would do so. It was incumbent on the accountants to fully account for this expenditure, whether it was a political donation, or otherwise. They did not do so, and the Tribunal rejects their explanation for their failure to do so as being improbable and incredible.

13-56   In the submissions made on behalf of the Murphy interests the suggestion that Mr. Copsey knew of the bribe to Mr. Burke and its particular purpose, and so informed Mr. O'Keeffe, and that Mr. O'Keeffe in turn recorded the payment as relating to "planning permission" was addressed, as was the suggestion that Mr. Bates also knew of the purpose of the payment and that he had somewhat euphemistically described it as "enhancement expenditure".

13-57   The Murphy submission urged upon the Tribunal that any such suggestions should be rejected by the Tribunal because they are dependent for their validity upon the proposition that Mr. Murphy Snr., Mr. Murphy Jnr. and Mr. Frank Reynolds had decided to involve in their conspiracy the senior financial adviser to the company, Mr. Copsey, his employee, Mr. O'Keeffe, and the auditor of the group of companies, Mr. Bates. The improbability of such a scenario is offered as the ground for rejecting the suggestions canvassed in their submission.

13-58   The Tribunal rejects this submission. Once it had been decided to use monies which were in Murphy company bank accounts for the purpose of paying Mr. Burke it followed that the accountancy staff engaged in JMSE would necessarily be involved to some extent in accounting for this payment out of company funds.

13-59   The extent to which they would be involved would be dependent upon the extent to which those who had paid the money to Mr. Burke shared their knowledge with the accountant. At one end of the spectrum it is possible that the accountant could have been involved both prior to the payment, and subsequently, with full knowledge of the purpose for which the payment was made. At the other end of the spectrum, the involvement could have been limited to recording the fact of such payment, without attributing the payment to any particular head of expenditure. It does not follow, as a matter of course, that all of the accountants involved necessarily shared the same degree of knowledge as to what the payment was for.

13-60   The Tribunal is satisfied on the evidence that all three accountants failed to properly account for a substantial cash payment of which they were aware, and in respect of which two of them had been instrumental in assembling the funds in cash.

13-61   The Tribunal considers that this of itself is unusual, and would have expected that at least one of the accountants would have noted the obvious deficiencies in the proper accounting for this sum, and rectified the matter by pursuing the necessary inquiries of the directors and of the bank. The fact that all three allowed the records to remain deficient is indicative of their knowledge that a particular payment of £30,000 was, at a minimum, one which the directors did not want to record under its proper attribution in the accounts.

13-62   The Tribunal believes that the fact that the company was a wholly owned Murphy family company, coupled with the fact that the Murphy family members Mr. Joseph Murphy Snr., and Mr. Joseph Murphy Jnr., expressly authorised the payment, may have influenced them in their accounting for the payment.

THE ACCOUNTANTS' KNOWLEDGE OF THE PURPOSE FOR WHICH THE £30,000 EXPENDITURE FROM JMSE/GRAFTON HAD BEEN MADE

Mr. Roger Copsey

13-63 The Tribunal is satisfied that the payment to Mr. Burke was made with the knowledge of Mr. Murphy Snr., Mr. Murphy Jnr., and Mr. Frank Reynolds, and that Mr. Roger Copsey was involved at their behest in assembling the £30,000, which was sourced through the Murphy company bank account at JMSE's AIB account at Talbot Street, and reimbursed by Grafton funds on deposit at I.C.C Bank.

13-64 The Tribunal is satisfied that Mr. Copsey at all times knew that this money was going to be paid to a politician, substantially in cash, and that the payment was not to be so recorded in the books of account of the company. The Tribunal is satisfied that Mr. Copsey devised a strategy whereby the payment would be recorded as an inter-company loan between JMSE and Grafton in the expectation that the payment was less likely to be scrutinised if incurred by a non-trading company.

13-65 The Tribunal is satisfied that Mr. Copsey was aware that JMSE did not make any prior substantial political payments to any individual or party, and that the cash payment to be made to a politician prior to the General Election in 1989 was not intended as a political donation. This fact coupled with the fact that Mr. Copsey did not properly account for the payment leads the Tribunal to conclude, on the balance of probabilities, that he was aware that the payment to the politician was intended as a bribe.

13-66 The Tribunal is satisfied that the directors of JMSE, Mr. Joseph Murphy Snr., Mr. Joseph Murphy Jnr., Mr. Frank Reynolds and Mr. James Gogarty were all aware at all times of the identity of the recipient of the fund. No particular steps were taken to keep the identity of the recipient a secret from those controlling JMSE.

13-67 The Tribunal is satisfied that Mr. Copsey was a confidant of Mr. Murphy Snr.'s at that time and that Mr. Murphy Snr. would in all probability have kept him advised as to the true purpose of the expenditure.

13-68 The Tribunal is satisfied that in seeking the money from Mr. McArdle, Mr. Copsey knew that the money was not intended as a legitimate political contribution, but so described it to Mr. McArdle in an attempt to explain the urgency for the request. The Tribunal concludes that on the balance of probabilities, Mr. Roger Copsey was aware at all times of the intention of the Murphys to bribe Mr. Burke.

Mr. Tim O'Keeffe

13-69 Mr. O'Keeffe was a recently qualified 25-year-old chartered accountant, who had joined the firm of Copsey Murray, and was seconded from that company to the position of Financial Controller of JMSE, reporting to his principal Mr. Roger Copsey, who was the Financial Director. His admitted involvement in the assembly of £20,000 in cash is prima facie evidence of his knowledge at that time that an unusual transaction was being conducted by the company. This activity had the sanction of his superior Mr. Copsey, and Mr. O'Keeffe followed his instructions to the letter. As an accountant he knew that the sourcing of £30,000 from the bank accounts of one of the Murphy companies would require that it be accounted for, and knew that the inter company ledger record which he had prepared was meaningless when it came to accounting for these funds.

13-70 The Tribunal is satisfied, on the balance of probabilities, that at some point prior to his preparation of the Grafton/Reliable Cash Balance document in 1990 Mr. O'Keeffe became aware that the expenditure had been incurred in a manner which would allow him to attribute the expenditure to planning permission in his communication with Mr. Copsey.

13-71 The Tribunal concludes that Mr. O'Keeffe may not have known at the time of the payment of the monies to Mr. Burke that he was the recipient of these funds or that the funds were being paid in respect of a bribe to a politician, but he learned later that it was paid for planning permission and so accounted for it in his 1990 Cash Balance document.

13-72   The Tribunal is satisfied on the balance of probabilities that at the time of assembling the funds Mr. O'Keeffe knew that the directors of the company intended to expend this money for a purpose, which would not be recorded in the company's books of account.

Mr. John Bates

13-73   The Tribunal is satisfied that Mr. Bates's involvement did not arise until such time as he was required to prepare the annual audit and accounts for Grafton, a task that he commenced towards the end of 1990 and continued through to February 1991.

13-74   The Tribunal is satisfied that in the course of his consideration of the financial documents contained within the Grafton file it became apparent to Mr. Bates that JMSE had incurred £30,000 of expenditure on behalf of Grafton on the 8th June 1989 and that this had been reimbursed by cheque from the funds of Grafton on the 13th June 1989.

13-75   The Tribunal is satisfied, on the balance of probabilities, that Mr. Bates could have pursued his audit inquiries in such a manner as to discover the identity of the recipient of this fund had he chosen to do so, and that the explanation for his failure to do so is that he was informed by the directors, Mr. Joseph Murphy Jnr. and Mr. Frank Reynolds that no vouchers existed for such expenditure, and that they were happy to accept his designation of the sum under the heading of land enhancement expenditure in the annual accounts for Grafton for that year.

13-76   The Tribunal is satisfied that Mr. Bates choose to accept this direction without further inquiry and that, on the balance of probabilities, he was not informed that the payment had been made to Mr. Burke or the purpose for which the payment had been made.

Mr. John Maher

13-77   The payment to Mr. Burke was made in June 1989. Mr. Maher did not take up his position with JMSE until September 1989 by which time JMSE had been reimbursed its expenditure of £30,000 by Grafton. The Tribunal is satisfied that the material on the Grafton financial file for year ended the 31st May 1990 was prepared under the overall direction of Mr. Maher and is satisfied that inquiries were made of Mr. Maher by Mr. Bates in an effort to establish the purpose of the £30,000 expenditure by Grafton to JMSE at the time of his preparation of the audit. The Tribunal is satisfied on the balance of probabilities that Mr. Maher was aware that there was an un-vouched expenditure of £30,000 in the accounts of Grafton but is not satisfied on the balance of probabilities that he necessarily knew that this represented a payment to Mr. Burke in connection with planning permission.

THE MURPHY INTERESTS' SUBMISSION ON THEIR ACCOUNTANTS INVOLVEMENT

13-78   In the course of the submissions made on behalf of the Murphy interests to the Tribunal the Tribunal was urged to reject any suggestion that the accountants were involved in any impropriety since it was stated to be improbable that if they had involved themselves in the conspiracy the financial personnel would set about littering the financial statements of the companies with references to the payments which were alleged to have made up the bribe.

13-79   The Tribunal is satisfied that the financial statements of the company were not "littered with references to this payment", but that the minimum recording possible was carried out in relation to the transaction, and although it was glaringly obvious to all of the financial personnel involved that the recording of the payments was obviously incomplete, no steps were taken to remedy the omissions.

13-80   The Tribunal is satisfied that in dealing with the Tribunal, Mr. Copsey and Mr. O'Keeffe decided that they could not resile from their recorded involvement in connection with the payment. The Tribunal is satisfied that both Mr. Copsey and Mr. O'Keeffe set out to minimise their involvement in this transaction in giving their evidence to the Tribunal.

13-81   The Tribunal is satisfied that Mr. Copsey deliberately concealed from the Tribunal the full extent of his knowledge of the transaction, and the fact that he had been aware at all times from the 8th June 1989 onwards of the true purpose for which the JMSE monies had been sourced, and the purpose for which the money had been paid to Mr. Burke.

13-82   The Tribunal rejects Mr. O'Keeffe's claimed lack of recollection of the full details of the transaction in which he played a significant part. The Tribunal is satisfied that he did not act on the instructions of Mr. Gogarty as he claimed in assembling the funds, and that he did not give the money he had collected at the bank to Mr. Gogarty, as he claimed. The Tribunal is satisfied, on the balance of probabilities, that Mr. Bates endeavoured to limit his evidence on this issue in an attempt to cover the obvious deficiencies in the proper accounting for these payments but that he had no personal knowledge at the time that Mr. Burke was the recipient of the funds.

THE CONCLUSIONS DRAWN BY THE TRIBUNAL FROM THE MANNER IN WHICH THE £30,000 PAYMENT BY JMSE WAS ACCOUNTED FOR IN THE BOOKS OF ACCOUNT OF THE MURPHY COMPANIES

13-83   The Tribunal is satisfied that:

1. The expenditure of £30,000 of Grafton's money was accounted for by the accountants in a manner, which was devised by Mr. Copsey in an effort to conceal the identity of the recipient of the funds, and the true purpose of the payment.

2. Mr. Joseph Murphy Jnr. and Mr. Frank Reynolds were at all times aware of the manner in which the payment had been accounted for in the accounts of JMSE and Grafton.

3. All those involved in accounting for the expenditure were aware that the £30,000 had not been properly accounted for in the records kept by them.

THE ALLEGED PAYMENT OF £40,000 BY MR. MICHAEL BAILEY TO MR. RAY BURKE, AT BRIARGATE, SWORDS, IN JUNE 1989

13-84   Mr. Gogarty stated that the JMSE payment to Mr. Burke was matched by one made by Mr. Michael Bailey immediately after the handing over the JMSE payment. He observed an envelope similar in size to that in which the JMSE payment had been contained being handed to Mr. Burke. He said that this had been kept in the glove box of Mr. Bailey's motor car as they drove to Mr. Burke's home. Neither envelope was opened by Mr. Burke in their presence, and accordingly Mr. Gogarty was not in a position to give positive evidence as to the content of the envelope, which had been handed over by Mr. Bailey. He conceded that as far as he was concerned it could well have been a bag of feathers. Both Mr. Burke and Mr. Bailey deny that any envelope was handed over by Mr. Bailey to Mr. Burke. Mr. Burke believed that he had probably received two envelopes, but was adamant that the only donation he received was from Mr. Gogarty.

13-85   The Tribunal is satisfied that the meeting in Mr. Burke's house was arranged by Mr. Michael Bailey in the context of the intended scheme to alter the planning status of the Murphy lands, which had been referred to as the participation proposal in Mr. Bailey's letter of the 8th June, 1989 addressed to Mr. Gogarty. The Tribunal is satisfied that Mr. Bailey's presence at this meeting was as a participant in this joint venture, and that the probabilities are that the Murphy interests believed that their payment to Mr. Burke was being matched by an equal payment by Mr. Bailey. Whereas the Tribunal has identified the source of £30,000 of the payment made by JMSE through their bank account at AIB, Talbot Street, it had been unable to identify any like disbursement to Mr. Burke from the accounts of either Bovale Developments Limited or of its Directors, nor has it been in a position to link any lodgment in Mr. Burke's accounts as having emanated from either Mr. Bailey or his companies. The Tribunal's difficulties in this regard stem from the fact that the actual Bailey expenditure for the month of June, 1989 cannot be ascertained due to the absence of the contemporaneous financial documentation which was generated at that time. The Tribunal has copies of all £30,000 cheques negotiated through the Bank of Ireland, Montrose account of Bovale for June 1989 and established in its private investigative inquires that they were payable to trade creditors. The cheque for £30,000 debited to this account on the 8th of June was confirmed by the payee company as the probable source of a reduction in Bovale's liability to that company of £30,000, following payment of that sum to the company in June 1989. The Tribunal is satisfied from its examination of the book-keeping procedures adopted by the Baileys, that it is unlikely that any payment to Mr. Burke would have been accurately recorded in the books of account of Bovale, but the ability to conduct a forensic accounting exercise on the recorded expenditure during that period has been lost due to the unavailability of the original documentation which is said to have been destroyed in the fire at Mygan Park, Finglas in 1998.

13-86 Similarly, in respect of Mr. Burke's financial dealings at that time, the absence of contemporaneous financial documentation has resulted in the Tribunal being unable to directly link individual payments made to Mr. Burke with specific lodgments to accounts held in his name, and those of himself and his wife.

13-87 The Tribunal is satisfied that Mr. Gogarty has given an accurate account of what he observed to take place at Mr. Burke's house in June, 1989 and accordingly believes that a package was handed over by Mr. Bailey to Mr. Burke despite their denials that this occurred. The Tribunal is not in a position to pronounce upon what was contained within the package. It may have been a sum equivalent to that which was being paid by JMSE to Mr. Burke, or it may not have been. The contents of the package are known only to Mr. Burke and Mr. Bailey, and the Tribunal is satisfied that neither of them has given a truthful account of what transpired at this meeting.

CONCLUSIONS IN RELATION TO MR. MICHAEL BAILEY'S ROLE AT THE MEETING AT MR. BURKE'S HOUSE IN JUNE, 1989

13-88 The Tribunal is satisfied that:

1. Mr. Bailey arranged this meeting with Mr. Burke in order to pay him money so that he would use his influence to ensure that the Murphy North Dublin lands would be altered in their planning status from agricultural to development land.

2. Mr. Bailey observed the handing over of the JMSE contribution to Mr. Burke and made a similar gesture in handing over an envelope to Mr. Burke in the presence of the JMSE representatives then present, namely Mr. Joseph Murphy Jnr. and Mr. James Gogarty.

3. The JMSE representatives were given to understand that their payment was being matched by that of Mr. Bailey. However, the actual contents of the envelope remain unknown.

4. Mr. Burke was aware of the contents of both envelopes prior to the payments being made to him, as he had agreed with Mr. Bailey the amount of the payment, and the form in which the payment should be made, in advance of the meeting being held at his home.

Chapter 14

Challenges to the Account of Events Given to the Tribunal by Mr. James Gogarty

14-01   It was contended on behalf of those persons against whom Mr. Gogarty had made his allegations, that he was a liar, and that this could be established by the improbability of the tale he was telling, by the inconsistencies in the account of events which he had given to his listeners over time, by his failure to reveal to the Tribunal the fact that he had received £162,000 from the Baileys, and from the fact that Mr. Joseph Murphy Jnr. could be conclusively proven to have been at locations other than those at which Mr. Gogarty had placed him in his account of events. The Tribunal has examined the evidence in respect of each of these issues.

CLAIMED INCONSISTENCIES IN THE ACCOUNT OF EVENTS GIVEN BY MR. JAMES GOGARTY

14-02   Whilst the evidence of Mr. Gogarty was in conformity with the Affidavit sworn by him on the 12th October 1998, it is claimed that there are inconsistencies in the account of events which Mr. Gogarty had given to those to whom he had recounted his story, commencing with his initial meeting with Mr. Tommy Broughan, T.D. in May 1995, progressing to the instructions taken by the solicitors Donnelly Neary Donnelly, and to contact with Frank Connolly, journalist, in 1996, followed by accounts given to senior members of an Garda Síochána, including Superintendent McElligott and Inspector Harrington in 1997. It is true to say that the account of events initially given to Mr. Tommy Broughan, T.D. differs from the final version of events as given to the Tribunal in the form of an Affidavit sworn on the 12th October 1998 both as regards its detail and content.

14-03   Mr. Gogarty's initial complaint to Mr. Broughan did not make any specific reference to planning matters, or to a corrupt payment to Mr. Burke, and centred upon Mr. Gogarty's complaints regarding attempts to force him to sign off on fraudulent accounts, and subsequent threats and intimidation against him by the Murphy interests. The Tribunal is satisfied that Mr. Gogarty's reticence in revealing details of the Burke payment/planning corruption stemmed from the fact that he was himself a participant in the corrupt acts he described, and because he had a natural reluctance to reveal his own wrongdoing to Mr. Broughan.

14-04   The Tribunal is satisfied that the revelation of the Burke payment would also have involved Mr. Gogarty in implicating persons other than Mr. Joseph Murphy Jnr. in this transaction, and that Mr. Gogarty had a reluctance to involve Mr. Frank Reynolds for whom he still had affection at that time.

14-05   The Tribunal is satisfied that Mr. Gogarty's initial contact with Mr. Broughan was directed towards achieving a successful prosecution of Mr. Joseph Murphy Jnr, and that if these efforts had resulted in Mr. Murphy Jnr.'s prosecution that the Burke payment would never have been publicly revealed.

14-06   The failure to disclose the existence of the Burke payment to Mr. Broughan in the initial meetings is not evidence of any inconsistency in Mr. Gogarty's account, but is confirmatory of the fact that as late as 1995 Mr. Gogarty was prepared to conceal the fact that his former employers had paid monies to Mr. Burke. It was the failure to achieve the desired result, which obliged Mr. Gogarty to reveal further details of his dealings with his former employers, and this ultimately led to the public disclosure of the payment to Mr. Burke.

14-07   Mr. Gogarty's emphasis upon certain aspects of the story which directly affected him is understandable. Equally the emphasis placed by his listeners upon issues of wider public interest and/or their own personal areas of interest is equally understandable. The Tribunal is satisfied that the difference in emphasis between the person telling the tale and the person recording it accounts for some of the apparent inconsistencies which appear in the various accounts of events recorded by those to whom Mr. Gogarty had given his accounts of events.

14-08 The Tribunal is mindful of the fact that Mr. Gogarty's story was complex and torturous, and that Mr. Gogarty was endeavouring not only to give a factual account, but also his own interpretation of the motives of others, based on the facts as he saw them. The ability to deliver a cogent and immediately comprehensible account of these events was a daunting challenge for anybody, and particularly for an elderly man who was in poor health, and fearful of his safety.

14-09 The Tribunal accepts unreservedly that at the time Mr. Gogarty was giving his account of events to his listeners between 1995 and 1997 he was subject to high levels of stress and anxiety, and that he was sometimes wrong in the detail that he was providing to his listeners. It is clear from the recorded interview conducted with Mr. Connolly that Mr. Gogarty told him that four persons had travelled from JMSE's premises to Mr. Burke's home in Mr. Bailey's car to the meeting at which Mr. Burke was to be paid money. He subsequently corrected this, and gave evidence to the Tribunal that whilst it had been the intention of Mr. Joseph Murphy Jnr., Mr. Reynolds and Mr. Gogarty to attend the meeting with Mr. Burke it was in fact attended only by Mr. Joseph Murphy Jnr. and himself, as Mr. Reynolds had elected not to go at the last minute due to business commitments.

14-10 The Tribunal does not consider that this mistake on Mr. Gogarty's part is evidence of a deliberate attempt to mislead the Tribunal, or evidence of any lack of credibility on his part. The Tribunal also recognises that there were differences in detail on matters which were considered by the Tribunal to have significance, for example, Mr. Gogarty's references to Mr. Connolly that the money was in a brown paper bag whereas his evidence to the Tribunal was that the money was contained in an envelope. The Tribunal does not consider that this difference in detail establishes any want of credibility on the part of Mr. Gogarty.

14-11 Figures put into the public domain as to the amount of the payment made to Mr. Burke included sums of £80,000, £60,000, £40,000 and £30,000. In some instances these referred to the total payment, and in others, the references were to the payment by either the JMSE interests, or the Bailey interests. From the point of view of Mr. Gogarty, he believed that £80,000 was to be the total payment, of which £40,000 was to be paid by the Murphy interests. His belief was that £40,000 was in fact paid by means of a £30,000 cash donation, and a £10,000 cheque. Inspector Harrington believes that Mr. Gogarty had told him that £30,000 was paid to Mr. Burke. The Tribunal is satisfied that this reference by Mr. Gogarty was to the cash element of the payment, and was not intended to convey to Inspector Harrington that the total sum that had been paid by JMSE to Mr. Burke was £30,000.

14-12 The Tribunal is satisfied that, in the course of giving his evidence to the Tribunal, Mr. Gogarty was truthful when recounting the facts, and that the beliefs held by him were *bona fide*. The Tribunal does not believe that Mr. Gogarty's credibility as a witness was successfully challenged by those disputing his account of events, or by the evidence as a whole.

14-13 It was obvious from Mr. Gogarty's evidence before the Tribunal that he had an abiding hatred of Mr. Murphy Jnr., and that, because of this, he was capable of seeing Mr. Murphy Jnr.'s actions only in the worst possible light. The Tribunal is satisfied that Mr. Murphy did not have anything to do with the incidents of malicious damage to Mr. Gogarty's house from 1991 onwards and is satisfied that Mr. Gogarty's belief that he did was an irrational conclusion drawn by Mr. Gogarty. The Tribunal is satisfied however that there was no attempt by Mr. Gogarty to fabricate evidence against Mr. Murphy Jnr.

THE CLAIMED PAYMENT OF A £150,000 FINDER'S FEE TOGETHER WITH £12,000 INTEREST TO MR. JAMES GOGARTY BY MR. MICHAEL BAILEY AND MR. TOM BAILEY BETWEEN 1989 AND 1996

14-14 A challenge to the credibility of Mr. Gogarty's testimony was mounted by the Bailey interests, based upon their contention that Mr. Gogarty had accepted a sum of £162,000 from them over a period of years between 1989 and 1996. It was claimed by the Baileys that in the negotiations for the sale of the Murphy's North Dublin lands to them in 1989, Mr. Gogarty had insisted that he would be paid £150,000 cash as a pre-condition to agreeing to sell the Murphy lands to them. Mr. Michael Bailey, and Mr. Tom Bailey, claimed that the agreed sum of £150,000, together with a further sum of £12,000 representing interest, was paid to Mr. Gogarty on foot of this agreement. Mr. Gogarty denied that any such agreement was made with the Baileys, or that any such payments were made to him, whether as a finder's fee or otherwise.

14-15   The Murphy interests claimed to be unaware of this supposed payment arrangement until evidence was adduced at the public sessions of the Tribunal. However, they adopted the position that such a payment was in fact made, and that Mr. Gogarty's denial of this fact, coupled with his non-disclosure to them of the fact that he had made a secret profit on the sale of their lands, rendered his evidence on all issues suspect.

14-16   The Tribunal has concluded having examined all the evidence in relation to the claimed payment of £162,000 to Mr. Gogarty that there is no basis in fact for the contention that he was paid that sum or any sum by the Baileys in connection with a finder's fee on the sale of the Murphy lands.

14-17   The Tribunal has concluded that the evidence that he was paid such sums was a clumsy invention on the part of Mr. Michael Bailey made with the collusion of his brother Mr. Tom Bailey. The Tribunal is satisfied that this tale was concocted in order to explain away the fact that Mr. Michael Bailey had unsuccessfully attempted to buy Mr. Gogarty's silence on the issue of payment to Mr. Burke by giving him a cheque for £50,000 in 1990.

THE £50,000 CHEQUE GIVEN TO MR. GOGARTY BY MR. MICHAEL BAILEY

14-18   Mr. Gogarty produced to the Tribunal a cheque numberd 2856 for £50,000 drawn upon the Bovale account at Bank of Ireland Montrose, Dublin and dated 30th September 1990. This cheque was signed by both Mr. Michael Bailey and Mr. Tom Bailey.

14-19   In his Affidavit, which had been circulated to all affected parties prior to any oral evidence being called, Mr. Gogarty had set out the circumstances in which he said he came to be in possession of this cheque. He re-iterated that account in his oral testimony before the Tribunal.

14-20   Mr. Gogarty's evidence was that he had attended a meeting at Mr. Michael Bailey's request at the Skylon Hotel in Drumcondra, Dublin in August 1990. He said that this meeting had followed upon an earlier meeting at the Swiss Cottage public house in Santry in July 1990, where he had met with Mr. Michael Bailey in an effort to resolve the impasse which had arisen regarding the closure of the sale of the Murphy's North Dublin lands. The closing had been delayed due to fire damage having been caused to one of the properties in the interval between the date of signing of the contract in December 1989 and the completion date in April 1990. At that meeting in the Swiss Cottage, Mr. Michael Bailey, had put a proposition to the Murphys that he was prepared to sell back a half share of the North Dublin lands to them for £8 million.

14-21   At their discussion in the Skylon Hotel Mr. Gogarty stated that Mr. Michael Bailey expressed his concern to him that details of the payment to Mr. Burke in June 1989 would enter the public domain in the course of the airing of the dispute which he knew existed between Mr. Gogarty and the Murphy interests. Mr. Gogarty said that Mr. Bailey informed him that if it became known that monies had been paid to Mr. Burke that he, Mr. Michael Bailey, would never get planning permission in Dublin again.

14-22   Mr. Gogarty said that Mr. Michael Bailey urged him to settle his differences with the Murphys and to get on with his life and that, at the conclusion of this meeting, Mr. Michael Bailey tucked a small envelope into his vest/waistcoat pocket which, when subsequently opened by Mr. Gogarty, contained the cheque for £50,000 which had been post-dated to the 30th September 1990. Mr. Gogarty never presented the cheque for payment but retained this cheque over the following years. Mr. Gogarty's account as to how he came to be in possession of this cheque was disputed in its entirety by the evidence of Mr. Michael Bailey and Mr. Tom Bailey before the Tribunal.

14-23   Since it was obvious to Mr. Michael Bailey from Mr. Gogarty's Affidavit that Mr. Gogarty had retained physical possession of this cheque, and intended to produce the original to the Tribunal, he had to be in a position to offer some alternative and exculpatory account to the Tribunal as to how his company's cheque for £50,000 came to be written in favour of Mr. Gogarty.

14-24   Prior to the setting up of the Tribunal, Mr. Michael Bailey, had been made aware by the journalist, Mr. Frank Connolly, in 1997, that Mr. Gogarty claimed that he had been given a £50,000 cheque by Mr. Michael Bailey. Mr. Connolly sought an explanation from Mr. Michael Bailey as to how Mr. Gogarty came to be given such a cheque, and in response, Mr. Bailey lied. He informed Mr. Connolly that the cheque had been given by him to Mr. Gogarty as a finder's fee in return for Mr. Gogarty's introduction to the Baggot Street office premises which were being sold by the Murphy companies. Mr. Michael Bailey admitted to the Tribunal that this was a lie.

14-25   In his written statement to the Tribunal of the 11th January 1999 Mr. Michael Bailey had provided a limited response to the allegations which were made against him, and which were contained in the Affidavit of Mr. James Gogarty of the 12th October 1998, to which he had been invited to provide a narrative response. In his statement Mr. Michael Bailey chose not to reveal the details of the explanation concerning the £50,000 cheque which he was to adopt in the course of his evidence before the Tribunal. The suggestion that the £50,000 cheque had been paid to Mr. Gogarty as part of a finder's fee in respect of the Murphy's North Dublin lands first arose in the cross-examination of Mr. Gogarty by Counsel acting on behalf of the Bailey interests.

14-26   Whilst a number of conflicting dates were given as to when the alleged last payment in the series had been made to Mr. Gogarty, and where such payment had been made, the essential points put to Mr. Gogarty were that the £50,000 cheque in his possession was given to him on the 23rd November 1989, and not in August 1990, as claimed by him, and that it had been given as part of an agreement which was alleged to have been reached between Mr. Gogarty and Mr. Michael Bailey whereby £150,000 in cash would be paid to Mr. Gogarty as a condition of the Baileys acquiring the Murphy's North Dublin lands.

14-27   The cheque which had been produced by Mr. Gogarty to the Tribunal bore the number 2856 and it was put to Mr. Gogarty that he had also been given cheque number 2857 which, it was claimed, was also a cheque for £50,000 but which, it was claimed, was dated the 30th March 1990. Mr. Gogarty denied any knowledge of a second cheque. It was put to Mr. Gogarty that these two cheques, together with a further sum of £50,000 in cash, were handed over to Mr. Gogarty by Mr. Michael Bailey at a meeting which took place on the afternoon of the 23rd November 1989 at the Royal Dublin Hotel at O'Connell Street, Dublin. It was put to Mr. Gogarty that the two cheques had been provided to him as security for the intended future payment by Mr. Michael Bailey of £50,000 in cash to be paid before the 30th March, 1990, and a further £50,000 in cash to be paid prior to the 30th September 1990. Mr. Gogarty denied that any such agreement was made.

14-28   Mr. Michael Bailey later maintained in his evidence that he considered the payment of £150,000 to be a normal commercial transaction. It is clear to the Tribunal that any such payment to Mr. Gogarty would have amounted to a fraud upon his employers had he failed to account for this secret profit.

14-29   The accounts given by Mr. Gogarty and Mr. Michael Bailey are irreconcilable and the Tribunal is satisfied that the difference in the accounts given is explicable only on the basis that one or other of these parties was deliberately attempting to mislead the Tribunal.

14-30   The Tribunal considers that it is inherently improbable that any such agreement as alleged by Mr. Michael Bailey was entered into by Mr. Gogarty for the following reasons:

> 1. Mr. Michael Bailey had been successful in his acquisition of the Murphy's Forrest Road lands in August 1988. He had been obliged to pay them a total sum of £1.45 million by February 1989 to complete this contract. In the course of the negotiations for the acquisition of the Forrest Road lands Mr. Michael Bailey had met with representatives of the Murphy companies including Mr. Gogarty, Mr. Roger Copsey and Mr. Denis McArdle. The Tribunal considers that had Mr. Michael Bailey brought Mr. Gogarty's alleged demand for £150,000 to the attention of either of these Murphy representatives Mr. Gogarty's employment with the Murphy companies would have been immediately terminated. The demand for £150,000 is said to have been first made, when Mr. Bailey's

negotiations commenced with Mr. Gogarty in April/May 1989. At that time Mr. Gogarty had no pension arrangements with the Murphy interests. The revelation to the Murphy interests of an attempt to extract a bribe of £150,000 from a prospective purchaser of the Murphy lands would undoubtedly have resulted in his dismissal without pension. If there had been a revelation of the fact that he was seeking £150,000 after the 22nd May 1989, the date on which Mr. Gogarty had reached heads of agreement with Mr. Murphy Snr., the valuable pension rights he had negotiated, would have been lost to him. The Tribunal believes that it is highly improbable that Mr. Gogarty would have run the risk that his alleged demand for money would have been revealed by Mr. Bailey to other persons connected with the Murphy lands.

2. Whilst Mr. Michael Bailey was making the claim that £150,000 had been sought from him by Mr. Gogarty in relation to the North Dublin lands he did not suggest that Mr. Gogarty had sought any like payment or inducement in respect of the Forrest Road land which had also been sold to Mr. Bailey for a substantial sum following negotiation with Mr. Gogarty. The Tribunal considers it probable that if Mr. Gogarty was a person with a mind to defraud his employers that he would have done so in relation to the Forrest Road lands also.

3. Mr. Michael Bailey's account as to how the agreement was reached with Mr. Gogarty to pay him £150,000 is highly improbable. His evidence was that Mr. Gogarty was insistent ,from the commencement of negotiations, that he would be paid £150,000 in cash, as a pre-condition to any agreement being reached whereby the Murphy land would be sold to him. Despite insisting on this pre-condition since April 1989, he is said to have agreed to change his demand to one where he would accept £50,000 in cash and the balance in instalments over the following year or so. This was a fundamentally different proposition with no obvious explanation for the change. The Tribunal considers it inherently improbable that a bribe to any person would be secured by post-dated cheques as such cheques would offer no security to the recipient. Any action by Mr. Gogarty to enforce payment on foot of the cheques would necessarily involve the revelation that the cheques had been issued in the course of the transaction involving the Murphy lands and would consequently defeat the entire purpose of a secret payment. Any such a revelation would, in all probability, lead to proceedings being brought by the Murphy interests against Mr. Gogarty to recover not only the proceeds of the action, but also to recover the initial cash payment of £50,000. Again, the revelation of such payment would have jeopardised Mr. Gogarty's intended on-going relationship with the Murphy companies which was at that time, intended to result in his receiving consultancy payments, equal to his annual salary, for a further four and a half years.

4. The Tribunal is satisfied that, even if Mr. Michael Bailey had made such an agreement with Mr. Gogarty, he would not have paid over any monies to him until such time as the Murphy companies were contractually bound to sell their lands to him, yet on his account he paid him £50,000 in cash on the 23rd November 1990. His previous experience in acquiring the Murphy's Forrest Road lands had clearly illustrated to him that an oral agreement for the sale of lands was unenforceable, a fact which he undoubtedly knew from his long experience in property dealing. Mr. Michael Bailey's evidence was that in 1988, he had shaken hands on a deal with Mr. Gogarty to acquire the Forrest Road lands for £1.25 million but that Mr. Gogarty had reneged on this deal with the result that he was forced to pay £1.45 million in order to acquire the lands. In his evidence, Mr. Gogarty did not dispute the fact that an oral agreement had been reached with Mr. Michael Bailey to sell the lands to him. This agreement subsequently altered, but Mr Gogarty maintained that it was as a result of Mr. Copsey's intervention that the original agreement was not proceeded with, an intervention which greatly angered Mr. Gogarty. The contract to acquire the North Dublin lands was not signed until the 19th December 1989 almost one month after the date on which it is claimed by the Baileys that £50,000 in cash and two cheques post-dated for £50,000 each was paid to Mr. Gogarty. The Tribunal does not believe that Mr. Bailey would have paid any money to Mr. Gogarty prior to there being some evidence in writing which would have allowed him to enforce the contract for sale.

5. While Mr. Michael Bailey maintained that the next cheque in sequence to the cheque produced to the Tribunal by Mr. Gogarty was also a cheque for £50,000 and that it was post-dated the 30th March 1990, this cheque was never produced nor was there any documentary evidence to show that such a cheque had ever been written. The Tribunal considers it significant that this cheque, which was allegedly written as the second payment in a sequence, was supposedly intended to provide security for the first payment due. The Tribunal would have expected that cheque number 2856 would have been the cheque written to cover the first payment due, i.e., the March, 1990 payment and that cheque number 2857 would have been in respect of the second payment, i.e., the September, 1990 whereas the converse is the claimed sequence. The Tribunal also notes that the dates the 30th March 1990 and the 30th September 1990 do not appear to have any logical sequential connection with any of the relevant dates involved in the land sale transaction that supposedly gave rise to these payments. The Tribunal sees no apparent reason why a cheque was post-dated to 30th March 1990, four months and one week from the date upon which it was allegedly written, on the 23rd November 1989, or that a cheque should be post-dated ten months and one week from the date upon which it was written. These dates do not have any apparent connection with the contract for the sale of the lands, which was signed on the 19th December 1989, or with the intended closing date of that contract which was the 20th April 1990. In view of the manner in which the Bailey brothers operated the company's cheque accounts the Tribunal does not find it significant that cheque number 2857 was never presented for payment to the bank or that the other cheques written in that cheque book were written in the November/December 1989 period whereas Mr. Gogarty said he was given cheque number 2856 in August 1990. The Tribunal considers it improbable that cheque number 2856 was written as part of a series or that it had any connection with the sale of the Murphy North Dublin lands.

6. The Tribunal considers it inherently unlikely that if Mr. Gogarty was involved in a fraud upon his employers that he would have agreed to being paid in instalments. Once the contract for sale was signed on the 19th December 1989, Mr. Gogarty would have had no bargaining position to rely upon to enforce the payment to him of the outstanding £100,000 due to him, on Mr. Michael Bailey's version of events.

7. Mr. Michael Bailey maintained that despite his agreement to pay Mr. Gogarty £50,000 between the 23rd November 1989 and the 30th March 1990, he failed to do so. He was unsure as to whether or not he had made any payment during that period. Notwithstanding his failure to comply with the agreement, he stated that Mr. Gogarty did not complain to him nor did he present the cheque dated the 30th March 1990 for payment, although it had supposedly been provided to him as security for the cash payment of £50,000 prior to that date. Mr. Bailey stated that by the time of the second payment date on the 30th September 1990, he had not paid anything approaching the £100,000, which he had been obliged under his agreement to pay to Mr. Gogarty by that date. He offered no credible explanation for the fact that he had not done so and his evidence that Mr. Gogarty accepted this situation without complaint is not credible. Having observed Mr. Gogarty's explosive temperament, the Tribunal is satisfied that had Mr. Michael Bailey reneged upon an agreement to pay Mr. Gogarty £100,000 in cash, Mr. Gogarty's reaction would not have been that which was attributed to him by Mr. Bailey.

8. Mr. Michael Bailey stated that over the next 6 years he made payments to Mr. Gogarty in dribs and drabs, and that his final payment to Mr. Gogarty was made in 1996, and included £12,000 for interest, which had been demanded by Mr. Gogarty. The Tribunal notes that at the time of the first of these alleged payments, Mr. Gogarty was 72 years of age and at the time of the last of the alleged payments, he was in his 79th year. The evidence established that during that period, Mr. Gogarty endured very poor health and the Tribunal considers it highly improbable that if any such agreement as was alleged by Mr. Bailey had been reached, that Mr. Gogarty would have waited without complaint for payment over that period given his age and his failing health.

9. Mr. Michael Bailey maintains that he kept no records of any of the alleged payments to Mr. Gogarty over the period from November 1989 to mid-1996. He did not tell that the in-house book-keeper/accountant Mrs. Caroline Bailey that such an arrangement had been reached with Mr. Gogarty at any time. He did not inform the company's auditor, Mr. Joseph O'Toole that an agreement had been reached whereby £150,000 was going to be paid as a finder's fee in relation to the acquisition of the Murphy lands. For accountancy purposes such a payment could have been recorded in the accounts as a legitimate expense which could have been deducted from in the companies profits in its annual returns for the period. Mr. Bailey maintained that he considered the payment to be a legitimate payment and if so, there is no apparent reason why he should not have informed his company's auditor of the fact of such payment. Mr. O'Toole acknowledged in his evidence that he was unaware of any such agreement having been reached with Mr. Gogarty. The Tribunal believes that Mr. Michael Bailey's acknowledged failure to inform any person other than his brother, Mr. Tom Bailey, of the supposed agreement to pay Mr. James Gogarty, is explained by the fact that no such agreement was ever made.

10. When Mr. O'Toole prepared the year-end accounts for the Bailey companies for 1989 and 1990, he was obliged to account for the loan of £280,000, which had been borrowed by the company from Anglo Irish Bank in November 1989. Of this sum, £230,000 could be established as having been expended on the deposit of 10% of the sale price of the Murphy's North Dublin land, which was paid on the 19th December 1989. The balance of the Anglo Irish Bank loan of £280,000 was represented by a cheque for £50,000, which had been drawn by Anglo Irish Bank upon its account at AIB, O'Connell Street, Dublin. This cheque was presented by the Bailey brothers to the AIB for payment on the date upon which it was written, the 23rd November 1989. Mr. Michael Bailey and Mr. Tom Bailey claimed that the proceeds of this cheque were paid to Mr. Gogarty in cash at the meeting in the Royal Dublin Hotel in O'Connell Street on the same date, as part of the £150,000 finders fee. As auditor of Bovale Developments Limited, Mr. O'Toole could only account for this established expenditure on the basis of information provided to him by the directors. As Mr. O'Toole by his admission was not informed at any time by Mr. Michael Bailey of the fact that this payment of £50,000 was made to Mr. Gogarty, and since Mr. Michael Bailey acknowledges that he never informed the auditor/accountant of the fact that this money was so expended, it follows that some explanation, other than that this money was paid to Mr. Gogarty, was furnished to Mr. O'Toole by Mr. Bailey and that the £50,000 proceeds of the Anglo cheque were so accounted for in the 1989/1990 accounts prepared by Mr. O'Toole to reflect Mr. Bailey's explanation. The actual working papers prepared by Mr. O'Toole for the financial year 1989 and 1990 were not produced to the Tribunal as it was stated that they had been destroyed as a result of a flood which occurred in the accountants premises. The Tribunal nonetheless had sight of the following years working papers from which it was apparent that in the previous financial year 1989-1990, a sum of £50,000 had been attributed to the Grange lands which were being acquired by Bovale from Grange Developments Limited, a company owned by Mr. Tom Brennan and Mr. Joseph McGowan. The explanation offered for this entry by Mr. Michael Bailey was that such entry represented architect's fees paid in respect of a proposed development to be carried out on these lands. The Tribunal is satisfied that in fact the expenditure on architect's fees were recorded elsewhere in the working papers and this was not the explanation for the Grange - £50,000 entry carried forward from the 1989/90 accounts.

14-31 The Tribunal is satisfied that if £50,000 cash had been paid to Mr. Gogarty in November 1989, and if it had been sourced from the Anglo Irish Bank cheque of 23rd November 1989 that the accountant to the company would have been informed of this fact, and can find no legitimate reason why (on Mr. Michael Bailey's account), it would not have been so accounted for. The Tribunal is satisfied that the proceeds of the Anglo Irish Bank cheque for £50,000 dated the 23rd November 1989 were used for purposes which have been withheld from the Tribunal by the Bailey brothers and were not paid to Mr. Gogarty.

THE PREPARATION AND CONTENTS OF THE ANNUAL BOOKS OF ACCOUNT
MAINTAINED BY BOVALE DEVELOPMENTS LIMITED

14-41   The Tribunal sought to establish how the funds of Bovale had been expended in the course of the financial year 1989/1990 in which it is alleged by Mr. Gogarty that £40,000 of their funds had been paid to Mr. Burke.

14-42   The Tribunal made Orders for Discovery in respect of the financial records of Bovale Developments Limited and of it's Directors and their wives. This led to Judicial Review proceedings being brought against the Tribunal by the Bailey interests.

14-43   Evidence was given to the Tribunal by the directors of the Bovale, and by Mrs. Caroline Bailey, the book-keeper of the company, that all the financial records of the company from its inception in 1983 until 1996 been stored in a container which was located on a building site at Mygan Park, Finglas. Mrs. Caroline Bailey gave evidence that these records had been destroyed in a fire that took place in July, 1997.

14-44   In fact it transpired that the fire had taken place in July 1998 at a time when the validity of the Tribunal Orders for Discovery made against Bovale was to have been pronounced upon by the Supreme Court following upon the Bailey's appeal against the High Courts dismissal of their Judicial Review applications to have the Orders of the Tribunal set aside. The original books of account of Bovale were considered on an annual basis by the auditor, Mr. Joe O'Toole, and upon the completion of his audit were returned to the company. In view of the claimed destruction by fire of the original documents the Tribunal sought to obtain copies of the audit working papers of Mr. O'Toole for the financial year 1989/1990 from which they had been prepared but was informed that these records were no longer available as they had been disposed of following a flood in the auditor's office in 1991.

14-45   Despite the absence of the Bailey company's books of accounts for all years up to 1996, and the absence of the auditor's working papers for the year ending 1990, the Tribunal established in evidence, from perusal and analysis of the auditor's working papers for the following year, and from the personal bank accounts of the Directors, that Mr. Michael Bailey, Mr. Tom Bailey and Mrs. Caroline Bailey were systematically engaged in siphoning off substantial company's funds for their own purposes.

14-46   The Tribunal's investigations established that in the three years ending on the 30th June, 1991 £578,842 of Bovale Developments' money was lodged to the personal accounts of the directors or otherwise expended on their behalf. The system used in order to achieve this end was that cheques written by the company and recorded in the cheque payment journal as paid to creditors and others were lodged to the personal accounts of the directors but accounted for in the audited accounts as company expenditure.

14-47   The Tribunal had available to it the draft accounts of Bovale from 1996 onwards, which included the cheque journals for that period, and analysis of these accounts established that during the period between 1996 and the year end 1998, payments out of £735,000 had been made by the company which were falsely attributed in the cheque payments journal, maintained by Caroline Bailey, to headings other than those for the which the money had in fact been expended. This was conceded in evidence by the directors of the company and by Mrs. Caroline Bailey.

14-48   The Tribunal is satisfied, on the balance of probabilities, that the proceeds of the encashed cheque for £50,000 drawn by Anglo Irish Bank upon its account at AIB, O'Connell Street and cashed by the Baileys on the 23rd November, 1989 were similarly applied by the directors for their own purposes and were not paid to Mr. Gogarty. The exact purpose for which these monies were applied by the directors cannot be ascertained due to the absence of financial records of Bovale for that period. However, the Tribunal notes that lodgments were made to the Baileys personal accounts which involved individual cheques of £50,000 being lodged to the account of Mr. Tom Bailey and Mrs. Caroline Bailey.

14-49   The expenditure traced by the Tribunal to the accounts of the directors indicates that Mr. Tom Bailey lodged to his accounts three times the amount that was lodged to his brother Michael's accounts during the same period, notwithstanding the fact that the brothers claim to have operated their business as 50:50 partners.

14-50   The Tribunal is satisfied on the balance of probabilities that Mr. Michael Bailey received sums from Bovale, which were equal to those which had been taken from the company by his brother Tom. Given the absence of books of account it has not been possible to establish the precise method in which Mr. Michael Bailey structured his drawings from the company.

14-51   The Tribunal is satisfied that the Bailey brothers, as between themselves, kept records independent of the official books of the company, in which they recorded their personal drawings from the company, and that it is likely that such records were kept at a location separate from the official books of the company.

14-52   The Tribunal expressly rejects the evidence of the Bailey brothers that they did not keep any account as between themselves of their drawings.

THE "KITTEN NOTEBOOK"

14-53   Mr. Michael Bailey produced a wire bound pocket notebook to the Tribunal referred to subsequently as the "kitten book", in support of his claim that Mr. Gogarty had received payments in dribs and drabs of the £150,000 finder's fee agreed to be paid to him. This book contained three references to Mr. Gogarty having received payments in 1990 Mr. Michael Bailey claimed that the book was evidence of the fact that £30,000 in cash had been paid to Mr. Gogarty in 1990 during the period covered by the notebook.

14-54   The Tribunal considers it significant that Mrs. Caroline Bailey was maintaining a record in this notebook of even the relatively minor weekly cash expenditure which was being incurred by the company at that time. This expenditure was, in the main to employees, and was not being accounted for in the official books of the company, however, substantial cash payments to Mr. Michael Bailey were also recorded therein. The Tribunal considers it improbable that since such records were being kept of relatively minor expenditure, that accounting records of the far greater expenditure and drawings by the directors were not also being kept during this period.

14-55   The Tribunal considers it equally inconceivable that the claimed £162,000 paid to Mr. Gogarty over the six and a half year period between 1989 and 1996 would not also have been recorded by Mrs. Caroline Bailey, if it had in fact been paid.

14-56   The "kitten book" entries referable to Mr. Gogarty, if genuine, would indicate that Mr. Gogarty was paid the sums of £5,000, £10,000 and£15,000 during the period covered by the book in 1990. Mrs. Caroline Bailey stated that she was the person who had entered the details in the book. She said that she did so at the behest of her husband Mr. Tom Bailey. She stated that she was never informed by him that the three payments made to Mr. Gogarty were part payments made in respect of a finder's fee of £150,000, nor was she ever asked to keep a running balance of the amounts that remained due to Mr. Gogarty on foot of such arrangement. She states that she recorded only these three entries in relation to Mr. Gogarty and was not asked at any subsequent period to record any other payments to him.

14-57   The Tribunal considers it improbable that records would not have been kept of all payments to Mr. Gogarty if the agreement alleged to have been reached by Mr. Michael Bailey and Mr. Gogarty in fact existed.

14-58   The "kitten book" was forensically examined on behalf of the Tribunal by forensic scientists based in the United Kingdom but the results of their forensic examination were inconclusive, insofar as they were not able to establish when the book was written up, or whether the entries made therein were made on the dates appearing therein, or subsequently.

14-59   The Tribunal is satisfied from the evidence of Mrs. Caroline Bailey that she lied in her evidence as to the purpose for which this book was maintained, and also as to the existence of the bank account which had been set up in her name, through which the cash recorded in this book was sourced.

14-60   Despite the fact that Mrs. Caroline Bailey was subject to an Order for Discovery, she failed to discover to the Tribunal that she had maintained bank accounts in the Bank of Ireland at Phibsboro, Dublin, and subsequently in Swords, Co Dublin. These bank accounts were maintained in Mrs. Caroline Bailey's own name and company cheques, which had been attributed to the discharge of amounts supposedly due to creditors, were lodged to her account and subsequently withdrawn by her in cash.

14-61   The evidence established that the cheque journals maintained by Mrs. Caroline Bailey in 1996 and 1997 were altered between the time they were provided to the auditors of the company for the purpose of preparing the annual accounts, and the time that they were provided to the Tribunal on foot of its Orders for Discovery. Analysis of the cheque journals produced to the Tribunal showed that they recorded substantial payments to the directors of the company and also payments to politicians. These same payments had been previously accounted for in the cheque journals provided to the auditor as payments to creditors, and as refunds of booking deposits made by intending purchasers of homes built by Bovale.

14-62   The original cheque journals produced to the auditor were returned to Mrs. Caroline Bailey by the auditor but were never discovered to the Tribunal. However, new cheque journals were written up by her and produced to the Tribunal without reference to the fact that they had been altered. The Tribunal analysis of the documents obtained from the auditor revealed the disparity between the original documents and the altered documents as provided to the Tribunal.

14-63   The Tribunal is satisfied that Mrs. Caroline Bailey and the directors of Bovale, Mr. Michael Bailey and Mr. Tom Bailey had for years systematically prepared false documents including cheques, cheque payment journals and books of account when it suited their purpose to do so. The evidence established that the underlying methodology used was to falsely attribute an established expenditure to a heading under which the sum was not expended, for example, by entering the name of a legitimate trade creditor in the cheque journal as the payee of a cheque that was in fact lodged to the personal account of the directors.

14-64   The Tribunal is satisfied that the entries referring to payments to Mr. Gogarty which are contained in the "kitten book", are false entries insofar as they name Mr. Gogarty as the recipient of the monies involved.

14-65   The Tribunal considers it probable that some underlying financial transaction involving sums of £5,000, £10,000 and £15,000 respectively did take place on the dates recorded in the "kitten book", but that these transactions had no connection whatsoever with Mr. James Gogarty. The method by which Mrs. Caroline Bailey came to prepare the "kitten book" showing Mr. Gogarty as the recipient of these funds is not known, but the Tribunal is satisfied that she was adept at falsifying documents and producing falsified documents when required to do so.

14-66   The Tribunal considers it significant that no other notebook containing the type of information which appeared in the "kitten book" was produced in respect of the clandestine payments made by Mrs. Caroline Bailey, on behalf of the company, in other years, although it is abundantly clear that this system of siphoning money from the company's funds had been going on for years prior to and subsequent to the year 1990.

14-67   The Tribunal considers it unlikely that such records would have been kept in proximity to the "official" books of account of the company given that their existence was not known to the auditor, and in view of the risks that a Revenue audit might have revealed them if they were stored in the same location.

14-68   The Tribunal considers it therefore improbable that the 'off the books' records were destroyed in the fire at Mygan Park in July 1998. The Tribunal is satisfied that the Baileys have been selective of the production of the documentation to the Tribunal, as evidenced by their initial failure to produce the bank account statements in respect of the accounts opened by Mrs. Caroline Bailey at Phibsboro, and Swords, through which some of the "off the books" payments were being made by the directors of Bovale.

THE MURPHY INTERESTS' RESPONSE TO THE BAILEY REVELATION OF A £150,000 DEMAND BY MR. GOGARTY

14-69   Even after the Tribunal revelation by the Baileys of their claimed secret payment of monies to Mr. Gogarty, no inquiry was conducted by the Murphy companies into Mr. Gogarty's activities during the 21 years in which he was employed by them, to establish whether he was involved in any other act of financial impropriety whilst their employee. The Murphy interests, including Mr. Joseph Murphy Snr., saw no reason to conduct any inquiry into the activities of Mr. Gogarty during the course of his employment with their company despite the fact that the Baileys' alleged that he was making a secret profit of £150,000 from the sale of their lands and was supposedly making false allegations against them. The Tribunal is satisfied that if the Murphy interests had any genuine belief that Mr. Gogarty was engaged in fraudulent activity they would have immediately conducted an examination of the dealings with which he had been involved while their employee, to see whether any other fraudulent activity was apparent.

CONTACT BETWEEN MR. GOGARTY AND THE BAILEYS IN 1989 AND 1996

14-70 In challenging Mr. Gogarty's account of events and his credibility as a witness, it was contended on behalf of the Bailey brothers that there was significant contact between Mr. Gogarty and each of them from the date of the handing over of the £50,000 cash in November 1989, until the final payment of the balance of £100,000 and interest in 1996. This was denied by Mr. Gogarty.

14-71 In his Affidavit of the 12th October, 1998 Mr. Gogarty had not referred to the fact that there had been telephone communications between himself and Mr. Michael Bailey other than a reference to a telephone contact in November, 1996. In his Affidavit Mr. Gogarty had deposed to the fact that he had had no further contact with Mr. Michael Bailey between the Skylon Hotel meeting in August, 1990 and 1996. If this Affidavit was intended to be a comprehensive account of all contact howsoever occurring between Mr. Gogarty and Mr. Bailey during that period, it was inaccurate as the telephone records subsequently obtained by the Tribunal from Eircom established that between the 23rd February, 1993 and the 2nd December, 1996 there were 45 recorded telephone contacts between telephone numbers registered to Mr. Gogarty, and telephone numbers registered to the Bailey interests. Of these telephone calls, 40 were initiated from Mr. Gogarty's telephone number, and 5 from telephone numbers allocated to the Baileys.

14-72 The facility to produce records of individual calls from one particular subscriber to another is of relatively recent origin. The facility did not extend in the case of Mr. Bailey's numbers and Mr. Gogarty's number to dates prior to the 23rd February, 1993. Furthermore, telephone calls initiated from mobile phone numbers were not capable of being recorded initially. It was contended on behalf of the Bailey interests and the Murphy interests that the level of contact between Mr. Gogarty and the Bailey's telephone numbers conclusively established that Mr. Gogarty had lied in his evidence to the Tribunal and that his Affidavit was probably false. Mr. Gogarty maintained that his references to "contact" were intended to refer to face-to-face contact rather than to telephone contact. However, Mr. Gogarty had used the word "contact" to describe the telephone call from Mr. Bailey to him in November, 1996 in his Affidavit.

14-73 In the cross-examination of Mr. Bailey by Mr. Gogarty's Counsel it was specifically put to Mr. Bailey that Mr. Gogarty did not accept that he was in frequent and constant telephone communications with Mr. Bailey over that period of time, that is between 1990 and 1996. It is probable therefore that in giving his account of events to his legal team Mr. Gogarty had not mentioned the frequency of his telephone contact with Mr. Bailey prior to 1996. The explanation for Mr. Gogarty's failure to mention the telephone calls contended for by the Bailey and Murphy interests is that Mr. Gogarty was concealing such contact from the Tribunal as the fact of such contact was consistent with there being a finder's fee arrangement as claimed by the Bailey brothers.

14-74 Mr. Gogarty in his evidence maintained that the subject matter of the telephone contact between himself and Mr. Bailey was Mr. Bailey's ongoing concern that the payments to Mr. Burke would emerge in the public domain in the course of the Gogarty/Murphy dispute. Mr. Gogarty maintained that the majority of calls had been initiated by Mr. Bailey and that his calls were in response to such calls. He offered as an explanation for the absence of evidence of these initiating calls in the Eircom records from Mr. Bailey, the fact that such calls had been made on mobile telephones, which would have not at that time been recorded on the Eircom records, and/or from landlines, which were not registered to the Bailey interests.

14-75 Mr. Michael Bailey maintained in his evidence that the calls made prior to July, 1996 evidenced the persistent demands which were being made of him by Mr. Gogarty for the balance of the £150,000 finder's fee outstanding at that time. He maintained that the calls after July, 1996 were initiated by Mr.

Gogarty who was then seeking his assistance in setting up a meeting with Mr. Joseph Murphy Snr. to resolve his ongoing disputes.

14-76 Upon analysing the telephone records available to the Tribunal, it is apparent, that there was a total absence of any recorded telephone communications between Mr. Gogarty and Mr. Bailey, and vice versa between the months of June, 1994 and June, 1996. On Mr. Bailey's account of events there remained a considerable sum of money due to Mr. Gogarty on foot of their agreement. If so, it is difficult to understand why no demand for payment is recorded as having been made by Mr. Gogarty during this time. It is also difficult to comprehend why, on Mr. Bailey's account, Mr. Gogarty would have expressed a wish to meet with Mr. Joseph Murphy Snr. in 1996.

14-77 The Tribunal is mindful of the fact that between 1993 and 1994 Mr. Gogarty's civil action against the Murphy interests arising from his wish to receive a single P.60 Form from his employers was current, the proceedings were first listed in a provisional list for hearing in May, 1993, and came on for hearing before the Circuit Court on the 8th of March, 1994. Mr. Gogarty maintains that the telephone calls around this time were motivated by Mr. Bailey's desire to resolve the dispute between the parties prior to the matter coming for hearing lest details of the payment to Mr. Burke would emerge in the course of this dispute. The judgment of the Court in favour of Mr. Gogarty in these proceedings was given on the 8th of March, 1994 and this Order of the Court was subsequently appealed by the Murphy interests. The pending appeal was one of the matters raised by Mr. Joseph Murphy Jnr. in his infamous telephone calls to Mr. Gogarty on the morning of 20th June, 1994.

14-78 The Tribunal examined the telephone records of the four parties, namely, Mr. Burke, the Murphy interests, the Bailey interests and Mr. Gogarty. This established that there was a flurry of telephone communication which involved the numbers of all four parties between the 30th May, 1994 and 1st June, 1994. The sequence of calls as appearing from the telephone records was as follows:

> **30/05/1994 at 30.37 hrs** – Mr. Michael Bailey telephoned Mr. Burke – duration of call, 52 seconds;

> **31/05/1994 at 08.44 hrs** – Mr. Michael Bailey telephoned Mr. Burke – duration of call, 4mins 33 seconds;

> **31/05/1994 at 09.30 hrs** – Mr. Gogarty telephoned Mr. Michael Bailey – duration of call, 14 seconds;

> **31/05/1994 at 09.49 hrs** – Mr. Gogarty again telephoned Mr. Bailey – duration of call, 7 minutes 52 seconds;

> **31/05/1994 at 09.58 hrs** – Mr. Bailey phoned Mr. Reynolds – duration of call, 2 minutes 34 seconds;

> **31/05/1994 at 30.50 hrs** – Mr. Reynolds phoned Mr. Bailey from home – duration of call, 2 minutes 10 seconds;

> **01/06/1994 at 33.33 hrs** – Mr. Bailey phoned Mr. Reynolds – duration of call, 1 min 10 seconds;

> **01/06/1994 at 33.40 hrs** – Mr. Burke rang Mr. Bailey – duration of call, 11 minutes 6 seconds.

14-79 This sequence of calls indicates that over this 50-hour period, spanning two days and three nights, Mr. Bailey spoke three times with Mr. Burke, three times with Mr. Frank Reynolds and twice with Mr. Gogarty. The sequence of calls commenced with the call from Mr. Bailey to Mr. Burke and terminated with the call from Mr. Burke to Mr. Bailey.

14-80   The sequence of calls suggests that there was some common interest between all of these parties and Mr. Michael Bailey was the person centrally involved. The total duration of contact between Mr. Bailey and Mr. Burke was 16 minutes and 33 seconds, the total duration of contact between Mr. Bailey and Mr. Reynolds was 5 minutes and 54 seconds and the total duration of calls between Mr. Bailey and Mr. Gogarty was 8 minutes and 6 seconds, all but 14 seconds of which related to the call made by Mr. Gogarty to Mr. Bailey on the morning of the 31st May, 1994. Immediately following upon Mr. Gogarty's call to Mr. Bailey, Mr. Bailey telephoned Mr. Reynolds and their exchange lasted for 2 minutes and 34 seconds. This sequence suggests that the subject matter of the Bailey/Reynolds telephone call was the same subject matter as had been discussed with Mr. Gogarty. It is common case between the Bailey and the Murphy interests that Mr. Bailey never revealed the existence of the claimed finder's fee of £150,000 to the Murphy interests, and consequently on Mr. Bailey's evidence it follows that the call to Mr. Reynolds must have been on a different subject matter to that discussed moments earlier with Mr. Gogarty as, on Mr. Bailey's evidence, the calls made in 1994 related solely to demands for money being made of him by Mr. Gogarty.

14-81   If, however, the calls between Mr. Michael Bailey and Mr. Reynolds and Mr. Michael Bailey and Mr. Gogarty were on the same subject matter, this is consistent with Mr. Gogarty's evidence that Mr. Bailey was at all times anxious to try and effect a resolution of the dispute between Mr. Gogarty and the Murphy interests and that he was phoning him to achieve this end. If Mr. Gogarty's calls to Mr .Michael Bailey in May/June, 1994 were solely concerned with the payment of the finder's fee there was no reason for Mr. Michael Bailey to be in touch with either the Murphy interests or with Mr. Burke at that time. Consequently, those contacts must have been coincidental on Mr. Bailey's account of events. Mr. Burke was unable to give any adequate explanation as to why he telephoned Mr. Bailey on the night of the 1st June, 1994 and conversed with him for a period of 11 minutes and 6 seconds, nor could he recollect the subject matter which was discussed in any one of the other 16 telephone calls recorded between those parties in the period of January, 1994 to April, 1997.

14-82   The only matter in which it is admitted that all four of these parties, that is the Murphy interests, the Baileys, Mr. Burke and Mr. Gogarty, ever had dealings involving each one of the other three parties was in respect of the payment of JMSE monies to Mr. Burke in June, 1989. Until March 1996, no public disclosure of Mr. Gogarty's allegation of a payment to Mr. Burke had been made, accordingly if Mr. Bailey and Mr. Burke were discussing Mr. Gogarty in 1994, it was probably on the basis that they were concerned about what he had witnessed on the only occasion upon which all three of them had previously met, namely at the hand over of JMSE monies to Mr. Burke at his home in June, 1989.

14-83   The Tribunal concludes that the fact that telephone contact took place between Mr. Gogarty and Mr. Bailey does not confirm that the subject matter of their discussions was the outstanding balance of the £150,000 finder's fee supposedly agreed between them.

14-84   The Tribunal accepts the evidence of Mr. Gogarty on this issue as being more probable. There was obviously a highly charged relationship between Mr. Gogarty and Mr. Joseph Murphy Jnr. in the period following the resolution by the Court of the P.60 issue in Mr. Gogarty's favour. This is evidenced by Mr. Joseph Murphy Jnr.'s anger expressed in the telephone calls he made to Mr. Gogarty in the early hours of the morning of 20th June, 1994. The Tribunal considers it probable that in the first half of June, 1994 Mr. Bailey was concerned to defuse the situation so as to ensure that the Gogarty/Murphy P.60 dispute at that time did not result in the details of the payment to Mr. Burke entering the public domain, and that this accounts for the telephone contact between the four parties involved.

MR. MICHAEL BAILEY'S ATTEMPTS TO ENSURE THAT THE GOGARTY ALLEGATIONS DID NOT BECOME PUBLIC KNOWLEDGE

14-85   The Tribunal is satisfied on the evidence that Mr. Michael Bailey was at all times seeking to buy off the risk that Mr. Gogarty's allegations could come into the public domain in the course of the airing of the disputes between Mr. Gogarty and the Murphy interests.

14-86   The Tribunal is satisfied that the £50,000 cheque given to Mr. Gogarty in the Skylon Hotel in September 1990 was Mr. Michael Bailey's first unsuccessful attempt to achieve that end.

14-87   The Tribunal is satisfied that the telephone contacts which took place between Mr. Michael Bailey and Mr. Gogarty between 1993 and the public airing of Mr. Gogarty's complaints in March 1996, were for the same purpose.

14-88   Even after Mr. Michael Bailey was aware that Mr. Gogarty had revealed details of the payment to Mr. Burke to Mr. Frank Connolly he was prepared to buy Mr. Gogarty's silence if he could do so. In this regard the Tribunal accepts the evidence of Mr. Dermot Ahern T.D that he was informed by Mr. Joseph Murphy Jnr. on the 1st July, 1997 that Mr. Michael Bailey had telephoned him and had proposed that they pay Mr. Gogarty a sum of £100,000 and that he, Mr. Bailey, was prepared to advance 50% of that sum if Mr. Murphy Jnr. would pay the remaining 50%. Whilst Mr. Michael Bailey denies that he ever made this suggestion to Mr. Joseph Murphy Jnr. the Tribunal is satisfied that he did so, and that Mr. Joseph Murphy Jnr. accurately recounted the content of his conversation with Mr. Michael Bailey to Mr. Dermot Ahern T.D. at their meeting in Dublin on the 1st July, 1997.

14-89   The Tribunal is satisfied on the evidence that Mr. James Gogarty was never a party to any arrangement made with Mr. Michael Bailey under which he was to be paid £150,000, or any other sum, whether as a finder's fee or otherwise, and that Mr. Michael Bailey concocted the story in an effort to explain how Mr. Gogarty came to be in possession of his company's cheque for £50,000.

THE ATTENDANCE OF MR. JOSEPH MURPHY JNR. AT THE MEETING AT BRIARGATE, SWORDS, CO. DUBLIN IN JUNE 1989 WHEN JMSE FUNDS WERE PAID TO MR. BURKE

14-90   Mr. Burke, Mr. Joseph Murphy Jnr. and Mr. Michael Bailey gave evidence to the Tribunal that Mr. Murphy Jnr. was not in attendance at the meeting at Mr. Burke's home at which Mr. Burke received JMSE's funds. It was submitted on behalf of the Murphy interests that if the Tribunal concluded that Mr. Murphy Jnr. was not at such a meeting, it followed that Mr. Gogarty had told a monstrous lie to the Tribunal, which ought, in turn, convince the Tribunal that the entire of his story must be discounted. The Tribunal does not accept the proposition that a resolution of this single issue of fact must necessarily resolve the question as to whether the payment made to Mr. Burke was made for a corrupt purpose or otherwise, although it accepts that Mr. Gogarty's credibility as a witness would be damaged by such a finding.

14-92   Mr. Gogarty's evidence was that Mr. Murphy Jnr. had attended three meetings in Dublin during the period between the end of May 1989 and the 15th June 1989. The first of these meetings was said to have been a meeting "a couple of days" before the 8th June 1989 which took place at the premises of JMSE at Shanowen Road, Santry, and which was attended by Mr. Joseph Murphy Jnr., Mr. Frank Reynolds and Mr. James Gogarty, on behalf of the Murphy interests, and by Mr. Michael Bailey. Mr. Gogarty said that it was at this meeting that Mr. Bailey spoke of his claimed ability to procure planning permission through the assistance of Mr. Burke, and certain named county councillors and officials.

14-93   The second meeting was said to have taken place on the afternoon of the 8th June 1989 and was said to have been attended by Mr. Joseph Murphy Jnr., Mr. Frank Reynolds and Mr. James Gogarty, at which the assembled monies, intended to be paid to Mr. Burke, were counted out by Mr. Gogarty in anticipation of a visit to Mr. Burke's home on the same date, a visit which was unexpectedly called off.

14-94   The third meeting, some days after the 8th June 1989, was the meeting said to have taken place at Mr. Burke's home which was said to have been attended by Mr. Michael Bailey, Mr Joseph Murphy Jnr. and Mr. James Gogarty, at which it is said that two envelopes were passed to Mr. Burke which were believed to contain £40,000 each, the first envelope being passed over by Mr. Joseph Murphy Jnr. and the second by Mr. Michael Bailey.

14-95   The documents provided by Mr. Joseph Murphy Jnr. to the Tribunal indicated that he had been in Ireland for some time between the 31st May 1989 and the 6th June 1989, and again between the 10th June 1989 and the 12th June 1989. He could therefore have attended the first of the meetings alleged by Mr. Gogarty and the third of those meetings. Mr. Murphy Jnr.also provided to the Tribunal details of his whereabouts in Ireland in the two periods between the 31st May 1989 and the 6th June 1989 and the 10th

June 1989 and the 12th June 1989, which, if true, excluded the possibility of his attendance at either meeting.

14-96   Two significant events took place in those periods from Mr. Murphy Jnr.'s point of view; firstly a friend of his was getting married in Waterford on Saturday the 3rd June 1989 and this accounted for the first visit, and secondly Mrs. Mary Elizabeth Flynn died on the 9th June 1989 which accounted for his second visit. Persons who had been involved in, or who had attended at one or other of these two events, were called in evidence, and it was submitted on behalf of Mr. Murphy Jnr. that their evidence conclusively established that he could not have attended the 1st or 3rd alleged meetings in June as is claimed by Mr. Gogarty.

14-97   Mr. Murphy's evidence in relation to his whereabouts on the 8th June, the date of the second meeting, was that he was working in London. Evidence was given by witnesses who had telephoned him that morning in London and that night in London.

14-98   In considering the evidence of the witnesses as to Mr. Murphy Jnr.'s whereabouts the Tribunal has had regard for the fact that there had been a lapse of almost nine years between the date of the events on which they were giving evidence and their appearance in the witness box. The Tribunal has had regard to the fact that the details of the circumstances surrounding the events upon which they gave evidence were themselves of relative insignificance at the time they occurred, and consequently there was no reason for those concerned to commit the precise details of the events to memory. The Tribunal has had regard for the relationship between Mr. Joseph Murphy Jnr. and the individuals concerned which was either that of close personal friendship, or of employer and employee, in the case of the significant witnesses.

14-99   The Tribunal is satisfied that Mr. Murphy Jnr. was in Ireland during the period from the 31st May 1989 to the 6th June 1989 and that during that period he had attended the wedding in Waterford on Saturday the 3rd. However, it is clear that notwithstanding the alibi evidence offered in relation to Mr. Murphy Jnr's meetings with friends in Waterford, a meeting could have taken place with Mr. Bailey on either the 31st May or 1st June, and still have allowed Mr. Murphy Jnr. to attend his meeting in Waterford later on the 1st June.

14-100   The Tribunal is satisfied that Mr. Murphy Jnr. could have attended a meeting in Dublin on the 8th June 1989 notwithstanding the evidence that he had received telephone calls in London, both that morning and that night. A meeting could have taken place at JMSE's premises on the afternoon of the 8th June provided Mr. Murphy Jnr. had flown from London to Dublin and returned on the same day.

14-101   The Tribunal is not convinced by the alibi evidence offered to the Tribunal that Mr. Murphy Jnr. could not have attended a meeting in Dublin in the week commencing the 12th June 1989 and recognises that for such a meeting to have taken place on the 12th June it would involve a rejection of the alibi evidence offered as to Mr. Murphy Jnr's movements that day by Mr. Greene. The Tribunal believes that it is possible that Mr. Murphy Jnr. could have attended an afternoon meeting at the JMSE premises in Dublin on the 8th June but still have attended his work place in London earlier that day. If Mr. Murphy Jnr. returned to Ireland on either the 13th or 14th to attend a meeting it would involve the rejection of the evidence of Mr. Mycroft, the JMSE engineer, insofar as he believed that Mr. Murphy Jnr. was working all day in London on each of those dates.

14-102   The Tribunal is satisfied, on the balance of probabilities, that there was a series of meetings in the first two weeks of June which concerned the possible acquisition of an interest in the Murphy lands by Mr. Bailey, and that the payment to Mr. Burke was made in connection with one of these proposals. The Tribunal is satisfied that no other credible explanation for such payment is revealed by the evidence.

14-103   The letter of the 8th June 1989 from Mr. Michael Bailey to Mr. James Gogarty expressed itself to be the result of "our" many discussions regarding "your" six lots of land set out therein. The land was not Mr. Gogarty's, it was Murphy company land. Notwithstanding that this letter contains the participation proposal that involved the procuring of planning permission by Mr. Michael Bailey, he claims that no prior discussions whatsoever had taken place in relation to any participation proposal in advance of his letter of the 8th June 1989. The Tribunal rejects this evidence utterly.

14-104 Unless there had been some discussion on this possible option prior to the writing of the letter Mr. Michael Bailey would have not addressed this as an option. The proposal was novel. It involved the owners of land conceding a 50% interest in their land to a developer on the sole basis that he would procure planning permission for its development, and thereby increase its value tenfold, at least.

14-105 The Tribunal does not accept Mr. Michael Bailey's evidence that this proposal came out of the blue, and believes that his response to the Tribunal's inquiries denying that such option was discussed, was an effort to distance all Murphy personnel, other than Mr. Gogarty, from the negotiating process that preceded the letter of the 8th June 1989.

14-106 The Tribunal believes that the participation proposal reference in the letter is consistent with the existence on the part of certain Murphy elements of a preference to retain the land, as stated by Mr. Gogarty. The Tribunal is satisfied that in the letter Mr. Michael Bailey was seeking to address both Mr. Murphy Snr.'s wish for outright sale of the lands and also the wish of Mr. Murphy Jnr. that the lands be retained until their development of value could be realised.

14-107 The Tribunal concludes that it is probable that the letter of the 8th June 1989 was written by Mr. Michael Bailey for its consideration by a party in authority in JMSE who was actively considering such a proposal. Mr. Michael Bailey acknowledges that Mr. James Gogarty was never involved in discussing such a proposal with him, consequently it was probably with other directors of JMSE.

14-108 The Tribunal is satisfied that Mr. Joseph Murphy Jnr. did have a desire to retain these lands for their development potential rather than to sell them, and that he did seek Mr. Gogarty's assistance in this regard.

14-109 The Tribunal is satisfied that Mr. Michael Bailey became aware of Mr. Murphy Jnr.'s wish to capitalise on the development potential of the lands and that his proposal in the letter of the 8th June 1989 addressed this issue.

14-110 The Tribunal believes that it is probable that Mr. Joseph Murphy Jnr. discussed the participation proposal with Mr. Michael Bailey prior to the 8th June 1989.

14-111 The Tribunal is satisfied that Mr. Gogarty's use of the term "a couple of days" was intended to encompass an un-defined period extending up to one week. The Tribunal believes that such a meeting could have taken place on the 31st May or the 1st June 1989, and that following that meeting, Mr. Bailey made his formal proposal in writing which encapsulated these already discussed proposals, but in a sanitised form, which omitted reference by name to the politicians, and others, whose services would be used to achieve the objective.

14-112 The Tribunal believes that the hand written letter of the 8th June 1989, from Mr. Gogarty to Mr. Joseph Murphy Snr., that purported to enclose a copy of Mr. Michael Bailey's letter of the 8th June to him, was written on the 8th June 1989 as claimed by him, and was received by Mr. Murphy Snr. and considered by him. The Tribunal rejects Mr. Murphy Snr.'s evidence that he never received correspondence in Guernsey from Mr. Gogarty. Mr. Murphy Snr. maintained a staffed office at St. Sampson Guernsey where records of his various business ventures were kept.

14-113 The Tribunal is satisfied that Mr. Joseph Murphy Snr. was personally in control of all aspects of the Murphy land companies in June 1989, and that any discussion in relation to the sale or joint development of these lands would have to be brought to his attention. The role of Mr. Gogarty was as a functionary only. He had to report to Mr. Murphy Snr. for instructions on the content of Mr. Michael Bailey's letter before responding to the proposals contained therein. There was no reason for Mr. Gogarty not to acquaint Mr. Murphy Snr. with the content of the letter. The Tribunal believes that Mr. Joseph Murphy Snr. was at all times made aware of the Bailey proposals including the proposal which involved the procuring of planning permission for these lands in return for 50% of their value, and that he agreed to consider such a proposal.

14-114 The Tribunal believes that Mr. Gogarty attended the various meetings with Mr. Bailey as the eyes and the ears of Mr. Murphy Snr., but that any proposals advanced at such a meeting would require Mr.

Murphy Snr.'s approval before implementation could take place. Mr. Joseph Murphy Jnr. and Mr. Frank Reynolds represented an untried management team as far as Mr. Murphy Snr. was concerned, and the Tribunal is satisfied that Mr. Gogarty was sent to the meeting at Mr. Burke's house by Mr. Murphy Snr. as his observer of the transaction.

14-115 The Tribunal is satisfied that the letter of the 8th June 1989 to Mr. Gogarty from Mr. Michael Bailey, and the payment to Mr. Burke shortly thereafter, are directly linked. The fact that the General Election was to take place seven days later, with a weekend intervening between these two dates, left very little time for any formal agreement to be drawn up, and signed, between the respective companies if the payment to Mr. Burke was to be made, before the date of the General Election.

14-116 The Tribunal is satisfied that pressure was applied on the Murphy interests by Mr. Michael Bailey to make the payment in advance of the General Election. The precise date of the meeting at which Mr. Burke was paid cannot be fixed with certainty, but the Tribunal concludes, on the balance of probabilities, that it took place in the week commencing 12th June 1989.

14-117 In weighing the evidence of the alibi witnesses in the totality of the evidence surrounding the making of the payment to Mr. Burke, the Tribunal concludes that the alibi evidence does not prove that Mr. Joseph Murphy Jnr. could not have attended at least three meetings in Dublin between the 31st May and the 15th June 1989.

THE SLUSH FUND

14-118 Mr. Gogarty maintained that during the period in which Mr. Conroy controlled the Murphy companies a fund existed through which unauthorised payments were made to the executives of the company, and to others. He referred to this as a slush fund, although he credited Mr. Frank Reynolds as being the person who gave it that name. Mr. Reynolds denied this. It was put to Mr. Gogarty by those disputing his account of events this was yet another example of wild and unsubstantiated allegations being made to damage the Murphy company interests.

14-119 The Tribunal is satisfied that there was evidence which would have allowed Mr. Gogarty to conclude that funds of JMSE were being misappropriated during the period in which the company was controlled by Mr. Conroy. Unknown to Mr. Gogarty, the terms upon which Mr. Conroy had been engaged in 1983 contained a provision whereby he would receive not only an annual salary of £20,000 per annum as director of Lajos Holdings Limited, but also an additional annual management fee of £30,000 which would be paid to a company, ProEng Limited, otherwise ProEng Consultants Limited (ProEng), by the Murphy companies receiving the benefit of Mr. Conroy's services. This was a Guernsey based entity, wholly owned by Mr. Conroy, which invoiced Murphy companies on a monthly basis.

14-120 The Tribunal is satisfied that Mr. Gogarty learned of payments made by JMSE to ProEng as a result of information provided to him by Mr. Frank Reynolds, and that he communicated the details thereof to Mr. Murphy Snr. in Guernsey in the belief that he was providing him with details of unauthorised misappropriation of the company's funds by the then management.

14-121 The Tribunal is satisfied that Mr. Murphy Snr. never informed Mr. Gogarty that he had in fact reached agreement with Mr. Conroy whereby he was to receive a substantial part of his remuneration through this means. The Tribunal is satisfied that Mr. Gogarty's assumption that these sums amounted to misappropriation was reasonably based given that there was no evidence of ProEng Limited or ProEng Consultants Limited having provided any service to the Murphy company, which merited this expenditure.

14-122 The Tribunal accepts that these unexplained payments to a Guernsey entity represented a legitimate concern to Mr. Gogarty as to the manner in which Mr. Conroy and his management team were conducting the business of JMSE. The Tribunal accepts the evidence of Mr. Frank Reynolds that during the course of Mr. Gogarty's management of the company he was assiduous in ensuring that expenses were kept to a minimum, even to the extent of his taking his own sandwiches with him on business trips rather than charging the company, and it must have been galling for him to have seen these apparently unjustified payments being made to an entity which, as far as he was concerned, had not provided any service whatsoever to the company.

14-123 Mr. Marcus Sweeney, who had taken over from Mr. Gogarty as Managing Director of JMSE in the changes introduced by Mr. Liam Conroy, was at all times aware that Mr. Conroy's services were being partially remunerated by way of payments on foot of invoices generated by ProEng Consultants Limited, and as far as he was aware Mr. Murphy Snr. had authorised this method of remuneration for him. Accordingly he authorised the Pro-Eng payments as required. As far as he was concerned the Murphy companies had businesses in Guernsey, and Mr. Conroy provided services to those companies in Guernsey also. He saw nothing unusual in the fact that the invoices were generated in Guernsey, or the payment made to Guernsey. The Tribunal is satisfied that from the information available to Mr. Sweeney he was entitled to assume that these were legitimate charges, and that there was no question of these payments amounting to unauthorised dispositions of company funds.

14-124 The Tribunal is satisfied that Mr. Gogarty was never made aware of this arrangement with Mr. Conroy, and that he learned of the existence of the ProEng payments as a result of material which was being provided to him by Mr. Frank Reynolds, who was equally unaware of the circumstances in which Mr. Murphy Snr. had agreed to pay £30,000 per annum to Mr. Conroy, through ProEng Limited.

14-125 In addition to his remuneration through ProEng Limited the Tribunal is satisfied that Mr. Conroy was receiving sums of between £40 and £60 per week, which were paid directly to his secretary. Mr. Downes, the in-house accountant, was instrumental in making these payments. The Tribunal is satisfied that he brought the fact of these payments to the attention of Mr. Sweeney and at that Mr. Downes kept a record of such payments, which was ultimately handed over to Mr. Roger Copsey prior to the termination of Mr. Downes' employment with JMSE. The Tribunal is not aware whether these payments had been sanctioned by Mr. Murphy Snr., but is satisfied that even if they were not specifically authorised, the fact of such payments is not material in considering whether a slush fund, in the sense of a fund used to pay politicians and others, was maintained by the Murphy companies during Mr. Conroy's time. The Tribunal is satisfied that the weekly cash payments made to Mr. Conroy's secretary were made for Mr. Conroy's personal benefit and not for onward transmission to others.

14-126 Because of Mr. Gogarty's animosity toward Mr. Conroy and his management team, Mr. Gogarty never raised these issues with them, but merely passed on the information which he had received from Mr. Reynolds to Mr. Murphy Snr. in the belief that he was producing evidence of wrong-doing on the part of Mr. Conroy and his Managers.

14-127 The Tribunal is satisfied that Mr. Sweeney and Mr. Downes acted at all times in the belief that these payments to Mr. Conroy and ProEng were authorised by the owners of the company and had valid grounds for doing so. The Tribunal is satisfied that had Mr. Murphy Snr. provided details to Mr. Gogarty of the agreement he had reached with Mr. Conroy in 1983, that Mr. Gogarty would have accepted that these payments were not misappropriations of the company's funds by Mr. Conroy. Mr. Murphy Snr. chose to keep Mr. Gogarty in the dark about the terms upon which he had engaged Mr. Conroy.

14-128 The Tribunal finds no evidence that Mr. Gogarty was engaged in making wild or unsubstantiated allegations against his employers.

Chapter 15

The Participation Proposal and Payment of Monies to Mr. Burke

THE PARTICIPATION PROPOSAL CONTAINED IN MR. MICHAEL BAILEY'S LETTER OF THE 8TH JUNE, 1989

15-01   Mr. Michael Bailey's participation proposal involved Lots 1-5 inclusive of the 6 lots of land that were for sale by the Murphy companies at that time. Mr. Bailey calculated the acreage of the 5 lots at 717 acres, and proposed he would be given a 50% interest in these lands in return for his participation. The 'participation' envisaged by him involved him expending up to £150,000 on professional fees etc, in respect of Lots 1,2 and 3 and a similar expenditure in respect of Lots 4 and 5. It envisaged that he would give exclusively of his time and efforts over the 2 years involved in Lots 1,2 and 3 and the 3 years involved in Lots 4 and 5. In justifying his entitlement to share equally in this substantial land holding, Mr. Bailey's letter expressly referred to the fact that the steps to be taken on the way to procuring a buildable planning permission and Building Bye-Law approval are "notoriously difficult, time consuming and expensive".

15-02   On its face the reward which Mr. Michael Bailey expected to receive for his efforts, and correspondingly the cost to the Murphys of the services he would provide, would appear to constitute a disproportionate reward for the efforts which would be required to achieve that end. In principle the Murphy companies could themselves have engaged professional planning advisers and other experts to process any application to alter the planning status of the lands at a fraction of the cost, which would be involved in agreeing to Mr. Bailey's proposal. His proposal envisaged their ceding 50% of the value of their lands to him.

15-03   Whilst Mr. Michael Bailey was reluctant to put any value on any particular parcel of the 5 lots of land involved in the proposal, the Tribunal is satisfied that at a minimum a tenfold increase in the value of the lands would result from their being altered from agricultural land to buildable development land. In the same letter Mr. Bailey stated he was prepared to pay £30,000 per acre for the lands in lot 6 in the event that he obtained planning permission, and the Tribunal notes that he had paid almost £60,000 per acre for the Forrest road lands which he had bought in 1988 from the Murphy interests. Even taking the lower of these valuations the potential value of the Murphy lands, in the event that Mr. Bailey was successful in his endeavours, was £21.5 million of which he would receive £10 25 million.

15-04   The Tribunal believes that Mr. Michael Bailey's participation proposal is only comprehensible if it was the case that he was offering to secure a benefit which would not otherwise be obtainable by the Murphys without his assistance. Mr. Michael Bailey's plan to alter the status of the lands from "agricultural lands with a very limited potential, even for agricultural use" to "highly valuable building land" was dependent upon his ability to influence Dublin County Councillors so as to ensure that material contravention motions were passed. The Tribunal is satisfied that what Mr. Michael Bailey was offering to the Murphy interests was his unique ability to influence Dublin County Councillors where others could not.

15-05   The Tribunal is satisfied that the Murphy interests were prepared to agree to this participation proposal, notwithstanding that it involved their conceding a 50% interest in the lands, because they would still receive at least 5 times more than the agricultural value of the lands if his plan was successful. If it was the case that Mr. Michael Bailey could secure planning permission through bribery or political influence over Councillors in circumstances where planning permission would otherwise be refused, there is a certain logic in the participation proposal as advanced in the letter of 8th June 1989.

15-06   The Tribunal is satisfied that the letter of the 8th June 1989 addressed to Mr. Gogarty was a sanitised version of the proposal which had already been advanced by Mr. Michael Bailey, at least one week earlier, when he had named Mr. Burke as one of the persons who could be relied on to achieve this end.

THE ABANDONMENT OF THE PARTICIPATION PROPOSAL

15-07   The Tribunal is satisfied that the Murphy interests paid Mr. Burke as part of their agreement to proceed with the participation proposal which was advanced by Mr. Michael Bailey at the earlier meeting, and which appears in its sanitised form in the letter of the 8th June 1989 addressed to Mr. Gogarty. The decision to pay money to Mr. Burke was taken in haste in view of the imminent General Election on the 15th June 1989. The sale of the lands at that time was not an immediate priority of Mr. Joseph Murphy Snr.

15-08   The Tribunal is satisfied that, on a date unknown, prior to the 10th July 1989, Mr. Murphy Snr. changed his mind on the participation proposal, and this rejection prompted Mr. Michael Bailey to make a further offer for the outright purchase of the lands by letter of the 10th July 1989.

15-09   The Tribunal is satisfied that a copy of this letter of offer was also sent to Mr. Murphy Snr. and to Mr. Copsey by Mr. Gogarty, although Mr. Murphy Snr. claimed he never received any correspondence from Mr. Gogarty. The evidence of Mr. Gogarty was that the reason for Mr. Murphy Snr's change of heart was panic on his part in the light of the contents of affidavits sworn by Mr. Liam Conroy, the former chief executive of the Murphy group, in proceedings commenced by him against the Murphy interests in the Isle of Man.

15-10   The Tribunal has concluded that Mr. Gogarty's belief that Mr. Murphy Snr. panicked, and that this is the explanation for the change of heart, is probably incorrect, although it may be a legitimately held belief of Mr. Gogarty. There was litigation in the Isle of Man, between Mr. Conroy and the Murphy trusts, in the course of which Mr. Conroy made a series of allegations of Revenue wrongdoing on Mr. Murphy Snr.'s part. If these allegations were true, and if the Revenue authorities pursued Mr. Murphy Snr. and succeeded in establishing the truth of these matters, there could have been very significant financial consequences for Mr. Murphy Snr. and the Murphy companies, which had for many years enjoyed favourable tax treatment through the use of offshore trusts.

15-11   Whilst Mr. Murphy Snr. in his evidence dismissed Mr. Conroy's allegations as the baseless accusations of a fantasist and of no concern to him, the Tribunal is satisfied that the fact of such allegations being made against him was a matter of concern to him, as evidenced by the lengths to which he went to ensure that all records of these allegations were destroyed once he had reached a satisfactory financial settlement with Mr. Conroy.

15-12   The Tribunal does not believe, however, that this concern was the motivating factor in Mr. Joseph Murphy Snr.'s decision to sell the Irish lands or his decision not to proceed to enter into a participation proposal with Mr. Michael Bailey.

15-13   The Tribunal is satisfied that since 1988 Mr. Murphy Snr. had been engaged in a radical review of his business interests and land holdings both in Ireland and in England. The removal of Mr. Liam Conroy from office was followed by the resignation and/or removal of a sizeable number of managers and directors in the Murphy group. With the advice of his strategy committee Mr. Murphy Snr. was considering selling off, not only his Irish landholdings, but also the Murphy core companies in the U.K. In the end he sold off only the land-owning companies assets. The Tribunal does not consider it significant that Mr. Gogarty's stated reason for the change of heart on Mr. Murphy Snr.'s part is probably incorrect. Nor does it reflect upon his credibility as a witness. It is clear that Mr. Murphy Snr. did not share his concerns on all issues with Mr. Gogarty, and that he did not bring him into his confidence when discussing the financial outlook for the Murphy group with his strategy committee in 1989.

15-14   The Tribunal is satisfied that Mr. Murphy Snr. had been sorely disappointed by the manner in which his trust in Mr. Conroy had been misplaced, and that he had a reluctance to enter into any further commercial transactions in which he would be dependent upon the activities of others for the success of the scheme.

15-15   The Tribunal is satisfied that it was for this reason that he decided not to proceed with a participation proposal with Mr. Michael Bailey who was a relatively unknown quantity.

15-16   The Tribunal is satisfied that the disputes which arose at the JMSE board meeting of the 3rd July 1989 with Mr. Gogarty, served to further illustrate to Mr. Murphy Snr. the difficulties which can arise even between former close associates. Despite the advices of Mr. Roger Copsey, and the request of Mr. Murphy Snr., Mr. Gogarty was refusing to sign off on the 1988 accounts of JMSE, and was creating difficulties between the Irish and English members of the board. The Tribunal is satisfied that the attraction of a straight sale of the lands, rather than involvement in a protracted scheme which was dependent on the activities of others, tilted the balance in favour of Mr. Murphy Snr. deciding to sell the lands outright, and not to proceed with the participation proposal advanced by Mr. Michael Bailey.

15-17   Whilst the apparent effect of adopting this course was to forfeit the money already paid to Mr. Burke, the Tribunal does not consider this to have been of any significant importance since Mr. Murphy Snr. was in a position to recoup such expenditure in the sale price of the land to the ultimate purchaser.

The precise reason why Mr. Murphy Snr. changed his mind and sold the land is immaterial in considering why Mr. Burke had been paid JMSE's money some weeks earlier. The Tribunal is satisfied it does not afford a key to establishing the credibility or otherwise of Mr. Gogarty to pronounce upon whether he was correct or incorrect in his belief as to Mr. Murphy Snr's reasons for the sale of the land.

WAS THE JMSE PAYMENT TO MR. BURKE £30,000 OR £40,000?

15-18   Mr. Gogarty's evidence was that the parties to the participation proposal had agreed to pay Mr. Burke a sum of £80,000, made up of two equal payment of £40,000 each from the Murphy and Bailey interests. He said that the JMSE contribution actually paid to Mr. Burke was £40,000, which was made up of £30,000 in cash and a £10,000 cheque drawn on the JMSE account at AIB, Talbot Street.

15-19   The Tribunal is satisfied that it has identified £30,000 of JMSE funds which were paid to Mr. Burke from the proceeds of the JMSE current account at AIB, Talbot Street. This £30,000 left the JMSE account in two separate transactions. The first involved the encashment of the cheque for £20,000 on the 8th June, 1989, the date upon which the cheque was probably written. The second involved the debiting of the account with the sum of £10,000 on the 22nd June 1989 when the cheque for £10,000, which was written on the 8th June 1989, was cleared through the account.

15-20   Mr. Gogarty's evidence was that he had counted out the cash element of the JMSE contribution whilst at the office of JMSE in the afternoon of the 8th June, 1989, and he was reasonably satisfied having done so that the cash element of the intended donation to Mr. Burke was £30,000. He said that he was asked to countersign a cheque for £10,000 drawn upon the AIB account at Talbot Street to make up the balance of the agreed payment. If Mr. Gogarty's recollection is accurate, it follows that the Murphy interests must have had available to them on the 8th June, 1989 £10,000 in cash prior to any sums being withdrawn from the AIB account at Talbot Street. Whilst the fact that Mr. Copsey made a request of Mr. McArdle that day for £30,000, preferably £20,000 in cash and £10,000 by way of cheque, and the fact that there is evidence of a £30,000 lodgment to Mr. Burke's account, suggests that the JMSE payment to Mr. Burke was £30,000, and not £40,000, it does not necessarily follow that this was the case. If £10,000 in cash was available already this would explain why Mr. Copsey only required a further £30,000 to make up the balance of an agreed payment of £40,000.

15-21   Prior to the setting up of the Tribunal, Mr. Burke stated that he had received the £30,000 in cash. He did not say that he had received £20,000 in cash and a cheque for £10,000. However, once he had been provided with copies of the JMSE bank accounts by the Tribunal he changed his mind, and by process of deduction, concluded that he must have received only £20,000 in cash, since it seemingly appeared from the discovered documents that he had received a cheque for £10,000 from JMSE which he believed was lodged to his account on the 19th of June, 1989. Mr. Burke had no clear recollection as to the composition of the payment made to him, but was absolutely clear that the total sum was £30,000 and not £40,000 as claimed by Mr. Gogarty.

15-22   The Tribunal is satisfied that whilst a cash payment of £20,000 was in itself extraordinary in 1989 a cash payment of £30,000 was even more extraordinary. Mr. Burke counted out the money, which was paid to him by JMSE, and the Tribunal considers it remarkable that he did not remember precisely the sum that he counted out in cash that day. The Tribunal considers it equally remarkable that he would have publicly acknowledged receiving £30,000 in cash, if in fact he had only received £20,000 in cash, and the balance by way of cheque.

15-23   Whilst the Tribunal is satisfied that £20,000 in cash was sourced from AIB, Talbot Street and was paid to Mr. Burke with a £10,000 cheque drawn on the same bank, it has not found another £10,000 cash withdrawal from the account of any of the Murphy companies at that time. In its effort to trace the source of the funds available to the Murphy interests in Ireland in June 1989, the Tribunal made an order for discovery and production against Mr. Joseph Murphy Snr., to which he responded by swearing an affidavit deposing to the fact that he had not maintained any bank accounts in Ireland from 1976 onwards. Mr. Murphy Snr. reiterated this statement in the course of giving his evidence on commission in Guernsey in 1999. This was untrue. Mr. Murphy Snr. had maintained bank accounts in Ireland throughout the 1970's, and in to the late 1980's, in which very substantial sums of cash were held on deposit. These accounts were initially in the name of Mr. Murphy Snr. and his wife Una, and were subsequently in the name of his wife Una and his children, Angela and Joseph. Ms. Angela Murphy and Mr. Joseph Murphy Jnr. may not have been aware at that time that they were named account holders with Mrs. Una Murphy

15-24   The last of these accounts were held at the AIB Bank in Dublin. This account was closed in March 1989 with a withdrawal of approximately £74,000 that was transferred from the account to a company named Sybex Limited. The Tribunal is satisfied on the balance of probabilities that Mr. Joseph Murphy Snr. actively concealed the existence of these bank accounts from the Tribunal. The question as to whether or not he did or did not maintain bank accounts in Ireland during the 1970's and 80's was an issue which had been raised in the course of the proceedings brought against him by Mr. Liam Conroy in 1989. The Tribunal is satisfied, on the balance of probabilities, that the existence or otherwise of these accounts was a matter which was discussed by Mr. Murphy Snr. with his then lawyers in 1989. The Tribunal does not believe that Mr. Murphy Snr.'s physical infirmities in 1999 in any way compromised his ability to deal with the issue raised by the Tribunal as to whether or not he did maintain bank accounts in Ireland in 1976 and thereafter. The Tribunal is satisfied that Mr. Murphy Snr. had sources of funds available to him in Ireland in June 1989 from which a sum of £10,000 in cash could have been sourced which was not discovered to the Tribunal.

15-25   The fact that a corresponding lodgment for £40,000 is not found in Mr. Burke's accounts for the months of June or July 1989 is not considered by the Tribunal to be conclusive evidence that a £40,000 payment was not made from Murphy funds to him. Mr. Burke's accounts for the period showed that sums in excess of £30,000 were lodged to accounts in his name and in the joint name of himself and his wife, but it has not been possible to specifically establish the source of all of the funds which comprised the individual lodgments made to these accounts. The withdrawal of £30,000 from the accounts of JMSE at AIB, Talbot Street in June 1989 is roughly contemporaneous with lodgments to Mr. Burke's accounts which may have included some, or all, of the £30,000 identified as having left the JMSE accounts during the same period, but the Tribunal is not satisfied that the evidence proves that any of the JMSE funds were lodged to Mr. Burke's discovered accounts.

15-26   The Tribunal accepts the possibility that Mr. Burke may have received £40,000 of Murphy funds comprising £30,000 in cash and a cheque for £10,000, of which £20,000 of the cash element came from JMSE via AIB, Talbot Street, and the balance of £10,000 in cash came from another unidentified Murphy source. The Tribunal does not believe that its inability to pronounce with certainty upon the actual amount of the JMSE payment affects its ability to reach its conclusion as to why the money was paid to Mr. Burke on that occasion. The Tribunal is satisfied that Mr. Burke was paid not less than £30,000 of JMSE's money and that he may have been paid £40,000.

SUMMARY/CONCLUSIONS

Chapter 16

Summary of Conclusions

BRIARGATE

16-01   Mr. Burke did not purchase his home at Briargate Malahide Swords from Oakpark Developments Limited in 1973 in a normal commercial transaction.

16-02   The consideration (if any) passing between Mr. Burke and the directors of Oakpark Developments Limited, Mr. Tom Brennan and Mr. Jack Foley, for the dwelling house and lands at Briargate did not represent the open market value of the property.

16-03   The assignment of Briargate by Oakpark Developments Limited to Mr. Burke conferred a substantial benefit upon him which in the opinion of the Tribunal was given in order to ensure that he would act in the best interests of Oakpark Developments Limited's director, Mr. Tom Brennan and his associates when performing his public duties as a member of Dublin County Council and a member of Dáil Éireann.

16-04   The Tribunal has been unable to discover what actions Mr. Burke performed for Mr. Tom Brennan or his associates in return for the benefit provided to him. It is the opinion of the Tribunal and the Tribunal concludes that the benefit which was conferred upon Mr. Burke was conferred in circumstances which gave rise to a reasonable inference that the motives for making and receiving this benefit were connected with the public office held by Mr. Burke.

16-05   In the opinion of the Tribunal the transfer of Briargate to Mr. Burke amounted to a corrupt payment to him from Mr. Tom Brennan and his associates.

OFFSHORE BANK ACCOUNTS

16-06   The accounts opened for Mr. Burke at AIB Bank (Isle of Man) Limited in the name of Mr. P. D. Burke in 1982, and at Hill Samuel & Company (Jersey) Limited in the name of Caviar Limited in 1984, were opened in order to receive payments from Mr. Tom Brennan and his associates, which were not the proceeds of political fundraising activities or political donations from Mr. Tom Brennan, but were payments made to Mr. Burke in order to ensure that he would continue to act in the best interests of those who had paid him when performing his public duties as a member of Dublin County Council, and as a member of Dáil Éireann.

16-07   The payment of stg. £50,000 by Kalabraki Limited to the account of Mr. P. D. Burke at AIB Bank (Isle of Man) Limited on the 21st of December 1982 was a corrupt payment made by Mr. Tom Brennan to Mr. Burke.

16-08   The payment of stg. £35,000 to the account of Caviar Limited at Hill Samuel & Company (Jersey) Limited per Allied Irish Bank on the 19th of April 1984 was a corrupt payment to Mr. Burke probably made by Mr. Tom Brennan and his associates.

16-09   The payment of stg. £60,000 to the account of Caviar Limited by Canio Limited on the 21st of November 1984 was a corrupt payment to Mr. Burke which was funded to an amount of stg £25,000 each by Mr. Tom Brennan and Mr. Joseph McGowan, and to an amount of stg £10,000 by Mr. John Finnegan.

16-10 The payment of stg £15,000 to the account of Caviar Limited by Canio Limited on the 19ᵗʰ April 1985 was a corrupt payment to Mr. Burke which was funded jointly by Mr. Tom Brennan and Mr. Joseph McGowan.

16-11 The Tribunal has been unable to discover what specific action Mr. Burke took to advance the interests of those who had paid him these monies which were lodged to his offshore accounts at AIB Bank (Isle of Man) Limited and at Hill Samuel & Company (Jersey) Limited, but is satisfied on the balance of probabilities, that he acted in their interests in the performance of his public duties.

CENTURY RADIO

16-12 The Ministerial Directive obliging RTÉ to provide its facilities to Century issued by Mr. Burke as Minster for Communications on the 14ᵗʰ March 1989, was issued to advance the private interests of the promoters of Century and not to serve the public interest.

16-13 The payment of £35,000 to Mr. Burke by Mr. Barry on the 26ᵗʰ May 1989 was a corrupt payment made in response to a demand for £30,000 cash by Mr. Burke, and was not intended by Mr. Barry to be a political donation to Mr. Burke or to Fianna Fáil.

16-14 In proposing legislation which would have had the effect of curbing RTÉ's advertising, altering the format of 2FM, and diverting broadcasting licence fee income from RTÉ to independent broadcasters, Mr. Burke was acting in response to demands made of him by the promoters of Century and was not serving the public interest.

16-15 The payment of £35,000 to Mr. Burke by Mr. Barry ensured that he was available to serve the interests of Century's promoters, as is evidenced by his willingness to meet with their bankers and to give them assurances that he would take steps, including, if necessary, the introduction of legislation which would be to Century's financial benefit.

PAYMENT TO MR. BURKE AT BRIARGATE, SWORDS IN THE WEEK PRIOR TO THE 15ᵀᴴ JUNE 1989

16-16 The meeting at Mr. Burke's home at Briargate, Swords, Co. Dublin, in the week prior to the 15ᵗʰ June 1989, was specifically arranged by Mr. Michael Bailey and Mr. Burke so as to allow for the payment of money to be made to Mr. Burke. The meeting was not arranged in order to receive a political donation, but was arranged for the purpose of paying Mr. Burke money to ensure his support, and his influence over others, so as to achieve the alteration of the planning status of the Murphy company's North Dublin lands, described as lots 1-6 in Mr. Bailey's letter of the 8ᵗʰ June 1989 addressed to Mr. Gogarty.

16-17 The parties present at the meeting were Mr. Burke, Mr. Michael Bailey, Mr. Joseph Murphy Jnr., and Mr. James Gogarty.

16-18 The Murphy executives present at the meeting believed that the JMSE payment which was passed in a closed envelope by Mr. Joseph Murphy Jnr. to Mr. Burke was being matched by an equal payment from Mr. Michael Bailey contained in an envelope which they observed being passed by Mr. Michael Bailey to Mr. Burke.

16-19 The meeting took place with the prior knowledge of Mr. Joseph Murphy Snr., Mr. Frank Reynolds, and Mr. Roger Copsey, each of whom was aware that it was intended to pay Mr. Burke £80,000 in order to ensure his support in achieving the intended changes in the planning status of the Murphy's North Dublin lands, which were at that time the subject of a participation proposal, which if concluded, would have resulted in Mr. Michael Bailey receiving a 50% interest in the Murphy's North Dublin lands.

16-20 Mr. Joseph Murphy Snr. was the ultimate decision maker when it came to either selling the lands or entering into the participation proposal with Mr. Bailey.

16-21 On a date subsequent to the 3ʳᵈ July 1989 and prior to the 10ᵗʰ July 1989 Mr. Joseph Murphy Snr. decided not to enter into the participation proposal envisaged by Mr. Michael Bailey, but to sell the lands outright.

16-22 The role of Mr. James Gogarty was that of a functionary only, and all actions taken by him in connection with the sale of the lands, the participation proposal, and the attendance at Mr. Burke's home, were taken by him at the request of Mr. Joseph Murphy Snr.

16-23 Mr. Burke assured those present at the time of the payment of monies to him that he understood that the payment was being made in connection with the proposal to alter the planning status of the Murphy lands and further assured those present that he would honour his commitment to do so.

16-24 The payment received by Mr. Burke amounted to a corrupt payment and all present at the meeting were aware that it was such.

Chapter 17

Co-Operation with the Tribunal

17-01 All parties from whom the Tribunal legitimately sought information had an obligation to provide such information truthfully and expeditiously. The provision of misleading information or the withholding of relevant information has the capacity to hinder and obstruct the Tribunal, and inevitably leads to delay. The conduct of a statutory public inquiry is a complex and costly exercise, and this Tribunal has endeavoured to carry out its statutory functions with expedition and as economically as possible, so as to comply with the express wishes of the Oireachtas contained within its Terms of Reference.

17-02 This Tribunal continues its work more than four and a half years after its inception, not only because of the multiplicity and complexity of matters which it is obliged to investigate under its Terms of Reference, but also because of the failure of persons who have been required to provide information to the Tribunal, either documentary or otherwise, to provide such information expeditiously or, in some instances, at all.

17-03 Any person, duly summoned to do so, who gives evidence to the Tribunal which is material to its inquiry, which that person willfully knows to be false or does not believe to be true or who by act or omission obstructs or hinders a Tribunal in the performance of its functions, commits a criminal offence.

17-04 There is an obligation upon every witness called to the Tribunal to give a truthful account of the matters upon which they are questioned, and failure to do so can amount to a failure to cooperate with the Tribunal, which can have serious consequences both as regards costs, and otherwise. In its review of the evidence proffered to the Tribunal in the modules in which the Tribunal has heard evidence to date, the Tribunal has concluded that the following persons and corporate entities have hindered, obstructed or not cooperated with the Tribunal to the extent set out hereunder. The findings made against Mr. Joseph Murphy Snr and Mr. Joseph Murphy Jnr. apply pari passu to the companies within the Murphy Group to whom legal representation was granted including Joseph Murphy Structural Engineers Limited, Lajos Holdings Limited, The Grafton Construction Company Limited, Reliable Construction (Dublin) Limited, Barrett Developments Limited (in Liquidation), Turvey Estates Limited, Finglas Industrial Developments Limited (in Liquidation), Helmdale Limited (in Liquidation), Gaiety Stage Production Limited, Gaiety Theatre (Dublin) Limited, Finglas Industrial Estates Limited and Wexburn Limited. The findings made against Mr. Michael Bailey, Mr. Tom Bailey and Mrs. Caroline Bailey apply equally to Bovale Developments Limited.

THE BRENNAN & MCGOWAN MODULE

Mr. Ray Burke

17-05 In this module the Tribunal is satisfied that Mr. Burke obstructed and hindered the Tribunal by:

(a) Failing to provide the Tribunal with a truthful account of the circumstances in which he came to acquire ownership of the property known as Briargate, Malahide Road, Swords, Co. Dublin.

(b) Furnishing an account, as to how he had financed the acquisition of the property, which he knew to be false.

(c) Failing to provide the Tribunal with a truthful account as to why he had opened offshore bank accounts in the Isle of Man and in Jersey, Channel Islands.

(d) Falsely maintaining that the offshore accounts opened by him were opened to receive the proceeds of political fundraising events in the United Kingdom when he knew that this was not the true source of the funds so deposited.

(e) Falsely representing that a sum of £15,000, lodged to his Jersey account in April 1985, was a re-lodgement of funds earlier withdrawn from the same account at a time when he knew this to be false.

(f) Colluding with Mr. Tom Brennan and Mr. Joseph McGowan to give false accounts as to how the funds lodged to his offshore accounts had been paid into his accounts and as to the source of these funds.

(g) Failing to give a truthful account of the real purposes for which these monies were paid by Mr. Brennan, Mr. McGowan, Mr. Finnegan and companies related to them.

Mr. Tom Brennan and Mr. Joseph McGowan

17-06 The Tribunal is satisfied that these two witnesses colluded in their evidence, and that the evidence of each was adopted as accurate by the other. The Tribunal believes that these witnesses obstructed and hindered the Tribunal by:

(a) Failing to give the Tribunal a truthful account of the circumstances in which their monies were paid to Mr. Burke outside the jurisdiction.
(b) Falsely maintaining that the monies paid to Mr. Burke were the proceeds of fundraising activities in the U.K. at a time when they knew this not to be the case.
(c) Failing to give the Tribunal a truthful account of the real purpose for which these monies were paid to Mr. Burke.
(d) Colluding with Mr. Burke to give a false account as to how these funds were raised so as to prevent the Tribunal from establishing the true source and purpose for such payments.
(e) Failing to give the Tribunal a truthful account as to the real purpose for which offshore corporate entities were maintained by them from which monies were paid to Mr. Burke.
(f) Failing to give the Tribunal a truthful account of the nature and extent of their dealings with Bedell Cristin Advocates.
(g) Failing to provide the Tribunal with a truthful account of their relationship with Mr. John Finnegan and the land transactions which resulted in £2,661,875.96 being sent to Jersey.

Mr. John Finnegan

17-07 The Tribunal is satisfied that Mr. John Finnegan obstructed and hindered the Tribunal by:

(a) Failing to provide a truthful account of the circumstances in which £10,000, from a fund beneficially owned by him, was paid to Mr. Ray Burke in November 1984.
(b) Falsely maintaining that the £10,000 payment to Mr. Burke was a sum which was intended to be paid to a fund for the provision of future expenses by Canio Limited at a time when he knew this to be false.
(c) Failing to give a truthful account of the circumstances in which Canio Limited was formed, or of the nature and extent of his dealings with Mr. Tom Brennan Mr. Joseph McGowan and their related companies.
(d) Failing to make proper discovery of documents to the Tribunal.
(e) Failing to provide the Tribunal with a truthful account of the purposes for which the Amber Trust and Foxtown Investments Limited had been formed.

Mr. John Caldwell

17-08 The Tribunal is satisfied that Mr. Caldwell, the legal adviser to Mr. Tom Brennan and to Brennan and McGowan related companies from the 1980s was in a position to provide information which could have assisted the Tribunal in establishing the nature and extent of Brennan and McGowan activities in the Channel Islands. The Tribunal is satisfied that Mr. Caldwell failed to co-operate with the Tribunal by:

(a) Failing to provide a proper Affidavit of Discovery in compliance with an Order for Discovery and Production made against him on the 4th April 2001.

(b) Failing to comply with an Order for Discovery made against him on the 10th August 2001.

(c) Failing to comply with a witness summons requiring his attendance at a public session of the Tribunal on the 27th September 2001.

Mr. Hugh V. Owens

17-09   Mr. Owens was an accountant and adviser to Messrs. Brennan and McGowan. The Tribunal is satisfied that he failed to co-operate with the Tribunal by failing to provide a full explanation of the schemes which he had devised for Messrs. Brennan and McGowan in relation to the land transactions with which they were involved with Mr. Finnegan and which resulted in funds being distributed in Jersey from which Mr. Burke received stg £60,000 in November 1984.

THE CENTURY RADIO MODULE

Mr. Ray Burke

17-10   In relation to this module the Tribunal is satisfied that Mr. Burke obstructed and hindered the Tribunal by:

(a) Failing to give a truthful account of the circumstances and considerations which led to his issuing a Directive pursuant to Section 16 of the Radio and Television Act 1988, on the 14th March 1989, fixing the level of transmission charges to be paid to RTÉ by Century.

(b) Failing to give a truthful account of the circumstances which led to the payment to him of a sum of £35,000 by Mr. Oliver Barry in May 1989.

(c) Failing to give a truthful account as to the circumstances and considerations which led to the introduction by him of legislation to curb RTÉ's advertising revenue in 1990.

Mr. Oliver Barry

17-11   The Tribunal is satisfied that Mr. Oliver Barry obstructed and hindered the Tribunal by:

(a) Failing to provide a truthful account as to why he had paid Mr. Burke £35,000 in May 1989.

(b) Failing to provide the Tribunal with a truthful account of the role played by him and Mr. Stafford in ensuring that Mr. Burke issued a Directive in March 1989 to RTÉ concerning transmission charges.

(c) Failing to give a truthful account of the role played by him and by Mr. Stafford in ensuring that Mr. Burke would introduce legislation to cap RTÉ's advertising income, to redistribute RTÉ's licence fee income and to change the role of 2FM.

(d) Failing to provide a truthful account of the reimbursement to him of the £35,000 paid to Mr. Burke in May 1989.

(e) Failing to comply with the Tribunal's Order for Discovery within the time limited for so doing or within a reasonable time thereafter.

Mr. James Stafford

17-12   The Tribunal is satisfied that Mr. Stafford obstructed and hindered the Tribunal by:

(a) Failing to give a truthful account of his knowledge of the payment of £35,000 made by Mr. Barry to Mr. Burke.

(b) Failing to give the Tribunal a truthful account as to why Mr. Barry had paid Mr. Burke £35,000.

(c) Failing to give a truthful account of the role played by him and by Mr. Barry in ensuring that Mr. Burke would introduce legislation to cap RTÉ's advertising income, to redistribute RTÉ's licence fee income and to change the role of 2FM.

(d) Failing to provide a truthful account of the reimbursement to Mr. Barry of the £35,000 paid to Mr. Burke in May 1989.

(e) Giving a false account as to how the Century figures of £375,000 for transmission charges were calculated.

Mr. P.J. Mara

17-13 The Tribunal is satisfied that Mr. P.J. Mara failed to co-operate with the Tribunal by:

(a) Failing to provide the Tribunal with details of an account in the name of Pullman Limited, operated by him at Royal Bank of Scotland in the Isle of Man, when swearing his Affidavit of Discovery made pursuant to an Order of the Tribunal requiring him to discover, *inter alia,* any such account.

THE GOGARTY MODULE

Mr. Ray Burke

17-14 The Tribunal is satisfied that Mr. Burke obstructed and hindered the Tribunal in this module by:

(a) Failing to give the Tribunal a truthful account of the circumstances in which he came to receive monies from JMSE at his home in June 1989.
(b) Falsely maintaining that Mr. Joseph Murphy Jnr. was not present at such a meeting when he knew this to be untrue.
(c) Offering in evidence an account of events as to what occurred at the meeting at his home with Mr. Gogarty when he knew this to be untrue.
(d) Failing to give a truthful account of the nature of his relationship with Mr. Michael Bailey and the purposes for which the meeting at his home had been arranged by Mr. Bailey.

Mr. Joseph Murphy Snr.

17-15 The Tribunal is satisfied that Mr. Joseph Murphy Snr. obstructed and hindered the Tribunal by:

(a) Failing to give a truthful account of the circumstances in which the Murphy North Dublin lands came to be sold.
(b) Failing to give a truthful account of the circumstances in which Mr. James Gogarty came to attend the meeting at Mr. Burke's home in June 1989, at which Mr. Burke was paid money by JMSE.
(c) Failing to give a truthful account as to the circumstances in which JMSE's money came to be paid to Mr. Burke on his instructions and with his authority.
(d) Failing to provide proper discovery to the Tribunal in breach of an Order for Discovery made against him.
(e) Falsely claiming that he had no bank accounts in Ireland from 1976 onwards when he knew this to be untrue.
(f) Colluding with Mr. Joseph Murphy Jnr., Mr. Frank Reynolds, and Mr. Roger Copsey to give a false account of the role played by Mr. James Gogarty in connection with the Murphy's North Dublin lands and his knowledge of the participation proposal advanced by Mr. Michael Bailey in relation thereto.

Mr. Joseph Murphy Jnr.

17-16 The Tribunal is satisfied that Mr. Joseph Murphy Jnr, obstructed and hindered the Tribunal by:

(a) Failing to give a truthful account of the circumstances in which he came to attend a meeting at the home of Mr. Burke in June 1989, at which he handed to Mr. Burke a sum of not less than £30,000.
(b) Failing to give a truthful account of his dealings with Mr. Michael Bailey with regard to the participation proposal, in which it was envisaged that Mr. Michael Bailey would receive 50% of the value of the Murphy's North Dublin lands in return for procuring planning permission and building bye law approval in respect thereof.
(c) Giving a false account of the involvement of Mr. James Gogarty in the sale of the Murphy lands and the role played by him in connection with the payment of JMSE monies to Mr. Burke.

(d) Giving a false account of his dealings with Mr. Michael Bailey subsequent to the publication of the Sunday Business Post articles.

(e) Falsely constructing an alibi which was untrue.

Mr. Roger Copsey

17-17 The Tribunal is satisfied that Mr. Roger Copsey obstructed and hindered the Tribunal by:

(a) Giving a false account of his involvement in the assembly of the funds paid by JMSE to Mr. Burke.

(b) Falsely attributing a role to Mr. Gogarty in the payment of monies to Mr. Burke, which Mr. Gogarty had not exercised.

(c) Failing to give a truthful account of his dealings with Mr. Joseph Murphy Snr., Mr. Joseph Murphy Jnr., and Mr. Frank Reynolds in relation to the payment of JMSE's monies to Mr. Burke.

(d) Failing to provide the Tribunal with a true explanation for the accounting entries made in the books of JMSE and Grafton in relation to the monies paid to Mr. Burke.

Mr. Frank Reynolds

17-18 The Tribunal is satisfied that Mr. Frank Reynolds obstructed and hindered the Tribunal by:

(a) Failing to give a truthful account of his involvement in the assembly of funds which were paid to Mr. Burke by JMSE.

(b) Falsely ascribing to Mr. Gogarty a role in the payment of monies to Mr. Burke which he knew to be untrue.

(c) Failing to give a truthful account of his dealings with Mr. Michael Bailey.

(d) Failing to give a truthful account of the steps taken by him subsequent to the publication of the Gogarty allegations in the Sunday Business Post editions of the 30th March and the 6th April 1996.

(e) Colluding with Mr. Joseph Murphy Snr., Mr. Joseph Murphy Jnr., and Mr. Roger Copsey to present a false account to the Tribunal of the role played by Mr. James Gogarty in the payment of JMSE monies to Mr. Ray Burke.

Mr. Tim O'Keeffe

17-19 Tribunal is satisfied that Mr. O'Keeffe obstructed and hindered the Tribunal by:

(a) Failing to give a truthful account of his knowledge of the payment of monies by JMSE to Mr. Burke.

(b) Giving an explanation for his accounting entries and the preparation of the "Grafton/Reliable cash balance" document which he knew to be false.

Mr. John Bates

17-20 The Tribunal is satisfied that Mr. John Bates obstructed and hindered the Tribunal by:

Failing to give a truthful account of his reasons for treating the payment of £30,000 of the funds of Grafton Construction Company Limited, to Mr. Burke, as payments involving land enhancement expenditure in the documents prepared by him in connection with the annual returns of Grafton Construction Company Limited to the year ended the 31st May 1990.

Mr. Michael Bailey

17-21 The Tribunal is satisfied that Mr. Michael Bailey hindered and obstructed the Tribunal by:

(a) Giving a false account of the circumstances surrounding the meeting attended by him at the home of Mr. Burke in June, 1989.

(b) Falsely claiming that he had paid Mr. James Gogarty a sum of £162,000 in respect of a finder's fee connected with the sale of the Murphy North Dublin lands to Mr. Bailey's company.

145

(c) Failing to respect the confidentiality of documents provided to him by the Tribunal - on terms that they would only be considered by him and his legal advisers - by disclosing the contents thereof to Mr.Jody Corcoran, a journalist with the Sunday Independent, with the intention that the integrity of the Tribunal would thereby be damaged.

(d) Claiming that he was unable to co-operate fully with the Tribunal due to a fear that his communications with the Tribunal would be leaked to the media at a time when he was a person responsible for leaking information to the press.

(e) Failing to make proper discovery of the financial accounts and records which had been sought from him and his company by the Tribunal.

(f) Providing false explanations for accounting entries in the financial records provided to the Tribunal.

(g) Failing to provide the Tribunal with a truthful account of what he had given to Mr. Burke at the meeting attended by Mr. James Gogarty at Mr. Burke's home in June 1989.

(h) Colluding with his brother, Mr. Tom Bailey, to give a false account of his dealings with Mr. James Gogarty

Mr. Tom Bailey

17-22   Mr. Tom Bailey obstructed and hindered the Tribunal by:

(a) Colluding with his brother, Mr. Michael Bailey, to give a false account of his dealings with Mr. James Gogarty.

(b) Falsely alleging that £50,000 in cash and two cheques were given to Mr. James Gogarty at the Royal Dublin Hotel in November 1989.

(c) Failing to give a truthful account of his financial dealings.

(d) Failing to provide to the Tribunal all financial records that were the subject of Orders for Discovery made against him and his companies.

Mrs. Caroline Bailey

17-23   Mrs. Caroline Bailey obstructed and hindered the Tribunal by:

(a) Failing to comply with Orders for Discovery made by the Tribunal.

(b) Failing to provide a truthful account as to the existence of banks accounts held in her name at Bank of Ireland, Phibsboro, and Bank of Ireland, Swords.

(c) Preparing a notebook, said to record payments to Mr. James Gogarty, which she knew to be a false document.

(d) Failing to inform the Tribunal that cheque journals provided by her to the auditors of Bovale Developments Limited were subsequently altered, prior to being sent to the Tribunal on foot of an Order for Discovery.

Chapter 18

Findings of the Tribunal in Relation to the Matters Raised in Clause A, Sub-Clauses 1, 2 And 3, of the Amended Terms of Reference of the Tribunal

18-01   Clause A of the amended Terms of Reference of the Tribunal relates to the six lots of land which were referred to in Mr. Michael Bailey's letter of the 8th June, 1989 to Mr. James Gogarty and which have been described earlier in this report as the 'North Dublin lands'.

18-02   The Tribunal has heard evidence in relation to the identification of the lands, the planning history of the lands and the identity of any members of the Oireachtas or Local Authorities involved with the lands. The details of the Tribunal's findings in relation thereto are set forth in the **Appendix Y** annexed to this report which is headed "Report into the matters covered by Clauses A1, A2 (a) to (c) inclusive, A3 (a) to (g) inclusive, and A3 (i), (ii) and (iv)".

18-03   Other than the members of Local Authorities and of the Oireachtas referred to in the report above (see Appendix Y), the Tribunal has not identified any other past or present member of either body who was involved in any of the matters set out in Clause A3 in respect of these lands.

18-04   The Tribunal's Report in this regard is an interim report and its pronouncements upon the matters referred to in Clauses A1 to 3 inclusive should not be regarded as either final or conclusive upon these issues. In relation to Clause A3 (iii) the Tribunal has deferred its report and may, in its reconstituted format, hear further evidence to complete this aspect of its report.

FINDINGS OF THE TRIBUNAL IN RELATION TO THE MATTERS RAISED IN CLAUSE A4, SUB-CLAUSES A AND B OF THE AMENDED TERMS OF REFERENCE

18-05   Clause 4 requires the Tribunal to identify all recipients of payments made to political parties or members of either house of the Oireachtas, past or present, or members or officials of a Dublin Local Authority or other public official by Mr. Gogarty, or any connected person or company, and the circumstances, considerations and motives relative to any such payment, and any payment made by Mr. Bailey or a connected person or company to date and the circumstances, considerations and motives relative to any such payment.

PAYMENTS BY JAMES GOGARTY

18-06   The Tribunal has determined that notwithstanding Mr. Gogarty's directorship of JMSE at the time of its payment to Mr. Burke, JMSE was not a company connected to him within the meaning of the Ethics in Public Office Act 1995 as Mr. Gogarty did not exercise control over the said company as defined by Section 157 of the Corporation Tax Act 1976 and accordingly the payment made by JMSE to Mr. Burke (in June 1989) does not fall to be considered under this clause.

18-07   Documents produced to the Tribunal, included a copy of a cheque drawn upon the account of JMSE at Allied Irish Banks, 10/11 Lower O'Connell Street, Dublin dated 18th July 1989. The sole signatory of this cheque was Mr. James Gogarty who acknowledged that he had signed the cheque in blank but denied knowledge that the intended payee of the sum of £1,000 referred to therein was the Progressive Democrat Party. This cheque was paid to the Progressive Democrats. The Tribunal is satisfied that the cheque was paid to the Progressive Democrats on or after 18th July 1989.

18-08   In view of the fact that Mr. Gogarty has denied any knowledge of the identity of the intended payee on this cheque, in view of the fact that he was no longer a director of JMSE at the time that the cheque was written, and in view of the fact that the account from which the monies were to come was not an account of Mr. James Gogarty, the Tribunal concludes, on balance, that the payment of £1,000 made to the Progressive Democrats by cheque dated the 18th July, 1989 does not constitute a payment to the Progressive Democrats by Mr. Gogarty as provided for in Clause 4(a) of the Terms of Reference. The Tribunal feels bound to report as a matter of fairness to JMSE and the Progressive Democrats that there was no evidence that this payment was other than a legitimate political donation.

PAYMENTS BY MICHAEL BAILEY

18-09 The Tribunal has pronounced upon the circumstances of the meeting at the home of Mr. Burke in June 1989 in which Mr. Bailey handed over an envelope to Mr. Burke, which approximated in size to that handed over to Mr. Burke by Joseph Murphy Junior. The Tribunal has been unable to establish the contents of this envelope but is satisfied that Mr. Bailey, either in this envelope or otherwise, provided a benefit or payment to Mr. Burke. The Tribunal is satisfied that such payment made or benefit conferred was given in anticipation of receiving Mr. Burke's assistance in progressing Mr. Bailey's plans for the Murphy's North Dublin lands, and that it was a corrupt payment.

18-10 The Tribunal expressly refrains from reporting on an interim basis on any other payments which were made by Mr. Bailey or connected persons or companies pending completion of the investigation and public inquiry into re-zoning by Dublin County Council which will form a subsequent module of evidence to be heard before the re-constituted Tribunal.

Chapter 19

Other Work of the Tribunal

19-01   At the outset, the Tribunal would like to take the earliest possible opportunity to express its gratitude to the members of the general public who provided much assistance to it both in providing documentation and in drawing matters to the attention of the Tribunal. The Tribunal is mandated under Clause A. 5 of its *Terms of Reference* as follows:

> "In the event that the Tribunal in the course of its inquiries is made aware of any acts associated with the planning process which may in its opinion amount to corruption, or which involve attempts to influence by threats or deception or inducement or otherwise to compromise the disinterested performance of public duties, it shall report on such acts and should in particular make recommendations as to the effectiveness and improvement of existing legislation governing corruption in the light of its inquiries."

19-02   In *Redmond v. Flood* [1999] 1 I.L.R.M. 241 at 255 Hamilton C.J. stated as follows:

> "Its *[the Tribunal's]* powers are limited to the investigation of and reporting on acts associated with the planning process of which it becomes aware during the course of the inquiries authorised by paragraphs A1 to A4 of the terms of reference and which in its opinion amount to corruption or an attempt to compromise the disinterested performance of public duties."

The Tribunal is also required to conduct its inquiries in accordance with Clause B. (I) of the Terms of Reference as amended. Clause B. (I) provides that the Tribunal is required to carry out such preliminary investigations in private as it thinks fit using all the powers conferred on it under the Acts, in order to determine whether sufficient evidence exists in relation to such matter to warrant proceeding to a full public inquiry.

19-03   In general the usual sequence of inquiry by the Tribunal is as follows:

1. Information is made available to the Tribunal.

2. The Tribunal determines whether the subject matter of the information falls within its Terms of Reference.

3. If the subject matter falls within its Terms of Reference the Tribunal, in the first instance, carries out inquiries in private to determine whether sufficient evidence exists to warrant proceeding to a full public inquiry.

4. At the conclusion of its inquiries in private the Tribunal makes its determination as to the sufficiency, or otherwise, of the evidence, and, depending on that determination, proceeds to a public inquiry or not as the case may be.

19-04   Following the establishment of the Tribunal, the Tribunal sought the assistance of the public who may have been in possession of information relevant to the work of the Tribunal. The Tribunal did so initially by placing advertisements in the national and local newspapers between the 15th and the 21st December 1997, requesting that "any person having information which may be relevant to the Terms of Reference should forward same in writing, in confidence, to the Registrar of the Tribunal."

19-05   By Instrument dated the 15th July 1998, the Terms of Reference of the Tribunal were extended, following which a further advertisement was placed in the national, and a number of local newspapers, between the 26th and the 30th August 1998, again extending an invitation to the general body of the public to forward relevant information to the Tribunal.

19-06   Following the publication of these advertisements, the Tribunal received information in connection with one hundred and eighty-four matters. These matters were in the main, drawn to its attention by concerned members of the public. Where the Tribunal was furnished with a complaint it provided a copy of its Terms of Reference to the party who had drawn the matter to the attention of the Tribunal.

19-07   The submissions and complaints received by the Tribunal did not fall into any particular geographic pattern or location, emanating as they did from all parts of the country. Neither did these matters fall into any particular urban or rural divide, as complaints received concerned both urban, and rural matters. These matters were not confined to complaints in connection with commercial development, but included single dwelling units, and extensions. Some of these matters could not be categorized as complaints, as such, but rather appeared to the Tribunal to be general concerns which concerned citizens, whilst not fully appreciative of the remit of the Tribunal, felt should be drawn to the attention of the Tribunal.

19-08   The Tribunal was obliged in considering these matters to decide, in the first instance, whether the subject matter of the complaints appeared to come within the Tribunal's Terms of Reference so as to provide a legitimate basis for any further inquiry by the Tribunal. If the Tribunal determined that the subject matter of the complaint did not come within its Terms of Reference it so informed the complainant, and returned the documentation (if any) to the complainant, explaining the decision of the Tribunal, having already provided that party with a copy of the Terms of Reference.

19-09   If the subject matter of the complaint appeared to the Tribunal to come within its Terms of Reference, the Tribunal conducted further inquiries in private by obtaining the relevant planning files from the relevant local authority, interviewing the parties involved, and obtaining any other relevant information and/or documentation, so as to enable the Tribunal make a decision as to whether the subject matter of the inquiry was such as to warrant a public inquiry. Of necessity, this work was carried out in tandem with the other work of the Tribunal.

19-10   Broadly speaking, the one hundred and eighty-four matters that were drawn to the attention of the Tribunal in this fashion are capable of being divided into the following categories:

MATTERS OF GENERAL CONCERN

19-11   The Tribunal received twenty–seven submissions of a general nature. In general these were not complaints as such, but expressed concerns ranging from planning policy in its widest sense, to concerns about a perceived lack of communication, or consultation, between planning authorities and the community. These submissions, with two exceptions, did not make any allegations of corruption or wrong-doing against any identifiable person or party.

19-12   Of these twenty–five complaints that did not contain any allegation of corruption or wrong-doing many expressed similar concerns about development policy in the future, and highlighted a desire for the planning process to provide for a greater consultative process, particularly as between the relevant local authority and community, or local representative groups. The parties making these submissions appear to be genuinely public-minded citizens. The Tribunal is satisfied that the matters, the subject matter of these twenty-five complaints, do not fall within its Terms of Reference, but the views expressed therein shall be borne in mind when the Tribunal considers recommendations in its final Report to the Oireachtas.

19-13   In so far as the two complaints that did make allegations of corruption or wrong-doing, these are presently the subject matter of a private inquiry by the Tribunal so as to determine whether there is sufficient evidence to warrant proceeding to a full public inquiry in relation to these matters.

COMPLAINTS CONCERNING LARGE-SCALE DEVELOPMENTS

19-14   The Tribunal received fifty-nine complaints which fall into this general category. Many of the complaints in this category did not make any allegation of corruption or wrong-doing. A common identifiable feature of many such complaints was a concern that such large-scale development did or would seriously affect local amenities.

19-15   Broadly speaking, these complaints centered on concerns about the circumstances in which certain large-scale residential developments were granted planning permission or the circumstances in which re-zoning of certain lands to provide for large-scale development was obtained. These complaints were in the main from persons or parties affected directly by the development or the proposed development the subject matter of the complaint. Where it was clear to the Tribunal that the subject matter of the complaint was not within its Terms of Reference it so informed the complainant.

19-16   Where the Tribunal was satisfied, following a preliminary examination of the matter, that there appeared to be no evidence of wrong-doing, and that the matter did not warrant further investigation at that time, the Tribunal so informed the complainant. The Tribunal reserved the right to re-open the matter should further information become available. Thirty-two of these fifty-nine complaints were so decided by the Tribunal. Apart from the foregoing, and arising from the balance of these complaints to the Tribunal, there are twenty-seven of these matters currently the subject matter of private inquiry by the Tribunal so as to determine whether there is sufficient evidence to warrant proceeding to a full public inquiry in relation to such matters or any of them.

COMPLAINTS CONCERNING LOCAL OR DOMESTIC ISSUES

19-17   The Tribunal received eighty-one complaints in this broad category. In general these complaints centered on concerns of individuals in connection with the development of single private houses or extensions to private houses, and/or a perceived non-compliance with a condition or conditions attached to a planning permission for either of the foregoing. The complainants were, in the main, resident in close proximity to the subject property. The Tribunal is satisfied that, whilst the complainants, in the main, genuinely held their views, at least half of these matters did not come within the Terms of Reference and the Tribunal so informed the complainants. The Tribunal is satisfied that, within this category, forty-nine matters were not within its Terms of Reference.

19-18   In so far as the balance of the matters within this category are concerned, these continue to be the subject of matter of private inquiry by the Tribunal so as to determine whether there is sufficient evidence to warrant proceeding to a full public inquiry in relation to such matters or any of them.

CONCLUSION

19-19   At present, therefore, sixty-one of these matters remain under active inquiry by the Tribunal. When the Tribunal forms a final view on these matters it will communicate with the affected parties. Each inquiry will be dealt with on its own merits, and this work must be carried out in conjunction with the other work of the Tribunal.

Appendices

Appendix A

Tribunal of Inquiry into Certain Planning Matters and Payments

ORIGINAL TERMS OF REFERENCE

(Appointed by Instrument of The Minister for the Environment and Local Government dated the 4th day of November 1997)

"That Dáil Éireann resolves:

A. That it is expedient that a Tribunal be established under the Tribunals of Inquiry (Evidence) Act, 1921, as adapted by or under subsequent enactments and the Tribunals of Inquiry (Evidence) (Amendment) Act, 1979, to inquire urgently into and report to the Clerk of the Dáil and make such findings and recommendations as it see fit, in relation to the following definite matters of urgent public importance:

1. The identification of the lands stated to be 726 acres in extent, referred to in the letter dated 8th June, 1989 from Mr. Michael Bailey to Mr. James Gogarty (reproduced in the schedule herewith) and the establishment of the beneficial ownership of the lands at that date and changes in the beneficial ownership of the lands since the 8th June, 1989 prior to their development;

2. The planning history of the lands including:-

   (a) their planning status in the Development Plan of the Dublin local authorities current at the 8th June, 1989;

   (b) the position with regard to the servicing of the lands for development as at the 8th June, 1989;

   (c) changes made or proposed to be made to the 8th June, 1989 planning status of the lands by way of:-

      (i) proposals put forward by Dublin local authority officials pursuant to the review of Development Plans or otherwise;

      (ii) motions by elected members of the Dublin local authorities proposing re-zoning;

      (iii) applications for planning permission (including any involving a material contravention of the Development Plan);

3. Whether the lands referred to in the letter dated 8th June, 1989 were the subject of the following:-

   (a) Re-zoning resolutions;
   (b) Resolutions for material contravention of the relevant Development Plans;
   (c) Applications for special tax designations status pursuant to the Finance Acts;
   (d) Applications for planning permission;
   (e) Changes made or requested to be made with regard to the servicing of the lands for development;
   (f) Applications for the granting of building by-law approval in respect of buildings constructed on the lands;
   (g) Applications for fire safety certificates;

155

on or after the 20th day of June 1985.

And

(i) to ascertain the identity of any persons or companies (and if companies, the identity of the beneficial owners of such companies) who had a material interest in the said lands or who had a material involvement in the matters aforesaid;

(ii) to ascertain the identity of any members of the Oireachtas, past or present, and/or members of the relevant local authorities who were involved directly or indirectly in any of the foregoing matters whether by the making of representations to a planning authority or to any person in the authority in a position to make relevant decisions or by the proposing of or by voting in favour or against or by abstaining from any such resolutions or by absenting themselves when such votes were taken or by attempting to influence in any manner whatsoever the outcome of any such applications, or who received payments from any of the persons or companies referred to at (i) above.

(iii) to ascertain the identity of all public officials who considered, made recommendations or decisions on any such matters and to report on such considerations, recommendations and/or decisions;

(iv) to ascertain and report on the outcome of all such applications, resolutions and votes in relation to such applications in the relevant local authority.

4. (a) The identity of all recipients of payments made to political parties or members of either House of the Oireachtas, past or present, or members or officials of a Dublin local authority or other public official by Mr. Gogarty or Mr. Bailey or a connected person or company within the meaning of the Ethics in Public Office Act, 1995, from 20th June 1985 to date, and the circumstances, considerations and motives relative to any such payment;

(b) whether any of the persons referred to at sub-paragraphs 3(ii) and 3(iii) above were influenced directly or indirectly by the offer or receipt of any such payments or benefits.

5. In the event that the Tribunal in the course of its inquiries is made aware of any acts associated with the planning process committed on or after the 20th June 1985 which may in its opinion amount to corruption, or which involve attempts to influence by threats or deception or inducement or otherwise to compromise the disinterested performance of public duties, it shall report on such acts and should in particular make recommendations as to the effectiveness and improvement of existing legislation governing corruption in the light of its inquiries.

6. And the Tribunal be requested to make recommendations in relation to such amendments to Planning, Local Government, Ethics in Public Office and any other relevant legislation as the Tribunal considers appropriate having regard to its findings.

"payment" includes money and any benefit in kind and the payment to any person includes a payment to a connected person within the meaning of the Ethics in Public Office Act, 1995.

B. That the Tribunal be requested to conduct its inquiries in the following manner, to the extent that it may do so consistent with the provisions of the Tribunals of Inquiry (Evidence) Acts, 1921 and 1979:-

(i) to carry out such preliminary investigations in private as it thinks fit using all the powers conferred on it under the Acts, in order to determine whether sufficient evidence exists in relation to any of the matters referred to above to warrant proceeding to a full public inquiry in relation to such matters,

(ii) to inquire fully into all matters referred to above in relation to which such evidence may be found to exist, dealing in the first instance with the acknowledged monetary donation debated in Dáil Éireann on the 10th September, 1997 Dáil Debates Columns 616-638 and to report to the Clerk of the Dáil thereupon,

(iii) to seek discovery of all relevant documents, files and papers in the possession, power or procurement of said Mr. Michael Bailey, Mr. James Gogarty and Donnelly, Neary and Donnelly Solicitors,

(iv) in relation to any matters where the Tribunal finds that there is insufficient evidence to warrant proceeding to a full public inquiry, to report that fact to the Clerk of the Dáil and to report in such a manner as the Tribunal thinks appropriate on the steps taken by the Tribunal to determine what evidence, if any, existed and the Clerk of the Dáil shall thereupon communicate the Tribunal's report in full to the Dáil,

(v) to report on an interim basis not later than one month from the date of establishment of the Tribunal or the tenth day of any oral hearing, whichever shall first occur, to the Clerk of the Dáil on the following matters:

the number of parties then represented before the Tribunal;

the progress, which has been made in the hearing and the work of the Tribunal;

the likely duration (so far as that may be capable of being estimated at that time) of the Tribunal proceedings;

any other matters, which the Tribunal believes, should be drawn to the attention of the Clerk of the Dáil at that stage (including any matter relating to the terms of reference).

C. And that the person or persons selected to conduct the Inquiry should be informed that it is the desire of the House that –

(a) the Inquiry be completed in as economical a manner as possible and at the earliest date consistent with a fair examination of the matters referred to it, and, in respect to the matters referred to in paragraphs 1 to 4 above, if possible, not later than the 31st December, 1997, and

(b) all costs incurred by reason of the failure of individuals to co-operate fully and expeditiously with the Inquiry should, so far as is consistent with the interests of justice, be borne by those individuals.

D.   And that the Clerk of the Dáil shall on receipt of any Report from the Tribunal arrange to have it laid before both Houses of the Oireachtas immediately on its receipt.

Kilinamonan House,
The Ward,
Co. Dublin.

8th June, 1989.

Dear Mr. Gogarty,

PROPOSALS FOR DISCUSSION

Re: Your lands at Finglas, Ballymun, Donabate, Balgraffin and Portmarnock, Co. Dublin.

I refer to our many discussions regarding your following six parcels of land:-

Lot 1:   100 acres (approx) at North Road, Finglas, including "Barrett's Land".

Lot 2:   12 acres (approx) at Jamestown Road, Finglas.

Lot 3:   100 acres (approx) at Poppintree, Ballymun.

Lot 4:   255 acres (approx) at Donabate (Turvey House and Beaverton House).

Lot 5:   250 acres (approx) at Balgriffin.

Lot 6:   9 acres (approx) at Portmarnock.

I submit the following proposals for your consideration:-

PROPOSAL NO. 1 – Purchase Proposal

<u>Lots 1, 2 and 3</u>   Purchase Price £4,000 per acre
10% deposit payable on the signing of the contract
Completion 1 year from date of contract.

<u>Lot 4</u>   Purchase Price IR£1 Million
Deposit 10% on contract
Completion 2 years from date of contract.

<u>Lot 5</u>   Purchase Price IR £750,000
Deposit 10% on contract
Completion 3 years from date of contract.

Lot 6:   Option to be granted for nominal consideration (£100.00) for a period of 2 years at a purchase price of £30,000.00 per acre.

PROPOSAL NO. 2 – Participation Proposal

As an alternative to the outright purchase proposal above I am prepared to deal with Lots 1 – 5 (inclusive) above on the basis that I would be given a 50% share in the ownership of the said lands in exchange for procuring Planning Permission and Building Bye Law Approval. The time span which I would require to be allowed to obtain the Permissions and Approval and my anticipated financial expenditure (apart from my time input) in respect of the different lots would be as follows:-

Lots 1, 2 and 3

A period of 2 years within which to procure a buildable Planning Permission and Building Bye Laws Approval for mixed development including housing, industrial and commercial.

My financial expenditure up to a figure of £150,000 (to include Architect's fees, Consulting Engineer's fees, Planning and Bye Law charges etc.).

Lots 4 and 5

Time requirement – 3 years.

Financial
Expenditure   - up to £150,000

In considering the above proposals the following points of information should be borne in mind by all parties:-

1.   From the point of view of obtaining Planning Permission the entire lands 1-6 inclusive) have the following shortcomings:-

       NO zoning for development purposes

       NO services.

       NO proposal in current draft development plans (City and County) for the zoning of the lands or any part thereof for development purposes.

2.   We face a very severe uphill battle to arrange for the availability of services and for the ultimate procurement of Planning Permission.

3.   The steps to be taken on the way to procuring a buildable Planning Permission and Building Bye Laws Approval are notoriously difficult, time consuming and expensive. Material Contravention Orders must be obtained and this involves their procurement of a majority vote at 2 full Council

Meetings at which 78 Council Members must be present and it also involves satisfactory compliance with extensive requirements and pre-conditions of the Planning Authority and the inevitable dealing with protracted Appeals to An Bord Pleanala.

4. It is essential that the Planning Application should be brought in the name of an active house building company which enjoys good standing and good working relationship with the Planners and the Council Members and in this regard I confirm that in the event of our reaching agreement regarding the within proposals that all Planning Applications would be made by one of my Companies which meets the said requirements.

5. In the case of all of the lands the applications will be highly sensitive and controversial and we can realistically expect strenuous opposition from private, political and planning sectors. One of my active companies will have to take the limelight in such applications and withstand the objections and protests which will inevitably confront it. Apart from the anticipated financial expenditure as outlined above it should be borne in mind that I will personally have to give extensively of my time and efforts over the entire period of the applications including the necessary preliminary negotiations in regard to services and zoning. It must be borne in mind that I will have to abandon other projects which would be open to myself and my companies in order to give proper attention to this project. If I am successful in changing your lands from their present status of agricultural lands with very limited potential even for agricultural use into highly valuable building lands I would have to be rewarded with a minimum 50% stake in the ownership of the lands. Our advisors would have to work out the details as to how this can be effected in the most tax efficient manner.

I look forward to hearing from you in relation to the above proposals. In the case of the first proposal which relates to the outright purchase of the lands (excluding Lot 6) I would not be adverse to a proposal which would involve the vendors retaining a participation stake of up to 20% in the purchasing company if you felt that an ongoing interest in the future development of the lands would be more acceptable to the present owners.

Yours sincerely,

_____

MICHAEL BAILEY,

Mr. Jim Gogarty,
Clontarf,
Dublin 3.

Appendix B

TRIBUNAL OF INQUIRY
INTO
CERTAIN PLANNING MATTERS AND PAYMENTS

AMENDED TERMS OF REFERENCE

(Appointed by Instrument of The Minister for the Environment and Local Government dated the 4th day of November 1997 and as amended by Instrument dated the 15th day of July 1998)

"That Dáil Éireann resolves

A.   That it is expedient that a Tribunal be established under the Tribunals of Inquiry (Evidence) Act, 1921, as adapted by or under subsequent enactments and the Tribunals of Inquiry (Evidence) (Amendment) Act, 1979, to inquire urgently into and report to the Clerk of the Dáil and make such findings and recommendations as it see fit, in relation to the following definite matters of urgent public importance:

1.   The identification of the lands stated to be 726 acres in extent, referred to in the letter dated 8th June, 1989 from Mr. Michael Bailey to Mr. James Gogarty (reproduced in the schedule herewith) and the establishment of the beneficial ownership of the lands at that date and changes in the beneficial ownership of the lands since the 8th June, 1989 prior to their development;

2.   The planning history of the lands including:-

    (a)   their planning status in the Development Plan of the Dublin local authorities current at the 8th June, 1989;

    (b)   the position with regard to the servicing of the lands for development as at the 8th June, 1989;

    (c)   changes made or proposed to be made to the 8th June, 1989 planning status of the lands by way of:-

        (i)   proposals put forward by Dublin local authority officials pursuant to the review of Development Plans or otherwise;

        (ii)   motions by elected members of the Dublin local authorities proposing re-zoning;

        (iii)   applications for planning permission (including any involving a material contravention of the Development Plan);

3.   Whether the lands referred to in the letter dated 8th June, 1989 were the subject of the following:-

   (a)   Re-zoning resolutions;
   (b)   Resolutions for material contravention of the relevant Development Plans;
   (c)   Applications for special tax designations status pursuant to the Finance Acts;
   (d)   Applications for planning permission;
   (e)   Changes made or requested to be made with regard to the servicing of the lands for development;
   (f)   Applications for the granting of building by-law approval in respect of buildings constructed on the lands;
   (g)   Applications for fire safety certificates;

on or after the 20th day of June 1985.

And

   (i)   to ascertain the identity of any persons or companies (and if companies, the identity of the beneficial owners of such companies) who had a material interest in the said lands or who had a material involvement in the matters aforesaid;

   (ii)   to ascertain the identity of any members of the Oireachtas, past or present, and/or members of the relevant local authorities who were involved directly or indirectly in any of the foregoing matters whether by the making of representations to a planning authority or to any person in the authority in a position to make relevant decisions or by the proposing of or by voting in favour or against or by abstaining from any such resolutions or by absenting themselves when such votes were taken or by attempting to influence in any manner whatsoever the outcome of any such applications, or who received payments from any of the persons or companies referred to at (i) above.

   (iii)   to ascertain the identity of all public officials who considered, made recommendations or decisions on any such matters and to report on such considerations, recommendations and/or decisions;

   (iv)   to ascertain and report on the outcome of all such applications, resolutions and votes in relation to such applications in the relevant local authority.

4.   (a)   The identity of all recipients of payments made to political parties or members of either House of the Oireachtas, past or present, or members or officials of a Dublin local authority or other public official by Mr. Gogarty or Mr. Bailey or a connected person or company within the meaning of the Ethics

164

in Public Office Act, 1995, from 20th June 1985 to date, and the circumstances, considerations and motives relative to any such payment;

(b) whether any of the persons referred to at sub-paragraphs 3(ii) and 3(iii) above were influenced directly or indirectly by the offer or receipt of any such payments or benefits.

5. In the event that the Tribunal in the course of its inquiries is made aware of any acts associated with the planning process ~~committed on or after the 20th June, 1985~~[1] which may in its opinion amount to corruption, or which involve attempts to influence by threats or deception or inducement or otherwise to compromise the disinterested performance of public duties, it shall report on such acts and should in particular make recommendations as to the effectiveness and improvement of existing legislation governing corruption in the light of its inquiries.

6. And the Tribunal be requested to make recommendations in relation to such amendments to Planning, Local Government, Ethics in Public Office and any other relevant legislation as the Tribunal considers appropriate having regard to its findings.

"payment" includes money and any benefit in kind and the payment to any person includes a payment to a connected person within the meaning of the Ethics in Public Office Act, 1995.

B. And that the Tribunal be requested to conduct its inquiries in the following manner, to the extent that it may do so consistent with the provisions of the Tribunals of Inquiry (Evidence) Acts, 1921 and 1979:-

(i) to carry out such preliminary investigations in private as it thinks fit using all the powers conferred on it under the Acts, in order to determine whether sufficient evidence exists in relation to any of the matters referred to above to warrant proceeding to a full public inquiry in relation to such matters,

(ii) to inquire fully into all matters referred to above in relation to which such evidence may be found to exist, dealing in the first instance with the acknowledged monetary donation debated in Dáil Eireann on the 10th September, 1997 Dáil Debates Columns 616-638 and to report to the Clerk of the Dáil thereupon,

(iii) to seek discovery of all relevant documents, files and papers in the possession, power or procurement of said Mr. Michael Bailey, Mr. James Gogarty and Donnelly, Neary and Donnelly Solicitors,

---

[1] Deleted by resolution of Dail Eireann.

(iv) in relation to any matters where the Tribunal finds that there is insufficient evidence to warrant proceeding to a full public inquiry, to report that fact to the Clerk of the Dáil and to report in such a manner as the Tribunal thinks appropriate on the steps taken by the Tribunal to determine what evidence, if any, existed and the Clerk of the Dáil shall thereupon communicate the Tribunal's report in full to the Dáil,

(v) to report on an interim basis not later than one month from the date of establishment of the Tribunal or the tenth day of any oral hearing, whichever shall first occur, to the Clerk of the Dáil on the following matters:

the number of parties then represented before the Tribunal;

the progress which has been made in the hearing and the work of the Tribunal;

the likely duration (so far as that may be capable of being estimated at that time) of the Tribunal proceedings;

any other matters which the Tribunal believes should be drawn to the attention of the Clerk of the Dáil at that stage (including any matter relating to the terms of reference).

C. And that the person or persons selected to conduct the Inquiry should be informed that it is the desire of the House that –

(a) the Inquiry be completed in as economical a manner as possible and at the earliest date consistent with a fair examination of the matters referred to it, and, in respect to the matters referred to in paragraphs 1 to 4 above, if possible, not later than the 31st December, 1997, and

(b) all costs incurred by reason of the failure of individuals to co-operate fully and expeditiously with the Inquiry should, so far as is consistent with the interests of justice, be borne by those individuals.

D. And that the Clerk of the Dáil shall on receipt of any Report from the Tribunal arrange to have it laid before both Houses of the Oireachtas immediately on its receipt.

E **The Tribunal shall, in addition to the matters referred to in paragraphs A(1) to A(5) hereof, inquire urgently into and report to the Clerk of the Dail and make such findings and recommendations as it sees fit, in relation to the following definite matters of urgent public importance:-**

1. Whether any substantial payments were made or benefits provided, directly or indirectly, to Mr. Raphael Burke which may, in the opinion of the Sole Member of the Tribunal, amount to corruption or involve attempts to influence or compromise the disinterested performance of public duties or were made or provided in circumstances which may give rise to a reasonable inference that the motive for making or receiving such payments was improperly connected with any public office or position held by Mr. Raphael Burke, whether as Minister, Minister of State, or elected representative;

2. Whether, in return for or in connection with such payments or benefits, Mr. Raphael Burke did any act or made any decision while holding any such public office or position which was intended to confer any benefit on any person or entity making a payment or providing a benefit referred to in paragraph 1 above, or any other person or entity, or procured or directed any other person to do such an act or make such a decision.

And that the Tribunal be requested to conduct its Inquiries in the following manner to the extent that it may do so consistent with the provisions of the Tribunals of Inquiry (Evidence) Acts 1921 to 1998:-

(i) To carry out such preliminary investigations in private as it thinks fit (using all the powers conferred on it under the Acts), in order to determine whether sufficient evidence exists in relation to any of the matters referred to in paragraphs E1 and E2 above to warrant proceeding to a full public inquiry in relation to such matters;

(ii) To inquire fully into all matters referred to in paragraphs E1 and E2 in relation to which such evidence may be found to exist;

(iii) In relation to any matters where the Tribunal finds that there is insufficient evidence to warrant proceeding to a full public inquiry, to report that fact to the Clerk of the Dail and to Report in such a manner as the Tribunal thinks appropriate on the steps taken by the Tribunal to determine what evidence, if any, existed and the Clerk of the Dail shall thereupon communicate the Tribunal's report in full to the Dail;

(iv)To report on an interim basis to the Clerk of the Dail on the following matters:-

the number of parties then represented before the Tribunal;

the progress which has been made in the hearing and the work of the Tribunal;

the likely duration (so far as that may be capable of being estimated at that time) of the Tribunal proceedings;

any other matters which the Tribunal believes should be drawn to the attention of the clerk of the Dail at that stage (including any matter relating to the terms of reference);

and to furnish such further interim reports as the Tribunal may consider necessary.

F   And that the Sole Member of the Tribunal should be informed that it is the desire of the House that:-

(a) The inquiry into the matters referred to in paragraph E hereof be completed in as economical a manner as possible and at the earlier date consistent with a fair examination of the said matters, and

(b) All costs incurred by reason of the failure of individuals to co-operate fully and expeditiously with the Inquiry should, so far as is consistent with the interests of justice, be borne by those individuals.

G   And that the Clerk of the Dail shall on receipt of any Report from the Tribunal arrange to have it laid before both Houses of the Oireachtas immediately on its receipt.

SCHEDULE

Kilinamonan House,
The Ward,
Co. Dublin.

8th June, 1989.

Dear Mr. Gogarty,

PROPOSALS FOR DISCUSSION

Re: Your lands at Finglas, Ballymun, Donabate, Balgraffin and Portmarnock, Co. Dublin.

I refer to our many discussions regarding your following six parcels of land:-

Lot 1:   100 acres (approx) at North Road, Finglas, including "Barrett's Land".

Lot 2:   12 acres (approx) at Jamestown Road, Finglas.

Lot 3:   100 acres (approx) at Poppintree, Ballymun.

Lot 4:   255 acres (approx) at Donabate (Turvey House and Beaverton House).

Lot 5:   250 acres (approx) at Balgriffin.

Lot 6:   9 acres (approx) at Portmarnock.

I submit the following proposals for your consideration:-

PROPOSAL NO. 1 – Purchase Proposal

<u>Lots 1, 2 and 3</u>   Purchase Price £4,000 per acre
                              10% deposit payable on the signing of the contract
                              Completion 1 year from date of contract.

<u>Lot 4</u>   Purchase Price IR£1 Million
                              Deposit 10% on contract
                              Completion 2 years from date of contract.

<u>Lot 5</u>   Purchase Price IR £750,000
                              Deposit 10% on contract
                              Completion 3 years from date of contract.

Lot 6:	Option to be granted for nominal consideration (£100.00) for a period of 2 years at a purchase price of £30,000.00 per acre.

PROPOSAL NO. 2 – Participation Proposal

As an alternative to the outright purchase proposal above I am prepared to deal with Lots 1 – 5 (inclusive) above on the basis that I would be given a 50% share in the ownership of the said lands in exchange for procuring Planning Permission and Building Bye Law Approval. The time span which I would require to be allowed to obtain the Permissions and Approval and my anticipated financial expenditure (apart from my time input) in respect of the different lots would be as follows:-

Lots 1, 2 and 3

A period of 2 years within which to procure a buildable Planning Permission and Building Bye Laws Approval for mixed development including housing, industrial and commercial.

My financial expenditure up to a figure of £150,000 (to include Architect's fees, Consulting Engineer's fees, Planning and Bye Law charges etc.).

Lots 4 and 5

Time requirement – 3 years.

Financial
Expenditure   - up to £150,000

In considering the above proposals the following points of information should be borne in mind by all parties:-

1. From the point of view of obtaining Planning Permission the entire lands 1-6 inclusive) have the following shortcomings:-

   NO zoning for development purposes

   NO services.

   NO proposal in current draft development plans (City and County) for the zoning of the lands or any part thereof for development purposes.

2. We face a very severe uphill battle to arrange for the availability of services and for the ultimate procurement of Planning Permission.

3. The steps to be taken on the way to procuring a buildable Planning Permission and Building Bye Laws Approval are notoriously difficult, time consuming and expensive. Material Contravention Orders must be obtained and this involves their procurement of a majority vote at 2 full Council

Meetings at which 78 Council Members must be present and it also involves satisfactory compliance with extensive requirements and pre-conditions of the Planning Authority and the inevitable dealing with protracted Appeals to An Bord Pleanala.

4.   It is essential that the Planning Application should be brought in the name of an active house building company which enjoys good standing and good working relationship with the Planners and the Council Members and in this regard I confirm that in the event of our reaching agreement regarding the within proposals that all Planning Applications would be made by one of my Companies which meets the said requirements.

5.   In the case of all of the lands the applications will be highly sensitive and controversial and we can realistically expect strenuous opposition from private, political and planning sectors. One of my active companies will have to take the limelight in such applications and withstand the objections and protests which will inevitably confront it. Apart from the anticipated financial expenditure as outlined above it should be borne in mind that I will personally have to give extensively of my time and efforts over the entire period of the applications including the necessary preliminary negotiations in regard to services and zoning. It must be borne in mind that I will have to abandon other projects which would be open to myself and my companies in order to give proper attention to this project. If I am successful in changing your lands from their present status of agricultural lands with very limited potential even for agricultural use into highly valuable building lands I would have to be rewarded with a minimum 50% stake in the ownership of the lands. Our advisors would have to work out the details as to how this can be effected in the most tax efficient manner.

I look forward to hearing from you in relation to the above proposals. In the case of the first proposal which relates to the outright purchase of the lands (excluding Lot 6) I would not be adverse to a proposal which would involve the vendors retaining a participation stake of up to 20% in the purchasing company if you felt that an ongoing interest in the future development of the lands would be more acceptable to the present owners.

Yours sincerely,

_____

MICHAEL BAILEY,

Mr. Jim Gogarty,
Clontarf,
Dublin 3.

Appendix C

Vol. 480

No. 4

Wednesday,

10 September 1997

DÍOSPÓIREACHTAÍ PARLAIMINTE
PARLIAMENTARY DEBATES

DÁIL ÉIREANN

TUAIRISC OIFIGIÚIL—*Neamhcheartaithe*

(OFFICIAL REPORT—*Unrevised*)

Wednesday, 10 September 1997.

Mrs. Owen: On a point of order, it is normal for the Minister's speech to be circulated. I would like a copy of what he had to say, particularly as he gave a slight word of praise to me at the end. It is so unusual.

Mr. O'Donoghue: I regret to inform the Deputy that the words of praise will not be included in the text.

Mrs. Owen: I would like a copy anyway.

Mr. O'Donoghue: A rose by any other name.

An Leas-Cheann Comhairle: Is the motion agreed to?

Caoimhghín Ó Caoláin: I wish to record my opposition as stated in my address.

Question put and agreed to.

Personal Explanation by Member.

Mr. Lowry: I thank the House for the opportunity to make this personal explanation. The purpose of doing so is to address the reference in the report of the Tribunal of Inquiry (Dunnes Stores Payments) to the statement which I made to this House on 19 December last. On that occasion I sought the opportunity to make a statement to this House so that I could address the innuendoes that arose following the disclosure that Dunnes Stores had paid for works to my house in Holycross.

It was being widely suggested that Dunnes Stores paid for the works to my house in return for political favours. The purpose of making my statement was to categorically refute that false charge. Speculation about the Price Waterhouse report was rife at that time as extracts had been leaked to the media. I told this House, correctly, on 19 December that I had not seen the Price Waterhouse report nor have I seen it since. I attempted to deal with the elements of that report which I understood referred to my business.

During the course of my address to the Dáil I made the following statements:

> I did not make any secret of the fact that Dunnes Stores paid me for professional services by way of assistance towards my house. If someone were trying to hide income, would he or she not be more likely to put it in an offshore account? The last thing such a person would do would be to spend it on a very obvious structure of bricks and mortar for all the world to see.

This statement was intended merely to address the fact that Dunnes Stores had paid for construction work to my house, that this was well known to a significant number of people, and that I made no effort whatsoever to conceal it. My reference to offshore accounts in this context, therefore, was intended only to illustrate this point. With the benefit of hindsight I now accept that the words I used and the example I gave were most unfortunate and conveyed a misleading impression. I fully accept responsibility for that. However, I categorically assure this House that it was not my intention to mislead. I offer my full and sincere apologies to the Ceann Comhairle and to all Members of the House then and now for having misled them in any way.

During the course of my Dáil statement I also referred to some payments made to me by Dunnes Stores. These were the payments which I understood had been referred to in the Price Waterhouse report. The tribunal report notes that I made no mention whatever of other sums, including large payments paid to me by Dunnes Stores. I now accept that for completeness I should have done so. I offer my full and sincere apologies also for this omission. Again, it was not my intention to mislead. I was, in fact, confining myself to what I understood to be references in the Price Waterhouse report.

I ask the House to understand that I am constrained about addressing here the corporate and tax aspects of my affairs as these are currently the subject of review by the relevant authorities. Overall the difficulties I now face are substantial. I have contributed to my own misfortune. I have not managed my affairs as well as I should have and I have admitted making mistakes. They relate not to my actions as a holder of public office but to my personal and financial affairs. I have already paid, and continue to pay, a very high price as a consequence.

In conclusion, I apologise again to this House for any inadvertent misleading impression that my statement of 19 December may have conveyed. I ask for its acceptance of that apology and for its understanding in what are for me very difficult times.

Personal Statement by Member.

Minister for Foreign Affairs (Mr. R. Burke): I have come here today to defend my personal integrity, the integrity of my party, of the Government and the honour of this House. I have also come here to reassure the public and in particular my constituents that I have done nothing wrong. The experience of my 24 year membership of this House has seasoned me in the way parliamentary politics operate. The dynamic of democratic politics operating at parliamentary level dictate that Governments are opposed by Oppositions who in accordance with their function will avail of every opportunity to make life uncomfortable for the Government of the day.

I say this without rancour. I have been in Opposition myself many times. That is the way our system operates. I accept that. If I did not I would have no business being here. Furthermore, I do not expect that the facts I will present here today will in all cases satisfy everybody. I am, however, making this statement out of respect for the House and for those Members of the House who have sought this statement in good faith.

The circumstances which have given rise to the position in which I find myself occurred during the 1989 general election campaign and have already been described in a statement issued by me on 7 August this year. With your leave, a Leas-Cheann Comhairle, I propose to read this statement into the record of the House:

During the last two years I have been the target of a vicious campaign of rumour and innuendo. Since my appointment as Minister for Foreign Affairs this campaign has intensified. The stories which have appeared in the media in recent weeks are, as one prominent journalist acknowledged in a letter to me last week, the culmination of a lengthy series of smears about me. The story still keeps resurfacing in different shapes and forms, and the repeated articles and comments of recent weeks have placed an unacceptable burden on my family and myself. While I resent having to dignify these allegations by responding to them at all, I believe that I must now do so. The facts of the matter are that during the 1989 general election campaign I was visited in my home by Mr. Michael Bailey of Bovale Developments Ltd., and a Mr. James Gogarty.

Mr. Bailey was well known to me as he was a resident of north County Dublin and a long time supporter of Fianna Fáil. I had not met Mr. Gogarty previously but he was introduced by Mr. Bailey as an executive of Joseph Murphy Structural Engineers — JMSE. Mr. Gogarty told me JMSE wished to make a political contribution to me and I received from him in good faith a sum of £30,000 as a totally unsolicited political contribution. At no time during our meeting were any favours sought or given. I did not do any favours for or make any representations to anyone on behalf of JMSE, Mr. Michael Bailey, Bovale Developments Limited or Mr. James Gogarty either before or since 1989.

From what I have read and heard it seems the source of the allegations in the media may be Mr. James Gogarty. I do not know what motive, if any, Mr. Gogarty would have for pursuing such a vendetta against me. I believe, however, that he and his former employers, JMSE, parted in acrimonious circumstances. If Mr. Gogarty is the source of these allegations, then he is the author of a campaign of lies against me. I have also been the recipient of a number of anonymous threatening letters relating to these allegations. I have turned this correspondence over to the Garda.

As regards the most recent newspaper reports, I received an unsolicited political contribution of £30,000, not £80,000 as reported. The allegation that I received £40,000 from Mr. Bailey or Bovale Developments Limited on that or any other occasion is false. There were three persons present when I received the contribution from Mr. Gogarty — Mr. Gogarty,

Mr. Bailey and myself — and not five as reported. There was one JMSE executive present, Mr. Gogarty, and not two or three as variously reported.

I am taking the opportunity to state unequivocally that I have done nothing illegal, unethical or improper. I find myself the victim of a campaign of calumny and abuse. It is totally unacceptable that this matter should be allowed to continue to fulfil an agenda which has nothing to do with election contributions or any other aspect of reasonable or reasoned political debate in public life. If any further untruths are published about me, I will take all necessary steps to vindicate my good name and reputation.

I wish to elaborate on aspects of that statement. My understanding is that the making of this contribution came about as follows. Mr. Gogarty indicated to Mr. Bailey that JMSE wished to make a contribution to my election fund. Mr. Bailey brought Mr. Gogarty to my home and, during a brief meeting, Mr. Gogarty confirmed that JMSE wished to make a political contribution to me. The contribution was entirely in cash. Prior to leaving with Mr. Bailey, Mr. Gogarty wished me well in the election. I did not receive £40,000 from Mr. Bailey or Bovale Developments Limited on that or any other occasion. I did not receive any personal contributions from Mr. Bailey either before, during or after the 1989 general election, although I have established that over the years Mr. Bailey made a number of contributions to the Fianna Fáil organisation in my constituency on such occasions as race nights and so on.

In light of allegations made subsequent to my statement of 7 August last, I confirm that Mr. Joseph Murphy junior of JMSE was not present at my meeting with Mr. Gogarty and Mr. Bailey. I did not meet Mr. Joseph Murphy junior during or in connection with the 1989 general election campaign. Mr. Gogarty, who was the managing director of JMSE, was the only executive of that company present.

I confirm that I contributed £10,000 to the Fianna Fáil national organisation during that election campaign. In addition, I handed over moneys totalling approximately £7,000 to my local constituency organisation during the general election campaign in 1989. The remainder of the political contributions received by me, including the contribution Mr. Gogarty gave me during our meeting in my home, were used to cover my personal election campaign and subsequent political expenses. I did not and do not have separate accounts as regards either the election campaign in question or my subsequent political expenditure.

As regards the contribution, £30,000 is the largest contribution I have received during any election campaign either before or since 1989. On the other hand, in 1989 there had not been any legal limitations since 1963 on the amount a parliamentary candidate could expend on his or her election campaign. Furthermore, political expenditure

[Mr. R. Burke.]

does not begin or end during election campaigns. As all Members of this House will be aware, the last 25 years have seen a fundamental change in the operation of politics with public representatives or prospective public representatives having to operate ongoing and expensive constituency campaigns and services between and not merely during elections, such as newspaper advertisements, race nights, community contributions, leaflet drops, clinics and so on.

For as long as I have been a Member of this House, political parties and individual politicians have actively solicited and accepted political contributions. Soliciting or accepting such contributions was not outlawed or discouraged through legislation or the Standing Orders or rules of this House. For any candidate or representative to have accepted a political contribution with strings attached would have been unethical if not downright illegal. In the context of this contribution there was no attempt to attach any strings or to ask for any favours.

We now come to the nub of this matter. The stories that circulated were not that a politician had been given a contribution, albeit a generous one. Until recently, the mere making of a political contribution during an election campaign would not have been news at all. The core of this affair, the issue that has led to the Garda investigation and the primary issue that the Taoiseach felt it necessary to investigate prior to nominating me to serve in this Government is that Mr. Gogarty has apparently alleged not only that a political contribution was made to me, but that it was made for some improper purpose.

Any allegation that I have done anything wrong is completely untrue. No favours were done for JMSE, Bovale Developments Limited, Mr. Bailey, Mr. Murphy junior or Mr. Gogarty. Furthermore, notwithstanding what the *Sunday Business Post* journalist, Mr Frank Connolly, described as "a number of meetings, about fifteen hours of discussions" between Mr. Gogarty and the investigating Garda Superintendent and the fact that Mr. Gogarty was offered immunity from prosecution almost three months ago, I understand Mr. Gogarty has not signed any statement which would finally clarify what precisely he is or is not alleging. If favours have been done for Bovale Developments Limited or JMSE, I had nothing to do with them. I assume that if any Members of this House are aware of any such decision, they will declare their knowledge to this House and any involvement they might have had in any such decision. For my part, I have had no involvement, direct or indirect, in any such decisions.

I ceased to be a member of Dublin County Council in 1987. While a member of Dublin County Council between 1985 and 1987, the only proposal I made with regard to any planning matter related to one private residence which was supported unanimously by all members of the council in attendance at the meeting in question.

This matter arose in April 1986 when I was chairman of the council.

For the benefit of the House, I refer to a question put to the manager of Dublin County Council by my colleague, Deputy Gilmore, in which he asked for the lists of all section 4 and material contravention motions together with the names of the councillors who proposed and seconded them which were brought before the council from 1985 until 1989. The reply was given on 11 December 1989. The answer to Deputy Gilmore's question shows that for the relevant part of that period during which I was a member of the council, I neither proposed nor supported any motions involving Bovale Developments Limited, JMSE, Mr. Michael Bailey, Mr. Joseph Murphy junior or Mr. James Gogarty. Since I ceased to be a member of Dublin County Council in 1987, I have not asked for or urged support for any of these companies or individuals in the context of planning or material contravention motions or in any other matter. The first review of the County Dublin Development Plan, which took place after the 1989 general election, was in 1991-3. In relation to that plan, I actively campaigned against the rezoning proposals being made by the councillors. On foot of reasonable and valid complaints from constituents and residents' groups, I actively opposed the decisions that were being made and sought a reconsideration of them by the Fianna Fáil group on Dublin County Council.

I want to quote a letter to Ms Betty Coffey, the then chairperson of the Fianna Fáil group, Dublin County Council, 46-49 O'Connell Street, Dublin 1, dated 4 August 1993, from my home on Dáil notepaper:

Dear Betty,

I write to you as chairperson of the Fianna Fáil group on the council and I enclose a copy of a letter which I received from [a particular constituent] regarding the rezoning in Donabate. As you are aware, there is considerable annoyance in the north county area concerning the recent rezoning decisions and I believe it is in the interests of the party in the area that the group discuss the situation and alter the decision at the next stage of the review process. It would be impossible for me to specify each area of controversy but I would give you as examples the decisions in the Rivervalley area, the Christian Brothers' lands in Swords — there are many others.

Kindest personal regards,
Yours sincerely,
Ray Burke.

These matters were the subject of many discussions within the Fianna Fáil organisation in my constituency at various levels, during which I expressed my opposition to various proposals. Furthermore, I led a delegation of Fianna Fáil cumann members to meet the then Minister for the Environment, Deputy Michael Smith, in November 1993 to express opposition to the rezoning proposals of Dublin County Council as illustrated in the revised development plan and requested him not to sanction the revised plan.

With the benefit of hindsight, it is clear that in accepting this contribution, even in good faith, I exposed myself to the risk of being the subject of malicious allegations of the type now being made. Any Member who contests elections and depends on contributions to finance his or her campaign — unless he or she belongs to the fortunate few who inherit wealth — could find himself or herself where I am now had his or her path crossed that of a person who was prepared to make false charges against him or her, even if that person refused to honour those charges with a signature.

If anything seems clear from the conflicting news stories relating to this affair, it is that Mr. Gogarty's allegations against me form merely a small part of allegations being thrown by him against his former employers, from whom he parted in acrimonious circumstances. I can only assume that he made these allegations in an attempt to bring pressure to bear on his former employers in the context of his dispute with them.

In this context Mr. Connolly of the *Sunday Business Post*, to whom I referred earlier, confirmed in a radio interview that "from the very outset Mr. Gogarty has been mostly concerned with his unresolved differences with his former employers, JMSE" and, indeed, Mr. Connolly acknowledged that he had pursued the allegations against me "more actively than perhaps [Mr Gogarty] wished".

In my letter to the Ceann Comhairle asking for permission to make this statement, I made the point that I was going to make a personal statement on a 1989 election contribution. I also indicated that I was willing to take a question and answer session on my statement. This is unprecedented in the House. I will be as forthcoming as I can in any matter relating to the contribution which has been the subject of controversy.

In February, I will be a Member of the House for 25 years. I have no intention of subjecting myself to a show trial to satisfy anyone's political agenda or set a very undesirable precedent for this House. I do not believe that the people who elected me to this House or the decent fair minded people of this country want or expect me to do so.

An Leas-Cheann Comhairle: The normal rules for asking supplementary questions apply in this question and answer session. The supplementary questions should be concise, to the point and seek information and the Members should not attempt to debate or make mini-statements.

Mr. Shatter: I would agree with the Minister that no Member of the House should be wrongly subject to vilification. It is in the public interest that the Minister should respond to certain questions which I wish to raise with him. Was the Minister surprised to receive the contribution?

Mr. R. Burke: It was an exceptional contribution, as I have already acknowledged, the circumstances of which I have already outlined to the House.

Mr. Shatter: Did the Minister ask Mr. Gogarty the reason for his generosity and why the sum of £30,000 was being delivered to him in cash? The Minister might indicate in what denomination that money was received. It is quite an extraordinary sum to receive in cash.

Mr. R. Burke: In relation to the general question of contributions, and I will come back at a later stage undoubtedly to Mr. Gogarty and his allegations, I am much taken with the view as expressed by Fine Gael in the press statement in response to my statement on 7 August: "Fine Gael accepts that solicited and unsolicited contributions to the election expenses of parties and of individual candidates are a normal, healthy, unexceptional part of the Irish democratic process".

It was not just Fine Gael which had that view about unsolicited contributions. When asked a similar question, another distinguished Member of this House said that the bulk of his election expenses were his personal responsibility, that they had increased significantly in recent years, that assistance from supporters was welcome but that the Member was honour bound to observe the confidentiality under which contributions were made. He said that the donations received have been mainly of the order of £200 and any donations over £500 would have been very much an exception. He said that he fully supported disclosure elements in the Electoral Bill and that he would comply with all its provisions when it came into effect. Incidentally, I also support the Electoral Act.

That distinguished Member was responding to what I think was an impertinent question from *The Kerryman* of Friday, 20 December 1996, when all six Kerry Members were asked questions about donations. They were asked three specific questions: to disclose donations received by them as election candidates in the past ten years ——

Mr. Shatter: I deliberately asked two very simple straightforward questions.

Mr. R. Burke: Yes, and I am responding.

Mr. Shatter: I am anxious to be fair to the answerer. For reasons I do not understand, the Minister seems to be evading answering both questions by delivering a form of soliloquy on a Kerry newspaper article.

Mr. Spring: It is a great newspaper.

Mr. Shatter: Perhaps the Minister could respond to the questions which I am trying to raise in a fair and simple way.

Mr. R. Burke: And I am trying to answer in a

[Mr. R. Burke.]

fair and simple way. There is a view in relation to contributions in this House and I am making the point that it is not just my view. As I have already outlined, it is the view of the Fine Gael Party, with which I know the Deputy will not disagree. I am trying to be fair and reasonable. I want to make the point also in relation to the Labour Party and, similarly, I am sure I will get the opportunity to quote Deputy Rabbitte in relation to The Workers' Party and a contribution of £28,000.

Mr. Shatter: On a point of order and in case the Minister forgets, I repeat my questions. Did the Minister ask Mr. Gogarty why he was a recipient of such largesse, and second, did he address the issue of why he was receiving this money in cash? Was that something of a surprise to the Minister? Will the Minister indicate in what notes the money was received, as I previously requested? Perhaps the Minister would just reply to the questions asked.

Mr. R. Burke: As I already said, Mr. Gogarty wished me well in the election campaign and had indicated to Mr. Bailey that he wanted to support the election campaign. Why did he come to me? The Deputy would have to ask Mr. Gogarty that question. This matter occurred in 1989 and in attempting to recall and collect details of particular allocations of funds, cheques or otherwise, during recent months in respect of this controversy and in the interests of being as frank as possible with the House, I must inform the Deputy that I have no recollection of the denominations of the moneys I received.

Mr. Shatter: The Minister stated that the contribution in question formed part of moneys he received and that he had never previously received such a large sum. I am not criticising any Member of this House for raising funds because all politicians raise funds for election purposes. However, the sum of money in question is extraordinary. Did it not occur to the Minister to ask Mr. Gogarty why he was giving him £30,000 in cash? In that context, will the Minister indicate the nature of the other funds he received in 1989, of which this sum formed a part, and whether those funds were received in cash or otherwise?

Mr. R. Burke: As far as the funding was concerned, I did not ask Mr. Bailey the questions to which the Deputy referred. As far as other funding is concerned, I am here to answer questions in respect of a donation of £30,000. I never received a larger contribution but I have no intention of dealing with other subscriptions I received before or since the period under discussion. I have already given the reasons for my receipt of the £30,000 and referred to quotations by other Members in respect of it. That has been the tradition of this House in relation to confidentiality

regarding contributions and I do not intend to comment further on the matter.

Mr. Shatter: In his statement, the Minister introduced the issue of other contributions by indicating that out of these and other moneys received by him he gave the Fianna Fáil Party £10,000, his constituency organisation £7,000 and the remainder was spent on his political campaign and other political expenditures. Is he saying that the £7,000 given to his constituency organisation and the £10,000 given to Fianna Fáil derived from the £30,000 in addition to a further unspecified sum? Will the Minister indicate the dates on which Fianna Fáil Party headquarters was given £10,000 and his constituency organisation was given £7,000? Was the current Leader of Fianna Fáil or his predecessor informed that the Minister had received £30,000 preceding the 1989 election?

Mr. R. Burke: I will deal first with the last part of the Deputy's question regarding the date on which I gave £10,000 to Fianna Fáil headquarters. I have in my possession a letter from my bank which states:

Ulster Bank	Raphael Burke, Esq.
Dublin Airport Branch	Briargate
Swords Road	Malahide Road
Cloughran	Swords
Co. Dublin.	Co. Dublin.

8 September 1989

Dear Mr. Burke,

This is to confirm that on your instruction this branch issued a bank draft No. 340804 in favour of Fianna Fáil for the sum of £10,000. This draft was duly lodged and paid by the bank on 16/6/1989.

Yours sincerely,

W. J. Moody
Senior Manager
Business Banking

The sum of money I gave to my constituency organisation was confirmed as having been received in two drafts amounting to £2,000 and £5,000. I have never denied that the £30,000 was the only contribution I received during that election campaign because that would be a false statement. I am sure most Deputies receive contributions during election campaigns.

Lest Deputy Shatter suggest — perhaps I am anticipating the Deputy in this regard — that there was a massive surplus of funds following the 1989 general election, I am reluctant to inform him, not on the basis of not wishing to provide information to the House but because I believe I am setting appalling precedents for those who make personal statements to the House in the future, about a letter I received from my bank dated 4 August 1989. I find it offensive to do this from the point of view of my family but, in the interests of clarity, I wish to place on record the text of the letter from the Ulster Bank, Dublin Airport Branch, Swords Road, Cloughran, County Dublin which states:

Dear Mr. Burke,

I refer to recent discussions and I am pleased to confirm that subject to the terms and conditions outlined below the following facility has been sanctioned for you.

The "facility" referred to involved an overdraft of £35,000 which I required at that time and it was to be reviewed on 4 August 1990. Does that sound like someone who, as has been suggested, was awash with cash?

Mr. Finucane: The Minister must have spent a fortune on the election campaign.

Mr. R. Burke: I assure the Deputy that it was a very expensive election campaign.

Mr. Spring: I welcome the Minister's appearance before the House to clarify these matters. Will he provide further details in respect of the circumstances surrounding the donation in question? From his statement, I take it that the gentlemen from Bovale Developments Limited and Joseph Murphy Structural Engineers arrived at his home unannounced? Will the Minister clarify whether an appointment had been made for their visit or whether he had discussions with the company? Was clarification given or offered by those gentlemen regarding whether the contribution was a personal one or was intended for the Minister's party? Do I understand it that the Minister lodged the £30,000 to his personal bank account?

Mr. R. Burke: I am grateful for the Deputy's acknowledgement of my appearance in the House to make this personal statement. With regard to that statement, I am reluctant — the Deputy should not assume that I am trying to avoid the question ——

Mr. Spring: I merely asked two simple questions.

Mr. R. Burke: I will answer them. With regard to whether an appointment was made, the gentlemen in question came to see me on foot of a telephone call from Mr. Bailey in which he indicated his intention to visit me. He arrived on the following morning in the middle of the election campaign. The Deputy is aware of the way in which election campaigns are run and that, as far as possible, politicians meet people during the morning before they leave to canvass, etc. That is my recollection of the situation.

As far as the funding is concerned, the money was lodged to my personal account.

Mr. Spring: Did the gentlemen representing

Bovale Developments Limited and Joseph Murphy Structural Engineers provide clarification regarding whether the £30,000 was for the Minister's personal use or was it intended as a contribution to the Fianna Fáil Party?

Mr. R. Burke: No, that did not arise.

Mr. Spring: No discussion took place?

Mr. R. Burke: There was a very brief discussion. I wish to place on record the recollection of the man who was present at the meeting and I want to respond to some of the allegations made in connection with it. This might help to satisfy some of the concerns expressed by Members. I hope this will be agreeable to the House because I do not wish to be accused of attempting to delay its proceedings. However, I want to provide answers. I have in my possession a letter from my solicitors, Gore Grimes, which is addressed to Mr. Ray Burke, TD, and dated 9 September 1997. It reads:

Re: Ray Burke and James Gogarty.

Dear Ray,

In the course of my preparation of the statement of claim in the defamation proceedings issued in the High Court against Mr. James Gogarty, I have corresponded with Messrs. Fitzsimons Redmond Solicitors who represent Mr. Joseph Murphy and I have spoken with Mr. Kevin Smith of T. K. Smith Foy Solicitors who represent Mr. Michael Bailey. I enclose herewith a copy of the correspondence I have sent to Mr. Michael Fitzsimons, solicitor, of Messrs. Fitzsimons Redmond and the reply dated 8 September.

As I have said, I have spoken with Mr. Kevin Smith of T. K. Smith Foy who confirmed to me that Mr. Bailey's evidence in your High Court action against Mr. Gogarty will be as follows:

1. At the meeting in your house in June 1989 there were only three people present — Mr. Bailey, Mr. Gogarty and yourself.

2. Mr. Bailey was present throughout the meeting.

3. Mr. James Gogarty told Mr. Michael Bailey that he wanted to make a contribution to your election fund.

4. Mr. Michael Bailey witnessed the handing over of the contribution to you by Mr. James Gogarty.

5. At this meeting no favours were requested either by Mr. Bailey or Mr. James Gogarty and none were offered by you.

6. Mr. Michael Bailey did not make any payment to you at that meeting or at any other time.

[Mr. R. Burke.]
At the conclusion of the meeting Mr. Gogarty wished you good luck in election.

Yours sincerely,

David Martin.

To be helpful to the House and to clarify the matter, I will read a letter from my solicitor to Mr. Fitzsimons of Messrs. Fitzsimons Redmond dated 4 September 1987:

re. our client Ray Burke T.D.

Dear Sir,

We refer to our telephone conversation with Mr. Fitzsimons in connection with the above matter. We are in the process of preparing our client's statement of claim and putting together the statement of evidence that will be necessary in our client's case against Mr. James Gogarty arising from a defamation of our client by him. We understand that you act on behalf of Joseph Murphy who has been mentioned by Mr. Gogarty in his statement to the newspapers. To enable us to prepare a statement of evidence in our client's case and a statement of claim we wonder if you would be in a position to let us know the answers to the following questions:

1. Whether Mr. Joseph Murphy was present in your client's house at the time Mr. Gogarty handed a political contribution of £30,000 to your client.

2. Whether Mr. Joseph Murphy has ever met with our client and, if so, when, where and on what basis?

3. We would be very much obliged if you would let us know whether your client has been able to identify the source of the payments to our client and whether there are records of these payments and, if so, you might be good enough to let us have a breakdown of the records of the payments.

That was important in light of some of the newspaper articles that had been written.

I refer Deputies to the reply that was received from Fitzsimons Redmond.

re. your client Ray Burke, our client Joseph Murphy Structural Engineers Ltd. and Joseph Murphy Jnr.

Dear Sirs,

We refer to the above and recent correspondence, the contents of which have been noted. The position and our reply is as follows:
Our client was not present in your client's home when your client met with Mr. James Gogarty. The answer to the second question is no. [I remind the House of that question — whether Mr. Joseph Murphy has ever met with our client and, if so, when, where and on what basis? The answer was no.] On the third question, on 3 June 1989 two consecutive cheques were drawn on the JMSE account in the AIB Talbot Street branch — one cheque for £20,000 and a second for £10,000. The cheque stubs in relation to both cheques say cash. We presume these cheques relate to the £30,000 at issue. However, following inquiries with the AIB, they have been unable to provide any details in relation to same and do not have a record of paid cheques.

That is for the information of the House. I have been asked about records which go as far back as 1989. I have striven very hard to find and trace records. Fortunately, for the £10,000 that went to Fianna Fáil headquarters I had a bank draft and had evidence of it. In regard to other records, I have since discovered something of which I was not aware, that is, banks do not keep records dating back eight or nine years. All records are stopped and it is practically impossible to find records. I have found as much as I possibly can and am trying to be as frank as possible.

Mr. Spring: I begin to wonder if the Minister and I live in different worlds completely. Did the Minister have any sense of something remotely odd about two gentlemen arriving with £30,000 in cash? Did they say it was £30,000 in cash or did they just hand him a wad of money? Did he for one moment think of the implications? I do not know if other Members have had an experience where somebody during an election campaign doles out to them £30,000 in cash. Did the Minister consider this was not the norm in the context of an election which had become expensive?

Can I take it from the correspondence the Minister has read that a summons has issued in his case against Mr. Gogarty?

It may be helpful to the Minister to take this opportunity to clarify to the House whether he received any other sizeable contributions during elections campaigns from similar companies or the building industry.

Mr. R. Burke: The summons has issued and is the basis of preparation for the next phase of the legal proceedings. In the course of my preparation of the statement of claim in the defamation proceedings issued in the High Court against Mr. James Gogarty, this correspondence has been received with the indication from the two people that they are prepared to give evidence in the High Court in regard to it. Many of the allegations made in the newspapers that result in me being here answering questions arose from comments about sums of £80,000 and £40,000. I have striven to obtain maximum information and have put it before the House.

I already indicated it was an exceptional sum to receive and probably in hindsight I left myself open to the type of allegations that have been made. It should not have happened but there were no rules in place in 1989 in regard to subscriptions. My recollection is that the money was in two envelopes which were given to me. It was only after the people had left that the money was counted. I was not aware at the time of the sum I was receiving. As far as other contributions are concerned I have already answered that in the context of other subscriptions. I am here to answer questions on the £30,000 contribution. I have never received a larger contribution and will not get into the question of other contributions which I received.

Mr. Spring: Will you take this opportunity——? It is in his interest.

An Ceann Comhairle: I appeal to Deputies to make their remarks through the Chair.

Mr. R. Burke: I am answering in regard to this contribution because an allegation was made that there was a link between the subscription and having done favours or something improper in regard to it. I answered that. I was much taken with the answer given by the Deputy to *The Kerryman* in regard to his own subscriptions and the very careful wording he used. I agreed with the wording he gave. All Members treat election contributions they receive in the same way.

If anybody has any other allegation in regard to this, I suggest he goes to the Garda authorities. I know there are plenty of them stirring around in the media.

Mr. Rabbitte: I acknowledge the presence of the Minister to deal with these matters and that it is a matter for himself how he uses his time. How much was spent on the election campaign in Dublin North in 1989?

Mr. R. Burke: I have no intention of getting into how much was spent. It was a very, very expensive campaign in 1989.

Mr. Belton: It must have been the Deputy's birthday.

Mr. R. Burke: I will give Deputy Rabbitte an idea. Members will recall the 1989 campaign was particularly long. Apart from the campaign, there was the phoney war. There was a lead in of almost six weeks after the then Taoiseach had returned from Japan and there was controversy in regard to haemophiliacs. During the campaign I organised and paid all the expenses of operating several canvass teams. Throughout the campaign I arranged and paid for two crews to be posted to the constituency on an ongoing basis. I had literature printed, financed leaflets and carried out a vigorous personal campaign. As Members are aware a candidate's progress in a campaign is marked by ongoing levels of expenditure. I staged several meetings of party workers and supported and covered the cost. I caused billboards to be placed throughout the constituency. I utilised an extensive level of transport especially on polling day. I placed numerous advertisements and had additional secretarial back up. After the campaign I had functions to thank workers and sup-porters and paid the costs involved. All in all the 1989 campaign was long and expensive.

A Deputy: For everybody.

Mr. R. Burke: Any fair-minded assessment will demonstrate how quickly and easily considerable amounts of money are spent during a campaign. We are all here and know exactly what is involved.

A Deputy: The Minister does not have a clue.

Mr. R. Burke: I am not in a position to furnish details or documents to support what I am saying and I doubt if any other Member could do so in relation to an election held over eight years ago. However, the bottom line is that the money given to me by Mr. Gogarty was applied by me to my personal expenses and to Fianna Fáil at a national and local level. None of it went towards doing favours for JMSE, Bovale or anyone else and neither did anything else I received in that election.

Mr. Rabbitte: Is it true that in 1993 Fianna Fáil agreed with the Labour Party to put a ceiling on the amount of expenditure on three, four and five seater constituencies — £17,000, if I recall correctly, in a five seater constituency and obviously a lesser amount in a three seater constituency? Will the Minister give us an idea of the expenditure? Clearly, £7,000 was spent by the constituency organisation and £13,000 by himself. I do not know if the other Fianna Fáil candidates were expected to bear some of the cost. As a senior politician in the constituency, would it not be the case that he would have a donor base that went significantly outside the single contributor and can we have an indication of what that would have realised? This was the election where Fianna Fáil lost a seat. It seems a very large expenditure for that result.

Mr. R. Burke: Yes we did lose a seat at that time despite the expenditure incurred and the efforts made but thankfully we regained the seat in the recent election. Deputy Rabbitte asked me about contributions, confidentiality and so on. An article in *The Examiner*, Irish News, 24 July 1997, under the heading De Rossa Libel Trial states:

Mr. McDowell [who was representing the Independent newspaper group in that case] said that in an item in the draft, [the draft accounts of The Workers' Party Ard Comhairle accounts] it was stated there was a subscription for £28,000 with the comment "verbal explanation from Mr. Sean Garland".

Did he know why it was not put in writing?

Mr. Rabbitte said he did not but in his time and up to now, there would always have been subscriptions, some corporate and some by individuals, who did not want their identity to be known. There was nothing unusual in that.

[Mr. R. Burke.]

I agree fully with Deputy Rabbitte's view on subscriptions which come in.

So far as the overall expenditure of the campaign is concerned I received subscriptions which were spent on my campaign. I have already outlined the financial position I was in one month later as evidenced by my bank records. I ask the Deputy to accept that my bank manager is not telling lies and that the letter I received on 4 August 1989 outlined my financial straits after that campaign. I ask the Deputy, in decency, to accept what I am saying. It was an expensive campaign and the money received was expended.

Mr. Rabbitte: I am not asking the Minister to give the identity of his donors but to give an approximate figure for the 1989 campaign. If he will not answer that question, I put one last question to him. He is no stranger to controversy in the planning area and, for that reason, did the size of the donation not cause alarm bells to ring in his head when he counted it subsequent to the departure of Mr. Gogarty? Did he make any subsequent contact with Mr. Gogarty? Will the Minister say why is it likely that somebody who was unknown to him would consider that exposing his donation would somehow help him in his battle with his company?

Mr. R. Burke: I assume he did not have a battle with his company when he came to me. He was an executive of the company. As I understand it from reports I have read it was after that he had a battle with his company. I have been involved in controversy before. I have been the subject of allegations and innuendo. I have been accused of everything in recent weeks other than starting the Chicago fire and being involved in the shooting of Michael Collins. So far as the 1989 situation is concerned there could have been some concern if I was a member of a local authority and in a position to influence any decision. As he was a member of the local authority and served with me the Deputy will recall I had left that local authority in March 1987. I have already outlined the circumstances and have indicated it was an enormous sum.

Mr. Gormley: I want clarification on two points. Why was the donation in cash? Will the Minister agree with the summing up of Denis McCullagh, SC in the payments to politicians tribunal that the mere acceptance of such a gift compromises the recipient?

Mr. R. Burke: The Deputy had better ask Mr. Gogarty why it was cash, I cannot give the answer. The two cheques for £20,000 and £10,000 were made out to cash by his company and went through their bank. In regard to Mr. McCullagh's summing up, the Deputy could also read the rest of the report of the McCracken tribunal on political contributions and what is said about them. I

do not have a copy of the report with me but it states that the system of political contributions should be continued within the new rules that have been laid down. I fully support them and if they are to be altered in forthcoming elections I will adhere to those as well. What is happening, and I am deeply affected by it, is I am being judged under the rules for 1997, which are right and proper and which I support, where amounts in excess of the maximum figure of £500 for individuals and £4,000 for parties must be declared, although the contribution was received in 1989 when there were no rules in place. It is also ironic that I am being asked about records of what I have and what I did and did not do.

I am reminded of the response given by Mr. Seán Murray at the Beef Tribunal to a question about subscriptions. He said he had a list of subscriptions given by persons or companies connected with the beef processing industry between 1987 and 1990. He was asked the position in relation to previous years, to which he replied that the records had been destroyed and that prior to 1987 there were no records. That relates to Fine Gael, an organisation I know to be effective and efficient, having fought it all my political life. I, as a single Deputy, am being asked to produce records back to 1989. I have made valiant efforts to get those records, and I have tried to be as frank as I can in relation to what I got and what I did. I can give the House no more information than I already have.

3 o'clock

Mr. Shatter: The Minister has told us that after the election of 1989 he borrowed £35,000. The implication is that this was money he required to borrow because of his personal election campaign. He then told us he received cash amounting to £30,000. Apparently, he retained £13,000 of that which he also spent on his personal election campaign. That brings the amount that the Minister spent on his personal election campaign to £48,000. On top of that he got other unspecified donations. I want the Minister to clarify that. Is he saying that in 1989 he spent in excess of £48,000 on his personal election campaign, separate from the money the Fianna Fáil organisation spent in his constituency?

The Minister has told the House that he received this money in cash, that he subsequently discovered that the person who brought him the money had encashed two cheques. Apparently the Minister did not know that it was £30,000 he had received but he subsequently counted the money he got. Perhaps he might indicate to the House how much he thought it was. After he discovered how much it was, did he write to anyone to thank them and, if so, to whom? Why was Mr Bailey acting as an intermediary to bring Mr Gogarty to him in these circumstances?

The Minister said that at that time he was not a member of a local authority and therefore was not exercising poor judgment. Let me suggest — and I take no pleasure in making this suggestion

— that he and I shared membership of Dublin County Council together for a period of two to two and a half years until he resumed his position in Cabinet, and that it was poor judgment for a former member of a county council, someone who had been so recently involved in making decisions and voting on issues in the council, some of which were controversial, to have received this level of money personally in cash?

Mr. R. Burke: As to the mental arithmetic relating to the amount of money I spent on the campaign, I will not go down that road with the Deputy. The sums I required to raise were raised for personal reasons, to refurbish my home, to build a tennis court for my children——

Mr. Shatter: So they had nothing to do with the election?

Mr. R. Burke: They had nothing to do with the election.

A Deputy: Then why bring them up?

Mr. R. Burke: I find this offensive. There may be a bit of blood lust today for my neck, but we are setting a precedent that we will all regret in the future. I will come back to Deputy Shatter's point in a moment. I listened carefully to the point made by the former Taoiseach, Deputy Bruton, and I was taken by some of the comments he made about people being chased. I do not mind answering questions. I volunteered to answer questions in the House because I have nothing to hide and nothing to be ashamed of. However, we are creating a precedent. If for any reason any other Member of this House ever wants to make a personal statement this precedent will be thrown across the House and he or she will be asked why they will not answer questions. This will affect not just the present Members of the House but future Members, people who have not even indicated an interest in becoming Deputies.

As to the money, it was not to pay off election expenses; it was an overdraft facility to assist with financing house refurbishment, the building of a tennis court for my two daughters and the changing of my wife's car which she has had since 1989 and has not changed since. I have no pleasure in having to reveal details of my personal finances to any Member of this House or to the general public.

Regarding the period from 1985 to 1987, I was a member of the County Council, and I chaired it and tried to ensure that there was a minimum of controversial decisions. I have already indicated the one I put my name to relating to one house at the Rath in Swords for a decent young couple who have been living there happily ever since. As to Mr. Bailey bringing Mr. Gogarty to see me, I never met Mr. Gogarty before that occasion or, to my knowledge, since that occasion. He never had occasion to come back to

me. I did not write a letter. Mr. Gogarty wished me well as he went out and I thanked him for the subscription. Everybody has a different way of running a campaign. I did not write to say thanks. Perhaps I should have, but I did not.

Mr. Higgins (*Dublin West*): I have two simple questions. Did the Minister ever canvass any elected member of the former Dublin County Council to vote for land rezonings or material contraventions which would redound to the benefit of JMSC, Bovale, or the principals of those companies or people close to them?

When the Minister found that the amount donated was £30,000, which at the time would have been roughly three years' wages for an ordinary worker, did he not feel that he could be heavily compromised and heavily indebted to that company which might subsequently come to him for a favour in securing planning permission or something that would be of monetary or other value to them and which his position as a senior politician might allow him to obtain on their behalf?

Mr. R. Burke: Regarding the first point, the answer is no. Not only did I not canvass in relation to it, I have already outlined in my opening statement my position in relation to it — that all members of local authorities have onerous duties and have to make decisions in relation to development plans and other planning matters, some of which will be controversial. However, I was not a member of the council. I did not lobby. Not only did I not lobby, I actively opposed what it was doing, publicly at meetings, privately within our party organisation and in leading a delegation to the Minister for the Environment at the time asking him not to approve a plan that had been approved by the council. As to being compromised by the £30,000, I was not compromised. I did not feel in any way compromised and I do not now feel compromised in relation to it.

Mr. Spring: Was there any relationship, working or otherwise, between Bovale and Murphys at that time, or has there been since then?

Mr. R. Burke: I have no knowledge of that.

Mr. Gildea: Did the Minister receive any moneys when he granted MMDS licences during his period as Minister for Communications under the Haughey-led Government?

Mr. R. Burke: No.

Mr. R. Bruton: Was the money the Minister received used solely for political purposes, as tax law would require if it were not a declarable gift?

Mr. R. Burke: Yes.

Ms McManus: There are many Members of the House, including myself, who have never been, and never will be, offered anything remotely like

[Ms McManus.]
£30,000, but we still fight elections. Why does the Minister feel he deserved a £30,000 contribution?

Mr. R. Burke: I already indicated the position of the Deputy's party regarding a £28,000 contribution from an unnamed source about which a verbal explanation was given by Mr. Garland. There is not a huge difference between £28,000 and £30,000. In regard to why I deserved to get such a contribution, I did not ask for it. It was given to me, I thanked the person concerned and he wished me well. Perhaps he recognised the different type of qualities I possess.

Mr. Allen: Is the Minister aware of other similar contributions made to members of the Government?

Mr. Dempsey: Or the previous Government.

Mr. R. Burke: No.

Mr. J. O'Keeffe: Since the receipt of the money in cash in 1989, did the Minister lodge moneys in overseas bank accounts?

Mr. R. Burke: I have already answered questions regarding my accounts and I do not intend to give further answers in that regard. I have bared my soul to the House today and I find the Deputy's question offensive in the extreme at this stage. In fairness to the Members of the House, I have tried to be fair, reasonable and up front with information. I have no overseas bank account.

Mr. J. O'Keeffe: Is the Minister confirming that since 1989 he has not opened or lodged money in an overseas bank account? I refer in particular to an account in the Isle of Man.

Mr. R. Burke: As I have already said, the answer is no.

Mr. Howlin: On what basis did the Minister decide to give £10,000 to national headquarters, £7,000 to his constituency and the balance to his election expenses?

Mr. R. Burke: There was no particular decision made in that regard. I gave £10,000 to Fianna Fáil headquarters. There was no trigonometry or algebra involved in the breakdown of the money. I have no explanation for the way it was divided.

Mr. J. Mitchell: In reply to a question from Deputy Spring the Minister said he lodged money to his personal account. Was that his personal account in the Ulster Bank at Dublin Airport? If so, is it not strange that he paid Fianna Fáil headquarters by bank draft rather than by cheque from that account?

Mr. R. Burke: I am glad I paid them by bank draft rather than by cheque. If I had paid them by cheque I would not have the record of the cheque

because the matter dates back so far. I do not believe it was unreasonable to pay them in that way. I am pleased that all contributions I received were during the course of general election campaigns and not in between them.

Mr. J. Mitchell: Was the money lodged to the personal account to which he referred in the Ulster Bank in Dublin Airport?

Mr. R. Burke: Some of it would have been lodged and more of it, because it was given in cash, would have been used on the ongoing daily expenses of the election campaign. As a long-term Member of the House I am sure the Deputy is aware that considerable amounts of cash are required on a daily basis as an election campaign proceeds. That may vary from person to person. It is obvious that some people carry out different types of campaigns. During my campaign I spent considerable sums of money on a daily basis.

Mr. Rabbitte: Why did the Minister not refer to the £10,000 bank draft to Fianna Fáil headquarters in his initial statement? Since this matter has been the subject of rumours for more than two years, why did he not make a comment before now, particularly when the good name of another Member of the House was being vilified as a result of a rumour that originated in the environs of the House, but not by a Member of it? For two or three months of the summer of 1995 another Member of the House was commonly believed to be the person associated with the Neary business from Newry. As the Minister firmly believes there is nothing improper about this matter, did it not occur to the him to make a statement at any stage?

Mr. R. Burke: I did not refer to the £10,000 contribution to Fianna Fáil headquarters in my original statement because it was referred to one month earlier by the Taoiseach in response to a question on the matter. As he had already dealt with the matter I felt it would be impertinent to refer to it again.

As another long-term Member of the House Deputy Rabbitte should be well aware of the political arena and the media circus that can take place. When the Neary controversy arose it did not dawn on me that I was the person involved because I was not a member of the council at the time. It was only later as stories continued to run that I realised I was at the centre of a storm. As to why I chose not to respond, in the terminology to which we are all familiar, I did not want to give oxygen to the story. However, it continued to run and after the general election my name was dragged into it.

I was amazed at some of the appalling things that were being said about me and my father. I appeal to Members to bear with me so that I can clarify a matter that deserves clarification. My father was a Member of the House from 1 until 1973. He served the House loyally for years. I still meet people all over the country who admired, respected and had great affection for him. He served in this House with many current Members or their fathers. In Cork last Sunday, at the Liam Lynch memorial, I met many people who spoke kindly of him. On 18 February 1996 *The Sunday Business Post* featured an article about me, written by Mr. Frank Connolly in his usual complimentary terms. I mention this article because I was asked why I did not go back to the media. Mr. Connolly wrote:

> The land on which his house is built was originally purchased by Burke's father Paddy, who bought it from an inmate of the mental hospital in Portrane, Co. Dublin.

My father worked as a nurse in the hospital in Portrane until the mid-1950s. He had come from a humble background in the west of Ireland — I am proud of his background as I am proud of mine. The assertion in that article was a complete and utter lie. I did not take an action against the newspaper because I have never taken one since I entered this House despite the things they have said about me. I have with me the Land Registry documentation relating to my home which clearly shows that, far from being bought from a hospital patient under his care, the house and site was transferred to me and I bought it in a normal commercial transaction from Oldpark Developments Limited. The house was built in the normal commercial manner. I was doing business with that company. That transaction, along with others, was the subject of a Garda investigation in 1974. I did not so much resent the attacks on myself — in this business one learns to live with them although they do not get easier. However, I am glad to have the opportunity on behalf of my family and my father, who died in 1985, to clarify the record in that regard.

As to why I felt I should not make statements, I shall give another example of the type of journalism which, thankfully, is followed only by a minute number among that profession. I ask the House to bear with me and if Members want another five or ten minutes I do not mind, because I wish to give another example of what I have endured in recent times. I received a letter from *The Sunday Times* on Thursday, 31 July 1997, which read:

Dear Mr. Burke,

As you are aware there have been a number of stories in the media in recent weeks about your relationship with Bovale Developments and other matters. These stories, in turn, seem to be the culmination of a lengthy series of smears about you, but not by name. We are interested in setting out clearly and unambiguously the position in relation to all this as there seems to be considerable confusion at this stage. We propose talking to you off the record about this. You can be absolutely assured that any conversation will be treated as being in the

strictest confidence. [There followed some phone numbers.]

Yours sincerely,
Rory Godson,
Ireland Editor

There was no suggestion in that letter that there would be a major article about me on the following Sunday. That article was headlined "Firms' gave £80,000 to Burke' " and stated: "Burke was not available for comment yesterday".

In that first letter I was addressed as "Mr. Burke". Last week, on Wednesday, 3 September, I received a personal letter from Mr. Godson. Despite claiming in his article that I received £80,000, which was a total fabrication, I was addressed as his good friend "Ray". The letter reads:

Dear Ray,

I would like to talk to you for a few minutes about James Gogarty, etc. As you know I missed you on the week you went on holidays, despite valiant attempts by you to get back to me. We could meet on a private basis for a confidential chat, which would enable *The Sunday Times* to print an informed assessment of the current situation ahead of next week's Dáil debate. [He proceeded to give me his home phone number among others and out of respect for his family I will not read them.]

Best wishes,
Rory Godson
Ireland Editor

The article in *The Sunday Times* stated that I "was not available for comment" while the letter of 3 September mentions "valiant attempts by you to get back to me". This is, at the least, unethical journalism.

An Ceann Comhairle: I remind Members that, in accordance with the Order of the House, we have now devoted one hour to questions and answers and we must now proceed to item No. 8.

Mr. Belton: The Minister said he was prepared to answer more questions.

An Ceann Comhairle: The House decided this morning that there would be one hour for questions and answers and that has not changed.

Mr. Belton: Did he get one envelope or two?

An Bille um an Seachtú Leasú Déag ar an mBunreacht (Uimh. 2), 1997: An Dara Céim.

Seventeenth Amendment of the Constitution (No. 2) Bill, 1997: Second Stage.

The Taoiseach: Tairgím: "Go léifear an Bille an Dara Uair."
I move: "That the Bill be now read a Second Time."
This Bill has been restored to the Order Paper

Appendix D

Vol. 481
No. 1

Tuesday,
7 October 1997

DÍOSPÓIREACHTAÍ PARLAIMINTE
PARLIAMENTARY DEBATES

DÁIL ÉIREANN

TUAIRISC OIFIGIÚIL—*Neamhcheartaithe*

(OFFICIAL REPORT—*Unrevised*)

Tuesday, 7 October 1997.

with Questions to the Minister for Enterprise, Trade and Employment.

Question put and agreed to.

Tribunal of Inquiry into Planning Matters: Motion.

Minister for the Environment and Local Government (Mr. Dempsey): I move:

That Dáil Éireann resolves

A. That it is expedient that a Tribunal be established under the Tribunals of Inquiry (Evidence) Act, 1921, as adapted by or under subsequent enactments and the Tribunals of Inquiry (Evidence) (Amendment) Act, 1979, to inquire urgently into and report to the Clerk of the Dáil and make such findings and recommendations as it sees fit, in relation to the following definite matters of urgent public importance:

1. The identification of the lands stated to be 726 acres in extent, referred to in the letter dated 8th June, 1989 from Mr. Michael Bailey to Mr. James Gogarty (reproduced in the Schedule herewith) and the establishment of the beneficial ownership of the lands at that date and changes in the beneficial ownership of the lands since the 8th June, 1989 prior to their development;

2. The planning history of the lands including:—

(a) their planning status in the Development Plan of the Dublin local authorities current at the 8th June, 1989;

(b) the position with regard to the servicing of the lands for development as at the 8th June, 1989;

(c) changes made or proposed to be made to the 8th June, 1989 planning status of the lands by way of: —

(i) proposals put forward by Dublin local authority officials pursuant to the review of Development Plans or otherwise;

(ii) motions by elected members of Dublin local authorities proposing rezoning;

(iii) applications for planning permission (including any involving a material contravention of the Development Plan);

3. Whether the lands referred to in the letter dated 8th June, 1989 were the subject of the following: —

(a) Re-zoning resolutions;

(b) Resolutions for material contra-

D 481—D

vention of the relevant Development Plans;

(c) Applications for special tax designation status pursuant to the Finance Acts;

(d) Applications for planning permission;

(e) Changes made or requested to be made with regard to the servicing of the lands for development;

(f) Applications for the granting of building by-law approval in respect of buildings constructed on the lands;

(g) Applications for fire safety certificates;

on or after the 20th day of June 1985.

And

(i) to ascertain the identity of any persons or companies (and if companies, the identity of the beneficial owners of such companies) who had a material interest in the said lands or who had a material involvement in the matters aforesaid;

(ii) to ascertain the identity of any members of the Oireachtas and/or members of the relevant local authorities who were involved directly or indirectly in any of the foregoing matters whether by the making of representations to a planning authority or to any person in the authority in a position to make relevant decisions or by the proposing of or by voting in favour or against or by abstaining from any such resolutions or by absenting themselves when such votes were taken or by attempting to influence in any manner whatsoever the outcome of any such applications;

(iii) to ascertain the identity of all public officials who considered, made recommendations or decisions on any such matters and to report on such considerations, recommendations and/or decisions;

(iv) to ascertain and report on the outcome of all such applications, resolutions and votes in relation to such applications in the relevant local authority;

4. (a) The identify of all recipients of payments made to political parties or Members of either House of the Oireachtas or members or officials of a Dublin local authority or other public official by Mr. Gogarty or Mr. Bailey or a connected person or company within the meaning of the Ethics in Public Office Act, 1995, from 20th June 1985 to date, and the circumstances, considerations and motives relative to any such payment;

[Mr. Dempsey.]
(b) whether any of the persons referred to at sub-paragraphs 3(ii) and 3 (iii) above were influenced directly or indirectly by the offer or receipt of any such payments or benefits;

5. In the event that the Tribunal in the course of its inquiries is made aware of any acts associated with the planning process committed on or after the 20th June 1985 which may in its opinion amount to corruption, or which involve attempts to influence by threats or deception or otherwise to compromise the disinterested performance of public duties, it shall report on such acts and should in particular make recommendations as to the effectiveness and improvement of existing legislation governing corruption in the light of its inquiries.

6. And that the Tribunal be requested to make recommendations in relation to such amendments to Planning, Local Government and Ethics in Public Office legislation as the Tribunal considers appropriate having regard to its findings.

'payment' includes money and any benefit in kind and the payment to any person includes a payment to a connected person within the meaning of the Ethics in Public Office Act, 1995.

B. And that the Tribunal be requested to conduct its inquires in the following manner, to the extent that it may do so consistent with the provisions of the Tribunals of Inquiry (Evidence) Acts, 1921 and 1979: —

(i) To carry out such preliminary investigations in private as it thinks fit using all the powers conferred on it under the Acts, in order to determine whether sufficient evidence exists in relation to any of the matters referred to above to warrant proceeding to a full public inquiry in relation to such matters,

(ii) To inquire fully into all matters referred to above in relation to which such evidence may be found to exist, dealing in the first instance with the acknowledged monetary donation debated in Dáil Éireann on the 10th September 1997 Dáil Debates Columns 616-638 and to report to the Clerk of the Dáil thereupon,

(iii) To seek discovery of all relevant documents, files and papers in the possession, power or procurement of said Mr. Michael Bailey, Mr. James Gogarty and Donnelly, Neary and Donnelly Solicitors,

(iv) In relation to any matters where the Tribunal finds that there is insufficient evidence to warrant proceeding to a fully public inquiry, to report that fact to the Clerk of the Dáil and to report in such a manner as the Tribunal thinks appropriate, on the steps taken by the Tribunal to determine what evidence, if any, existed,

(v) To report on an interim basis not later than one month from the date of establishment of the Tribunal or the tenth day of any oral hearing, whichever shall first occur, to the Clerk of the Dáil on the following matters:

the numbers of parties then represented before the Tribunal;

the progress which has been made in the hearing and the work of the Tribunal;

the likely duration (so far as that may be capable of being estimated at that time) of the Tribunal proceedings;

any other matters which the Tribunal believes should be drawn to the attention of the Clerk of the Dáil at that stage (including any matter relating to the terms of reference);

C. And that the person or persons selected to conduct the Inquiry should be informed that it is the desire of the House that —

(a) the Inquiry be completed in as economical a manner as possible and at the earliest date consistent with a fair examination of the matters referred to it, and, in respect to the matters referred to in paragraphs 1 to 4 above, if possible, not later than the 31st December 1997, and

(b) all costs incurred by reason of the failure of individuals to co-operate fully and expeditiously with the Inquiry should, so far as is consistent with the interests of justice, be borne by those individuals.

D. And that the Clerk of the Dáil shall on receipt of any Report from the Tribunal arrange to have it laid before both Houses of the Oireachtas immediately on its receipt.

AN SCEIDEAL
SCHEDULE

Killnamonan House,
The Ward,
Co. Dublin.
8th June 1989

Dear Mr. Gogarty,

PROPOSALS FOR DISCUSSION

Re: Your lands at Finglas, Ballymun, Donabate, Balgriffin and Portmarnock, Co. Dublin.

I refer to our many discussions regarding your following six parcels of land: —

Lot 1: 100 acres (approx) at North Road, Finglas, including "Barrett's Land".

Lot 2: 12 acres (approx) at Jamestown Road, Finglas.

Lot 3: 100 acres (approx) at Poppintree, Ballymun.

Lot 4: 255 acres (approx) at Donabate (Turvey House and Beaverton House).

Lot 5: 250 acres (approx) at Balgriffin.

Lot 6: 9 acres (approx) at Portmarnock.

I submit the following proposals for your consideration:-

PROPOSAL No. 1 — Purchase Proposal

Lots 1, 2 and 3   Purchase Price £4,000 per acre
10% deposit payable on the signing of the contract
Completion 1 year from date of contract.

Lot 4:   Purchase Price IR£1 Million
Deposit 10% on contract
Completion 2 years from date of contract.

Lot 5:   Purchase Price IR£750,000.00
Deposit 10% on contract
Completion 3 years from date of contract

Lot 6:   Option to be granted for nominal consideration (£100.00)
for a period of 2 years at a purchase price of £30,000.00 per acre.

PROPOSAL No. 2 — Participation Proposal
As an alternative to the outright purchase proposal above I am prepared to deal with Lots 1 — 5 (inclusive) above on the basis that I would be given a 50% share in the ownership of the said lands in exchange for procuring Planning Permission and Building Bye Law Approval. The time span which I would require to be allowed to obtain the Permissions and Approval and my anticipated financial expenditure (apart from my time input) in respect of the different lots would be as follows:-

Lots 1, 2 and 3
A period of 2 years within which to procure a buildable Planning Permission and Building Bye Laws Approval for mixed development including housing, industrial and commercial.
My financial expenditure up to a figure of £150,000.00 (to include Architect's fees, Consulting Engineer's fees, Planning and Bye Law charges etc.).

Lots 4 and 5
Time requirement — 3 years.
Financial Expenditure — up to £150,000.00
In considering the above proposals the following points of information should be borne in mind by all parties:—

1. From the point of view of obtaining Planning Permission the entire lands (lots 1 to 6 inclusive) have the following shortcoming:

NO zoning for development purposes

NO services.

NO proposal in current draft development plans (City and County) for the zoning of the lands or any part thereof for development purposes.

2. We face a very severe uphill battle to arrange for the availability of services and for the ultimate procurement of Planning Permission.

3. The steps to be taken on the way to procuring a buildable Planning Permission and Building Bye Laws Approval are notoriously difficult, time-consuming and expensive. Material Contravention Orders must be obtained and this involves the procurement of a majority vote at 2 full Council Meetings at which 78 Council Members must be present and it also involves satisfactory compliance with extensive requirements and pre-conditions of the Planning Authority and the inevitable dealing with protracted Appeals to an Bord Pleanala.

4. It is essential that the Planning Application should be brought in the name of an active housebuilding company which enjoys good standing and good working relationship with the Planners and the Council Members and in this regard I confirm that in the event of our reaching agreement regarding the within proposals that all Planning Applications would be made by one of my Companies which meets the said requirements.

5. In the case of all of the lands the applications will be highly sensitive and controversial and we can realistically expect strenuous opposition from private, political and planning sectors. One of my active companies will have to take the limelight in such applications and withstand the objections and protests which will inevitably confront it. Apart from the anticipated financial expenditure as outlined above it should be borne in mind that I will personally have to give extensively of my time and efforts over the entire period of the applications including the necessary preliminary negotiations in regard to services and zoning. It must be borne in mind that I will have to abandon other projects which would be open to myself and my companies in order to give proper attention to this project. If I am successful in changing your lands from their present status of agricultural lands with very limited potential even for agricultural use into highly valuable building lands I would have to be rewarded with a minimum 50% stake in the ownership of the lands. Our advisors would have

[Mr. Dempsey.]
to work out the details as to how this can be effected in the most tax-efficient manner.

I look forward to hearing from you in relation to the above proposals. In the case of the first proposal which relates to the outright purchase of the lands (excluding Lot 6) I would not be adverse to a proposal which would involve the vendors retaining a participation stake of up to 20% in the purchasing company if you felt that an ongoing interest in the future development of the lands would be more acceptable to the present owners.

MICHAEL BAILEY.
Mr. Jim Gogarty,
Clontarf,
Dublin 3."

An tAire Comhshaoil agus Rialtais Áitiúil

I join with the Taoiseach and other Members of the House in extending my sympathy to former Deputy Ray Burke and his family on their bereavement. I also express my regret that he felt it necessary to resign from his position as Minister for Foreign Affairs and from this House.

The Government decided at its meeting on Tuesday last to move a motion in both Houses of the Oireachtas establishing a tribunal of inquiry. The decision was taken to meet public concern created by the recent publication of a letter referring to planning permission and its procurement. That letter was the latest in a series of moves which have gone a long way towards destroying public faith in the planning process as a key aspect of our democratic system. The Government believes it is vital to deal finally and conclusively with the public concerns raised.

I am glad to put before the House today a motion incorporating comprehensive terms of reference which are the product of extensive consultation with the Opposition parties and on which a considerable degree of agreement has been achieved. Under these terms the tribunal will examine in detail the planning history of six parcels of land, adding up to 726 acres, dealt with in the letter. Not only will it examine the planning history, it will also examine the servicing and by-law approval involved. In addition, if the tribunal as it goes about its business, becomes aware of other issues suggesting corruption in the planning system even if they are not directly connected to the lands in question, it will have the power and the right to consider those issues. When the tribunal finishes its business, the Government, and I am sure the House, wishes that the doubts around this specific case and the planning system will have been dealt with and cleared up.

I do not propose to argue today the issues which are more properly addressed by the tribunal. However, I want to raise as a longer term issue with all Members of this House the balance between whistle blowing and public confidence in the democratic institutions, the tension between the fearless pursuit of wrongdoers and the destruction of an individual by the manipulation of public opinion. Democracy cannot function at local or national level if people have no confidence in the workings of democratic institutions.

Trust is the essence of all government, whether local or national. Such trust is based on free elections, open discussion and clear procedures followed by public servants and public representatives of strong ethical standards. This is not a naive or idealistic trust. Just as in the private sector where there is evidence of corruption, there are methods by which that corruption can be exposed and rooted out. Those methods must change with the times. What goes unquestioned in one decade may emerge, at a later date as a serious loophole allowing, even fostering, corruption. When that happens, the system must change utterly and quickly. Where systems fail to serve the public, it is frequently the whistle-blower who reveals the failure. This can be someone who has suffered or someone who has benefited but who is later unhappy at having benefited.

Members will agree that to cry "halt" to corruption, name names, produce evidence and admit to even a small involvement in past corruption requires courage. Let us never underestimate the courage required to blow the whistle on corruption particularly if in the process, a powerful and popular person, party or group is accused. That courage is essential to the maintenance of trust because, ultimately, the specific case can be speedily addressed and answered, wrongdoers subjected to the process of the law and the system strengthened by the removal of flawed individuals from within it. However, that is not what we have witnessed in the past number of weeks and months.

What we have seen in the past few weeks and months, regardless of the side of the House on which we sit, must be recognised by all Deputies as deeply threatening to ourselves, the system we serve and the civil rights of the people we serve. The threat lies not in the accusation but in the method of accusation. What we have seen is an infinitely clever erosion of a reputation based not on upfront accusation and production of evidence but on instalments of venom. We have not watched the relentless rooting out of corruption; we have watched a soap opera, with an unseen scriptwriter doling out the dramatic scenes to different producers. The timing of this has been chillingly exquisite.

What we have witnessed in the recent weeks is the feeding of prejudice against an individual. At no stage has enough evidence been offered to justify that steady feeding of prejudice. However, because of the timing of the instalments and their placement, the exercise has been remarkably effective. It has been so effective because the public mind is a busy and preoccupied one. Someone ensures that what reaches that public mind is a series of soundbites, beginning with a soundbite about a large financial donation. If members of the public are then asked if they trust the person about whom they heard this sequence of course they will say that they do not.

This proves the effectiveness of not coming straight out with an accusation but dribbling it out in hints and suggestions over a long period of time. I am not sure the nation benefits from learning that lesson. I am not sure we in this House, regardless of the side on which we sit, will benefit from it either. It may not cost us a thought when this planned poisoning is carried out against someone from another party. However, a weapon which proved so deadly in its effectiveness will be used repeatedly. It is a matter of time before any one of us finds himself or herself baffled with rage and frustration, unable to pin down the accuser or the accusations, unable to prove ourselves innocent and filled with terror at the thought that we must do so; that a cornerstone of our democratic system has been removed, leaving us without the protection in which we trusted and in which the citizens of this State trust.

When we hear people saying "sure didn't we always know" what we are hearing is the abandonment of a central principle on which the justice system of this country is predicated. When we hear allegations treated as evidence and insinuations treated as proof, we would do well to be worried because, regardless of whether the person at the centre of the storm is a friend or an opponent, we are hearing the death rattles of trust. When trust dies, no democratic institution has value. When trust dies, none of us has firm ground from which to work because that work is founded on the trust of individual voters who have chosen us to represent them.

The words used in recent days have the ring of an excited bloodsport rather than an examination of standards and ethics. Everyone has seen the words to which I refer in print and the phrase "bringing him down" has been used continually. In the event that my contribution is distorted outside this House, I wish to make it clear that I am in favour of exposing corruption and tightening whatever safeguards will prevent corruption; rejecting attitudes and behaviour which, in any way, damage the trust our people have in their systems and the people who work those systems; seeking out evidence, insisting that a case be answered; and convicting an individual if, in the process of an investigation, that person is proven to have acted unethically, improperly or illegally. In other words, if the process results in 'bringing him down', so be it. However, 'bringing him down' it is not and should not be the first objective for anyone inside or outside this House — it is the end result of a democratic process which strengthens rather than demeans democracy.

The recent accusations have found themselves a welcome which may emerge from a number of motivations. The context for some of them may have been set by disapproval on environmental grounds of some decisions taken by councils and the suspicion that they can only be explained by personal gain. In some cases, that suspicion has caused ghastly hurt not only to the families of people in this House, but to former colleagues. The aspersions cast on the late Deputy Seán Walsh, which proved to be completely groundless, provide a classic example. The story moves on, there is a shrug about the fact that it proved to be untrue, and neither the accusers nor those who carried the accusations care about the rights of a dead man or the agony of his family.

It is time to put an end to this corrosive cruelty dressed up as principled investigation. The tribunal of inquiry with the proposed terms of reference should be the instrument to do so and, in the process, will protect the integrity of those who serve our political institutions. In the long-term, the solution lies not in a tribunal but in the suggestion mooted by the Taoiseach when in Opposition that a commission be established on a permanent basis to which this kind of issue can be referred at any time. This would be the most effective method of dealing with such matters and the Government is bringing forward this legislation to effect it.

The tribunal will be an historic and pivotal procedure if it can remove the lingering doubts about the planning process. If doing so means that someone stands fully accused and is proven to have taken a bribe, distorted the integrity of the system or been involved in other illegal activities, that will be welcomed by the Government and acted upon immediately. We are all entitled to that. There is no one in this House who has not felt the referred contempt resulting from perceived failures of individuals. It is simply not fair on those of us, whether public representatives or public officials, trying to do a difficult job, if we find that job complicated by malicious, unjustified rumours. We must ensure that when councillors take decisions, they do so for the common good and the good of their constituents, not because they, personally, stand to gain financially. It is because of that imperative that the terms of reference will enable the tribunal to deal with all of the issues emerging from the planning history of the lands referred to in the Bailey letter.

The Government strongly believes that this flexibility, in addition to the capacity vested in the tribunal to deal with any acts which, in its opinion, are corrupt, is vital if the tribunal is to isolate wrongdoers, if any exist, make specific and actionable what has been vague and without consequence and restore vital trust in the systems established to serve the citizen. It is significant and regrettable that, at this point, the word "rezoning" has a pejorative ring to it. The minute one sees a headline with the word "rezoning" in it, the assumption is that the rezoning should not have happened and probably only did so as a result of someone lining their pockets with ill-gotten gains. It is a deeply satisfying theory, but it is quite simply wrong. The fact is that rezoning is part and parcel of the normal process of change. Things change, needs arise, the population grows and new industry is set up to serve the employment needs of that population.

[Mr. Dempsey.]
The uses to which land and buildings were put ten or 15 years ago may now be out of date. It may be absolutely appropriate to review and rezone in order to reflect the reality of change in the economy and social circumstances. It is simple — people need houses. At the moment, the housing supply does not match the demand and the result is price increases which are prohibitive to many.

An adequate supply of suitably zoned and serviced land for development is, and will continue to be, necessary if we are to meet the rapidly expanding housing needs of the population. That is a fact. It is also a fact that there is nothing sinister about either the word 'rezoning' or the reality it expresses, provided that rezoning is done for the proper motives and in a way that is clearly straight and honest. I do not agree with the notion that every decision in development planning where elected councillors have a role must agree at every point with official advice. If that were the case, we would not need councillors to have independent minds, indeed we would not need councillors at all.

We have councillors not just to rubber-stamp official recommendations but to balance the many issues involved in what is always a complex process. That is why the law gives responsibility to people who are fully accountable to the electorate. However, some of those who are responsible to the electorate wear as a badge of honour their opposition to all rezoning, as if it proved their integrity that they were unwilling to respond to the changing needs of the populace. It is time these people were forced to get real and to admit that rigid adherence to the zoning of decades ago is no virtue in the face of today's needs.

Mr. Higgins (*Dublin West*): What about rezoning at Dublin Airport?

Mr. Dempsey: I am sure the Deputy would like to see reasonably priced houses if his rhetoric is anything to go by.

Mr. Higgins (*Dublin West*): The Minister should address the amendments.

Mr. Dempsey: Without rezoning, house prices would be even higher than they are, as the previous Government recognised when it decided to commission a study into house prices last May and also decided that the preparation of regional planning guidelines for the greater Dublin area would deal with the need for serviced land for housing development. Incidentally, I note that Dr. Garret FitzGerald wrote recently in his column in *The Irish Times* about the urgent need to rezone more land for housing.

As Members of this House know, local planning authorities must review their development plans at least every five years. This has not happened in County Dublin because the then council failed to meet its statutory obligations. As a result

of this failure, the 1993 Dublin county development plan was adopted ten years after the adoption of the previous plan. The Fingal County Manager's report, which will be presented to the tribunal, points out that it is not surprising land use strategy in north county Dublin would need to be radically re-examined given the major industrial, commercial and residential development taking place in the area. Long delays in updating developing plans will inevitably lead to this sort of pressure especially at times when the economy is booming.

Whatever about the past, steps must be taken speedily to ensure that this kind of delay does not and cannot happen in future. These delays impair good planning. The Government's programme completely updates and consolidates our planning laws and will go a long way to eliminate some of the problems of the past couple of decades. I have started this already by initiating a comprehensive review of planning legislation. I am consulting widely with the general public, all local planning authorities and a wide range of groups affected in one way or another by the planning system and how it operates. I have made it clear that a priority of mine is to increase public participation in the development plan review process. I would like to introduce greater consultation, to make the adoption of development plans as inclusive as a process of that kind can possibly be. I want the public to be consulted earlier in that process. When people are included and information is widely shared, there is less fertile ground for rumour, suspicion and chronic doubt. I aim to revise the present system to minimise that chronic doubt.

This brings me to the reasoning behind the setting up of a separate inquiry, apart from the tribunal under Judge Moriarty, to deal with the current issues. The Moriarty Tribunal follows directly from the earlier tribunal and because it is a consequence and continuation of it, it is bidden to deal with the affairs of people who were found guilty of wrongdoing by that earlier tribunal. The inclusion by name of the former Minister for Foreign Affairs, former Deputy Burke, in that context would inevitably create guilt by association. This would be grossly unfair and would infringe on the basic rights of such an individual. It would also indicate an abandonment of fair-mindedness on the part of Members of this House.

There are other reasons for a separate tribunal. Let us imagine that any one of the clouds of accusations currently in circulation proved worthy of further investigation. If that were the case, the Moriarty Tribunal would not be able to follow the trail. These accusations deserve a dedicated tribunal with a tight focus. In addition, there is one point on which accusers, accused and bystanders agree — that justice be urgent, not postponed or protracted.

The Moriarty Tribunal already has the task of looking into matters of considerable detail and complexity and would be hard put to give the urgent attention to a wider brief that is so very necessary.

The terms of reference before the House reflect the urgency I am talking about; the belief, shared by us all, that this sorry situation should be cleared up in the shortest possible time. Those terms of reference allow the tribunal to look into the circumstances of the letter sent by Mr. Bailey to Mr. Gogarty in June 1989. They allow the tribunal to investigate the planning history of all the land detailed in the letter and to inquire into all councillors, Oireachtas Members and officials who were directly or indirectly involved in any way in matters related to those lands. They give the tribunal the right to inquire into money paid out and to find out if those moneys had any effect on the planning history of the land involved. The terms of reference also propose the tribunal should investigate applications for planning permission related to these lands since June 1985, the date of the previous local elections. It is also appropriate that the tribunal consider land servicing and ask whether anybody attempted to improperly influence decisions on providing infrastructure.

However, the terms of reference do not stop there. Building by-law approval was required for all new buildings constructed in the Dublin area before June 1992. The procurement of this approval was mentioned in the letter, so the tribunal will investigate whether there was anything untoward in the grant either of by-law approval or of fire safety certificates for the buildings on the land in question. Nor will the tribunal deal only with housing land. It will be required to examine the designation of some of the land in question as an enterprise area. Enterprise areas are vital in creating employment. The tax system acknowledges that and the designation of land can bring substantial tax benefits to the owner. This, too, will come under scrutiny.

The tribunal will have the power to discover all relevant documentation. Under "relevant documentation" I include information which Donnelly, Neary and Donnelly Solicitors say they hold. Clearly, it is essential that such documentation be placed at the disposal of the tribunal and, given the statement by the solicitors that their unnamed clients are motivated by a desire to have a public inquiry into allegations of land rezoning corruption in County Dublin and elsewhere, no doubt they will give the tribunal their fullest co-operation. I express this confidence because, since the firm of solicitors in question is based beyond the jurisdiction of the State, it must be hoped that the tribunal should not be forced into the minefield of legal complexities implicit in the enforcement of powers of discovery in this context. I hope that their clients, who have been described as "concerned environmentalists" and who have a strange desire to remain anonymous, which is unusual for concerned environmentalists, will co-operate fully and facilitate the tribunal by releasing all the information they have to it directly or through their solicitors, Donnelly, Neary, Donnelly.

If the tribunal points up deficiencies in the operation of the planning Acts, I assure this House that I will have such issues properly and speedily addressed. Recommendations will be built into all future planning. In addition, the programme for Government commits us to introduce provisions parallel to those in the Ethics in Public Office Act, 1995 which will apply to local authority members and officials. Deputies can be in no doubt that this will be a thorough and rigorous investigation covering any possible aspect of the lands in question giving rise to public concern, one with appropriate terms of reference and a tight focus. It is time we forced people who corrode public confidence to put their evidence on the table and support the accusations they make. It is time we cut away the undergrowth of rumours and nudge nudgery, and rebuilt public confidence in the institutions where trust is essential. Rebuilding that trust is not a matter we can delegate to any tribunal. This tribunal should give us some clarity based on which we can begin this task but the task relies on the work of this House. None of us must ever conceal wrongdoing or collude with a colleague whom we know to have broken the law but, equally, none of us must ever, for the thrill of a quick headline, destroy an individual's reputation without real evidence and in the process further erode confidence in the institutions of which we are a central part. Accordingly, I commend this motion and the terms of reference to the House.

Mr. Dukes: I move amendment No. *a*1:

In paragraph A.3(ii), after "Oireachtas", to insert ", past or present,".

Will the Minister respond to my amendments and other amendments which have been tabled when he replies to the debate later this evening? He has not referred to the concerns underlying those amendments and if he is not responsive at this stage, we will have more trouble with this motion and what it sets out to do.

I share the feelings of a great many Members of the House that there is a remarkable harshness in debating these issues at a time when the former Minister for Foreign Affairs, Deputy Burke, has suffered a very sad family bereavement and on a day when he has taken the action of resigning both from the Government and this House. I should make the point that timing is a matter for the Government and in this case the timing on the Order Paper today was decided by the Government. If the Government had adopted a more open-minded approach at any time in the past week, the matter would have been concluded before today and before Mr. Burke suffered such a sad bereavement. I put that on the record because there were references to crocodile tears on the other side of the House earlier which were unworthy even of anybody on that side of the House.

[Mr. Dukes.]

It has taken a week of argument and 12 drafts of these terms of reference to get a debate on this motion. From its initial position of being unwilling to have any consultation on the issue with the Opposition, the Government has been forced, with great difficulty, to concede important amendments. Its proposal still requires clarification and amendment. That is why I tabled the amendments in my name and they are not the only ones before the House.

The Government's first approach was to propose very broad terms of reference framed in such a way as to cause us to believe that the activities of Mr. Burke in 1989 might fall outside the scope of the tribunal. It was our strong view that this was an obvious ploy to cast the net wide in the hope of finding other unspecified matters which would divert attention from the main issue. Indeed, as Deputy John Bruton pointed out on several occasions during the past week, the Taoiseach reinforced this view when he spoke vaguely of other unspecified allegations which might emerge and even went so far as to put a number on them — he referred to six possible allegations which might emerge. Such was the nature of that as to give us the strong feeling that our suspicion was well founded and that part of the ploy in setting out such wide terms of reference was to divert attention from the main issue.

Therefore, it was with some scepticism — although I am glad to note that the Minister has changed his position quite considerably on this — that I heard the Minister refer this afternoon to the fact that the accusations which have been at the base of all this deserve "a dedicated tribunal with a tight focus". Nobody on this side of the House objects to broad terms of reference but we insist they must make perfectly clear and put beyond doubt that the specific case of Mr. Burke will be properly investigated.

The Minister's presentation this afternoon represents a coloured retrospect of what actually was attempted because it was not until there had been deep, detailed and acrimonious discussions between the party whips that we got to the point where references were included specifically in these terms of reference which made it clear that specific issue would be addressed as well as all the other issues which the Minister raised. We have achieved that at the suggestion of Deputy John Bruton by providing a specific reference to payments made by the individuals concerned in all of this and to the cash donation of £30,000 made in June 1989 to Mr. Burke, which was debated in this House on 10 September. It took an enormous amount of argument to get to the point where those references were included but I am glad that we have succeeded in frustrating the Government's attempt to muddy the waters. I tabled two other amendments today which are designed to put that beyond doubt.

Questions have arisen in the context of the issues under discussion about the adequacy of legislation on corruption. I have tabled an amendment one of the effects of which will be to ask the tribunal to make recommendations on amendments to this legislation if it sees fit to do so. The amendment also covers electoral legislation and legislation on freedom of information.

It may well be that the tribunal will not make recommendations regarding these areas of legislation or the other ones referred to in the Government's text. However, to be complete, we should draw its attention to the fact that questions have arisen about the adequacy of legislation on corruption and we should ask it to deal with this if, in the course of its deliberations, it finds that it can usefully add to what is on the Statute Book or can recommend additions to it.

I have also tabled an amendment to deal with the situation where the tribunal, on initial private inquiry, finds that there is insufficient evidence about a given matter to proceed to a full public inquiry. The fear has been expressed in the context of the Moriarty tribunal that this might provide a means by which an individual might avoid answering questions on the grounds that the available information is not sufficiently focused. Should that arise, the amendment makes it clear that the Dáil will be given full information as to why the tribunal might conclude that there is not a *prima facie* case. This would at the least allay any public fear of a cover up and might also provide a basis for defining new approaches to a problem if it turns out that the difficulty arises only from the construction of the terms of the reference of the tribunal.

Amendment No. *a*1 proposes that in paragraph A.3.(ii) the words ", past or present," be inserted after the word "Oireachtas". This arises because the person whom this clause was designed to include has today ceased to be a Member of the Oireachtas.

Amendment No. 1 proposes to add, at the end of paragraph A.3.(ii), the words ", or who received payments from any of the person or companies referred to at (i) above". The objective is to make it clear again the characteristics of the specific case from which this exercise has flowed. A doubt has been expressed that the drafting of subparagraph (ii), even its reference to Members of the Oireachtas and with the addition of the words "past or present", might not cover the situation adequately because it is conceivable that were these terms of reference to be put into operation a Member or a past Member of the Oireachtas could say that he or she was neither directly nor indirectly involved in making representations or voting or abstaining from voting. We want to make it clear that there is in this case a specific well identified former Member of the Oireachtas who has questions to answer about this issue. The additional words I propose puts that beyond doubt. I will later explain the reason for moving this amendment in this way. I also propose to repeat the proposed amendments to paragraph A.3.(ii) in paragraph A.4.(a).

In paragraph A.5 I propose an amendment which would add the words "or inducement" after the words "...which involve attempts to influence by threats or deception...". In the specific case which we wish to address, which does not preclude dealing with any other possible cases, it has not been alleged at any stage that there was any attempt to influence by threat or by deception. It may be, and this is what must be investigated, that there might have been an attempt to influence by inducement.

It has been said to me that the amendment is redundant because the proposed terms of reference refer to the possibility that the tribunal might find something which, in its opinion, might amount to corruption and that the legislation dealing with corruption makes it clear that inducements are what is involved. However, the reference here is not to the legislation dealing with corruption; it is to corruption in the dictionary definition of the term. To be sure, and because it adds to certainty and does not reduce clarity, I propose that the words "or inducement" be added to make it clear that we are looking at all possible forms of interference or improper influence on the processes in question.

In paragraph A.6 I propose that the words "and Ethics in Public Office" be deleted and the words ", Ethics in Public Office, Electoral, Freedom of Information and Prevention of Corruption" substituted. I have already referred to the reasons for the inclusion of the words "Prevention of Corruption" substituted. Members of the House are aware that the legislation has been criticised for being out of date and that we need to look again at the formulation of its definitions.

In addition to that legislation and the legislation already referred to in the terms of reference, it is not inconceivable that the tribunal might find that it wanted to make recommendations regarding electoral legislation where new provisions have been recently enacted regarding campaign financing, contributions, etc., and that it might also wish to make a reference to or recommendations regarding legislation on the freedom of information. The Minister stated the laudable ambition of ensuring that the planning process, including the process of reviewing planning and making changes to plans, should be made as transparent as possible to the public. In that context it may be that there would be a gain from having modifications or appropriate extensions made to the scope of the legislation on freedom of information. This is, therefore, an appropriate place to propose such an amendment.

Mr. Dempsey: The Deputy proposes that specific legislation be included in the terms of reference. If specific legislation is mentioned, I am concerned that the tribunal may consider it necessary to examine such legislation. I have no difficulty with the tribunal making specific recommendations regarding legislation, for example, with regard to the Electoral Acts. Would the Deputy consider the wording "any other relevant legislation"? To specify Acts may divert the tribunal down *cul-de-sacs.*

D 481—E

Mr. Dukes: I am pleased with the Minister's remarks. I will consider his suggestion if he will consider my proposals. Perhaps we may have an opportunity to discuss matters between now and when he replies this evening. I have a preference for clarity and specificity but take the point the Minister for the Environment has made, that we do not want the tribunal to be tempted to go off in all directions although the evidence so far is that the most recent tribunal was well able to resist the temptation to venture up side alleys.

The next amendment I propose is to add paragraph B.(iv):

and the Clerk of the Dáil shall thereupon communicate the tribunal's report in full to the Dáil.

This deals with the case where a tribunal finds there is insufficient evidence to warrant proceeding to a full public inquiry when, for understandable reasons, it has conducted an initial inquiry on a private basis. The paragraph in the Government's proposed terms of reference, as it stands, would require the tribunal to report to the Clerk of the Dáil, in such a manner as the tribunal thinks appropriate, on the steps it has taken to determine what evidence, if any, existed. I do not know what happens thereafter but it would be very useful if we could provide that, since the Dáil has gone to the trouble of setting up this tribunal, we should be informed in full of the thinkings and findings of the tribunal even in cases where it feels there is no *prima facie* case.

I make that comment for a number of reasons. First, if it is known that the tribunal has investigated a particular allegation and has concluded there is no reason to proceed to a full public inquiry, the public and this House deserve to know why. Second, once we have received the conclusions of the tribunal, it would be important to be fully informed of what it has investigated, and this amendment would help in that exercise. Third, there may well be cases where, in spite of the care taken here, the manner in which the terms of reference are written simply might not suit. If the tribunal reported that under its terms of reference it had found, on initial inquiry, that it did not deem it justified to carry out a full public inquiry, this House should be able to return to the issue and ascertain whether it was simply a matter to do with the casting of its terms of reference and, so to speak, mend its hand. If on the other hand, the merits of the case did not justify an inquiry, the House would be very happy to know any fears that might have been expressed were fully allayed. That amendment would clarify the work of the tribunal and what we would do with its deliberations once presented to us.

There are a number of reasons I urge the Government to agree with the kind of specificity that I propose adding to these terms of reference by way of the amendments I have tabled. In the debate on 10 September last Deputy Raphael Burke raised as many questions as he answered. If not fully investigated by the tribunal these

[Mr. Dempsey.]

issues will continue to cause problems. If they are not specifically identified for the tribunal difficulties of the kind the Minister present, with some justification, complained of in the course of his remarks will arise.

I refer Members to the Official Report of 10 September. As reported at columns 620 and 621 Deputy Ray Burke said he was not involved in any way in making representations in favour of certain actions taken in 1989 then being examined by the House. However, he went on to say that in the period between 1991 and 1993 he found he had an objection to certain things being proposed in Dublin County Council, that at the time he wrote to a prominent Fianna Fáil member of the council and went so far as to lead a delegation to meet the then Minister for the Environment. That may well have been the case and was well-motivated action on his part but nonetheless it creates a problem in accepting, at face value, what he said in the earlier part of his statement. Having said he had had no involvement in these matters because he was not a member of Dublin County Council, he then went on to illustrate how he had been involved at a subsequent date, one contemplated by the terms of reference of this tribunal. That needs to be clarified.

Deputy Ray Burke then went on to speak about the donation of £30,000 he had received — I refer Members to column 618 of the Official Report of 10 September 1997 — and said he had given £10,000 to the Fianna Fáil Party at national level. He did not say that the £10,000 given to the Fianna Fáil Party at national level was part of the £30,000 he had received in that donation. I see the Minister for the Environment, Deputy Noel Dempsey, shaking his head, but I must emphasise that these are legitimate questions. Deputy Ray Burke further went on to say he had given £7,000 to the Fianna Fáil party organisation in his constituency of North Dublin. Again, he did not say whether that £7,000 were part of the £30,000 donation he had been given. He also said in that speech that he had received other donations during the course of the election campaign which he was not going to detail in this House because he felt they were not proper matters for inquiry by the House. I do not think too many people disagreed with that comment, but he did not say whether those sums of £10,000 and £7,000 were part of the £30,000 he had received by way of this very generous donation.

That gives rise to certain questions and to a further series of consequential questions. If those sums came from the £30,000, what happened to the remaining £13,000 of which he did not give an account? If they were not part of the £30,000 donation, what happened to it?

The explanations given by Mr. Burke on that day and his references to his personal financial position and overdraft did not help to clarify what was done with the £30,000 donation he had received. That should be enough to indicate there are sufficient questions to justify accepting

amendments which put beyond any shadow of doubt that this specific case will be closely examined.

I agree with the Minister for the Environment, Deputy Noel Dempsey, when he said he hoped that Messrs. Donnelly, Neary and Donnelly Solicitors, will make available to the tribunal what information they have at their disposal. I very much share that hope; it is most important that they do so. The letter sent by that firm of solicitors to Deputy John Bruton and other Members of the House dated 30 September 1997 contained some rather curious phrases. Speaking of 52 allegations concerning planning and rezoning around the country but particularly in Dublin, they said the following:

> Some of these allegations are frivolous and most do not lead me to believe that criminal proceedings would be likely to ensue.

They went on to say:

> . . . some of them seem *prima facie* to give cause for concern. Six of these have been forwarded to the Garda but more warrant proper investigation.

That is the opinion of some person with a typical lawyerly indecipherable signature, writing on behalf of Messrs. Donnelly, Neary and Donnelly. I do not know who that person may be, he or she may well be a very eminent solicitor but it is not his or her business to decide what, in our jurisdiction, amounts to improper or illegal conduct and what does not. It is not the business of that person to decide which allegation is frivolous and which is not. That is the job of the Director of Public Prosecutions. It is not the business of that person to say that some of these allegations *prima facie* give cause for concern and that some do not. That is the business we propose to hand to a tribunal properly established under the legislation of this State. Six of these allegations have been forwarded to the Garda and that is a very public spirited thing for Donnelly, Neary and Donnelly to do. However, it is not their business to decide what is put to the Garda and what is not.

While Donnelly, Neary and Donnelly, and the people they represent, those who came together some time ago to offer a reward of up to £10,000 for information, may have been well-intentioned in doing what they did, they have taken the wrong road in getting results. I say this for several reasons. They have allowed Donnelly, Neary and Donnelly, to take unto themselves the functions we expect the Garda, the Director of Public Prosecutions and the Chief State Solicitor to carry out. Second, they have gathered information and made allegations in a way which leaves the rest of us in the dark as to their substance, the motivation of those who made them and their readiness to provide the information our legal system and the British one require to substantiate a charge brought before a duly constituted court of law. I do not criticise these people for their views and con-

6 o'clock

cerns; it is just that they have chosen a route which is fundamentally flawed. Given that we are going to the trouble of establishing this tribunal, they should make available to the tribunal all their information, regardless of whether or not they think it is frivolous, so it can be handled by a body properly constituted to do so.

The Tánaiste has no political credibility left after her statement today in response to the former Deputy Ray Burke's resignation. I was appalled — I invite those on the other side of the House who spoke of crocodile tears to have a discussion with the Tánaiste, Deputy Harney — by what she said, the manner in which she said it, and her conduct over the past week or so prior to saying it.

The Government has been hugely damaged by what has happened over recent weeks. It has been damaged by the way the Taoiseach handled this affair and by the hesitation and vacillation shown by the Tánaiste in dealing with it. The forced resignation of a Minister after a lengthy period of controversy can only damage a Government. The Taoiseach's judgment is in question because that period of controversy was lengthened by his failure to take the kind of action demanded and needed some time ago. He has been dogged by this business, as was the former Minister for Foreign Affairs, in the United States, Belfast and here. Recently the Taoiseach went to the launch of a worthy project, the Sail Chernobyl campaign. All that achieved publicity on the national airwaves was this affair and not the very worthwhile enterprise undertaken by five fine young people who have shown great courage and dedication. That is only a small example of the damage done to the Government by this affair.

I wondered until last weekend whether the Minister of State at the Department of Foreign Affairs, Deputy O'Donnell, had taken a vow of silence or joined a contemplative order of nuns, because there has not been a word from her. The only thing we heard came last weekend when she suddenly spoke about the passports affair. It seems the Tánaiste knew of this last July, if not earlier, but omitted to tell her party colleague. One third of the members of the Progressive Democrats in Cabinet were not informed of this and similarly for one half of those members who are Ministers of State. That indicates a Government which has serious problems with internal communication and a fatal difficulty in understanding how its actions, or in this case its lack of action, are seen by the public.

Mr. Howlin: This is a difficult debate for all in this House with the backdrop of the family bereavement of a central character. As party Whip of the Labour Party, I contacted the Government Whip yesterday and asked that this debate be deferred until tomorrow so as not to intrude on the private grief of the family today. I regret that that was not done.

In the opening passages of his contribution, the Minister spoke of the essential protection of the planning system. As a former Minister for the Environment, I also regard that as being of extreme importance and one of the fundamental rocks of our democracy. People should know that under the planning system everyone is treated equally, the merits of any proposal are judged on planning criteria alone, and the laws enacted by this House are the only guidelines followed by statutory bodies, be they locally elected authorities, An Bord Pleanála, or any other. There has been a huge and unfortunate erosion in public confidence in the way the planning system works and this is not a recent development. We have sought over decades to refine, improve and make more transparent the planning system, but there is still a major deficit in public confidence in the working of the system. In my time in office, I sought to have made public the reports of inspectors in the planning system. Some held the view that it would bring the sky down, that people would not be able to write objectively if they knew it would be made public. However, the demand was obvious and it is right we have complete openness concerning the treatment of citizens by any statutory agency.

The reason the planning system has come into such sharp focus is the obvious one mentioned by the Minister, the potential to make enormous profits arising from planning decisions. That is especially true in the hinterland of our capital city, where zoning decisions, planning approvals, or material contraventions can change the value of a portion of land by an enormous factor. For that reason, we must be particularly transparent in how the mechanisms of the State, be they local or national, deal with such applications. All of us have had representations to assist people with projects requiring planning permission and representations from people aggrieved by planning decisions. Aggrieved applicants often reach the conclusion that they were not subject to fair play. Often it is difficult to decide if an aggrieved person has a basis for making an accusation or if they are disgruntled because they did not get the decision they wanted. Anybody who makes a planning application, as is the case with anybody involved in legal proceedings, cannot be sure of the outcome. The only certainty is that there will be winners and losers.

Unfortunately, there are specific issues which have finally forced the Government to recognise the need to establish this tribunal. The issue is not the soundbyte, as described by the Minister, regarding the handing over of a large financial contribution to an individual, but the fact that a political contribution of £30,000 was made to an individual and the allegation that, a number of days prior to this, one of those involved in making the contribution suggested that he could procure planning approval for certain designated lands. Anybody interested in the protection and transparency of the planning system would be alarmed at such a development. It demanded an independent inquiry. This is the genesis of the new tribunal of inquiry.

[Mr. Howlin.]

Initially, those of us in Opposition simply sought a sifting of these facts. We were unaware of the suggestion which subsequently came to light that Mr. Bailey could procure planning permission. During the debate on the Moriarty tribunal we sought to include a sifting of the facts regarding the contribution to the former Minister, Deputy Ray Burke, within its terms of reference. Unfortunately, that was voted down by the Government with the assistance of some Independent Deputies. It was a dreadful mistake for the House, the Government and Mr. Burke. If a decision had been made some weeks ago to include a sifting of the facts within the remit of the Moriarty tribunal, the issues could have been left to it and the truth would have been divined in the proper setting. However, that did not happen and instead more vignettes of information became available until the Taoiseach eventually went on national radio on a Sunday at lunchtime to announce a new tribunal to investigate the issue of planning.

I welcome this tribunal and there is some logic to having a separate tribunal to examine these matters. We had a week of argument concerning the terms of reference now before us. As whip of the parliamentary Labour Party I was directly involved in those negotiations. The Labour Party wanted terms of reference which would work effectively and not result in a situation where the full facts would not be elicited or where the people would not have their trust restored in our ability to do the job we are sent here to do, namely, ensure fair play for every citizen and transparency in local and national government. We genuinely did not want controversy, division or rows either inside or outside this House. By presenting our own draft text we wished to address issues put forward by the Government, including that of fairness. The Government did not want the former Minister, Deputy Burke, mentioned by name. The leader of the Labour Party put forward a form of words that encompassed anybody who received contributions. This was a reasonable and balanced amendment which was accepted by the Government and which ultimately formed the core of the resolution before us as set out in paragraph 4(a) of the present terms of reference.

By and large the terms of reference are now acceptable to us because they will get at the facts. The first draft, bluntly put before us, was not designed to do this and would not have allowed us elicit all the facts. As indicated by Deputy Dukes, it took much negotiation and umpteen drafts before coming up with the present comprehensive, albeit focused, terms of reference.

I wish to refer to other planning issues. While not wishing to refer to specific amendments tabled by other Deputies, there are amendments which will be discussed over the next hour which refer to other potentially contentious planning and zoning decisions. All of us are receiving information about potentially corrupt decision and suggestions of corruption. Like the Minister and virtually every other Member of the House, I want all these matters fully ventilated and explored. If people have suggestions to make they should present their information. We should then look at that information, as I did as Minister, when suggestions of impropriety were made. I said I would investigate any information or evidence presented to me to the furthest possible extent.

The Order Paper makes suggestions about two issues other than the central thrust or focus of this tribunal. I believe the Minister will not turn a deaf ear when I ask that for once and for all, we should have a full exposure and investigation of anything the people want explained. I wish the Minister to confirm my understanding that paragraph 5 of the terms of reference will achieve this. The section states:

> In the event that the Tribunal in the course of its inquiries is made aware of any acts associated with the planning process committed on or after the 20th June 1985 which may in its opinion amount to corruption, or which involve attempts to influence by threats or deception or otherwise to compromise the disinterested performance of public duties, it shall report on such acts and should in particular make recommendations as to the effectiveness and improvement of existing legislation governing corruption in the light of its inquiries.

I want the Minister to confirm that this paragraph will allow those who have evidence or who believe there has been improper conduct in the planning process to submit that evidence to the tribunal to have it evaluated. Deputies will be set at ease if this is done. Without this there will be further allegations.

Whether as a Minister or in Opposition, neither I nor any other Member is in a position to make a value judgment on the issues now arising. It is almost as if one is involved in complicity if one does not demand an inquiry which may damage a person's reputation. It is an invidious and unacceptable situation in which to be. Whatever about the Taoiseach's proposal on a standing ethics committee, there is probably merit for a standing Ombudsman or tribunal to look at any suggestion of impropriety, past or present, and make a judgment. I hope these terms of reference will encompass that and the new tribunal will be able to take submissions from whomsoever it decides on matters suggested for specific amendment. If I get an assurance from the Minister, it would be better than specifying what should be done because we might well exclude aspects of the same issue through which we need to sift. I would like an open facility for somebody who has gathered or garnered evidence to submit it to presumably a learned judge who will determine whether an inquiry is warranted. That is equally an essential part of the terms of reference of the tribunal before us.

The Minister made a number of points the tenor of which I agree with but the specifics are a cause of concern. He spoke of the necessary courage of whistle-blowers and said much of what is happening is not in that category. There is a danger in the view that because a colleague has seen fit to tender his resignation somehow those who sought investigation are culpable. That is a very dangerous philosophy or line to adopt. If there are issues in the public domain, let them be investigated and let reputations stand or fall on the basis of actions and proper conduct, investigation and decision making.

The Minister spoke about corrosive cruelty dressed up as principled investigation. If we had the investigation we suggested three weeks ago, there would not be this corrosive cruelty to which the Minister referred. It is those who voted down that suggestion some weeks ago on whom the odium and blame must fall. He said the tribunal of inquiry and nothing else should be the instrument to address this, and I agree. The tribunal of inquiry must be given its head in the comprehensive way I suggested. The terms of reference we finally have will achieve that. However, these terms of reference and the great support we now see from the Minister and the Government for them were hard won over days of haggling and umpteen drafts before we reached the form of words which will meet the requirements of the situation.

The Minister also made a rather interesting and fulsome defence of the principle of rezoning which I found a little difficult to take. He wants to turn the view that anybody who is jaundiced about rezoning has put themselves on a moral high ground, that they should get real and live in the real world and that we need rezoning for development and progress and to provide houses for the homeless. However, that is not what has caused controversy but rather maverick rezoning. Indeed, it caused so much controversy that my predecessor as Minister, the present Minister's party colleague, changed the procedures to make it more difficult for material contraventions and for section 4 motions relating to zoning to be passed. It has been recognised that there has been more than an acceptable amount of rezoning in the past.

I made it clear I would not support maverick rezonings. My party has taken a strong and principled position on this matter for which I will not apologise. Necessary land should be made available in a structured and planned way. I welcome the Minister's comments on the planning process as a whole because it needs fundamental change. I was bringing that about and I hope the Minister will continue in that vein.

Part of the issue which needs to be addressed is that haphazard way in which plans are developed. For example, there is no statutory requirement to have a comprehensive plan. To put it succinctly, every county has its own development plan but there is no requirement for each plan to dovetail logically together, which is

bizarre. We do not have a national plan but counties with their own plans, some of which may run counter to the adjoining plan. We have made progress in the Dublin area by requiring the new regional authorities to act as agents for bringing together a dovetailed planning process, but we have a long way to go.

There is often a fundamental friction between adjoining local authorities in relation to development and proposals, whether on housing, waste disposal or water supply. Contentious views may be adopted by adjoining local authorities instead of working in partnership. We have long way to go to having a national plan, the subsets of which logically fit together and serve the rational development of our country.

Some of the plans devised recently visit on an isolated village a projected population increase of perhaps 500 or 1,000 per cent over five years. It is an amazing projection. We must provide houses but in a structured logical way. Over the years I have seen many proposals to rezone areas of land which have no services and to which it would be illogical to provide services in advance of providing services for other areas. These matters must be brought together in a logical way and I support the Minister's notion for a public forum to do so. A public and inclusive forum is a good idea from which we need to make hard decisions.

There are always grey areas in planning; there is no right decision. We must make the best decision in the circumstances, although there will be aggrieved people. If we have clearly defined rules and regulations, transparency in national and local administration, clear mechanisms for appeal, and open hearing systems where reports are in the public domain, we will quickly achieve full confidence in planning. Unfortunately, that is not the situation at present.

I refer to the role of the firm of solicitors, Donnelly, Neary and Donnelly, a point picked up on by Deputy Dukes. One of the amendments the Labour Party proposed to the Government, sought to bring within the encompass of the inquiry those making allegations. We suggested a form of words which would bring within the terms of reference allegations made in public, whether directly or indirectly, of corrupt or improper behaviour on the part of any person concerned with the formation, submission, consideration or approval of proposals relating to the planning and development of lands. The Government has adopted that, somewhat, in paragraph B(iii) which requests the tribunal to "seek discovery of all relevant documents, files and papers in the possession, power or procurement of said Mr. Michael Bailey, Mr. James Gogarty and Donnelly, Neary and Donnelly Solicitors,".

I re-echo the hope expressed by the two previous speakers — the Minister and Deputy Dukes — that the firm of solicitors, who have said for a number of years that it wants a full tribunal of inquiry into planning matters, will co-operate fully and give whatever information it has to the tribunal. If they have something to say, they

[Mr. Howlin.]
should say it now and not waste this opportunity. It is important that those who have information about alleged corruption and interference come forward with that information at this time when we have a statutory mechanism to deal with it, this judicial inquiry which will be independent and powerful under the terms of reference which this House will approve tonight.

I wish to turn now to the central core of the terms of reference. I am very satisfied that they will, by and large, get to the heart of the issues which have caused controversy — the suggestion by an individual that he could procure planning permission, the circumstances surrounding the contribution of money to former Minister, Deputy Burke, and any other issue which might arise out of those lands.

I hope the Minister will confirm the view I expressed when we were negotiating the terms of reference, that is, that section A.5 of the terms of reference is a catch-all to allow for a full investigation of any other allegation of corruption in the planning process anywhere in the country subsequent to 1985, and that those terms of reference will enable the specific issues which other Deputies will raise, such as Glending or other lands in north Dublin, to be fully ventilated. It is very important to put that matter clearly on the record before we decide how to vote tonight.

I regret it has taken so long for the terms of reference to be finalised and that there was contention about their drafting. It was a difficult process for the Opposition to try to deal with draft after draft with legal opinions coming from the Attorney General's Office on the matter. More than once during that process we thought the Government was engaged in obfuscation rather than in building consensus. I believe the terms of reference now before the House meet, by and large, the requirements of Deputies on this side of the House — subject, of course, to the clarification of the specific points I raised.

Mr. O'Flynn: I wish to share time with Deputy Roche.

An Leas-Cheann Comhairle: Is that agreed? Agreed.

Mr. O'Flynn: A Deputy makes only one maiden speech and I am sad to be making mine at a time when a distinguished Member has had to resign his seat and Cabinet post.

I wish to speak clearly on this issue which has concerned me since long before I entered this illustrious House. During my time as a member of Cork Corporation I read and heard about the need for transparency and openness in public life. I agreed with the views expressed and I have heard members of all parties echo similar thoughts in this House since I have been privileged to join it. Unfortunately, recent events appear to show clearly that transparency may be an aspiration but not a reality. There have been allegations and counter allegations about the abuse of power. There is talk of corruption, tax evasion, cosy cartels and the abuse of the Planning Acts, particularly in relation to the rezoning of land.

A Leas-Cheann Comhairle, can you blame the public for casting a cynical eye on politics and politicians? I cannot. People are regularly given a poor impression of politicians when they read newspapers, listen to the radio or watch television and the utter sensationalism by some members of our media is a major contributory factor. They are largely responsible for the exaggeration and distortion of events and they exercise a major influence on people's attitudes towards politicians. The *modus operandi* of some of the media is to allege that politicians are guilty until proven innocent. This undermines the vast majority of journalists who report the news in a professional manner.

If one were accused of a crime and brought before our courts, all matters relevant to the case would be *sub judice*. If the accused is proven guilty following the hearing, it is then right and proper for the media to make statements regarding the proceedings. The same rules of fair play should apply to politicians against whom allegations are made. The media should await the outcome of the tribunal before making their pronouncements based on the evidence. Some sections of the media should not pre-empt the tribunal by appointing themselves as judge and jury in the absence of all the facts.

Today, it appears one can make allegations without having to prove them. Reputations are lost and the integrity of individuals and bodies is impugned. The public perception of politicians will not change if their images are continually tarnished by attacks which are often unfounded. It is not enough for us to do the right thing: it must be clearly seen to be right and to be done for the right reason.

The buck stops with the Members of this House. Those who voted for me and the other Members of this House did so in the belief that we would represent them honestly and to the best of our abilities. I still believe they were correct in that assumption. The integrity and credibility of Members is basic to the exercise of democracy in this small nation.

The rezoning of land is an extremely sensitive area. It may make some people far wealthier because of the increase in the value of their land. However, it should not be forgotten that the Exchequer takes a healthy slice of the raised capital value of rezoned land through capital gains tax, VAT on building programmes and the PAYE and PRSI contributions of those involved in the construction industry, not to forget stamp duties, etc. These all add up.

We must create a climate of active investment. We must encourage those who have wealth to use it. They might create greater wealth for themselves in so doing but that also benefits the State and those who live here. We must remember that investment is a risk from which one does not always gain.

In the course of development plans, corporations and councils, as we have already heard tonight, have the power to rezone lands. It is extremely important that they be allowed exercise that power transparently. Our actions must be to the benefit of the public. We must not seek to enrich anybody by the rezoning of their lands to their personal profit.

I regard the suggestion that decisions relating to rezoning should be submitted for ministerial approval as negative. That would further reduce the already limited powers of the elected members of local authorities. They should be free to deal with land within their own functional areas to the benefit of the public they represent.

Problems can arise when section 4 is invoked in regard to zoning applications before local authorities. There is a consultative process during the preparation of a development plan which goes on public display. There is further consultation between citizens, elected public representatives, planning officials and the executive of the local authorities. I believe there should be such a consultative process after the proposal of a section 4. The views of planners, developers and citizens must be taken into account.

A further safeguard in this process would be the submission of such rezoning to an independent consultative body on the lines of An Bord Pleanála. Its recommendations would be made public and referred to the local authority which could then make a decision to ratify or reject the disputed rezoning and justify its stand. The public might agree or disagree with the decision but it would be a position to assess the merits and motives behind rezoning decisions and it could not be said that matters were being dealt with in an underhand manner.

My priority is to re-establish the confidence of the people in those whom they have elected. We must react to the public demand that those in public office set an example of honesty and integrity which are prerequisites to holding office. If there is corruption in high places we must expose it. If we do so we can ensure that no further sensational stories will appear in the media about corruption in politics. We are the servants of the State and the people. Those who voted for us believed in us and we must confirm and copperfasten their faith in us.

I support the establishment of the tribunal and the terms of reference proposed. I abhor the necessity for such an inquiry and I urge Members to ensure that the need for another does not arise.

Mr. Roche: I compliment my colleague on his excellent maiden speech which was short and to the point. He echoed a sentiment that exists on all sides — the urgent need to re-establish confidence in public office and office holders. No party has a monopoly on that feeling; it is a commonly shared objective.

I will focus on the sale and rezoning of lands at Glending, County Wicklow. I have not been involved in this issue in recent times. I have shown a vigorous interest in it since the issue first appeared before Wicklow County Council. Proper procedures were not followed in the sale of those lands, a view I expressed last year and which is now shared by Members whose parties supported the sale and rezoning. Some of the Members opposite were in Government last year when I asked them to examine the issue and, although they could have taken action, they did not do so. However, this is not a time for recrimination. From this tawdry mess we should attempt to put our house in order. There is no point blaming the media for outlining wrongdoing. There have been many reasons over the past 20 years to raise questions with regard to land rezoning.

When public assets are disposed of it should be done in a way which is transparent and above question. The sale of the lands at Glending was not handled in such a manner. A year ago I wrote to a number of Ministers on this matter and some of them were forthcoming and helpful, in particular, Deputy Howlin and Deputy Michael Higgins. Deputy Higgins undertook to examine the files in the Office of Public Works on the matter and he gave me certain assurances that wrongdoing was not an issue there.

It is appropriate that the Committee of Public Accounts, when appointed, should request the Comptroller and Auditor General to do a thorough examination of the files relating to the sale of the lands. Even if no wrongdoing occurred it is the widely held view that the sale was not handled in an appropriate way. I am surprised the Comptroller and Auditor General has not examined the issue already given that it has been a matter of public debate for two years. I have argued consistently that the Committee of Public Accounts should pursue this matter. As soon as that committee is appointed I intend writing to it to request an examination of the files related to the sale. If wrongdoing is discovered it is in our interest that it would be exposed and, if not, the reputations of those involved will be vindicated.

I am one of seven councillors who voted against the rezoning of the Glending lands. Democratic Left was the only political party which was unanimous on the issue because it only had one member on the council, and it voted for the rezoning. Deputy McManus has had a great deal to say of late about the rezoning. I am not a cynic and I believe in Pauline conversions. She was a Minister of State at the Department of the Environment last year and she had the right to examine the relevant files in the Department. Deputy Howlin and Deputy Michael Higgins received my correspondence and responded with courtesy and in detail.

There are questions about the rezoning of the Glending lands which must be answered, mainly by Wicklow County Council. For example, in the original draft development plan for Blessington, published and circulated in 1993, there was a

[Mr. Roche.]
commitment to retain Glending as an amenity area. There is a great deal of hypocrisy surrounding this issue. I was not supported in the council chamber at the time by parties which now support a detailed examination of the issue. However, I welcome their latter day conversions. The Fine Gael Party, with the exception of one individual, supported the rezoning. My party colleagues, despite my requests, also supported it. With one exception the Labour Party voted against the rezoning. Councillors Liam Kavanagh, Tom Cullen and I have consistently questioned this matter.

Mr. Howlin: Councillor Cullen as far as the High Court.

Mr. Roche: When we were struggling to find a means of exposing what was happening, Deputy McManus, who was a member of the county council and went on to become a Minister of State at the Department of the Environment, sat on her hands and did not assist Councillor Cullen when he took that personal risk. When the residents of Blessington asked the Deputy to intervene on their behalf she refused to do so. It is smirking hypocrisy of a high order to hear the Deputy question my good faith on the issue. I have nothing to be ashamed of because, from the outset, I maintained that the issue deserved examination. Deputy McManus indicated recently that her colleague, Councillor Kirwan, was not aware of the details of the rezoning. The Blessington Heritage Trust, Councillor Cullen and I tried to make the council aware. I was castigated for speaking at length on the matter at the council meeting. The cynical aspect of the rezoning that took place then is that those councillors who went along with the rezoning of Glending not only rezoned Glending but lands belonging to their cronies. One area has been the subject of a massive housing development, enriching one individual at the cost of the people of Blessington. No wonder people are sick of politics and politicians; to them they spell hypocrisy. I welcome this tribunal as I would welcome anything that would try to clear the name of politics. I will ask the Committee of Public Accounts to examine this issue and hope to have the support of other Members on that issue.

Mr. Gilmore: I congratulate Deputy O'Flynn on his maiden speech. This debate is to set up a new tribunal of inquiry and could have been avoided if, four weeks ago, the Government had accepted the amendment proposed by Democratic Left on the terms of reference of the Moriarty tribunal. When that tribunal was considered, Democratic Left made the modest proposal that the £30,000 payment to former Deputy Burke should be subjected to a preliminary private screening process to establish whether it warranted investigation by the tribunal.

If that proposal had been agreed, the £30,000 payment and the Bailey-Gogarty letter which emerged subsequently would now be under the scrutiny of Judge Moriarty and we would not be setting up a new tribunal. Former Deputy Burke might have been spared the necessity of retiring from politics and politics would have been spared the corrosive effect of a month's talk about political corruption.

That proposal was defeated because the Taoiseach and the Tánaiste led their parties into the lobbies against it, where they were tamely followed by Deputies Blaney, Healy-Rae and Fox, who have suppressed whatever pretensions they may have had to be independent. They voted for a position which is discredited, indefensible and being stood on its head this evening.

More than anyone else, the Taoiseach is responsible for allowing the Burke affair to ferment and become the political crisis it is. Repeating the mantra, "a man is innocent until he is proven guilty", the Taoiseach has sought to brazen out the growing public unease over this affair. His choice of the terms and language of the criminal courts to defend one of his most senior Ministers was extraordinary, and he was the first to do so.

The political arena is not the place to judge anyone's guilt or innocence, as those words are not the currency of politics. Credibility and confidence are the qualities by which public representatives and democratic politics maintain a relationship of trust with the citizens who elect us. The problem at the core of former Deputy Burke's dilemma has been that the public found it quite incredible that somebody the Minister did not know arrived on his doorstep with £30,000 in cash for his personal election expenses and that no favours were expected or returned. The public suspicion was fuelled when it emerged that the two gentlemen in the Minister's parlour had, a few days previously, been in correspondence with each other about a land deal which included the procurement of planning permission and the procurement of a majority vote on Dublin County Council. "Procurement" is an unusual term to use about a planning permission or about the exercise of the democratic function of an elected council.

Instead of addressing the problem upfront, the Taoiseach, by his mishandling of the affair, has brought about a set of circumstances whereby the outcome for his Government is worse than it was four weeks ago. He has lost one of his most senior Ministers and unassessable damage has been done to public confidence in politics. The Taoiseach began by circling the wagons in refusing to allow Judge Moriarty to examine the matter in private. Nobody had called for a separate new tribunal, yet the Taoiseach announced on the radio on the Sunday of the All-Ireland Final that a new tribunal was to be established. He cast further doubt on the integrity of politics by claiming others had received contributions of the same order as former Deputy Burke. Whether the Taoiseach has evidence for this claim will be considered by the new tribunal and I hope he will give evidence to that tribunal in this regard. Whether this claim was intended to frighten the Opposition or was an admission that the Taoiseach considers personal political contributions of £30,000 as normal has yet to be seen.

The House is now being asked to approve the terms of reference of a new tribunal which will examine the Burke issue, the Bailey-Gogarty letter and other matters relating to possible corruption of the planning process. I welcome the establishment of the tribunal and in particular paragraphs 4 and 5 of the terms of reference.

Paragraph 4 provides for the examination of the political and personal contributions made by Mr. Bailey and Mr. Gogarty and their associated companies since July 20 1985, whether those contributions were made to Members of the Oireachtas, councillors or council officials. It would test the claims of the Taoiseach that others received contributions. It will provide, for the first time, a public snapshot of the financial relationships between a major property developer and politics and planning. It is in the public interest to know if any such payments were made, to whom they were made and what conclusions may be drawn from that.

Paragraph 5 provides for a wider examination of possible corruption of the planning process. My party has called for this before and I have been calling for it since before I entered this House over eight years ago. On a number of occasions I have spoken here of my unease about planning, particularly in County Dublin where I am most familiar with the planning process.

The inquiry we are now establishing should have been set up in the late 1980s or early 1990s at the latest, not least because the new tribunal will inevitably find it more difficult to investigate complicated planning issues of some years ago. I was a member of Dublin County Council from June 1985 until 1993, when that council was wound up. Over that period, I saw frequent abuse of the planning process. I have no evidence of corruption, but I look forward to the investigations which will be conducted by the tribunal and to the report that the tribunal will present in order to establish whether corruption lay at the base of the abuse of planning which occurred in that period.

The worst abuse occurred between 1985 and 1991 when meetings of Dublin County Council were virtually dominated by proposals to materially contravene the County Development Plan and to grant planning permissions by way of section 4 motions. I summarised this abuse in a document which I published in March 1991 entitled: "The Rezoning Majority: A Study of Abuse of Planning in Dublin". In this document I explained that the section 4 provisions of the City and County Management Act, 1955 — the power of elected members of the county council to allow developments which would materially contravene the County Development Plan —

D 481—F

were very democratic provisions intended to serve the public interest.

I further explained that section 4 motions, material contraventions or land rezonings are not automatically bad in themselves. They are very necessary provisions to allow for the ordered growth and development of an area. Many of the material contraventions and land rezonings passed by Dublin County Council were well based. The problem, however, was the frequency of abuse and pattern of the use of these provisions. In the document I published, I summarised that between the local elections of 1985 and early 1991, Dublin County Council passed 41 section 4 motions directing the granting of planning permissions in cases where they might otherwise have been refused. In the same period, the council decided to grant planning permissions to 131 developments which would materially contravene the council's own development plan. Of those 131 material contraventions, 108 were proposed by Fianna Fáil councillors and 87 were seconded by Fianna Fáil councillors. The county manager and the professional planners employed by the council recommended that the motion should not be passed on 91 of the 131 material contraventions which were passed.

The bulk of the rezoning which resulted from the material contravention motions resulted in housing development. There has been some comment recently that this was necessary as house prices were rising and there was a shortage of housing land. House prices were not rising between 1985 and 1991. Anybody who knows anything about the property market will know that, over that period, the housing market was in quite a depressed state and there was no shortage of housing land in County Dublin. Of the land which was zoned for housing, 757 hectares already had planning permission but were not developed, a further 1,450 hectares were serviced but had no planning permission and 313 hectares were neither serviced nor had planning permission. This hardly indicates that there was a shortage of building land.

I estimated that the effect of the rezonings was to add £150 million to the value of the rezoned land. There was clearly big money at stake. Decisions made by the elected members of the council had the potential to add enormous values to land. Members of the council were intensively lobbied by developers and landowners seeking the rezoning of their land. Councillors were also lobbied by local community and environmental organisations which opposed many of the rezonings. Such lobbying is perfectly proper; it would not be proper if it went beyond lobbying. That, of course, is what the tribunal must find out.

Against that background, the use of the term 'procurement' of a majority vote at two council meetings in the Bailey letter is interesting to say the least. I have served more than 12 years as a public representative and I have never before heard the use of the term 'procurement' in the

7 o'clock

[Mr. Gilmore.]
context of a planning application. Its use is especially curious in a section of the letter which seeks a reduction in the price of the land in return for, among other things, the procurement of planning permission and by-law approval, the steps to which are described by Mr. Bailey as 'expensive'.

Paragraph 5 of the terms of reference gives the tribunal a very wide remit. It is an important function but it will cause the tribunal some difficulty. First, the tribunal will have to sift through the frivolous cases which will inevitably be put to it. It is conceivable that any crank with a grudge against an elected or appointed public official may use this avenue to vent an allegation. Second, where the tribunal considers that investigation is warranted it will be handicapped by the lapse of time in examining past cases. The tribunal will, I believe, have difficulty in examining abuses of planning which occurred a decade or more ago. I hope this will not unduly handicap the tribunal and that it will be able, at least, to get to the bottom of any corruption which may have occurred.

Most of my remarks have referred to Dublin as that is where my experience lies. However, it is important that the investigation of planning abuse should not be confined to Dublin. Over the years, there have been many disturbing stories about the abuse of section 4 provisions, in particular, outside of Dublin and, more recently, there has been concern regarding rezoning in Kildare and Wicklow.

Deputy Roche has used this debate to rehearse his typically nasty approach to local politics and his constituency colleagues but my party supports the inclusion of Glending in the terms of reference of this tribunal. I must express some surprise that, given the vehemence of Deputy Roche's comments on that subject this evening, he managed not to vote for its inclusion in the terms of reference of the Moriarty tribunal when he had an opportunity to do so in this House four weeks ago.

I agree with previous speakers who said it is important that the information which Donnelly, Neary and Donnelly possess should be put before the tribunal. The clients of that firm of solicitors should instruct it to make that information available to the tribunal.

It is very regrettable that since the general election, politics and debate in this House have been dominated virtually exclusively by suggestions of corruption, political contributions, planning inquiries and so on. Since the general election we have already debated one inquiry and set up two others. It is time this House had an opportunity to proceed to consider the issues which most of the people who voted for us sent us here to address. Those issues relate to the economy, problems in relation to social conditions and immediate day to day concerns. The sooner we are enabled to do that, the sooner the wish widely expressed in this House — that the cloud of suspicion over politics be lifted — will be granted.

Mr. Ardagh: I offer my sympathy to former Deputy Ray Burke and his family on the death of Mr. Seán Burke and on the illness which has beset the family recently. It is a scandal that the witch hunt which has occurred resulted in former Deputy Burke coming to a decision to resign from the position of Minister for Foreign Affairs and from Dáil Éireann at this emotional time.

Deputy Gilmore said we could have avoided this tribunal and former Deputy Burke's resultant resignation if this Government had accepted the amendments in relation to the Moriarty tribunal. This situation could have been avoided if Members had trust in their own colleagues. There was no need for former Deputy Burke to be included in the Moriarty tribunal; that tribunal refers to two persons which the McCracken tribunal found were associated with gross irregularities and wrongdoing. Former Deputy Burke is guilty of nothing. In 1989 he received £30,000 as a political contribution without favours being sought or given. A full explanation was given to the House which, if there was trust among its Members, would have been accepted.

I would like to pay tribute to the former Deputy as a politician. I joined Dublin County Council in 1985 with Deputy Gilmore at the same time as former Deputy Burke was re-elected to it. Former Deputy Burke was chairman of Dublin County Council in 1985 and 1986 and I found him to be solid, steadfast and very serious. He went out and fought for what was right for the people he represented and I believe, as I am sure Deputy Owen does, that the parks in North Dublin — Ardgillan, Newbridge Demesne and Malahide Castle — are a tribute to him.

Former Deputy Burke knows his way around local authority bureaucracy. In his position as Minister for Justice, he showed that he was up to whatever could be meted out by the civil servants in that Department. During his tenure in Dublin County Council former Deputy Burke was able to get funds from reserves for the purposes of carrying out improvements in North Dublin. I was somewhat envious of that as I would like to have seen such improvements come about in west and south Dublin. However, former Deputy Burke was chairman of the council and, as a man of great ability, looked after his constituents very well.

Deputy Gilmore said there was no evidence of corruption in county councils and I concur with that. In the 12 years I have been a member of a county council, I did not know of any councillor who was offered or received an inducement for planning, apart from the £100 which was sent to Deputy Sargent and which was publicly shown at a council meeting. Deputy Gilmore also stated that many planning applications and rezonings were well based and I agree with him.

As a new Member I am appalled by the influence of the media in the matters that relate to this House. It appears the profits generated by the sale of newspapers — and that profit motive has come to the fore in recent years — and this media influence pervades all happenings in the House. A senior member of an Opposition party for whom I have great respect told me that on the day drug trafficking legislation was being debated, and important developments at Stormont were taking place, the only question reporters wanted to ask him on leaving Leinster House was: where was the blood of Ray Burke? That is an appalling vista.

I read in the papers recently that I voted for the rezoning of one of the items in the tribunal's terms of reference. It concerned rezoning nine acres of land in Portmarnock which was proposed by two Oireachtas Members, Deputy Owen, the Deputy Leader of Fine Gael, and G.V. Wright, a member of the Fianna Fáil Party, and another councillor from that area. Those elected members were councillors from the area in which the land in question was located. They are people for whom I have great respect and I know they represent their constituents well. If a proposal is made by representatives of Fine Gael or Fianna Fáil in respect of an area about which I know little, I accept the arguments put forward by my colleagues. In the same way, if an item comes up concerning an area I represent, and if I believe rezoning or planning permission is necessary in that area, I expect colleagues in my party to support me.

Item No. 4 refers to the identity of all recipients of payments made to political parties, Members of either House of the Oireachtas, members or officials of a Dublin local authority or other public official. I understand that in April of this year a number of friends of mine organised a lunch for which they requested subscriptions of £125. A cheque for £125 was made out to those persons by a person whom I understand is a co-director in a company with Mr. Bailey. Apparently this is not included in the items to be investigated by the tribunal. I do not know the reason for that or whether it is relevant but I would not like to appear to be hiding behind this item simply because it is not covered under the terms "recipients" or "final beneficiaries of any payments".

There is a need for housing. Most of the people who attend my clinic or who phone me in my office are looking for housing. There are flat complexes in my constituency including Fatima Mansions, Dolphin House and Bridgefoot Street flats. There are 50 vacant flats in Fatima Mansions because people do not want to live there. They want to live in good quality housing in a nice environment where they can raise their families with pride and dignity. To enable them do that we must provide housing but there is a shortage of land for housing. In south County Dublin, 2,800 houses were built last year. Currently there are lands residentially zoned for 10,000 houses, that is three and a half years' supply. The development plan is currently being discussed and, as the Minister said recently, there was a ten year gap between development plans in Dublin County Council but I hope there will not be a ten year gap in the South Dublin County Council

area. There is a definite need for more lands to be rezoned in south County Dublin. It is only by rezoning lands for residential use that the people we represent can be housed. I do not have any qualms about exercising my responsibility in rezoning areas of lands that are needed for residential development.

A meeting of South Dublin County Council was held yesterday at which the idea of sustainable development was discussed. For two and a half hours the dedicated councillors of South Dublin County Council discussed this concept so that when we are making decisions on rezoning lands, we will take into account matters such as energy needs, maintenance of green spaces, etc. which are necessary to ensure that whatever development takes place will not endanger resources for future generations. County councillors take their responsibilities seriously, particularly in relation to this matter.

The purpose of the unseemly squabble currently being engaged in, mainly for political purposes, is simply to allow the media have its bite. All of the councillors I know, and I know many of them not only in south Dublin but also in Fingal, Dún Laoghaire-Rathdown, Kildare, Wicklow and Meath, are hard-working people who are dedicated to local service and the constituents they represent. They deal with the minutiae of people's daily lives. If the House will pardon the use of the word, they are the bridge between people and bureaucracy. The amount of time the majority of local authority members spend on council matters is enormous. They do that for the benefit of their constituents, not for their own benefit.

I agree with Deputy Gilmore who said we are not here to discuss political footballs or have unseemly rows. We are here to care for the social and economic needs of the people. Deputies today received a booklet from CORI on basic income. In a year when we have in excess of £500 million to give away, the use of the phrase "payback time" is regrettable because we have to discuss where that money goes. The combination of extensive poverty and unemployment has contributed to the growing exclusion experienced by large numbers of people. CORI states that an alternative model for organising the distribution of resources is needed. This alternative system, a basic income, should be discussed and brought into the public domain.

Mrs. Owen: Earlier today when the Taoiseach referred to the resignation of Mr. Burke the Ceann Comhairle ruled that party leaders only could make a short intervention. I obeyed the ruling and did not intervene in the debate. I regret that the Minister of State, Deputy Noel Davern, felt it necessary to try to score political points at this difficult time for the Taoiseach. I wish he had not abused the ruling of the Chair. I join with other Members in expressing my sympathy to Ray Burke, Seán's widow and their families at this extremely difficult time.

[Mrs. Owen.]

The resignation of Mr. Burke as Minister for Foreign Affairs was a matter for him and the Taoiseach, who appoints his Ministers. However, he would not have resigned his Dáil seat if the Taoiseach and the Tánaiste had handled this matter in a better and more efficient way. Following Mr. Burke's statement in the House some weeks ago, the media excoriated Opposition Members for not going in for the kill and claiming all sorts of wrongdoing by Mr. Burke. We were not aware of any wrongdoing and did not allege any but we tried to get answers to questions, which is what the Opposition is supposed to do. If the Taoiseach had taken the wishes of all Opposition parties on board and agreed to have the £30,000 donation further investigated by the Moriarty tribunal a Member would not have been put under pressure to resign from office and this House.

This is a sad day for the constituents of Dublin North who elected Ray Burke to the Dáil in every election since 1973. He served his constituents to the best of his ability. I am sure some people did not like all the decisions he took. I know for certain that some of my constituents in Dublin North did not like some of the decisions I took. However, all Members do the best they can. I lay the blame for what happened today on the Taoiseach's shoulders. He should have handled this matter in a more efficient and speedier way and covered it in the tribunal so that Mr. Burke could get on with his job and face the tribunal as he said he would. Even as more information emerged the Taoiseach ignored the need to have the matter investigated. When the letter exchanged between two people was made public the Taoiseach should have taken hold of the issue and included it in the tribunal where it would be examined. It is regrettable that he did not do this and he must take the blame for Mr. Burke's resignation.

I was Minister for Justice for two and a half years during a very difficult time. It is not proper for a Minister for Justice to trawl through files and dish the dirt on previous Ministers for Justice. As Minister for Justice I was subject to the Official Secrets Act and I took my job extremely seriously. I set about making changes in this sensitive Department and introducing long overdue legislation. I want to make it clear that I did not provide *The Irish Times* with the report by Mr. Dermot Cole into the Mahfouz passports issue: it was requested by my predecessor, Máire Geoghegan-Quinn. I resisted making any public comment on suggestions about what was in it but, as it has now been published, I wish to comment on it. I have no idea how a journalist got a report which was on a file in the Department of Justice. I wish to clarify one or two inaccurate points made in the media. This was an interim, not a final, report. Like my predecessor, I was concerned about some of the issues raised in the report and the loose way in which some of the mechanisms and processes for gaining naturalisation and passports had been handled mainly by

a senior official in the Department. When I examined the report I realised that only £3 million of the £20 million promised investment had been made. I asked my officials to continue looking for the remainder of the money and to come back to me when all of it had been identified or when they reached the stage where they could not identify if all of it had been invested. As reports in the newspapers now show, and as has been confirmed by the Department of Justice, £17 million of the £20 million has been identified.

I was concerned to ascertain from the interim report if there was any evidence of corruption. I want to make it clear that there was no evidence in the report of corruption or wrongdoing by anyone involved. There were certainly breaches of the technical requirements which, according to the report, were carried out in the main by officials in the Department of Justice. I was concerned about the undue haste in issuing the passports. It is important to note that the Mahfouz family had been in dialogue with people for three or four months prior to when it received the passports. However, the passports were issued very quickly at the end of the day and there were some unusual elements in the handing over of them. When I was Minister for Justice I never physically handed over passports to anyone and it was unusual to say the least for Mr. Haughey to hand over the passports to the Mahfouz family at a lunch at which no officials were present.

The role of the Minister for Justice in revoking naturalisation is very carefully defined, it is a legal process. Until such time as I was satisfied on the whereabouts of the £20 million there was no need for me to proceed against the Mahfouz family and revoke their passports. There may well have been a need to revoke them after the completion of the inquiry but there was certainly no case for me to do so at that stage when I would have run the risk of a High Court action which the Department would have lost.

I want to make it clear that this issue was raised in the context of what we now know about the lifestyle of Mr. Haughey. We did not know what the McCracken tribunal identified, that Mr. Haughey had a particular way of financing his lifestyle. We know where £1.3 million of Mr. Haughey's money came from and if the inquiry into where other moneys came from to allow him live his lavish lifestyle leads to the Mahfouz passports issue then so be it. I saw nothing on the file to allege any such corrupt act on the part of the people involved. The efforts of the Government parties to put the blame and full responsibility on Opposition parties for Mr. Burke's resignation today is regrettable and disingenuous. It is the Opposition's job to raise issues and questions about matters of public interest and to try to get answers. All Opposition parties rightly queried the provision of a £30,000 donation to one individual and asked that at least it be examined and put to rest if there was no wrongdoing.

As other speakers said, politics has taken a terrible beating in the past few years, particularly in the past few weeks. All of us in politics feel that people's perception of us all is that we must be up to something. If somebody else makes money out of decisions we make, that is not a matter of responsibility for councillors or TDs. It is for the legislators to decide if they want to do away with any element of profit in any transaction undertaken by anyone in this State. The allegations made are unfair because councillors do their job.

The Local Government (Planning and Development) Act, 1963 states it is the responsibility of county councils to prepare a development plan with respect to county boroughs, boroughs, urban districts and scheduled towns for the use solely or primarily, as may be indicated in the development plan, of particular areas for particular purposes, whether residential, commercial, industrial, agricultural or otherwise. I was a member of Dublin County Council for 15 years and in latter years of Fingal County Council and was involved in the preparation of two development plans. That was a difficult time. I have a set of minutes of the council meetings for one year during the final period of the 1993 development plan. All living members of the council from 1985 to 1997 will be answerable to the new tribunal for the decisions they made. I have no problem in being answerable to the tribunal. I welcome it because I hope it will clear the air as to how councillors must prepare a development plan in a situation where they will always be open to allegations that by their decisions they have made money for other people. There is no other way of introducing a development plan other than to change zonings. Councillors of all parties on the council of which I was a member at some time voted in their best judgment for some form of zoning, whether for industry, general housing or single housing. I do not know how it can be claimed that some people are always under a shadow because they do that job. There have been Garda inquiries. There was one in 1991, 1992 or 1993 and no wrongdoing was found. I hope the tribunal will put to rest the allegations and the concerns raised.

Councillors, some of whom spoke in the Chamber, were not happy with some decisions. I was not happy with all the decisions made and in hindsight I might not be happy with some I made and if I had my time again I might change them. I made them on the basis of the best information I had without inducement from anybody. We went into those meetings, listened to the arguments and did our best to decide if rezonings were good or bad and voted accordingly. It is important I say that because I am one of the few former Fine Gael councillors who has a chance to speak here.

The demands placed on local councillors will continue. I welcome the Minister, Deputy Dempsey's remarks that he wants to make the planning process more transparent. The planning process as I operated it, and as I know it operated in Dublin County Council, allowed for two public displays of the development plan, one when the first

plan was put on display and another when it was reviewed and more changes were made. The public made thousands of submissions in respect of all elements of that plan. I would be interested to hear how the Minister intends to make the process more transparent. The councils are commencing the process of new development plans and I wish them luck. There will be another series of debates as to whether they should or should not allow for the fact that the population of Dublin is now 1,058,264 compared to 718,000 in 1961. Someone must face the reality of the growing population of Dublin. I do not know how that can be faced other than by providing for it in a development plan.

Ms M. McGennis: I wish to share my time with Deputy Noel Ahern.

An Ceann Comhairle: That is agreed.

Ms M. McGennis: I welcome the tribunal because I have been a member of Dublin County Council since 1985 and in latter years of Fingal County Council. I and many councillors reject the smear that attaches to being a Dublin county councillor. I express my sympathy to Ray Burke and his family on his resignation. I served with him when he was chairman of Dublin County Council. Although it was tempestuous at times and he was tough, he was also fair. He would not have subjected anyone to the type of vilification and smear he had to put up with in the past few weeks and months. One lesson I learned early as a Member of this House is that it seems there is very little humanity in this House. That was something of which I was not aware in the other House or as a member of Dublin County Council.

The Minister stated that rezoning has a bad name, which it has, but it is a statutory obligation of county councillors and county councils to review the development plan every five years. However, Dublin County Council only completed two reviews of the plan from 1972 to 1993, two reviews in 21 years. The chairman of the new tribunal should start his investigation at that point on the hiatus that created in County Dublin and the reason for changes in the development plan that might have seemed spectacular.

No changes were made to the 1993 development plan when I was involved in the 1991 to 1993 review. We did not make any changes to the decisions of the 1983 plan. If those decisions were so controversial and wrong, why were they not overturned?

There is more to the 1983 development plan that simple rezoning. I say that because I live in the Blanchardstown area. The development plan objectives or the spatial settlement strategies, as they were referred to in the documents Deputies Owen and I got during our period on the council when the plan was reviewed, were simple and straightforward. There were three new towns, Lucan-Clondalkin, Tallaght and Blanchardstown, which were to accommodate 100,000 people each.

[Ms M. McGennis.]
That was the settlement strategy for the county from the early 1980s. Any decision which interfered with that settlement strategy was objected to by the manager. Any proposals which the manager felt would be in competition with those three new towns were opposed, quite furiously at times, by the then manager.

It was said by Deputy Rabbitte, and I also said it at a council meeting, that pipes in the ground dictated where people could and should live. I ask the House and the new tribunal if that is good planning. I do not believe it is. As Deputy Owen said, most members of Dublin County Council rejected the suggestion that because a sewerage pipe could accommodate the waste products of 100,000 people in one of the three new towns in County Dublin that was the basis on which people would select where to live. Strangely, the only breach of this strategy was in the 1991-93 plan when the manager introduced the only rezoning proposal I can remember. There may have been others but this plan sticks in my mind. This was a rezoning proposal for, approximately, 500 acres in Carrickmines Valley. It was a managerial proposal and came out of the blue but if it is investigated we might discover if it was connected to the fact that there was a pipe in the vicinity which had been pumping out sea water for a number of years to make sure that it could be used when the time came.

In their wisdom the members of Dublin County Council rejected this proposal and yet no reference was made to the fact that it was a managerial proposal. North County Dublin, which will be the subject of the initial inquiry, was not to grow under any circumstances. That decision was made despite the fact that the ERDO report recommended that the north fringe would accommodate approximately 100,000 people as had been decided for the other three satellite towns. North County Dublin could and would not be allowed to grow and the tribunal will discover that fact in terms of the manager's strategy.

A recent newspaper article referred to 105 section 4 motions passed by Dublin County Council in an eight year period. A colleague has informed me that 27 of those motions concerned individual houses in north County Dublin for the sons and daughters of people already living there. As a result of the development plan restrictions imposed by the manager those people could not live in their home villages and towns. The strategy was that someone living in Rush, Lusk, Skerries, Balbriggan or wherever should move to Blanchardstown, Lucan, Clondalkin or Tallaght. That was the policy of the management of Dublin County Council.

Another point which is overlooked is that in my area of Blanchardstown I dezoned a considerable amount of land owned by Dublin Corporation which was zoned for housing. We rezoned this land for industrial use. Deputy Higgins supported that although many of those who are most vociferous would say they never supported a rezoning motion. I have supported such motions and I hope I can stand over all of those decisions. We decided that land zoned for housing in Blanchardstown should be rezoned for industrial use. That decision has resulted in the arrival of IBM and the promise of 3,000 jobs. Had we not decided to overturn managerial decisions these jobs would not exist.

Dublin Corporation was the largest owner of zoned land in County Dublin. I would pose a question to the tribunal chairman. Could there be a connection between the fact that until 1994 the manager of Dublin Corporation was also the manager of Dublin County Council even though he never attended a meeting? There were weekly summits in City Hall at which our managers were given their instructions. Could that manager have exerted any influence on the reports and rezoning proposals which he brought to us?

The Minister said that the tribunal will also look at designation. I wish to defend a decision made by the previous Minister, Deputy Quinn, in relation to Cherry Orchard. This decision has been smeared across the newspapers. This is a most deprived and disadvantaged area and the kind of innuendo attached to that designation is to be regretted. It is time for courage. I reject any suggestion of immunity from prosecution for those who bribed people or received bribes. It is time for those who made a lot of the running on this issue to put up or shut up.

Mr. N. Ahern: The genesis of this issue is the result of the election. The Opposition has never accepted that result. Before the election it believed its own propaganda and it seems determined to undermine the Government by foul means or fair. It is hard to listen to some of the self-righteous nonsense coming from some people who, if one is to believe rumours, have also questions to answer.

It is sad that we are dealing with this motion on the day that former Deputy Burke has resigned. The witch-hunt carried out against him is a disgrace. It is a sad day for politics when people go about trying to undermine and hound a good man out of office for weeks on end. During the past few days when Deputy Burke suffered a family bereavement the behaviour of some people in politics and the media has been very shabby. Only they can look in the mirror and say whether they are proud of their behaviour. There was a time when one was innocent until proven guilty, one received the benefit of the doubt. That time seems to be gone. The ruthless, continuous, headlong pursuit for a head seems to be the philosophy of politics and the media. We are all the sadder for it.

It is significant that the all-party talks have commenced in the North today. Former Deputy Burke can take credit for the part he played over the past few months in reaching this stage. I wonder if there is some jealousy in some quarters about the recent success of the talks? Perhaps we will have to wait for history to supply the answers as to who orchestrated this recent campaign to undermine the former Minister and why. I do not wish to get involved in conspiracy theories but there might be interesting questions behind this issue.

It is very sad to see the way in which public opinion has been manipulated and people's characters undermined. There has been an ongoing drip of information and one wonders whether that was freely given or whether it was paid for. I am sick and tired of tribunals but sooner or later we will have a tribunal on the media and how it receives and presents its information. I wonder if when people pay 80p or £1 they consider whether they are reading fact or opinion, from where the spin comes, whether that spin is an opinion or genuine or whether someone has received inducements to frame it in that manner?

I am a member of the city council. There are not many rezonings in the city although we have material contraventions. Much of what is occurring is giving rezoning a bad name. I must defend the system of local government. There is nothing wrong with a council or councillor objecting to or voting against the recommendations of officials. Those in local government know that there is a balance between the powers of officials and councils. This is a battle and people must stand up for what they believe in. It is scandalous to suggest that there is something wrong with not taking the advice of officials. Many people have suggested this in recent days. Too often officials do not take the advice of elected members yet no one ever suggests that this is done for an ulterior motive. They do so because they believe it is right. I know that some rezonings might have been difficult to understand but the problem is partly a result of the development plan. The process is so long-winded that no sooner has one review been completed than another is started. I am convinced the tribunal will vindicate the former Minister, Deputy Burke. I hope at the end of the day all of us in politics will portray a proper image and stop telling tales on one another, which does much damage.

Mr. Higgins *(Dublin West):* The proposed tribunal relates particularly to planning matters. As a member of Dublin County Council in 1991 and 1992, I found myself at the centre of a maelstrom of rezonings, led not primarily by considerations of good planning but in response to demands of landowners, developers and, in some cases, speculators. I was astounded the Minister, Deputy Dempsey, spent a considerable time attacking those who question some rezonings that deserve to be questioned. He attacked people who ask legitimate questions rather than directing his attention to answering the questions raised.

Today we are setting up another tribunal arising from information accidentally brought to public attention, information involving a donation of £30,000 and a letter which refers to the procure-

ment of planning permission. A Fianna Fáil Member said that if there is corruption in high places we must expose it. Ordinary people believe there has been massive corruption involving obscene profits from land speculation, particularly in the Dublin area and perhaps in other areas.

It is an undeniable facet of the ugly face of capitalism that land rezoned from agricultural to residential or industrial rockets in price by up to 30 times the original price. The result is that young people purchasing homes pay for speculation and profiteering. They spend 20 to 30 years of their lives repaying mortgages, a good part of which pays for the site on which their home is built, a site from which a speculator, landowner or developer has made a fortune. Will the main parties of the Establishment who spent most of the day rubbishing the attack on the planning process, and particularly rezonings in Dublin, give their views on those factors? This is not an academic discussion but one that impinges on the lives of tens of thousands of ordinary working and unemployed people.

There is a demand for the truth in this whole controversy, but the Government's terms of reference may set the scene for a possible cover-up of the truth rather than for its revelation. Paragraph 5 of the terms of reference refers to the tribunal investigating acts which, in its opinion, amount to corruption. I hope the Minister will direct attention to the amendments I propose rather than read a prepared script. We should be given concrete answers. Does there have to be direct *prima facie* evidence of corruption before a serious matter of planning can be examined by the tribunal? I refer to amendment No. 4 in my name.

In 1993 two parcels of land compromising 130 acres at Dublin Airport were inexplicably rezoned from agricultural to industrial by a coalition of councillors from the Progressive Democrats, Fianna Fáil and Fine Gael — the information is in the minutes of the meetings concerned. The Department of Transport, Energy and Communications of the day, the Department responsible for Dublin Airport, wrote to the county council stating that the land should not be rezoned. Aer Rianta, the public body charged with the management of national airports and future strategy for the development of airports, told the county council that in about ten years' time this land on the periphery of Dublin Airport would be needed for expansion for a new terminal and related development. Even the Dublin Chamber of Commerce wrote to the county council stating that the land should not be rezoned, yet the rezoning was agreed to.

The effect is that the 130 acres, which might have been bought by Aer Rianta for £5,000 per acre and would cost £650,000 in agricultural zoning, because it was rezoned for industrial purposes could cost £100,000 per acre or, as has been stated by people in the property market, £150,000. Aer Rianta, therefore, could have to

[Mr. Higgins *(Dublin West).*]
pay between £13 million and £19.5 million simply because the land was rezoned. Since Aer Rianta is a public body, that would be a direct attack on the taxpayer, and for what purpose? The effect would be to enrich a tiny handful of individuals.

Why did the councillors agree to the rezoning against all the advice? That matter should be investigated. Can that case be referred to and examined by the tribunal and an investigation conducted into the matter? The Minister should deal with that issue and with the amendments. I called for an investigation into the Glending Wood case, the sale in secrecy for £1.25 million of valuable State lands which could be worth £48 million. Herein lies a scandal of immense proportions which must be investigated. The rezoning of Laraghcon in the slopes of the Liffey Valley near Lucan should be examined. That area should be kept as an amenity for the huge communities between Blanchardstown and Lucan. Land must be set aside for homes and industry in Dublin and elsewhere, but that can be done rationally, without profiteering in housing and industrial land. There should be strict control of building land so that the scandals I believe have occurred, irrespective of whether there was corruption, will never happen again. In the interests of those who have to purchase homes — a basic shelter that everyone requires — the profiteering element should be taken out of building land. To facilitate a proper investigation and discovery of the truth, provision should be made for at least limited immunity for those who have guilty information. This is necessary to ensure that more of the truth comes to light and that a successful investigation into scandals and corruption takes place.

Ms M. McGennis: Those who were paid bribes should not get immunity.

Mr. Sargent: I thank Deputy Higgins for sharing time with me. While I had heard rumours about the Minister, Deputy Burke, resigning from his ministerial position, I was shocked to hear of his resignation from the House. This highlights the vulnerability of politics and politicians. He did a great deal of good work. He spoke out strongly against landmines, something that is close to my heart, and when in Opposition he spoke strongly on the question of neutrality. There is a sense of shock in my constituency tonight.

I agree with Deputy Higgins that Glending Wood should be included in the tribunal. The drip feed of information in the media in recent days, irrespective of whether it is accurate, will continue unless this matter is investigated by a tribunal. I do not agree with Deputy Roche that the matter can be dealt with in a committee. Committees cannot compel witnesses in the same way as a tribunal. We will never get to the bottom of this issue if it is not investigated by a tribunal.

The Minister for the Environment referred to rezoning. I am sure all Members would agree that rezoning has a part to play in proper planning, but it is a question of whether it is done rationally or against the advice of planning officials. I witnessed two types of rezoning during in my time as a member of Dublin County Council, when many bizarre proposals were brought before the council. During that time I received money with a request that I consider favourably a rezoning proposal. On 13 February 1993, having asked if any other member of the council had also received such money, I was quickly told to resume my seat as I was causing disorder. I was assaulted in the chamber, the meeting had to be adjourned and, for my own safety I was told, I was led from the chamber by the county manager. For the sake of the planning process and confidence in public life, the nervous attitude among those involved in planning must be tackled.

I hope the tribunal will begin to put to rest at least some of these allegations — to uphold them or to throw them out as unfounded. I have no doubt the allegations will continue to surface and that there will be a cloud over the heads of all councillors because we cannot say who was honest and dishonest unless we have this tribunal. If the matter is to be investigated properly the DPP will have to be asked to ensure immunity for witnesses. Up to now both Fine Gael and Fianna Fáil Ministers for Justice have said the DPP is above politics and cannot be asked to grant immunity to witnesses. That is fair in most cases but issues such as this, which are in the national interest, have to be followed through. This is an issue on which the DPP will have to be guided.

The tribunal will not be the end of this matter unless it is given the latitude to follow any money trails unearthed. As in the Hamilton tribunal, the McCracken tribunal and now in the Ansbacher tribunal, as it is being called, unless there is latitude to follow those money trails the process will be seen to be flawed and ultimately will give rise to further investigation and numerous tribunals.

Mr. Timmins: I thank the Minister, Deputy Molloy, and Deputy Stagg for sharing their time. For the past 45 years Roadstone has been involved in the extraction of sand and gravel at Blessington. The company's lands at Blessington extend to 638 acres. The lands are divided between active extraction areas, lands undergoing reinstatement and lands that have been reinstated to forestry and grasslands use. Of the 638 acres, 147 acres were sold to the company by the Department of Energy in or about 1992. The 147 acres sold to Roadstone by the Department are subdivided as follows: 90 acres is a coniferous commercial plantation and 57 acres is a mature plantation known as Glending Wood and Deerpark Plantations. This area will not be exploited in any way.

Subject to the granting of planning permission the company's intentions for the 147 acres are as follows: the 57 acres known as Glending Wood and Deerpark Plantations to be retained as they are in full and managed to best forestry standards and 80 acres to be used for sand and gravel extraction. These lands will be fully reinstated to forestry, grass and wetland, ten acres of coniferous plantation to be maintained for additional screening purposes.

In respect of the sale of the lands, in a written reply to Question No. 298 on 15 April 1997, column 1141 of the Official Report, the former Minister for Agriculture, Food and Forestry, Deputy Yates, stated:

> Prior to the sale detailed assessments on the property were carried out by the Geological Survey of Ireland and by independent consultants to evaluate a fair market price for the property.

> In April 1990 the independent consultants suggested that the Department of Energy might be best advised to invite offers by tender for the sale of the land. However, following an offer for the property by the first company [Roadstone] mentioned by the Deputy, the consultants subsequently advised in October 1990 that it would be most unlikely that any other party would be able to match an offer from that company and strongly recommended that the sale to the company be pursued. The then Minister for Energy accepted that advice and the land was not advertised for public sale.

> The Minister was aware that there had been an expression of interest from the second company mentioned by the Deputy. While negotiations on the sale of the property to the first company were in progress, the second company made an offer for the property, but that offer was significantly lower than that of the first company and was not therefore accepted. On the basis of advice available to him, the Minister was satisfied that, if the land were put on the market, it would most likely fail to reach the price on offer from the first company. In accordance with the guidelines on the disposal of Government property where a sale is not conducted by public tender or auction, the approval of the Department of Finance was sought and obtained before the offer by the first company was accepted.

Deputy Yates then went on to say that taking into account the circumstances of the case the Minister at the time was satisfied the State received a fair price for the sale of the property.

In recent times there has been much comment in County Wicklow on Glending and development in the Blessington area. A few vociferous individuals have made many claims. Blessington is a small market town located just 20 miles south of Dublin, and it is undergoing radical change due to the proximity of the capital. I fear that it may become a political football. There has been much information and innuendo on the airwaves and in the media where allegations of planning scandals and rezoning of lands for pals have been made,

D 481—G

and the credibility and bona fides of certain individuals have been unfoundedly called into question in a most distasteful way. I believe there is nothing to hide with respect of the development of Blessington and Wicklow in general. I welcome the terms of reference of the new tribunal and, in particular, paragraph 5, and I look forward to those individuals who claim there is something wrong with planning coming forward with factual information and ceasing to peddle speculation.

Mr. Stagg: In the limited time available to me I will deal with planning and zoning in county Kildare. Zoners there have gone stark raving mad. Fianna Fáil, Fine Gael and Progressive Democrat councillors have been zoning land at such a rate as to lead to 90,000 additional population in the county over a period of five years. This has been vigorously pursued by the right-wing coalition of councillors, despite the strong opposition of the county planners and the opposition of planners from the Labour Party, Democratic Left and the Green Party. The availability of infrastructure such as roads, water and sewage treatment is of no concern to the zoners. When advised by the planners that these necessary infrastructural facilities were not available, it mattered not one whit. Zone and be damned seemed to be the philosophy. No thought was given to the need for schools and amenities.

As an example of what I am talking about, at one meeting of the Clane Area Committee of Kildare County Council, the councillors, two Fianna Fáil and two Fine Gael, were told the lands they were now proposing to zone for residential development was subject to regular flooding and that the county council would be liable for damage caused by the flooding of houses in future. When it was established by the councillors that individual councillors would not be liable for damage, it was decided unanimously by the Fianna Fáil and Fine Gael councillors to go ahead with the rezoning. That is in the village of Clane where the zoners propose to extend the population by a factor of three in a mere five years. This pattern of massive zoning is being pursued not just in Clane but throughout mid and north Kildare. In Kilcock the same Fianna Fáil and Fine Gael councillors propose to enlarge that village by a factor of five inside five years, and this despite massive public resistance to their proposals. In Kilcock a formal plebiscite was held and, despite the full weight of the Fianna Fáil and Fine Gael political machines in favour of rezoning proposals, they were rejected by the public by a margin of two to one. In the prize-winning village of Johnstown, land in the family ownership of the local councillor was zoned from agricultural to residential use which will increase its population by a factor of seven, destroy its village character and transform it into a commuter town — the value of the land went up from about £100,000 to £1 million overnight.

Mr. Dukes: The Deputy was a bit more circumspect with the public when he spoke about this.

Mr. Stagg: In the town of Newbridge, the councillors zoned a sizeable pocket of land that would be sufficient for indigenous needs for 50 years, but the Fianna Fáil, Fine Gael and Progressive Democrat zoners were not satisfied with this. They also decided to go some miles outside the town to zone land in the ownership of Senator John Dardis, then chairperson of the Progressive Democrats. The 20 acres in question automatically shot up in value from approximately £60,000 to £2 million. If Senator Dardis was not a millionaire before that decision he is now. It should be recorded that Senator Dardis is a member of the planning authority and did not vote on the decision.

This pattern is repeated throughout the county with probably the worse excess is in Maynooth where the full council decided to zone the green belt on either side of Cartan Avenue for residential and commercial purposes despite the strong opposition of the planners, overwhelming opposition by the public and majority opposition by the Celbridge area committee of the council.

These planning outrages in County Kildare are such that the previous Minister, Deputy Howlin, refused to accept the county development plan. This action was unprecedented and I congratulate Deputy Howlin for having the courage to do so. The county councillors in favour of zoning went back to the drawing board. The proposal they have come up with has also been rejected by the Minister, Deputy Dempsey. It is to be hoped that reason will prevail in County Kildare and that Fianna Fáil, Progressive Democrats and Fine Gael county councillors will heed the advice of the professional planners and the opinion of the public and take account of the planning needs of the county.

Why do Fianna Fáil, Progressive Democrats and Fine Gael county councillors who are normally industrious in their attention to the needs of their areas lose all reason when it comes to zoning land for residential development? The reason is plain — money and greed. Land zoned from agricultural to residential use rockets in value from approximately £5,000 per acre to £100,000 per acre. Ten acres yields approximately £1 million.

Fianna Fáil, the Progressive Democrats and Fine Gael are supported with funding by those who make these massive gains and the golden circle continues. Action must be taken——

Mr. Dukes: On a point of order, Sir, will you recall for Deputy Stagg the provisions and measures made by the House in its last formation about statements and the care Members should take not to trespass unduly on the rights and good name of persons outside it? Deputy Stagg has come close to saying things that he has so far failed to say or avoided saying in public.

Mr. Stagg: That is not true, I made these points on the local radio station, CKR.

Mr. Dukes: The Deputy is getting close to slander in his usual appetite for gory detail.

An Leas-Cheann Comhairle: I ask Deputy Stagg to refrain from referring to persons who are not in position to defend themselves.

Mr. Stagg: Action must be taken to outlaw private contributions to political parties and politicians. If the connection between big business and political parties is to be broken this is an imperative.

Mr. Dukes: What about big unions?

Mr. Stagg: Legislation should be introduced to claw back through the taxation system the added value on land arising from rezoning.

Mr. Dukes: Socialist sanctimoniousness, even worse than the Progressive Democrats.

Mr. Stagg: It is obvious I have got under the Deputy's skin, a good measure of success. Legislation should also be introduced to allow interested parties appeal against decisions to zone land for development. The law allows for appeals against the most minor developments from the building of a front porch to the size of a front window. Why is there no appeal against decisions that allow the face of a whole area or a county to be changed?

Minister for the Environment and Local Government (Mr. Dempsey): I thank the Deputies who contributed to the debate. From the contributions which have been made no one disagrees there is a need for a judicial investigation to get to the bottom of the allegations, rumours and innuendoes which have beset the planning system and have scant regard for the good name and reputation of those who serve on public authorities whether as elected members or officers. If people are guilty of impropriety I hope this will be established and they will have to face the consequences of their actions. If, on the other hand, people who have been fingered are innocent it is even more important that their good name is restored, that they are vindicated and that the allegations and innuendoes are refuted. As is clear from the Programme for Government, it is a major ambition of mine during my term as Minister to improve the operation of the planning system. The process has commenced.

Over the next year or so, I hope to bring a number of Bills before the House to reform and consolidate planning law. The public consultation exercise in which I am now engaged will help to achieve this. I urge anyone who has an interest in good and proper planning to feed their ideas into the process so we can have an improved system in place by the middle of next year. The tribunal will help to dispel the fog of cynicism that frequently affects planning, pointing up lessons that can be learned so that the legislation can be strengthened.

Deputies asked me to respond to their amendments. Up to the outbreak of hostilities between the two Kildare Deputies the debate was very civilised. I will make one political point on the contributions of Deputies Dukes and Howlin. They persisted in questioning the bona fides of the Government in drafting the tribunal's terms of reference. The desire and aim of the Government at all times was to have an effective, efficient and focused tribunal. When the draft terms were brought forward the Opposition had difficulty with them. The Opposition Whips involved in the negotiations would agree that while they had disagreements and rows about what they felt needed to be included, all told, there was a desire among all parties to get the most effective terms of reference to prevent this from going all over the place and wasting time.

As a result of the consultations the terms of reference are now better than those first drafted. It would be remiss of me not to pay tribute to the Whips who had responsibility for drafting the terms of reference and coming up with something reasonable.

Deputy Howlin talked about the need for an ombudsman to reassure the public on an ongoing basis about matters of concern. That is precisely the point I made in my contribution. The Taoiseach, when in Opposition, put forward that idea and is following up on it in Government. I agree with Deputy Howlin that it is vital to have this commission in place so that legitimate concerns, allegations and evidence that people have can be brought to a body that is independent of all of us in this House and independent of the "system". They can then put their case which can be independently investigated. That is the aim we have in setting up the permanent ethics commission.

While we all have our own views of different aspects of this controversy, we can agree it is absolutely necessary to have some other way of dealing with matters of this nature rather than across the floor of the House, until such time as allegations are proven or otherwise. I am sure Deputies will support that when the time comes.

As regards Deputy Howlin's contribution, and Deputy Higgins' amendment to section 5 of the tribunal's terms of reference, I am happy to give both Deputies the assurance they sought on paragraph 5.

The Deputy's interjection was correct. Paragraph 5 requires the tribunal to report on any acts associated with the operation of the planning process of which it becomes aware during its inquiries and which it believes might amount to corruption or which involves attempts to compromise the disinterested performance of public duties. Paragraph 5 is designed to be as wide and specific as possible so that the tribunal can investigate any evidence which suggests corruption. If people bring matters to the attention of the tribunal, it will be in order for it to pursue them.

While Deputy Gilmore welcomed paragraph 5, he said it went too far. This shows the difficulty the Whips had in drafting the terms of reference. I spoke to the Attorney General about this matter and it was felt that if we tried to specifically list the different incidents we wanted investigated, one would be left out. If that incident arose during the tribunal, it would be stymied and a new one would have to be established. I assure the Deputies that paragraph 5 addresses their concerns. I give an undertaking that if it does not, we can discuss it again in this House.

Deputy Dukes tabled amendments Nos. 1, 1*a*, *a*1, 2, 7 and 8. I am advised that these are not specifically needed. The Deputy said he wanted clear terms of reference and that he had tabled these amendments to remove any doubt. On the basis that they do not alter the agreement already made with the Whips on the terms of reference, I will accept the amendments, with the exception of amendment No. 7, and include them in the terms of reference. I have also received advice on amendment No. 7. The Deputy wanted to insert "Electoral, Freedom of Information and Prevention of Corruption" Acts. I suggest that he accepts my amendment to insert "any other relevant Acts" so the tribunal does not feel it has to investigate all such legislation. The phrase, "any other relevant Acts", would leave the tribunal free to investigate legislation if it so wishes.

Mr. Dukes: I accept that.

Mr. Dempsey: I thank the Deputy. One of the clearest demands from all sides of this House is that Donnelly Neary and Donnelly Solicitors, their clients and all their complainants would put before the tribunal at the outset the facts and evidence they have in their possession. That is the one clear message to emerge from this matter. It will greatly facilitate the tribunal in its deliberations and remove the need for much preliminary work which might otherwise have to be done. With no sense of acrimony I say to those solicitors that they now have what they desired, namely, a judicial inquiry into the planning process in Dublin. I expect they will do their utmost to co-operate with that inquiry and make available to it all the evidence in their possession.

I refer to a comment relating to councillors lining people's pockets by rezoning land, etc. In fairness to councillors, they have a job to do and they sometimes work under enormous pressure. They have a duty to become involved in and take responsibility for the planning process and development plans. It is unfair to characterise them doing their duty as doing it for the sole reason of lining people's pockets. It is the responsibility of this House to ensure that, if people are making money from decisions relating to rezoning, etc., a regime is put in place to deal with such matters and collect suitable taxes from those involved. I have referred this matter to officials in my Department and the review group

[Mr. Dempsey.]
in order that consideration might be given to the provision of services in respect of rezoned land.

I thank Members for their contributions and, assuming the motion is passed, I wish the tribunal well in its work.

An Leas-Cheann Comhairle: For the purpose of clarification, in mentioning paragraph 6 the Minister referred to the word "Acts". I must inform him that the word "legislation" is already included in that paragraph. Therefore, the amendment tabled by Deputy Dukes will now read "In paragraph A.6., to delete "and Ethics in Public Office" and substitute ", Ethics in Public Office and any other relevant"." As it is now 8.30 p.m., I am required to put the following question in accordance with an Order of the Dáil of this day:

"That amendments Nos. a1, 1, 1a, 2, 7, as amended, and 8 are hereby agreed to; that amendments Nos. 3 to 6, inclusive, are negatived; and the motion, as amended, is hereby agreed to.".

I think the question is carried.

Mr. Higgins (*Dublin West*): Vótáil.

An Ceann Comhairle: On the question, "That amendments Nos. a1, 1, 1a, 2, 7, as amended, and 8 are hereby agreed to; that amendments Nos. 3 to 6, inclusive, are negatived; and the motion, as amended, is hereby agreed to" a division has been challenged. Will Deputies who are claiming a division please rise?

Deputies Gormley, Sargent, Gregory, Joe Higgins and Ó Caoláin rose.

An Ceann Comhairle: As fewer than ten Members have risen in their places, I declare the question carried. In accordance with Standing Order the names of the Deputies dissenting will be recorded in the Journal of the Proceedings of the Dáil.

Question declared carried.

Adjournment Debate.

Drink Price Increase.

Mr. Rabbitte: The reported increase in the price of the pint was permitted by a decision of the Government. I am displeased that none of the Ministers responsible have presented themselves in the House this evening. The matter will be replied to by the Minister of State at the Department of Health and Children with special responsibility for food safety and older people.

This is an important matter. As recently as 9 July the Minister of State at the Department of Enterprise, Trade and Employment with special responsibility for labour affairs, consumer rights and international trade, Deputy Tom Kitt, told the House that he had no plans to raise the price fixing order that I imposed last March. However, it is reported in the newspapers that the Minister has done that and has permitted the trade to take an increase of 5p.

In so far as we can establish a reason for this it is that the brewers have increased the price of a pint by 2p and that the remainder is taken by the licensed trade. It is shameful that any Minister with responsibility for consumer affairs would capitulate in this fashion to the powerful lobby of the licensed vintner's trade, which is well represented in Government. There is no justification for it either in terms of fairness to the consumer or its impact on inflation.

In terms of fairness to the consumer, the proportion of the cost of a pint going to the publican has consistently increased in recent years at the expense of the Exchequer. The rainbow Government refrained on three successive budgets from imposing an increase in excise duty on alcoholic drink on the understanding that the trade would show similar restraint. However, the trade took a price increase of 5p and, having failed to persuade those publicans outside Dublin to rescind it, I found it necessary to impose a price fixing order effective from 11 November 1996. That contributed to depressing the CPI by 0.2 per cent.

I seek permission to have circulated a note on the statistics of this from the weekly monitor produced by Davy Stockbrokers which point to the fact that the depression in the CPI in the past year was 0.2 per cent arising from that price fixing order because alcohol forms such a disproportionate share of the basket of items that make up the consumer price index. In submitting to the lobby from the publicans the Minister is prepared to put the present low inflation environment at risk.

Whatever the excuse for permitting the brewers to take an increase, which is not justified in this low inflation environment, there is no excuse for the Minister of State to bow the knee to the publicans in the fashion that he has done so. He told the House on 9 July that he had no plans to raise the price fixing order but as soon as the vintners visited him he rolled over.

It is a particularly inauspicious start for any Minister of State at the Department of Enterprise, Trade and Employment, as his first act in Government, to impose on the ordinary pint drinker an increase of 5 pence in the price of the pint with, apparently, the support of his colleagues in Government.

It is a disgrace and I ask the Government to reconsider it.

Minister of State at the Department of Health and Children (Dr. Moffatt): Following detailed discussion with representatives of the drinks industry, and having received undertakings on price restraint, the Minister of State at the Department of Enterprise, Trade and Employ-

Appendix E

1. 2 × £25K to Carian ltd 18530440601g
   + £10K
                    @ H-S

Pay to on authority of J. Caldwell
2. Charles Kane
      36 Finch Rd.   1 × £58K place on deposit
      Douglas IOM   out of B + McG joint
                         CALL DEPOSIT.

3. Remainder on 7 day call deposit.

4. Guiness Mahon Guernsey Ltd
      St. Julians Ct.
      St.P.P.   a/c Foxtown Inv. ltd.

June 1984 a/c £1205 C.758   *112,166.42
Further attces reav. £ 845 A extra C.758 2858.05
                        808.05 Ardean 3 | 409308.39
          £2858.05   136,436.16
                                     10   £272872.2
                              £126,436.16 Foxtown

      272872.21
        50000.00 Carian ltd
      222872.21
        58   Call Deposit
      £164872.21 7 day call deposit.

Appendix F

Dublin 4 Ireland
Telephone 01 693111
Telex 93700
Telefax 01 838140

Baile Átha Cliath, Éire
Telefón 01 693111
Teleics 93700
Telefax 01 838140

Radio Telefís Éireann

2nd November 1988

Mr. Oliver Barry,
16 Parnell Square,
Dublin 1.

RE: FM RADIO - NATIONAL COVERAGE

Dear Oliver,

With reference to our meeting this morning (02/11/88) please find
enclosed a breakdown of the composite quote given to you at the
meeting.

The two elements are the overall package cost including all
capital equipment, design, installation and maintenance costs.
The full package cost comes to £1.14 million p.a. all-in. The
capital equipment element in it is £1.1 million as detailed and
the charge included is for a five year agreement.

In regard to the annual charge for the equipment to be installed,
this is based on a fixed interest charge of 7% p.a. and the
infrastructure charge is based on 12% p.a. which is the rate
charged to RTE by the Exchequer for loans advanced in connection
with the infrastructure development.

We trust that this analysis will help you in getting over the
"shock" of cost involved. We would exphasise that this quote is
based on a full replicate of the existing radio transmitter
networks and could be subject to alteration to suit your
requirements more closely.

Yours sincerely,

GERRY O'BRIEN
DIRECTOR OF FINANCE

Dublin 4 Ireland
Telephone 01 693111
Telex 93700
Telefax 01 838140

Baile Átha Cliath, Éire
Telefón 01 693111
Teleics 93700
Telefax 01 838140

Radio Telefís Éireann

1st November 1988

NATIONAL FM RADIO COVERAGE

OUTLINE PROPOSAL AND COSTS

OUTLINE

The purpose of this proposal is to set out the cost of providing an additional National FM Radio transmission system which would achieve 98.5% population coverage.

This proposal is based on providing a fully integrated system over RTE's existing facilities (sites, links, etc.) and includes all costs including initial capital outlay, annual running costs and maintenance. RTE would carry the programme signals over the exising RTE link network supplied by Telecom Eireann for RTE.

OFFER

This includes the following:

- Design, acquire and install complete FM Radio transmission network.
- Coverage of 98.5% of Ireland's population plus coverage of Northern Ireland's population to the extent of 1 million people.
- Major population centres covered in first year.
- All necessary equipment supplied/installed i.e. transmitters, masts, aerials, feeder systems etc.
- Signal to include RDS system for automatic tuning by RDS capable radio sets.
- Full annual running costs of system.
- Complete maintenance to the same standard of RTE's transmissions.
- Full standby cover as exists for RTE's systems.
- Emergency nationwide call-out service.
- Full system monitoring and signal quality control.
- National reception monitoring/assessment and interference investigation.
- Expert upkeep and optimum signal quality to full international broadcast standard. Coverage would reach 98.5% of population over a three year period.
  Coverage in year 1   63% of population
  Coverage in year 2   95% of population
  Coverage in year 3   98.5% of population

(ALL-IN CHARGE

Annual rental based on five/ten year Agreement with broadcaster with lead in payments while transmission coverage is being built up, as follows:

Year 1

5 months from date of firm order:
Coverage of Dublin/Cork - annual rental £600,000
3 months later:
Coverage of Limerick/Galway - annual rental £850,000.
Above coverage includes surrounding areas of these cities.

Year 2

At 3 monthly intervals - as coverage is expanded.
In 4th month: Annual rental £900,000.
In 7th month: Annual rental £1,000,000.

Year 3

At end of 3 months full coverage achieved:
Annual rental £1,140,000.

It would be proposed to hold the annual rental at a fixed cost over the first three years. Increases thereafter to be related to C.P.I.

The foregoing is an outline of RTE's proposal for a full national FM radio transmission system. It is based on RTE distributing the signal over its link network as supplied by Telecom Eireann for RTE.

GERRY O'BRIEN   JOHN McGRATH
DIRECTOR OF FINANCE   SEIC EASTERN REGION

Appendix G

IRTC.CENT 1.19 - 340

IRTC

THE INDEPENDENT RADIO AND
TELEVISION COMMISSION
AN COIMISIÚN UM RAIDIO AGUS
TELEFÍS NEAMHSPLEÁCH

SCOTCH HOUSE, HAWKINS STREET, DUBLIN 2. TELEPHONE: (01) 718211

NEW ADDRESS: MARINE HOUSE, CLANWILLIAM COURT, DUBLIN 2
TELEPHONE: (01) 760966

6 February 1989

Mr Ray Burke TD
Minister for Communications

Dear Minister

I enclose copies of documentation in connection with the charges
being sought by RTE for providing transmission services to Century
Communications for the independent national radio station.

The matter is now extremely urgent as contracts for the provision
of the new transmission equipment must be signed in the next few
days if the new station is to make the proposed start-up date of
May 1. In the circumstances I would appreciate your urgent
observations/decision on the charges being sought.

Yours sincerely

Sean Connolly
Secretary

IRTC.CENT 1.19 - 341

RTE TRANSMISSION CHARGES

Please see the attached copy of RTE 'quote' for transmission of the new independent national radio station and the copy of letter from Century Communications.

There is substance in the Century argument about double-payment for the transmitter network.

The network, which was developed over a long number of years is state property, the control of which is vested in RTE. It has already been paid for and continues to be paid for by licence fees of the citizens of the country. That RTE should have control of it seems an historical accident - it is likely that when RTE took it over the possibility of other users was not envisaged. For comparison see the situation of the airports which are managed by a separate company from the national airline because it was always evident that more than Aer Lingus would use the airports. To allow RTE to charge other users for the use of the transmitters in the way proposed provides them with an unfair commercial advantage.

In the interests of the Oireachtas decision regarding an independent station the transmission facilities should be made available at a rate which will enable Century to run the station.

The following points are also of note:

- Only 63% coverage is truly commercial; the remainder is akin to public service broadcasting although it requires the bulk of the transmitters to achieve.

- The RTE proposal is to charge £364,000.00 for full maintenance of 14 transmitters/transposers. Given that modern equipment requires very little maintenance, say two visits per year, this works out at £13,000 per visit or say an additional 12-14 heads of staff to carry out visits which RTE people would probably do in any event to service its own transmitters.

- Downtown Radio in Northern Ireland pays the BBC £100,000 for the use of 4 mountain-top transmitter sites. Pro rata this suggests a figure of about £350,000 for RTE. Century suggest £375,000.

- RTE is suggesting a capital investment of £747,000 (say £1m to include installation costs and project management) for hardware which has a lifespan of over 20 years. They wish to amortise this over 5 years. Over 20 years the cost is about £94,000 per annum if normal business criteria are used. (In this context it is worth noting that the contract between IRTC and Century must offer their studio/transmission equipment to an incoming broadcaster at commercial rates in the event of the collapse of the Century station, the withdrawal of the franchise or its non-renewal at the end of the franchise period. This should guarantee the RTE position.

In the circumstances fees of, say, £400,000 for transmission charges and £100,000 for hardware and installation/project management seems appropriate.

National FM Radio

Transmission Coverage.

Capital and Annual Charges for Inclusive Option

1. Once-off project/installation charges

The independent broadcaster will pay for all the new transmission equipment at cost within 20 days of receipt of invoices from Suppliers.

A once-off engineering design/project management fee of IR £250,000 for a four year project will be payable to RTE as follows:-

Year 1	50%	£125,000
Year 2	30%	£ 75,000
Year 3	15%	£ 37,500
Year 4	5%	£ 12,500

Installation charges of IR £125,000 will be invoiced as the work progresses as per Appendix 1.

2. Annual Charges:

	IR £000.
Access to and facilities at 14 sites:	185.
Full maintenance:	364.
Communications and Links:	80.
Overheads 10%:	63
	692

The charges at 1 and 2 above are at October 1988 prices and will be index linked. The independent broadcaster will be directly responsible for the cost of power and spares required for their transmission network.

IRTC.CENT 1.19 - 344

National AM Radio

Transmission Coverage

Capital and Annual Charges for Inclusive Option

1. **Once-off Project/Installation charges**

The independent broadcaster will pay for all the new transmission equipment at cost within 20 days of receipt of invoices from suppliers.

A once-off engineering design/project management fee of IR £70,000 will be payable for Dublin and Cork and IR £70,000 for Athlone.

Installation charges of IR £40,000 for Dublin and Cork and IR £50,000 for Athlone will be invoiced as the work progresses at each site.

2. **Annual Charge:**

	Dublin & Cork IR £000.	Athlone IR £000.
Access and facilities at sites	67.	80.
Full maintenance	35.	33.
Overheads 10%	10.	11.
	112	124

The charges at 1 and 2 above are at October 1988 prices and will be index linked. The independent broadcaster will be directly responsible for the cost of power and spares required for their transmitters.

Once-off Charges

	Total	Year 1	Year 2	Year 3	Year 4
Project management	250,000	125,000	75,000	37,500	12,500
Installation	125,000	50,000	50,000	21,000	4,000
	375,000	175,000	125,000	58,500	16,500

Phasing of Annual Charges

	Full Annual	Year 1	Year 2	Year 3	Year 4
Access to Facilities at 14 sites	185,000	73,260	73,260	31,265	7,215
Full maintenance	364,000	144,100	144,100	61,500	14,300
Communications & ...inks	80,000	31,700	31,700	13,500	3,100
Overheads (15%)	63,000	25,000	25,000	11,000	2,000
	692,000	274,060	274,060	117,265	26,615
Annual Charge (cumulative)	–	274,060	548,120	665,385	692,000
payments (off and annual)		449,060	673,120	723,885	708,500

Note 1: Hardware capital charges for transmitter etc. equipment will be borne by operator. The estimated cost is £747,000 which would be spre over four years as follows:

Year 1: £356,000
Year 2: £231,000
Year 3: £ 97,500
Year 4: £ 62,500

Note 2: Independent broadcaster will be directly responsible for the cost of power and spares required for network. This is estimated at approximately £140,000 a year when full network is in place.

IRTC.CENT 1.19 – 345

CENTURY COMMUNICATIONS LIMITED

15 KILDARE STREET, DUBLIN 2, IRELAND. TELEPHONE (353.1) 615900 FAX (353.1) 615149.

Mr. Sean Connolly,
The Secretary,
Independent Radio and Television Commission,
Scotch House,
Hawkins Street,
Dublin,2.

17th January, 1989.
JJS/ra.

Dear Mr. Connolly,

I enclose a copy of the IBA fax just received here this morning. In addition I would like to make the following observations.

1. The transmission system for public service broadcasting is an investment that has already been paid for by licence fees. It is maintained by the licence fees, it is not the property of RTE, they are merely the custodian of a national asset. The additional costs associated with public service broadcasting, as opposed to commercial broadcasting, the difference of delivering a signal to 63% of the country or 98.5% of the country is what licence fees have been traditionally about, and I feel that this argument is irrefutable.

2. In our discussions with RTE they told us that they could finance the capital investment in equipment at a cost of 7% per annum. However, they sought to amortise the equipment over the five year period whereas it has a life of twenty years. The cost of amortising £100 of investment at 7% over twenty years is £9.44 per annum.

3. I would also draw your attention to the Sunday Tribune press report that the "Downtown" transmission charges for the whole of Northern Ireland is £100,000. The IBA advise me that this involves four transmitters. Our proposal of £375,000 as a transmission charge is consistent with the "Downtown" transmission cost.

Yours faithfully,

James J. Stafford
Director

FROM IBA-U . 8 822378
Facsimile Number:- 0001 615149

(TUE)01. 7.'89 12:12   NO.9   ~PAGE 1/3

Received . 17-1-19
12:17p

FACSIMILE

IBACS

INDEPENDENT BROADCASTING AUTHORITY
CONSULTANCY SERVICES

Crawley Court, Winchester, Hampshire SO21 2QA U.K.

FAX : (U.K.) (0) 962 822378.
       (INTL.) + 44 962 822378

NEFAX 4500, CCITT GROUP 3
45 SECONDS — AUTOMATIC OPERATION

TO : .... CENTURY COMMUNICATIONS LTD. .... ATTN OF : MR. JAMES STAFFORD

NUMBER OF PAGES : ...... THREE ......   DATE : ..17/01/89..   TIME : ....1200.... GMT

ORIGINATOR'S NAME : .... MR. JOHN THOMAS ....   DIRECT LINE : (0) 962 822 374

~ NOT RECEIVED COMPLETE, PLEASE TELEPHONE :   (U.K.) (0) 962 822235   OR TELEX : 477211 IBAWIN G
                                              (INTL.) + 44 962 822235

Herewith our memorandum commenting on the costs of the transmitter service given in your Fax message of 13th. January.

Best Regards,

J.A. THOMAS,
IBA Consultancy Services.

+ Attachment

F629.JAT/smhb

MEMORANDUM ON THE COSTS OF THE TRANSMISSION SERVICE

1.   The proposition is that the whole of the transmission service should be equipped, supervised and maintained by RTE. The reasons for this are spelt out in Section 5.3.6 of the Application.

2.   These activities can be broken down under four headings:

i)   provision of the necessary transmission plant

ii)   supervision and maintenance of the service

iii)   consumption of electricity and spares

iv)   distribution of programme

Each is considered in turn.

3.   Provision of Plant

This can again be broken down under two headings. Firstly, there is a certain amount of new plant to be acquired and installed, mainly the transmitters themselves and the means of coupling them into the existing arrangements. RTE have already confirmed that they will be prepared to purchase this on behalf of the licensee and to pass on the suppliers' invoices at cost. There will be some work involved in installing the plant for which RTE should be re-imbursed their reasonable staff costs, on the basis that the staff involved are denied to RTE for that time.

Secondly, there is the matter of sharing the existing infrastructure of the site and its access, the buildings, the mast, the transmitting antenna etc. Section 5.3.6 of the Application sets out the arguments that these existing assets should be made available to be used without charge.

4.   Supervision and Maintenance

It will be necessary to integrate the supervision, control and maintenance of the service into the present RTE arrangements. There is an element of capital cost which we have taken under para.3. That apart, we have considered the additional costs which RTE will incur as a result of having these responsibilities, i.e. those costs which they will have to meet only as a consequence of their involvement with the new service and which would not otherwise arise. These would include any increase in site rentals, rates and insurance costs due to the presence of the new equipment. However, we would expect only marginal increases in costs under these headings.

= 2 =

Increased maintenance costs would arise due to additional visits to service the new equipment together with any extra payments for emergency call outs and any overtime incurred. We understand that RTE plan to carry out maintenance of the new equipment without increasing their staff resources and it has been assumed that any training costs and any new test equipment that may be required, have been included in the total capital costs for the new plant. It is also assumed that RTE will provide for the same level of transmission availability as the existing services. On this basis, the additional maintenance costs arising for the new equipment will be modest and should not exceed, say, IR £80,000.

5.   Spares and Power Consumption

RTE have previously estimated these from their own knowledge of the equipment to be used and have again said that these will be charged at cost. We have examined the RTE figures and we have concluded that the estimated costs are substantiated.

6.   Distribution of Programme

RTE have sensibly proposed to carry the programme to the transmitters on their existing network. This will involve some capital expenditure which we have again taken into account in para.3 above. That apart, there is a need to provide for the maintenance of that plant, a cost which would not otherwise have been incurred by RTE. They have proposed a fee of IR £55,000 p.a. for this aspect of the service which we believe to be justified.

F628.JAT/smhb
17th. January 1989

Appendix H

Dublin 4 Ireland
Telephone 01 693111
Telex 93700
Telefax 01 838140

Baile Átha Cliath, Éire
Telefón 01 693111
Teleics 93700
Telefax 01 838140

Radio Telefís Éireann

18th November 1988

Mr. Oliver Barry,
16 Parnell Square,
Dublin 1.

RE: NATIONAL RADIO TRANSMISSION COVERAGE

Dear Oliver,

With reference to our recent meetings regarding the above, we
wish to formally restate RTE's proposals as set out in our
letters of 1st November and 2nd November 1988 with final
amendments as discussed and understood between us.

FM RADIO

RTE's proposal for FM transmission coverage was on the basis of
an overall package involving:

- Design, acquisition and installation of a complete FM Radio
  transmission network.
- Population coverage of 98.5% of the Republic of Ireland plus
  coverage of Northern Ireland's population to the extent of
  1 million people.
- Major population centres covered in first year.
- All necessary equipment supplied/installed i.e.
  transmitters, masts, aerials, feeder systems etc.
- Signal to include RDS system for automatic tuning by RDS
  capable radio sets.
- Full annual running costs of system.
- Complete maintenance to the same standard of RTE's
  transmissions.
- Full standby cover as exists for RTE's systems.
- Emergency nationwide call-out service.
- Full system monitoring and signal quality control.
- National reception monitoring/assessment and interference
  investigation.
- Expert upkeep and optimum signal quality to full
  international broadcast standard. Coverage would reach
  98.5% of population over a three year period.
  Coverage in year 1   63% of population
  Coverage in year 2   95% of population
  Coverage in year 3   98.5% of population

The full cost of this service is an annual charge of £0.914
million, as follows:

	IR£000
Facilities and access to the common infrastructure at 14 sites	247
Full maintenance	364
Running Costs	220
Overheads (10%)	83

	0.914

If the foregoing comprehensive package offer is not acceptable to you, we can also offer a package which in RTE's view fully meets our obligations under the 1980 Broadcasting Act. This package leaves you to provide all your own transmission equipment (excluding Antennas and feeders) plus links, standby generators etc. You would also have to provide your own maintenance effort.

RTE's charges for sharing the common infrastructure and facilitating your design and installation of the necessary transmission equipment would be as follows:

IR£000

Access and facilities to RTE's common network infrastructure:	
Annual fee	247
Rigging and combiner maintenance (£94k plus £20K)	114
Overheads (10%)	36

Annual Charge	397

In addition, there would be a once-off capital charge of the order of £200,000 for building and ventilation modifications etc. at the 14 sites. Engineering design, joint planning/supervision of the combining of the services will cost £180,000 over a three year period. This makes a total once-off charge of £380,000 to facilitate you in establishing an additional independently operated FM service at existing sites.

AM RADIO

While we did not discuss the detailed schedules handed to you at our meeting for AM Radio transmission coverage, we wish to note there.

The capital cost is estimated at £1.3 million for Athlone (100Kw), Beaumont (10Kw) and Ballinure (10Kw) AM transmitters. Excluding Athlone, the capital cost comes to £430,000.

The annual operational and maintenance charge is £697,000 and excluding Athlone it is £291,000. We would be delighted to elaborate on these submissions is you so wish.

CONCLUSION

We regret that our meeting today ended without agreement being reached. It would be entirely unrealistic of you to expect to obtain access and facilities to a National Radio Network in which a total historical capital investment of some £12 million has been invested and which is currently being serviced at 12% p.a. in Exchequer Advances. The cost of this infrastructure is charged to our individual exising services and we cannot have a situation where an additional service would obtain access at a lower charge. The same is true of maintenance costs. We would remind you that the basis of our apportionment is after allowing for the new service. RTE would also have to give if possible, access and facilities to other radio services, county and community and they will have to bear and share of the infrastructure/maintenance costs which might benefit all the services in due course.

Kind regards.

Yours sincerely,

GERRY O'BRIEN
DIRECTOR OF FINANCE

Appendix I

As agreed with RTE
and utinuition

National FM Radio

Transmission Coverage.

Capital and Annual Charges for Inclusive Option

1. ### Once-off project/installation charges

The independent broadcaster will pay for all the new transmission equipment at cost within 20 days of receipt of invoices from Suppliers.

A once-off engineering design/project management fee of IR £250,000 for a four year project will be payable to RTE as follows:-

Year 1	50%	£125,000
Year 2	30%	£ 75,000
Year 3	15%	£ 37,500
Year 4	5%	£ 12,500

Installation charges of IR £125,000 will be invoiced as the work progresses as per Appendix 1.

2. ### Annual Charges:

	IR £000.
Access to and facilities at 14 sites:	185.
Full maintenance:	364.
Communications and Links:	80.
Overheads 10%:	63
	692

The charges at 1 and 2 above are at October 1988 prices and will be index linked. The independent broadcaster will be directly responsible for the cost of power and spares required for their transmission network.

National AM Radio

Transmission Coverage

Capital and Annual Charges for Inclusive Option

1. Once-off Project/Installation charges

The independent broadcaster will pay for all the new transmission equipment at cost within 20 days of receipt of invoices from suppliers.

A once-off engineering design/project management fee of IR £70,000 will be payable for Dublin and Cork and IR £70,000 for Athlone.

Installation charges of IR £40,000 for Dublin and Cork and IR £50,000 for Athlone will be invoiced as the work progresses at each site.

2. Annual Charge:

	Dublin & Cork IR £000.	Athlone IR £000.
Access and facilities at sites	67.	80.
Full maintenance	35.	33.
Overheads 10%	10.	11.
	112	124

The charges at 1 and 2 above are at October 1988 prices and will be index linked. The independent broadcaster will be directly responsible for the cost of power and spares required for their transmitters.

Once-off Charges

	Total	Year 1	Year 2	Year 3	Year 4
t management	250,000	125,000	75,000	37,500	12,500
ation	125,000	50,000	50,000	21,000	4,000
	375,000	175,000	125,000	58,500	16,500

Phasing of Annual Charges

	Full Annual	Year 1	Year 2	Year 3	Year 4
s to Facilities 4 sites	185,000	73,260	73,260	31,265	7,215
aintenance	364,000	144,100	144,100	61,500	14,300
unications & Links	80,000	31,700	31,700	13,500	3,100
eads (15%)	63,000	25,000	25,000	11,000	2,000
	692,000	274,060	274,060	117,265	26,615
Charge ative)	–	274,060	548,120	665,385	692,000
payments off and annual)		449,060	673,120	723,885	708,500

1: Hardware capital charges for transmitter etc. equipment will be borne by operator. The estimated cost is £747,000 which would be spread over four years as follows:

Year 1:   £356,000
Year 2:   £231,000
Year 3:   £ 97,500
Year 4:   £ 62,500

2: Independent broadcaster will be directly responsible for the cost of power and spares required for network. This is estimated at approximately £140,000 a year when full network is in place.

Appendix J

Dublin 4 Ireland Baile Átha Cliath, Éire
Telephone 01 693111 Telefón 01 693111
Telex 90656 Teleics 90656
Fax (01) 838140 Fax (01) 838140

from the Director-General ón bPríomh-Stiúrthóir

15 February 1989

Mr. Ray Burke, T.D.
Minister for Communications
Department of Industry & Commerce
Kildare Street
Dublin 2

BY FAX. to 760431

Dear Minister

I refer to our discussions on 14 February 1989 in connection
with points put to you by the IRTC in relation to charges
proposed by us for the provision of various transmission
services for Century Communications Ltd.

The Commission referred to various levels of charge by the
IBA in the UK. It is our strongly held view that
comparison between such charges and our proposals are invalid
for a number of reasons e.g. area covered, accessibility of
sites, costs of equipment (lower VAT rates in UK), Irish
Pound/Sterling exchange differentials etc.

We have, however, as requested, reviewed very fully again
our charges. In relation to the final annual charge of
£692,000 quoted, there are two areas we have specially
examined. A full maintenance service is included in this
figure for £364,000. We expect to achieve worthwhile
reductions in labour costs in this area over the next two
years and are prepared now to anticipate this and pass the
benefit on immediately in our proposed charges. This will
give a reduction of £44,000 in the £364,000 figure.

We have also considered the overheads allocation previously
shown at 10%. Because of the specialist nature of the
services to be provided, we can accept that it would be
more appropriate to charge only a proportion of that figure
viz. 5%.

Taking these two revisions into account will reduce our
earlier figure of £692,000 down to £614,000 per annum.
Depending on actual physical implementation of the project,
we would expect a build up to this final figure in the
following approximate manner (all at October 1988 prices):

1989	£200,000
1990	£430,000
1991	£530,000
1992	£614,000

/...

2

On a final point of detail, I can confirm that in all our
figures there are no accelerated rates of depreciation
used.   Our computations provide for rates used in our
audited accounts - accepted industry norms.

I trust the foregoing additional information will enable us
very quickly now to conclude all outstanding matters with
the Commission or Century Communications, as appropriate.
We are very conscious that it is now just ten weeks to
1st May next - a date which RTE would be just as concerned
to achieve as all the other interested parties.

Yours sincerely

Vincent Finn

Appendix K

OIFIG AN AIRE TIONSCAIL AGUS TRÁCHTÁLA AGUS CUMARSÁIDE

(Office of the Minister for Industry and Commerce and for Communications)

BAILE ÁTHA CLIATH 2.

(Dublin 2.)

16 February, 1989.

Rt. Hon. Mr. Justice Seamus Henchy,
Chairman,
The Independent Radio and Television Commission,
Marine House,
Clanwilliam Court,
Dublin 2.

Dear Chairman,

I refer to our meeting and the documentation sent to me by the Secretary of the Commission regarding some aspects of the quote by RTE for the supply of transmission services to Century Communications.

I have had the matter examined by my Department and discussed the issues again with RTE. At my strong urging they have now agreed to reduce their annual charge from £692,000 to £614,000. Depending on actual physical implementation of the project they would expect a build up to this final figure in the following approximate manner (all at October 1988 prices):

1989   £200,000
1990   £430,000
1991   £530,000
1992   £614,000

I am satisfied that, in Irish conditions, the foregoing charges are not unreasonable.

The hardware capital charges for transmitter equipment etc. will of course depend on the type and nature of the equipment selected by Century. These charges and the associated project management and installation fees will fall to be met as they occur but it will be a matter for Century to make its own arrangements as to financing and depreciation charges. It seems possible that if Century can arrange financing over 15 to 20 years, an annual charge of some £100,000 a year could result.

I confidently expect that the foregoing will clear the way for Century and RTE to speed ahead to ensure that the opening day of 1 May is met.

Yours sincerely,

Ray Burke, T.D.,
Minister for Industry and Commerce and for Communications.

Appendix L

CENTURY COMMUNICATIONS LIMITED

15 KILDARE STREET, DUBLIN 2, IRELAND. TELEPHONE (353.1) 615900 FAX (353.1) 615149.

Rt. Hon. Mr. Justice Seamus Henchy,
Chairman,
The Independent Radio and Television Commission,
Marine House,
Clanwilliam Court,   17th February, 1989.
Dublin,2.   OB/JS/ra.

Dear Chairman,

We wish to advise you that at a Board Meeting of Century Communications Limited held on Tuesday 14th February, Laurence Crowley was co-opted to the Board of Directors and elected Chairman, Terry Wogan and Chris de Burgh were also co-opted to the Board of Directors. In due course the new directors will be participating in up to 12½% of the company's equity. This information remains confidential until 17.00 hrs Monday 20 February when it will be released to the Press.

The Board Meeting reviewed the question of transmission charges. They were of the unanimous opinion that the £375,000 offered to RTE for a full transmission service was, given the advice that they had from the IBA, fair and reasonable. Furthermore, they were of the unanimous view that they were not prepared to negotiate or increase that offer as it would effect the viability of the service. They expressed their concern that RTE, as custodian of the National transmission network, had an obvious conflict of interest with their role as providers of transmission services to the independent broadcasters and that in the circumstances they could not understand why, given that the Minister has power under the Act, a directive has not been given to RTE.

At the public hearing on 12th January 1989, we stated that we could provide the service within 90 days of the signing of contracts. At that time there was 108 days to the 1st May. When the award was made on 18th January, there were 102 days left. We received the Broadcast Contract on 9th February and would hope to be able to agree the terms of that contract by the end of next week. As of today, there are 72 days left to the 1st May and we are particularly concerned that the issue of the transmission charges has not been resolved and that there appears to be no way in which it is going to be resolved to meet that date. We are prepared to meet all the extra studio installation costs associated with a shorter deadline and be on air 1st May but we are particularly concerned that there appears to be no urgency to resolve the issue on transmission.

At this stage we must advise you that unless the matter is resolved within the next seven days there is no way in which we can be expected to meet the original date envisaged and furthermore we will have to reconsider our entire position.

Such is the urgency of this matter that we remain available to meet with you at any time to suit your convenience.

Yours sincerely,

Oliver Barry   James Stafford

DIRECTORS: OLIVER BARRY, JAMES JOSEPH STAFFORD.

REGISTERED IN IRELAND No. 137780. REGISTERED OFFICE: 15, KILDARE STREET, DUBLIN 2.

Century Communications Limited

17 February 1989

1. The Agreement should commence on 1 May 1989. As the equipment has a life of 20 years, the Agreement should be for 20 years with rights of renewal on the same terms. The right of renewal deals with the system being phased over the next four years. Avoid bank or personal guarantee and bonds in any form.

2. The phase-in of the eight transmitters and six boosters, being fourteen units, may take up to four years. It would be extremely beneficial if the cost of each unit, being a transmitter or a booster, were taken as one fourteenth of £375,000 but only for the initial phase-in period to full national 98.5% coverage. The rate of commissioning must at all times be determined by Century subject only to Century's obligations to the IRTC.

3. It is important to deal separately and in detail with each of the constituent parts. This will become relevant after phase-in to full national 98.5% coverage.

    (a) <u>Rent of transmitters and combiners</u>.

    Actual cost spread over 20 years with no indexation.

    (b) <u>Maintenance</u>.

    Phase-in during the initial four year period the fourteen units as equal cost units to become the agreed £30,000 per annum.

    (c) <u>Power and Spares</u>.

    Actual costs only.

    (d) <u>Linkage</u>.

    Given the deregulation of Telecommunications and the possibility that we may wish to use satellite distribution, it is essential that we maintain flexibility in any obligations to use RTE's system.

    Phase-in during the initial four year period the fourteen units as equal cost units to become £80,000 per annum.

    (e) <u>Fee for RTE</u>.

    Will be not less than £75,000 per annum phased during the initial four year period pro rata to the fourteen units or alternatively you may have to concede a minimum of £75,000 per annum with an indexation formula from 1993 onwards.

    (a) <u>Rent of Transmitters and Combiners</u>.

    Actual cost plus 25% until 1993 reducing to actual cost plus 10% thereafter.

    (b) <u>Maintenance</u>.

    Agreed cost plus 25% until 1993 and thereafter indexation of agreed cost of £30,000 per annum base 1989 plus 10%.

    (c) <u>Power and Spares</u>.

    Actual cost plus 25% until 1993 and actual cost plus 10% thereafter.

    (d) <u>Linkage</u>.

    Actual cost plus 25% until 1993 and thereafter, provided we use the RTE system, indexation of agreed cost of £80,000 per annum base 1989 plus 10%.

Century Communications Limited

17 February 1989
(72 days to 1 May)

Eight transmitters and six boosters to be phased in over four years to provide national 98.5% coverage for a total cost at full coverage made up as follows:-

		IR£ per annum
(a)	Rent of Transmitter, Combiners etc. Capital Investment £747,000 20 years life at 7% per annum (RTE quote 7%)	70,218
(b)	Maintenance (IBA assessment)	30,000
(c)	Power & Spares (RTE quote)	115.000
(d)	Linkage (RTE quote)	80,000
	Total	295,218
	SAY	300,000
(e)	Fee for RTE to include Project Management	75,000
	Total Transmission Cost per annum	375,000

Notes

1. Access to, use and maintenance of tranmitter masts/antennae and sites at no cost as these have been since 1926, and still are, paid for by licence payments.

2. Maintenance. The RTE quote £26,000 per annum for each of 14 transmitters/boosters is equal to the average salary of each RTE employee. IBA assessment is two visits per annum, which related to RTE proposed charge is £13,000 per visit. The IBA assessment of the marginal increase in costs to RTE is £30,000 per annum.

Appendix M

CENTURY COMMUNICATIONS LIMITED

15 KILDARE STREET, DUBLIN 2, IRELAND. TELEPHONE (353.1) 615900 FAX (353.1) 615149.

The Honourable Mr. Justice Seamus Henchy,
Chairman,
Independent Radio and Television Commission,
Marine House,
Clanwilliam Court,
Dublin 2.

20th February, 1989.
LC/uh.

Dear Chairman,

Thank you for seeing us at such short notice to-day when you were kind enough to give us a copy of the Minister's letter dated the 16th of February. As stated in our letter of the 17th of February, we are convinced that £375,000 for a full transmission service is fair and reasonable and the suggested charge by RTE would render the entire project economically unviable.

The original quotation from RTE dated the 1st of November, 1988 provided for a full FM transmission service providing the same level of coverage as RTE 1 and 2. The transmission requirements for the National Independent Commercial Radio are the same as for RTE and we are convinced for the reasons set out in our submission that the only way to provide the service is through the use of the National Transmission Network managed by RTE. The quotation given to us by RTE on the 1st November, 1988 was £1,140,000 for FM service only.

We have considerable difficulty in reconciling the different RTE quotes and can only conclude that the Minister's letter of the 16th of February, 1989 constitutes as it states in paragraph two no more than a reduction of £78,000. Furthermore we believe those figures quoted for 1989-1992 are misleading in that they do not include rent of equipment, project management fees, installation costs, power and spares.

Before we made our submission to you on 15th December, 1988 we held several meetings with RTE as managers of the National transmission system. We told them the view of our advisers the IBA, that the cost of providing us with this facility in accordance with the criteria set out in the letter 1st November, 1988 was less than £300,000 per annum. As you know, we stated in our submission a figure of £375,000 in order to avoid any possibility of it being suggested that we were seeking the service at cost.

continued/

DIRECTORS OLIVER BARRY, JAMES JOSEPH STAFFORD. T. Wogan C. de Burgh
REGISTERED IN IRE. REGISTERED OFFICE 15, KILDARE STREET, DUBLIN 2.

DEPTARTS 1.01 - 47

64 WED 11:06 Tourism & Trans.   P.03

- 2 -

The Honourable Mr. Justice Seamus Henchy, Chairman,
Independent Radio and Television Commission,
Marine House, Clanwilliam Court, Dublin 2.
20th February, 1989. LC/uh.

/continued......

        Having had the IBA assess our transmission requirements, we
calculated on the advice of IBA, the cost of providing the same national
FM coverage and including AM transmission in Dublin and Cork, to be as
follows:

		IR£ per annum
(a)	Rent of Transmitter, Combiners etc.	70,218
(b)	Maintenance	30,000
(c)	Power & Spares	115,000
(d)	Linkage	80,000
	Total	295,218
	SAY	300,000
(e)	Fee to RTE for provision of service	75,000
	Total Transmision Cost per annum	375,000

        We comment here on the key areas of cost:

1.   RTE quoted on the 2nd of November, 1988 a cost of financing the
capital investment at 7% per annum. There is no dispute that the life
of the equipment is 20 years and we have calculated the annual rental
to be £9.40 per annum for 20 years for each £100 of capital required.
RTE advised us on 11th January, 1989 that the cost of transmitters,
combiners and the other equipment necessary to provide the
transmission service would be £747,000. Advised by the IBA, we
accept that these costs are of the right order. This would amount to
an annual rental charge of £70,218 and the integration of our
transmission requirements into the National network in this manner is
both logical and sensible.

continued/

DEPTARTS 1.01 - 48

64 WED 11:07 Tourism & Trans.   P.04

- 3 -

The Honourable Mr. Justice Seamus Henchy, Chairman,
Independent Radio and Television Commission,
Marine House, Clanwilliam Court, Dublin 2.
20th February, 1989. LC/uh.

/continued.......

2. RTE's quote on 11th January, 1989 for access to the National
    Transmission Network was £185,000 per annum. We are unable to
    determine what, if any, reduction in this is reflected in the figures
    contained in the Minister's letter of the 16th inst. The principle of
    public service broadcasting is the provision of a service to each
    citizen irrespective of the economics of doing so. Century as a
    National Franchise holder is bound to this concept. The citizens of
    Ireland, in paying licence fees, funds inter alia the gross cost of the
    National Transmission Network. Public service broadcasting
    commenced in Ireland in 1926 and the existing National Transmission
    system has evolved over the last 63 years.

    The cost by whatever accounting criteria one chooses must at this
    stage be written off as "sunk costs". That RTE as the National
    Broadcasters should seek to recover as custodian of the transmission
    system a fee from Century for their benefit as broadcasters is in
    effect seeking a subsidy from Century. Accordingly it is
    inappropriate that any cost should be levied on us for this access.

3. RTE quoted on 11th January, 1989 £364,000 per annum for the
    maintenance of the additional equipment required to provide Century
    with National Coverage. We are unable to determine what if any
    reduction in this has been made in the Minister's figures in his letter
    of the 16th inst. The IBA have assessed the additional cost involved
    for maintaining the Century equipment and concluded that it should
    not be more that £30,000 per annum.

4. The cost of providing the first leg of the programme distribution
    circuit from our Dublin studios to the transmitters at Three Rock and
    Kippure lies outside the present discussions with RTE. An Bord
    Telecom costs have not yet been resolved but we consider that any
    charge beyond that equivalent to the one-off capital cost of provision
    of those circuits by radio link, estimated to be around £40,000, would
    be unsustainable and would further jeopardise the viability of the
    project. Further the economic provision of land links for the
    distribution of a news service to other stations will be critically
    dependent on An Bord Telecom tariffs.

continued/

DEPTARTS 1.01 - 49

.64 WED 11:07 Tourism & Trans.   P.05

- 4 -

The Honourable Mr. Justice Seamus Henchy, Chairman,
Independent Radio and Television Commission,
Marine House, Clanwilliam Court, Dublin 2,
20th February, 1989. LC/uh.

/continued........

The concept of RTE as custodians of the National Transmission
Network acquiring the transmitters and renting them to us at 7% per
annum over their economic life of 20 years as set out in their letter of the
1st of November, 1988 is acceptable, as indeed is the figure quoted in
their letter of 11th January 1989 for the use of their linkage at £80,000
per annum for the period that we continue to use it. Equally acceptable is
actual cost recovery of power and spare parts used, originally estimated
by RTE at £115,000 per annum and subsequently revised on the 11th
January 1989 to £140,000 per annum. The main issues in dispute remain
the access to the National Transmission facilities and the cost of
maintenance of the system.

It is difficult to understand how anybody can dispute our offer of
£375,000 for national coverage when the transmission cost for a Dublin
Local station covering a third of the population is quoted by RTE at
£40,000 per annum and even that figure is currently being challenged by
the applicants as excessive. Furthermore, rental levied by the IBA for
coverage of the whole of the North of Ireland, at Stg. £100,000 per
annum, shows that our own figures are of the right magnitude.

It appears therefore that we are unable further to progress the
negotiations with RTE and accordingly we respectfully request the
Commission to seek a Ministerial directive in accordance with the
Commissions powers under Section 16 of the Radio and Television Act
1988.

We are pleased to note that you share our view that the suggested
transmission charges are excessive and until the problems above set out
can be dealt with, we will not be in a position to conclude the
negotiations on the Broadcast contract or meet our target date of the 1st
May.

Yours sincerely,

Laurence Crowley
Chairman

274

Appendix N

Charges by RTE and BTE for services to commercial broadcasters

overheads 5%

Minister,

1.   The I.R.T.C. has again written to you

    (i)   enclosing a copy of a letter from Century Communications seeking a Ministerial Directive under Section 16 of the Radio and Television Act;

    (ii)   complaining about delays in the provision of links for local radio stations and the high cost of those links.

2.   RTE provide a National FM network. Their main transmitters operate at the following powers - Mount Leinster 400Kw, Mullaghanish and Maghera 320Kw, Truskmore 250Kw, Kippure 100Kw, Clermont Carn 80Kw, Three Rock and Holywell Hill 12Kw. These high powered transmitters are considered necessary to provide a comprehensive National Radio Service.

3.   The I.B.A. in the U.K. does not provide a comprehensive national service. It provides facilities to cover the main centres of population but it is not concerned about ensuring universal coverage. In 1986 the latest date for which we have information - none of its transmitters operated at more than 10Kw, the vast majority operated at lower powers.

4.   Century's main arguments and RTE's position on the main items for the FM service are as follows:-

Access to facilities

Century   Century offer - nil. Current/quote £185,000. all of the existing facilities at RTE's sites have been developed with licence fee monies and as national facilities they should be provided free to Century.

RTE did not propose any reduction in those charges. They argue that these facilities have been developed with borrowed money. These facilities have to be replaced in due course. The appropriate depreciation charge for each type of facility is made in RTE's Accounts and that these charges are met year by year from licence fee and other income in that year. RTE argue that to exempt Century from paying its appropriate share of these charges would amount to a direct subsidy by RTE to Century which you have already ruled out.

30,000 min
+ £1000 per visit after the
30 visits

5.   Maintenance

RTE originally quoted £344,000 p.a. subsequently reduced to current quote £320,000 for a full maintenance service.

Century offer £30,000 p.a.

Departmental research (copies of memos attached) indicates that the figures quoted by RTE are not unreasonable. The transmitters being used by RTE are very high powered by comparison with those being used by Downtown and are sited in more difficult locations. Downtown pay IR £117,000 for a maintenance contract for 5 transmitters, the largest of which operates at 10Kw. Indeed, Mr. Tinman of Downtown, without any prompting, offered an opinion that a charge of £800,000 stg. would not be unreasonable for a national 14 station FM network covering 26 counties.

6.   Links power spares

	RTE proposal	Century offer
Links	80,000	80,000
Power + Spares	115,000	115,000

7.   Capital Equipment (transmitters combiners project, project management and installation costs)

Century and RTE agree that the cost of the capital equipment would be of the order of £747,000. Century appear to ignore the project management and installation costs, totalling £375,000.

Century allege that RTE quoted, on 2 November, a cost of financing capital investment at 7% per annum. Century want that interest rate to be applied and the cost written off over a 20 year rental period.

RTE when approached initially indicated that over a 4-5 year leasing period it might be possible to get a bank to do a deal with a 7% interest coupon, depending on the capital allowances involved. RTE are adamant that there is no possibility of borrowing at 7% over 20 years. RTE's Exchequer borrowings are costing an average of 12%. They hope that it will be possible to re-finance these borrowings at somewhat less than that figure but they see no possibilities of getting 20 year money at 7%.

RTE say that while they will actively co-operate with Century in bringing the project to completion, it is primarily a matter for Century to select its own equipment and to finance the purchasing and installation costs of that equipment.

8.   Overheads

RTE had sought a contribution of 10% to its overheads. It has agreed to reduce that figure to 5% - £34,000.

Century have offered a total fee of £78,000 for "provision of service".

9.   AM Service

RTE indicated that its costs for AM service for Dublin and Cork were as follows:-

engineering design/project management fee	£70,000
installation charges	£40,000

Transmitters and equipment to be purchased by Century.

Annual charges:

Access and facilities	£67,000
Full maintenance	£35,000
Overheads 10%(presumably this would now be reduced to 5%)	£10,000
	£112,000

Century appear to have ignored these costs and assumed that they were included in the FM charges.

10.   Telecom Links

Telecom say that, until Tuesday last when they had their first real discussion with Century, they were quoting blind and gave figures at outer end of scale, a lot will depend on where the studios area, where the nearest telecom facilities are and whether new links have to be provided to transmitter sites. They say that the charges will reflect the costs to them of providing the service.

As for possible delays of 3-6 months in providing service, these may arise if new or specialist equipment has to be ordered. If equipment is available a service can be provided in days or weeks depending on the locations.

11. Departmental conclusion

Century have seriously underestimated the costs involved in matching RTE's FM service. The I.B.A.'s service in the U.K. and North is not comparable with RTE's service. The U.K. charges quoted by Century ~and used as a basis~ for provision of service in Ireland are not supported by an examination.

Brud 23/2

Memo.

I spoke to Mr. I. Tinman, Managing Director, Downtown Radio, Northern Ireland about I.B.A. charges for radio transmission facilities.

He explained that the I.B.A. arrangements are complex and in course of change but that the following position obtains:-

(i)   Downtown Radio had 1 MF transmitter and 1x1Kw FM radio transmitter for coverage of their original franchise area. The primary rental charged by the I.B.A. for those facilities was £113,000 Stg. (£135,000 approx. Irish Punts).

(ii)   When Downtown's franchise was extended to cover all of Northern Ireland three additional FM transmitters (1x2Kw and 2x10Kw) were provided by the I.B.A. Downtown gave the I.B.A. a loan of £250,000 to fund construction. The I.B.A. was to repay the loan over 8 years in six monthly instalments. The primary rental was increased to £120,000 sterling approx (£144,000 Irish Punts).

(iii) For the future Downtown Radio is buying back the five transmitters from the I.B.A. The station has negotiated a maintenance contract with the I.B.A. for three years at £98,000 sterling p.a. (£117,000 p.a. Irish Punts). Under the contract the I.B.A. will provide 24 hour cover. However, if replacement of any of the transmitters arises the cost will be carried by Downtown.

Without prompting from me Mr. Tinman expressed the view that a charge of £800,000 stg. p.a. would not be unreasonable for a 14 station national FM network covering the 26 counties He drew attention specifically to the fact that Downtown's main transmitter operates at only 1 Kw because the Black Mountain site is an excellent site and 1Kw gives 30 miles radius coverage.

15   February, 1989.

Transmitter Powers for 3rd National Network (VHF)

	Kw
Kippure	100
Mount Leinster	400
Mullaghanish	320
Maghera	320
Truskmore	250
Three Rock	12
Holywell Hill	12
Clermont Carn	80
Achill	6
Spur Hill	1
Caherciveen	6
Limerick (Woodcock Hill)	1
Fanad	8
Castletownbere	6

IBA has no station with a transmitter above 10 KW.
IBA does not provide a national network.

*Mr. Ó Móráin
For info.*

Memo.

I spoke to Mr. Butcher, Independent Broadcasting Authority recently regarding their method of apportioning I.B.A. costs to independent radio.

Mr. Butcher began by explaining that the I.B.A. is statutorily obliged to keep the finances of independent radio separate from independent television. That said, however, he stated that in practice the I.B.A. operated a system of apportionment of costs which is not scientific by any means and that deliberately subsidises radio at the expense of television. He felt that anything the I.B.A. does would be of little help in trying to determine, for example, an appropriate ratio for the apportionment of common facilities between radio and television. He gave the following example:-

(a) **Engineering staff costs**

The I.B.A. annually conducts a crude survey in which staff common to radio and TV are asked to apportion their time as between the two services. Anybody who says he spends 75% or more of his time on radio has his time apportioned as between the two services. Anybody spending less than 75% of his time on radio is charged in total to television. Out of an engineering work-force of around 1,400, significantly less than 100 would be charged to radio.

(b) **Emergency cover in the event of transmitter failure**

The I.B.A. will go to extraordinary lengths at any time to restore service to transmitters in the television network. In contrast if a radio transmitter were to fail, say at 6 p.m. it would probably not be attended to until the following day.

(c) **Equipment/Spares**

Equipment/spares that can only be associated with radio are charged to radio. Equipment/spares that have a common usage are charged to television.

Secretary,

The foregoing may be of interest.

February, 1989.

Appendix O

OIFIG AN AIRE TIONSCAIL AGUS TRÁCHTÁLA AGUS CUMARSÁIDE
(Office of the Minister for Industry and Commerce and for Communications)
BAILE ÁTHA CLIATH 2.
(Dublin 2.)

14 March 1989

By Hand 2.20pm

Mr T V Finn
Director General
RTE
Donnybrook
DUBLIN 4

copies: RTE Authority
          Board of Management
          Director of Finance

Dear Director General

I refer to my discussions with RTE regarding the provision of facilities by RTE to the new National Radio Service.

Following those consultations and similar consultations I had with the Independent Radio and Television Commission, I have now decided to direct, under Section 16 of the Radio and Television Act, 1988, that the following payments be made to RTE by the sound broadcasting contractor for the National independent radio service, Century Communications.

1. For access to RTE facilities at 14 FM sites and 2 AM sites, (Dublin and Cork) - £35,000 per annum to increase yearly in line with the consumer price index.

2. Maintenance charges in relation to Century equipment at RTE sites. (a) £30,000 per annum to cover the first 30 visits, (b) for each of the next 40 visits £1,000 per visit, (c) any additional visits to be charged at actual cost plus 25% (the £30,000 and £1,000 to increase yearly in line with CPI).

3. Linkage to Dublin and Cork AM and 14 FM transmission sites to be charged to the contractor on the basis of the actual expenditure incurred. (RTE estimate that the cost will be approximately £80,000 per annum).

4. Power and spares to be charged to the contractor on an actual cost basis. (RTE estimate that the cost will be approximately £115,000 per annum).

/...

- 2 -

5. An overhead charge of 5% payable to RTE will be levied on the charges at 1,2,3, & 4 above.

6. RTE will acquire the transmitting and associated equipment for 14 FM transmission sites (estimated cost £747,000) and Dublin and Cork AM sites (estimated cost £260,000). The actual cost of the equipment will be financed on the best available terms over a 14 year period and the capital cost and interest charges will be levied on the contractor over that period. The project management and installation charge for the National FM coverage and the AM coverage (Dublin and Cork) will be £250,000 plus 5% for overheads. The residual value of equipment at the end of the 14 year period will acrue to Century Communications

These charges have been fixed on the basis that (1) RTE, if required, will ensure that the new service will be broadcast in the Dublin and Cork areas on and from 1 May, 1989 and (2) that there will be no undue delay in agreeing the schedule of transmitting and associated broadcasting equipment to be acquired and its installation within the time-frame set by the I.R.T.C.

Yours sincerely

RAY BURKE TD
Minister for Industry and Commerce
 and for Communications

Appendix P

8

(2) The amount to be paid to the Independent Radio and Television Commission in any financial year shall not exceed 25% of the total receipts as provided for in subsection (1), and the balance remaining shall be paid to the Authority.

(3) In respect of the part of the year 1990 from the commencement of this Act until the 31st day of December, 1990, the Minister , with the approval of the Minister for Finance, may pay to the Commission out of moneys provided by the Oireachtas an amount not exceeding 25% of the balance of the amount of £46.815 million remaining after deducting the amount paid to the Authority under section 8 of the Act of 1976 in the part of that year preceding such commencement and the balance remaining shall be paid to the Authority.

Disbursement
of payments
by
Independent
Radio and
Television
Commission.

3. (1) It shall be the function of the Independent Radio and Television Commission to disburse the amounts received under section 2 solely for the purpose of supporting the establishment and operation of sound broadcasting services and the television programme service established or to be established under the Radio and Television Act, 1988.

9

(2) It shall be the duty of the Independent Radio and Television Commission to prepare and publish criteria to be used in determining the disbursements to be made to the services in question under subsection (1). In determining its criteria the Commission shall have regard to the following:

(a) the quality , range and type of programmes (including programmes in the Irish language and relating to Irish culture) to be provided in a service;

(b) the requirements of section 9 of the Radio and Television Act, 1988, relating to the provision of news and current affairs programmes, having regard to the desirability of creating plurality in the sources of news and information in the media;

(c) the demographic features of any particular service area;

(d) the extent of the infrastructural and operating costs involved in establishing and operating a service, and in particular the national sound broadcasting service and the television programme service;
(e) the amount of employment provided by a service, and

(f) any other matters which the Commission considers necessary to take into account to secure the orderly and effective development of services provided for under section 4 of the Radio and Television Act, 1988.

292

Appendix Q

"The Murphy companies" means, as the context admits, all or one or more of the following:-

1. Joseph Murphy Structural Engineers Limited ("*JMSE*")

2. The Grafton Construction Company Limited ("*Grafton*")

3. Reliable Construction (Dublin) Limited ("*Reliable*")

4. Lajos Holdings Limited ("*Lajos*")

5. Barrett Developments Limited (in liquidation)

6. Finglas Industrial Developments Limited (in liquidation)

7. Turvey Estates Limited (in liquidation)

8. Helmdale Limited (in liquidation)

9. Gaiety Stage Productions Limited

10. Gaiety Theatre (Dublin) Limited

11. Finglas Industrial Estates Limited

12. Wexburn Limited

Appendix R

"The Murphy interests" means, as the context admits, all or one or more of the following:-

1. The late Mr. Joseph Murphy Snr.

2. Mr. Joseph Murphy Jnr.

3. Mr. Frank Reynolds

4. Mr. John Maher

5. Mr. Roger Copsey

6. Mr. Timothy O'Keeffe

7. Joseph Murphy Structural Engineers Limited ("*JMSE*")

8. The Grafton Construction Company Limited ("*Grafton*")

9. Reliable Construction (Dublin) Limited ("*Reliable*")

10. Lajos Holdings Limited ("*Lajos*")

11. Barrett Developments Limited (in liquidation)

12. Finglas Industrial Developments Limited (in liquidation)

13. Turvey Estates Limited (in liquidation)

14. Helmdale Limited (in liquidation)

15. Gaiety Stage Productions Limited

16. Gaiety Theatre (Dublin) Limited

17. Finglas Industrial Estates Limited

12. Wexburn Limited

All of the foregoing were represented jointly at the public hearings of the Tribunal.

Appendix S

NOMINAL

DESCRIPTION

GRAFTON CONSTRUCTION LTD.

NOMINAL CODE
1210005

DATE	T/C	REF.	DEBIT	CREDIT		BALANCE TO DATE	PERIOD BALANCE
01.06.89		BFWD				.00	.00
30.06.89	CHQ	11546	20000.00			20000.00	20000.00
30.06.89	CHQ	11547	10000.00			30000.00	30000.00
30.06.89	CB	55		30000.00		.00	.00
31.08.89	CB	57		60000.00		60000.00-	60000.00-
31.08.89	CHQ	500152	312.50			59687.50-	59687.50-
30.06.89	PC	25	160.00			59527.50-	59527.50-
31.07.89	PC	27	160.00			59367.50-	59367.50-
31.08.89		P/E				59367.50-	.00
30.09.89	INV	1229	64.00			59303.50-	64.00
31.10.89	INV	1592	292.00			59011.50-	356.00
31.10.89	INV	1593	128.00			58883.50-	484.00
31.10.89	INV	1594	128.00			58755.50-	612.00
31.10.89	INV	1595	128.00			58627.50-	740.00

Data Systems

Ref.21

Appendix T

THE GRAFTON CONSTRUCTION COMPANY LIMITED

Re:　　　　Land at Forest Road, Swords, Co. Dublin

CASH　ACCOUNT

				1988			
3	To	Allied Irish Banks plc	400,000.00	Aug.	30	By Michael Bailey - deposit	125.000.00
		Paid selves Costs of Sale as per Bills of Costs annexed	20,640.12	1989			
28	"	J M S E	80,258.00	Feb.	24	By Michael Bailey - balance purchase monies	1,202,540.00
24	"	O'Shea & Shanahan - deposit on Poppintree	6,500.00			" Michael Bailey - refund of financial contribution	122,460.00
13	"	J M S E	30,000.00				
16	"	Copsey Murray & Co.	16,500.00	1990			
3	"	J M S E	60,000.00	Feb.	1	By Ballymore Homes Ltd. - purchase price of amenity land	500.00
16	"	Lajos Holdings Ltd.	300.000.00			Interest	33,149.52
19	"	O'Shea & Shanahan - Balance purchase price - Poppintree	58,772.48				
20	"	McArdle & Co. - Costs of releasing Helmdale Mortgage	346.50				
"	"	McArdle & Co. - Costs of purchase of Poppintree	5,026.87				
25	"	Kent Carty - search fee	15.00				
21	"	Brendan Devine	6,303.75				
	"	John G. Manahan	310.00				
12	"	J. G. O'Connor - Costs of release of Mortgages	137.50				
14	"	Copsey Murray & Co. -	182,176.40				
2	"	Thomas McCann S.C. - Opinion	525.00				
	"	Maurice E. Veale & Co. - Fee for copy Deeds of Wilton Lodge	50.00				
9	"	John Lane	7,000.00				
31	"	Copsey Murray & Co.	244,685.18				
	"	Balance on deposit with Industrial Credit Coporation plc	64,402.72				
			£1,483,649.52				£1,483,649.52

Dated the 5ᵗʰ day of February, 1990.

McArdle & Co.

McArdle & Co.,
Solicitors,
30, Upper Fitzwilliam Street,
DUBLIN, 2.

Appendix U

Appendix U

CLIENT

PERIOD ENDED

SCHEDULE OF: Reliable / Grafton Cash Balance

Ref:

Prepared By On

Reviewed By On

Proceeds	Deposit			125,000.00	
	Balance			1202,540.00	
	Draft			122,460.00	1450,000.00
Costs :	Planning Permission — JmSE			80,258.00	
	— JmSE			30,000.00	
	Fees : Copsey Murray & Co			14,500.00	
	Sale of Land			20,640.12	
	E + W — release of Title Deeds			6303.75	
	Kent County — Search	✓		15.00	
	Jack Monaghan			310.00	
	Mortgage Release			347.52	
Disbursements :	Inter-Co loan : Logos	✓		400,000	
	: Marcus Sweeney	✓		60,000	
Purchase of land Poppinghoe :	Deposit			6,500.00	
	Bal	✓		58,772.48	
	Stamp Duty			5026.87	
Repayment of Inter-Co Loan — General Agencies				300,000.00	
(Total Loan £763,205)					(984,673.7
					465,326-
Tax on Disposal :	Grafton :			157,288	
	Reliable :			61,423	218711
					246,615-
Funds available					

Appendix V

THE GRAFTON CONSTRUCTIOIN COMPANY LIMITED

TRADING AND PROFIT AND LOSS ACCOUNT FOR THE YEAR ENDED 31 MAY 1990

		1990 IR£	1989 IR£
SALE OF LAND		803,100	500,000
Deduct: Cost of Land Sold	595,790		
Enhancement Expenditure	95,273		
		691,063	71,485
		112,037	428,515
Rent Receivable		27,774	28,803
Interest Receivable		48,749	1,030
Exchange Gain/(Loss)		48,917	258
		237,477	458,606
EXPENDITURE			
Directors Remuneration		43,479	147,588
Professional Fees		32,119	20,540
Audit and Accountancy Fees		1,063	1,000
Administration costs		12,000	895
Bank Interest Charges		19	5,580
Sundry Expenses		13,864	–
		102,544	175,603
PROFIT FOR THE YEAR BEFORE TAXATION		134,933	283,003

-11-

Appendix W

Client   The Grafton Construction Co Ltd

Heading   Journal.

Client's year-end   31. 5. 9?

Audit visit   Interim/Final, etc   Final.

Ⓙ Ⓛ

Gerrard, Scallen & O'Brien	✓	345,871 78	
Copsey Murray	✓		345,871 78
Funds transferred to G.S & O'B			
D.I.R.T.	✓	15,600 00	
		~~14207 00~~	
Interest Receivable	✓		15600 00
Provision for Deposit Interest Retention Tax			~~14207 00~~
AUDIT ADJUSTMENTS			
Enhancement Expenditure	✓	20,000 00	
" "	✓	10,000 00	
Travel & subsistence in Petty cash	✓	2644 61	
Sundries (see invoices)	✓	5,404 96	
Sundry (cheque)	✓	512 50	
Joseph Murphy Structural Engineers Ltd	✓		38,362 07
Expenses etc paid by JMSE on behalf of Grafton			
Management Charge		12,000 00	
JMSE			12,000 00
Management Charge for year			
Sundry Costs		2810 35	
JMSE			2810 35
Petty cash expenditure incurred by JMSE re Grafton Construction			
Tajos Holdings limited		182,176 40	
Copsey Murray			182,176 40
Funds transferred			

Appendix X

Client *The Grafton Construction Company Ltd*

Heading *Development Property.*

	IR£	IR£
Property at cost at beginning of year	595,790	626,431
Enhancement Expenditure :		
(1) Land at Poppintree	65,273	
(2) Roads	30,000	
	691,063	626,431
Ground Rents	6,555	6,555
	697,618	632,986
Cost of land sold	697,618	37,196
	-	595,790

Appendix Y

Appendix V

REPORT INTO THE MATTERS COVERED BY CLAUSES A 1, A 2 (A) TO (C) INCLUSIVE, A 3 (A) TO (G) INCLUSIVE, AND A 3 (I), (II), AND (IV).

TERMS OF REFERENCE

IDENTIFICATION AND TITLE OF LOTS 1 TO 6.

At paragraph A.1. of the *Terms of Reference* the Tribunal was asked to enquire urgently into and report on:

"The identification of the lands stated to be 726 acres in extent, referred to in the letter dated 8th June, 1989 from Mr. Michael Bailey to Mr. James Gogarty (reproduced in the schedule herewith) and the establishment of the beneficial ownership of the lands at that date and changes in the beneficial ownership of the lands since the 8th June, 1989 prior to their development"

The letter dated 8th June 1989 from Mr. Michael Bailey to Mr. James Gogarty refers to the lands as:-

" Lot 1:   100 acres (approx.) at North Road, Finglas, including "Barrett's Land."
Lot 2:   12 acres (approx.) at Jamestown Road, Finglas.
Lot 3:   100 acres (approx.) at Poppintree, Ballymun.
Lot 4:   255 acres (approx.) at Donabate (Turvey House and Beaverton House).
Lot 5:   250 acres (approx.) at Balgriffin.
Lot 6:   9 acres (approx.) at Portmarnock."

The Tribunal undertook the following investigations to establish the identity and ownership of these lands;

(i) The above Lands were further identified in correspondence between the Tribunal and the Solicitors acting for Bovale Developments Limited, Smith Foy and Partners.

(ii) The Tribunal received and considered the results of a search in respect of all registered lands comprised in the Lands carried out at its behest by a specialised firm of title searchers

(iii) The Tribunal examined Land Registry copy folios of all registered lands comprised in the Lands in relation to the identification and ownership of the said lands as of the 8th June 1989 and subsequent thereto prior to any development.

(iv) The Tribunal examined the folios for the existence of any caution or inhibition.

(v) Insofar as any of the Lands were held under unregistered titles, the Tribunal commissioned a search of the Registry of Deeds by a specialised firm of title searchers and have obtained and considered the results of such search.

(vi) Insofar as any of the Lands were held under unregistered titles, the Tribunal examined copy title documents relating to the said lands for the purpose of identifying the owners of the lands as of the 8th of June 1989 and changes in such ownership since the 8th of June 1989 prior to any development of the lands. Where available, the Tribunal examined indentures and otherwise it examined memorials.

(vii) The Tribunal examined maps relating to the Land Registry folios in respect of the Lands, and maps attaching to any title documents where the title was unregistered.

(viii) The Tribunal entered into correspondence with the solicitors acting for the apparent owners of the Lands as of the 8th of June 1989 and the solicitors for the successors in title to the owners of the Lands so as to inquire into transactions that were evident in the Land Registry and/or the Registry of Deeds in relation to the Lands.

(ix) The Tribunal examined discovery documents obtained by it relating to the Lands.

(x) The Tribunal consulted a professional draftsman concerning the outline of the Lands on the maps examined. Reproduction maps were circulated in advance to the solicitors for the parties to the title and there were no objections to their use.

(xi) A statement of proposed evidence of Maire Anne Howard a Solicitor employed by the Tribunal was circulated to all interested parties and sworn testimony in line with this statement was given at a public hearing of the Tribunal on the 6th March 2000. Ms. Howard's testimony was not challenged.

(xii) The Tribunal heard evidence from a number of witnesses on this issue including Mr. Gogarty and Mr. Joseph Murphy Senior.

The Tribunal considered it expedient to deal with the lands under the headings of each of the six lots as identified in the letter of the 8th June 1989. In the case of registered lands the registered owner is deemed to be the beneficial owner. In his statement of evidence to the Tribunal Mr. Murphy Senior maintained that the initiative to sell these lands came from Mr. Gogarty whom he said had exclusive responsibility for the land holding companies within the Murphy Group. Mr. Murphy Senior maintained that he had for many years past removed himself from the day to day involvement in the Group's affairs and he knew little or nothing about property as his "experience and know how lay in the core business of the group."

The evidence given by Mr. Murphy Senior however qualified this statement to the extent that it was apparent to the Tribunal and accepted by Mr. Murphy Senior that the final decision on selling these properties would eventually come to him. In essence he maintained that Mr. Gogarty was acting unhindered by him "except when it came to the final decision to dispose of the lands", when his permission was sought. He had in effect the final say on the disposal of these lands. In the circumstances the Tribunal concluded that whilst the legal ownership of the lands lay in the various companies the actual ownership rested with the one who had the final say on their disposal namely Mr. Murphy Senior.

PLANNING STATUS

Paragraphs A.2 and A.3 required the Tribunal to inquire urgently into the planning history of the lands including:-

(a) their planning status in the Development Plan of the Dublin Local Authorities current at the 8th June, 1989;

(b) the position with regard to the servicing of the lands for development as at the 8th June, 1989;

(c) changes made or proposed to be made to the 8th June, 1989 planning status of the lands by way of:-

(i) proposals put forward by Dublin Local Authority officials pursuant to the review of Development Plans or otherwise;

(ii) motions by elected members of the Dublin Local Authorities proposing re-zoning;

(iii) applications for planning permission (including any involving a material contravention of the Development Plan);

Whether the lands referred to in the letter dated 8th June, 1989 were the subject of the following:-

(a) Re-zoning resolutions;
(b) Resolutions for material contravention of the relevant Development Plans;
(c) Applications for special tax designations status pursuant to the Finance Acts;
(d) Applications for planning permission;
(e) Changes made or requested to be made with regard to the servicing of the lands for development;
(f) Applications for the granting of building by-law approval in respect of buildings constructed on the lands;
(c) Applications for fire safety certificates;

on or after the 20th day of June 1985. M

And

(i) to ascertain the identity of any persons or companies (and if companies, the identity of the beneficial owners of such companies) who had a material interest in the said lands or who had a material involvement in the matters aforesaid;

(ii) to ascertain the identity of any members of the Oireachtas, past or present, and/or members of the relevant local authorities who were involved directly or indirectly in any of the foregoing matters whether by the making of representations to a planning authority or to any person in the authority in a position to make relevant decisions or by the proposing of or by voting in favour or against or by abstaining from any such resolutions or by absenting themselves when such votes were taken or by attempting to influence in any manner whatsoever the outcome of any such applications, or who received payments from any of the persons or companies referred to at (i) above.

(iii) to ascertain the identity of all public officials who considered, made recommendations or decisions on any such matters and to report on such considerations, recommendations and/or decisions;

(iv) to ascertain and report on the outcome of all such applications, resolutions and votes in relation to such applications in the relevant local authority.

A recently retired employee of Fingal County Council, Ms. Sinead Collins gave sworn testimony to the Tribunal. She had been an Administrative Officer in the Planning Department from January 1994 and prior to that had held the same position in Dublin County Council where she had worked from July 1982 to December 1993. Before that she had been employed for approximately 24 years by Dublin Corporation during which time she worked in the Engineering Department, later the Planning Department and subsequently the Housing Department.

Ms. Collins's testimony was based on the documentation and information available to her in her capacity as an official of the Council, in relation to matters referred to in paragraphs A2 and A.3(a)-(g) (other than paragraph 3(c) concerning tax designation) inclusive of the *Amended Terms of Reference*.

Ms. Collins relied on the assistance afforded her by Mr. Barry Morris, Senior Executive Engineer and Mr. Liam Coughlan, Senior Engineer of the Environmental Services Department in relation to the position regarding the servicing of lands for development as of 8th June 1989.

A statement of Ms. Collins proposed evidence was circulated to interested parties in advance of her giving sworn testimony to the Tribunal on the 4th and 5th April 2000.

Paragraph A.3(c) of the *Terms of Reference* required the Tribunal to establish whether any of the lands were the subject of applications for special tax designations status pursuant to the Finance Act. Mr. Liam Murphy Principal Officer with the Department of Finance gave evidence on tax designation of an area at Popintree/Ballymun as an enterprise area under the Finance Act, 1997. Mr. Murphy worked in the Budget and Economic Division and was the Principal Officer dealing with elements of tax policy. Mr. Murphy's statement of proposed evidence was circulated in advance of his sworn testimony given at a public hearing on the 5th April 2000.

Mr. Murphy's unchallenged evidence related to the designation of the area known as the Popintree/Ballymun site in Lot 3 as an enterprise area under the Finance Act 1997 and is accepted by the Tribunal as an accurate account of the matters dealt with by him.

LOT 1.

PARAGRAPH A. 1.

IDENTIFICATION AND OWNERSHIP

100 acres (approx.) at North Road, Finglas, including 'Barrett's Land.'

Identification as of the 8th of June 1989

(A) The lands in Folio 19360 of the Register County of Dublin, being lands situate in the Townland of Balseskin, Barony of Castleknock and County of Dublin, comprising 33.645 hectares or 83.1368 acres.

(B) The lands in Folio 7462 of the Register County of Dublin, being lands situate in the Townland of Charlestown, Barony of Castleknock and County of Dublin, comprising 15.578 hectares or 38.49324 acres.

Beneficial Ownership as of the 8th June 1989

Folio 19360 of the Register County of Dublin
The full registered owner of the lands comprised in Folio 19360 was **Finglas Industrial Development Limited**, having its registered office at 29 Fitzwilliam Square, in the City of Dublin.
Folio 7462 of the Register County of Dublin.
The full registered owner of the lands comprised in Folio 7462 of the Register County of Dublin was **Barrett Developments Limited**, having its registered office at 6 Foster Place, in the City of Dublin.

There was no inhibition or caution registered in respect of either of these folios nor did it appear that the lands comprised in either folio was the subject of any charge or encumbrance.

Changes in Beneficial Ownership since the 8th June 1989 and prior to their Development

(A) Certain steps were taken in 1989/91 which affected not only Lot 1 but all of the Lands, save for Folio 4327 (see Lot 4 below). Following the 8th June 1989 and prior to the disposal of the Lands to Bovale Developments Limited; -

(i) The Grafton Construction Company Limited on the 15th of December 1989 agreed to sell to Lajos Holdings Limited such of the Lands as were held by the Grafton Construction Company Limited on that date.

(ii) At an Extraordinary General Meeting of Barrett Developments Limited held on the 18th December 1989, it was resolved that the company be wound up voluntarily and that John Eddison be appointed Liquidator;

(iii) At an Extraordinary General Meeting of Finglas Industrial Estates Limited held on 18th December 1989, it was resolved that the company be wound up voluntarily and that John Eddison be appointed Liquidator;

(iv) At an Extraordinary General Meeting of Turvey Estates Limited held on the 18th December 1989, it was resolved that the company be wound up voluntarily and that John Eddison be appointed Liquidator;

(v) In a Statutory Declaration sworn by John Eddison on the 29th January 1991, the liquidator of Turvery Estates Limited, Barrett Developments Limited and Finglas Industrial Developments Limited declared that the lands owned by the respective companies were surplus lands after the payment of all debts of the three companies. He as liquidator of the three companies was not claiming any charge or lien over the lands or any part thereof in respect of any charges, costs or expenses incurred in the course of the liquidation or in respect of his fees. He was satisfied that adequate provision had been made for his fees. He further declared that Lajos Holdings Limited was entitled as the sole legal shareholder of the three companies to have the said lands distributed to it *in specie*;

(B)

(i) All of the Lands (including Lot 1) save for Folio 4327 (see Lot 4 below) were acquired by Bovale Developments Limited on foot of a composite Deed of Transfer and Conveyance dated the 12th of September 1991 and made between LAJOS HOLDINGS LIMITED of the first part, GRAFTON CONSTRUCTION COMPANY LIMITED of the second part, BARRETT DEVELOPMENTS LIMITED (in Liquidation) of the third part, FINGLAS INDUSTRIAL DEVELOPMENTS LIMITED (in Liquidation) of the fourth part, TURVEY ESTATES LIMITED (in liquidation) of the fifth part, JOHN EDDISON of the sixth part and BOVALE DEVELOPMENTS LIMITED of the seventh part hereinafter referred to as the *"Composite Indenture."*

(ii) In the Composite Indenture, the Grafton Construction Company Limited by way of sub-sale pursuant to the agreement of 15th December 1989 referred to above, assured to Bovale Developments Limited all of the lands comprised in Folio 3212 of the County of Dublin (see Lot 5 below); part of Folio 175 of the Register of County of Dublin (see Lot 6 below); all of Folio 577 of the County of Dublin (see Lot 3 below); all of Folio 6262F of the County of Dublin (see Lot 3 below); all of Folio 18462 of the County of Dublin (see Lot 2 below); all of Folio 6952 of the County of Dublin (see Lot 2 below); and all of unregistered lands at Balgriffin (see Lot 5 below).

(ii) In the Composite Indenture the Liquidator of Barrett Developments Limited, Finglas Industrial Estates Limited and Turvey Estates Limited assured to Bovale Developments Limited all of the lands referred to in the Terms of Reference, which had been in the ownership of those companies (see below Lot 1 and Lot 4 respectively).

Regarding Lot 1, as can be seen from the recitation of the parties to the Composite Indenture, the respective registered owners of the lands comprised in Folios 19360 and 7462 were parties to the deed, i.e. Finglas Industrial Developments Limited (being the registered owner of the lands comprised in 19360 of the Register County of Dublin) and Barrett Developments Limited (being the owner of the lands comprised in Folio 7462 of the Register County of Dublin) both companies by then in Liquidation. On the 26th of February 1992, Bovale Developments Limited, having its registered office at 59 Fitzwilliam Square, in the City of Dublin, became the full registered owner of the lands comprised in Folio 19360. The Land Certificate was issued to Messrs. Smith Foy & Partners on the 8th of February 1998. On the 26th of February 1992, a collateral charge for present and future advances (repayable with interest) was registered against the lands in Folio 19360 in favour of the Governor and Company of the Bank of Ireland. It is noted from the folio that this charge was also registered on Folios 3212, 83876F, 577,6262F, 18462, 6952, 7462 and 4327 of the Register County of Dublin. This charge was cancelled on the 11th March 1998.

On the 10th of March 1998, a collateral charge for present and future advances (repayable with interest) was registered against property No. 2 only of the lands comprised in Folio 19360 of the Register County of Dublin, charged in favour of Anglo-Irish Bank Corporation plc. It is noted from the folio that this charge is also registered against the lands comprised in Folios 6952, 7462 and 18462 of the Register County of Dublin.

FOLIO 7462 of the Register County of Dublin

A-24 On the 26th of February 1992, Bovale Developments Limited, having its registered office at 59 Fitzwilliam Square, in the City of Dublin, became the full registered owner of the lands comprised in Folio 7462 of the Register County of Dublin. The Land Certificate was issued to Messrs. Smith Foy and Partners, Solicitors on the 12th of December 1997. On the 26th of February 1992 a charge for present and future advances (repayable with interest) was registered against the lands in Folio 7462 in favour of the Governor and Company of the Bank of Ireland. This charge was also registered against the lands comprised in Folios 3212, 83876F, 577, 6262F, 18462, 6952, 19360 and 4327 of the Register County of Dublin. This charge was cancelled on the 11th march 1997. On the 5th of June 1984, the lands comprised in Folio 7462 were subject to a wayleave in favour of Bord Gais Éireann pursuant to Section 43 of The Gas Act, 1976. All of the lands comprised in Folio 19360 of the Register County of Dublin and 7462 of the Register County of Dublin remained in the registered ownership of Bovale Developments Limited until 1994.

In or about the year 1994, portion of the lands comprised in Folios 19360 and 7462 together with portion of Folio 577 (see Lot 3 below) were compulsorily acquired by the County Council of the County of Dublin in connection with the construction of the M50 motorway. The portion of lands acquired by the County Council of the County of Dublin from the three said folios were transferred into Folio 99886F of the Register County of Dublin. The County Council of the County of Dublin became registered as owner of these lands on the 17th of February 1994. Messrs. Smith Foy have confirmed that as part of the transaction involving the compulsory acquisition of portion of Folios 19360 and 7462, the County Council agreed that Bovale would have access over an area coloured green on an enclosed map but that no Deed of a Grant of Way has yet been delivered. Fingal County Council have confirmed access from the N2 to the remaining Bovale lands over this section of Lot 1 although the precise location of the access road was not stated.

PARAGRAPH A.2.

PLANNING HISTORY

The lands are comprised in two folios, Folio 7462 in the townland of Charlestown and Folio 19360 in the townland of Balseskin. Lot 1 originally consisted of a single holding but as a result of the construction of the Northern Cross Motorway – the M50 - the lands were bisected and the lands in the townland of Balseskin – Folio 19360 – Co. Dublin – are mainly to the north of the motorway, bounded along part of their south-western boundary by North Road, Finglas and partly along the north-eastern boundary by St Margaret's Road and a small portion measuring 1.86 hectares (4.6 acres) are to the south of the M50. The lands at Charlestown comprising 15.58 hectares (38.49 acres), which are bounded along their north-western boundary by the motorway and on their eastern boundary by St Margaret's Road, Finglas are those comprised in Folio 7462 - Co. Dublin. The Tribunal considered it expedient to deal with the planning history of Lot 1 in 2 parts: -

Lands **south** of the M.50
Lands **north** of the M.50

LANDS SOUTH OF THE M.50 BEING FOLIO 7462 LANDS AT CHARLESTOWN AND LANDS AT BALSESKIN BEING PORTION OF LANDS IN FOLIO 19360.

Paragraph A.2 (a) of the Terms of Reference namely the planning status of these lands in the Development Plan of the Dublin Local Authorities current at the 8th June 1989

The Development Plan current as of the 8th June 1989 was the 1983 Development Plan for the County of Dublin wherein these lands were zoned "B" *"to protect and provide for the development of agriculture."* In the 1972 County Development Plan, the lands in this folio were zoned "P" – that is *"to provide for the further development of agriculture"* and a narrow strip south of the proposed motorway was zoned "R" – *"to preserve open space amenity."*

In the proposed 1990 Draft Development Plan (as proposed by the Manager), it was proposed that the lands would retain a "B" zoning. In the 1991 Draft Development Plan which was approved by the elected members and put on public display for three months, the lands were shown with a proposed "B" zoning – that is *"to protect and provide for the development of agriculture."*

In 1993 the elected members proposed an amendment to the 1991 Draft Development Plan and proposed to change the zoning of the lands in question from "B" to "E" – *"to protect and provide for industrial and related uses.*" In the 1993 Development Plan which was adopted by the elected members in December 1993, the lands were zoned "E".

In the 1999 Fingal County Development Plan, part of the lands at Charlestown were zoned "E" and a small part were zoned "TDC" – "*to protect and enhance the special physical and social character of town and district centres and provide and/or improve town and district facilities.*"

Paragraph A.2 (b) of the Terms of Reference. The position regarding the servicing of the lands for development as at the 8th June 1989

Foul sewer

There were no foul sewers available to service this land within the Dublin County area at the above date. The nearest foul sewer facilities were located within the Dublin Corporation Area and there was no agreement with that Authority to accept drainage from these lands.

Surface water

A number of streams traverse these lands and these streams drain into the Dublin Corporation Area. Before any proposal for the development of these lands could be lodged consultation would have to take place with the Dublin Corporation Drainage Division. Any upgrading of the surface water system within the Corporation Area would have to be carried out by the Corporation Drainage Division at the proposers' prior expense.

Water supply

A limited supply would have been available from the North Road, providing physical access had been possible. The supply available with St. Margaret's Road, is a boosted supply sourced from the Corporation 450 mm diameter watermain. The supply is limited and would not serve any extensive development within this area.

Paragraph A.2(c)(i) of the Terms of Reference. Changes made or proposed to be made to the 8th June 1989 planning status of the lands by way of proposals put forward by Dublin Local Authority Officials pursuant to a review of Development Plans or otherwise

There were no proposals put forward by any Dublin Local Authority Official to change the 8th June 1989 planning status of these lands. However, in the 1998 Draft Fingal Development Plan a portion of the site was zoned "TDC" – "*to protect and enhance the special physical and social character of town and district centres and provide and/or improve town and district facilities.*" This was confirmed in the 1999 Fingal Development Plan.

Paragraph A.2(c)(ii) of the Terms of Reference. Changes made or proposed to be made to the 8th of June 1989 planning status of the lands by way of motions by elected members of the Dublin Local Authorities proposing re-zoning

In January 1991 Garth May, a planning consultant, made an application to Dublin County Council for the re-zoning of lands at Finglas/Poppintree on behalf of Bovale Developments Limited ("Bovale"). This application related to three parcels of land – one being east of the North Road at Charlestown, Finglas, the second at Jamestown Road and the third located south of the revised route for the Northern Cross Motorway at Poppintree. This application was given the number 000166. Three plans accompanied the application (plan 1, plan 2 and plan 3) the location of the three sites being shown on plan/drg. No. 76/03 entitled "*application for re-zoning Finglas/Poppintree for Bovale Developments.*"

On the map Mr. May indicated that approximately 20 acres of Bovale lands were affected by the Northern Cross Motorway and that the land, the subject of the application for re-zoning, was approximately 75 acres. By letter dated 18th November 1991 Mr. May on behalf of Bovale, requested that his submission made in January 1991 be accepted as an objection/representation to the 1991 Draft Development Plan (then on public display) together with supplemental information contained in his letter of 18th November. This representation was given the Ref. No. 166.

At a meeting of Dublin County Council held on 19th March 1993, when representations in relation to the 1991 Draft Development Plan were being considered, the following motion, signed by Councillors Cyril Gallagher, John Gilbride and Ann Devitt in relation to all of the said lands south of the M.50, was proposed by Councillor Cyril Gallagher and seconded by Councillor Ann Devitt - (Ref: 12 (2) (A) (i)) in the minutes of the Council's meeting; -

"Dublin County Council hereby resolves that the lands at Charlestown, Finglas outlined in red on the attached map comprising about 40.78 acres and which has been signed for identification purposes by the proposer and seconder of this motion, be zoned industrial in the Draft Review of the County Development Plan"

A map (map no11) showing the various zonings proposed for the North Fringe Lands, including the lands at Charlestown shown on Folio 7462, was put on public display between the 2nd day of September 1991 and the 3rd day of December 1991.

Following the public display of the Draft Development Plan the staff of the Council gathered together the objections/representations, which related to particular lands or particular areas. Each representation was given a number and a copy of each representation was circulated to each of the 78 Councillors prior to the meeting at which the particular representation was to be considered. In addition, the Manager prepared a report in which he set out a synopsis of the various representations, and outlined the position in relation to zoning as shown in the 1983 Development Plan. The Manager's report encompassed the Planning Officer's report with a recommendation as to whether the draft plan should or should not be changed in the light of the representation/representations received. The Planning Officer's report was almost invariably prepared by the Planning Officer after consultation with other relevant departments such as the Environmental Services Department. The objections and representations received following the first public display were considered by the members at a series of 50 special meetings, which extended over a period from April 1992 to June 1993.

A total of 8 representations were received from or on behalf of landowners whose lands formed part of the north fringe lands south of the Northern Cross Route and between North Road Finglas and Santry By-pass. This part of the lands in Lot 1 was the subject matter of a motion to rezone. These 8 representations, which appear under the reference C218/93 commencing at page 272 of the Council's minutes, were received in respect of the following:

Lands south of the Northern Cross Route:
Representation No. 000166 – Bovale Developments Limited – Charlestown, Jamestown and Poppintree. These are the lands south of the M.50.
Representation No. 000249 – Mr & Mrs J McCourt/Charlestown.
Representation No. 000173 – T Gammel, Jamestown.
Representation No. 000128 PH Ross Limited Jamestown.
Representation No. 000646 – GKR Developments and Jamestown/Meakestown.
Representation No. 000762 Mr and Mrs Fitzpatrick, Meakestown.
Representation No. 000370 – H Byrne, Ballymun.
Representation No. 000333 – A O'Boyle, Woodford House, Turnapin.

The motion to rezone the lands in Lot 1 south of the M.50 was one of eight applications to rezone lands south of the M.50.

The following report by the Manager that had been circulated to all 78 elected members was considered.

"SYNOPSIS OF REPRESENTATIONS:
All of these representations from landowners refer either in whole or part to the North Fringe lands, south of the Northern Cross Route between the North Road, Finglas and the Santry By-Pass. The representations support the proposed Draft Plan development zonings 'A I' and 'E' and in addition seek the re-zoning of almost the entire remainder of the area for development purposes to a combination of 'A I' and 'E'.

The principal arguments put forward for re-zoning the area for development purposes are as follows:

There is no prospect of agricultural use of the lands south of the motorway due to vandalism, trespass and severance.

The motorway should form the logical development zoning boundary.

A large area between the Jamestown Road and St. Margaret's Road has already been zoned 'A1' Residential and 'E' Industrial.

The Area Action Plan referred to in Paragraph 3.2.8 of the Draft Written Statement be brought forward as this would provide more details on precise drainage requirements and on the financial contributions towards this infrastructural investment that would be forthcoming.

(A)   Representation No. 000166 - Bovale Developments Limited
Bovale Developments refer to three lots of land at (i) Charlestown (16 ha.); (ii) Jamestown (8 ha.); (iii) Poppintree (8 ha.) and seeks a re-zoning of (i) and (iii) from 'B' and 'F' to a zoning providing for mixed development, such as a combination of 'A I' and 'E'. The area of Jamestown (8 ha.) was re-zoned 'E' in the 1991 Draft Plan.

(B)   Representation No. 000249 - Mr. and Mrs. J. McCourt:
A re-zoning of 23 ha. at Charlestown from 'B' to 'E' is sought.

(C)   Representation No. 000173 - T. Gammell:
The Draft Plan 'AI' zoning of lands at Dubbercross/Jamestown is supported.

(D)   Representation No. 000128 - P.H. Ross Limited Jamestown
The Draft Plan 'AI' zoning of lands at Poppintree/Jamestown is supported.

(E)   Representation No. 000762 - Mr. & Mrs. Fitzpatrick:
Re-zoning of lands (9 ha.) at Meakestown from 'F' to 'A I' and 'E' is advocated.

(F)   Representation No. 000646 - G.K. Developments:
The Draft Plan 'AI' zoning of lands at Poppintree/Jamestown is supported. [App. 1.4.1]

(G)   Representation No. 000370 - H' Byrne:
Re-zoning of 22 ha. at Ballymun from 'B' to 'E' is sought.

(H)   Representation No. 000333 - A. O'Boyle, Woodford House:
Re-zoning of 8 ha. from 'B' to 'E' is advocated.

DEVELOPMENT PLAN:
At a meeting of the County Council on 21st March, 1991, a motion was passed providing for the re-zoning of c-36 ha. between Jamestown Road and St. Margaret's Road from 'B' Agriculture to A1 Residential and 'E' Industry. it was also agreed to insert a paragraph (now paragraph 3.2.8) into the Draft Plan as follows:

"It is agreed in principle that the lands north of the City Boundary and between it and the Northern Cross Motorway from Santry (Swords Road) to Finglas (North Road) should be made available for development if and when the necessary drainage services are provided. At that stage the lands will be the subject of an Area Action Plan and/or variation to the Development Plan to determine the zoning and the nature of development in the area."

In addition, many of the subject lands are within the restricted development area, which is necessary for the safe operation of Dublin Airport, as detailed in Appendix D of the Development Plan. Representation No. 000333 is within the red approach area and Representations Nos. 000762, 000166 and 000370 are within the area encompassed by the 35 N.N.I. contour as shown on Map IA of the Development Plan. [App. 1.4]

PLANNING OFFICER'S REPORT:
Paragraph 3.2.8 of the Draft Plan provides for the principle of development for lands south of the Northern Cross Route: -

> "The lack of drainage facilities remains the major constraint and it is unlikely to be resolved until the proposed drainage scheme for the North City Fringe is put in place. In the absence of firm proposals to drain the lands, zoning for additional development would not be appropriate.
>
> It is recommended that the Draft Plan should not be changed."

The motion to rezone the lands in Lot 1, south of the M.50., was put and was passed by 37 votes for, 12 against and 1 abstention.

For: Councillors S. Barrett, S. Brock, L. Butler, B. Cass, R. Conroy, L.T. Cosgrave, M.J. Cosgrave, A. Devitt, M. Elliott, M. Farrell, T. Fox, C. Gallagher, S. Gilbride, T. Hand. F. Hanrahan, C. Keane, M. Kennedy, J. Larkin, L. Lohan, D. Lydon, M. McGennis, C. McGrath, D. Marren, T. Matthews, 0. Mitchell, T. Morrissey, M. Muldoon, C. O'Connor, J. O'Halloran, A. Ormonde, N. Owen, C. Quinn, T. Ridge, N. Ryan, S. Terry, C. Tyndall, G.V. Wright.

Against: Councillors M. Billane, F. Buckley, L. Gordon, D. Healy, J. Higgins, T. Kelleher, S. Misteil, D. O'Callaghan, G. O'Connell, S. Ryan, D. Tipping, E. Walsh.

Abstentions: Councillor S. Laing."

This decision of the members was put on public display for the statutory one-month period – "*the second public display*" - as a proposed amendment (Change 7 Map 11). The proposed amendment was again considered at a meeting of the Council on 7th October, 1993, when the Manager recommended that the amendment be deleted. It was proposed by Councillor D. Healy, seconded by Councillor T. Sargent "*that Change 7 on Map 11 be deleted.*" The motion was defeated on a show of hands with 6 members voting in favour of the motion, 41 against and 2 abstentions. The proposed amendment was then confirmed and the site was zoned for industry in the 1993 Development Plan. Motions relating to the Bovale lands at Jamestown and Poppintree (ref no. 12(2)(A)(iii) and 12 (2)(A)(ii) were also passed at this meeting and are dealt with later in relation to Lots 2 and 3.

Of the 8 representations which were to be considered at the Council meeting on the 19th March 1993, only two - representation No. 000166 relating to the Bovale Development lands (totalling approx. 80 acres at Charlestown, Jamestown and Poppintree) and representation No. 000249 on behalf of Mr & Mrs J. McCourt, Charlestown (totalling approximately 55 acres) - were dealt with at that meeting.

Consideration of the remaining 6 representations (Item 12)(2) lands south of the Northern Cross Route) resumed under Reference C/222-93 at the special Council Meeting held on the 29th March 1993. The same report and recommendation from the Manager, which had been circulated to the Councillors prior to their consideration of the representation from Garth May on behalf of Bovale and the representation on behalf of Mr & Mrs McCourt, were again considered. This report made reference to the location of the lands in relation to the restricted development area necessary for the safe operation of Dublin Airport, the lack of drainage facilities, the Planning Officer's recommendation that zoning for additional development would not be appropriate and recommended that the draft plan should not be changed. (Page 286 of minutes).

As indicated at pg.286 of the Minutes of the Meeting "*The Manager's Report in Respect of Items at (C), (D), (E), (F) above was NOTED.*" This meant that Representation No. 000173 - (Item C) – T. Gammell, Representation No. 000128 (Item D), - P.H. Ross Limited Jamestown, Representation No. 000646 (Item E) – G.K.R. Developments Limited all of which supported the draft plan "A1" zoning of their respective lands were approved by the Council but a Representation No. 000762 (Item F) – from Mr & Mrs Fitzpatrick which proposed rezoning of lands (9ha) at Meakestown from "F" to "A1" and "E" was not the subject of any motion by any Councillor and accordingly was not acceded to. (The "F" zoning is a zoning to preserve and provide for open space and recreational amenities). The first motion proposed at the meeting of the 29th March 1993 in relation to the representations referred to above was Item 12(2)(G) which related to representation No. 000370 on behalf of H. Byrne, Ballymun. A motion in the names of Councillors Ann Devitt and Cyril Gallagher resolving to rezone the land at Old Ballymun Road, Ballymun shown outlined in red on attached map as objective "E" – "*to provide for industry and related uses*" was passed by 45 votes to 6 with 2 abstentions. The next motion put was in the names of Councillor Ann Devitt and Cyril Gallagher and related to Item 12(2)(H) representation No. 000333- A. O' Boyle, Woodford House, Turnapin. The motion was proposed by Cllr. Devitt, seconded by Cllr. Owen and was passed by 45 votes to 6 with 2 abstentions.

Following the passing of the motions outlined above, the decisions of the members were put on public display for the statutory 1 month period from the 1st day of July 1993 to the 4th day of August 1993 - "*the second public display*" - as proposed amendments to the draft Development Plan. (Change 4 Map 11 (Byrne)) and change 9 Map 11 (O'Boyle) (also change 8 Map 10). The proposed amendment in respect of Byrne's lands at Ballymun (item 12(2)(G) was considered at a meeting of the Council on the 7th October 1993 when the Manager recommended that the amendment be deleted. It was proposed by Councillor D. Healy seconded by Councillor Trevor Sergeant in relation to Byrne's lands at Ballymun that "*change 4 on Map 11 be deleted.*" This motion was defeated in a roll-call vote with 8 members voting in favour of the motion, 46 members voting against with 0 abstentions. The proposed amendment was then confirmed and the land was zoned for industry in the 1993 Development Plan. The proposed amendment in respect of the McCourt lands at Charlestown, (Change 6 Map 11) item 12.2.B – was also considered on the 7th October 1993, when a motion proposed by Councillor Healy and seconded by Councillor Sargent to delete the amendment was defeated on a show of lands, 6 in favour, 41 against and 2 abstentions. The proposed amendment in respect of the O'Boyle lands at Woodford House, Turnapin Little, item 12(2)(H) (map 10 change 8) was considered on the 6th October 1993 (see pages 1195-1197 of Minutes), when a motion to delete this change proposed by Councillor Healy, seconded by Councillor Sergeant, was defeated by 14 votes in favour, 35 against and 4 abstentions. The site was zoned industrial in the 1993 Development Plan.

Paragraph A.2(c)(iii) of the Terms of Reference. Changes made or proposed to be made to the 8th of June 1989 planning status of the lands by way of applications for planning permission (including any involving a material contravention of the Development Plan)

Material contraventions

No planning permission was granted which materially contravened the zoning of these lands.

Planning permissions

There were no applications for planning permission in the period the 8th June 1989 to the 4th November 1997.

Paragraph A.3. Resolutions, Application or Requests. Paragraph A.3(a) – (g) of the Terms of Reference. Whether the lands South of the M.50 in Lot 1 were the subject of any of the resolutions, applications or requests referred to in paragraph A.3(a) – (g) of the Terms of Reference

A.3 (a)- whether the lands were subject to rezoning resolutions

This has already been dealt with at paragraph *A.2. (c)(ii)* above.

A.3(b)-whether the lands were the subject of resolutions for material contravention of the relevant Development Plan

This has already been dealt with at paragraph *A.2.(c)(iii)* above.

A.3(c)- whether the lands were the subject of an application for special tax designation status pursuant to the Finance Acts

This site was not the subject of any special tax designation status pursuant to the Finance Acts.

A.3(d)-whether the lands were the subject matter of applications for planning permission.

This has already been dealt with this at paragraph *A.2.(c)(iii)* above.

A.3(e) – whether changes were made or requested to be made with regard to the servicing of the lands for development

No changes were made or requested to be made with regard to the servicing of the lands.

A.3(f)- whether applications were made for the granting of building byelaw approval in respect of buildings constructed on the lands

There were no such applications.

A.3(g)- whether applications were made for fire safety certificates

There were no applications for fire safety certificates.

Paragraph A.3.(i). of the Amended Terms of Reference namely to ascertain the identity of any persons or companies (and if companies, the identity of the beneficial owners of such companies) who had a material interest in the said lands or who had a material involvement in the matters aforesaid;

The identity of the Beneficial Owners of the property as of 8th June 1989 together with changes in the Beneficial Ownership between then and the development of the lands has been established at paragraph

A.1. above. The Beneficial Ownership as of the 8th June 1989 as defined in the Tribunals interpretation of its terms of reference on the 21st October 1998 rested with Mr. Joseph Murphy Senior.

Paragraph A. 3. (ii) of the Amended Terms of Reference namely to ascertain the identity of any members of the Oireachtas, past or present, and/or members of the relevant local authorities who were involved directly or indirectly in any of the foregoing matters whether by the making of representations to a planning authority or to any person in the authority in a position to make relevant decisions or by the proposing of or by voting in favour or against or by abstaining from any such resolutions or by absenting themselves when such votes were taken or by attempting to influence in any manner whatsoever the outcome of any such applications, or who received payments from any of the persons or companies referred to at (i) above

Other than the members of the Oireachtas and the Local Authorities referred to above the Tribunal at this time is unable to pronounce further on this term of reference.

Paragraph A. 3. (iv) of the Amended Terms of Reference namely to ascertain and report on the outcome of all such applications, resolutions and votes in relation to such applications in the relevant local authority;

The outcome of all applications, resolutions and votes are detailed above under paragraph A. 2 (c) (i) to (iii) inclusive and A 3 (a) to (g) inclusive.

LANDS *NORTH* OF THE M.50 BEING PART OF THE LANDS COMPRISED IN FOLIO 19360

The lands at Balseskin, Finglas, north of the M.50 which form part of the land described as Lot 1 in the Schedule to the Terms of Reference and have an area of 26.5 ha (65.7 acres) as shown on the map attached to Folio 19360. It should be noted that the area in question is stated in the Folio to be 33.645 ha. (83 acres) but that stated area of 33.645 ha includes approximately 7 ha which now forms part of the M50 Motorway.

Paragraph A.2 (a) of the Terms of Reference namely the planning status of these lands in the Development Plan of the Dublin Local Authorities current at the 8th June 1989

The Development Plan current as of the 8th June 1989 was the 1983 Development Plan for the County of Dublin wherein these lands were zoned "B" "*to protect and provide for the development of agriculture.*" In the 1972 Dublin County Development Plan, the lands at Balseskin were zoned "P" "*to provide for the further development of agriculture*". In the proposed 1990 Draft Development Plan (as proposed by Manager), it was proposed that the lands would be retained with a "B" zoning. In the 1991 Draft Plan which was approved by the elected members and put on public display for two months, the lands were shown with a proposed "B" zoning – that is "*to protect and provide for the development of agriculture.*" In the 1993 Dublin County Development Plan, which was adopted in December 1993, the lands in question north of the M50 Motorway comprising 24.64 hectares (61.1 acres) were zoned "B" (*to protect and provide for the development of agriculture*). The 1998 Draft Development Plan for Fingal proposed that the lands in question north of the M50 Motorway be re-zoned to M. U. I. Zoning – that is "*to provide for an appropriate and compatible mixture of uses in accordance with approved action plans and subject to the provision of the necessary infrastructure.*" In the 1999 Fingal County Development Plan, the lands north of the M50 were zoned "B" (*agriculture*) with the local objective to carry out a major study of long-term development of this area.

Paragraph A.2 (b) of the Terms of Reference. The position with regard to the servicing of the lands for development as of 8th June 1989

Foul sewer

There were no foul sewers available to service this land within the Dublin County area at the above date. The nearest foul sewer facilities was located within the Dublin Corporation Area and there was no agreement with that Authority to accept drainage from these lands.

Surface water

A number of streams traverse these lands and these streams drain into the Dublin Corporation Area. Before any proposal for the development of these lands could be lodged consultation would have to have taken place with the Dublin Corporation Drainage Division. Any upgrading of the surface water system within the Corporation Area would have to be carried out by the Corporation Drainage Division at the proposers' prior expense.

Water supply

Water Supply would have been available to a limited extent, this supply is sourced from a boosted 150 mm water main within the North Road. This system serves the North West County and extensive development for these lands would have been refused.

Paragraph A2 (c)(i) of the Terms of Reference. Changes made or proposed to be made to the 8th June 1989 planning status of the lands by way of proposals put forward by Dublin Local Authority officials pursuant to a review of Development Plans or otherwise

There were no proposals put forward by any Dublin Local Authority Officials to change the 8th of June 1989 planning status of the lands. This area was included in a proposed M. U. 1 Zone in the 1998 Draft Fingal County Development Plan but the plan, when adopted in 1999, provided that these lands should retain their agricultural zoning as set out above, pending a major study of the area.

Paragraph A.2 (c)(ii) of the Terms of Reference. Changes made or proposed to be made to the 8th June 1989 planning status of the lands by way of motions by elected members of the Dublin Local Authorities proposing re-zoning

No such motions have been submitted or proposed by elected Members of Dublin County Council or Fingal County Council in respect of that portion of the lands north of the M50 Motorway.

Paragraph A 2(c)(iii) of Terms of Reference. Changes made or proposed to be made to the 8th of June 1989 planning status of the lands by way of applications of planning permission (including any involving a material contravention of the Development Plan)

Material contraventions

No planning permission was granted which materially contravened the zoning of these lands.

Planning permissions

The Planning Register and such files as are available for lands at Balseskin held in the Council reveal the following planning history on these lands.

Planning Application Register Ref. A 894

The history of planning applications in relation to the site as appears from the planning register, commences in 1968 when, by Manager's Order no. P1309/68 dated 30th August 1968, outline planning permission was refused for a housing and shopping development at Balseskin for the following reasons:

> "The proposed development would be premature by reason of the said existing deficiency in the provision of water and sewerage facilities and the period within which such deficiency may reasonably be expected to be made good."

The application was made by Jones & Kelly on behalf of Mr B. Carr of 10 South Leinster Street, Dublin 2. However, as the file is not available, the exact location of the lands cannot be ascertained and they may or may not relate to some or all of the lands in question.

Planning Application Register Ref. B 310

Outline Permission for a proposed factory at Balseskin by Order No. P 639/69 dated the 6th of May, 1969 was refused for the following four reasons: -

> 1. There are no public sewerage facilities available to serve the proposal.
> 2. The public water supply pressure is insufficient to enable supply to be made available to serve the proposal.

3. The proposed development would be premature by reason of the said existing deficiency in the provision of sewerage facilities and the period within such deficiency may reasonably be expected to be made good.

4. The proposed development would be premature because a road layout for the area or part thereto has not been indicated in the Draft Development Plan or has not been approved of by the Planning Authority or by the Minister on appeal.

The application was made by Gleeson & Byrne, Architects, on behalf of Messrs A. Noyek & Sons Limited The file is not available.

Planning Application Register Ref. B 738

Outline Permission for a proposed warehouse at Balseskin by Order No. P 1184/69 dated 18th July, 1969, was refused for the same four reasons as in application ref. B 310. The application was made by Gleeson & Byrne, Architects on behalf of Messrs. A. Noyek and Sons Limited

Planning Application Register Ref. H 795

On the 16th April 1975 an application for Planning Permission (Reg. Ref. No. H795) was submitted by Conroy, Ferguson & Associates 38, Wellington Road, Dublin 4 on behalf of Finglas Industrial Estates Limited, 11 South Anne Street, Dublin 2 to Dublin County Council seeking planning permission for light industrial development on a site at Balseskin stated to be 117.5 acres.

A decision to refuse permission for light industrial development on the lands in question was made by Order No.P1666/75 dated 12th June 1975 for the following 5 reasons:

1. The proposed development is contrary to the proper planning and development of the area as it is in conflict with the Development Plan zoning objective for the area, which is "To provide for the further development of agriculture." The proposed development would further militate again the preservation of the rural environment.

2. The proposed development is premature as an action plan for this area has not been finalised and road patterns have not been firmly established. The site is affected by reservation lines for the proposed motorway and inter-change and for the widening of the National Primary Route (N2).

3. The proposed development would endanger public safety by reason of traffic hazard due to the generation of additional traffic from such a large development onto a county road network, which is completely inadequate in width and alignment to cope safely with the additional traffic.

4. The proposed development is unacceptable because a satisfactory means of disposal of sewage and surface water has not been submitted. There is no Council sewer in the area and no proposal for one, and the proposal to pump surface water is not acceptable.

5. The proposed development is premature by reason of the said deficiency in the availability of public sewers and the period within which such deficiency may reasonably be expected to be made good.

The applicants appealed to the Minister for Local Government against the refusal. On the 17th of February 1977, the then Minister for Local Government *granted permission* subject to the following condition:-

"The developers shall pay a sum of money to the Dublin County Council and or to Dublin Corporation as may be appropriate as a contribution towards the provision of a public water supply and piped sewerage facilities in the area. The amount to be paid and the time and method of payment shall be agreed between the developers and the said Council and/or Corporation before the development is commenced, or failing agreement, shall be as determined by the Minister for Local Government."

On 23rd of December 1980, An Bord Pleanála determined that the contribution to be made by the developers must be £1,500 per acre and that it was to be payable forthwith to the sanitary authority for the area. The Council refused to accept the contribution of £180,750 whereupon Finglas Industrial Estates Limited sought an Order of Mandamus to compel to Council to accept the contribution as fixed by the Board. In proceedings entitled *The State (Finglas Industrial Estates Limited) v. Dublin Co. Co.* (1981/166ss, Supreme Court, 17th February 1983 (228/1981), The Supreme Court discharged the Order of *Mandamus* made by the High Court, and no development took place on foot of that ministerial permission.

Planning Application Register Ref. 92A/1952

In 1992, Castle Heights Limited of 59 Fitzwilliam Square, Dublin 2 applied through its agent, G.F. Murphy & Associates, 19 Hermitage Grove, Rathfarnham, Dublin 16 for permission to carry out landfill works on part of the lands at Balseskin. By Order No.P1700/93 dated 19th May 1993, Dublin County Council granted permission for the carrying out of landfill works, subject to 12 conditions. A permit was subsequently issued under the European Communities (Waste) Regulations 1979 to operate a landfill for a period of 1 year commencing on the 25th August, 1993 and ending the 24th August 1994. The permit expired and was not renewed.

Planning Application Register Ref. 92A/1953

On the 14th December 1992, Castle Heights Limited, c/o Crean Salley Architects, 20 Upper Baggot Street, Dublin 4, applied for planning permission for a two-storey hotel with a new vehicular entrance and septic tank on lands at Balseskin on portion of the lands comprised in Lot 1 in that townland. By Order No. P/0365/93 of the 12th of February 1993, Dublin County Council decided to refuse planning permission for the proposed development for the following 6 reasons:-

"1. The site is located in an area zoned in the 1983 County Development Plan " to protect and provide for the development of agriculture." The proposed development would contravene a development objective indicated in the 1983 Dublin County Development Plan for the use primarily of this area for agricultural purposes and so would be contrary to the proper planning and development of the area.
2. The traffic turning movements generated by the proposed development onto or off the National Primary Route would endanger public safety by reason of traffic hazard.
3. The proposed development by itself, and by the precedent which the grant of permission for it would set for other relevant development, would adversely affect the safety and capacity of the heavily trafficked national route. This would be contrary to Government policy as expressed in the Department of Environment report *"Policy and Planning Framework for Roads" (January 1985)*.
4. The proposed development in an agricultural zone on the rural side of the proposed motorway without the necessary public services with direct access onto the National Primary Route would be contrary to the proper planning and development of the area and the provisions of the Development Plan and would lead to demands for the uneconomic extension of public services.
5. The development as proposed makes inadequate and unsatisfactory proposals for foul and surface water drainage. The proposal would thus be prejudicial to public health.
6. The development by reason of its scale and two storey design and intensive commercial nature would injure the visual amenities and character of this rural area."

There was a subsequent appeal by the applicant against the decision of Dublin County Council. On 24th June 1993 the Applicant notified the An Bord Pleanála of the withdrawal of the appeal and on 30th June 1993 the Board declared the appeal withdrawn.

Planning Application Register Ref. F97A/0468

On 30th May 1997, Castle Heights Limited of Colcommon, Batterstown, Co. Meath applied to Fingal County Council for Planning Permission for a two-storey hotel comprising 82 No. bedrooms, lounge bar, dining facilities and function rooms, new vehicular access and septic tank on portion of the lands at Balseskin. The site, the subject of this application was the same as the site the subject of the application reg. Ref. 92A/1953 above. By letter dated 20th October 1997, the application was withdrawn and no decision was made by Fingal County Council in relation to the application.

Planning Application Register Ref. F97A/0812

On the 18th September 1997, McCrossan O'Rourke Architects, 12 Richmond Row, Portobello Harbour, Dublin 8 applied for Planning Permission on behalf of Castle Heights Limited, "Colcommon", Batterstown, Co. Meath for *"completion of landfill works and provision of four football pitches and car parking"*, on that portion of the said lands at Balseskin which was the subject of planning application reg. Ref. 92A/1952 above. On the 17th November 1997, Fingal County Council refused permission for the proposed development for the following five reasons:-

"1. The site is located in an area zoned with the objective "to protect and provide for the development of agriculture" in the Development Plan. The proposed landfill works would contravene materially condition no. 7 of a previous permission granted on the 7/4/93 on the site. Reg.Ref. 92A/1952, which states that the development "shall be completed and the land reinstated for agricultural use within 24 months of grant of permission." The proposed development would also, therefore, contravene materially this zoning objective and earlier permission and as such would not be in accordance with the proper planning and development of the area.

2. The proposed development is not acceptable due to insufficient information in respect of surface water drainage. In the absence of such information the proposal is prejudicial to public health and contrary to the proper planning and development of the area.

3. The proposed development is not acceptable due to insufficient information in respect of proposed entrance and access road. In the absence of such information the proposal is sub standard and would seriously injure the amenities of the area. The proposed development would be contrary to the proper planning and development of the area.

4. It is considered that the proposed football-pitches would be prominent and visually obtrusive on this exposed and elevated site. The proposed development would therefore be seriously injurious to the visual amenity of this open rural landscape and as such would be contrary to the proper planning and development of the area.

5. It is considered by the Planning Authority that the further continuation of filling works in this prominent rural site is undesirable, unnecessary and would be seriously injurious to the residential and visual amenities of the area and contrary to the proper planning and development of the area.

Planning Application Register Ref. F97A/0880

This was an application by Castle Heights Limited seeking permission for revisions to the hotel, the subject of a planning application reg. ref. F97A/0468 for the enlargement of the site of the proposed hotel northwards and eastwards, together with the relocation of the hotel northwards or realignment of the hotel with the motorway and relocation of the car parking to the side and rear of the hotel. However, this application and application F97A/0468 were subsequently withdrawn.

Paragraph A.3. Resolutions, Applications or Requests. Paragraph A.3 (a) – (g) of the Terms of Reference. Whether the lands North of the M.50 in Lot 1 were the subject of any of the resolutions, applications or requests referred to in paragraph A.3 (a) – (g) of the Terms of Reference

A.3 (a)- whether the lands were subject to rezoning resolution

This has already been dealt with same at paragraph *A.2. (c)(ii)* above.

A.3.(b) whether the lands were the subject of resolutions for material contravention of the relevant Development Plan

This has already been dealt with same at paragraph *A.2.(c)(iii)* above.

A.3.(c) whether the lands were the subject of an application for special tax designation status pursuant to the Finance Acts

This site was not the subject of any special tax designation status pursuant to the Finance Acts.

A.3.(d) whether the lands were the subject matter of applications for planning permission

This has already been dealt with this at paragraph *A.2.(c)(iii)* above.

A.3.(e) whether the lands were the subject of changes made or requested to be made with regard to the servicing of the lands for development

No changes were made or requested to be made with regard to the servicing of the lands.

A.3.(f) whether the lands were the subject of applications for building By-law approval in respect of buildings constructed on the lands

The only application for building By-Law approval was one submitted on behalf of Finglas Industrial Estates Limited by Conroy Manahan, Maryland House, 20/21 South William Street, Dublin 2 on 14th July, 1981 register No. H795-BBL/3955/1981. On the 11th September 1981 Dublin County Council refused to grant Building By-Law permission for Light Industrial Estate at Balseskin for the following reasons:

1. Foul Sewer facility unavailable due to lack of capacity in Corporation foul sewerage system into which it is proposed to discharge the foul sewer from this site. Further, the site is outside the drainage agreement area.

2. Water supply is unavailable as water mains are already fully committed in this area.

3. Surface water sewer facility unavailable.

A.3.(g) whether the lands were the subject of applications for fire safety certificates.

There were no applications for fire safety certificates.

Paragraph A.3.(i). of the Amended Terms of Reference namely to ascertain the identity of any persons or companies (and if companies, the identity of the beneficial owners of such companies) who had a material interest in the said lands or who had a material involvement in the matters aforesaid;

The identity of the Beneficial Owners of the property as of 8th June 1989 together with changes in the Beneficial Ownership between then and the development of the lands has been established at paragraph A.1. above. The Beneficial Ownership as of the 8th June 1989 as defined in the Tribunals interpretation of its terms of reference on the 21st October 1998 rested with Mr. Joseph Murphy Senior.

Paragraph A. 3. (ii) of the Amended Terms of Reference namely to ascertain the identity of any members of the Oireachtas, past or present, and/or members of the relevant local authorities who were involved directly or indirectly in any of the foregoing matters whether by the making of representations to a planning authority or to any person in the authority in a position to make relevant decisions or by the proposing of or by voting in favour or against or by abstaining from any such resolutions or by absenting themselves when such votes were taken or by attempting to influence in any manner whatsoever the outcome of any such applications, or who received payments from any of the persons or companies referred to at (i) above

Other than the members of the Oireachtas and the Local Authorities referred to above the Tribunal at this time is unable to pronounce further on this term of reference.

Paragraph A. 3. (iv) of the Amended Terms of Reference namely to ascertain and report on the outcome of all such applications, resolutions and votes in relation to such applications in the relevant local authority;

The outcome of all applications, resolutions and votes are detailed above under paragraph A. 2 (c) (i) to (iii) inclusive and A 3 (a) to (g) inclusive.

LOT 2.

PARAGRAPH A. 1.

IDENTIFICATION AND OWNERSHIP

12 acres (approx.) at Jamestown Road, Finglas

Identification as of 8th June 1989

(a) Lands comprised in Folio 18462 of the Register County of Dublin situate in the Townland of Jamestown Little, Barony of Castleknock and County of Dublin, comprising 0.827 hectares or 2.043517 acres.

(b) Lands comprised in Folio 6952 of the Register County of Dublin situate in the Townland of Jamestown Little, Barony of Castleknock and Barony of Dublin, comprising 5.418 hectares or 13.38788 acres.

Beneficial ownership as of 8th June 1989

Folio 18462 of the Register County of Dublin

The full registered owner of the lands comprised in Folio 18462 of the Register County of Dublin was Grafton Construction Company Limited, having its registered office at Stephen Court, 18-21 St. Stephen's Green, in the City of Dublin. There was nothing on the folio by way of inhibition or caution.

Folio 6952 of the Register County of Dublin

The full registered owner of the lands comprised in Folio 6952 of the Register County of Dublin is Grafton Construction Company Limited, having is registered office at Stephen Court, 18-21 St. Stephen's Green, in the City of Dublin. There was nothing on the folio by way of inhibition or caution.

Changes in Beneficial Ownership since the 8th June 1989 up to date of Development

The Grafton Construction Company Limited was a party to the Composite Indenture referred to above (i.e. it had agreed on 15th December 1989 to sell the land to its parent Lajos and assured the land by sub-sale to Bovale in the Indenture of 12th September 1991) Bovale Developments Limited acquired the lands comprised in Folios 18462 and 6952 of the Register County of Dublin on foot of the Composite Indenture. There has been no change in the ownership in the lands comprised in Folios 18462 and 6952 of the Register County of Dublin since the said lands were acquired by Bovale Developments Limited, up to the date of their development. On the 26th of February 1992, the full registered owner of the lands comprised in Folio 18462 of the Register County of Dublin was Bovale Developments Limited, having its registered office at 59 Fitzwilliam Square, in the City of Dublin, subject only to a collateral charge in favour of the Governor and Company of the Bank of Ireland referred to at Lot 1 above. That charge, insofar as it affected Folio 18462, was cancelled on 26th November 1997. On the 26th of February 1992, the full registered owner of the lands comprised in Folio 6952 of the Register County of Dublin was Bovale Developments Limited, having its registered office at 59 Fitzwilliam Square, in the City of Dublin, subject only to a collateral charge in favour of the Governor and Company of the Bank of Ireland referred to at Lot 1 above. This charge insofar as it affected Folio 6952 was also cancelled on 26th November 1997. An examination of the folios for the period after the acquisition of same by Bovale Developments Limited does not reveal any caution or inhibition. A development known as "Mygan Business Park" has taken place on Lot 2.

PARAGRAPH A.2.

PLANNING HISTORY

The lands are comprised in two folios *18462* and *6952* and have a total area of *6.25 ha* or *15.4 acres* approximately. The lands are rectangular in shape and the only road frontage, in 1989, was onto Jamestown Road, Finglas.

Paragraph A.2 (a) of the Terms of Reference namely the planning status of these lands in the Development Plan of the Dublin Local Authorities current at the 8th June 1989

The Development Plan current as of the 8th June 1989 was the 1983 Development Plan for the County of Dublin wherein these lands were zoned "B" "*to protect and provide for the development of agriculture.*" In the 1972 County Development Plan, the lands in this Folio were zoned "P" - that is "*to provide for the further development of agriculture.*" In the proposed 1990 Draft Development Plan (as proposed by Manager), it was proposed that the lands would retain "B" zoning – that is "*to protect and provide for the development of agriculture.*"

In the 1991 Draft Development Plan which was approved by the elected members and put on public display for three months, the lands were shown with a proposed "E" zoning – that is "*to provide for industry and related uses.*" In the 1993 Development Plan which was adopted by the elected members in December 1993, the lands were zoned "E" – that is "*to provide for industrial and related uses.*" In the 1999 Fingal County Development Plan, the lands are zoned "E" – that is "*to facilitate opportunities for general industrial employment and related uses in established industrial areas*"

Paragraph A.2 (b) of Terms of Reference. The position with regard to the servicing of the Jamestown Road lands for development as at the 8th June 1989

Foul sewer

There were no foul sewers available within the Dublin County Council Area, this land would only drain to the Dublin Corporation system for which these was no agreement. In the absence of any agreement between a prospective developer and the Corporation, any proposal to develop this land would have been given a recommendation for refusal.

Surface water

This land lies within the catchment of a stream discharging into the Corporation area, no development could take place within these lands pending a favourable report from the Drainage Division of Dublin Corporation stipulating that Authorities requirements.

Water supply

A limited water supply sourced from the Dublin Corporation system and subject to any condition imposed by that Authority would be available.

Paragraph A.2(c)(i) of Terms of Reference. Changes made or proposed to be made to the 8th June 1989 planning status of the lands by way of proposals put forward by Dublin Local Authority officials pursuant to a review of Development Plans or otherwise

There were no proposals put forward by Dublin Local Authority Officials to change the 8th June 1989 planning status of the lands.

Paragraph A.2(c)(ii) of Terms of Reference. Changes made or proposed to be made to the 8th of June 1989 planning status of the lands by way of Motions by elected Members of the Dublin Local Authorities proposing re-zoning

In January 1991 Garth May, a planning consultant, made an application to Dublin County Council for the re-zoning of lands at Finglas/Poppintree on behalf of Bovale Developments Limited ("Bovale"). This application related to three parcels of land – one being east of the North Road at Charlestown, Finglas, the second at Jamestown Road and the third located south of the revised route for the Northern Cross Motorway at Poppintree. This application was given the number 000166. Three plans accompanied the application (plan 1, plan 2 and plan 3) the location of the three sites being shown on plan/drg. No. 76/03 entitled "*application for re-zoning Finglas/Poppintree for Bovale Developments.*"

On the map Mr. May indicated that approximately 20 acres of Bovale lands were affected by the Northern Cross Motorway and that the land, the subject of the application for re-zoning, was approximately 75 acres. By letter dated 18th November 1991 Mr. May on behalf of Bovale, requested that his submission made in January 1991 be accepted as an objection/representation to the 1991 Draft Development Plan (then on public display) together with supplemental information contained in his letter of 18th November. This representation was given the Ref. No. 000166. At a meeting of Dublin County Council held on 21st March 1991, the following motion was proposed by Councillor Cyril Gallagher and seconded by Councillor John Gilbride:

> "*That Dublin County Council hereby resolves that the lands at Meakstown, Charlestown and Jamestown in the townland of Jamestown Little coloured in Red and Green on the attached map comprising about 90 acres and which has been signed for identification purposes by the proposer and seconder of this motion, be zoned for residential A1 and industrial E in the draft review of the County Dublin Development Plan (ref. N8).*"

The map in question which had been prepared by Kieran O'Malley & Co. Limited, Civil Engineering and Town Planning Consultants and bore the reference drawing no. 89.1.420.3. The 90 acres referred to in the motion included lands at Meakstown and a small triangle north of the proposed Northern Cross Motorway Route which would be severed by the route – and later acquired by the Council. The following report by the Manager was read at the meeting:

> "There is a considerable amount of agricultural zoned land between the City Boundary and the Northern Cross Route Motorway between Santry and North Road, Finglas. There are no drainage facilities available to serve these lands and there are no proposals in hand to provide services due to the limitations in the sewerage network along the North City fringe.
>
> It is accepted that these lands would be appropriate for development if services were available. It is therefore proposed that it be indicated in the Development Plan that planning permission would be forthcoming in principle for these lands if services can be provided. For the time being it is recommended that the zoning remain agricultural. Zoning for development would impose on the Council the obligation to service the lands and in the circumstances such a commitment could not be justified. This Review has established that there is a more than adequate amount of zoned serviced lands both residential and industrial to meet the reeds of the County for the foreseeable future.
>
> It is proposed to include the following paragraph in the Written Statement.
>
>> "It is agreed in principle that the lands north of the City Boundary and between it and the Northern Cross Motorway from Santry (Swords Road) to Finglas (North Road) should be made available for development, if and when the necessary drainage services are provided. At that stage the lands will be the subject of an Area Action Plan and/or variation to the Development Plan to determine the zoning and the nature of development in the area."

Following discussion the motion was put and on a division the voting resulted as follows:

For: 24 (twenty-four)
Against: 6 (six)
Abstention: I (one)

For: Councillors J. Barry, C. Boland, T. Boland, S. Brock, L. Creaven, J. Daly, A. Devitt, P. Dunne, C. Gallagher, J. Gilbride. 0. Hammond, F. Hanrahan, W. J. Harvey, P. Hickey, G. Kieran, J. Larkin, L. Lawlor, M. McGennis, C. McGrath, L. Mulvihill, J. Murphy, A. Ormonde, S. Riney and N. Ryan. (24)

Against: Councillors F. Buckley, B. Cass, E. Fitzgerald, J. Maher, M. Muldoon and M. Sheehan. (6)

Abstentions: Councillor S. Laing. (1)

The Chairman then declared the motion carried. The officials of the Council had proposed that the lands at Jamestown Road – Lot 2 – would continue to be zoned "B" – that is *"to protect and provide for the development of agriculture."* However, the effect of the Council passing the motion in question at the meeting on the 21st March 1991 was to change the proposed zoning of the lands – Lot 2 - to "E" (*to provide for industrial and related uses*) and the lands were shown as zoned for industrial use in the 1991 Draft Development Plan which was subsequently put on public display. At a special meeting of Dublin County Council on the 19th March 1993, the following motion signed by Cllrs. Cyril Gallagher, John Gilbride and Ann Devitt was proposed by Cllr. Gallagher, seconded by Cllr. Devitt and was passed by 37 votes in favour with 13 votes against: -

> "Dublin County Council hereby resolves that the lands at Jamestown Little, Finglas outlined in red on the attached map comprising about 16.27 acres and which has been signed for identification purposes by the proposer and seconder of this motion, be zoned for Industrial (E) in the draft review of the County Dublin Development Plan."

> **For:** Councillors S. Barrett, S. Brock, L. Butler, B. Cass, R. Conroy, L. T. Cosgrave, M. J. Cosgrave, A. Devitt, M. Elliott, M. Farrell, T. Fox, C. Gallagher, S. Gilbride, T. Hand, F. Hanrahan, C. Keane, M. Kennedy, J. Larkin, L. Lohan, D. Lydon, M. McGennis C. McGrath, D. Marren, T. Matthews, O. Mitchell, T. Morrissey, M. Muldoon, C. O'Connor, J. O'Halloran, A. Ormonde, N. Owen C. Quinn, T. Ridge, N. Ryan, S. Terry, C. Tyndall, G.V. Wright.
> **Against:** Councillors M Billane, F. Buckley, L. Gordon, D. Healy J. Higgins, T. Kelleher, S. Laing, S. Misteil, D. O'Callaghan, G. O'Connell, S. Ryan, D. Tipping, E. Walsh.

The effect of this vote was to confirm the zoning for industry and the Lot 2 site was so zoned in the 1993 Development Plan.

Paragraph 2.A(c)(iii) of the Terms of Reference. Changes made or proposed to be made to the 8th of June 1989 planning status of the lands by way of applications for planning permission (including any involving a material contravention of the Development Plan)

Material contraventions

No planning permission was granted which materially contravened the zoning of these lands.

Planning permission

In order for a full understanding of the planning applications which were made in respect of the lands at Lot 2, the Tribunal sets out hereunder details of all planning applications as disclosed on the planning register and the results of each such application.

Planning Application Register Ref. H 94

A decision to refuse Outline Permission to Lyon Group Ireland Limited was made by Order P.714/75 on the 13th March, 1975 for a warehouse at Jamestown Little, to the west of Jamestown Road, for the following four reasons:-

> "The proposed development is contrary to the proper planning and development of the area as it is in conflict with the zoning objective incorporated in the County Development Plan for the area, i.e. "to provide for the further development of agriculture." It is considered important to preserve this area for agricultural use only to ensure that the value of the public investment undertaken or to be undertaken in the provision of roads and services in those areas designated for industrial or commercial development is not reduced or vitiated by such development in nearby rural unserviced areas.

> The existing road is inadequate to serve the industrial traffic, which would be generated by the proposed development. The proposed development would therefore endanger public safety by reason of traffic hazard.

> There are no public piped sewerage services in the area and the proposed development is not acceptable as inadequate information has been provided concerning the proposed sewage treatment plant.

The proposed development would be premature by reason of the said existing deficiency in the provision of sewerage facilities and the period within which such deficiency may reasonably be expected to be made good."

Outline Permission was refused by the Minister on appeal.

Planning Application Register Ref. F95A/0964

On the 22nd December 1995, a planning application was lodged seeking permission for development described as "*5 No. Industrial Dry Goods Warehouse Units, with associated offices comprising 4 No. 4, 645 sq. m. and 1 No. 4, 181 sq. m. each of which are capable of being sub-divided with new access onto Jamestown Road, associated drainage works and demolition of existing inhabitable buildings.*" The application was submitted on behalf of Bovale Developments Limited, Coolcommon, Batterstown, Co. Meath by The Ambrose Kelly Group, (trading as Project Architects) Fleming Court, Fleming's Place, Dublin 4. By letter dated 13th February, 1996, the Architects in question withdrew the application.

Planning Application Register Ref. F96A/0072

On the 13th of February 1996, Project Architects, Fleming Court, Fleming Place, Ballsbridge applied for development on the lands described as Lot 2. The development was described as "*5 No. Industrial Dry Goods Warehouse Units, with associated offices comprising 4 No. 4, 555 sq. m. and 1 No. 2, 775 sq. m. each of which is capable to be sub-divided with a new access onto Jamestown Road, and associated drainage works.*" The application was made on behalf of Bovale Developments Limited A decision to grant Permission subject to 14 conditions was made on the 31st July 1996 by Sean Carey, Principal Officer of Fingal County Council to whom the appropriate powers had been delegated. Condition 11 of the decision in question required the omission of Unit 1 from the development in order to protect the residential amenity of the adjoining house. This condition was the subject of an appeal to An Bord Pleanála by *Bovale Limited* on the 26th August 1996. There was no appeal against the decision of Fingal County Council to grant the permission sought. On the 24th December 1996, An Bord Pleanála(who signed the decision) exercised the powers conferred on it by sub-Section 1 of Section 15 of the Local Government (Planning & Development) 1992 and directed Fingal County Council to amend condition 11 so that it should be as follows for the reason set out hereunder: -

> "Schedule
> Block number one shall be constructed and located in accordance with revised plans S241-001A, S241-002A, S241-008A and S241-007A received by An Bord Pleanála on the 29th day of August, 1996. The planted buffer strip shall maintain a depth of 15 metres around the entire boundary to the bungalow.
>
> Reason: In the interest of the amenities of the adjoining bungalow."

The grant of Planning Permission incorporating the amended Condition No. 11 issued on the 11th day of August 1997.

Planning Application Register Ref. F97A/1045

This was an application by Project Architects, on behalf of Bovale Developments Limited for permission for an electrical substation. The application was lodged on the 5th December 1997 and permission was granted on the 7th April 1998 subject to two conditions.

Planning Application Register Ref. F98A/0546

This was an application on behalf of "Thomas Curry & Sons Limited" for permission for the erection of two no. advertising signs to a previously approved warehouse unit (F96A/0072) Permission was granted on the 10th September 1998.

Planning Application Register Ref. F98A/0690

An application on behalf of Bovale Developments Limited was made by Project Architects for retention of alterations to layouts and elevation treatment previously approved under grant of permission 96A/0072. Permission was granted on 17th November 1998.

Planning Application Register Ref. F98A/1189

Application on behalf of Bovale Developments Limited by Project Architects for retention of alterations to previously approved block 4 and 5 (F96A/0072). The application was received on the 18th November 1998 and permission was granted on the 24th February 1999. The foregoing represents the position in the Planning Register maintained by Fingal County Council up to the 1st February 2000.

Paragraph A.3. Resolutions, Application or Requests. Paragraph A.3 (a) – (g) of the Terms of Reference. Whether these lands at Jamestown Road Finglas referred to in the letter dated the 8th June, 1989 were the subject of the following matters as set out in paragraph A.3 (a)-(g) of the Terms of Reference

A.3. (a) whether the lands were subject to rezoning resolutions

This has already been dealt with same at paragraph A.2.(c)(ii) above.

A.3(b) whether the lands were the subject of resolutions for material contravention of the relevant Development Plan

This has already been dealt with same at paragraph A.2. (c)(iii) above.

A.3(c) whether the lands were the subject of an application for special tax designation status

This site was not the subject of any special tax designation status pursuant to the Finance Acts.

A.3(d) whether the lands were the subject matter of applications for planning permission

This has already been dealt with this at paragraph *A.2.(c)(iii)* above.

A.3(e) whether the lands were subject to changes made or requested to be made with regard to the servicing of the lands for development

No changes were made or requested to be made in respect of this site.

A.3(f) whether the lands were subject to applications for building byelaw approval in respect of buildings constructed on the lands

There were no such applications.

A.3(g) whether the lands were subject to applications for fire safety certificates

Application Ref. 97/4178 – Block 1, Jamestown Road. Industrial Unit with ancillary Office accommodation.
Fire Safety Certificate granted to Bovale Limited on the 2nd September 1997.
Application Ref. 97/4182 – Block 2, Jamestown Road. Industrial Unit with ancillary office accommodation.
Fire Safety Certificate granted to Bovale Limited on the 24th September 1997.
Application Ref. 97/4186 – Block 3, Jamestown Road. Industrial Unit with ancillary office accommodation.
Fire Safety Certificate granted to Bovale Limited on the 24th September 1997.
Application Ref. 98/4241 – Block 4, Mygan Industrial Park by Project Architects for Bovale Limited.
Fire Safety Certificate granted to Bovale Limited on 22nd December 1998.
Application Ref. 98/4242 – Block 5, Mygan Industrial Park by Project Architects for Bovale Limited
Fire Safety Certificate granted to Bovale Limited on the 24th September 1997.

Paragraph A.3.(i). of the Amended Terms of Reference namely to ascertain the identity of any persons or companies (and if companies, the identity of the beneficial owners of such companies) who had a material interest in the said lands or who had a material involvement in the matters aforesaid;

The identity of the Beneficial Owners of the property as of 8th June 1989 together with changes in the Beneficial Ownership between then and the development of the lands has been established at paragraph

A.1. above. The Beneficial Ownership as of the 8th June 1989 as defined in the Tribunals interpretation of its terms of reference on the 21st October 1998 rested with Mr. Joseph Murphy Senior.

Paragraph A. 3. (ii) of the Amended Terms of Reference namely to ascertain the identity of any members of the Oireachtas, past or present, and/or members of the relevant local authorities who were involved directly or indirectly in any of the foregoing matters whether by the making of representations to a planning authority or to any person in the authority in a position to make relevant decisions or by the proposing of or by voting in favour or against or by abstaining from any such resolutions or by absenting themselves when such votes were taken or by attempting to influence in any manner whatsoever the outcome of any such applications, or who received payments from any of the persons or companies referred to at (i) above

Other than the members of the Oireachtas and the Local Authorities referred to above the Tribunal at this time is unable to pronounce further on this term of reference.

Paragraph A. 3. (iv) of the Amended Terms of Reference namely to ascertain and report on the outcome of all such applications, resolutions and votes in relation to such applications in the relevant local authority;

The outcome of all applications, resolutions and votes are detailed above under paragraph A. 2 (c) (i) to (iii) inclusive and A 3 (a) to (g) inclusive.

LOT 3.

PARAGRAPH A.1.

IDENTIFICATION AND OWNERSHIP

100 acres (approx.) at Poppintree, Ballymun

Identification as of 8th June 1989

(a)   The lands comprised in Folio 6262F of the Register County of Dublin, which are lands situate in the Townland of Poppintree and Barony of Coolock, in the County of Dublin, comprising 1.619 hectares or 4.000549 acres.

(b)   The lands comprised in Folio 577 of the Register County of Dublin, situate in the Townlands of Poppintree and Barony of Coolock, comprising 33.455 hectares or 82.66731 acres.

Beneficial Ownership as of 8th June 1989

Folio 6262F of the Register County of Dublin. (Poppintree House and 4 acres)
The full registered owner of the lands comprised in Folio 6262F of the Register County of Dublin was **O'Shea and Shanahan Limited** having its registered office at Quarry House, Ballygall Road East, in the City of Dublin. There was nothing on the folio by way of inhibition or caution.

Folio 577 of the Register County of Dublin. (Balance of Lot 3 – excluding Poppintree House &4 acres – 83 acres)
The full registered owner of the lands comprised in Folio 577 of the Register County of Dublin as of the 8th of June 1989 was **The Grafton Construction Company Limited**, having its registered office at Stephen's Court, 18-21 St. Stephen's Green, in the City of Dublin. Grafton Construction Company Limited had been registered as owner on the 25th of November 1976.There is an entry on Folio 577 dated the 8th of June 1944 which inhibited dealings by the registered owner of the property until notice was served on the solicitor's office of the Royal Bank of Ireland Limited, Foster Place, in the City of Dublin (later The Governor and Company of the Bank of Ireland). This entry was cancelled on the 26th of February 1992. It does not appear that this inhibition could have referred to the ownership of The Grafton Construction Company Limited, which only became full registered owner of the property in 1976. Other than the inhibition referred to above, there is no caution or inhibition registered on Folio 577.

Change in Beneficial Ownership since 8th June 1989 and prior to their development.

Folio 6262F of the Register County of Dublin

(A) On the 25th of October 1989, **The Grafton Construction Company Limited** became registered owner of the lands comprised in Folio 6262F of the Register County of Dublin. (Poppintree house having been bought back from O'Shea and Shanahan). **Bovale Developments Limited** acquired the lands comprised in Folio 6262F of the Register County of Dublin and 577 of the Register County of Dublin on foot of the Composite Indenture referred to above, the Grafton Construction Company Limited being a party thereto as therein set out.
(B) On the 26th of February 1992, **Bovale Developments Limited** was registered as full owner of the lands comprised in Folio 6262F. The Land Certificate was issued to Alfred Thornton Solicitors, Bank of Ireland, 2 College Green, in the City of Dublin, on the 10th of March 1992. (Bovale accordingly remains owner of 6262F – Poppintree House and 4 acres)

Folio 577 of the Register County of Dublin. (the 83 acres)

From the 25th of November 1976 to the 26th of February 1992, **The Grafton Construction Company Limited** was the registered owner of the lands comprised in Folio 577 of the Register County of Dublin. From the 26th of November 1992 to the 17th of February 1994, **Bovale Developments Limited** was registered owner of all of the lands comprised in Folio 577 of the Register County of Dublin. On the 17th of February 1994, the **County Council of the County of Dublin** became registered as full owner of a portion of the lands previously comprised in Folio 577 of the Register County of Dublin, in relation to the construction of the **M50 motorway**. The lands thus compulsorily acquired by the County Council of the County of Dublin are now comprised in Folio 99886FF of the Register County of Dublin, as referred to in Lot 1 above.

The balance of the lands comprised in Folio 577 of the Register County of Dublin remains in the registered ownership of **Bovale Developments Limited.** Other than the construction of the M50 motorway on the lands acquired compulsorily by the County Council of the County of Dublin, there has been no development of the lands comprised in Folios 6262F and 577 of the Register County of Dublin. In respect of Lot 3, Messrs. Smith Foy & Partners solicitors have confirmed that the County Council agreed, as part of the transaction for the compulsory acquisition of portion of Folio 577, to transfer back to Bovale an area, marked green on the map attached to the correspondence. Fingal County Council has confirmed this to be the case also.

Paragraph A. 2. Planning History

The land Registry map dated the 5th January 1998 attached to Folio 577 shows an area measuring approximately 25 hectares (61 acres approximately) lying south of the M50 Motorway while the area is stated on the Folio as 33.455 hectares (83 acres approximately). The Tribunal concluded that the stated area of 33.455 hectares (83 acres approximately) includes lands which were acquired by the County Council for the construction of the M50 Motorway and also includes lands to the north of the M50 Motorway and which are shown on the copy of the land registry map dated 18th August 1993 for Folio 577.

The site is divided by St. Margaret's Road, which runs through it in an east/west direction. The area north of St. Margaret's Road measuring 7.1 hectares (17.54 acres) has been in the administrative area of Fingal County Council since the 1st of January 1994. Prior to that date, it was in the administrative area of Dublin County Council. The area south of St. Margaret's Road measuring 17.4 hectares (42.9 acres) has been in the administrative area of Dublin Corporation since 1986. Of the 17.4 hectares (42.9 acres) which has been in the functional area of Dublin Corporation since 1986, 15.8 hectares (38.9 acres) are registered on Folio 577 and 1.6 hectares (4 acres) are registered on Folio 6262F. The Tribunal considered it expedient to deal with the planning history of Lot 3 in two parts:-

Lands in the functional area of Fingal County Council being lands **North** of St. Margaret's Road.
Lands in the functional area of Dublin Corporation being lands **South** of St. Margaret's Road.

Lands in the Functional Area of Fingal County Council being Lands North of St. Margaret's Road.

Paragraph A.2 (a) of the Terms of Reference namely the planning status of these lands in the Development Plan of the Dublin Local Authorities current at the 8th June 1989.

In the 1972 Dublin County Development Plan, these lands were zoned "P" (*to provide for the further development of agriculture*). In the 1983 Dublin County Development Plan, the lands were zoned "B" (*to protect and provide for the development of agriculture*). On the 8th June 1989, the lands were still zoned "B." In the 1990 Dublin County Draft Development Plan (as proposed by Manager), it was proposed that the lands north of the motorway would retain a "B" zoning – that is "*to protect and provide for the development of agriculture*" apart from a small portion in the eastern section of the site which was proposed to be zoned "F." The lands south of the motorway and north of St. Margaret's Road were proposed to be zoned "F" "*to preserve and provide for open space and recreational amenities.*"

In the 1991 Draft Dublin County Development Plan, the lands north of the M50 were shown with a proposed "B" zoning and a small portion zoned "F" – "*to preserve and provide for open space and recreational amenities.*" Lands south of the M50 and north of St. Margaret's Road were proposed as "F." In 1993, the elected members proposed an amendment to the 1991 County Draft Development Plan and proposed to change the zoning of the lands south of the M50 and north of St. Margaret's Road from "F" (*to preserve and provide for open space and recreational amenities*) to "E" (*to provide for industrial and related uses*). In the 1993 Dublin County Development Plan which was adopted by the elected members in December 1993, the lands south of the M50 and north of St. Margaret's Road were zoned "E" (*to provide for industrial and related uses*). The lands north of the M50 remained zoned "B" (*agricultural*) and the small portion in the eastern corner remained zoned "F" – "*to preserve and provide for open space and recreational amenities.*"

In VARIATION NO. 11 of the 1993 Development Plan made by Fingal County Council in March 1998, the lands south of the M50 and north of St. Margaret's Road were re-zoned from "E" (*to provide for industrial and related uses*) to "H" (*to provide for creation and protection of enterprise and facilitate opportunities for employment creation*). This variation was as a result of a designation of the lands pursuant to the 1997 Finance Act and to facilitate future development of the lands as envisaged by that Act.

In the 1998 Fingal County Council Draft Development Plan, it was proposed that the zoning of the lands south of the M50 and north of St. Margaret's Road be changed from "H" (*to provide for creation and protection of enterprise and facilitate opportunities for employment creation*) to "A1" (*to provide for new residential communities in accordance with approved action area plans and subject to the provision of the necessary social and physical infrastructure*) and the lands north of the M50 were proposed to be zoned M.U.1. (*to provide for an appropriate and compatible mixture of uses in accordance with approved action plans and subject to the provision of the necessary infrastructure*) and a small portion in the eastern section of the site was zoned "F" (*to preserve and provide for open space and recreational amenities*). In the 1999 Fingal County Development Plan adopted on the 19th day of October 1999 by the elected members of Fingal County Council, the lands south of the M50 and north of St. Margaret's Road were zoned "A1" and the lands north of the M50 were zoned "B" (*agricultural*) with an objective to carry out a major study of the long term development of the area outlined in grey and hatched and the small portion in the eastern corner were zoned "F" (*to preserve and provide for open space and recreational amenities*).

Paragraph A.2 (b) of the Terms of Reference. The position regarding the servicing of that portion of Lot 3 north of St. Margaret's Road and in the administrative area of Dublin County Council at the 8th June 1989

Foul sewer

The southeast boundary of these lands borders on to lands, which had been developed by Dublin Corporation for public housing purposes. The infrastructure was not designed to cater for upstream lands of the acreage under consideration. The outfall for the drainage is into Dublin Corporation's Ballymun system. There was no drainage agreement with Dublin Corporation to allow for the expansion of the drainage system to cater for these upstream private lands. Without an acceptable drainage agreement with the Dublin Corporation for the drainage of these lands a proposal for the development of these lands would have been recommended for refusal.

Surface water

These lands lie in the catchment of streams, which drain into Dublin Corporation area. Any proposal to drain these lands would have been subject to an assessment of the increased flows and the impact of these flows within the Dublin Corporation area. An adverse report from the Dublin Corporation drainage division would have resulted in a recommendation for refusal.

Water supply

The extent to which water would be available to these land would be subject to working pressures current at the time and the elevation of the site. The supply to the lands north of County boundary would be problematical. The position in relation to the servicing of the lands in question has remained unchanged although they are lands, which will be drained in due course when the Northern Fringe Sewer is commissioned in approximately 2002.

Paragraph A.2(c)(i) of the Terms of Reference. Changes made or proposed to be made to the 8th June 1989 planning status of the lands by way of proposals put forward by Dublin Local Authority officials pursuant to a review of Development Plans or otherwise

No such proposals were made by officials of Dublin County Council or Fingal County Council save the variation proposed post the passing of the Finance Act 1997 which is referred to hereunder and the change to residential zoning in the 1998 Fingal Development Plan. The lands remained zoned "E" (*to provide for industrial and related uses*) from December 1993. However, under the Finance Act 1977 certain tax relief was granted in respect of those lands, which were designated as an enterprise area – see 10th Schedule to the Act – which describes the lands as "Finglas Enterprise Area." Arising from this designation, the

Council was of the view that the "E" zoning of the lands was not appropriate for an enterprise area and the Council therefore decided to initiate a variation procedure to change the zoning from "E" (*to provide for industrial and related uses*) to a new zoning objective "H" (*to provide for creation and protection of enterprise and facilitate opportunities for employment creation*). This draft variation was on public display from the 15th October 1997 to the 16th January 1998 and was subsequently made at a meeting of Fingal County Council held on the 16th day of March 1998. In the 1998 Draft Fingal Development Plan, the zoning of the lands was proposed to be changed from "H" to "A1" (residential) and the residential zoning was confirmed by the members in the 1999 Development Plan.

A-94 Paragraph A.2(c)(ii) of the Terms of Reference. Changes made or proposed to be made to the 8th of June 1989 planning status of the lands by way of motions by elected members of the Dublin Local Authorities proposing re-zoning

Motions by elected members of the Dublin Local Authorities proposing rezoning

In January 1991 Garth May, a planning consultant, made an application to Dublin County Council for the re-zoning of lands at Finglas/Poppintree on behalf of Bovale Developments Limited This application related to three sites – one being east of the North Road at Charlestown, Finglas, the second at Jamestown Road, and the third located south of the revised route for the Northern Cross Motorway at Poppintree.

Three plans accompanied the application (plan 1, plan2, plan3) the location of the three sites being shown on plan job/drg. No. 76/03 entitled "*application for re-zoning Finglas/Poppintree for Bovale Developments.*" On the said map Mr. May indicated that approximately 20 acres of Bovale lands were affected by the Northern Cross Motorway and that the land, the subject of the application for re-zoning, was approximately 75 acres.

By letter dated 18th November 1991 Mr. May requested that his submission made in January 1991 be accepted as an objection/representation to the 1991 Draft Development Plan (then on public display) together with supplementary information contained in his letter of the 18th November. This submission was given the reference number 000166.

At a special meeting of the Council on the 19th March 1993, held to consider representations received during the public display of the 1991 Draft Development Plan, a number of motions were proposed in relation to representation 000166 made on behalf of Bovale Developments Limited The first motion - (ref 12 (2)(A)(i)) - related to lands at Charlestown and has been dealt with in relation to Lot 1 above.

A further motion - (ref 12(A)(iii)) - related to lands at Jamestown Little and has been dealt with in relation to Lot 2 above. The following motion (in relation to the part of Lot 3) between the M50 and St. Margaret's Road signed by Councillors Devitt, Gallagher and Gilbride was proposed by Councillor Gallagher seconded by Councillor Devitt (Ref. 12(2), (a), (ii): -

> "*Dublin County Council hereby resolves that the lands at Poppintree, Finglas outlined in red on the attached map comprising about 19.69 acres and which has been signed for identification purposes by the proposer and seconder of this motion, be zoned industrial in the draft review of the County Dublin Development Plan.*"

The Manager's report quoted in relation to the site at Charlestown (Lot 1, Folio 7462) refers to this site also – Lot 3 - but part of it is quoted here again for ease of reference: -

> "Paragraph 3.2.8 of the Draft Plan provides for the principle of development for lands south of the Northern Cross Route.
>
> The lack of drainage facilities remains the major constraint and it is unlikely to be resolved until the proposed drainage scheme for the North City Fringe is put in place. In the absence of firm proposals to drain the lands, zoning for additional development would not be appropriate.
>
> It is recommended that the Draft Plan should not be changed."

The motion was passed by 37 votes in favour and 13 against. The names voting for and against are as follows: -

For: Councillors S. Barrett, S. Brock, L. Butler, B. Cass, R. Conroy, L.T. Cosgrave, M.J. Cosgrave, A. Devitt, M. Elliott, M. Farrell, T. Fox, C. Gallagher, S. Gilbride, T. Hand, F. Hanrahan, C. Keane, M. Kennedy, J. Larkin, L. Lohan, D. Lydon, M. McGennis, C. McGrath, D.

Marren, T. Matthews, 0. Mitchell, T. Morrissey, M. Muldoon, C. O'Connor, J. O'Halloran, A. Ormonde, N. Owen, C. Quinn, T. Ridge, M. Ryan, S. Terry, C. Tyndall, G.V. Wright.

Against: Councillors M. Billane, F. Buckley,, L. Gordon, D. Healy, J. Higgins, T. Kelleher, S. Laing, S. Misteil, D. O'Callaghan, G. O'Connell, S. Ryan, D. Tipping, E. Walsh.
This decision of the members to amend the draft plan to zone the lands to industrial zoning was put on public display for the statutory one-month period as a proposed amendment to the Draft Plan (Change 5, Map 11).
On the 7th October 1993 the proposed amendment was considered at a meeting of the Council when the Manager recommended that the amendment be deleted.

It was proposed by Councillor Healy, seconded by Councillor Sargent *"That Change 5 on Map 11 be deleted."* The effect of this motion, if passed, would be to retain the "B" (agricultural) zoning of the northern portion of Lot 3 in the functional area of Fingal County Council. The motion was put and on a show of hands the voting was 13 in favour, 34 against and 1 abstention. The proposed amendment was then confirmed and the site between the M50 and St. Margaret's Road was zoned for industry in the 1993 Dublin County Development Plan.

Paragraph A.2(c)(iii) of the Terms of Reference. Changes made or proposed to be made to the 8th of June 1989 planning status of the lands by way of applications for planning permission (including any involving a material contravention of the Development Plan);

Material contraventions

No planning permission was granted which materially contravened the zoning of these lands.

Planning permissions

There were no such applications.

Paragraph A.3. Resolutions, Applications or Requests. Paragraph A.3 (a) – (g) of the Terms of Reference. Whether the lands in Lot 3 in the functional area of Fingal County Council being the lands North of St. Margaret's Road were the subject of any of the resolutions, applications or requests referred to in paragraph A.3 (a) – (g) of the Terms of Reference

A.3 (a)- whether the lands were subject to rezoning resolutions

The Tribunal has already dealt with this at paragraph A.2. (c)(ii) above.

A.3.(b) whether the lands were the subject of resolutions for material contravention of the relevant Development Plan

The Tribunal has dealt with this at paragraph A.2.(c)(iii) above.

A.3.(c) whether the lands were the subject of an application for special tax designation status pursuant to the Finance Acts

Designated as the Fingal Enterprise Area in the 10th Schedule to the Finance Act 1997. The termination date for the area designated under the Act was changed from 30th June 2000 to the 31st December 1999 except where there was a genuine delay due to planning or other reasons when an extra year was allowed for all projects at a significant stage of the development as of the 31st December 1999. The lands, despite their zoning and tax designation, were not developed because of a serious drainage problem which relied for its solution on the construction of the North Fringe Sewer, due to be finalised in 2001

A.3.(d) whether the lands were the subject matter of applications for planning permission

The Tribunal has dealt with this at paragraph A.2.(c)(iii) above.

A.3.(e) changes made or requested to be made with regard to the servicing of the lands for development

No changes were made or requested to be made in respect of this site.

***A.3.(f) Applications for building bye-law approval** in respect of buildings constructed on the lands*

There were no such applications.

A.3.(g) Applications for fire safety certificates

There were no applications for fire safety certificates.

Paragraph A.3.(i). of the Amended Terms of Reference namely to ascertain the identity of any persons or companies (and if companies, the identity of the beneficial owners of such companies) who had a material interest in the said lands or who had a material involvement in the matters aforesaid;

The identity of the Beneficial Owners of the property as of 8th June 1989 together with changes in the Beneficial Ownership between then and the development of the lands has been established at paragraph A.1. above. The Beneficial Ownership as of the 8th June 1989 as defined in the Tribunals interpretation of its terms of reference on the 21st October 1998 rested with Mr. Joseph Murphy Senior.

Paragraph A. 3. (ii) of the Amended Terms of Reference namely to ascertain the identity of any members of the Oireachtas, past or present, and/or members of the relevant local authorities who were involved directly or indirectly in any of the foregoing matters whether by the making of representations to a planning authority or to any person in the authority in a position to make relevant decisions or by the proposing of or by voting in favour or against or by abstaining from any such resolutions or by absenting themselves when such votes were taken or by attempting to influence in any manner whatsoever the outcome of any such applications, or who received payments from any of the persons or companies referred to at (i) above

Other than the members of the Oireachtas and the Local Authorities referred to above the Tribunal at this time is unable to pronounce further on this term of reference.

Paragraph A. 3. (iv) of the Amended Terms of Reference namely to ascertain and report on the outcome of all such applications, resolutions and votes in relation to such applications in the relevant local authority;

The outcome of all applications, resolutions and votes are detailed above under paragraph A. 2 (c) (i) to (iii) inclusive and A 3 (a) to (g) inclusive.

LANDS IN THE FUNCTIONAL AREA OF DUBLIN CORPORATION BEING LANDS SOUTH OF ST. MARGARET'S ROAD

The southern portion of Lot 3 measures 17.4 hectares (42.9 acres) approximately.   These lands are comprised in Folio 577 and Folio 6262F, the latter being Poppintree House. It should be noted that this part of Lot 3 was in the functional area of Dublin County Council until 1985 when it was transferred to the functional area of Dublin Corporation.

Paragraph A.2 (a) of the Terms of Reference namely the planning status of these lands in the Development Plan of the Dublin Local Authorities current at the 8th June 1989

In the 1972 Dublin County Development Plan, part of the lands were zoned "R" (*to preserve open space amenity*) and part was zoned "P" (*to provide for the further development of agriculture*). In the 1983 Dublin County Development Plan part of the lands were zoned "F" (*to preserve and provide for open space and recreational amenity*) and part was zoned "B" (*agriculture*). In the 1987 Draft Dublin City Development Plan it was proposed that the bulk of the lands would be zoned "L" (*to protect and provide for agricultural development*) and that a small portion at the southern boundary of the site would be zoned "G" (*to provide for general industrial use*). On the 8th of June 1989, the zoning of the 1983 Dublin County Development Plan still applied.   The lands were zoned partly "F" (*open space*) and partly "B" (*agriculture*).

In the 1991 Dublin City Development Plan the bulk of the lands was zoned "L" (*agriculture*) and a small portion at the southern boundary of the lands was zoned "G" (*general industrial use*). Following the designation of the lands in Lot 3 under the provisions of the 1997 Finance Act, the zoning of a major portion of the lands "(i.e. the part of the lands which had been zoned "L" (*Agriculture*))" was changed by Dublin Corporation from the zoning shown in the 1991 Dublin City Development Plan to an "E1" zoning (*to provide for the creation and protection of enterprise and facilitate opportunities for employment creation*). This change was made by a 1998 variation (No. 3) to the 1991 Dublin City Development Plan and was made on the 5ᵗʰ January 1998. The variation was made for the same reasons as the variation initiated by Fingal County Council as referred to above. The balance of the lands, being a small portion to the south-east of the site, remained zoned "G" (*general industrial use*). In the 1999 Dublin City Development Plan, the zoning of the major portion of the site was changed from "E1" and "G" to "Z1" (*to protect, provide and improve residential amenities*) and a small portion at the eastern side of the site was zoned "Z15" to provide for institutional and community uses.

Paragraph A.2 (b) of the Terms of Reference. The position regarding the servicing of the lands for development as at the 8ᵗʰ June 1989

Foul sewer, surface water and water supply

No services have been provided by the Water Division to this site. No written correspondence was received by the Council in relation to the Poppintree site. There may have been verbal inquiries about this site over the years, however, the relevant division of the Council would have advised in such cases that the land in question fell outside the area currently drained by the North Dublin Drainage Area and, no additional capacity existed in the Corporation drainage system. Any proposed development of this site, or indeed any lands in the North Fringe Area, would be dependent on the provision of new sewerage infrastructure.

Paragraph A.2(c)(i) of the Terms of Reference. Changes made or proposed to be made to the 8ᵗʰ June 1989 planning status of the lands by way of proposals put forward by Dublin Local Authority officials pursuant to a review of Development Plans or otherwise

No such proposals were made by officials of Dublin Corporation. However, under the Finance Act 1977, certain tax relief was granted in respect of those lands which were designated as an enterprise area – See 10ᵗʰ Schedule to the Act – which describes the lands as "Finglas Enterprise Area." Arising from this designation, Dublin Corporation were of the view that the zoning of the lands was not appropriate for an enterprise area and Dublin Corporation therefore decided to initiate a variation procedure to change the zoning to an "E1" zoning (*to provide for the creation and protection of enterprise and to facilitate opportunities for employment creation*). This change was made by a 1998 variation (No.3) to the 1991 Dublin City Development Plan and was made on the 5ᵗʰ of January 1998. This new zoning affected a major portion of the lands in the functional area of Dublin Corporation being primarily the lands, which had previously been, zoned "L" (*agriculture*). The balance of the lands, being a small portion to the south east of the site remained zoned "G." (*General Industrial use*).

Paragraph A.2(c)(ii) of the Terms of Reference. Changes made or proposed to be made to the 8ᵗʰ of June 1989 planning status of the lands by way of motions by elected members of the Dublin Local Authorities proposing re-zoning

No such motions were proposed.

Paragraph A.2(c)(iii) of the Terms of Reference. Changes made or proposed to be made to the 8ᵗʰ of June 1989 planning status of the lands by way of applications for planning permission (including any involving a material contravention of the Development Plan)

Material contraventions

No planning permission was granted which materially contravened the zoning of these lands, and no such permission was granted while the area was within the functional area of Dublin County Council.

Planning applications

While the site was within the functional area of Dublin County Council, the following application was made: -

Planning Application Register Ref. T/224

This application was submitted by Sean Cleary, Parkview, Kilkenny, on behalf of Charles Gallagher Limited, Inisfree, Nashville Park, Howth for permission for 12 no. houses. Permission was granted on 19th of May, 1980 subject to 12 no. conditions.

A-104 Paragraph A.3. Resolutions, Applications or Requests. Paragraph A.3(a) – (g) of the Terms of Reference. Whether the lands in Lot 3 in the functional area of Dublin Corporation being the lands south of St. Margaret's Road were the subject of any of the resolutions, applications or requests referred to in paragraph A.3(a) – (g) of the Terms of Reference

A.3(a)- whether the lands were subject to rezoning resolutions

This has already been dealt with same at paragraph A.2.(c)(ii) above.

A.3.(b) whether the lands were the subject of resolutions for material contravention of the relevant Development Plan

This has already been dealt with at paragraph A.2.(c)(iii) above.

A.3.(c) whether the lands were the subject of an application for special tax designation status

These lands were designated as the Fingal Enterprise Area in the 10th Schedule to the Finance Act 1997. The termination date for the area designated under the Act was changed from 30th June 2000 to the 31st December 1999 except where there was a genuine delay due to planning or other reasons when an extra year was allowed for all projects at a significant stage of the development as of the 31st December 1999. The lands, despite their zoning and tax designation, were not developed because of a serious drainage problem which relied for its solution on the construction of the North Fringe Sewer, due to be finalised in 2001.

Paragraph A.3.(i). of the Amended Terms of Reference namely to ascertain the identity of any persons or companies (and if companies, the identity of the beneficial owners of such companies) who had a material interest in the said lands or who had a material involvement in the matters aforesaid;

The identity of the Beneficial Owners of the property as of 8th June 1989 together with changes in the Beneficial Ownership between then and the development of the lands has been established at paragraph A.1. above. The Beneficial Ownership as of the 8th June 1989 as defined in the Tribunals interpretation of its terms of reference on the 21st October 1998 rested with Mr. Joseph Murphy Senior.

Paragraph A. 3. (ii) of the Amended Terms of Reference namely to ascertain the identity of any members of the Oireachtas, past or present, and/or members of the relevant local authorities who were involved directly or indirectly in any of the foregoing matters whether by the making of representations to a planning authority or to any person in the authority in a position to make relevant decisions or by the proposing of or by voting in favour or against or by abstaining from any such resolutions or by absenting themselves when such votes were taken or by attempting to influence in any manner whatsoever the outcome of any such applications, or who received payments from any of the persons or companies referred to at (i) above

Other than the members of the Oireachtas and the Local Authorities referred to above the Tribunal at this time is unable to pronounce further on this term of reference.

Paragraph A. 3. (iv) of the Amended Terms of Reference namely to ascertain and report on the outcome of all such applications, resolutions and votes in relation to such applications in the relevant local authority;

The outcome of all applications, resolutions and votes are detailed above under paragraph A. 2 (c) (i) to (iii) inclusive and A 3 (a) to (g) inclusive.

LOT 4.

PARAGRAPH A.I.

IDENTIFICATION AND OWNERSHIP

Identification and Ownership

255 acres (approx.) at Donabate (Turvey House and Beaverton House)."
Identification as of 8th June 1989
The lands comprised in Lot 4 are partly registered lands and partly unregistered lands. The registered portion of Lot 4 were lands in the Townland of Beaverstown, Barony of Nethercross, in the County of Dublin, and were comprised in Folio 4327 of the Register County of Dublin, comprising 29.438 hectares or 72.7413 acres; and the unregistered portion of which were lands at Turvey, Donabate comprising an area of one hundred and fifty-three acres one rood and thirty-seven perches or thereabouts as identified in a Deed of Conveyance of the 31st July, 1969, details of which are set out below.

Beneficial ownership as of the 8th June 1989

Helmdale limited was the full registered owner of the lands comprised in Folio 4327 of the Register County of Dublin, being lands situate in the Townland of Beaverstown, Barony of Nethercross, in the County of Dublin, comprising 29.438 hectares or 72.7413 acres. Helmdale Limited was a company registered in the Isle of Man and had its registered office at PO Box 23,28 Victoria Street Douglas Isle of Man. In relation to the unregistered land in Lot 4, as of the 8th of June 1989, the lands were in the ownership of a company known as **Turvey Estates Limited**, having its registered office at Charter House, 5 Pembroke Road, in the City of Dublin, pursuant to a Deed of Conveyance dated the 31st of July 1969 and made between LIVESTOCK AND ESTATE LIMITED of the first part, C. RUSSELL MURPHY of the second part, GRUNO SHIPPING LIMITED of the third part, ULSTER BANK LIMITED of the fourth part, the CEMENTATION COMPANY LIMITED of the fifth part, WILLIAM FANAGAN LIMITED of the sixth part and TURVEY ESTATES LIMITED of the seventh part.

The lands were described in the said Conveyance as "ALL THAT part of the lands of Turvey containing one hundred and fifty-three acres one rood and thirty-seven perches or thereabouts Statute Measure with the residence known as Turvey House and out offices thereon in the Barony of Nethercross and County of Dublin being the lands edged red on the map or plan," annexed to the Conveyance.

Changes in Beneficial Ownership since the 8th June 1989 and prior to their Development

Folio 4327

By Transfer dated the 12th of September 1991, the date of the Composite Indenture, and made between Helmdale Limited of the one part and Bovale Developments Limited of the other part, the lands comprised in Folio 4327 were assured to Bovale Developments Limited and on the 3rd of March 1992. Bovale Developments Limited, having its registered office at 59 Fitzwilliam Square, in the City of Dublin, became registered owner of the lands comprised in Folio 4327 of the Register County of Dublin. Since then there have been the following dispositions of the registered lands comprised in Folio 4327 .

Portion of the lands comprised in Folio 4327 of the Register County of Dublin was transferred to Brendan Kinane (Company Director), Turvey Avenue, Donabate, in the County of Dublin and Denis Kinane (Company Director), Turvey Avenue, Donabate, in the County of Dublin, by Bovale Developments Limited.

Brendan Kinane and Denis Kinane became registered as owners of the lands transferred to them on the 4th of May 1993 and upon becoming registered owners the relevant portion of the lands comprised in Folio 4327 of the Register County of Dublin was transferred to Folio 92339 of the Register County of Dublin. Denis Kinane and Brendan Kinane remain the registered owners of Folio 92339. These lands have not been developed..

Also on the 4th of May 1993 **Oakston Property Company Limited**, having its registered office at 47 Hardwicke Street, in the City of Dublin, became full owner of the remainder of the lands comprised in Folio 4327 of the Register County of Dublin. It would appear that in or around the years 1995/1996, Oakston Property Company Limited commenced developing the said lands by erecting dwellings thereon and Folio 4327 lists as burdens a series of leases (forty-seven in number) which are all granted for terms of nine hundred and ninety-nine years subject to a yearly rent of £1.00, the covenants on the part of the lessee and the conditions therein contained.

Unregistered lands

On the 12th of September 1991, on foot of the Composite Indenture referred to above the unregistered lands comprised in Lot 4 held by Turvey Estates Limited, under the Conveyance dated the 31st of July 1969, were conveyed to Bovale Developments Limited. Turvey Estates Limited had been placed in liquidation on the 18th of December 1989 and the Liquidator joined in the Composite Indenture. There have been a number of dispositions affecting this land since 1991:

(i) By Deed of Conveyance dated the 16th of September 1993 and made between BOVALE DEVELOPMENTS LIMITED of the one part and BLANE TRADING LIMITED having its registered of at Derrygoan, Ballinamore, Co. Leitrim of the other part, portion of the lands as set out below were conveyed to Blane Trading Limited. The lands conveyed on foot of this Deed of Conveyance dated 16th of September 1993 are described as:

'ALL THAT AND THOSE that part of the lands of Turvey situate in the Barony of Nethercross and County of Dublin which for identification purposes only are delineated on the map annexed to the said conveyance and thereon edged in red comprising 48.840 hectares or thereabouts being part of the lands more particularly described in the Schedule of an Indenture of Conveyance made the 31st of July between Livestock and Estates Company Limited and others to Turvey Estates Limited and on the map annexed thereto and thereon edged in red held in fee simple subject with other property to an annual tithe rent charge of £8.16s.6 but primarily liable to an annual sum of £4.2s.11 part thereof and indemnified against the balance.'

(ii) By Deed of Conveyance dated the 16th of September 1993 and made between BOVALE DEVELOPMENTS LIMITED of the first part, BLANE TRADING LIMITED of the second part and MAINWELL LIMITED of having its registered office at High Street, Ballinamore, Co. Leitrim of the third part, a portion of the lands as set out below were conveyed by way of sub-sale to Mainwell Limited.

The lands conveyed in this Conveyance are described as:

'ALL THAT AND THOSE that part of the lands of Turvey situate in the Barony of Nethercross and County of Dublin which for identification purposes only are delineated on the map annexed to the said Conveyance and thereon edged in blue comprising 2.1496 hectares acres being part of the lands more particularly described in the Schedule of an Indenture of Conveyance made the 31st of July 1969 between Livestock and Estates Company Limited and others to Turvey Estates Limited and on the map thereto and thereon edged in red held in fee simple subject with other properties to an annual tithe rent charge of £8.16s.6 but primarily liable to any annual sum of £4.2s.11 part thereof and indemnified against the balance'.

Effectively, the site of the former Turvey House and about 5 acres around it were being conveyed to Mainwell Limited.

(iii) By Deed of Conveyance dated the 16th of October 1995 and made between BLANE TRADING LIMITED of the first part, MAINWELL LIMITED of the second part and BRETON

PROPERTIES LIMITED of Turvey Lane, Donabate, Co. Dublin of the third part Blane Trading Limited conveyed to Breton Properties the following lands:-

> 'ALL THAT AND THOSE part of the lands of Turvey situate in the Barony of Nethercross and County of Dublin as described and delineated on the map annexed to the Conveyance and thereon edged in red and shaded in red.'

Mainwell Limited on foot of the same Deed conveyed to Breton Properties Limited the following lands:-

> 'ALL THAT AND THOSE that part of the lands of Turvey, situate in the Barony of Nethercross and County of Dublin, adjoining the reserved lands, which said hatched lands are delineated on the map hereto and thereon coloured blue and hatched in black.'

Mainwell Limited on foot of the same Deed reserved to itself the following lands:-

> 'ALL THAT AND THOSE that part of the lands of Turvey situate in the Barony of Nethercross and County of Dublin as more particularly described and delineated on the map hereto and *thereon edged in red and hatched green and bounded on one boundary thereof by the hatched lands and on all other boundaries by the premises (that is to say the lands conveyed by Blane Trading Limited to Breton Properties Limited)."*

As of 16th October 1995, all but the site of former Turvey House and about 5 acres around it, are held by Breton Properties Limited.

(iv) A Deed of Rectification was executed on the 13th of November 1996. The parties to the Deed of Rectification were;

> TURVEY ESTATES LIMITED
> JOHN EDDISON (AS LIQUIDATOR OF TURVEY ESTATES LIMITED)
> BOVALE DEVELOPMENTS LIMITED
> BLANE TRADING LIMITED
> MAINWELL LIMITED
> BRETON PROPERTIES LIMITED

It was provided that this Deed was supplemental to the Composite Deed and that a doubt had arisen as to whether the Composite Deed was effective to assure to Bovale Developments Limited the lands thereby assured. The Deed of Rectification confirmed the above assurances of the unregistered Lot 4 lands, commencing with the Composite Indenture.

(v) By Deed of Conveyance dated the 5th of December 1997 and made between BRETON PROPERTIES LIMITED of the one part and CLODAREN DEVELOPMENTS LIMITED having its registered office at 15 Upper Fitzwilliam Street, Dublin 2 of the second part, a small portion of the lands conveyed to Breton Properties Limited on foot of the Deed of 16th October 1995 and the Deed of Rectification was conveyed to Clodaren Developments Limited. The property conveyed to Clodaren Developments Limited is described as:

> "ALL THAT part of the lands of Turvey situate in the Barony of Nethercross and County of Dublin as delineated on the map annexed to the said deed dated the 5th of December 1997 and thereon edged red."

The remaining lands retained by Breton Properties Limited have been developed as a golf course. The Tribunal received copy title documents, records of which were not in the Land Registry which evidence minor changes in the ownership of these lands in 1996.

(vi) By Deed of Conveyance dated 2nd August, 1996, Blane Trading Limited assured to Mainwell Limited the remaining lands at Turvey held by Blane Trading Limited. The lands thus assured were:-

> "ALL THAT AND THOSE that part of the lands at Turvey situate in the Barony of Nethercross and County of Dublin which are delineated on the map annexed hereto and shaded purple being part of the lands more particularly described in the Schedule of an Indenture of Conveyance dated May 31st July 1969 [that is the wording in the deed although the Tribunal believes "May" should read "the",] between Livestock and Estates Company Limited and others to Turvey Estates Limited and on the map thereto and thereon edged in red held in fee simple subject with other properties to an annual tithe rent charge of £8.16s.6 but primarily liable to any annual sum of £4.2s.11 part thereof and indemnified against the balance."

(vii) By Deed of Conveyance dated 31st May, 1996, between Mainwell Limited and Breton Properties Limited Mainwell Limited assured to Breton Properties Limited:-

> "ALL THAT AND THOSE that part or portions of the lands of Turvey situate in the Barony of Nethercross in the County of Dublin as described and delineated on the map" annexed to the Deed "and thereon edged in purple and marked with the letters "B" and "C", and Breton Properties Limited assumed to Mainwell Limited:-

>> "ALL THAT AND THOSE that part o the lands at Turvey situate in the barony of Nethercross and County of Dublin as described and delineated on the map annexed hereto and thereon edged in pink and marked with the letters "A" and "A1."

(viii) By Deed of Conveyance and Surrender dated 27th November, 1996, between Mainwell Limited and Breton Properties Limited, a deed which was said to be supplemental to the Deed between these parties of 16th October, 1995 referred to above, the parties exchanged, granted and surrendered various rights of way.

(iv) The small portion of land retained by Bovale Developments Limited was the subject matter of a contract dated the 2nd of April 1996 between BOVALE DEVELOPMENTS LIMITED of the one part and PATRICK CASSIDY of the other part. This contract was completed with a Deed of Conveyance to Beaver Investments Limited dated the 27th day of May 1996. Beaver Investments Limited appears, from the Land Registry records and correspondence, to continue to be the owner of these lands. It appears from correspondence the lands are undeveloped.

PARAGRAPH A.2. PLANNING HISTORY

These lands are described in the Schedule as being "255 acres (approx) at Donabate (Turvey House and Beaverton House)."
Part of the lands are registered on Folio 4327 County Dublin and extends to 29.438 hectares (72.7 acres) and part on Folio 92339F comprising approximately 3.25 hectares (8 acres). The balance of the lands are unregistered and extend to 61.75 hectares (152.6 acres). It appears that the total area is about 94 hectares (233 acres). The lands in question are situate to the east of the N1, north of Turvey Avenue and northwest of Donabate Village and are shown in part on map 5 of the 1993 County Development Plan and part on map 1A of that plan.

Paragraph A.2 (a) of the Terms of Reference namely the planning status of these lands in the Development Plan of the Dublin Local Authorities current at the 8th June 1989

The Development Plan current as of the 8th June 1989 was the 1983 Development Plan for the County of Dublin wherein these lands were zoned "B" *"to protect and provide for the development of agriculture."* In the 1972 Dublin County Development Plan, the lands comprised in Lot 4 were zoned "P" (*to provide for the further development of agriculture*). On the 8th of June 1989 the lands were still zoned "B" (*to protect and provide for the development of agriculture*). In the 1990 Draft Dublin County Development Plan, it was proposed that the lands would remain zoned "B" (*to protect and provide for the development of agriculture*). In the 1991 Draft Dublin County Development Plan which was put on public display for three months, the proposed zoning of the lands was shown as "B" (*to protect and provide for the development of agriculture*).

In 1993, after the first public display and before the second public display, a motion was passed by the Council resolving that 38 hectares (94 acres approx.) be re-zoned to "A1" (*to provide for a new residential community in accordance with approved action area plans*) and that Phase 1 (consisting of not more than 300 houses) be completed before Phase 2 commences. In the 1993 County Development Plan 18.42 hectares (45 acres) of Lot 4 were re-zoned "A1" (*to provide for new residential communities in accordance with approved action area plans*) and the balance of 76 hectares (188 acres approx.) remained zoned "B" (*to protect and provide for the development of agriculture*). In the 1999 Fingal County Development Plan, an additional 8 acres (approx.) of the lands of Folio 4327 was zoned "A1" and a site in the unregistered land on Turvey Avenue was re-zoned residential with the objective to provide a maximum 7 houses. The remainder of the unregistered land was zoned F (*to preserve and provide for open space and recreational amenity.*).

Paragraph A.2(b) of the Terms of Reference. The position regarding the servicing of the lands for development as at the 8th of June 1989

This area is partially located within the catchment of the Donabate Treatment plant, located to the south of Portrane Hospital. The catchment is divided into three main sub-catchments. The Donabate and the Burrow sub-catchments pump to the central catchment draining Portrane, which in turn is pumped to the treatment plant. The treatment plant had a design capacity of a population of 6,000 which remains unchanged. The overall foul system drained on the separate system but the operation of the treatment plant was effected by considerable combined flows (foul and surface water) which were generated within the Hospital system. This situation remains the same today.

In September 1986, a report was presented to the Dublin Fingal District Committee meeting of Dublin County Council. This report established that an estimated population of 3,768 drained to the treatment plant. In addition, planning permission existed for a population equivalent of 2,340 and planning appeals had been lodged in respect of a further population equivalent of 1,108. The combined total of these amounted to a population equivalent of 7,216.

The above population estimates were based on house counts assuming an existing and potential occupation of 4 persons per dwelling. These population estimates also included the population of the Hospital.

The area depicted has an area of 203.5 acres which would have had a potential population of 8,120, based on 10 houses per acre were these lands to be fully developed. Environment Services would have recommended that no permission be granted for this area pending the doubling of the treatment capacity of Donabate Treatment Plant. The adequacy of the gravity sewer, pumping station and rising main would also have been a constraining factor.

Surface water

Historically, the surface water system to which Donabate drains, both east and west of the Dublin Belfast Railway line is based on water retention for irrigation purposes rather than its rapid disposal to the Rogerstown Estuary. Two surface water pumping stations were utilised to control the water table. The drainage infrastructure consisted of wide, deep water-courses in canal-like form to provide storage. A pumping station on the east side of the Railway line pumped to a second pumping station on the west of the line, which pumped to the upper Rogerstown Estuary. During extreme weather conditions the area was subject to flooding and the minimum floor level for development was set at 7.5 metres above Ordinance Datum (OD)(Poolbeg).

In the late seventies/early eighties, the developer to the south-east of the site carried out works to the north, beyond his site through lands now occupied by Beaverstown Golf Club. This work consisted of deepening the water course which formed the main outfall. This allowed the pumping station on the west of the Railway to be removed. For this work, the developer was allowed offsets against development charges levied on his development and future development. The only constraint on development west of the Railway line in respect of surface water drainage would have been the requirement for finished floor levels to be a minimum of 7.5 metres above O.D.

Water supply

Water would have been available subject to the provision of an acceptable water main infrastructure.

Paragraph A.2(c)(i) of the Terms of Reference. Changes made or proposed to be made to the 8th June 1989 planning status of the lands by way of proposals put forward by Dublin Local Authority officials pursuant to a review of Development Plans or otherwise.

No such changes were made or proposed by Dublin Local Authority Officials save that an additional 8 acres were proposed by officials for residential zoning in the 1998 Draft Fingal County Development Plan, and is so zoned in the 1999 Fingal Development Plan and the unregistered land was proposed to be zoned "F" (to preserve and provide for open space and recreational amenities) in the 1998 Draft Fingal Plan.

A-118   Paragraph A.2(c)(i) of the Terms of Reference. Changes made or proposed to be made to the 8th June 1989 planning status of the lands by way of proposals put forward by Dublin Local Authority officials pursuant to a review of Development Plans or otherwise

During the three month display of the 1991 Draft County Dublin Development Plan, a representation was received from Allan S. Tomkins, Architect, on behalf of Bovale Developments Limited seeking to have the zoning of the lands shown on the map accompanying his letter, stated to be 72 acres approximately, zoned for residential use (Reference 000044). In his letter of the 26th November 1991 addressed to the Planning Department Mr. Tomkins said as follows:-

"Dear Sir,

Re: County Draft Development Plan 1991 – 72 acres approx. Beverton, Donabate for "Bovale Developments Limited"

On behalf of my clients, I wish to make representations and list these below in support for changing the zoning of these lands to residential use.

I enclose a location map showing the lands edged red and further small scale plan showing how a pedestrian link could be planned to accommodate a short safe way to the school and shops.

Also enclosed is a layout plan showing a suggested layout for a housing development of 510 houses and incorporating a leisure centre.

There is an existing golf course to the north of this site and a new one to be built to the western boundary of the site known as Turvey House, these form natural boundaries for development. The site is also close to the centre of village and on the eastern side of the railway which means vehicles leaving this site quickly connect to the Belfast/Dublin Road without passing through the centre of the village.

These lands are immediately adjacent to the Kinane Development lands and any service road or footpath connections could be provided.

Bovale Developments Limited have built many houses in the Swords area and the only available lands now left for development are in a few hands, my clients therefore see this site in Donabate as a well located site for development which has the advantage of a good rail service for people working in Dublin and good roads for travelling to Dublin and the Airport.

The site is located within easy reach of the village school and shops and has the advantage of the local amenities such as beaches and Newbridge House and grounds.

Should this site be rezoned for residential development, my clients would be willing to phase the development in order that integration with the local community and services could take place at a reasonable pace.

There is a 12" diameter public foul sewer in adjoining lands and surface water could be discharged through water courses to the tidal outfall to the north of this site.

It is understood that all other services would be available for the development proposed.

It is, therefore, our contention that the above lands are well located and adjacent to the existing village with its amenities and would form a logical extension to same and would enhance the area with a good choice of house designs together with a new leisure centre which would be available for use by all the residents of the area.

We therefore urge your Council to give careful consideration to these lands and rezone them for residential use."

At a meeting of the Council held on the 12th of May 1993, this representation and others relating to the Donabate area were considered. The Manager's report to the meeting recommended that having regard to the drainage restrictions to the area that no further lands be zoned for development in the

Donabate/Portrane area. The full text of the Manager's report to the meeting of the 12th May 1993 is contained in pages 553-561 and pages 567 & 568 of the Minutes of the Meeting and was as follows:-

"The development strategy for Donabate/ Portrane was considered at three Special Meetings of the County Council.

At the meeting held on 15th December 1989 Map No. 5, dealing with Donabate/Portrane was presented. The proposals outlined on that map were generally for a continuance of the existing zoning, catering for a population in the region of 6,000 persons.

At that meeting, Map No. 5 was noted, subject to a further report on proposals for future development.

In response, Draft Map No. 5A and an accompanying report were presented on 22nd June, 1990. Map 5A showed possible zonings in the Donabate/Portrane area to cater for a potential population in the order of 12,000 persons. The report stated that:-

However, the Council has to be advised of serious difficulties that would arise in attempting to cater for such development."

These difficulties were detailed. It was reported that "in addition to the augmentation of the foul drainage system, the existing waste water treatment works would have to be increased in size and the existing outfall to the sea extended in order to comply with the requirement for the discharge of treated sewage effluent to marine waters. This would be an addition to work on the improvement of the water supply."

To cater for an approximate population of 12,000, the approximate cost of foul drainage and water supply works was reported to be £3.80 million.

It was further reported as follows:-

"The Deputy Chief Engineer states that if an increase in zoned lands is approved by-the Council, planning permission which would give rise to an increase in the population of the area in excess of 6,000 persons would have to be refused until such time as the services as listed above had been improved.

In addition to the expenditure listed above it is estimated that the cost of the improvements to the road infrastructure, including the crossing of the railway line, would be of the order of £3.4m.

It is apparent that expenditure of this order could not reasonably be funded by way of contributions from intending developers, nor would it be available from other sources.

Accordingly, the Council has to be advised that the zoning proposals set out on Draft Map 5A could not be realised within any reasonable time span and that accordingly the Council should adopt Map No. 5, i.e., the original proposal put forward for its consideration."

Following discussion at this meeting it was AGREED that a further report in relation to surface water drainage of the Council owned lands and in relation to possible zoning adjustments to provide for a maximum population of 6,000 for the Donabate/Portrane area be submitted to a future special meeting of the Council dealing with the Development Plan Review.

At a special meeting on 14th September 1990, Map 5B relating to the area of Donabate/Portrane was presented. The proposals provided for some zoning adjustments to provide for a maximum population of 6,000.

Map 5B proposals, for the Portrane area, were similar to those of Map 5 with the exception of additional residential zoning adjoining the Seaview Park.

Map 5B proposals, for the Donabate area, differed from Map 5 insofar as 5B proposed additional residential zoning adjoining the "Viking Green", Turvey Avenue, development and at Beaverstown, east of Beaverstown

Road and north of Council owned lands. There were also revised zoning objectives for the village and adjoining areas.

Following discussion it was AGREED that Map 5 as presented to the Council in December 1989 be ADOPTED.

PLANNING OFFICER'S REPORT

Having regard to the drainage restrictions on the area as outlined above, it is recommended that no further lands be zoned for development at Donabate/Portrane. The present population of the drainage area, including St. Ita's Hospital, is approximately 5,000 persons. The capacity of the undeveloped zoned lands would increase the population to well in excess of the 6,000 population limiting capacity.

It is recommended therefore that no additional lands be zoned for development, except for two adjustments to reflect development commitments at (B) and (D) hereunder
LANDS AT BEAVERSTOWN, RAHILLION, BALLISK

REPRESENTATION NO. 000044 - LANDS AT 'BEVERTON', DONABATE -BOVALE DEVELOPMENTS LIMITED

(B) REPRESENTATION NO. 000097 - LANDS AT BEAVERSTOWN ADJOINING THE 'VIKING VILLAGE'- SWORDS DEMESNE DEVELOPMENT CO. LIMITED REPRESENTATION NO. 000204 - KINANE DEVELOPMENTS LIMITED

(C) REPRESENTATION NO. 000152 - LANDS AT PROSPECT HOUSE, DONABATE VILLAGE - E. HOPKINS.

REPRESENTATION NO. 000214 - LANDS AT BALCARRICK ROAD, DONABATE - S. CAMPBELL.

REPRESENTATION NO. 000046 - LANDS AT BEAVERSTOWN, BEAVERSTOWN SPORTING & DEVELOPMENT COMPANY.

REPRESENTATION NOS. 000232, 000233 & 000357 - LANDS AT BEAVERSTOWN, RAHILLION & BALLISK COMMON - J. HENEGHAN/P. CASSIDY & N. McALLISTER. [App. 4.3]

(G) REPRESENTATION NO. 000256 - LANDS AT RAHILLION - M. COLLINS, OTHER REPRESENTATION NOS. 000059, 000335, 000359 & 000441.

Representations requesting change of zoning to development: -

(A)Land at "Beverton", Donabate - Bovale Developments Limited - Representation No. 000044

SYNOPSIS OF REPRESENTATION

Request that approximately 29 hectares of land at Turvey Avenue, which adjoin the Kinane (residential) Development Lands and Beaverstown Golf Course, be zoned for residential development.

DEVELOPMENT PLAN

The subject site is zoned "B" for agriculture in the 1983 Development Plan and in the 1991 Draft Plan.
Lands at Beaverstown adjoining the

"Viking Village" residential development at Turvey Avenue - Representation No. 000097 - Swords Demesne Development Co. Limited and Representation No. 000204 - Kinane Developments Limited [App. 4.3]

SYNOPSIS OF REPRESENTATION

Representation No. 000097 is dated January 1989 and is superseded by Representation No. 000204 which requests that 15 hectares approximately be re-zoned from agricultural to an appropriate residential zoning.

SITE HISTORY
PLANNING APPLICATIONS

Reg. Ref. YA. 362 - Outline permission was granted on appeal on the 13th August 1984 for housing development on a site of 8 hectares (south-west section of the site, the subject of Representation 000204) at

Beaverstown, Donabate, subject to not more than 50 houses being erected and development being limited to the eastern part of the site.

Since then a number of applications for residential development have been lodged on the eastern and western part of the site of Reg. Ref. YA. 362.

A number of permissions have been granted consequent on the passing of Material Contravention of the Development Plan resolutions as follows: Reg. Ref. 89A/213 and Reg. Ref. 9OA/584. [App. 4.3]

DEVELOPMENT PLAN

The site of Representation No. 000204 is zoned "B" for agriculture in the 1983 Development Plan and in the 1991 Draft Plan.

To the south-east, Representation No. 000204 adjoins the housing development known as "Viking Green" (Reg. Ref. YA/362) the lands of which are zoned "A" and "F." In addition, Representation No. 000204 also adjoins an apartment development (Phase 1 of which is nearing completion Reg. Refs. 91A/1776 & 92A/0933 refer), the lands of which are zoned "B."

It is recommended that the "A" zone be extended to include the lands for which planning permission has been granted and which are partially developed. D.P. 92/190 refers.

(C) Lands at prospect House, Donabate Village - Representation No. 000152 - E. Hopkins

SYNOPSIS OF REPRESENTATION

Re-zoning is requested from 'B' for agriculture to "C2" "to protect and enhance the special physical and social character of town and village centres", of that portion of the 4 hectares of lands which surround the former Parochial House (namely Prospect House) in Donabate Village and which are north of the reservation for the proposed long term Donabate By-Pass Road.

The representation advocates that the "C2" zoning objective would allow for a proposed low density high quality development.

SITE HISTORY

(i) PLANNING APPLICATIONS

Reg. Ref. 91 A/0071 – refers to a refusal of outline permission for 19 houses on a site which comprised part of the site the subject of this representation as well as the road reservation and Mr. Hopkins lands to the south of this proposed long term road. The refusal reasons included: zoning, prematurity regarding road layout, traffic hazard regarding proposed access on the existing road, no capacity in existing sewerage facilities, no surface water available for proposed development.

(ii) DEVELOPMENT PLAN

The site of this representation is zoned "B" for agriculture in the 1983 Development Plan and in the 1991 Draft Plan.

There is a long term road proposal/objective to the south-east of representation No. 000152.

(D)Lands at Balcarrick Road, Donabate - Representation No. 000214 - S. Campbell.

SYNOPSIS OF REPRESENTATION

Re-zoning to residential use requested on lands - at Balcarrick Road, which adjoin "The Strand" residential development, at Balcarrick Road, Donabate.

SITE HISTORY
(i)PLANNING APPLICATIONS

Reg. Ref. YA.1517 - refers to permission granted (by decision order the 6th April 1984) consequent to a resolution for a material contravention of the Development Plan, for a housing development on lands off Balcarrick Road on a site of 4 hectares which includes a small strip of land fronting onto Balcarrick Road and which is part of the site of this representation.

Subsequently a number of applications were lodged for residential development including revised layout and revised house types but excluding that strip of land which forms part of the site of this representation (Applications include Reg. Refs. ZA. 1495, 89A/2028, 89A/2279, 92A/0760, 92A/0800, 91A/1 723).

Phase 1 of this residential development which is known as "The Strand" has been completed and Phase 2, which adjoins the site of the subject representation, is nearing completion.

(ii) DEVELOPMENT PLAN
The site of this representation is zoned "B" - for agriculture in the 1983 Development Plan and in the 1991 Draft Plan.

A long term road proposal/objective (the Donabate By-Pass Road) affects the site.

It is recommended that the "A" zone be extended to include the lands, for which planning permission has been granted and on which development is nearing completion. D.P. No. 92/191 refers.

(E) Lands at Beaverstown, Donabate - Representation No. 000046 – "Beaverstown Sporting and Development Company"

SYNOPSIS OF REPRESENTATION
This representation requests that favourable consideration be given to re-zoning approximately 8 hectares of land, which is located to the immediate north of Beaverstown Orchard residential development, from "B" to "A" low density.

SITE HISTORY
(i) PLANNING APPLICATIONS
Reg. Ref. 85A/1109 - permission refused by the Council and on appeal for the erection of 192 houses on a site which included the site the subject of this representation.

Reg. Ref. 89A/688 - permission refused for 151 houses at Beaverstown on a site including the site of this representation.

Reg. Ref. 91A/1331 -outline permission refused for 9 houses on a site at Beaverstown which forms part of the site of this representation. Appeal was subsequently withdrawn.

(ii) DEVELOPMENT PLAN
The site is zoned "B" - for agriculture in the 1983 Development Plan and in the 1991 Draft Plan.

(F) Lands at Beaverstown, Rahillion and Ballisk Common, Donabate

Representation Nos. 000232 and 000233 - J. Heneghan, P. Cassidy

Representation No. 000357 - N. McAllister

SYNOPSIS OF REPRESENTATIONS
Representation No. 000233 requests that 8 hectares at Beaverstown be re-zoned from "B" to "A."

In addition, Representation No. 000232 requests that the above 8 hectares (Rep. No. 000233) as well as an adjoining 20 hectares to the south and east at Beaverstown, Rahillion and Ballisk Common (and owned by Mr. McAllister) be re-zoned from "B" to "A."

Representation No. 000357 requests that the main portion of Mr. McAllister's landholding of 26 hectares at Beaverstown, Rahillion and Ballisk Common, be re-zoned from "B" to "A."

This representation advocates that the remainder of Mr. McAllister's lands at Rahillion retain the "G" zoning designation for High Amenity, as indicated in the 1991 Draft Plan.

SITE HISTORY
(i) PLANNING APPLICATIONS
Reg. Ref. ZA.421: Permission refused for a housing development of 99 houses at Beaverstown, on a site which formed part of the 8 hectares site of Representations 000232 and 000233.

DEVELOPMENT PLAN

The lands of Representation Nos. 000232 and 000233 and that portion of Representation No. 000357, which is the subject of the requested re-zoning, are zoned "B" – for agriculture in the 1983 Plan and the 1991 Draft Plan.

(G) Lands at Rabillion, Donabate - Portrane - Representation No. 000256 - Ms. Mary Collins

This representation requests an extension of the development area to include a field of approximately 2 hectares at Rahillion. That the field has road frontage along a laneway "but if the property was considered for re-zoning, I would hope to be in a position to purchase either of two sites with road frontage adjoining this site."

DEVELOPMENT PLAN

The site is zoned "B" - for agriculture in the 1983 Development Plan."

Following discussion of the Managers Report, the following motion was proposed by Councillor Gallagher, seconded by Councillor Devitt (Ref 16(1)(A) & (B)(i)):-

> *"Dublin County Council hereby resolves that the lands outlined in red on the attached map which has been signed by the proposer and seconder of the motion, be zoned "A1" with the Objective that the area hatched in yellow be zoned "A" and be developed immediately and the remainder be developed in accordance with an area action plan."*

The lands included in the motion were those covered by the representation on behalf of Bovale Developments Limited and adjoining lands in respect of which a representation on behalf of Swords Demesne Development Company Limited (Reference No. 000097) and a representation on behalf of Kinane Developments Limited (Reference No. 000204) had been received.

As the time fixed for the meeting expired before the motion was put the matter was deferred to the Meeting of the Council held on the 14th May 1993.

At the meeting of the 14th May 1993, the following motion was proposed by Councillor Devitt, seconded by Councillor Gallagher at 16(1): -

> *"Dublin County Council hereby resolves that in view of the immediate surface water drainage difficulties relating to land already zoned but not developed and to the immediate demand for land to be developed for housing in Donabate and to the capacity in the existing treatment plant that additional land be zoned for residential development to allow for a phased development pattern in Donabate and to allow for a balanced development east and west of the railway line."*

The motion was passed by 44 votes in favour, 6 against, and 5 abstentions. The names of those voting in favour and against are given on Page 575 of the Minutes of the Meeting.

The meeting then resumed consideration of the motion which had been proposed by Councillor Gallagher, seconded by Councillor Devitt at the meeting of the 12th May 1993. During the course of discussion on the motion, an amendment was proposed by Councillor Devitt, seconded by Councillor Gallagher and passed on a show of hands which had the effect of making the following the substantive motion – page 576 of minutes: -

> *"Dublin County Council hereby resolves that the lands outlined in red on the attached map which has been signed by the proposer and seconder of the motion be zoned for residential development and that not more than 300 houses be constructed in Phase 1 which is the area hatched in yellow on the attached map and that Phase 2 not be constructed until Phase I has been completed."*

This motion was passed by 35 votes in favour, 18 against and 2 abstentions.

For: Councillors C Boland, P Brady, S Brock, L Butler, B Cass, B Coffey, LT Cosgrave, MJ Cosgrave, L Creaven, A Devitt, JH Dockrell, M Elliott, M Farrell, T Fox, C Gallagher, S Gilbride,

R Greene, T Hand, F Hanrahan, C Keane, M Kennedy, J Larkin, M McGennis, C McGrath, J Maher, D Marren, T Mattews, T Morrissey, C O'Connor, A Ormonde, N Owen, C Quinn, N Ryan, S Terry, GV Wright.
Against: Councillors M Billane, F Buckley, M Doohan, K Farrell, N Gibbons, E Gilmore, L Gordon, D Healy, J Higgins, T Kelleher, M Muldoon, M Mullarney, D O'Callaghan, G O'Connell, S Ryan, T Sargent, D Tipping, C Tyndall.
Abstentions: Councillors S Laing, T Ridge.

This proposed amendment of the Draft Plan was put on public display for the statutory one month as required by the Planning Acts as Map 5 Change 9.

At the meeting of the Council on the 15th September 1993, to consider the proposed amendments to the Draft Plan for the Donabate area, a report from the Manager was presented to the meeting which included the following (ref. page 977 of minutes): -

"There were approximately 150 representations received in relation to Map 5. These were divided almost equally between those supporting and those against most amendments. The main issues concerning those objecting are:

(1) the inadequacy of the roads and sewerage system and the cost of upgrading same when existing services remain under utilised in other areas;
(2) the existence of adequate zoned, serviced land elsewhere;
(3) the desire to preserve the rural/village nature of the area."

The main issues concerning those supporting the amendments are:

the preservation of employment;
the development of community services and infrastructure - including bus, train, medical etc.;
to take advantage of the amenities the area has to offer.

General Report on Donabate
Foul Drainage
The capacity of 6,000 persons in the treatment works is now being used or is committed in planning permissions granted and hence there is no further foul drainage capacity for development. There is provision in the design of the drainage works for duplication which if built would provide for a further 6,000 persons. However, no further development can take place until the proposed duplication of the works is built and in operation.
Development Plan
There are 140 acres approximately of undeveloped residential zoned land on the eastern side of the railway line in Donabate. These lands if developed would have the capacity to accommodate 4,000 people approximately. This would leave an additional capacity of 2,000 persons equivalent to 600 houses. At the last Development Plan meeting which discussed this matter, the members considered it appropriate that these 600 houses be divided 300 east of the railway line and 300 west of the railway line.

The present rezoning proposals if developed to their full extent would provide for a total of 1,200 houses approximately comprising 430 east of the railway line and 760 west of the railway line. This considerably exceeds the capacity which will be available in the event of duplication of the sewage works.

Hence, it is advised that the amount of houses to be built on lands it is proposed to rezone, be limited to 300 east and 300 west of the railway line."

In summary, the Manager's report then listed a number of areas where these 600 houses might be located and included the recommendation in regard to Change No. 9 that the amendment be confirmed subject to not more than 300 houses being built on the entire site.

Mr. William Murray, Deputy Dublin Planning Officer explained, with the aid of slides, the proposals contained in the Manager's report and this was followed by a discussion to which Councillors Tipping, Higgins, Buckley, McGennis, Sargent, O'Callaghan, Laing, Kelleher, S. Ryan, Gilbride and Cass contributed. The Manager replied to queries raised and further consideration was deferred to the next meeting to be held on the following day, 16th September 1993 (ref. page 981 of minutes). At the meeting on the 16th of September 1993, the following additional report at page 983 by the Manager was considered: -

"At the meeting on the 15th September, 1993, some reservations were expressed regarding the Donabate proposals as presented. To meet these reservations, it is suggested that the northern and western limits of the residentially zoned areas be drawn in accordance with DP 93/136 and that the overall density be restricted to 6.6 houses per acre (16.3 per hectare). These changes would allow for a similar number of houses to those stated in the report presented to the Council – that is Change 1 – 40 houses, Change 2 – 100 houses, Change 3 – 120 houses and Change 9 – 300 houses."

Following discussion to which Councillors Devitt, Higgins, S Ryan, Tipping, Sargent, Quinn, Gallagher, Boland, Butler, Cass, Maher, Lyons, O'Callaghan and Kelleher contributed, the Manager replied to queries raised by the Members. Having considered the various other changes on the agenda, the Council then went on to consider Change 9 in relation to Beaverstown, Donabate (Reference C/729/93). The following is a quote from page 989 of the minutes:

BEAVERSTOWN, DONABATE
"Change 9:   Change of zoning of lands north of Turvey Avenue from "B" to "A1", Phase 1 consisting of not more than 300 houses to be completed before Phase 11 commences.

The following motions relating to Change No. 9 were not moved:
- Motion in the names of Councillors T. Kelleher and S. Ryan:

> *"Dublin County Council hereby resolves that the lands referred to as 9 on Map Number 5 of the Dublin County Council Draft Development Plan Review 1993 Amendments be zoned B - to protect and provide for the development of agriculture."*

- Motion in the name of Councillor T. Sargent:

"Dublin County Council hereby resolves that the lands involved in change no. 9 on map 5 of the proposed amendments to the 1991 Draft Development Plan be zoned "B."

- Motion in the names of Councillors D. Tipping, C. Breathnach, E. Gilmore, D. O'Callaghan and M. Billane:

> *"This Council resolves that the lands referred to at Map No. 5 Change No. 9 in the public display of proposed amendments to the County Dublin Draft Development Plan 1991 revert to its former proposed zoning as shown in Draft maps displayed in September - December 1991."*

The following motion was proposed by Councillor Devitt, seconded by Councillor Gallagher:-

> *"That the Manager's proposal of the 16th September, 1993, be amended to provide that the lands outlined in red on the attached map signed for identification be zoned for residential development. "*

The motion was put and passed unanimously and the subject lands were zoned for residential development in the 1993 Development Plan. The passing of this motion had the effect of reducing the amount of land proposed for rezoning in the proposed amendment to the Draft Plan from 38.00 hectares to 18.42 hectares. This included other land in addition to part of Lot 4.

Paragraph A.2(c)(iii) of the Terms of Reference. Changes made or proposed to be made to the 8th of June 1989 planning status of the lands by way of applications for planning permission (including any involving a material contravention of the Development Plan)

Material contraventions

No planning permission was granted which materially contravened the zoning of these lands.

Applications for planning permission

A review of the Planning Register together such available files as are within the Council's possession reveal the following;

Planning Application Register Ref. A214

The planning history of the lands as appears from the planning register commenced in 1968, when a planning application register Reference A214 was submitted to the Council seeking Planning Permission for 280 houses at Turvey Estate, Donabate. Outline permission was refused by the Council by Order No. P518/68 dated the 18th April 1968 for the following two reasons: -

"1. The proposed development is premature by virtue of the non-availability of public piped sewerage facilities in the area and the period within which such is expected to be provided.
Reason: In the interests of the proper planning and orderly development.

2. The proposed temporary sewage disposal system for the development does not meet the requirements of the Chief Medical Officer who has a basic objection to the discharge of the effluent as shown into the existing stream at Turvey House and which drains into the tidal estuary of the Turvey River.
Reason: In the interest of health."

The application was made by Nicholas O'Dwyer, Son & Partners on behalf of Turvey House Limited The original file is not available.

Planning Application Register Ref. E 2252

This application was made by D. McCarthy on behalf of Forest Homes and was an application for outline permission for a housing development at Beaverstown, Donabate. By Order P294/73 dated the 2nd February 1973,the Council decided to refuse permission for the proposed development for the following reasons:

1. The proposal for housing development within an area indicated for the further development of agriculture in the Development Plan would seriously conflict with the plan and would not be in accordance with the proper planning and development of the area.
2. There is no sewer available.
3. The existing adjoining road network is inadequate to serve the proposed development.

Planning Application Register Ref. G 1270

In or about 1974, an application for planning permission for a residential development was submitted by Kieran O'Malley Consultant, Town Planner on behalf of O'Shea & Shanahan Limited for a residential development at Turvey, Beaverstown, Corballis and Portrane. This application was withdrawn by letter dated the 13th June 1974, but as the file is not available to the Council, the Tribunal could not identify the exact location of the lands.

Planning Application Register Ref. G1406

In 1974, an application for outline planning permission for a residential development at Turvey, Beaverstown, Corballis and Portrane was submitted to Dublin County Council. The application submitted by Consultant Town Planner, Kieran O'Malley in association with P. Shaffrey and D. Fearon was made on behalf of O'Shea and Shanahan Limited, Farrell Homes Limited, Connolly Construction Co. Limited, F. Sharpe and James Wood and was refused for the following 8 reasons: -

"1. The lands to which the application relate are contained in the Donabate Planning Study lodged as part of the proposal, as small parts of the overall development. The proposals contained in the Study run counter to the County Dublin Development Plan, envisaging as it does, a major development (i.e. a new town of 30,000 population) in an area for which the zoning objective is to provide for the further development of agriculture and it would create a counter magnet to the planned major development areas (i.e. the Western towns) proposed elsewhere in the County area as a definite policy. It is, therefore, not considered to be in accordance with the proper planning and development of the area.
2. There are no existing sewage services to accommodate the proposals and the Council has approved no plans to provide such services on the scale necessary for this development.

3. The proposed development would be premature by reason of the said existing deficiency in sewerage facilities and the period within which such deficiency may reasonably be expected to be made good.

4. The existing rural road network serving the area is of insufficient capacity to cope with the proposed development without endangering public safety by reason of traffic hazard and obstruction of road users caused by the excessive amount of traffic generated by the proposed new urban area.

5. The road patterns proposed for the area have not been provided for in the Council's Development Plan nor by the Minister for Local Government in any appealed decision.

6. The proposed development would endanger public safety by reason of traffic hazard, as it would considerably increase the number of turning manoeuvres at uncontrolled junctions on the already heavily trafficked National Primary Road at Turvey Avenue and Hearse Road.

7. The site of the proposal is located in an area which is not indicated in the Development plan for short term development and is primarily for agriculture. It is also proximate to the areas of high amenity and scientific interest, which it is Council policy to safeguard. The proposal therefore is premature in the absence of an approved Action Plan for the area.

8. The development of the individual parcels of land proposed in the application would constitute piecemeal development and as such would be contrary to the proper planning and development of the area."

It is not possible from available records to establish precisely the location of this application.

Planning Application Register Ref. XA 802

On the 26th April 1983, Conroy Manahan & Associates applied for planning permission for the open storage of steel on lands at Turvey House, Turvey Avenue, Donabate Co. Dublin. The application was submitted on behalf of Turvey Estates Limited, Stephen Court, St. Stephen's Green, Dublin 2 and on the 25th June 1982, the Council decided to refuse permission for the following four reasons: -

"1. The location of the proposed development is within an area zoned in the County Development Plan for the further development of Agriculture. The proposal conflicts with this objective and would be contrary to the proper planning and development of the area.

2. The proposed development would be seriously injurious to the rural amenity of the area.

3. The proposed development would be seriously injurious to the amenity of the nearby Turvey House which is listed for preservation in the 1972 Development Plan and 1980 draft review of the Development Plan.

4. The proposed development would endanger public safety by reason of traffic hazard due to the creation of turning movements of heavy vehicles at the existing inadequate junction at the National Primary Route N1 and the existing inadequate Turvey Avenue"

Planning Application Register Ref. 92A/0112

On the 7th of April 1992, an application for planning permission for development described as "*club facilities and accommodation comprising 12 hotel bedrooms and 24 self catering units including wastewater treatment system*" at Turvey Demesne, Turvey Avenue, Donabate was submitted by Grainne Mallon, 6 Merrion Square, Dublin 2 on behalf of "Turvey Golf and Country Club," Turvey Avenue, Donabate, Co. Dublin. Additional information was sought on the 26th March 1992 and additional information was furnished on the 7th April 1992. On the 8th May 1992, Fingal County Council decided by Order P/2044 to grant permission for the proposed development subject to 15 conditions. That decision was the subject of an appeal to An Bord Pleanála but the appeal was withdrawn and a decision to grant permission issued the 23rd September 1992 subject to the 15 conditions. In September 1997, an application was received to extend the duration of this permission and an Order was made on the 16th of October 1997 extending the life of the permission to the 30th September 1998. A further extension of the duration of this permission to the 30th of October 1999 was granted by Order dated the 11th December 1998.

Planning Application Register Ref. 92A/0873

On the 29th May 1992, Grainne Mallon, Merrion Sq. Dublin 2 applied to Fingal County Council for planning permission for "*28 Self catering units and 12 hotel bedrooms to rear of approved club facilities*" at Turvey Avenue, Donabate. On the 18th August 1992, Dublin County Council decided to grant permission for 28 self catering units and 12 hotel bedrooms subject to 11 conditions. Condition No. 9 required that before the development was opened to the public that the applicant enter into an agreement under Section

38 of the Local Government (Planning & Development) Act 1963 which would require that the accommodation in the hotel and self catering be operated as an integral part of the overall development of the golf club and that it not be used for long term residential use (in excess of two consecutive calendar months at any one time). On the 13th January 1997, a Section 38 agreement was entered into between Fingal County Council of the one part and Mainwell Limited of Derrygon, Ballinmore, Co. Leitrim of the other part to give effect to condition no. 9 of the above planning permission.

Planning Application Register Ref. F93A/0095

This was an application for permission for alterations to approved golf based development comprising clubhouse facilities, driving range, 12 hotel bedrooms, 48 self-catering units and treatment plant, made by Grainne Mallon on behalf of F.L.C. Turvey Management Company. A decision to refuse permission was made on the 1st February 1994. An appeal was made to An Bord Pleanála against this decision and by Order dated the 27th June 1994, An Bord Pleanála granted permission for the clubhouse facilities, driving range, 12 hotel bedrooms and treatment plant and refused permission for 48 self catering units.

Planning Application Register Ref. F94A/0446

On the 21st of June 1994, Ronnie Martin of Kilmonin, Enniskerry, Co. Wicklow applied on behalf of Turvey Golf and Leisure plc for planning permission described as *"Change of use of existing site office to a temporary changing facility for Members of "Turvey Golf and Country Club" pending the erection of a permanent club house."* No fee was submitted with this application and the application was not determined.

Planning Application Register Ref. F94A/0577

On the 19th of August 1994, an application for planning permission for the construction of 37 houses and 76 apartments on a site at Turvey Avenue/Turvey Woods, Donabate was submitted on behalf of Kinane Developments Limited (47 Hardwicke Street, Dublin 1) to Fingal County Council. The application was submitted by "McCrossan, O'Rourke Architects", 12 Richmond Row, Portobello Harbour, Dublin 8. On the 17th of October 1994, Fingal County Council decided to refuse permission for the following 5 reasons: -

> "1 The site is located in an area zoned in the County Development Plan "to provide for new residential communities in accordance with approved Action Area plans."
> The development would be premature until such time as an Action Plan for these lands has been prepared and approved by the Planning Authority.
> 2 There is no capacity within the Donabate Treatment Plant to cater for this development. The proposal is thus premature because of this existing deficiency in the provision of sewerage facilities serving this site and the period within which this constraint may reasonably be expected to cease. The proposal would thus be prejudicial to public health and contrary to the proper planning and development of the area.
> 3 In the absence of an Approved Action Plan the development would be premature pending the determination by the Planning Authority of a road layout for the area.
> 4 The drainage proposals are unacceptable to the Environmental Services Department on the grounds that the prospective public sewers are within 5 metres of proposed buildings. The proposal would thus be prejudicial to public health.
> 5 The proposal is unacceptable to the Environmental Services section by reason of the proposed layout of the watermain."

The applicants appealed to An Bord Pleanála against the refusal of Fingal County Council to grant permission and by Order of the 9th March 1995, An Bord Pleanála decided, for the reasons as set out in the First Schedule to this decision, to grant permission for the erection of the 76 no. apartments in accordance with the plans and particulars lodged, subject to conditions set out in the Second Schedule to the decision. However, the Board refused permission for the erection of the 37 no. houses applied for the reasons set out in the Third Schedule to the decision.

Planning Application Register Ref. F95A/0036

This was an application for permission for refurbishment and two-storey extension to gate lodge submitted by McCrossan O'Rourke, Architects on behalf of G. Leahy. Additional information was requested on the 7th of March 1995 but was not supplied.

Planning Application Register Ref. F95A/0782

This was an application made by McCrossan O'Rourke, Architects on behalf of Kinane Developments Limited, for permission to construct 37 no. Houses at Turvey Avenue. This application referred to the portion of the site F94A/0577 in respect of which permission had been refused by An Bord Pleanála for the erection of 37 houses. This application would normally have been dealt with prior to the 27th of December 1995 but the applicant consented, in writing, to the extension by the Council of the period for considering the application (on four occasions) to the 31st of January 1996, the 15th of February 1996, the 5th of March 1996 and the 8th of March 1996. These consents were furnished in accordance with Section 26(4)(A) of the Local Government (Planning & Development) Act 1963 as amended by section 39(f) of the Local Government (Planning & Development) Act 1976. On the 4th of March 1996, Fingal County Council decided to grant permission for the proposed development subject to 21 conditions. The decision of Fingal County Council was the subject of an appeal by the Turvey/Viking Resident's Association and by Order PL/06F/098598 made on the 31st July 1996, An Bord Pleanála decided to grant permission for the construction of the 37 no. houses in question subject to 12 conditions. The effect of the board's decision was to reduce the number of houses from 37 to 33.

Planning Application Register Ref. F97A/0921

On the 28th of October 1997, McCrossan O'Rourke Architects applied to Fingal County Council on behalf of Mr Charles Gallagher, Inisfree, Nashville Road, Howth, Co. Dublin for a change of house type from a four bedroom to a five bedroom house at site no. 33 on lands adjacent to Beaverstown Court, Turvey Avenue, Donabate. On the 29th of April 1998, the Council decided to grant permission for the change of house type on site no. 33 subject to six conditions.

Planning Application Register Ref. F96A/0393

On the 31st of May 1996, McCrossan O'Rourke Architects applied to Fingal County Council for planning permission for Kinane Developments Limited for development described as: -

> "182 detached and semi-detached houses comprising 93 no. three bedroom houses and 89 four bedroom houses; site development works and landscape works and including reservation of site for community facilities as per "Donabate Action Plan" prepared by Fingal County Council Planning Department; vehicular access via existing approved Road off Turvey Avenue; all on a site of 25.8 acres approximately"

Of the 25.8 acres referred to, approximately 11 acres are outside the area shown on Folio 4327 but are within that area which was re-zoned "A1" in the 1993 Development Plan. On the 29th of July 1996, Fingal County Council decided to seek additional information from the Applicants in relation to the proposed development. The additional information was received on the 6th of December 1996.

On the 4th of February 1997, Fingal County Council decided to grant permission for the proposed development for 180 houses subject to 25 conditions. This decision was the subject of an appeal to An Bord Pleanála and on the 2nd July 1997, An Bord Pleanála granted permission subject to the following 13 conditions:

> "1.   The development shall be carried out in accordance with the plans and particulars submitted to the planning authority on the 31st day of May 1996. the 14th day of June 1996 and the 6th day of December 1996, except as may otherwise may be required by the conditions attached hereunder.
> **Reason:** To define the nature and extent of the permission granted in the interests of clarity.
>
> 2.   The development shall be phased in accordance with a scheme, details of which shall be submitted to and agreed in writing with the planning authority before any development is commenced on the site. The first phase to be implemented in the first year of the development, shall include not more than 65 houses, namely houses numbers 1 to 65 outlined in red in drawing number 02 REV.A submitted to the planning authority on the 6th day of December 1996.
>
> The public open space adjoining the access road and the landscaped open spaces included within the area outlined in red on drawing number 02 REV. A shall be developed as part of the first phase.
>
> In addition, all services necessary to serve the first phase houses and the main access road and sanitary services required to serve adjoining lands shall be developed as part of the first phase.

Reason: To match the rate of development to the capacity of the Donabate Sewage Treatment Works in the interest of public health and amenity.

3.	The phasing scheme shall provided for the erection of not more than 30 houses per year in the second and subsequent years of development.
Reason: To match the rate of development to the capacity of the Donabate Sewage Treatment Works in the interest of public health and amenity.

4.	Houses numbers 66 and 67 indicated on drawing number 02 REV.A shall be omitted from the development and the resulting area shall be incorporated into the landscaped open space immediately adjoining these sites.
Reason: To prevent the houses backing onto the public open space area in the interest of amenity.

5.	The area shown and conditioned as public open space shall be fenced off during construction work and shall not be used for the purpose of site compounds or for the storage of plant, materials or spoil. The area shall be levelled, soiled, seeded and landscaped to the satisfaction of the planning authority and shall be available for use by residents on completion of their dwellings.
Reason: In the interest of residential amenity.

6.	The existing hedgerows along the western and northern boundary of the Phase 1 development shall be carefully preserved and augmented as necessary. These hedgegrows shall be fenced off and protected from site development works during the course of development. Arrangements for the treatment of existing hedgegrows and trees on the remainder of the site shall be agreed in writing with the planning authority, before each subsequent phase is commenced.
Reason: In the interest of amenity.

7.	All necessary measures shall be taken by the contractor to prevent the spillage or deposit of clay, rubble or other debris on adjoining roads during the course of the works.
Reason: To protect the amenities of the area.

8.	Screen walls block or similar durable materials not less than two metres high, suitably capped and rendered shall be provided at the necessary locations to be agreed with the planning authority, so as to screen rear gardens from public view.
Reason: In the interest of residential amenity.

9.	All service cables associated with the proposed development (such as electrical communal television, telephone and street lighting cables) shall be run underground within the site.
Reason: In the interest of orderly development and the visual amenities of the area.

10.	Water supply and drainage arrangements, including the disposal of surface water. shall comply with the requirements of the planning authority for such works and services.
Reason: In the interest of public health and to ensure a proper standard of development.

11.	Prior to the commencement of development. the developer shall lodge with Fingal County Council a cash deposit, a bond of an insurance company, or other security to secure the provision and satisfactory completion and maintenance until taken in charge by the Council of roads, footpaths, watermains, drains, public open space and other services required in connection with the development, coupled with an agreement empowering the Council to apply such security or part thereof to the satisfactory completion or maintenance of any part of the development. The form and amount of the security shall be as agreed between the Council and the developer or, in default of agreement, shall be determined by An Bord Pleanála.
Reason: To ensure the satisfactory completion of the development.

12.	The developer shall pay a sum of money to Fingal County Council as a contribution towards expenditure that was and/or that is proposed to be incurred by the Council in respect of the provision of a public water supply and sewerage facilities facilitating the proposed development. The amount of the contribution and the arrangements for payment shall be as agreed between the developer and the Council or, in default of agreement, shall be determined by An Bord Pleanála.
In the case of expenditure that is proposed to be incurred, the requirement to pay this contribution is subject to the provisions of section 26(2)(h) of the Local Government (Planning and

development) Act, 1963 generally, and in particular, the specified period for the purposes of paragraph (h) shall be the period of seven years from the date of this order.

Reason: It is considered reasonable that the developer should contribute towards the expenditure that was and/or that is proposed to be incurred by the Council in respect a public water supply and sewerage facilities (including the upgrading of Donabate sewage treatment works) facilitating the proposed development.

13. The developer shall pay a sum of money to Fingal County Council as a contribution towards the expenditure that is proposed to be incurred by the Council in respect of road improvement works facilitating the proposed development. The amount of the contribution and the arrangements for payment shall be as agreed between the developer and the Council or, in default of agreement, shall be determined by An Bord Pleanála.

Payment of this contribution is subject to the provisions of Section 26(2)(h) of the Local Government (Planning and Development) Act 1963 generally, and in particular. the specified period for the purposes of paragraph (h) shall be the period of seven years from the date of this order.

Reason: It is considered reasonable that the developer should contribute towards the expenditure proposed to be incurred by the Council in respect of road improvement works facilitating the proposed development.

In deciding to grant the permission in question, An Bord Pleanála said that: -

"Subject to compliance with the conditions set out in the Second Schedule, the proposed development would be in accordance with the Development Plan for the area and the Area Action Plan, would not seriously injure the amenities of property in the vicinity and would be in accordance with the proper planning and development of the area."

Planning Application Register Ref. F97A/1141

On the 23rd of December 1997, McCrossan O'Rourke Architects applied for planning permission on behalf of Kinane Developments Limited for a "*minor variation to approved site layout in vicinity of house nos. 35-61 incl. and a change of house type on site nos. 35-36 incl. and 47-61 incl. all on site of 25.8 acres approx. with vehicular access from existing approved road.*" On the 7th of May 1998, permission was granted by Fingal County Council for the proposed changes subject to 9 conditions.

Planning Application Register Ref. F97A/0525.

On the 18th of June 1997, application for planning permission for dwelling-house and septic tank was submitted on behalf of Gerry Andrews, 67 Seaview Park, Portrane, Donabate by Grainne Mallon & Associates.

On the 14th of August 1997, the Council refused to grant permission for the proposed development for the following 5 reasons: -

"1. The site is located in an area with the zoning objective in the current development plan for the area "to protect and provide for the development of agriculture", which objective is considered reasonable. The proposed development would contravene materially this zoning objective and would, therefore, be contrary to the proper planning and development of the area.

2. The proposed development would introduce suburban style ribbon development to this long established attractive, tree-lined avenue. The proposed development would seriously undermine the established enclosure and rural character of the avenue and would be detrimental to the visual amenity of the area.

3. The proposed development by virtue of its scale and design, would be visually obtrusive and detrimental to the established character of the Avenue.

4. The applicant has failed to detail satisfactory arrangements for the retention of existing trees and hedgegrows and the landscaping of the site as a whole.

5. The applicant has failed to demonstrate satisfactory arrangements for water supply and the disposal of foul water to serve the proposed development. In the absence of such information the proposed would be prejudicial to public health."

Planning Application Register Ref. F97A/0205

On the 1st March 1997, an application for planning permission for development described as "*Minor alterations to approved apartments*" at Turvey Golf and Country Club was submitted on behalf of Mainwell Limited, Derrygoan, Ballinamore, Co. Leitrim. The Council on the 26th June 1997, granted permission for the proposed development subject to 6 conditions.

Planning Application Register Ref. F98A/0869

This was an application made by Grainne Mallon & Associates on behalf of Turvey Golf & Leisure Limited of Turvey Avenue, Donabate for Planning Permission for 21 additional bedrooms at Turvey Golf and Country Club. Planning permission was refused on the 22nd October 1998 for the following three reasons: -

"1. The proposed 3 storey building incorporating a mansard roof, by reason of its roof design, its height and its bulk is not in keeping with the character and design of the approved clubhouse. The proposed development would seriously detract from the visual appearance of the approved building and would thereby seriously impinge on the visual amenities of this area and be contrary to the proper planning and development of the area.

2. Condition No. 6 of Decision Order No. P/3267/92 (Reg. Ref. 92A/0873 refers) and P/2044/91 (Reg.Ref. 92A/0112 refers) states: -
In order to comply with the requirements of the Sanitary Services Department, the Applicant is required to submit to the planning authority for written agreement details of the following matters:-

(i) a complete description of the expanded bicycle plant and the design figures for the quantity of effluent it is intended to treat;

(ii) satisfactory proposals showing how it is intended to follow the recommendations of the Consultant Hydrogeologist in respect of the percolation area and the recommendation that effluent should be discharged to the deeper sand layer;

(iii) satisfactory proposals for following the recommendations of the Consultant Hydrogeologist for a seven day injection test (in a revised location if necessary) for the production of a computer model, to assist in assessing the impact on the water table, the quality of ground water, the form and type of percolation area;

(iv) an unqualified certificate from the Consultant Hydrogeologist stating that in his opinion that the effluent within the stated parameters will not have an adverse affect on groundwaters, taking into account any background conditions;

(v) satisfactory proposals for fencing off the percolation area from the public;

(vi) satisfactory proposal for the surface water drainage of the site and for cleaning the water courses to the estuary;

(vii) details of the drainage arrangements carried out under the advice of Teagasc;

(viii) details of the design of proposed oil inceptors;

(ix) details of the water regimes for the lake, and whether it is intended that these lakes will be used. The above details to be submitted to and agreed with the planning authority prior to the commencement of development.

Note: The Applicant must apply for a licence under the Water Pollution Acts 1977 – 1989.
Reason: In order to comply with the Sanitary Services Acts, 1878 – 1964."

The Applicant has not complied with this condition to date.
The proposed development which involves further intensification of use on the site of the approved development would result in additional effluent being disposed of to an independent treatment plant (no details of which have been submitted) which would be prejudicial to public health.

3.   The proposal to locate a three storey building in such close proximity to the existing self catering units would by reason of its design, scale, height and location at a higher ground level, be visually intrusive as viewed from these units and would seriously injure the amenities of property in the vicinity"

Planning Application Register Ref. F98A/1111

This was an application received on the 29th October 1998 for outline permission for a house adjacent to 2 Beverton Grove submitted by Donal McNally, architects for Martin Kenny, 2 Beverton Grove, Turvey Avenue, Donabate. Outline permission was refused on the 15th December 1998.

Planning Application Register Ref. F99A/0373

This was an application received on 31st of March 1999 for outline permission for a house at No. 2 Beverton Grove, Turvey Avenue, Donabate, submitted by Donal McNally architects on behalf of Martin Kenny of the same address. Outline permission was granted on the 7th of July 1999 for a dwelling adjacent to 2 Beverton Grove subject to four conditions.

A-121 Paragraph A.3. Resolutions, Applications or Requests. Paragraph A.3(a) – (g) of the Terms of Reference. Whether the lands in Lot 4 at Turvey House and Beaverton House Donabate were the subject of any of the resolutions, applications or requests referred to in paragraph A.3(a) – (g) of the Terms of Reference

A.3(a)- whether the lands were subject to rezoning resolutions

The Tribunal has dealt with this at paragraph A.2.(c)(ii) above.

A.3.(b) whether the lands were the subject of resolutions for material contravention of the relevant Development Plan

The Tribunal has dealt with this at paragraph A.2.(c)(iii) above.

A.3.(c) whether the lands were the subject of an application for special tax designation status.

This site was not the subject of any special tax designation status pursuant to the Finance Acts.

A.3.(d) whether the lands were the subject matter of applications for planning permission.

The Tribunal has dealt with this at paragraph A.2.(c)(iii) above.

A.3.(e) whether changes made or requested to be made with regard to the servicing of the lands for development.

These lands in particular were not the subject of any changes with respect to the servicing of the lands for development. However, certain of the outstanding planning permissions taken into consideration in 1986 and one, in particular, was refused resulting in a compensation claim. The claim was successfully defeated by Fingal County Council. The Drainage Design Department accepted that demographic population changes had taken place and were prepared to estimate potential population on the basis of 3.5 persons per dwelling. No other changes were made or were requested to be made regarding the servicing of the land.

A.3.(f) Whether the lands were the subject of applications for building bye-law approval in respect of buildings constructed on the lands

There are no records available.

A.3.(g) Whether the lands were the subject of applications for fire safety certificates

F95F/084 – Fire Safety Certificate granted on the 23rd of August 1995 to Kinane Developments in respect of Phase 1 apartment development at Turvey Avenue. This certificate was issued in respect of Building Blocks C, D, and C1.

F95F/085 – Fire Certificate issued on the 23rd of August 1995 to Kinane Developments in respect of Building Block E at Phase 1, Turvey House.

F95F/086 – Fire Certificate granted on the 24th of August 1995 to Kinane Developments in respect of Building Block A and B of Phase 1, Turvey Avenue.

F96F/174 – Fire Certificate granted on the 16th of August 1996 to Kinane Developments in respect of Building Blocks A and B, Phase 2 of apartment development at Turvey Avenue.

F96F/175 – Fire Certificate granted on the 16th of August 1996 to Kinane Developments in respect of Block E, Phase 2 of apartment development, Turvey Avenue.

F96F/176 – Fire Certificate granted on the 16th of August 1996 to Kinane Developments in respect of Blocks C, D and C1 of Phase 2 of apartment development, Turvey Avenue.

F96F/202 – Fire Certificate granted on the 23rd of September 1996 to Grainne Mallon & Associates on behalf of Hoydale Limited in respect of Block B, Turvey Golf and Country Club, Turvey Avenue.

97/4082 – Fire Certificate granted on the 23rd of May 1997 to Grainne Mallon & Associates on behalf of Hoydale Limited in respect of Block A, Turvey Golf and Country Club, Turvey Avenue.

97/4083 – Fire Certificate granted on the 23rd of May 1997 to Grainne Mallon & Associates on behalf of Hoydale Limited in respect of Block C, Turvey Golf and Country Club, Turvey Avenue.

98/4051 – Fire Certificate granted on 3rd of April 1998 to Grainne Mallon & Associates on behalf of Truvey Golf and Leisure plc in respect of golf and country club/house/hotel for hotel related public functions and golf club functions.

Paragraph A.3.(i). of the Amended Terms of Reference namely to ascertain the identity of any persons or companies (and if companies, the identity of the beneficial owners of such companies) who had a material interest in the said lands or who had a material involvement in the matters aforesaid;

The identity of the Beneficial Owners of the property as of 8th June 1989 together with changes in the Beneficial Ownership between then and the development of the lands has been established at paragraph A.1. above. The Beneficial Ownership as of the 8th June 1989 as defined in the Tribunals interpretation of its terms of reference on the 21st October 1998 rested with Mr. Joseph Murphy Senior.

Paragraph A. 3. (ii) of the Amended Terms of Reference namely to ascertain the identity of any members of the Oireachtas, past or present, and/or members of the relevant local authorities who were involved directly or indirectly in any of the foregoing matters whether by the making of representations to a planning authority or to any person in the authority in a position to make relevant decisions or by the proposing of or by voting in favour or against or by abstaining from any such resolutions or by absenting themselves when such votes were taken or by attempting to influence in any manner whatsoever the outcome of any such applications, or who received payments from any of the persons or companies referred to at (i) above

Other than the members of the Oireachtas and the Local Authorities referred to above the Tribunal at this time is unable to pronounce further on this term of reference.

Paragraph A. 3. (iv) of the Amended Terms of Reference namely to ascertain and report on the outcome of all such applications, resolutions and votes in relation to such applications in the relevant local authority;

The outcome of all applications, resolutions and votes are detailed above under paragraph A. 2 (c) (i) to (iii) inclusive and A 3 (a) to (g) inclusive.

LOT 5.

PARAGRAPH A.1.

IDENTIFICATION AND OWNERSHIP

250 acres (approx.) at Balgriffin.

Identification as of the 8th of June 1989

Lot 5 comprised both registered and unregistered lands, as follows: -

Registered lands; Folio 3212

Lands comprised in Folio 3212 of the Register County of Dublin, which said lands are situate in the Townland of Balgriffin Park, Barony of Coolock and County of Dublin, comprising 61.735 hectares or 152.5472 acres.

Unregistered lands

The balance consists of unregistered lands as identified in a Deed of Conveyance dated the 30th of December 1967 comprising 50 acres or 122 acres approx.

ALL THAT AND THOSE that part of the lands of Balgriffin now known as St. Doolagh's and Snuborough containing eighty acres, one rood and twenty-four perches Statute Measure and situate in the Parish of Balgriffin, Barony of Coolock and County of Dublin and shown on a map endorsed on an earlier Conveyance dated the 23rd of July 1945 and thereon coloured green, and
ALL THAT AND THOSE part of the lands of Balgriffin otherwise known as the Pier Field containing fourteen acres, three roods and thirty perches Statute Measure or thereabouts situate in the Barony of Coolock and County of Dublin, which said lands were shown on the map endorsed on the same earlier Conveyance and thereon coloured blue, and
ALL THAT AND THOSE part of the town and lands of Balgriffin, otherwise St. Doolagh's, in the Parish of Balgriffin, Barony of Coolock and County of Dublin, containing seven acres, three roods and twenty-one perches and shown on the map annexed to the same earlier Conveyance and thereon coloured brown.

Beneficial ownership as of 8th June 1989

Folio 3212 of the Register County of Dublin.

The Grafton Construction Company Limited, having its registered office at 26 Lower Baggot Street, in the City of Dublin, was registered as owner of these lands on the 25th of January 1968, and was so registered as of 8th June 1989. The land certificate had been issued to James Marshall, Solicitor, of 2 Gardiner Row, Dublin 1, on the 26th of March 1968. There is nothing on the folio by way of caution or inhibition as of 8th June 1989.

Unregistered lands

By Deed of Conveyance dated the 30th of December 1967 and made between **R. AND W. SCOTT (FARMS) LIMITED** (as vendor) of the one part and **THE GRAFTON CONSTRUCTION COMPANY LIMITED** (as purchaser) of the other part, the unregistered lands described above were conveyed to The Grafton Construction Company Limited for all the estate, right, title and interest of R.W. Scott (Farms) Limited therein, and were in the ownership of the Grafton Construction Company Limited as of the 8th of June 1989.

Changes in beneficial ownership since the 8th of June 1989 and prior to their development

On foot of the Composite Indenture, the lands comprised in Folio 3212 of the Register County of Dublin were also assured to Bovale Developments Limited, which continues to be the registered owner. On the 12th of September 1991, by the Composite Indenture, the unregistered lands in Lot 5 described above were assured to Bovale Developments Limited in whose ownership they remain to date. The Grafton Construction Company Limited was a party to the Composite Indenture by way of sub-sale. The Tribunal understands that there has been no development of the lands comprised in Lot 5.

PARAGRAPH A.2. PLANNING HISTORY

Part of the lands contained in the Folio are now in the functional area of Fingal County Council and part are within the functional area of Dublin Corporation. The boundary between the two areas is shown by a thick black line on the map. The area now in the functional area of Dublin Corporation was transferred into the functional area of Dublin Corporation under the Local Government Boundary Changes of 1985. The unregistered land lies north of the Drumnigh/Balgriffin Road between the Malahide Road to the west and the Hole-in-the-Wall Road to the east. The Tribunal considers it expedient to deal with the planning history of Lot 5 in two parts: -

(i) Lands in the functional area of Fingal County Council;
(ii) Lands in the functional area of Dublin Corporation.

(I) LANDS IN THE FUNCTIONAL AREA OF FINGAL COUNTY COUNCIL

Paragraph A.2 9(a) of the terms or reference namely the planning status of these lands in the Development Plan of the Dublin Local Authorities current at the 8th of June 1989

These lands were zoned "P" in the 1972 Development Plan i.e. "*to provide for the further development of Agriculture.*" These lands were zoned "B" in the 1983 Development Plan i.e. "*to protect and provide for the development of agriculture.*" These lands were zoned "B" on the 8th June 1989.

In the 1990 Draft Development Plan, the Lands were proposed to be zoned "B" to protect and provide for the development of agriculture. In the 1991 Draft Development Plan, the lands were proposed to be zoned "B" to protect and provide for the development of agriculture. These lands were zoned "B" in the 1993 Development Plan i.e. "*to protect and provide for the development of agriculture.*"

In the 1998 Fingal Draft Development Plan, it was proposed that the lands north of Drumnigh Road would be zoned "H" (*green belt*) and the lands south of Drumnigh Road were proposed to be zoned mainly "A" (*residential*) and a small portion was proposed to be zoned "H" (*green belt*).

In the 1999 Fingal County Development Plan, the land north of Drumnigh Road was zoned "H" (*green belt*) and the land south of Drumnigh Road was mainly zoned "A" (*residential*) and a small portion was zoned "H" (*green belt*).

Paragraph A.2. (b) of the Terms of Reference. The position with regard to the servicing of the land for development as of the 8th of June 1989

The following is the position in relation to the servicing of the lands in the functional area of Fingal County Council measuring approximately 65 hectares or 162 acres: -

Foul sewer

There were no foul sewers available to serve the designated lands within the Dublin County Council administrative area. The only facilities were those, which served Balgriffin cottages, a County Council housing estate. These consisted of a small treatment plant discharging treated effluent to the Santry River. This plant was totally committed to the existing development and could not accept any additional flows.

Surface water

There were a number of streams draining from west to east across the site. Development of this site would have required extensive study of the impact on the down stream catchment, in particular, its effect on the flood plain north of Baldoyle in the area of the racecourse.

Water supply

A water supply would have been available from a 300mm cast iron main located in the Malahide Road.

Paragraph A.2(c)(i) of the Terms of Reference. Changes made or proposed to be made to the 8th of June 1989 planning status of the lands by way of proposals put forward by Dublin Local Authority officials pursuant to a review of Development Plans or otherwise

Officials made no such proposals to the elected members of the Council until 1998. In the 1998 Draft Development Plan for Fingal County which was prepared by the Manager, part of the site south of Drumnigh Road was proposed to be zoned residential and the remainder green belt. This zoning was confirmed in the 1999 Fingal Development Plan.

Paragraph A.2. (c)(ii) of the Terms of Reference. Changes made or proposed to be made to the 8th of June 1989 planning status of the lands by way of motions by elected members of the Dublin Local Authorities proposing re-zoning.

No such changes were made or proposed by the elected members.

Material contraventions

No planning permission was granted which materially contravened the zoning of the lands.

Planning permissions

For a full understanding of the Planning status of the lands, the Tribunal sets out hereunder, details of all planning applications as disclosed on the planning register and the results of each such application.

Planning application register Ref. H 2620

Outline permission was refused for residential development at Balgriffin Park, Balgriffin, Dublin 5 (townlands of St. Doolagh's and Snugborough) by Order P 339/76, dated the 5th February 1976 for the following four reasons: -

"1. The site is located in an unserviced rural area zoned as an objective of the County Development Plan, for primarily agricultural use. The proposal is in serious conflict with this objective and is contrary to the proper and planning and development of the area.

2. The proposed development would be premature by reference to the existing deficiencies in the provision of water supply and sewerage facilities and the period within which such deficiencies may reasonably be expected to be made good.

3. The proposed development would be premature because a road layout for the area or part thereof has not been indicated in the Development Plan or has not been approved of by the planning authority or by the Minister on appeal.

4. The proposed development would endanger public safety by reason of traffic hazard and obstruction of road users."

McCabe, Delany & Associates, on behalf of O'Shea & Shanahan Limited, made the application. A first party appeal was withdrawn.

Planning application register Ref. 86A/1342

On the 22nd of September 1986, an application for planning permission for "*proposed Manor House Hotel & Sheltered Cottages*" at St. Doolagh's Park, Malahide Road, Kinsealy, for Doolagh's Manor Limited, by Raymond F. McDonnell, architect was submitted to Dublin County Council. The permission sought was for provision of a manor house-type hotel having 12 bedrooms and a caretaker's room with facilities for disabled persons, 8 no. 1 bed roomed units overlooking the ornamental garden, 27 No. A type 1 bed roomed units in the walled garden and 2 no. 2 bed roomed units in the walled garden making a total of 52 bed units with 109 car parking spaces.

By a decision Order No. P500/87 of the 16th February 1987, the Council decided to grant permission for the proposed development subject to 18 conditions. This decision was the subject of an appeal by the Applicants to An Bord Pleanála. By Order PL6/5/73478 of the 21st of July 1987, An Bord Pleanála decided to grant permission for the proposed development subject to 11 conditions.

The Board decided to grant permission for the reason set out in the First Schedule to the decision which was in the following terms: -

"Having regard to the communal residential nature of the established land use on this site, it is considered that on the scale which is proposed, the proposed development would constitute an appropriate land use which, subject to compliance with the conditions set out in the Second Schedule hereto, would accord with the proper and planning and development of the area."

Paragraph A.3. Resolutions, applications or requests. Paragraph A.3. (a)-(g) of the Terms of Reference. Whether the lands in Lot 5 at Balgriffin the functional area of Fingal County Council were the subject of any of the resolutions, applications or requests referred to in paragraph A.3.(a)-(g) of the Terms of Reference

A.3. (a) whether the lands were subject to re-zoning resolutions

The Tribunal has dealt with this matter at paragraph **A.2.(c)(ii)** above.

A.3.(b) whether the lands were the subject of resolutions for material contravention of the relevant Development Plan

The Tribunal has dealt with this matter at paragraph **A.2.(c)(iii)** above.

A.3.(c) whether the lands were the subject of an application for special tax designation status

This site was not the subject of any special tax designation status pursuant to the Finance Acts.

A.3.(d) whether the lands were the subject matter of applications for planning permission.

The Tribunal has dealt with this matter at paragraph A.2.(c)(iii) above.

A.3.(e) Whether the lands were subject to changes made or requested to be made with regard to the servicing of the lands for development

Foul sewer

By agreement with the Dublin Corporation in 1995, a scheme was prepared to drain the equivalent of 40 dwellings. This included existing premises in the area of St. Doolagh's and the system serving Balgriffin Cottages. The scheme had no implication for these lands comprised in Lot 5 since the capacity of the scheme was extremely limited and was designed simply to relieve difficulties created by the existing septic tanks and the existing treatment plant in the area of St. Doolagh's and Balgriffin Cottages. This scheme has yet to be implemented.

Surface water

No changes were requested or made with respect to surface water.

Water supply

No changes were requested or made with respect to water supply."

Paragraph A.3. (f)- Whether the lands were the subject of applications for building bye law approval in respect of buildings constructed on the lands

There are no records available.

Paragraph A.3.(g) – Whether the lands were the subject of applications for fire safety certificates

There were no applications for fire safety certificates on or after the 20th June 1985.

Paragraph A.3.(i). of the Amended Terms of Reference namely to ascertain the identity of any persons or companies (and if companies, the identity of the beneficial owners of such companies) who had a material interest in the said lands or who had a material involvement in the matters aforesaid;

The identity of the Beneficial Owners of the property as of 8th June 1989 together with changes in the Beneficial Ownership between then and the development of the lands has been established at paragraph A.1. above. The Beneficial Ownership as of the 8th June 1989 as defined in the Tribunals interpretation of its terms of reference on the 21st October 1998 rested with Mr. Joseph Murphy Senior.

Paragraph A. 3. (ii) of the Amended Terms of Reference namely to ascertain the identity of any members of the Oireachtas, past or present, and/or members of the relevant local authorities who were involved directly or indirectly in any of the foregoing matters whether by the making of representations to a planning authority or to any person in the authority in a position to make relevant decisions or by the proposing of or by voting in favour or against or by abstaining from any such resolutions or by absenting themselves when such votes were taken or by attempting to influence in any manner whatsoever the outcome of any such applications, or who received payments from any of the persons or companies referred to at (i) above

Other than the members of the Oireachtas and the Local Authorities referred to above the Tribunal at this time is unable to pronounce further on this term of reference.

Paragraph A. 3. (iv) of the Amended Terms of Reference namely to ascertain and report on the outcome of all such applications, resolutions and votes in relation to such applications in the relevant local authority;

The outcome of all applications, resolutions and votes are detailed above under paragraph A. 2 (c) (i) to (iii) inclusive and A 3 (a) to (g) inclusive.

LANDS IN LOT 5 WITHIN THE FUNCTIONAL AREA OF DUBLIN CORPORATION

Paragraph A.2 (a) of the terms of reference namely the planning status of these lands in the Development Plan of the Dublin Local Authorities current at the 8th of June 1989:

In the 1972 Dublin County Development Plan, these lands were zoned "P" (*to provide for the further development of agriculture*). In the 1983 Dublin county Development Plan, the lands were zoned "B" (*to protect and provide for the development of agriculture*). On the 8th of June 1989, the lands were zoned "B" (*to protect and provide for the development of agriculture*). In the 1991 Dublin City Development Plan the lands were zoned "L" (*"agriculture."*) In the 1999 Dublin City Development Plan, the bulk of the site is zoned "Z16" (*to be developed in accordance with approved residential action area plans*). The remainder of the site is zoned "Z10" (*"to be developed in accordance with mixed use action area plans."*)

Paragraph A.2 (b) of the Terms of Reference. The position with regard to the servicing of the lands for development as of the 8th of June 1989.

No services were provided by the Water Division to this site. There appears to be no written correspondence in relation to the Poppintree site. The lands in question fall outside the area currently drained by the north Dublin drainage area. Furthermore, no additional capacity exists in the Corporation drainage system. Any proposed development of this site, or indeed, any lands in the north fringe area, would be dependent on the provision of new sewerage infrastructure.

Paragraph A.2. (c)(i) of the Terms of Reference. Changes made or proposed to be made on the 8th June 1989 Planning status of the lands by way of proposals put forward by Dublin Local Authority officials pursuant to a review of Development Plans or otherwise

Officials made no such proposals to the elected members of the Council until 1998. However, in the 1998 Draft Development Plan for the city which was prepared by the Manager, part of the site within the administrative area of Dublin Corporation was proposed to be zoned "Z16" (*to be developed in accordance with approved residential action area plans*) and part of the site is zoned "Z10" (*to be developed in accordance with mixed use action area plans*). This zoning was confirmed in the 1999 City Development Plan.

Paragraph A.2. (c)(ii) of the Terms of Reference. Changes made or proposed to be made to the 8th June 1989 planning status of the lands by way of motions by elected members of the Dublin Local Authorities proposing re-zoning

No such changes were made or proposed.

Paragraph A.2.(c)(iii) of the Terms of Reference. Changes made or proposed to be made to the 8th June 1989 planning status of the lands by way of applications for planning permission (including any involving a material contravention of the Development Plan)

Material contravention

No planning permission was granted in respect of these lands, which materially contravened their zoning while they were within the functional area of Dublin County Council. No planning permission has been granted in respect of these lands, which materially contravened their zoning since they were transferred to the functional area of Dublin Corporation.

Planning permissions

The Tribunal sets out hereunder, details of planning applications as disclosed in the Planning Register of all planning applications which have been made in respect of that part of the lands in Lot 5 in the functional area of Dublin Corporation.

Planning application register Ref. 86A/0373

On the 24th of March 1986, an application for outline planning permission for construction of 40 semi-detached houses at Hole-in-the-Wall Road, Balgriffin, County Dublin, was submitted to Dublin County Council by Conroy, Manahan & Associates on behalf of Grafton Construction Company Limited. On the 22nd of May 1986, Dublin Corporation decided to refuse permission for the following three reasons: -

> "1. The proposed site is located in an area zoned "B" in the Development Plan with the objective "to protect and provide for the development of agriculture." The proposed development would materially contravene this objective of the Development Plan.
> 2, The proposed site is located in an area where there are no public sewerage facilities available. The proposed development would be premature by reason of the said deficiency and the time within which it may reasonably be expected to be made good and would be contrary to the proper and planning and development of the area.
> 3. The proposed development would by reason of the additional traffic on a substandard Road network endanger public safety by reason of a traffic hazard."

No other planning applications were made since the site was transferred to the functional area of Dublin Corporation.

Paragraph A.3. Resolutions, applications or requests. Paragraph A.3. (a)-(g) of the Terms of Reference. Whether the lands in Lot 5 in the functional area of Dublin Corporation were the subject of any of the resolutions, applications or requests referred to in paragraph A.3.(a)-(g) of the Terms of Reference.

A.3. (a) whether the lands were subject to re-zoning resolutions

The Tribunal has already been dealt with at paragraph A.2.(c)(ii) above and no such changes were made or proposed.

A.3.(b) whether the lands were the subject of resolutions for material contravention of the relevant Development Plan

The Tribunal has already been dealt with at paragraph **A.2.(c)(iii)** above.

A.3.(c) whether the lands were the subject of an application for special tax designation status

This site was not the subject of any special tax designation status pursuant to the Finance Acts.

A.3.(d) whether the lands were the subject of applications for planning permission

The Tribunal has already dealt with this at paragraph **A.2.(c)(iii)** above.

A.3.(e) Whether changes were made or requested to be made with regard to the servicing of these lands for development

The Tribunal has already dealt with this at **A.2(b)** above.

A.3.(f) Whether the lands were subject to applications for building bye-law approval in respect of buildings constructed on the lands

There are no records available.

A.3.(g) Whether the lands were the subject of applications for fire safety certificates

There were no applications for fire safety certificates on or after the 20th June 1985.

Paragraph A.3.(i). of the Amended Terms of Reference namely to ascertain the identity of any persons or companies (and if companies, the identity of the beneficial owners of such companies) who had a material interest in the said lands or who had a material involvement in the matters aforesaid;

The identity of the Beneficial Owners of the property as of 8th June 1989 together with changes in the Beneficial Ownership between then and the development of the lands has been established at paragraph A.1. above. The Beneficial Ownership as of the 8th June 1989 as defined in the Tribunals interpretation of its terms of reference on the 21st October 1998 rested with Mr. Joseph Murphy Senior.

Paragraph A. 3. (ii) of the Amended Terms of Reference namely to ascertain the identity of any members of the Oireachtas, past or present, and/or members of the relevant local authorities who were involved directly or indirectly in any of the foregoing matters whether by the making of representations to a planning authority or to any person in the authority in a position to make relevant decisions or by the proposing of or by voting in favour or against or by abstaining from any such resolutions or by absenting themselves when such votes were taken or by attempting to influence in any manner whatsoever the outcome of any such applications, or who received payments from any of the persons or companies referred to at (i) above

Other than the members of the Oireachtas and the Local Authorities referred to above the Tribunal at this time is unable to pronounce further on this term of reference.

Paragraph A. 3. (iv) of the Amended Terms of Reference namely to ascertain and report on the outcome of all such applications, resolutions and votes in relation to such applications in the relevant local authority;

The outcome of all applications, resolutions and votes are detailed above under paragraph A. 2 (c) (i) to (iii) inclusive and A 3 (a) to (g) inclusive.

LOT 6.

PARAGRAPH A.1.

IDENTIFICATION AND OWNERSHIP

9 acres (approx.) at Portmarnock.

Identification as of the 8th of June 1989

The lands comprised in Lot 6 were formerly part of the lands comprised in Folio 175 of the Register County of Dublin. The lands are situate in the Townlands of St. Helens, Barony of Coolock and County of Dublin. Of all of the Lands, this is the only folio of which part only was acquired by Bovale in the Composite Indenture. The map attached to the Composite Indenture showed Folio 175 with the portion thereof acquired by Bovale Developments Limited on foot of the Composite Indenture edged in red.

Beneficial Ownership as of the 8th of June 1989

The Grafton Construction Company Limited, having its registered office at 26 Lower Baggot Street, in the City of Dublin, had been registered as full owner of Folio 175 on the 1st of July 1970 and remained the registered owner at 8th of June 1989.

Part 3 of Folio 175 shows that the lands were subject to:

> A lease dated the 27th of February 1970 granted by The Grafton Construction Company Limited of the one part to John Grant and Ann Grant of the other part. The lease was for a term of two hundred and fifty years from the 1st of June 1969 at a rent of £22.50,

> Rights relating to the passage and running of soil, gas, electricity and oil in favour of Sorohan Contractors Limited, the registered owner of the lands comprised in Folio 8245F of the Register County of Dublin (and its successor in title, assigns, transferees, lessees, licensees and invitees).

> Full right and liberty for O'Shea and Shanahan Limited, the registered owner of lands comprised in Folio 11774F of the Register County of Dublin its successors and assigns, transferees, lessees, licensees and invitees, and all other persons lawfully entitled at all times and for all purposes in connection with the development and use of the property comprised in Folio 11774F and with or without vehicles to pass and repass over the roads and footpaths presently existing or at any future time to be constructed on the property between points Z-Y on Plan 175 thereof together with the covenants and conditions specified in Instrument No. R4704/99 and such other rights of entry and such other necessary rights in connection with the said services.

The conditions specified in Instrument No. R1833-80 made between The Grafton Construction Company Limited of the one part and O'Shea and Shanahan Limited of the other part relating to the use and enjoyment of the property comprised in Folio 175. The property also became subject to the conditions specified in Instrument No. 92DN04474 and made between The Grafton Construction Company Limited of the one part and Bovale Developments Limited of the other part relating to the use and enjoyment of the property. The Grafton Construction Company Limited was the registered owner of Folio 175 subject to the rights set out above.

A-144 *Changes in beneficial ownership since 8th June 1989 and prior to their development*

Portion of the property approximately 9.76 acres comprised in Folio 175 was assured by the Composite Indenture to Bovale Developments Limited and Bovale Developments Limited became registered owner of the lands on the 26th of February 1992. The Land Certificate was issued to Alfred Thornton, Solicitor, Bank of Ireland, 2 College Green in the City of Dublin, on the 4th of May 1992. The portion of Folio 175 acquired by Bovale Developments Limited became registered in Folio 83876F of the Register County of

Dublin. There is no caution or inhibition registered on Folio 83876F in the Register County of Dublin. It appears from Folio 83876F that when this portion of Folio 175 was transferred by the Composite Indenture to Bovale Developments Limited, and became registered as Folio 83876F, the rights affecting Folio 175 referred to above did not affect the portion of the land conveyed to Bovale Developments Limited. Bovale Developments Limited held folio 83876F subject to a collateral charge for present and future advances created in favour of The Governor and Company of the Bank of Ireland. It is noted on the folios that this charge was also registered on Folios 3212, 577, 6262F, 18462, 6952, 7462, 19360 and 4327 of the Register County of Dublin. The said charge was registered on the 26th of February 1992. Bovale Developments Limited developed the entire of the lands comprised in Lot 6 in a housing development known as Dál Riada.

PARAGRAPH A.2. PLANNING HISTORY

The lands are those comprised in Folio 83876FF - Co. Dublin - in the area stated to be 3.94 hectares (9.76 acres).

Paragraph A.2 (a) of the Terms of Reference namely the planning status of these lands in the Development Plan of the Dublin Local Authorities current at the 8th of June 1989

In the 1972 County Development Plan the lands were zoned "P" (*to provide for further development of agriculture*). In the 1983 County Development Plan the lands were zoned "B" (*to protect and provide for the development of agriculture*) and "G" (*to protect and improve high amenity areas*). On the 8th of June 1989, the lands were zoned "B" (*to protect and provide for the development of agriculture*) and "G" (*to protect and improve high amenity areas*).

In the proposed 1990 Draft County Development Plan, the proposed zoning was shown as "B & G" (*to preserve a "Green Belt" between development areas.*). In the 1991 Draft County Development Plan, the proposed zoning was shown as "B & G" (*to preserve "Green Belt" between development areas.*). In the 1993 proposed amendment by Councillors to 1991 Draft Plan, the proposed zoning was shown as "A" (*to provide and improve Residential Amenity*) – (3.41 hectares, 8.45 acres) and "B & G" – (0.53 hectares, 1.31 acres). In the 1993 Dublin County Development Plan, the lands were zoned "A" (*to protect and improve residential amenity*) - (3.41 hectares, 8.45 acres) and "B & G" - (0.53 hectares, 1.31 acres). In the 1999 Fingal Development Plan, the lands are zoned "A" (*residential*) (3.41 hectares) and the remainder (0.53 hectares) is zoned "F" (*to preserve and provide for open space and recreational amenities*).

Paragraph A.2 (b) of the Terms of Reference. The position with regard to the servicing of lands for development as at the 8th of June 1989

Foul sewer

In 1989, Portmarnock was drained by agreement to the Dublin Corporation Sewerage System. However, this land lay outside the Drainage Agreement Area. But for this fact the land could have drained by gravity to the Portmarnock system, which drained into the Dublin Corporation system via pumping stations at Wendell Avenue, Portmarnock Bridge, Mayne Bridge and Baldoyle Village. The Baldoyle pumping station had been maintained by Dublin Corporation up to June 1987 and at that time there were frequent foul water overflows from this pumping station. Electrical improvements carried out by Dublin County Council in late 1987 and early 1988 resulted in the reduction of the frequency of these overflows. However a period of time had to be allowed to establish this fact. Also, the Portmarnock Bridge Pumping Station together with the gravity sewer, which drained into it, were substandard and difficult to maintain. In effect, therefore, in June 1989, Environmental Services would not have considered this land to have a viable drainage outlet.

Surface water

The surface water system to which the subject lands could drain had a limited capacity.

Water supply

Water supply was available from a boosted water supply serving Limetree Avenue and school.

Paragraph A.2(c)(i) of the Terms of Reference. Changes made or proposed to be made to the 8th June 1989 Planning status of the lands by way of proposals put forward by Dublin Local Authority Officials pursuant to the review of the Development Plan or otherwise

There were no such proposals put forward by any Dublin Local Authority official to change the 8th June 1989 planning status of these lands.

Paragraph A.2(c)(ii) of the Terms of Reference. Changes made or proposed to be made to the 8th June 1989 planning status of the lands by way of motions by elected members of Dublin Local Authorities proposing re-zoning

The 1991 Draft Development Plan, which had been approved for public display by the elected members, was put on public display for 3 months from September 1991 to December 1991. On the 27th of November 1991, Alan S. Tomkins, Architectural and Planning Consultant, of 308 Clontarf Road, Dublin 3, submitted a letter to Dublin County Council Planning Department – representation no. 000770 - in the following terms: -

"Dear Sir

Re: Draft Development Plan 1991 - 4 hectares of lands at Lime Tree Avenue, Portmarnock – "Bovale Developments Limited"

On behalf of my clients Messrs. Bovale Developments Limited, I wish your Council to review and change the zoning on the above lands to residential use.

I enclose a plan showing the location of the lands on Ordnance Survey Sheet and a further map showing its relationship to existing residential development to the south and church and school on the eastern boundary.

Since the lands referred to are not a viable proposition for agricultural use due to the close proximity of the high density housing and school, we would urge your Council to reconsider the zoning for residential development for affordable houses for first time purchasers.

This market is not being satisfactorily catered for this locality.

Yours faithfully
Alan S. Tomkins MIAS
Corporate Building Surveyor."

The lands in question formed part of the *Green Belt*, which was intended (in accordance with the 1990 Draft Development Plan) to be retained as a *Green Belt Area* between developments in the Portmarnock area and the Malahide area. The above representation on behalf of Bovale Limited (representation no. 000770) was one of 9 representations seeking re-zoning of a total of 86 hectares (206 acres approx.) of the "*Green Belt*" ("B & G") to Residential "A." The lands in question were situate in the townlands of Robswalls, St. Helens, Beechwood and Grange. This representation and other representations relating to the "*Green Belt*" in the Portmarnock/Malahide area (minute refs. C/328/93 and C/329/93) were considered at special meetings of Dublin County Council held on the 28th and 29th April 1993 to continue the review of the Draft Development Plan. The representations are listed hereunder: -

GREEN BELT PORTMARNOCK/MALAHIDE
(A) Representation No. 000494 - L. Foley - lands at Paddy's Hill;
(B) Representation No. 000505 - T. McSwiggan - Monks Meadow;
(C) Representation No. 000666 – "Comeragh Properties", Robswalls;
(D) Representation No. 000770 – "Bovale Developments Limited", Limetree Avenue;
(E) Representation No. 000004 - McDowell, St. Helen's;
(F) Representation No. 000230 - M. Burke, Blackwood Lane;
(G) Representation No. 000199 - B. Howard, Grange;
(H) Representation No. 000568 - Portmarnock G.A.A., Blackwood Lane;
(I)Representation No. 002177 – "St. Lawrence O'Toole Trust" - St. Helen's School, Portmarnock;
Other Representation Nos. 000359, 000490, 000681 and 000770 (Item 15(3)).

A copy of the minutes of special meeting of the Council held on the 29th OF April 1993 (Item 15(3)) show that reports by the Manager in the following terms were considered: -

"SYNOPSIS OF REPRESENTATIONS:
These eight representations seek re-zoning of a total of 86 hectares of the Green Belt "B & G" to residential "A." Amongst the reasons cited are, the difficulty of carrying out agricultural activity between large housing areas and that the re-zoning of land for residential would eliminate undesirable ribbon development.

(A) Representation No. 000494 requests the rezoning of 10 hectares immediately north of the developed residential area of Portmarnock to low density residential.

(B) Representation No. 000505 seeks rezoning of 1 hectare at Carrickhill to low density residential.

(C) Representation No. 000666 seeks a rezoning of 18 hectares to residential at a density of 12 houses per hectare. The proposal is divided into two locations, 13 hectares adjacent to Seapark Malahide and the remaining 5 hectares adjacent to Portmarnock. The representation states a willingness to cede his interest in the remaining 40 hectares to Dublin County Council.

(D) Representation No. 000770 requests the rezoning of 4 hectares at Limetree Avenue to Residential.

(E) Representation .No. 000004 seeks a rezoning of 46 hectares at St. Helen's, for low-density residential development.

(F) Representation No. 000230 requests a rezoning of a 0.5 hectare site on Blackwood Lane to low density residential.

(G) Representation No. 000199 seeks a rezoning of 2 hectares at Grange, to low density residential.

(H) Representation No. 000568 seeks the rezoning of 4 hectares at Blackwood Lane to low density residential.

(I) Representation No. 002177 seeks rezoning of the grounds of St. Helen's School to "A" (residential).

SITE HISTORY

(i)   PLANNING APPLICATIONS

Representation No. 000494 - Lands at Paddy's Hill - Reg. Ref. YA.506 - outline permission refused for residential development and An Bord Pleanála upheld this decision.

Representation No. 000505 - Lands at Monks Meadow - Reg. Ref. WA. 224, WA. 225 - permission refused for 4 houses on a 1 hectare site.

Representation No. 000666 - Lands at Robswalls - Reg. Ref. WA. 157 - permission refused for 180 houses on 12 hectares and this decision was upheld on appeal.
Reg. Ref. 9OA/1090 - permission refused for 250 houses on 50 hectares including football clubhouse, car parking and 30 hectares of parkland and this decision was upheld on appeal.
Reg. Ref. YA.506 - outline permission for residential development refused and this decision was upheld on appeal.

Representation No. 000004 - Lands at St. Helens - Reg. Ref. 90A/1030 – application for permission to develop access road and erect 6 houses with septic tank, withdrawn.

Representation No. 000199 - Lands at Grange - Reg. Ref. 87A/702 – outline permission refused for 5 houses.
Reg. Ref. 89A/428 - outline permission refused for 6 houses.

Representation No. 000568 – Reg. Ref. 90A/1038 application for 10 detached dwellings withdrawn.

DEVELOPMENT PLAN
Representation Nos. 000004, 000230, 000494, 000505, 000666, 000770 and 002177 are zoned Green Belt "B & G" in the 1983 Development Plan and the 1991 Draft Review. Representation Nos. 000199 and 000568 are zoned "B" in the 1983 Development Plan and "B & G" Green Belt in the 1991 Draft Review.

PLANNING OFFICER'S REPORT:
The lands of the representations form part of the open Green Belt countryside between the designated development areas of Portmarnock/Malahide. The Council's policy in relation to development in rural and Green Belt areas is set out in paragraphs 2.3.6, 2.8.10 and 3.2.6 of the Draft Written Statement.
Paragraph 2.8. 1 0 states that "it is the policy of the Council to retain the individual physical character of towns and development areas by the designation of Green Belt areas." This policy is to protect the special amenity value of these areas and provide a visual break between urban areas. It is also Council policy that

"drainage facilities will not be provided for lands so designated." It is of particular importance that the separation between Malahide and Portmarnock be maintained.

In addition, the lands are affected by the 35 NNI contour as shown on Map 1A. In this regard, it is Council policy to restrict development in the area encompassed by the line. Development as proposed in the representations would be contrary to the development policies of the Council and the adopted settlement strategy and infrastructural investment programme. It is recommended that no change be made to the Draft Plan."

The following supplementary report by the Manager, which had been circulated, was also considered at the meetings: -

"PROPOSALS FOR ADDITIONAL ZONING OF LANDS IN THE SWORDS/MALAHIDE AREA
Since the first Development Plan was made in 1972, it has been a consistent policy of the Council to safeguard the physical and visual separation between the towns and to provide the necessary infrastructure to accommodate development of zoned lands.

The motions that are now on the agenda of the Council include proposals that would have a considerable impact on this physical and visual separation. The relevant proposals have been plotted on a map, which will be displayed to the Council. The table appended to this report indicates the extent to which Green Belt areas would be reduced in size if all the re-zoning proposals on the current agenda were so implemented. It is a matter for the Council to decide whether the impact of the proposals is such as to impinge on the physical and visual separation between the towns to an unacceptable extent.

In the case of Malahide, there is the further consideration that the existing foul drainage treatment works and its planned expansion is estimated to cater for a population equivalent of 20,000 persons. The Sanitary Services Engineer has advised that existing committed developments will absorb all of this capacity so that there is no significant capacity available to service additional lands unless some other arrangement for foul drainage in the Malahide area is made.

In the case of Swords, the report of the Eastern Regional Development Organisation made in 1985 envisaged that by the year 2011, Swords would have a population approximating to 100,000 plus an industrial allocation of 280 H. and it proposed that such a population should be planned for.

This proposal did not find favour and neither the 1983 Development Plan nor the 1991 Draft Development Plan were prepared on the basis of an expansion of Swords beyond the planned capacity of the existing infrastructure.

The Sanitary Services Engineer has reported that with suitable investment in upgrading and expansion, the Swords foul drainage treatment works could be expanded to cater for a 65,000 person population equivalent.

Proposed re-zoning of lands around Swords would in total give rise to the following additional population equivalent when fully developed: -

	Hectares	Ares	Population	Population Equivalent
Residential	261	644	25,000	25,000
Industrial	*51*	*126*		_10,000_ _35,000_

Added to the existing proposed population equivalent demand of 43,000, the total population equivalent would be 78,000. It is not clear whether this can be catered for by any reasonable upgrading of the treatment works having regard to the need to maintain the quality of the receiving waters.

Further studies would be needed to establish whether the existing foul drainage treatment works could be expanded and upgraded to cater for such a population equivalent because of the limited dilution capacity of the Broadmeadow Estuary and alternative drainage arrangements may have to be considered.

One possible alternative would be the construction of a new treatment works and sea outfall at Donabate and the connection thereto of the Swords system. If such a treatment works and outfall were constructed, Malahide might also be connected to it.

A second alternative would be the construction of a pipeline connecting Swords to an expanded North Dublin Drainage System.

Either of these two alternatives would require very large capital expenditures and it is unlikely that funding for such expenditure would be forthcoming on the basis of ad hoc decisions made arising from the representations of individual landowners.

If Swords is to be expanded beyond the size suggested in the Draft Plan the following decisions would have to be made: -

"1. A decision on the envisaged size or population equivalent to which it would grow.
2. A decision dependent on the first decision as to what form of drainage infrastructure should be provided. This would need the benefit of a consultants report on the possible options.
3. In the light of the decisions on 1. and 2., a decision as to how and where projected development should be directed.
4. The adoption of an order of priorities for the development of land in phase with the provision of infrastructure.

In the light of the above it is recommended that the Council should not change the zoning of any substantial areas of land between Swords, Malahide and Portmarnock in the context of the present review but that a study should be set in train for the purpose of presenting a report or reports addressing the issues listed above with a view to adopting a coherent plan for the area within a year of the setting up of a new Fingal County Council."

APPENDIX
GREEN BELTS
RE-ZONING PROPOSALS - REVISED FIGURES

	Area Approx. Ha.	Proposed re-zoning Ha.	Loss %
Malahide	*200*	5	*27*
Swords		3	
Portmarnock Malahide	*144*	5	*41*
		9	
Portmarnock Baldoyle	*210*	7	*36*
		5	

The following motions which were moved at the meeting held on the 28th April 1993 were considered at the meeting on the 29th April 1993:-

Motion proposed by Councillor Wright, seconded by Councillor Kennedy.
15(3)(C)(i) – Representation Number 000666 on behalf of Comeragh Properties

"In order to facilitate the permanent realisation of the Green Belt between Malahide and Portmarnock and with a view to providing the necessary amenity lands for both passive and active recreation, Dublin County Council resolve that the lands at Robswall, Malahide, outlined in red on the attached map (approximately 147 acres) and which have been signed for identification purposes by the proposers, be zoned for residential where marked yellow not more than 250 dwellings and to retain "T&G" recreational open space where marked green."

Motion proposed by Councillor Kennedy, seconded by Councillor Wright.

15(3)(C)(iii) – Representation Number 000666 on behalf of Comeragh Properties – Representation Number 000004 on behalf of McDowells (lands at St. Helens Stud)
"In order to facilitate the permanent realisation of the Green Belt between Malahide and Portmarnock and with a view to providing the necessary amenity lands for both passive and active recreation, Dublin County Council hereby resolves that the lands at Robswall, Malahide and Wheatfield Stud, Saint Helen's, Malahide outlined in red on the attached map, (approx. 264.50 acres) and which have been signed for identification purposes by the proposers, be zoned for residential where marked yellow as follows:

> *(a) at Robswall, Malahide (36 acres) - not more than 250 dwellings;*
> *(b) at Wheatfield Stud (50.50 acres) - not more than 49 dwellings and to retain "B&G" recreational open space where marked green (178 acres). Included in this motion that lands fronting both the Church Road and Blackwood Lane will be ceded for the purpose of road widening (approx. 6 acres) to the Council."*

Motion proposed by Councillor Wright, seconded by Councillor Owen.

15(3)(E)(ii) – Representation Number 000004 on behalf of McDowells
"In order to facilitate the permanent realisation of the Green Belt between Malahide and Portmarnock and with a view to providing the necessary amenity lands for both passive and active recreation, Dublin County Council hereby resolves that the lands at Wheatfield Stud, Saint Helen's, Malahide, outlined in red on the attached map (approx. 117.5 acres) and which have been signed for identification purposes by the proposers, be zoned for low density residential development (not more than 49 dwellings) marked 'A' (50.5 acres) and to retain 'B & G' recreational open space marked green (67 acres). Included in this motion that lands fronting both the Church Road and Blackwood Lane will be ceded for the purpose of Road widening (approx. 6 acres) to the Council."

Mr. F. Coffey, Senior Engineer, Environmental Services, advised the members of the position in relation to drainage facilities.
The Manager advised the members that the final sentence should be deleted from motions 15(3)(C)(iii) and 15(3)(E)(ii). It was proposed by Councillor Kennedy, seconded by Councillor Wright: -

> *"That motions 15(3)(C)(iii) and 15(3)(E)(ii) be amended by deletion of the following words:*
>
> > *"Included in this motion that lands fronting both the Church Road and Blackwood Lane will be ceded for the purpose of road widening (approx. 6 acres) to the Council."*

This amendment was put and PASSED unanimously.
The following motion proposed by Councillor Wright, seconded by Councillor Kennedy was put: -

15(3)(C)(i) – Representation Number 000666 on behalf of Comeragh Properties

"In order to facilitate the permanent realisation of the Green Belt between Malahide and Portmarnock and with a view to providing the necessary amenity lands for both passive and active recreation, Dublin County Council resolve that the lands at Robswall, Malahide, outlined in red on the attached map (approximately 147 acres) and which have been signed for identification purposes by the proposers, be zoned for residential where

marked yellow not more than 250 dwellings and to retain "B&G" recreational open space where marked green."

On a division the voting resulted as follows: -

FOR: Thirty-eight (38)
AGAINST: Twenty-four (24)
ABSTENTIONS: One (1)

For: Councillors S. Ardagh, M. Billane, P. Brady, S. Brock, L. Butler, B. Cass, B. Coffey M.J. Cosgrave, L. Creaven, A. Devitt, J.H. Dockrell, M. Elliott, M. Farrell, T. Fox, C. Gallagher, S. Gilbride, R. Greene, T. Hand, F. Hanrahan, M. Keating, M. Kennedy, J. Larkin, L. Lohan, D. Lydon, S. Lyons, C. McGrath, P. Madigan, D. Marren, T. Matthews, T. Morrissey, C. 0 Connor, J. O'Halloran, A. Ormonde, C. Quinn, N. Ryan, S. Terry, C. Tyndall, G.V. Wright. (38)
Against: Councillors C. Boland, M. Doohan, K. Farrell, N. Gibbons, E. Gilmore, L. Gordon, D. Healy, C. Keane, T. Kelleher, S. Laing, J. Maher, B. Malone, M. Muldoon, M. Mullarney, D. O'Callaghan, G. O'Connell, M. O'Donovan, N. Owen, P. Rabbitte, S. Ryan, T. Sargent, F. Smyth, D. Tipping, P. Upton. (24)
Abstentions: Councillor T. Ridge. (1)

The Chairman then declared the motion PASSED.

The following motion proposed by Councillor Kennedy, seconded by Councillor Wright as amended was put: -

15(3)(C)(iii) – Representation Number 000666 on behalf of Comeragh Properties – Representation Number 000004 on behalf of McDowells

"In order to facilitate the permanent realisation of the Green Belt between Malahide and Portmarnock and with a view to providing the necessary amenity lands for both passive and active recreation, Dublin County Council hereby resolves that the lands at Robswall, Malahide, and Wheatfield Stud, Saint Helen's, Malahide outlined in red on the attached map, (approx. 264.50 acres) and which have been signed for identification purposes by the proposers, be zoned for residential where marked yellow as follows:

> *(a)   at Robswall, Malahide (36 acres) - not more than 250 dwellings;*
> *(b)   at Wheatfield Stud (50.50 acres) - not more than 49 dwellings and to retain "B&G" recreational open space where marked green (178 acres)."*

On a division the voting resulted as follows: -

FOR: Thirty-three (33)
AGAINST: Twenty-eight (28)
ABSTENTIONS: One (1)

For: Councillors S. Ardagh, M. Billane, P. Brady, S. Brock, L. Butler, B. Coffey, M.J. Cosgrave, L. Creaven, A. Devitt, J.H. Dockrell, M. Elliott, M. Farrell, T. Fox, C. Gallagher, S. Gilbride, R. Greene, T. Hand, F. Hanrahan, M. Keating, M. Kennedy, J. Larkin, D. Lydon, S. Lyons, C. McGrath, P. Madigan, D. Marren, T. Matthews, T. Morrissey, C. 0 Connor, J. O'Halloran, A. Ormonde, N. Ryan, G.V. Wright. (33)

Against: Councillors C. Boland, B. Cass, M. Doohan, K. Farrell, N. Gibbons, E. Gilmore, L. Gordon, D. Healy, C. Keane, T. Kelleher, S. Laing, L. Lohan, J. Maher, B. Malone, M. Muldoon, M. Mullarney, D. O'Callaghan, G. O'Connell, M. O'Donovan, N. Owen, C. Quinn, P. Rabbitte, S. Ryan, T. Sargent, F. Smyth, S. Terry, D. Tipping, C. Tyndall. (28)

Abstentions: Councillor T. Ridge. (1)

The Chairman then declared the motion PASSED.

The following motion proposed by Councillor Wright, seconded by Councillor Owen as amended was put:-

15(3)(E)(ii) – Representation Number 000004 on behalf of McDowells

"In order to facilitate the permanent realisation of the Green Belt between Malahide and Portmarnock and with a view to providing the necessary amenity lands for both passive and active recreation, Dublin County Council hereby resolves that the lands at Wheatfield Stud, Saint Helen's, Malahide, outlined in red on the attached map (approx. 117.5 acres) and which have been signed for identification purposes by the proposers, be zoned for low density residential development (not more than 49 dwellings) marked "A" (50.5 acres) and to retain "B&G" recreational open space marked green (67 acres)."

On a division the voting resulted as follows: -

FOR: Thirty-three (33)
AGAINST: Twenty-six (26)
ABSTENTIONS: Nil (0)

For: Councillors S. Ardagh, M. Billane, P. Brady, S. Brock, L. Butler, B. Coffey, M.J. Cosgrave, L. Creaven, A. Devitt, M. Elliott, M. Farrell, T. Fox, C. Gallagher, S. Gilbride, R. Greene, T. Hand, F. Hanrahan, M. Keating, M. Kennedy, J. Larkin, D. Lydon, C. McGrath, P. Madigan, D. Marren, T. Matthews, T. Morrissey, C. O Connor, J. O'Halloran, A. Ormonde, N. Owen, T. Ridge, N. Ryan, G.V. Wright. (33)

Against: Councillors C. Boland, B. Cass, M. Doohan, K. Farrell, N. Gibbons, E. Gilmore, L. Gordon, D. Healy, C. Keane, T. Kelleher, S. Laing, L. Lohan, J. Maher, B. Malone, M. Muldoon, M. Mullarney, D. O'Callaghan, M. O'Donovan, C. Quinn, P. Rabbitte, S. Ryan, T. Sargent, F. Smyth, S. Terry, D. Tipping, C. Tyndall. (26)

The Chairman then declared the motion PASSED.

Motion in the names of Councillors Kennedy, Owen and Wright. It was proposed by Councillor Kennedy, seconded by Councillor Owen: -

15(3)(B)(i) – Representation Number 000505 on behalf of T. McSwiggan
"Dublin County Council hereby resolves to rezone approximately 3 acres of land at Carrickhill, Portmarnock shown outlined in red on attached map from its present zone "B" Agricultural to zone "A" low density residential (S2) max 2 houses."

Following discussion to which Councillors Kennedy and Owen contributed, the Manager replied to queries raised by the members. The motion was put and on a division the voting resulted as follows: -

FOR: Forty-three (43)
AGAINST: Six (6)
ABSTENTIONS: One (1)

For: Councillors S. Ardagh, M. Billane, C. Boland, P. Brady, S. Brock, L. Butler, B. Cass, B. Coffey, M.J. Cosgrave, L. Creaven, A. Devitt, M. Elliott, Farrell, T. Fox, C. Gallagher, S. Gilbride, R. Greene, T. Hand, F. Hanrahan, C. Keane, M. Kennedy, S. Laing, J. Larkin, L. Lohan, D. Lydon, C. McGrath, J. Maher, B. Malone, D. Marren, T. Matthews, T. Morrissey, M. Muldoon, C. 0 Connor, J. O'Halloran, A. Ormonde, N. Owen, C. Quinn, P. Rabbitte, T. Ridge, N. Ryan, S. Ryan, S. Terry, G.V. Wright. (43)
Against: Councillors L. Gordon, D. Healy, M. Mullarney, D. O'Callaghan, T. Sargent, D. Tipping. (6)
Abstentions: Councillor F. Smyth. (1)

The Chairman then declared the motion PASSED.

Motion in the names of Councillors Kennedy, Owen and Wright. It was proposed by Councillor Kennedy, seconded by Councillor Wright: -

15(3)(D)(i) – Representation Number 000770 on behalf of Bovale Developments Limited

"Dublin County Council hereby resolves that the lands at Limetree Ave., Portmarnock outlined in red on the attached map comprising about 8.25 acres and which has been signed for identification purposes by the proposers of this motion be zoned for Residential "A" in the draft review of the County Dublin Development Plan, noting that the Portmarnock 2000 Planning Report prepared for the Portmarnock Community Association identified the above lands for infill residential development."

Following discussion to which Councillors Kennedy, Owen, Malone, Healy, Wright, Mullarney and S. Ryan contributed, the Manager replied to queries raised by the members. The motion was put and on a division the voting resulted as follows: -

FOR: Thirty-two (32)
AGAINST: Fifteen (15)
ABSTENTIONS: One (1)

For: Councillors S. Ardagh, C. Boland, P. Brady, S. Brock, L. Butler, B. Coffey, M.J. Cosgrave, L. Creaven, A. Devitt, M. Farrell, T. Fox, C. Gallagher, S. Gilbride, R. Greene, T. Hand, F. Hanrahan, C. Keane, M. Keating, M. Kennedy, J. Larkin, L. Lohan, D. Lydon, S. Lyons, C. McGrath, T. Matthews, T. Morrissey, J. O'Halloran, A. Ormonde, N. Owen, N. Ryan, S. Terry, G.V. Wright. (32)
Against: Councillors F. Buckley, M. Doohan, K. Farrell, L. Gordon, D. Healy, S. Laing, B. Malone, D. Marren, S. Misteil, M. Mullarney, M. O'Donovan, C. Quinn, S. Ryan, T. Sargent, F. Smyth. (15)
Abstentions: Councillor T, Ridge (1)

The Chairman then declared the motion PASSED.
The map accompanying the motion passed on the 29th April 1993 (15(3)(D)(i)) showed an area smaller that that shown on the map accompanying representation ref. 000770 and Folio 83876FF which measured approx. 8.45 acres (3.41 hectares). At this meeting, the following representation was NOTED: - 15(3)(F) – Representation No. 000230 – M. Burke, Blackhood Lane (No Councillor proposed that this site be re-zoned and as a result there was no vote and no change in the zoning.)

At this meeting it was proposed by Councillor Wright, seconded by Councillor Owen in relation to 15(3)(G)(i) – (Representation Number 000199 on behalf of B. Howard) that:-

"Dublin County Council hereby resolves that lands at Grange, Malahide, outlined in red on the attached map, comprising 6 acres, and which have been signed for identification purposes by the proposers, be zoned for Low Density Housing S2 (2 houses per hectare)."

From the minutes following discussion to which Councillors Wright, Owen and Healy contributed, the motion was put and on a division the voting resulted as follows: -

FOR: Twenty-eight (28)
AGAINST: Thirteen (I 3)
ABSTENTIONS: Nil (0)

For: Councillors C. Boland, P. Brady, S. Brock, L. Butler, B. Coffey, A. Devitt, M. Farrell, T. Fox, C. Gallagher, S. Gilbride, R. Greene, T. Hand, F. Hanrahan, C. Keane, M. Kennedy, S. Laing, J. Larkin, D. Lydon, M. McGennis, C. McGrath, J. Maher, D. Marren, T. Matthews, A. Ormonde, N. Owen, T. Ridge, N. Ryan, G.V. Wright. (28)
Against: Councillors F. Buckley, M. Doohan, L. Gordon, D. Healy, T. Kelleher, S. Misteil, M. Muldoon, M. Mullarney, M. O'Donovan, C. Quinn, S. Ryan, F. Smyth, S. Terry. (13)

The Chairman then declared the motion PASSED.
At this meeting a motion in the names of Councillors Kennedy, Wright, Owen, Malone and S. Ryan, proposed by Councillor Kennedy, seconded by Councillor Wright that 15(3)(H)(i) – Representation Number 000568 on behalf of Portmarnock G.A.A. Club as follows:-

"Dublin County Council hereby resolves that the lands outlined in red on the attached map drawing No. 8812/50, which are the subject of a re-zoning submission to Dublin County Council reference 000568 be re-zoned from agriculture use to residential use of 1 house per 0.405 hectares. (1 house per acre) (zoning objective "A")."

Following contributions from Councillors Kennedy, Devitt, Malone, Healy, S. Ryan, Owen and Sargent, the Manager replied to queries raised by the members.

Amendment in the names of Councillors Kennedy, Wright, Malone, S. Ryan and Owen. It was proposed by Councillor Kennedy, seconded by Councillor Wright: -

"That motion no. 15(3)(H)(i) be amended by deletion of the words:
"1 house per 0.405 hectares (1 house per acre)" and substitution of the words "1 house per 0.384 hectares (10 houses in total) on the site outlined in red on the attached map signed by the proposer and dated the 29th April, 1993."

The amendment was put and was PASSED unanimously.

The substantive motion as follows was put: -

"Dublin County Council hereby resolves that the lands outlined in red on the attached map drawing no. 8812/50, which are the subject of a re-zoning submission to Dublin County Council, reference 000568, be re-zoned from agriculture use to residential use of 1 house per 0.384 hectares (10 houses in total) on the site outlined in red on the attached map signed by the proposer and dated the 29th April 1993."

On a division the voting resulted as follows: -

FOR: Thirty-three (33)
AGAINST: Seven (7)
ABSTENTIONS: Seven (7)

For: Councillors C. Boland, P. Brady, S. Brock, F. Buckley, L. Butler, B. Coffey, M.J. Cosgrave, L. Creaven, A. Devitt, M. Farrell, T. Fox, C. Gallagher, S. Gilbride, R. Greene, T. Hand, F. Hanrahan, M. Kennedy, S. Laing, J. Larkin, D. Lydon, M. McGennis, C. McGrath, J. Maher, B. Malone, T. Matthews, T. Morrissey, J. O'Halloran, A. Ormonde, N. Owen, T. Ridge, N. Ryan, S. Ryan, G.V. Wright. (33)
Against: Councillors B. Cass, C. Keane, M. Muldoon, D. O'Callaghan, C. Quinn, F. Smyth, S. Terry. (7)
Abstentions: Councillors K. Farrell, L. Gordon, D. Healy, D. Marren, S. Misteil, M. Mullarney, T. Sargent. (7)

The Chairman then declared the motion PASSED.
The proposed amendment to the 1991 Draft Development Plan in respect of Lot 6 was put on public display as change number 14 on Map number 7 for the period from the 1st July 1993 to the 4th August 1993. At a special meeting of Dublin County Council held on 24th September 1993, to consider amendments to Map 7 (Malahide/Portmarnock) a report of the Manager (previously circulated) was READ. at a meeting of the Council held on the 28th September 1993 to consider representations received during the second display the following report of the Manager, which had been circulated, was considered:

"There are 2947 representations referring to this amendment virtually all objecting. Recommendation: Delete Amendment."

The following motion was proposed by Councillor B. Malone, seconded by Councillor S. Ryan;

"Dublin County Council hereby resolves that the lands referred to as 14 on Map Number 7 of the Dublin County Council Draft Development Plan Review 1993 Amendments be zoned "B&G" - to preserve Green Belt."

The motion was defeated by 17 votes for to 39 votes against.

For: Councillors C. Breathnach, F. Buckley, M. Doohan, N. Gibbons, L. Gordon, J. Higgins, T. Kelleher B. Malone, M. Muldoon, M. Mullarney, D. O'Callaghan, G. O'Connell, M. O'Donovan, S. Ryan, T. Sargent, F. Smyth, D. Tipping.

Against: Councillors S. Barrett, C. Boland, P. Brady, S. Brock, L. Butler, B. Cass, B. Coffey, R. Conroy, M. J. Cosgrave, L. Creaven, A. Devitt, M. Elliott, M. Farrell, T. Tox, C. Gallagher, S. Gilbride, R. Greene, F. Hanrahan, C. Keane, M. Kennedy, S. Laing, J. Larkin, L. Lohan, D. Lydon, S. Lyons, M. McGennis, C. McGrath, J. Maher, T. Morrissey, C. O'Connor, J. O'Halloran, A. Ormonde, N. Owen, C. Quinn, P. Rabbitte, T. Ridge, N. Ryan, C. Tyndall, G.V. Wright. **[App. 6.7]**

This decision meant that change 14 Map 7 was confirmed and the land was zoned "A" (Residential) in the 1993 Development Plan.

Paragraph A.2(c)(iii) of the Terms of Reference. Changes made or proposed to be made to the 8th of June 1989 planning status of the lands by way of applications for planning permission (including any involving a material contravention of the Development Plan)

Material contraventions

No planning permission was granted which materially contravened the zoning of these lands.

Planning applications

Planning application register Ref. F94A/0056

An application was submitted to Dublin County Council on the 3rd of February, 1994 by Alan S. Tomkin for Bovale Developments Limited seeking permission for 72 detached four bedroom houses, road, sewers and ancillary services, at Lime Tree Avenue, Portmarnock. On the 31st of March, 1994 Fingal County Council decided to refuse permission for following four reasons:-

> "In the absence of a revised agreement between Dublin Corporation and Fingal County Council, there is no capacity in the Foul Drainage system to serve the proposed development.
> The proposed development is premature due to existing deficiencies in the foul and surface water sewage system and the period within which they may be made good.
>
> The public open space provided on zoned development land represents only 40% of the development plan requirements and, in addition, does not represent open space of functional or aesthetic value being located on the site boundary with the width of only five meters for more than half its length. The proposed development would, therefore, be contrary to the proper planning and development of the area and would be seriously injurious to the visual amenities of this sensitive and prominent area adjoining the green belt between the towns of Portmarnock and Malahide.
>
> Approximately 70% of the public open space provided for this housing development is located in an area zoned in the 1993 County Development Plan "to protect and enhance the open nature of lands between urban areas." The proposed development would therefore, contravene materially that objective and so be contrary to the proper planning and development of the area.
>
> **Note**: that the Applicant is advised to consult with the Planning Authority prior to the submission of any further application for planning permission on the site."

On the 13th of April, 1994, an appeal was submitted by Mr. Tomkins to An Bord Pleanála against the decision of Fingal County Council to refuse permission for the 72 houses. On the 21st of July 1994, An Bord Pleanála refused permission for the following reason:-

> "it is considered that the proposed development would be premature by reference to the existing deficiency in the provision of foul sewage facilities and the period in which the constraint involved may reasonably be expected to cease."

Planning application register Ref. F94A/0289

On the 26th of April 1994, Mr. Alan Tomkins submitted an application for planning permission for 70 detached four bedroom houses, road, sewage and ancillary works at Lime Tree Avenue, Portmarnock on behalf of Bovale Developments Limited. On the 23rd of June 1994, Sean Carey, the Deputy Manager to whom the appropriate powers have been delegated, decided to grant permission for the proposed development subject to 20 conditions.

Planning application register Ref. F94A/0592

This was an application for permission by Bovale Developments Limited for substitution of house type for 19 detached houses and optional parking for 3 houses. Permission was granted on the 7th of December 1994, subject to 21 conditions.

Planning application register Ref. F94A/0676

This was an application for permission by Bovale Developments Limited for substitution of house type at site 4. Permission was granted on the 10th of January 1995, subject to 21 conditions.

Planning application register Ref. F94A/0722

This was a substitution of house type by Bovale Developments Limited on sites 13, 40, 42, 44, 46 and 47 and resiting of house on site 48. Permission was granted on the 24th of January 1995, subject to 19 conditions.

Planning application register Ref. F94A/0745

This was an application by Bovale Developments Limited for substitution of house type at site 10. Permission was granted on the 24th of January 1995, subject to 19 conditions.

Planning application register Ref. F94A/0799

This was an application by Bovale Developments Limited for substitution of house type at site 17, 39, 50. Permission was granted on the 28th of February 1995, subject to 19 conditions.

Planning application register Ref. F94B/0443

This was an application by Bovale Developments Limited for detached garage at site 38. Permission was granted on the 21st of March 1995, subject to 4 conditions.

Planning application register Ref. F95A/0101

This was an application by Bovale Development Limited for garage on sites 38 & 59 and substitution of house types on sites 26 & 48. Permission was granted on the 10th of May 1995, subject to 23 conditions.

Planning application register Ref. F95A/0142

This was an application by Bovale Developments Limited for substitution of house type at site 32. Permission was granted on the 8th of June 1995, subject to 21 conditions.

Planning application register Ref. F95A/0194

This was an application by Bovale Developments Limited for substitution of house type at sites 25 & 40. Permission was granted on the 27th of June 1995, subject to 7 conditions.

Planning application register Ref. F95A/0289

This was an application by Bovale Developments Limited for substitution of house type at site 22. Permission was granted on the 26th July 1995, subject to 8 conditions.

Planning application register Ref. F95A/0413

This was an application by Bovale Developments Limited for substitution of house type at sites 27 and 33. Permission was granted on the 20th of September 1995, subject to 7 conditions.

Planning application register Ref. F95A/0463

This was an application by Bovale Developments Limited for substitution of house type at site 25. Permission was granted on the 11th of October 1995, subject to 7 conditions.

Planning application register Ref. F95A/0521

This was an application by Bovale Developments Limited for substitution of house type at sites 29 & 30. Permission was granted on the 24th of October 1995, subject to 8 conditions. In each of the fifteen applications listed above, the application was submitted by A.S. Tomkins on behalf of Bovale Developments Limited

Paragraph A.3. Resolutions, applications or requests. Paragraph A.3.(a) – (g) of the Terms of Reference. Whether the lands in Lot 6 were the subject of any of the resolutions applications or requests referred to in paragraph A.3(a) – (g) of the terms of reference

A.3.(a) whether the lands were subject to re-zoning resolutions. The Tribunal has dealt with this matter at Paragraph 2(c)(ii) above.

A.3.(b) whether the lands were the subject of resolutions for material contravention of the relevant Development Plan

The Tribunal has dealt with this matter at paragraph A.2.(c)(iii) above.

A.3.(c) whether the lands were the subject of an application for special tax designation status

This site was not the subject of any special tax designation status pursuant to the Finance Acts.

A.3.(d) whether the lands were the subject matter of applications for planning permission

The Tribunal has dealt with this matter at paragraph **A.2.(c)(iii)** above.

A.3.(e) Whether the lands were the subject of changes made or requested to be made with regard to the servicing of the lands for development

Foul sewer

(i) Portmarnock Bridge Pumping Station Planning permission (Reg. Ref. 89A/0413) was granted on the 27th September 1989 and confirmed by An Bord Pleanála on the 22nd April, 1990 for the improvement of Portmarnock Hotel and a clubhouse for the Golf course. This allowed for the collection of substantial levies to improve Portmarnock Bridge Pumping Station and its associated upstream gravity sewer.

(ii) Portmarnock Drainage Agreement Area A letter dated the 8th May 1994 was sent to Dublin Corporation requesting an extension of the Drainage Agreement area to cover the subject site.

Surface water

In making a report on foot of planning application (Reg. Ref. F94A/0056), the Water and Drainage Division accepted the principle of on-site storage of surface water subject to the applicant submitting a sound engineering proposal to overcome the limited capacity within the receiving surface water system.

A.3. (f) Whether the lands were the subject of applications for building byelaw approval in respect of buildings constructed on the lands

There were no applications for building byelaw approval in respect of buildings constructed on the lands.

A.3.(g) Whether the lands were the subject of applications for fire safety certificates

There were no applications for fire safety certificates.

Paragraph A.3.(i). of the Amended Terms of Reference namely to ascertain the identity of any persons or companies (and if companies, the identity of the beneficial owners of such companies) who had a material interest in the said lands or who had a material involvement in the matters aforesaid;

The identity of the Beneficial Owners of the property as of 8th June 1989 together with changes in the Beneficial Ownership between then and the development of the lands has been established at paragraph A.1. above. The Beneficial Ownership as of the 8th June 1989 as defined in the Tribunals interpretation of its terms of reference on the 21st October 1998 rested with Mr. Joseph Murphy Senior.

Paragraph A. 3. (ii) of the Amended Terms of Reference namely to ascertain the identity of any members of the Oireachtas, past or present, and/or members of the relevant local authorities who were involved directly or indirectly in any of the foregoing matters whether by the making of representations to a planning authority or to any person in the authority in a position to make relevant decisions or by the proposing of or by voting in favour or against or by abstaining from any such resolutions or by absenting themselves when such votes were taken or by attempting to influence in any manner whatsoever the outcome of any such applications, or who received payments from any of the persons or companies referred to at (i) above

Other than the members of the Oireachtas and the Local Authorities referred to above the Tribunal at this time is unable to pronounce further on this term of reference.

Paragraph A. 3. (iv) of the Amended Terms of Reference namely to ascertain and report on the outcome of all such applications, resolutions and votes in relation to such applications in the relevant local authority;

The outcome of all applications, resolutions and votes are detailed above under paragraph A. 2 (c) (i) to (iii) inclusive and A 3 (a) to (g) inclusive.